After Effects® 5
Bible

After Effects® 5 Bible

J. J. Marshall and Zed Saeed

Hungry Minds™

Best-Selling Books • Digital Downloads • e-Books • Answer Networks • e-Newsletters • Branded Web Sites • e-Learning

New York, NY✦ Cleveland, OH ✦ Indianapolis, IN

After Effects® 5 Bible

Published by
Hungry Minds, Inc.
909 Third Avenue
New York, NY 10022
www.hungryminds.com

Library of Congress Control Number: 2002100342

ISBN: 0-7645-3655-9

Printed in the United States of America

10 9 8 7 6 5 4 3 2 1

1B/ST/QU/QS/IN

Distributed in the United States by Hungry Minds, Inc.

Distributed by CDG Books Canada Inc. for Canada; by Transworld Publishers Limited in the United Kingdom; by IDG Norge Books for Norway; by IDG Sweden Books for Sweden; by IDG Books Australia Publishing Corporation Pty. Ltd. for Australia and New Zealand; by TransQuest Publishers Pte Ltd. for Singapore, Malaysia, Thailand, Indonesia, and Hong Kong; by Gotop Information Inc. for Taiwan; by ICG Muse, Inc. for Japan; by Intersoft for South Africa; by Eyrolles for France; by International Thomson Publishing for Germany, Austria, and Switzerland; by Distribuidora Cuspide for Argentina; by LR International for Brazil; by Galileo Libros for Chile; by Ediciones ZETA S.C.R. Ltda. for Peru; by WS Computer Publishing Corporation, Inc., for the Philippines; by Contemporanea de Ediciones for Venezuela; by Express Computer Distributors for the Caribbean and West Indies; by Micronesia Media Distributor, Inc. for Micronesia; by Chips Computadoras S.A. de C.V. for Mexico; by Editorial Norma de Panama S.A. for Panama; by American Bookshops for Finland.

For general information on Hungry Minds' products and services please contact our Customer Care department within the U.S. at 800-762-2974, outside the U.S. at 317-572-3993 or fax 317-572-4002.

For sales inquiries and reseller information, including discounts, premium and bulk quantity sales, and foreign-language translations, please contact our Customer Care department at 800-434-3422, fax 317-572-4002 or write to Hungry Minds, Inc., Attn: Customer Care Department, 10475 Crosspoint Boulevard, Indianapolis, IN 46256.

For information on licensing foreign or domestic rights, please contact our Sub-Rights Customer Care department at 212-884-5000.

For information on using Hungry Minds' products and services in the classroom or for ordering examination copies, please contact our Educational Sales department at 800-434-2086 or fax 317-572-4005.

For press review copies, author interviews, or other publicity information, please contact our Public Relations department at 317-572-3168 or fax 317-572-4168.

For authorization to photocopy items for corporate, personal, or educational use, please contact Copyright Clearance Center, 222 Rosewood Drive, Danvers, MA 01923, or fax 978-750-4470.

Hungry Minds™ is a trademark of Hungry Minds, Inc.

About the Authors

J. J. Marshall is a born and bred resident of New York City and makes his living there as a broadcast designer and a digital video consultant. Most recently, he assisted in developing a nationwide broadband news-on-demand network called The FeedRoom. Prior to that, he helped introduce Oxygen Media to the joys of Final Cut Pro and After Effects while editing a weekly two-hour show. In addition, his past efforts have included freelance projects for the New York New Media Association (NYNMA), Liz Claiborne, NetShoot, and the Center for Neurobiology and Behavior at Columbia University, as well as independent documentary productions that have aired on PBS. Teaching credits include courses in digital video at open-I Media and the School of Visual Arts (SVA). While writing this book, he served as a beta tester on the latest version of After Effects. A self-proclaimed refugee from the world of theater, J. J. has long been creating data-driven art in one form or another.

Zed Saeed lives and works in New York City as a freelance digital-media consultant specializing in editing, compositing, and workflow issues. Zed served as a senior post-production consultant for Apple Computer and Oxygen Media on Final Cut Pro and digital-video workflow design and has worked with Media 100 and Adobe Systems on video-related products. He has also worked as an editor, producer, compositing artist, and broadcast designer at Showtime Channels, Sundance Channel, and ESPN Classics. Zed has written articles on digital media technologies for magazines and has served on the faculty of NYU Graduate School, Parsons School of Design, and New School University. Zed has written, produced, and edited videos that have received awards and recognition by the Academy of Television Arts and Sciences and the American Film Institute. Zed is also the author of *Final Cut Pro 2 Bible*.

Credits

Acquisitions Editor
Tom Heine

Project Editor
Melba Hopper

Technical Editor
Alan Hamill

Copy Editor
Jerelind Charles

Editorial Manager
Rev Mengle

Permissions Editor
Laura Moss

Media Development Specialist
Angela Denny

Project Coordinator
Regina Snyder

Graphics and Production Specialists
Beth Brooks
Melanie DesJardins
Joyce Haughey
Gabriele McCann
Laurie Petrone
Betty Schulte
Jacque Schneider
Jeremey Unger

Quality Control Technician
Laura Albert
Andy Hollandbeck
Charles Spencer

Proofreading and Indexing
TECHBOOKS Production Services

No lake so still but that it has its wave;

No circle so perfect but that it has its blur.

I would change things for you if I could;

As I can't, you must take them as they are.

-Han Fei Tzu, noted Chinese Realist

Foreword

It was once said of science that the more we know, the less we know; or to quote Shakespeare, "There are more things in heaven and earth, Horatio, Than are dreamt of in your philosophy."

A rather strange statement indeed when applied to the subject matter of this book, a software application called Adobe After Effects. However, in the six years that I've been using and teaching the application, this often describes the way I feel. Because every day I'm learning some new technique, some unique design concept, a different method of expressing a creative impulse, of communicating a point via animated graphics. . . .

One can never know it all.

At my seminars, I amuse the audience when someone raises a hand and asks, "Can After Effects do . . . ?" and before they continue, I preempt the questioner by saying, "Yes. It can!" And that isn't far from the truth, because almost any visual concept you can imagine can be implemented in After Effects.

Go watch a major movie. After Effects was probably used in the production. Check out TV commercials—more After Effects. From something as subtle as changing the color of an actor's hair to elaborately conceived spaceship battles in far-off galaxies; from creating animated graphics for display on a Web page to polishing up the latest entry to Sundance. Power, flexibility, precision, grace. After Effects exhibits all these characteristics, and more.

But what about the human element and the interface between imagination and implementation? How do you get to that stage? How do you become *expert* (or expert enough)? Some learn by example, others by rote. Efficient learning, though, comes through comprehension and practice, then adaptation and improvement. If you see something, you'll remember some of it, but if you see *and* do, your mind and body develop a synergy of understanding.

Which brings us to the ideal teaching process—this book. Instruction and example are all rolled up into the *After Effects 5 Bible,* which combines meticulous text with practical examples provided on the DVD-ROM. I consider this to be one of the best After Effects books I've seen. Why so, especially? Well, for me, it is J. J. and Zed's specific approach. Just the right amount of instructional *gravitas* balanced with a gentle sense of humor. Indeed, akin to a fine gourmet meal, let this reference educate and satisfy, until you, too, develop the means to express through art, with the *After Effects 5 Bible* providing your guidance.

Alan Hamill
Dana Point, CA
March 2002

Preface

While it's easy to learn, After Effects takes time and passion to master. If an artist has a real vision, passion for seeing that vision realized, and a mastery of this fantastic tool, the final results will be gratifying indeed. We've written the *After Effects 5 Bible* with practical applications in mind. Our primary focus has been to provide you with a set of concrete steps for all the production scenarios you might encounter. When we were getting started in this field, we were confounded when experts would say something such as, "I did that with a displacement map." While everyone nodded in what appeared to our eyes as a somewhat unbelievable collective understanding, we'd be thinking, "Well, how *exactly* did you do that with a displacement map?" Basically, we tried to write a book that we wished we had years ago.

For most of us who use it regularly, After Effects is something of a religion. It's a joy to use, and the people who make a living from it seem happy to while away entire portions of their lives manipulating the controls of its well-designed interface. Certain software applications develop an extremely devoted following, and After Effects is a prime example of this phenomenon. More importantly, After Effects devotees form a community that's mostly comprised of visual artists. It's so well engineered that its audience can look past the vexing nature of computers and immediately start throwing clay on the wheel. Strength as a channel for creativity is its distinguishing trademark.

After Effects has revolutionized the broadcast industry. The mid-nineties showed the public a dazzling array of visual artistry in ad campaigns and television network promotions, the quality and the quantity of which were unprecedented. All corners of the market have been dramatically affected. On one hand, Academy award winner John Gaeta, special effects supervisor for the immensely popular movie, *The Matrix*, makes mention of his use of the application in a documentary about the technical aspects of his work on that film. On the other hand, wedding videos have started appearing with suddenly high production values. After Effects contributed to the rise of the so-called "digital video revolution," and there are numerous professionals whose careers stem completely from the widespread use of this indispensable tool.

So What Is After Effects, Anyway?

After Effects 5.5 is Adobe's latest overhaul of this enormously successful motion graphics software. In years past, it has become a widely used tool in post-production, regardless of a facility's size or budget. Its use is prevalent at all levels of the film, broadcast, and Web industries, yet After Effects is noteworthy in that it is truly *software*. The application doesn't rely on any proprietary hardware; instead, it requires only the inherent resources of a personal computer. With the advent of After Effects, the balance of power has shifted. High-end studios with large quantities of bulky and expensive analog equipment now share the market with talented artists whose "studio" consists of a single machine. Vital and important work is as likely to originate from the realm of the desktop as it is from any other production environment, and this is due in large part to the accessible power of this highly user-friendly application.

Version 5.5 is a major upgrade, and the Adobe After Effects development team is to be commended for their amazing work. Truly phenomenal software, this build of After Effects boasts a variety of new features as well as vast enhancements of its user interface. There are numerous new filters for concretizing any effect that your mind can envision. Additionally, 5.5 includes native 3D-compositing capabilities as well as vector paint tools, both of which were possible only a short time ago with the purchase of expensive additional software. Considering that the 3D tools include lights, virtual cameras, and shadows, version 5.5 represents a huge leap forward for a product that had already filled its niche in the market.

Every release of an Adobe graphics product allows for greater integration with their other offerings, and After Effects is no exception. After Effects 5.5 impressively imports work created in the latest builds of Premiere (6.0), Photoshop (6.0), and Illustrator (10.0). Real-time dynamic previews of compositions allow for instant visual gratification as your work evolves over the course of a project. Masks can now be manipulated directly in the Comp window. Multiple layers can be simultaneously animated with the addition of a hierarchical parenting switch in the Timeline window. The list goes on.

Further still, Adobe has continued its efforts in bringing the power of procedural animations to your work by adding something new called *expressions*. Based on JavaScript, expressions are scripts that you can use to dynamically control the values of different properties so that you don't have to lose time setting tons of keyframes. Finally, your output options have been greatly enhanced. Compositions can be rendered for the versatile Flash (SWF) file format just as easily as they can be prepared with 16-bit color for HDTV or film.

How This Book Is Organized

If you've read all the way up to this point, we're hoping that you want to look into this whole thing a bit further. We've put this book together in an attempt to give you a complete tour of how After Effects works, as well as to describe some of the ways you'll actually use it in production. We've also designed it so that it can be read from front to back or, if you prefer, as a desktop reference. In either case, there's some logic to the order of the chapters, and we talk a little bit about that development in the following description of the book's parts.

Part I: Welcome to After Effects 5

Part I acquaints you with the basics of the After Effects interface and gets you started on creating your own animations. In essence, there's an After Effects "headspace," or thought process, and the point of the first few chapters is to fully introduce you to this way of thinking. Once you know the basics of importing elements and animating them, you will find it much easier to approach the more sophisticated aspects of compositing.

Part II: Keyframes and Rendering

Part II looks into the different kinds of keyframe interpolation you can incorporate into your animations. Perhaps more importantly, this section of the book takes a good look at the Render Queue, that all-important "oven" where you bake your creations once you've thrown them together. Lastly, this part of the book will introduce you to the wonders of applying effects. After all, the application is called After Effects, and it hardly seems like fun to have to wait to see what the Big Fun is all about.

Part III: Broadening Animation Skills: Masks, Transparency, and Time

Part III looks closely at the various ways you can work with transparency in After Effects. Usually, budding motion graphic artists are too busy plotting the ways in which they might overthrow the industry before getting overly concerned with details such as alpha channels. Nonetheless, an understanding of transparency is absolutely critical to comprehending After Effects as a whole. Even better than that, acquiring such an understanding is usually fun, at least when it's compared to the kind of tooth pulling some folks imagine the topic to be. Additionally, because After Effects deals with a succession of images over time, it's also important to know how to control the way time unfolds in your projects. Do you want your clips to play slowly or quickly, or perhaps both at different points in their playback?

Part IV: Using Effects: The Big Fun

Part IV looks at the myriad of effects that you can apply to your moving images. Sometimes, this aspect of the application seems a bit overwhelming in light of the fact that the Production Bundle of After Effects now boasts of having more than 90 plug-ins to enhance your work. Still, the effects make up the reason why a good number of After Effects aficionados initially sought out the software. Perhaps your humble aim is to change the distribution of color in a clip of film that wasn't lit exactly right. Maybe you happen to be interested in creating your own dramatic weather full of blizzards or lots of lightning. Either way, the effects offer you the means to make it happen.

Part V: Aiming Higher: Advanced Techniques

Part V goes into what some people think of as the "hard" stuff. At this point, we cover topics such as Motion Math, expressions, 3D compositing, as well as tracking and stabilizing your footage. We've also included a couple of chapters on the use of text and typography, because so many folks who use After Effects initially come to it from the need to make a title sequence.

Part VI: Rendering for All Media

Part VI considers After Effects in the context of the greater realm of video production. What did you shoot on? What are you editing on? What's your delivery format? How do all the pieces fit together? This part of the book briefly touches on the role of After Effects in a production workflow that might run the gamut from miniDV to HDTV.

Part VII: Appendixes

In the appendixes, we've given you a list of resources on the World Wide Web. These include sites that offer After Effects goodies that range from tutorials to stock footage to free plug-ins. Additionally, we've given you a list of keyboard short-cuts for users of both the Macintosh and Windows platforms. Lastly, we include an appendix that tells you what's on the DVD-ROM in the sleeve on the back cover.

How to Use This Book

It seems a little strange to have to explain how to use this book, but I guess some explanation is needed (typically, when people ask us how to use a book, our response is to politely tell them to read it). As we mentioned earlier, you can read this book sequentially just as easily as you can jump from place to place while using it as a reference. In each chapter, we did our best to debunk topics that might appear complicated, and we also tried to give you a matching step-by-step exercise to accompany each explanation.

Conventions Used in This Book

We tried to keep the explanations from being overly technical in nature, but because we're talking about software, sometimes there's no way to avoid *digibabble*. Hopefully, the only parts of the book that will seem as though they've been written in *computerese* are the keyboard shortcuts in the step exercises. Just so you know, whenever we refer to a keyboard shortcut, we first provide the Mac instructions, which are followed by a forward slash and the corresponding Windows instructions. For example, the keyboard shortcut for Undo is Command+Z/Ctrl+Z.

The DVD-ROM

Yep, it's a DVD-ROM, not a CD-ROM. All that means is that there is a lot more room for us to put stuff. In other words, it holds more data than a CD-ROM, but it's not a DVD that you can pop into the DVD player on your home entertainment system. Most computers sold in the past couple of years ship with DVD-enabled drives, so you shouldn't have any problems getting the data into your system.

Throughout the chapters of the book, we consistently refer to the After Effects projects that we put on the DVD-ROM for you to refer to as you work your way through the step exercises. If you want to get the most out of the lessons in the chapters, you'll definitely want to copy the project files and their related media onto your own computer. Of course, if you want to work with your own material, you're welcome to do that instead.

In addition to the projects and their media, we've also put a bunch of other goodies on the disc, and we've given you a detailed listing of these in Appendix D.

Icons and Sidebars

In a number of places, we found it useful to point out some important information by highlighting it with these nifty little icons.

 Anywhere you see a Caution icon, just know that you might do some damage to your project or your peace of mind.

 We used the Note icon to separate what we hope are useful bits of information related to the topic under discussion.

 A Tip usually denotes a technique that saves a lot of time or is otherwise imminently useful in production.

 We placed Cross-Reference icons in spots where we mention a subject that is covered in greater detail in another chapter. We even go so far as to tell you the chapter number in the reference!

Lastly, we've included a number of sidebars devoted to the topic of what's new in After Effects 5.5. They are sprinkled throughout the book wherever the update to the application is relevant to the topic.

Contacting the Authors

Feel free to drop us a line at *aebible@earthlink.net*. We'd be happy to hear any insights and observations you might have. While we read every message we receive, just remember these two caveats: First, depending on the nature of our schedule in addition to the volume of e-mail we receive, we may not be able to get back to every one of you. Secondly, if you're looking for any type of tech support for either your hardware or software, you should directly contact the vendor in question.

So, get to it. We sincerely hope that learning After Effects will be as much fun for you as it was for us.

Acknowledgments

J. J. Marshall — Above all, I want to thank my wife, Christine. If not for her continual and unswerving support, this book wouldn't even be a remote possibility. For her love, and the grace with which it is always and unconditionally given, I am profoundly grateful.

Even though he's my coauthor, I feel it necessary to express my gratitude to Zed. Years ago, he took me to my first After Effects User Group meeting, and the rest, as they say, is history. More than that, I'm lucky to consider him a great friend. It's my hope that we continue our "vision quest" in one form or another.

Much love and many thanks to the "folks" — my mother and father continue to serve as the core members of a small, but devoted, fan club. Everyone should be so lucky.

If it weren't for the support of friends like these, difficult deadlines would have been impenetrable walls. Thanks to Eric Morrissey, Dan Sherman, Aaron Fein, Louie Berk, Mukesh Vasvani, and TJ Shea.

Zed Saeed — It has been my privilege to be involved with the development of After Effects for many years. I have had the support and ear of many good people from Adobe Systems: Steve Kilisky, Erica Schisler, David Trescot, Christie Evans, Dan Wilk, Richard Pelzar, Bruce Bowman, Kim Platt, Marcus Chang, Phil Nelson, and many others have over the years put up with my nagging and harassment and responded with nothing but kindness. It seems like a foregone conclusion now, but I have long held that After Effects would take over the world, as it so rightfully has.

Special thanks to Showtime Channels and Sundance Channel for all the time they granted me to be their After Effects artist, designer, and usurper of resources for all-night beta testing. Thanks also to visionary art directors like Tony Castellano and Crystal Hall-Aurnhammer, who spoiled me for anything else for the rest of my living days.

As always my gratitude goes to my mentor Dirk Van Dall, Vice President of Digital Video at Showtime Channels. Dirk, an artist at heart and hands-down the most knowledgeable person on digital media issues, got me started on this path and gave me the access and direction to get where I am today. As we like to say, "It's Dirk's world. We all just live in it."

The authors join together in expressing their gratitude to the following people.

We'd like to express our appreciation to the people at Hungry Minds for all their help preparing this book. Thanks to Tom Heine, our acquisitions editor, for providing steady support and looking out for us from the time the book was no more than a concept.

Also, many thanks are due to Melba Hopper, our project editor, whose tireless efforts have resulted in making this book a reality. Early in the process, she told us that she didn't like to work after 8 p.m., in the interest of preserving her sanity. We could hardly disagree, but the number of late night e-mails we received from her were a testament to her dedication. We also want to express our gratitude to the copy editor, Jerelind Charles, for her careful editor's eye.

We owe a great deal of credit to Adobe Systems, Inc. — first, for creating and releasing After Effects, thereby providing us with the opportunity to even write this book; second, and far more importantly, for continuing to develop After Effects as beautifully as they do. Extra special thanks go to Steve Kilisky and Erica Schisler for their kindness in finding the time to go out of their way to support us in the midst of their extremely hectic schedules.

We particularly want to express our appreciation for the work of Alan Hamill, our technical editor. It's a privilege to write about After Effects when you know that a member of Adobe's superb digital video team is watching out for you.

A number of companies kindly provided us with some gorgeous stock footage. We deeply appreciate the contributions made by John Davis from bestshot.com; Sam Bartlett from Digital Juice, Inc.; Steve Gianfermo from Videometry; Charlie Patton from EyeWire by Getty Images; Dave Hill from Creatas; Barry Dagestino, Michael Pixley, and Domenic Rom from Sekani; and Julie Hill from ArtBeats. If you need production-quality elements, look these guys up.

Thanks to Victoria Hamilton from The Foundry in the U.K. They make fantastic plug-ins, and Vikki is a highly valued ally.

As we began putting this book together, many colleagues graciously answered the call to contribute some of their work to the cause. For this, we deeply thank Adam Helfet Hilliker of HelfetHillikerGormley Designs (say that 10 times!), Steve Fein of Big Ripple Multimedia, Axel Baumann, and Mark Magnus. All of them are great artists.

As some of you may know, there are a number of very talented folks who prepare top-notch training materials for After Effects. Brian Maffitt and Trish and Chris Meyer have set the bar in this particular field. We owe them our thanks for their inspiration and our respect for their contributions.

Last, but certainly not least, everything changed one morning during the second week of writing this book. The atrocity of September 11 hit so close that it literally shook the windows of our homes. We were spared, but thousands were not. Writing about After Effects suddenly seemed frivolous when compared to the harrowing reality that too many of our neighbors had to face. Our hearts go out to those who were lost and to those who lost them on that day. Despite its wounded soul, New York City is still a great place to live, and we do so with pride.

Contents at a Glance

Contents

Part III: Broadening Animation Skills: Masks, Transparency, and Time   297

Part IV: Using Effects: The Big Fun   387

Part V: Aiming Higher: Advanced Techniques   603

Making a Movie with After Effects

✦ ✦ ✦ ✦

In This Chapter

Creating and saving
a project

Importing different
media types

Creating a
composition

Animating Layers
with keyframes

Applying effects

Using Basic Text

Using Markers
with sound

Enabling Motion Blur
and continuously
rasterizing EPS files

Exporting a
QuickTime movie

✦ ✦ ✦ ✦

Greetings, folks! Welcome to the amazing creation known as After Effects. If you've never used it before, then this Quick Start chapter will introduce you to the basic workings of the application. If you're a graphics professional, you may have worked with some of Adobe's excellent contributions to the field, and After Effects deserves its place in the company of great programs like Illustrator and Photoshop. Others among you may be getting more deeply immersed in the rapidly expanding world of digital video and are wondering what the hype surrounding After Effects is all about. No matter how you ended up here, there's no question that the application can take your dynamic media productions to a higher level. By the time you're finished with this brief chapter, you'll be familiar with its basic animation techniques and be able to create your own QuickTime movie as the result of your efforts.

This chapter assumes that you've pulled up a chair next to your happily humming workstation and want to get down to work. Armed with a copy of After Effects and this Bible, it's time to see what a few clicks of the mouse will yield. Getting up and running involves familiarizing yourself with some rudimentary compositing techniques. If you aren't clear as to exactly what it is, *After Effects* is visual effects and compositing software that gives you tight control over your motion graphics productions. For the most part, that means that you can use it to make preexisting elements move through space over time while directly controlling their appearance. You'll be able to see this for yourself very quickly.

Adobe Systems, Inc., has recently unleashed version 5.5 of After Effects upon the world. This means a number of things, such as support for Mac OS X, enhanced 3D controls, new effects, smart mask interpolation, and a whole host of enhancements and goodies. Version 5.0 was a quantum leap in and of itself, introducing 3D animation into what had always been a 2D environment, as well as offering the control afforded by expressions, which are based on JavaScript. These are great developments, and by the time you make your way through this book, you'll know a good deal more about them than you do now. If you're new to this corner of the universe, don't worry. We'll tell you what all these things mean a bit later. For the moment, you should focus your attention on the basics of this program that have made it such a powerful tool from the very beginning.

Note

The Quick Start "chapter" is our introduction to new users of After Effects. If you're an After Effects veteran, you probably don't have much to gain from the following exercises. If that's the case, you may want to use the book as a desktop reference. We leave it up to you.

Building an After Effects Project

Without any more drum rolls, go ahead and fire up your machine and start After Effects by double-clicking its application icon. When you open up the program for the first time, you are greeted with the splash screen while the application loads, and then you see an empty Project window and some palettes. Before you get overly concerned with exactly what these are, start building good habits by saving your project.

On the DVD-ROM

In order for these opening exercises to work properly, you need to copy the *Source Material* folder from the DVD-ROM to your hard drive. Over the course of the Quick Start chapter, you'll be working with a number of files that we put in this folder. We provide you with a QuickTime movie that we rendered from our own project using the same elements. The movie is called *QS Rendered.mov*, and we suggest that you look at it to get a sense of the composition you'll be building. Also, if you want to look at the finished version of the After Effects project that you're going to create in this chapter, take a look at the one called *Quick Start.aep*. You can find both the finished project file and the QuickTime movie in the *Project Files/Quick Start* folder. If you want to get the most out of the chapter, you may not want to open the finished After Effects project until you've tried to complete the project on your own.

Saving a project

After you initially open the application, by default, After Effects creates a project called *Untitled Project.aep*. Change that and give this project a name. Choose

File ⇨ Save As and the Save Project As dialog box opens up. Name the file something such as *My Quick Start project.aep* and save it in a location where you plan on saving your After Effects work.

Caution

You should make a habit of keeping the .aep file extension on the tail-end of all your After Effects project files. There are a couple of good reasons for this. First of all, if you're working on a Windows-based PC, your system may not recognize the file without the correct extension. Secondly, if you're working on a Mac, while it doesn't matter because the OS will recognize the file whether or not you add the extension, if you ever want to bring your project into a PC environment, the .aep file extension will suddenly become an issue. In short, we recommend that you get in the habit of ending your project filenames with .aep. See Figure QS-1.

Figure QS-1: An After Effects project file uses the .aep extension and contains links to various media, not the actual media.

After Effects project files are interesting animals, because they don't contain any actual media. If you're a video editor, you're used to this concept because video-editing applications work in a similar fashion. This may not seem overly remarkable when you first think about it, but we should mention that most other programs handle the job of saving their respective files somewhat differently. For example, when you save a Photoshop or word-processor file, you're writing the contents of that file to disk. When you save an After Effects project, you're saving a file that contains links to the media that are used by the project, not the actual media itself. For example, imagine that you've brought a QuickTime movie into your After Effects project. After you save the project file, if for some reason it is inadvertently deleted, the QuickTime movie won't be lost. What's lost is the project file containing the link to the QuickTime movie. This will make more sense as you move through the chapter, but that's the basic idea behind the actual contents of an After Effects project file.

Importing media

Now that you saved your project file, it's time to move on to the fun stuff. Before you can start moving elements around, you need to bring some into your project. After you complete the following steps, you'll have everything you need to start animating.

STEPS: Bringing Elements into Your Project

1. **Choose File ⇨ Import ⇨ Multiple Files.** This opens up the Import Multiple Files dialog box shown in Figure QS-2.

Figure QS-2: Choose File ⇨ Import ⇨ Multiple Files
to open the Import Multiple Files dialog box.

2. **Navigate your way to the location where you copied the files from the DVD-ROM to your hard drive and select the *Quick Start Media* folder by clicking it.**

3. **Click the Import Folder button above the Open button at the lower-right corner of the Import Multiple Files dialog box.**

4. **After you successfully do this, click the Done button to the left of the Open button.**

5. **In the Project window, twirl open the *Quick Start Media* folder by clicking the small triangle to the left of it.** Doing this displays the contents of the folder you just imported.

Okay, mission accomplished. You successfully brought in all the media you're going to use to create your animation.

Select any of the footage items under the *Quick Start Media* folder by clicking them once, and a thumbnail sketch of the item appears at the top of the Project window, along with some information describing the file's vital statistics. Look at Figure QS-3 to see what After Effects has to say about some of the media you imported.

You may have noticed the asterisk following your project name at the top of the Project window. This is After Effects' way of telling you that your file has been modified since the last time you saved it. Because you just imported all that media, you should save your project. As a general rule, anytime you make significant changes to your project file, you should save them. Go ahead and choose File ⇨ Save and do it regularly in the future. You'll be glad you did.

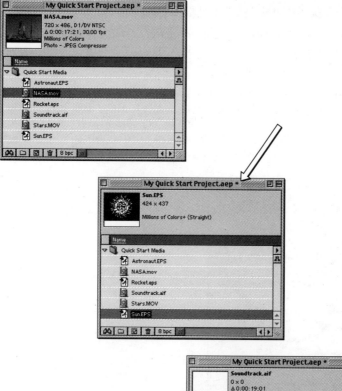

Figure QS-3: If you click a footage item in the Project window, After Effects will show you a thumbnail of the file and tell you everything it knows about it.

Caution

If you remember what we told you earlier, then you'll know that your project file now contains links to the media you just imported. This is an important detail, and we'll explain why. If you were to quit After Effects and move any of the media files you just imported to a different location on your hard drive, the next time you opened up the project, After Effects would report the moved files as missing. Later on in the book, we explain how to relink your project to files that have been moved, but at this point, you should at least be aware of the fact that moving media around the different folders of your hard drive can result in problems.

Creating and developing a composition

Now it's time to take the elements you just imported and place them in a composition. In order to animate the various footage items in the Project window, you need to create a composition, more commonly known as a *comp*.

In this particular project, the two movie clips and the soundtrack provide the backdrop for the entire animation. If you want to look at a footage item in more detail, hold down the Option/Alt key and double-click it. Try this with the file called *NASA.mov,* and the QuickTime movie opens up in its own Footage window (see Figure QS-4).

Figure QS-4: If you want to take a closer look at a footage item in the Project window, hold down the Option/Alt key and double-click it to open it in its own Footage window.
Image courtesy of ArtBeats (NASA — The Early Years)

After you open up the file in its own Footage window, press the spacebar to play the file's contents. It won't play in real time, but all the frames will play, so you can see what's in it. After you finish previewing the contents of the clip, press the spacebar again to stop playback and close the window by clicking the button at its upper-left corner. If you're curious, take a look at the other elements in the Project window by using the same method.

At this point, you want to create a 15-second composition that's built to properly contain the footage that you'll be using as the backdrop for your animation. Complete the following steps to set up your new comp.

Tip

"To err is human." Before you race ahead, take comfort in the fact that After Effects is very forgiving. If you make a few mistakes as you work your way through this introduction, know that you can always undo your last action by choosing Edit ⇨ Undo. Don't be gun shy. If things don't work out as you intended, invoke the Undo command. By default, you can actually undo your last 20 actions! In other words, try and complete the exercises without fearing that you might make some destructive and irrevocable error. Have a good time, and go forward with confidence. If only life were so easy.

STEPS: Setting Up Your Comp

1. **Choose Composition ⇨ New Composition.** This opens up the Composition Settings dialog box shown in Figure QS-5.

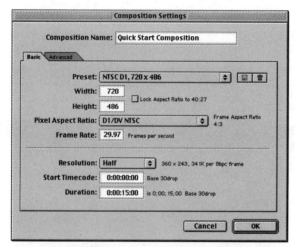

Figure QS-5: The Composition Settings dialog box defines the dimensions, duration, pixel aspect ratio, and frame rate of your comp, among other details.

2. **Click in the Composition Name field and type the name that you want to use for your new comp.**

3. **From the Preset menu, select the NTSC D1, 720 x 486 option.** This matches the dimensions of the clips you use as the backdrop for the animation.

4. **Click in the Duration field and specify a value of 0:00:15:00 for 15 seconds.**

5. **From the Resolution menu, select Full.**

6. **Click OK.**

After you click OK, you'll see a pretty dramatic change in the appearance of the After Effects interface. The three main windows that comprise the After Effects workspace should now be visible: the Project window, the Comp window, and the Timeline window. Your new comp also appears as its own footage item in the Project window. If you want, you can move the various windows wherever you want to on your desktop. Stay tuned; the fun begins pretty soon.

Adding footage to your composition

Let's get right to it. Click and drag the *NASA.mov* footage item from the Project window to the Timeline, releasing the mouse after it's positioned over the left area underneath the Source Name column. After you finish doing this, you'll see that the *NASA.mov* QuickTime movie is centered in the Comp window, and it also appears as a layer in the Timeline. Your workspace should now resemble Figure QS-6. You're on your way, gang.

Project window   Comp window

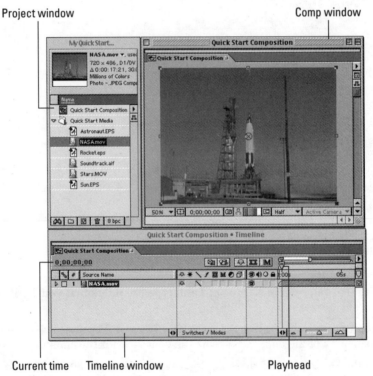

Current time   Timeline window   Playhead

Figure QS-6: After you finish placing the *NASA.mov* QuickTime movie into your new comp, you see that it's centered in the Comp window and also appears as a layer in the Timeline.

Image courtesy of ArtBeats (NASA — The Early Years)

Trimming and animating layers

Now it's time to start layering and animating your composition. First, you're going to put a couple of layers of video into the comp to serve as a backdrop. Then you add a soundtrack. As soon as you put together this basic setup, you add some line art and begin animating the layers and adding a couple of effects to them. Before long, you will have a small production on your hands.

STEPS: Trimming a Layer in the Timeline

1. **Click and drag the current time marker or the playhead as some of us like to call it, toward the right.** This displays a dynamic preview of your comp in the Comp window, which in this case reveals the frames of the *NASA.mov* layer, because it's the only item you added to the mix so far.

2. **Position the playhead about nine seconds from the beginning of the comp.** For visual reference, that's about one second into the dissolve from the rocket lifting off to the shot of the one and only John Glenn. You want to trim the layer so that it stops playing at this point.

3. **Select the layer by clicking the layer's name in the Timeline, which gives it a highlighted appearance.**

4. **Hold down the Option/Alt key and then press the right bracket key.** This trims the layer's Out point at the current time. Look at Figure QS-7 to make sure that you did this correctly.

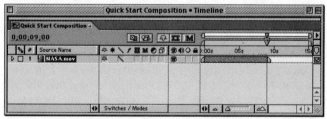

Figure QS-7: With the *NASA.mov* layer selected in the Timeline and the playhead positioned at approximately nine seconds into the comp, hold down the Option/Alt key, and then press the right bracket key to trim the layer's Out point.

Tip

Setting a layer's In point to the current time simply involves holding down the Option/Alt key and then pressing the left bracket key.

Well done. Now you want to add another layer of video to the comp and create a simple transition between the two layers.

STEPS: Animating Opacity

1. **In the Timeline, drag the playhead back roughly one second so that the Current Time is about eight seconds into the comp.**

2. **In exactly the same way you added the *NASA.mov* layer to the Timeline, drag the *Stars.MOV* layer from the Project window into the Timeline.** Be careful not to release the mouse until you've positioned it underneath the *NASA.mov* layer. This is indicated by a thick black line appearing under, not over, the *NASA.mov* layer. When you add a layer to the Timeline, you see that its In point is set to the current time, as indicated by the position of the playhead. When you add a layer to a comp in this manner, After Effects gives you control over where you want to position it in the layer stacking order of the Timeline. If you release the mouse while the thick black line is above the *NASA.mov* layer, the *Stars.MOV* layer is placed above the *NASA.mov* layer.

3. **Twirl open the properties of the *NASA.mov* layer by clicking the little triangle to the left of the layer name.** This reveals three categories of layer properties: Masks, Effects, and Transform.

4. **Twirl open the transform properties, which are the following: Anchor Point, Position, Scale, Rotation, and Opacity.**

5. **Click the stopwatch icon to the left of the Opacity property name.** This sets an opacity keyframe at the current time, which is represented by the little diamond-shaped object on the same line as the Opacity property in the Timeline. The idea here is that you're going to fade this layer out over the course of about one second, and you're going to accomplish that by setting two opacity keyframes for the layer that are one second apart and have values of 100% and 0%, respectively.

> **Note**
>
> Not everyone knows what Opacity means. It's better to think of it in terms of transparency. By default, a layer is set to 100% Opacity, meaning that it's fully opaque. If you change a layer's opacity to 0%, then it's completely transparent, or invisible.

6. **Press O to go to the layer's Out point, which you just trimmed at approximately nine seconds.**

7. **Click the numerical field to the right of the Opacity property name, which presently indicates a value of 100%.** The field becomes highlighted after you click it, indicating that you can now edit this value.

8. **Type the number 0 and press Return.** This sets a second opacity keyframe with a value of 0%. Your Timeline should resemble Figure QS-8.

9. **Drag the playhead through the area in the Timeline where you just set the keyframes, and you should see that the image of John Glenn fades into a background of stars as the comp progresses from roughly eight to nine seconds.**

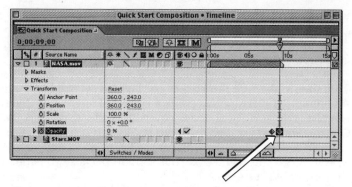

Figure QS-8: By now, you created an opacity keyframe animation for the *NASA.mov* layer, fading it from 100% to 0% over the course of approximately one second.

By now, you're picking up a lot of skills that are universal in the realm of After Effects. This brief exercise is your introduction to creating keyframe animations. This is what After Effects is really all about on some level, because the power of the software lies in its capability to change the properties of a layer by interpolating between different keyframe values over a specifically defined timeframe. As soon as you know how to set keyframes, basically, you've got the keys to the kingdom. Welcome! We wish you many happy returns.

So far, this may seem more like traditional video editing than anything else. Hang on. We still have a few tricks left to show you.

Adding an effect to a layer

Now that you've set up a pretty visual backdrop with the two crossfading layers of video, it's time to add some more elements to your composition. Next up on your list are the EPS files in the Project window. The next phase in building your composition involves adding these files as well as learning how to apply an effect to a layer. After all, an introduction to After Effects wouldn't seem right without including at least an effect or two.

STEPS: Applying Effects

1. **Drag the playhead so that it lies somewhere between the two opacity keyframes that you just set (between eight and nine seconds, approximately).**

2. **Click and drag the *Rocket.eps* file from the Project window to the top of the layer stacking order in the Timeline.** Again, when you add a layer to the Timeline, you see that it's In point is set to the current time, as indicated by the position of the playhead. This particular file happens to be black, and you need it to be white in order to blend well in front of a black backdrop full of stars. You may have guessed that there's a fix for this particular problem.

EPS files are vector graphics, and you can create them with applications such as Illustrator or Freehand. Vector graphics differ from bitmap images like those you might create using Photoshop, because their image quality remains consistent regardless of how much you enlarge them.

3. **In the Timeline, make sure the *Rocket.eps* layer is selected and choose Effect ➪ Channel ➪ Invert.** At this point, a couple of interesting things happen. First of all, the layer you just added is now white instead of black, and the Effect Controls window for the *Rocket.eps* layer opens up (see Figure QS-9). Inside it, you'll see the Effect Controls for the Invert effect you just applied. For now, you can go ahead and close this window because you don't need to modify any of the effect's properties.

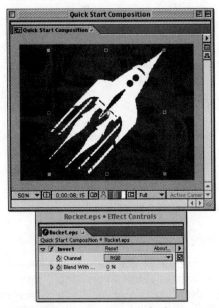

Figure QS-9: After you apply the Invert effect, the *Rocket.eps* layer is now white instead of black. Also, notice the Effect Controls window, which opens up when you apply an effect.

Image courtesy of ArtBeats (NASA – The Early Years), Creatas, and EyeWire by Getty Images www.gettyimages.com (Cosmic Moves)

Another noteworthy aspect to the *Rocket.eps* layer is the fact that it contains transparency, more commonly known as an *alpha channel.* To see exactly which part of the file is transparent, Option/Alt+double-click on the *Rocket.eps* file in the Project window to open it in its own Footage window and then click the Show Alpha Channel button, as shown in Figure QS-10. Working with alpha channels will become critical as you continue learning After Effects. The art of compositing, or blending multiple layers, wouldn't amount to much without transparency.

Figure QS-10: To see exactly which part of the file is transparent, Option/Alt+double-click the *Rocket.eps* file in the Project window to open it in its own Footage window and then click the Show Alpha Channel button.

Image courtesy of Creatas

4. **Because EPS files don't look so great at Draft quality, set the layer to Best quality by clicking the switch that looks like a jagged line to the right of the layer's name in the Timeline.** Doing this changes the switch from a jagged line to a smooth line, and more importantly, the layer will look much cleaner in the Comp window.

That's a very brief introduction to effects, but at the very least, now you know how to actually apply them. That's it; just select a layer in the Timeline and then choose an effect from the Effect menu. You have a lot of them at your beck and call, and even more if you invest in the Production Bundle of After Effects.

Now that you've got this unwieldy cartoon rocket sitting in the middle of the frame, it's time to scale it down and rotate it so that it's pointing up.

Animating a layer's Transform properties

We already mentioned the Transform properties: Anchor Point, Position, Scale, Rotation, and Opacity. You already adjusted and animated a layer's opacity. Now it's time to adjust the Rocket's Scale and Rotation, and when you're done with that, you animate its Position.

STEPS: Adjusting Rotation and Scale

1. **In the Comp window, click and drag one of the corners of the Rocket's bounding box in toward its center.** As you drag, press and hold down the Shift key to guarantee that the change in scale happens evenly across height and width. The Info palette tells you how much progress you're making as you scale it down. Release the mouse when the Info palette tells you that you've reached 25% of the file's original scale.

Tip   If, for some reason, the Info palette isn't visible, choose Window ➪ Info.

2. **Select the Rotate tool from the Tools palette (it looks like a circle made from an arrow), and click and drag on one of the corners of the Rocket.** In much the same way you constrained the proportions of the Rocket's scale, press and hold down the Shift key as you drag, and this locks changes to the layer's rotation in 45 degree increments. When the Rocket is pointing up (which it will after you rotate it by –45 degrees), you can release the mouse. If you twirl open the Transform properties for the Rocket layer, your Timeline and Comp window should resemble Figure QS-11.

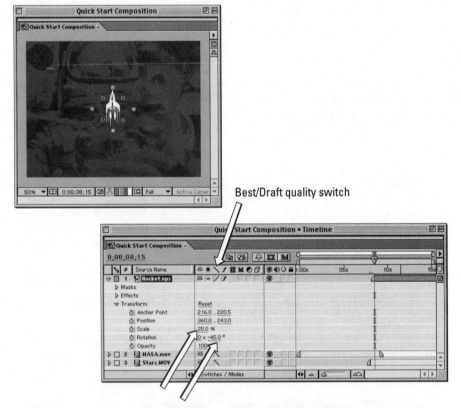

Figure QS-11: After you apply the Invert effect to the Rocket, you want to scale it down to 25% of its original size and rotate it by –45 degrees.

Images courtesy of ArtBeats (NASA — The Early Years), Creatas, and EyeWire by Getty Images www.gettyimages.com (Cosmic Moves)

Tip   If, for some reason, the Tools palette isn't visible, choose Window ➪ Tools.

Okay. Now it's time for you to make this rocket fly through space.

STEPS: Animating Position

1. **Choose the Selection tool (the one that looks like a regular mouse pointer) from the Tools palette and click and drag the little Rocket down off the bottom edge of the comp.** As you drag, hold down the Shift key to limit the positional change to the vertical plane, or Y-axis. After it's positioned just out of view, release the mouse. The rocket's bounding box should still be visible underneath the comp.

2. **If you haven't already, twirl open the Transform properties for the Rocket layer and click the stopwatch next to the Position property name to set an initial positional keyframe.**

3. **Drag the playhead forward by a couple of seconds (this is approximately 10 or 11 seconds into the comp).**

4. **Now, click and drag the Rocket up off the top edge of the comp.** As you drag, hold down the Shift key to continue limiting the positional change to the vertical plane, or Y-axis. After it's positioned just out of view, release the mouse. This sets a second keyframe and creates an animation in which the rocket comes on from the bottom of the comp and flies off at the top.

5. **Drag the playhead back and forth through the timeframe of the positional animation to see what you did.** See Figure QS-12.

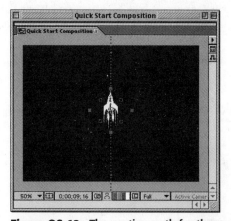

Figure QS-12: The motion path for the rocket is made visible by the dotted line running through it. Each dot represents the Rocket's position at a given frame of the comp.
Image courtesy of EyeWire by Getty Images
www.gettyimages.com (Cosmic Moves)

The overall idea here is to jump from the literal world of John Glenn's lift-off into a cartoon-like realm in which you'll create the rest of the animation.

Duplicating layers

After you bring a file into a comp, getting a lot of mileage from it is easy because you can duplicate any layer to your heart's content. In the next exercise, you add another EPS file, apply the Invert effect to it once again, scale it down as you did with the Rocket, and duplicate it so that you can animate multiple copies of it in the Comp window.

STEPS: Making Two Astronauts from One

1. **Drag the playhead to the frame in which you added the Rocket layer.** If you look at the Timeline, you'll see that you set the In point of the Rocket roughly halfway between eight and nine seconds.

2. **From the Project window, drag the *Astronaut.EPS* footage item into the Timeline.**

3. **Apply the Invert effect to it like you did with the Rocket layer.** Remember that the layer needs to be selected in order for you to apply an effect to it.

4. **In a manner similar to the way you transformed the Rocket, set the Astronaut layer to Best quality and scale it down to about 25%.**

5. **With the Astronaut layer selected in the Timeline, choose Edit ⇨ Duplicate.** This makes a copy of the layer.

6. **In the Comp window, drag the Astronaut to a location on either the left or the right side of the comp.** As you do so, you'll notice that a duplicate of the Astronaut is left behind in its original position.

7. **Move the second Astronaut to the side opposite to where you just positioned the last one.** See Figure QS-13 for reference.

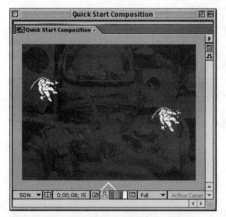

Figure QS-13: After you add a layer to a comp, you can duplicate it as many times as you like. In this animation, there are two instances of the Astronaut—one on either side of the comp.

Image courtesy of ArtBeats (NASA – The Early Years), Creatas, and EyeWire by Getty Images www.gettyimages.com (Cosmic Moves)

8. **Create your own positional animations for the Astronaut layers by using the same method you learned with the Rocket in the last set of steps.** This time, you don't have to constrict the layer's movement to either the horizontal or vertical planes, and for that matter, the animations don't have to begin or end off-screen.

You have some creative license here. Animate the positions of the Astronauts in any way you see fit.

On the DVD-ROM Remember, if you want a loose guideline, look at the QuickTime movie we rendered from our project. It's called *QS Rendered.mov*, and if you're curious, you can find it in the *Project Files/Quick Start* folder.

Adding a soundtrack to your comp

Animations often derive some added punch from a soundtrack, especially if key parts of your animation coincide with cymbal crashes or other dramatic high points in the audio. Now that your animation is starting to come together, it's time to add an audio file to your comp. After you do this, we show you how to mark the points in the soundtrack that might benefit from a matching visual.

STEPS: Previewing Audio and Adding Layer Markers

1. **Press the Home key to return the playhead to the first frame of the comp.**

2. **Drag the *Soundtrack.aif* footage item from the Project window to the bottom of the stacking order in the Timeline.** After you line it up so that it is the bottom layer, release the mouse.

3. **Choose Edit ⇨ Preferences ⇨ Previews.**

4. **Click in the Audio Preview duration field, enter a value of "1500," and click OK.** This changes the length of the Audio Preview from the default of four seconds to 15.

5. **Make sure that the audio layer is selected in the Timeline and then press the period key on the numeric keypad to hear an audio preview of your comp.** Be forewarned: The audio loops continuously until you press a key to stop it.

6. **At the key points during the progression of the soundtrack, add markers to the built-in climaxes by pressing the asterisk key on the numeric keypad.** We found the points at approximately 10 and 14 seconds to be the most dramatic and added markers in those spots.

Caution If you didn't select the soundtrack layer in the last step, then no markers will be added.

7. To stop the audio preview, press any key. The markers you added during the preview are now visible on the Soundtrack layer in the Timeline. If you want to delete any of them, Control+click/right-click them and choose Delete this marker.

Just as a point of interest, twirl open the Soundtrack layer's properties and then twirl open the Audio and Waveform properties. The audio waveform of the soundtrack is visible in the Timeline, and this information often provides an invaluable guide when you're setting keyframes for dramatic effect. Look at Figure QS-14 for reference.

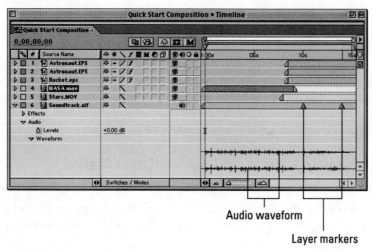

Audio waveform

Layer markers

Figure QS-14: In addition to previewing an audio track and adding markers to it in real time, you can "see" an audio layer by opening up its waveform in the Timeline.

Timing your animations to coincide with sound cues

You only need to add a couple more finishing touches, and you are all set. Now that you've gotten familiar with the feel of the audio track, you must admit that there's something begging to be done with that rousing cymbal crash/horn blast finale at about 10 seconds. The following is a suggestion. As is always the case with anything we show you how to do in this book, what really matters is your own creativity. We're merely providing you with techniques. That said, keep going, because you're almost done.

Enlarging the scale of vector graphics

We want to mention another detail about using EPS graphics in After Effects. If you ever need to scale an EPS vector graphic (such as an Illustrator file or a Freehand file) past 100%, you need to turn on its Continuously Rasterize switch to make sure that it scales cleanly. This is made clear in the following steps.

STEPS: Animating on a Big Scale

1. **Drag the playhead to the marker that you added to the audio layer at approximately 10 seconds into the comp.**

   Note   We're assuming that you added a marker here. The rest of the steps are designed to create a scale animation to coincide with the musical climax of the audio file. Even so, the concept of scaling vector graphics is universal.

2. **Drag the *Sun.EPS* footage item from the Project window to the top of the layer stacking order in the Timeline.** This sets its In point to the current time.

3. **Set the Sun layer to Best quality.**

4. **In the Timeline, twirl open the Sun layer's Transform properties.**

5. **Click the stopwatch next to the Scale property name to set an initial keyframe.**

6. **Position the mouse over the numerical field indicating the value for the Sun's scale.** When the pointer turns into a hand with an outstretched finger, click and drag to the left until the scale value reads 0%. This method of changing a property's value is known as *scrubbing*.

7. **Drag the playhead forward by approximately two seconds.**

8. **Scrub the Sun's scale value up to 600%.** This sets a second keyframe. Only problem is that it looks pretty poor. At 600% scale, the Sun looks blurry and artifacted, if not downright ugly.

9. **Turn on the Sun layer's Continuously Rasterize switch.** This neat switch enables you to scale up an EPS file to outrageous proportions while maintaining razor sharp image quality. See Figure QS-15 for reference.

Now that you've got a scale animation that's timed to go with the soundtrack, we can show you two more tricks. No introduction to After Effects is complete without some mention of text, so we're going to cover that next.

Continuously Rasterize switch

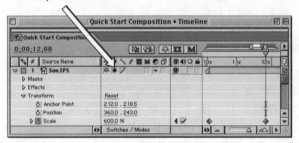

Figure QS-15: Before you turn on the Sun's Continuously Rasterize switch, it looks pretty crummy when it's scaled up to 600%. By contrast, its detail is remarkable once you turn this switch on.

Images courtesy of Creatas

Using the Basic Text effect

A great deal of the work you do in After Effects will involve the use of typography. You have a number of ways to work with text in the application, and you look at all of those a bit later in the book. In the meantime, we show you how to quickly add text to your comp by creating a solid and applying the Basic Text effect to it.

STEPS: Creating a Solid as a Vessel for Text

1. **Choose Layer ⇨ New ⇨ Solid.**

2. **In the Solid Settings dialog box that opens up, name the solid *Text*, click the Make Comp Size button, and then click OK.** For the moment, this new addition completely obscures the other layers of you comp. Don't worry. You fix that in a second.

3. **With the new solid *Text* layer selected in the Timeline, choose Effect ⇨ Text ⇨ Basic Text.**

4. **Next, you are presented with a dialog box in which you can enter whatever text you want by using whatever font suits your taste.** After you finish, click OK. At this point, the solid layer which hid all your work a moment ago is replaced with a bright red and rather pixelated rendering of the text that you just entered, and the Effect Controls window for the Basic Text effect pops open.

5. **In the Effect Controls window, twirl open the groups of properties to see what this effect can do for you (see Figure QS-16).** There are various properties you can control, such as the color and size of the text. For example, to change the color of the text from the default red, click once on the dropper, drag it over anything you want, and click again to set the color to the area of the desktop that you clicked on.

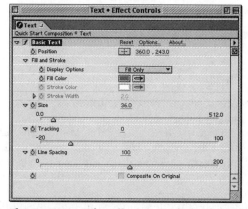

Figure QS-16: The Effect Controls for the Basic Text effect enable you to change the color and size of the text you entered in Step 4, among other properties.

6. **Set the solid Text layer to Best quality.** This fixes the pixelated look of the characters.

For more control, you can move the position of this layer wherever you want in the Comp window, and you can also use opacity keyframes to control when to fade the text in and out.

Enabling Motion Blur

We have one last little introductory production trick to tell you about. If you create any high-speed positional animations for any of the layers, you can add a "realistic" look to them by enabling Motion Blur. For example, you've already sent the Rocket across the vertical length of the comp, and if you want to blur it in relation to its speed, you can turn on its Motion Blur switch. The only caveat is that you also need to enable Motion Blur for the entire comp. Figure QS-17 explains how you can incorporate this trick into your animation.

Individual Motion Blur switch for a layer

Enable Motion Blur in the Comp

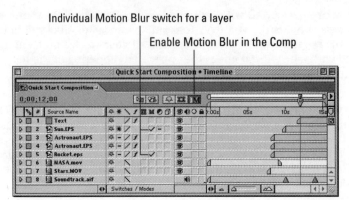

Figure QS-17: If you want to add a realistic Motion Blur to fast-moving objects in your comp, enable Motion Blur at the composition level by clicking the Motion Blur switch at the top of the Timeline as well as turning it on for any individual layers that you want to blur.

Putting on the finishing touches

By now, you know enough to create some pretty solid animations. You can create a composition, import media into your project, add elements to your comp, animate their properties, apply effects to layers, use text, and enable Motion Blur, among other things. Again, if you're at a loss for creative ideas (which we highly doubt), you can reverse engineer the QuickTime movie we rendered from our own project called *QS Rendered.mov,* or you can take a look at our project file called *Quick Start.aep.*

Now that you've got a few animation techniques under your belt, finish building out your comp in any way that suits your own creative drive. After you're done, it's time to render a QuickTime movie from your work.

Rendering Your Creation

Now that your animation is finished, it's time to finish your production. The next series of steps net you a QuickTime movie, and your After Effects initiation is complete.

STEPS: Making Your Own QuickTime Movie

1. **Choose Composition ⇨ Make Movie.**

2. **In the Output Movie To dialog box, name the file whatever you want and save it wherever you like.** If you're on a PC, make sure that you keep the .mov file extension. After you finish, click Save. This opens the Render Queue.

3. **Using the pull-down menus to the right of your composition name, select Best Settings from the Render Settings options and select Lossless from the Output Module options.**

4. **Click the blue words that read Best Settings, and you are presented with the Render Settings dialog box.** Select Half from the Resolution pop-up menu, accept the remaining defaults, and click OK.

5. **Click the blue word that reads Lossless, and you are presented with the Output Module Settings dialog box.** Click the Format Options button, which opens the Compression Settings dialog box. Move the Quality slider to Low and click OK. Back in the Output Module Settings dialog box, click the Audio Output check box to turn it on, accept the remaining defaults, and click OK.

6. **Click the Render button in the upper-right corner of the Render Queue, and After Effects puts together your QuickTime movie.** It tells you when it's finished by sounding off like happy bells. At that point, you can play your newly rendered QuickTime movie. It is a relatively large file, but that's okay for your purposes right now.

Congratulations! You're on your way. From these humble beginnings, you can already see how much you can accomplish with After Effects, and the best is certainly yet to be.

✦   ✦   ✦

Welcome to After Effects 5

Working in After Effects: Finding Your Way Around the Interface

Before revolutionizing the world's understanding of art history with your work in After Effects, you'll probably benefit from investing a bit of time learning the actual logic behind the software. After you learn the fundamentals, you'll find the program to be a clear channel for your creativity rather than a stumbling block on the way to realizing your vision. In this chapter, we explain the basics on working in After Effects.

What do you use After Effects for, anyway? In case you don't know the answer, the idea behind the software lies in its name. "After" you've imported QuickTime movies, Illustrator and Photoshop files, and whatever other elements you've prepared for a project, you can apply "Effects" to them before rendering your final masterpiece. Such a description is admittedly vague and general, but it serves as a useful starting point for a more detailed explanation. Going from there, you might ask, "How does it do that?"

The answer lies in learning the functions of the various windows and palettes in the application's interface. By the time you finish reading this chapter, you should know what the Project, Comp, and Timeline windows are. You'll also know what the tools in the Tools palette actually do. Better than that, you'll know how to import elements into a project, create a composition, and save your project. Along the way, you'll pick up a few tips that will save you time as you make your way through the latter parts of the book. Don't sweat it; the folks at Adobe have done such a great job designing the application, you'll find that most things work intuitively.

Establishing Home Base: The Project Window

All your work in After Effects begins with the project file. The project file references all the media you import in order to create your design. It also contains compositions that you create by using that imported media. When you start After Effects, it opens an empty project by default. Figure 1-1 displays the empty Project window.

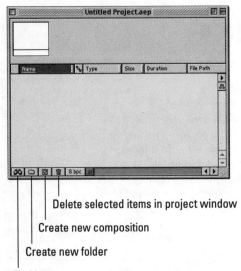

Delete selected items in project window

Create new composition

Create new folder

Find item

Figure 1-1: The Project window contains no media when you start After Effects.

Looking ahead: What are you making?

Before starting an After Effects project, you should think about exactly what you're trying to accomplish. Specifically, you need to know your delivery format. Ultimately, how are you going to deliver the goods? Are you making film titles, or are the fruits of your labor going to be viewed as NTSC video on tape? Maybe you've been asked to create a video that will be streamed on the Web or viewed on a DVD. Perhaps you're creating a flash animation or an animated GIF for a Web page. You need to be clear on these details first, because they will determine important aspects of your compositions.

We cover the specific meaning of terms such as NTSC video in Chapter 28.

Regardless of the delivery format, you make your compositions from various footage items. Before layering footage into compositions, let's look at the various kinds of footage that After Effects handles. In terms of After Effects, footage is really a synonym for your source material.

Footage can come in the shape of video clips, still images, and sounds. Within those basic descriptions, you can use many different kinds of these media types. As far as After Effects is concerned, video clips can be enormous film files that run at 24 fps (frames per second), or they may be somewhat smaller NTSC video clips that run at 30 fps. A video clip can just as easily take the shape of tiny 160 x 120 pixel files that run at 15 fps. The point is that After Effects can handle almost any variant in the video world, and the term "video clip" is a very open-ended definition for this kind of footage item.

In the realm of still images, After Effects recognizes just as many different kinds of formats. Independent of resolution, your project can include TIFFs, PICTs, JPEGs, and GIFs to name but a few. Actually, you are limited to footage items beneath the threshold of 30,000 x 30,000 pixels (!), but we're guessing that you're probably going to stay under this limit for the moment.

Other footage elements include audio files, 3D graphics files, Photoshop files, Illustrator or other vector-based EPS files, and so on. The basic premise is that you can load up your After Effects project with all manner of digital creations. What matters in the end is how you layer those footage items into compositions.

Importing Footage Items into the Project Window

Now that we've established that you need footage items to create compositions in After Effects, you should import some media into an After Effects project.

The following exercise uses footage items, which are located on the DVD-ROM in a folder called *Source Material*. Note that you need to copy the *Source Material* folder from the DVD-ROM to your hard drive.

Feel free to import any items you like. We've provided you with some items to get you going, but if you have your own elements, by all means, use them. These general concepts apply regardless of the media you import.

STEPS: Learning How to Import Footage

1. **Open After Effects by double-clicking its shortcut on your desktop if you haven't already.** An empty project named *Untitled Project.aep* opens.

2. **Choose File ⇨ Import ⇨ File (Command+I/Ctrl+I).** You are presented with a dialog box.

3. Select the *Source Material* **folder and click Open.**

4. Select the *QuickTime* **folder and click Open.**

5. Select the *ArtBeats* **folder and click Open.**

6. Select the *NA103.mov* **clip and click Import (as shown in Figure 1-2).**

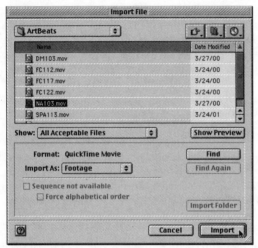

Figure 1-2: The Import File dialog box enables you to import footage into your After Effects project.

7. **Choose File ➪ Import ➪ Multiple Files (Command+Option+I/Ctrl+Alt+I). This** method allows you to import more than one file at a time.

8. **Using the dialog box, navigate your way to the *Title.ai* file located inside** **the *Illustrator* folder and click Import.** The *Illustrator* folder is contained in the *Stills* folder, which is also in the *Source Material* folder. After you finish importing this file, the dialog box remains open, enabling you to continue importing files.

9. **Using the dialog box, navigate your way to the *BlynBrg.pict* file located** **inside the *Photoshop* folder and click Import.** The *Photoshop* folder is contained in the *Stills* folder, which is also in the *Source Material* folder.

10. **Click Done to close the dialog box (as shown in Figure 1-3).** This returns you to your After Effects Project window.

Now that three footage items are in this After Effects project, you can examine each individual item's various properties in detail.

11. **Click the *NA103.mov* clip in the Project window.** The file is highlighted, and many of its details are carefully explained to the right of its thumbnail picture in the Project window, as shown in Figure 1-4.

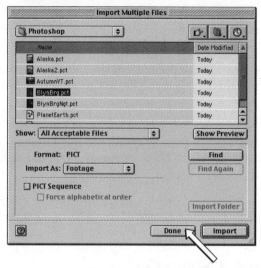

Figure 1-3: Clicking Done returns you to your After Effects project after you have finished importing files in the slightly different Import Multiple Files dialog box.

Selected file   File properties

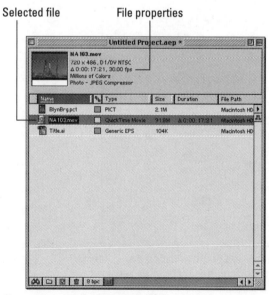

Figure 1-4: The selected file's properties are laid out in detail next to the file's thumbnail sketch in the Project window.

According to After Effects, this is a 91.8MB QuickTime file that runs for 17 seconds and 21 frames with a given frame rate of 30 frames per second. Going further, the movie is sized at 720 by 486 pixels, and those pixels are not square but rectangular as indicated by the D1/DV NTSC aspect ratio listed next to its dimensions. Lastly, the QuickTime file uses the Photo-JPEG codec and contains millions of colors. Go ahead and click any of the individual items in the Project window and read up on each file's details.

Note   If you're new to the world of digital video, don't be scared by words like *codec, aspect ratio,* and *frame rate.* We go into more detail on all these subjects throughout the various chapters of the book. At this point, we only want to introduce you to these terms.

Compositions are also footage items, and they contain other footage items, including other compositions. Next, you create a couple of simple compositions containing some of the files you just imported.

STEPS: Creating a Basic Composition

1. **Choose Composition ➪ New Composition (Command+N/Ctrl+N).** This brings up the Composition Settings dialog box, which explains a number of different options with regard to your composition. See Figure 1-5.

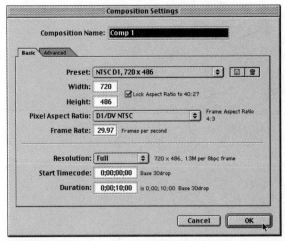

Figure 1-5: The Composition Settings dialog box contains a number of options including Preset comp dimensions, Pixel Aspect Ratio, and Resolution.

Tip   You can also create a new composition by clicking the New Composition button at the bottom of the Project window indicated in Figure 1-6.

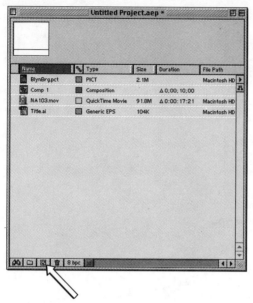

Figure 1-6: Click the New Composition button.

2. **Choose NTSC D1, 720 x 486 from the Preset pull-down menu and choose Full from the Resolution pull-down menu.**

3. **Click OK.** This adds a composition called Comp 1 to your Project window. Comp 1 also appears in the newly visible Comp and Timeline windows.

Tip

After Effects names a new composition Comp 1, Comp 2, and so on by default. You can call your comps whatever you like, but it's a good idea to name them sensibly. Because we're only taking you on a walking tour of the interface, you needn't worry about it too much at this point. As you begin building more sophisticated projects, your naming schemes will become a lot more important as a means of organization.

4. **Drag and drop the *BlynBrg.pct* file on top of the Comp 1 composition in the Project window, as shown in Figure 1-7.**

Your composition called Comp 1 now includes a footage item, which is reflected by the Comp and Timeline windows. See Figure 1-8.

Note

Using this method to add footage to a composition centers the item being added. We show you how to move this added element a little bit later in the chapter.

Tip

You also have a very quick and easy way to create a composition in the Project window. Drag and drop a footage file on top of the New Composition button to create a comp with the exact dimensions (and running time if it's a video clip) of the footage item that you drag onto the button.

Figure 1-7: In the Project window, you can add any item to a composition by dragging and dropping the item on top of the composition.

Comp window   Timeline window

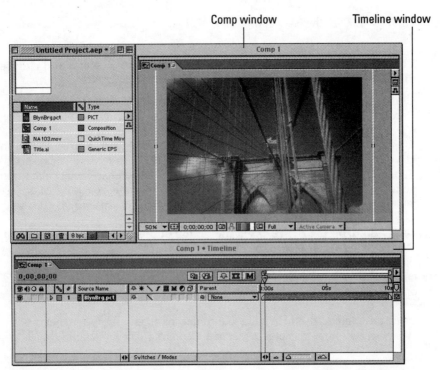

Figure 1-8: The Comp and Timeline windows reflect the addition of a footage item to your new composition.

STEPS: Creating a Composition the Easier Way

1. **Click and drag *NA103.mov* on to the New Composition button in the Project window.** See Figure 1-9.

Figure 1-9: Drag a footage item from the Project window onto the New Composition button to create a comp with the exact dimensions and running time of the footage item being added.

2. **Release the mouse.** Your new composition should appear in the Project, Comp, and Timeline windows.

The new comp is set to the same dimensions, frame rate, and running time of the clip that was used to create it. When created this way, the comp is named after the clip inside it.

Pushing more buttons in the After Effects Project window

You get considerable mileage from the New Composition button at the bottom of the Project window, but you might be curious as to the function of the other ones located there. As you might have guessed, they're not too difficult, and like their New Composition counterpart, they make your work in After Effects more efficient.

Finding the lost clip

You can find footage items in a project window by pressing the button that looks like a pair of binoculars. This invokes the Find command, which you can also bring up by choosing File ➪ Find (Command+Option+G/Ctrl+Alt+G). In a complicated project teeming with footage items, tracking down what you're looking for is easy by entering the first few letters of the footage item's name in the dialog box, as shown in Figure 1-10.

Figure 1-10: The Find command expedites your search for that phantom clip in a project that has grown past the limits of your control.

Don't underestimate the importance of good file-naming habits. Good filenames will make your searches less plentiful and more successful. File-naming conventions are of the utmost importance when working in the PC space. The three-letter file extensions, which represent the various file types, are essential if After Effects is going to properly recognize various footage items. This comes into play in production environments that involve both PCs and Macs. When you import After Effects projects into a PC, things only work as planned if you appropriately name all your source material with the correct file extension, such as MOV, PCT, EPS, and so on.

What's new in After Effects 5.5: Creating a new composition from a selection

When working in After Effects 5.5, you can drag multiple footage items in the Project window to the New Composition button and specify whether you want to create a single composition or multiple compositions in the resulting dialog box shown in Figure SB 1-1. You can also select which footage item's dimensions to use for the new composition settings.

Figure SB 1-1: The New Composition From Selection dialog box offers a number of handy timesaving options.

Tip

As is becoming clear, keyboard shortcuts provide a far more efficient way to work than using menu-driven commands. If you're just getting started, our suggestion is that you begin by working with the menus because the requisite keyboard shortcuts are clearly laid out right next to the commands listed in any menu (see Figure 1-11). Simply by virtue of using the menus again and again, the keyboard shortcuts will slowly but surely become ingrained in your mind. At that point, you'll probably start working almost exclusively with the keyboard shortcuts, because you'll be getting around the interface far more quickly. That beats the prospect of memorizing the six-page foldout of keyboard shortcuts from scratch, doesn't it?

Figure 1-11: Use the menus and start noticing the keyboard shortcuts to the right of the commands.

Good housekeeping

Good housekeeping is an easy way to earn the admiration of your clients and co-workers, maybe even make your mother proud (assuming that she's a neatnik). Make folders. Label them clearly. Keep your footage organized. Fastidious friends and Martha Stewart fans aside, you'll thank yourself for doing this in the end.

How might we bring about this small, albeit important, bit of self-confidence? Press the button that looks like a folder. This invokes the New Folder command, which you can also bring about by choosing File ➪ New ➪ New Folder (Command+Option+Shift+N/Ctrl+Alt+Shift+N). This command makes a new folder in your Project window, which you can rename after creating it (see Figure 1-12). You would be wise to take advantage of folders, sometimes called *bins* in the industry, in order to separate your elements so that your mind remains clear as your project becomes complex.

Figure 1-12: Create new folders and give them sensible names in order to organize your project.

Click the new folder button to create a new folder.

Caution

No reference to clean living is complete without mentioning the delete button. That little trash can at the bottom of the Project window can help rid you of the clutter in your project. Use it carefully. You can drag and drop footage items onto it, or you can click it with items selected in the Project window. You're protected by the Undo command in case you throw out something you need. Nonetheless, be careful here. After Effects warns you if you're deleting items that are actually used in your project.

Sifting and sorting through the footage in the Project window

You can organize the Project window to suit your needs. Click the various columns to organize your view according to the properties of those columns. For example, click Name, and all the items in the Project window are organized in descending alphabetical order. Click Type to organize the items by their file type.

What's new in After Effects 5.5: Replacing one project item with another

Here's a great new one in After Effects version 5.5: Now you can Option/Alt+drag one footage item onto another in the Project window to replace all instances of the original throughout the entire Project. That includes compositions.

You can also set up the view you want. Click and drag the various columns to the left or right and arrange them according to your own priorities. Control+click/ Right-click on the column headings to pull up a contextual menu that enables you to hide or show the various columns that give you details about a file's properties (see Figure 1-13). Finally, you can click and drag the edges of the columns to make them wider or narrower in the Project window.

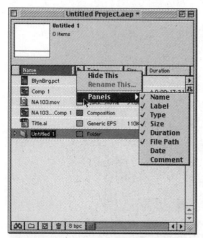

Figure 1-13: Control+click/Right-click on the column headings and choose any category from the contextual menu to add that column to your Project window.

Saving your project

By now, you've made numerous changes to this Untitled Project of yours, and you're running the risk of losing your work the longer you go without saving your project. A quick look at the top of the Project window shows you an asterisk to the right of the project name. This asterisk warns that you've made changes to your project that you haven't saved. So hurry up and save your work by choosing File ➪ Save (Command+S/Ctrl+S), which brings up a Save Project dialog box. Give your project file a name and save it in a handy location, remembering to give it the AEP three-letter file extension if you're working on a PC (or if you're working on a Mac and planning on collaborating with someone working on a PC).

A brief word on this topic might be useful in developing an understanding of the After Effects thought process. Project files contain references to the media they contain. They don't actually hold the source media files. Take a look at the properties of the project file you just created. Project file sizes are usually quite small. This first project is considerably smaller than 1MB. This makes project files perfect for backing up, and it makes a good deal of sense to back up your critical After Effects projects on removable media, such as a Zip disk. Now that you've saved your work, notice how the asterisk is gone from the Project window, as shown in Figure 1-14.

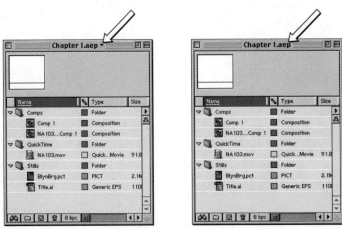

Figure 1-14: The asterisk is gone from the Project window in your newly saved After Effects project. Also, look at the folders and the organization they lend to a project.

Knowing Your Tools

The Toolbox enables you to manipulate layers in a variety of ways. If you're at all familiar with the Adobe way of thinking as expressed in programs such as Photoshop and Illustrator, the notion of the Toolbox will be quite familiar. Ultimately, if you know your way around the Toolbox, you can do anything from creating sophisticated motion paths and masks to moving virtual cameras in three-dimensional space. Before we reach this higher plane of compositing, check out these tools and see what they do. Look at the Toolbox in Figure 1-15.

Tip   Click a tool to make it active or hold the mouse over the tool to get a tool tip. Tool tips tell you what each tool is and give you the tool's keyboard shortcut as well.

The tools in the Toolbox can be divided into separate categories. Table 1-1 describes each tool in detail.

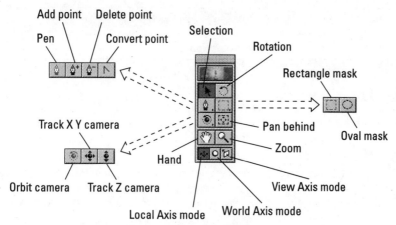

Figure 1-15: The Toolbox contains more tools than you can see. The miniature arrows in the lower-right corner of some tools indicate whether other related tools are available.

	Table 1-1 **The Toolbox**	
Tool	***Name***	***Description***
	Selection	Use to select items.
	Pen	Creates points, which comprise a mask or path. Can be used in either a Footage window or the Comp window.
	Add Point	Adds points to an existing mask or path in either a Footage window or the Comp window.
	Delete Point	Removes points from an existing mask or path in either a Footage window or the Comp window.
	Convert Point	Changes the points of a mask from Bezier to Linear and vice versa. Can be used in either a Footage window or the Comp window.
	Orbit Camera (3D)	Rotates the current view around the point of interest.

Continued

Table 1-1 *(continued)*

Tool	Name	Description
	Track XY Camera (3D)	Adjusts the view horizontally or vertically.
	Track Z Camera (3D)	Adjusts the view along the line leading to and from the point of interest.
	Hand	Moves your view of a comp into the Comp, a Footage, or the Timeline window when the view is scaled beyond the boundaries of the window.
	Rotate	Rotates a layer in the Comp window.
	Rectangular Mask	Creates a rectangular mask on a layer in a Footage window or the Comp window.
	Oval Mask	Creates an oval mask on a layer in either a Footage window or the Comp window.
	Pan Behind	Moves a masked layer behind an existing mask. Also moves a layer's anchor point.
	Zoom	Magnifies a layer or view in a Footage, Comp, or Timeline window.
	Local Axis Mode (3D)	Aligns the axes to the surface of a particular 3D layer.
	World Axis Mode (3D)	Aligns the axes to the absolute coordinates of the composition.
	View Axis Mode (3D)	Aligns the axes to the view you have selected.

Knowing Your Palettes

In addition to the Project, Comp, and Timeline windows are three palettes, the Time Control palette, the Info palette, and the Audio palette. You can view the Info palette by choosing Window ⇨ Info (Command+2/Ctrl+2). Figure 1-16 shows you the other palette selections in the Window menu as well as their keyboard shortcuts.

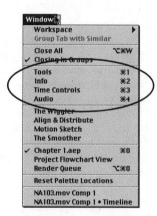

Figure 1-16: The Window menu shows you the various palettes you can display or hide according to your preference. Windows users can substitute Ctrl for the Command symbol when using keyboard shortcuts.

Tip   Pressing the Tab key hides whatever palettes are visible, and pressing it again makes them reappear. Sometimes screen real estate gets a little cramped, and you might find this useful if you want to view your Comp window at a higher magnification.

Decoding the Info palette

The Info palette is a rather nifty aid that tells you color information about a composition in the Comp window as you move the mouse over your artwork. With the Info palette visible and a composition open in the Comp window, drag the mouse across the composition while paying careful attention to the activity in the Info palette (see Figure 1-17). The palette displays Red, Green, Blue, and Alpha channel color values according to the position of your mouse pointer. In and of themselves, these numbers are grayscale values. Each pixel in the Comp window is the visual result of the combined RGBA values visible in the Info palette.

Note   An *alpha channel* refers to the part of an image that is transparent. We cover this subject in far greater detail throughout the book. For the time being, just know that an alpha channel value of 255, or white, is opaque. Conversely, an alpha channel value of 0, or black, is transparent. Values between 0 and 255 represent partial transparency. If a layer contains pixels with alpha channel values that are less than 255, all layers underneath will be visible.

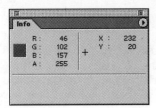

Figure 1-17: The Info palette gives you Red, Green, Blue, and Alpha Channel color information on your composition as well as the X- and Y-coordinates of your mouse.

When not working in the Comp window, the Info palette provides information relevant to other functions in After Effects. For example, if you're moving a layer in the Time Layout window, the Info palette indicates the layer's In and Out points. If you move a layer in the Comp window, the Info palette tells you the X- and Y-coordinates of the layer's center point relative to the composition, the offset from the layer's last position, and the X- and Y-coordinates of that layer's anchor point. This kind of information allows you to position a layer with the utmost precision. As you work in After Effects, you can perform several Undo commands if you've made a mistake and need to retrace your steps. In this case, the Info palette will tell you the steps you are undoing in exact detail. Clicking directly on the Info palette cycles you through the various Color Display modes. All of these uses for the Info palette are shown in Figure 1-18.

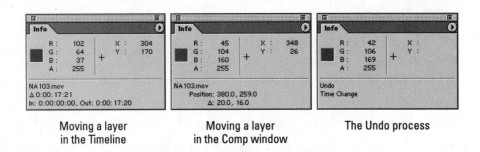

Moving a layer
in the Timeline

Moving a layer
in the Comp window

The Undo process

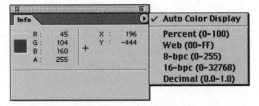

Color Display modes

Figure 1-18: The Info palette returns all kinds of information that are relevant to the task you are performing.

Tip   Only a keyboard shortcut can access another very useful feature involving the Info palette. To reveal a layer's source filename, select a layer in the Timeline window and press Command+Option+E/Ctrl+Alt+E.

Jumping in time with the Time Control palette

The Time Control palette enables you to preview your composition in a number of ways. We rarely use the buttons on the palette to navigate our way through the running time of a composition, but we extensively use the keyboard shortcuts, which invoke the functions of those buttons. Look at Figure 1-19 and the requisite keyboard shortcuts in Table 1-2.

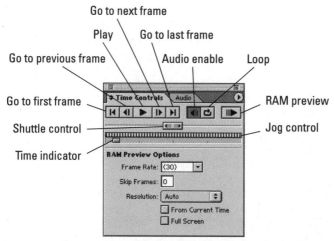

Figure 1-19: The Time Control palette is revised considerably in After Effects 5, especially in its RAM Preview Options.

Table 1-2	
Time Navigation Keyboard Shortcuts	
Function	**Keyboard Shortcut**
First Frame	Home
Back One Frame	Page Up
Play*	Spacebar
Forward One Frame	Page Down
Last Frame	End
RAM Preview	0 (Numeric Keypad)

*As fast as After Effects can play a composition given its resolution.
Usually slower than real-time; sometimes faster.

To us, the most important button in this palette is the RAM Preview button, located all the way to the right at the top row of buttons. Rather than clicking this button, pressing 0 on the numeric keypad is much easier.

We cannot underestimate the importance of the RAM Preview. It is one of the functions of After Effects that you use almost all the time. Because After Effects is not a real-time system, this preview is the only way you can see what your composition will actually look like in real-time before actually rendering it. Go ahead and try it out.

In the Project window, double-click NA103.mov Comp 1 composition. Press 0 on the numeric keypad. After you press 0, look at the information displayed in the lower portion of the palette. Figure 1-20 displays a typical progress report of a RAM Preview in progress.

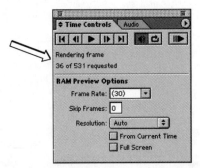

Figure 1-20: The Time Controls palette displays the number of frames rendered from the specified work area, which in this case is the length of the composition.

Making RAM Previews

As soon as After Effects has loaded as many frames into RAM as it has room for, it plays the composition in the Comp window in real-time. This preview gives you a very clear idea of how your composition is coming along and whether your animations and effects are working as designed.

First, you can specify the number of frames that After Effects will skip when creating a RAM Preview. Try entering different numbers in the Skip Frames field and pressing 0 to look at the results. The higher the number, the more jerky the playback, but a higher skipped frame count enables you to see much more of your composition.

The resolution menu is another timesaver. Click the resolution pull-down menu in the Time Control palette and select the Quarter setting. Press 0 on the numeric keypad and view the new RAM Preview. The results in the Comp window should appear pixelated at the lower resolution setting. Lowering the resolution in the Time Control palette enables After Effects to build a longer RAM Preview. This can be useful if you're trying to get a general sense of the motion and flow of your work.

This feature knocks down the resolution of your playback, but After Effects can also load four times as many frames into the RAM Preview. As with the Skip Frames field, this feature enables you to establish a larger framework of reference when checking the entirety of your work.

Leveraging Shift+RAM Previews

The good news is that you aren't relegated to only one set of RAM Preview options. You also have the Shift+RAM Preview at your disposal. As its name suggests, the Shift+RAM Preview is invoked by pressing Shift+0 on the numeric keypad. Unless you change the settings, the only initial difference between the two is that the Shift+RAM Preview plays back every other frame, but you can change its settings however you like. If you're consistently working with high-resolution footage while under the pressure of a tight deadline, it can prove useful to set your RAM Preview settings to production-quality levels and your Shift+RAM Preview settings to draft settings. The Shift+RAM Preview yields quickly rendered sketches of your developing compositions. To switch between the RAM and the Shift+RAM Preview settings, click the arrow at the upper-right corner of the palette.

The two check boxes are fairly self-explanatory. From Current Time starts a RAM Preview from the current location of the playhead as opposed to the beginning of the work area. Full Screen is a convenient new feature that can be thought of as "client mode," or a showier way of displaying the RAM Preview. To see what we mean, check the Full Screen box and press 0 on the numeric keypad. When the RAM Preview plays, it's the only thing visible on the screen regardless of the actual composition's display size.

Tip

The Full Screen feature is a handy aesthetic enhancement in version 5 that gives you the capability to show your work to a client/manager/producer/boss standing over your shoulder or looking at a projection screen. You can show your work without worrying that anyone will get distracted or deterred by After Effects' many windows.

Peeking at the Audio palette

First of all, if you click the Audio palette tab when the Time Control palette is in the foreground, it will probably be rather small. To get a better look at its detail, resize it by clicking and dragging its lower-right corner down. After you release the mouse, you'll see quite a bit more detail in the distance between the top and bottom (see Figure 1-21). At this point, that's about as deeply as we need to delve into the subject.

Cross-Reference   You can learn how to mix audio and add effects to it in Chapter 26, entitled *Improving Your Visuals with Sound*.

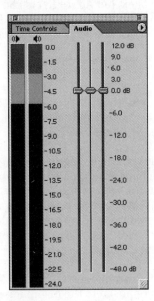

Figure 1-21: The resized Audio palette now contains quite a bit more detail than when you first selected it.

Working Within a Composition

After you create a composition, you do the bulk of your work in both the Comp and Timeline windows. The composition, or "comp" in After Effects-speak, is the application's common denominator. In After Effects, you render your comps to create finished work for broadcast, CD, or the Web. You already learned how to create new compositions by using the New Composition button at the bottom of the Project window. Now you discover a little bit about how to actually work with these new creations. The Comp window is where you layer artwork into position and move your elements around. The Timeline window is where you set keyframes for your animations and navigate your way through time. Both of these windows are shown in Figure 1-22.

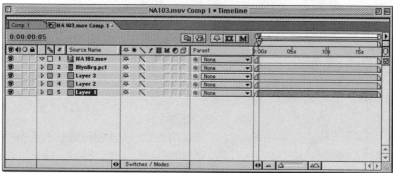

Figure 1-22: The Comp and Timeline windows — This is Motion Graphics Central. It all happens here.

Moving layers in the Comp window

Now you're going to move elements around the Comp window to get a clear idea of how the Comp window works.

STEPS: Dragging Pictures Through Space

1. **Create a new comp by clicking the New Composition button at the bottom of the Project window.**

   This time, choose 320 x 240 as your frame size and Square Pixels from the Preset and Aspect Ratio menus in the Composition Settings dialog box.

2. **In the field called Composition Name, type Put Stuff In Here.**

3. **Click and drag the *BlynBrg.pict* file from the Project window over to the Comp window, as shown in Figure 1-23.** Don't release the mouse just yet.

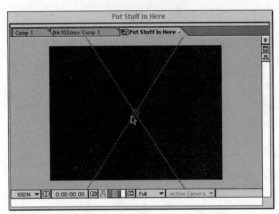

Figure 1-23: Drag a still image from the Project window over to your new composition in the Comp window. Before releasing the mouse, move it around to see where After Effects "wants" to place it.

You can tell when the picture is centered, because After Effects "wants" to place the image at the center of the composition. The picture, which is shown as a wireframe until you actually drop it in, should snap into place when you move its center near the comp's center.

4. **After the picture has snapped into the center in the comp, release the mouse.** You see that the image you're dropping into the comp is much larger than the comp itself.

After you drop the picture in the comp, you actually can see the image you just placed (as opposed to only its wireframe). If you're using the *BlynBrg.pict* file from the DVD-ROM, it's clear that the image is quite a bit larger than the canvas of the Comp window. Next, you see how to scale the image down and adjust its position so that it looks better in a comp of this size.

To change the position of the image in the frame, click and drag it in the Comp window to move it around. For your information, the Selection tool is enabled by default, and that's the tool you're using to move the image around the canvas. The Info palette tells you exactly how much you're moving the image relative to the dimensions of the composition. After you try moving the image around the space of the comp a little bit, change your Comp window Magnification ratio pop-up settings to reduce the scale of your view to 25% (see Figure 1-24). Adjust your magnification more or less until you can see the edges of your newly placed picture.

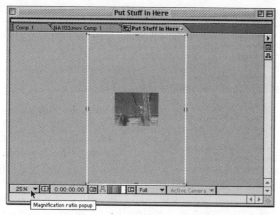

Figure 1-24: This image has many more pixels than afforded by the 320 x 240 dimensions of this particular composition.

Click one of the corner control points of the picture (its boundaries are delineated by the white border). Drag it toward the middle of the comp and hold down the shift key as you scale the image down in order to maintain its original proportions. After you experiment with this technique a little, reset your comp's magnification to 100% and position the scaled-down image so that it sits in the frame more elegantly than it did before. Check out Figure 1-25 for reference.

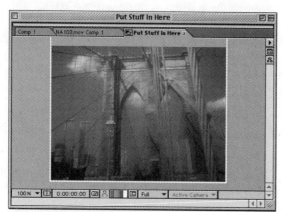

Figure 1-25: The picture looks better in this 320 x 240 comp now that it's been scaled down and repositioned.

These examples should begin to shed light on the Comp window. Essentially, this window is a canvas or main staging area where you can manipulate artwork on your way to finishing your composition.

Working with layers in the Timeline window

The Timeline window is every bit as important as the Comp window. You work with layers of footage in the Timeline, and together these layers appear as a composite in the Comp window. For those of you who are just getting acquainted with After Effects and the larger context of digital video as a whole, you might have wondered why After Effects is referred to as excellent special effects and *compositing* software. *Compositing* is literally the presence of more than one image source on a screen at any given time. Newly enlightened as you may or may not be with this information, you're going to learn how to work with layers in the Timeline window.

Note If you can't or don't want to use the footage on the DVD-ROM, bring a piece of your own footage into a comp, and you can perform the rest of the steps without a hitch.

STEPS: The Layers' Lair

1. **In the Timeline window, click the NA103.mov Comp 1 tab to make it active.** This will bring it to the foreground in the Comp window as well. If the NA103.mov Comp 1 is closed, double-click it in the Project window to make it active.

2. **Choose Composition ⇨ Composition Settings (Command+K/Ctrl+K).** This brings up the Composition Settings dialog box.

3. **Rename the comp Intro to Layers and click OK.** This step is here for two reasons. One is to show you how to call up the Composition Settings dialog box. The other is in the interest of developing good organizational habits early in the game.

Note Once more, if you can't or don't want to use the files we provide on the DVD-ROM, go ahead and use your own typography in the form of an Illustrator or other EPS file as a substitute.

4. **Drag the *Title.ai* file from Project window directly into the Timeline window.** Release the mouse after the black line is positioned above the NA103.mov layer, not below it. Figure 1-26 shows both potential layering order states in the Timeline window. When bringing artwork from the Project window into the Timeline or simply reordering layers within the Timeline, you can click and drag a layer to any position in the layering order of the Timeline window.

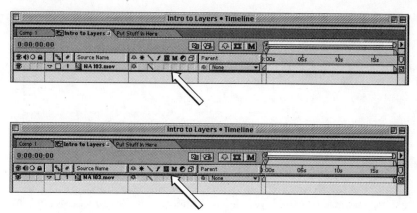

Figure 1-26: You can add a layer to the Timeline and place its layer anywhere in the stacking order. Just keep an eye on the black line, which tells you where you're placing the layer.

Now two layers are in your Timeline window, and your Comp window should have footage residing behind some type in the foreground. In the Timeline, click, drag, and drop the Title.ai layer so that it's under the footage layer. It disappears from the Comp window simply because it's sitting behind the video clip. Drag and drop it back to the top again so that it reappears. Your Comp window should resemble Figure 1-27.

Figure 1-27: Your typography should be visible in front of the footage behind it.

Image courtesy of ArtBeats (NASA — The Early Years)

Cross-Reference

When you first bring in the Title.ai layer, the text appears a little ugly on the screen. Working with Illustrator or other vector-based files has its own science. Rather than get caught up in it now, we cover that in the next chapter. Let's just say that if you aren't fond of the type's crude appearance, turn on the Best quality switch next to the Title.ai layer in the Timeline by clicking it, as shown in Figure 1-28.

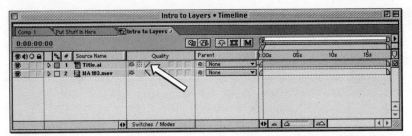

Figure 1-28: Clean up the appearance of your type with the Quality switch if you prefer.

Next, you manipulate the layers in the Timeline window to transform the appearance of the layers in the composition.

STEPS: Tweaking in the Timeline

1. **In the Timeline, click the twirler to the left of the Title.ai layer.** This will reveal various layer properties that you're about to adjust.

2. **Click the Transform twirler.** Under the word Transform are numerous properties, the values of which you can adjust. See Figure 1-29.

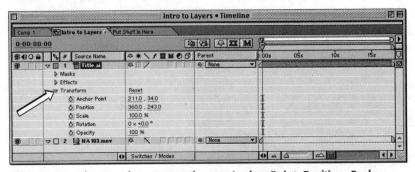

Figure 1-29: The Transform properties are Anchor Point, Position, Scale, Rotation, and Opacity (more easily understood as transparency).

Next, you manipulate the Transform properties of the layers in the Timeline window to change the appearance of the composition.

3. **Click in the number of the Scale field (100%) and drag the pointer to the right and left while watching the results in the Comp window.**

4. **After getting a sense of how this function works, set the value to 50%.** This is known as *scrubbing*, a new feature in After Effects 5. See Figure 1-30.

5. **Click once in the Opacity number field so that the value is highlighted.**

6. **Enter a value of 50 so that the Text.ai layer is 50% opaque/transparent and press Return.**

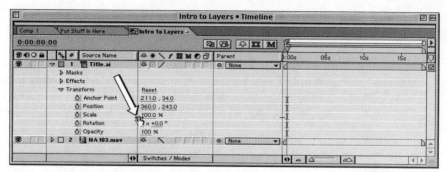

Figure 1-30: Scrubbing the Scale value gives your pointer a slightly different appearance in the Timeline.

7. **If it isn't already highlighted, select the Title.ai layer by clicking it in the Timeline.**

8. **In the Comp window, click and drag the Title.ai layer toward the top of the Comp window to position the text near the top of the frame.** As you drag the layer, hold down the Shift key to keep it centered as it moves up. Holding the Shift key after you begin dragging the layer upward allows the layer to move vertically only. The same is true if you press the Shift key after moving the layer horizontally. This step covers an important concept; as a general rule, you must select the layer you want to modify in the Timeline before altering it in the Comp window. This is especially true when you begin working with compositions that contain many layers.

The Timeline is the only place where you can modify the Opacity property, and it's also the only means by which you can enter specific values of your choosing. For example, you can move a layer's position in the Comp window, but you can enter only exact numerical values in a layer's property fields by using the Timeline window. Most important, though, the Timeline window enables you to single out specific layers for modification.

Using the Timeline to navigate time

It's important to remember that the Timeline's primary function is to enable you to drag the playhead through your composition so that you can animate the properties of layers over the course of your composition's running time. There are different ways to get to a specific point in time using the Timeline window.

✦ **Click and drag the playhead back and forth through the composition.** Look at the dynamically updated Comp window to see your movement through time.

✦ **Click directly on the Current Time field and enter a specific value.** Try this and enter a value of 100. This moves the playhead directly to the point in time that you specify; in this case, that's one second into the piece. Another way to achieve this is to choose View ⇨ Go To Time (Command+G/Ctrl+G).

Scaling your view of the Timeline and setting a work area

You can focus in on a smaller part of the timeline of your composition just as easily as you can change the magnification of it in the Comp window. This can be very helpful if you only want to work on a given set of frames in a comp. Additionally, you can set the boundaries of a work area in your composition. Doing this will tell After Effects to render only the frames inside this work area when you create a RAM Preview. By default, the work area includes the entire running time of a comp.

In the next exercise, you make a work area comprised of only the first two seconds of the composition. Also, you magnify that work area so that only those two seconds are visible.

STEPS: Setting a Work Area and Zooming In on It

1. **Choose View ➪ Go To Time (Command+G/Ctrl+G) and enter a value of 200.** This takes you to the two-second mark in your composition.

2. **Press N to set the end point of the work area.** By default, the beginning of the work area is set to the first frame of the composition, so you don't need to set it. If you need to set it somewhere else, you press B.

3. **Magnify your Timeline view by clicking and dragging the Right-edge Time View Bracket on the right side of the Timeline window toward the middle of the comp.** Ultimately, your Timeline should look like Figure 1-31.

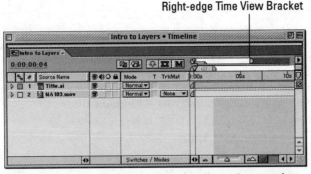

Right-edge Time View Bracket

Figure 1-31: Dragging the Right-edge Time View Bracket will enable you to magnify the work area that you have specified in the Timeline window.

Defining a work area and zeroing in on parts of your Timeline give you greater control over your animations as you move toward creating animations in After Effects. This is especially true when setting keyframes that fall within a range of a small number of frames. The next exercise shows this fully.

Control+clicking/Right-clicking in After Effects

It should not go unmentioned that After Effects contains tons of contextual menus that are enormously useful in helping you get the most out of the program. With all the various windows and palettes open (Project, Comp, and Timeline windows, Info, RAM Preview, and Tool palettes), start Control+clicking/Right-clicking your way around the interface and see what you find. We give you a couple of examples in the two figures in this sidebar.

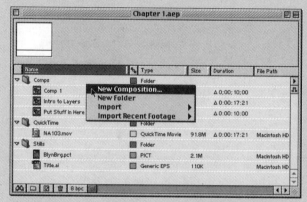

Figure SB 1-2: Contextual menu in the Project window

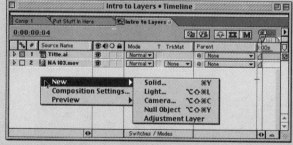

Figure SB 1-3: Contextual menu in the Timeline window

Setting a keyframe in the Timeline

Setting a couple of animation keyframes yields your first glimpse of the power of After Effects. This basic concept will be repeated time and again as your mastery of animation techniques begins to develop, but for now, you take a small step toward reaching that goal.

STEPS: Fading Out the Title Layer

1. **In the Intro to Layers comp in the Timeline window, click the layer and transform twirlers of the Title.ai layer so that you can see its Transform properties.**

2. **Drag the playhead until the Current Time reads 0:00:01:00 (one second).**

3. **Set an Opacity keyframe by clicking the stopwatch icon to the left of the Opacity Transform property.** See Figure 1-32 for reference.

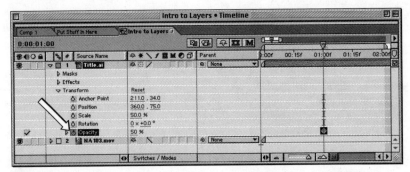

Figure 1-32: Set an Opacity keyframe for the Title.ai layer at 0:00:01:00.

4. **Drag the playhead until the Current Time reads 0:00:01:15 (one second, 15 frames).**

5. **Set another Opacity keyframe by clicking the numerical property value to the right of the Opacity Transform property.**

6. **Enter a value of 0.** Your Timeline window should resemble Figure 1-33.

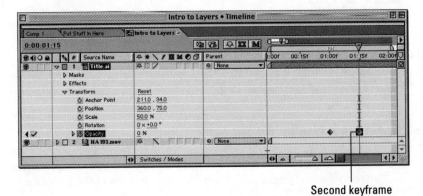

Second keyframe

Figure 1-33: Set another Opacity keyframe for the Title.ai layer at 0:00:01:15.

7. **Press 0 on the numeric keypad to preview the first two seconds of your composition**. You defined the length of the RAM Preview by the work area you set in the last exercise.

Watch the text fade out before John Glenn heads into orbit. While it's a basic animation that's certainly less momentous than the Mercury 7 mission behind the text layer, it does serve to show you how to work across the windows of the After Effects interface.

What's new in After Effects 5.5: Native Mac OS X support

After Effects 5.5 has been added to the list of applications that have been revamped for Mac OS X. As you may know, Apple's new Mac OS X has been the biggest and most radical change in the Macintosh operating system since the original Macs arrived in 1984. Mac OS X boasts a Unix back end, on top of which lies a new and beautiful graphical user interface (GUI). Familiar in some ways, new in others, and absolutely gorgeous in its looks, Mac OS X promises such long-awaited features as memory protection, preemptive multitasking, and stronger support for multiprocessing. The most visible feature of OS X is, of course, the design of its beautiful new interface, called "Aqua" by Apple. Apple's CEO, Steve Jobs, claims that he wanted his designers to create an interface that users would want to lick. You be the judge.

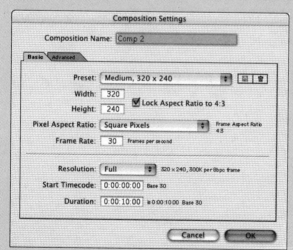

Figure SB 1-4: In addition to running on UNIX and offering the benefits of true multiprocessing, running After Effects 5.5 on Apple's OS X is, quite literally, something to see.

Tip   If you managed to get into some kind of trouble at any point in the last exercise, it would be of great service for us to tell you about the wonderful world of Undo, which you can invoke by choosing Edit ➪ Undo (Command+Z/Ctrl+Z). Don't forget its friendly sibling Redo, which you can bring about by choosing Edit ➪ Redo (Command+Shift+Z/Ctrl+Shift+Z). By default, After Effects allows for 20 levels of Undo. You can reset this in the preferences, which will be covered in Chapter 4.

Saving Your Workspace

One more important note on this grand tour of the interface is that you can set the positions of the windows in your workspace and have After Effects remember these positions so that you don't have to spend the first minute of every session aligning your windows to suit your taste (or available screen real estate). This feature is new in After Effects 5, and a lot of motion graphic designers couldn't be happier about it.

Experienced After Effects artists are sometimes lucky enough to have the benefit of dual monitors or a huge flat-panel LCD display. Others who are less fortunate must make do with less. Regardless, given your available space, set up the various windows of the interface to your liking. After you have an arrangement that you're happy with, choose Window ➪ Workspace ➪ Save Workspace and name your new arrangement. Now you can revert to this workspace whenever you like by once again choosing Window ➪ Workspace and the name of your new arrangement. See Figure 1-34.

Onward budding compositors, onward. . . .

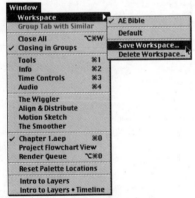

Figure 1-34: Save your favorite workspace configuration.

✦   ✦   ✦

Importing Media: Bringing Things In

Almost all the glory of After Effects depends on bringing previously prepared elements into the application. This isn't always the case. After all, you can create original artwork from within the application, but more often than not, you'll be working with preexisting artwork. That's where this chapter comes in.

After Effects works with lots of different media types, and you'll want to know the specifics of working with them, whether someone has prepared elements for you or you've made them yourself. Before your gorgeous stuff can emerge from the render queue, you'll benefit from knowing all the ways you can bring different files into a project.

Figuring Out the Import Business

After Effects is amazing in its capability to recognize and import an incredibly wide variety of graphics file formats. You can gather all kinds of disparate elements in your quest to create compelling motion graphics. Just look at the range of formats accepted, as shown by the Import File dialog box in Figure 2-1. Importing images of high quality is generally a good idea, the prevailing wisdom being that if you bring pretty things in, the chances are high that pretty things will come out. In this sense, "high quality" can sometimes mean detail or pixel resolution.

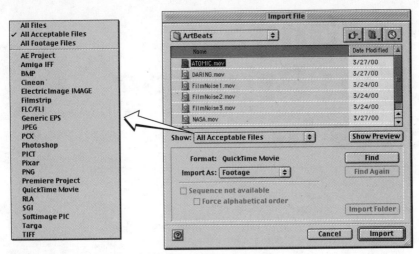

Figure 2-1: The pull-down menu in the Import File dialog box gives you an idea of the range of images that After Effects can use in a composition.

Whether you're new to After Effects or not, you probably realize that you're going to be using a variety of applications in completing a video project, regardless of whether it ends up on CD or HDTV. At the very least, you'll need to use some kind of vector graphics software, such as Adobe Illustrator or Macromedia FreeHand. Additionally, you have no way around the need to have a working knowledge of a bitmap image editing application, such as Adobe Photoshop. Examples of integrating these applications might include panning across a large photograph while layering text over the panned image. In this sense, After Effects is not one-stop shopping, but no need to despair. By no means do you have to become an expert in these applications in order to create good motion design.

Understanding image size

As far as still images are concerned, After Effects concerns itself with a graphics file's pixel count, not its printing dimensions. In other words, the application doesn't treat an 8-x-10-inch picture as such. After Effects looks only at the number of pixels contained in the image and treats it accordingly. If a 1000-x-1000-pixel image is placed into a 720 x 486 composition at 100% scale, that image will extend well beyond the borders of the composition into which it is placed whether it's actually a 1-x-1-inch film negative when held in your hand.

When gathering still image elements as you develop a project, definitely concern yourself with the pixel counts of those files. In this case, low quality can be thought of as not enough pixels. Specifically, if you take a non-vector bitmap image that is smaller than your comp and scale it up to fill the canvas, the results will be pixelated. Unless that's the look you're working on, this count is something to keep in mind.

In the domain of moving images, the same logic applies. As you might already be aware, a large number of video formats are in the world of video production. One look at the preset composition sizes in the Composition Settings dialog box makes this clear (see Figure 2-2). On one end of the spectrum, you're offered small 160-x-120-pixel dimensions for multimedia production, and at the other, you've got a full-sized frame of film topping the scales at a whopping 3656 x 2664 pixels. The huge range of dimensions in these presets literally reflects the different kinds of environments in which designers use After Effects. Remember, when you're thinking of elements to use in your comps, it's pixels that count.

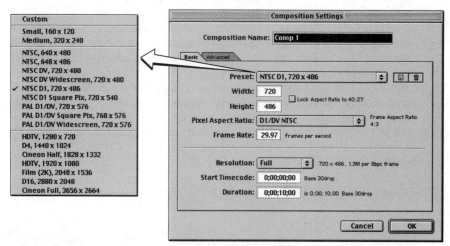

Figure 2-2: One look at your options in the Preset pull-down menu in the Composition Settings dialog box gives you a clue as to the number of different video and film formats that exist in the production world.

The logic of project files

Before we get too deeply involved in the process of prepping and importing lots of different files, we should explain the means by which After Effects deals with imported media. You never actually move or copy an entire file into After Effects when you import it. Rather, when you import a file into the project window, After Effects starts building a table of information on the file paths or locations of the files you imported. These locations can be thought of as pointers, links, or references. With regard to a project file, media listed in the Project window is merely a listing of these file paths. Actual source media used in a project stays put while After Effects makes use of it. Be careful not to move or delete any of the source media you import. Doing so makes "dead links" of the pointers in an After Effects project.

STEPS: Understanding Pointers in an After Effects Project

Rather than say much more about these principles, you'll probably get a better understanding of these aspects of After Effects if you look into a couple of features of the Project window. Create a new project or open an existing project. If you haven't already, import a few still images and video files into it; or if you prefer, you can work with the *Chapter 2.aep* project for this exercise.

The following exercise uses footage items, which are located on the DVD-ROM in a folder called *Source Material*. Just as a reminder, you need to copy the *Source Material* folder from the DVD-ROM to your hard drive.

Feel free to import whatever items you like. We provide you with some items to get you going, but if you have your own elements, by all means, please use them. These general concepts apply regardless of whatever media you import.

1. **Click and drag the lower-right corner of the Project window to expand your view of the Project window.** This gives you a clear view of all of its columns, as shown in Figure 2-3. The file path column shows the source file's location on the hard drive. If you rename, move, or delete a source media file, the reference link to that file will be broken and After Effects will report the file as missing.

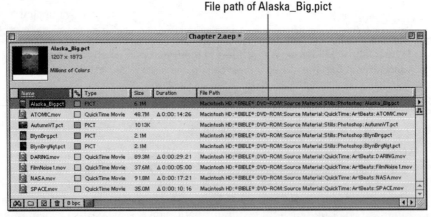

Figure 2-3: A larger view of the Project window shows the complete file paths of any imported media.

2. **Control+click/Right-click on a footage item in the Project window and select Reveal Source (or in Finder for Mac OS).** This brings you to the location of the original source file as well as select the file.

3. **Give the source file a new name.**

4. Return to After Effects.

5. Create a new composition.

6. Add the footage item whose source name you just changed to the new comp by dragging it from the Project window directly to the Timeline window. This generates an error message (see Figure 2-4). The file path that is contained in the Project file now refers to a file that no longer exists.

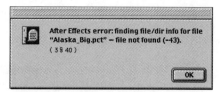

Figure 2-4: After Effects generates an error message after you change the name of a source file.

7. Click OK. The layer in the Timeline window is now a placeholder. This is clear on two levels. First, nothing is visible in the Comp window to show for the newly added layer. Second, the layer's icon in the Timeline is a thumbnail of color bars, indicating that this layer refers to a placeholder, not a file.

8. Control+click/Right-click on another footage item in the project window and select Reveal Source (or in Finder for Mac OS). If you have to, do this until you arrive at a folder on your system where a number of your footage items reside in the same place. In our example, the QuickTime files are all located in one folder.

9. Move several of the source files to your desktop (see Figure 2-5).

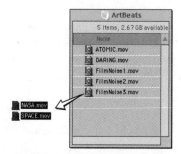

Figure 2-5: Move several of your project's source files from their original location.

10. Return to your *Chapter 2.aep* **After Effects project.**

11. Look at the Project window and select each of the footage items to see what After Effects tells you about each file. Some files are no longer listed as their native file types, but as placeholders instead. Their thumbnail sketches are shown as color bars and the text representing them in the Project window is italicized (see Figure 2-6).

Thumbnail for a missing file appears as color bars.

Type for a missing file changes to Placeholder.

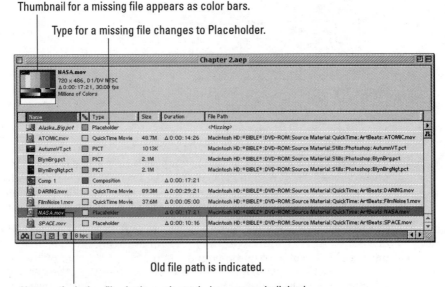

Old file path is indicated.

Names of missing files in the project window appear italicized.

Figure 2-6: The Project window informs you of its missing links with the Placeholder file type. If you select a placeholder, its thumbnail is shown as color bars.

As you can see, moving or renaming source files causes all sorts of problems in After Effects. Still, the program retains all the information about a given source file prior to its disappearance from radar. Should these mishaps ever happen, and they just might, all you need to do is relink your files.

STEPS: Relinking Files

1. In the Project window, Control+click/right-click the still image file whose name you changed.

2. Choose Replace Footage ➪ File (Command+H/Ctrl+H).

3. Select the renamed file by using the Replace Footage File dialog box, as shown in Figure 2-7. As far as After Effects is concerned, you are replacing the file even though all you really did was rename it.

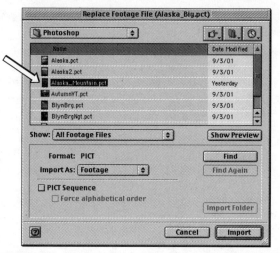

Figure 2-7: Replace the footage file with the renamed version.

4. **At the system or finder level, move the QuickTime files back to their original locations.**

5. **Relink the files by using the method learned in Steps 1–3.**

Tip If you move all of a project's media files to a new location, they'll all be listed as missing in the Project window. Double-click one of the missing links and navigate your way to the file's new location. If all the other media related to the project are in the same location as the newly relinked file, then After Effects will automatically relink all the missing files instead of forcing you to manually relink each file one by one. You'll learn that this is a real blessing.

Working with Still Images

Considering the need to work across various applications, the difference between broadcast and other design media is pretty vast and complicated. You have to be vigilant and constantly aware of the idiosyncrasies involved in prepping a still image made of square pixels for use in video. Broadcast resolution is thought of as 72 dpi (dots/pixels per inch), but this term is a bit misleading. First, the term "inch" has no meaning like it does in the world of print. Second, these are not square pixels. These are D1 pixels, and they're rectangular. They're a little bit taller than they are wide (.9:1 ratio), giving still images the appearance that they have been squished from the sides when brought into video. You've heard whiny subjects complain that the camera "adds a few pounds," but After Effects gives images a slimmer appearance, initially. To continue the metaphor, you'll be adding the pounds back! The following sections explain these differences in detail, at which point you can work across different media.

Drag-and-drop importing

Funnily enough, very few seasoned After Effects users import files by using the Import File or Import Multiple Files commands. There is a much easier and more efficient way. With the Project window open, navigate your way to the location of files that you want to import on the desktop. From there, simply drag and drop the files that you want to add to your project directly on to the Project window (see Figure SB 2-1).

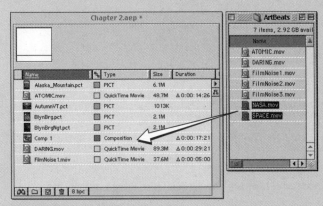

Figure SB 2-1: Drag files directly from the desktop onto the Project window, which is much faster than using an Import File command.

One word of warning in using this method, however — if you drop a folder full of elements onto the Project window, unless you specify otherwise, After Effects considers the contents of the folder as though they were a sequence of still images. Try dragging a folder full of QuickTime video files into the Project window, and After Effects returns the message seen in Figure SB 2-2.

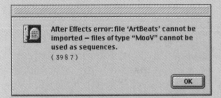

Figure SB 2-2: Adding a folder of elements from the desktop to the Project window generates an error message if the contents of that folder are anything other than still images.

Here's how you can avoid this problem: Click and drag the folder full of QuickTime files over to the Project window just as you did before, only this time press the Option/Alt key and hold it down as you release the mouse. A word of caution here: Add the Option/Alt key *after* you click the folder and start dragging it, not before. Try it out a few times to get the hang of it. The results of a successful effort here resemble Figure SB 2-3.

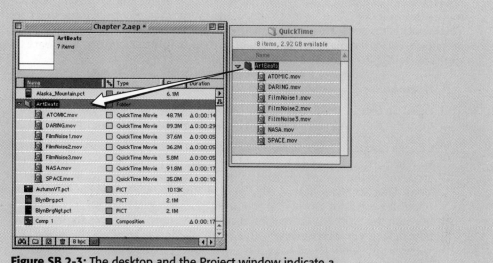

Figure SB 2-3: The desktop and the Project window indicate a successful import of a folder full of QuickTime video files.

Prepping still images to import into After Effects

We've established that it's the number of pixels that determines the size of an image in an After Effects composition. To broaden your understanding of this concept, get your feet wet with the following exercises. In them, you prepare two still images. One is for a pan across a large scan, and the other is set to the dimensions of the composition while being careful to avoid any image distortion.

STEPS: Scan for a Pan

You're probably familiar with documentaries as a mode of visual storytelling. Often, the only way in which filmmakers can bring motion to visual subjects that only exist as still images is to pan across a large scan of a photographic image. Before After Effects added to the list of options available to moving picture artists, the only way you could move across a photo was to put your camera up close to the photo and slowly move from one part of the image to another. Try out the following exercise and experience digital progress firsthand!

Note

The following exercise involves using both Photoshop and After Effects. For best results, use Photoshop 6, because that's the version we used to create the following exercise and related figures. Features in version 6 allow for better integration between the two applications. We explain these later in Chapters 13 and 14 after we address the issue of importing layered Photoshop files.

In the following steps, we use scans that we created in our studio. If you prefer, feel free to use your own. The larger the scan, the more room you have for a long pan. The hypothetical scenario for this creation is to create the pan for inclusion in a broadcast video, the dimensions of which are compatible with video hardware that works at D1 NTSC 720 x 486 screen resolution.

1. **Open Adobe Photoshop.**

2. **Open an image.** If you're working from the DVD-ROM, open *Alaska_Big.pct* from the *Photoshop* folder located in the *Source Material* folder.

3. **Choose Image ➪ Image Size.** Looking at the picture's pixel count in Figure 2-8, you have a lot of room to work with here. As we mentioned previously, pay attention to the number of pixels and disregard the document size dimensions. We scanned a slide at 300 dpi to ensure that we would have a lot of breathing room for our pan. If you bring in an image whose pixel count is beneath the 720 x 486 dimension threshold, you won't be able to perform a pan. In fact, you won't even be able to use the image to reach the edges of your composition. If you have a scanner, adjust its resolution settings to experiment with scans that have different pixel counts. Doing this will familiarize you with how much real estate you'll need from project to project. The pixel limit in After Effects is 30,000 x 30,000. The sky is pretty much the limit.

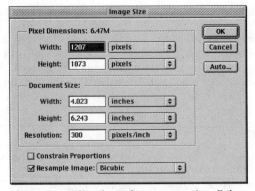

Figure 2-8: The Photoshop Image Size dialog box contains information about the dimensions of still image not available in After Effects.

4. **Click OK.**

5. **Choose Edit ➪ Preferences ➪ Units & Rulers.** Be sure to select pixels as the default unit in the Unit pull-down menu.

6. **Click OK.**

7. **Choose View ➪ Show Rulers if they're not already shown.** This enables you to view the image strictly in terms of pixels. You want to crop the image so that you can perform a horizontal pan across the mountain range. This is best

accomplished by leaving the width dimension and cropping the height to roughly 600 pixels so that there's room for a little vertical movement if you decide you want any. Using pixels as a unit of measurement gives you a clear idea of exactly how much of the image you're going to be bringing into After Effects.

8. **Select the Photoshop Rectangular Marquee tool.** Click and drag it across the image to create a frame that contains those parts of the image you want included in your pan. For reference, see Figure 2-9.

9. **In the docked palette at the top of the interface, select Fixed Dimensions from the Style pull-down menu and then enter the following dimensions: Width 1207 and Height 600.** Click and drag from inside the selection you've made to frame the part of the image you're going to include in your pan. The edges of the selection snap to the sides of the image. The current state of affairs in Photoshop looks similar to Figure 2-9.

Figure 2-9: Prepping a cropped image in Photoshop for a future pan in After Effects.

10. **Choose Image ⇨ Crop.** The newly cropped image displays the portion that you prepared for After Effects.

11. **Choose File ⇨ Save As.** Save the new image as a PCT, JPEG, or TIFF with an appended filename (such as *Alaska_Big_Cropped.pct*). Remember where you save it; in fact, make a habit of keeping your elements organized and located in the same area.

Granted, we claimed that we would only show you how to prep the image, but a simple pan is easy to execute, so here's how to pull one off in After Effects. Of course, it will be the ultimate no-frills pan. Later on, the range of your techniques will grow and improve, but you probably wanted a somewhat instant return on that last Photoshop investment.

STEPS: A Quick and Dirty Pan

1. **Open After Effects.**

Note

Depending on your available RAM, you might need to close Photoshop to open After Effects. If need be, go ahead and do so.

2. **Drag and drop your image from the desktop into the Project window.**

Note

If you like, open *Chapter 2.aep* from the files located on the DVD-ROM. The *Alaska_Bigger.pct* file is already imported into this project.

3. **Click the New Composition button at the bottom of the Project window.**

4. **Select the NTSC D1, 720 x 486 setting from the Preset pull-down menu.** Specify a composition length of 10 seconds and give the comp a name relevant to the exercise.

5. **Drag the footage item prepared for the pan from the Project window into the Timeline window.** If you use our image from the last exercise, *Alaska_Big_Cropped.pct* will appear in the Comp window, but we need to greatly reduce the magnification of the composition to see the pixel footprint of the scan.

6. **Select 25% from the Magnification pop-up menu in the Comp window.** This shows you the limits of your cropped scan.

7. **In the Timeline window, twirl down both the image layer and its transform twirler.**

8. **Set an Anchor Point keyframe by clicking the stopwatch next to the Anchor Point property.** Make sure the current time is at the beginning of the composition.

9. **Scrub the x value of the Anchor Point property in the Timeline window until the right edge of the photo is lined up with the right edge of the composition in the Comp window (see Figure 2-10).**

10. **Press End to go to the end of the composition in the Timeline window.**

11. **Scrub the x value of the Anchor Point property in the Timeline window until the left edge of the photo is lined up with the left edge of the composition.** Changing the anchor point value automatically sets up another keyframe, as shown in Figure 2-11.

12. **Press 0 on your numeric keypad to preview your pan.**

Outline of image file   Right edge of image

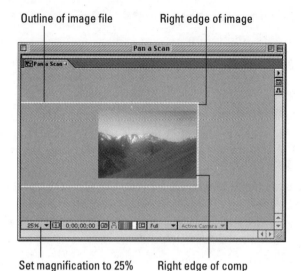

Set magnification to 25%   Right edge of comp

Figure 2-10: Line up the right edge of the image with the right edge of the comp.

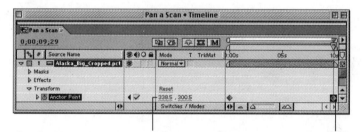

Scrub with pointer to change this value   New anchor point keyframe

Figure 2-11: Changing the anchor point value in the Timeline sets another keyframe.

There you have it. A brief and fleeting glimpse of animation techniques to come. Remember, the important part of the exercise deals with pixels and image size. No resolution is necessarily the "right" one when working through these issues. If you're going to be prepping a still for a pan, make sure that you include enough pixels. Crop it in Photoshop if the image contains portions you don't plan on using.

The next part of the chapter deals with aspect ratio problems when moving between square and D1 pixels. You perform a series of steps that illustrate these differences by preparing square pixel still image for use in a D1, NTSC 720 x 486 composition without distorting the image. It's a little trickier than you might think, but plunge in and solve this pixel business once and for all.

STEPS: Squeezing and Stretching Pixels

1. **Once again, open Adobe Photoshop.**

2. **Choose File ⇨ Open and open up an image.** The image needs to be at least 720 by 540 pixels. We use *BlynBrg.pct* from the *Photoshop* folder located in the *Source Material* folder located on the DVD-ROM.

3. **Select the Rectangular Marquee tool.**

4. **In the docked palette at the top of the interface, choose Fixed Dimensions from the Style pull-down menu and then enter the following dimensions: Width 720 and Height 540.**

5. **Click the image and move the marquee selection to frame the part of the image you want to crop.**

6. **Choose Image ⇨ Crop.** Now that you have cropped a 720 x 540 image, you resize it and then it is ready to import into After Effects.

7. **Choose Edit ⇨ Image Size.**

8. **Uncheck Constrain Proportions if it's checked and enter a value of 486 in place of 540.** Also, make certain that Resample Image is checked with the Bicubic option selected. See Figure 2-12 to make sure that eveything's right.

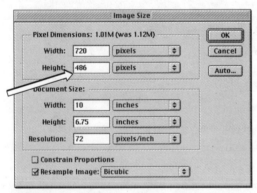

Figure 2-12: Make sure that you enter the right settings in the Image Size dialog box.

9. **Click OK.** Look at the difference in the image before and after you resize it in Figure 2-13.

10. **Choose File ⇨ Save As.** Name your newly cropped image and save it with your other media elements.

Figure 2-13: Look carefully at the difference between the two images. The original scan is on the left, and the resized, resampled image that you prepared for After Effects is on the right.

If you look at Figure 2-13, you'll notice that the image being prepped for After Effects is squashed from the top and bottom and is somewhat fatter looking. You have no way around it. Preparing an image for NTSC video involves jumping through these hoops, but the only way you can get a still image to appear on an NTSC monitor the way it appears on the left of Figure 2-13 is to complete these steps.

To better illustrate this point, a more compelling example involves the use of a perfect circle. This gives unequivocally clear results in terms of directly and concretely understanding pixel aspect ratio problems and pitfalls.

One final comment here—you don't have to resample your 720 x 540 image in Photoshop. Instead, you can save your file at those dimensions (before resizing and resampling is done in Steps 7–9). In After Effects, import your 720 x 540 still image and use the shrink to fit keyboard shortcut (Command+Option+F/Ctrl+Alt+F) on the image layer. Shrinking gives it scale dimensions of 100% width and 90% height. On your computer monitor, the image will look squashed; but as you discovered, in video, it will look right.

Cross-Reference

We cover all the possible aspect ratios in Chapter 28. If you're just getting started, you may not want to jump ahead just yet.

Importing a sequence of still images

As you may have noticed when learning how to import files the quick-and-easy way, unless you hold down the option key, After Effects wants to import a folder and its contents as a series of still images, which it treats as video. Take a folder full of still images and drag and drop it onto the project window. No need to add the option key as you click and drag the folder this time.

Note   On the DVD-ROM, we provide you with a TIFF sequence located in the *Photoshop* folder inside the *Stills* folder, which, in turn, is located under *Source Materials.*

Look at the Project window after you complete this. The window should resemble Figure 2-14. In order for this kind of import to go smoothly, however, a few conditions must be met:

✦ Obviously, make sure that all the stills reside in the same folder.

✦ If you don't want any annoying problems down the line, make certain as you prepare these files that they remain consistent in their properties. Stick with 720 x 486 if that's how you initially prepared them and don't change formats in the middle of the stack (in other words, go from TIFF to JPEG back to TIFF, and so on).

✦ The stills comprising the sequence all need to have the same name. The only difference from file to file should be the number following the underscore in the filename, such as *Now Playing_001.tif, Now Playing_002.tif,* and so on.

Imported TIFF sequence

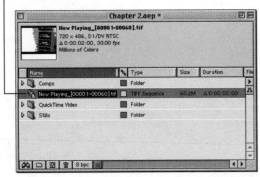

Figure 2-14: The Project window reflects the newly imported TIFF sequence. The "folder" that the TIFFs came in is gone.

When you import a folder full of stills, After Effects runs a spot check on its contents. It looks for discrepancies in the sequence of numbers and generously informs you if it perceives anything as missing, as shown in Figure 2-15. Of course, if you want to go back to importing files the old-fashioned way (by choosing File ⇨ Import ⇨ File Command+I/Ctrl+I), you can run a check on the filenames and numbers yourself in the Import File dialog box. Why wouldn't you take advantage of this well-designed drag-and-drop import feature? Well, there is one reason.

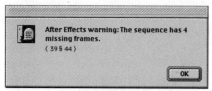

Figure 2-15: After Effects can head off a lot of future troubles by diligently checking the numbers in a still sequence and cluing you in if anything's missing.

If you have tons of stills and only want to make a sequence out of a few of them, there is a method for creating a sequence from a selection of the images as opposed to using all of them.

1. **Choose File ⇨ Import ⇨ File and navigate your way inside a folder of still images.**

2. **After you're inside that folder, Shift+click the stills you want to use as your first and last frames, check the TIFF sequence box, and click Import (see Figure 2-16).**

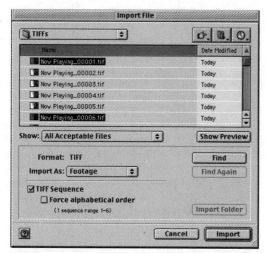

Figure 2-16: The Import File dialog box indicates the options you have when importing a TIFF sequence. You can shorten the sequence by selecting fewer stills with the Shift+click option.

This method of importing serves to show you that the drag-and-drop method isn't a perfect fit for every time.

Leading the Adobe Family Reunion

No assessment of After Effects' strengths would be complete without mentioning the fantastic integration that Adobe Systems has engineered across its suite of graphics software. In some sense, a lot of motion graphic designers think of After Effects, Photoshop, and Illustrator as one master application. As we mentioned previously, After Effects is rarely ever a complete solution unto itself. Once you have created and gathered all your elements for a project, that's when After Effects truly shines.

Typically, you've captured video with a high-end board such as the Digital Voodoo or Aurora Igniter card. You could also have gotten good stock footage on CDs from one of the many companies that sell gorgeous royalty-free footage. Just as easily, you might have some DV footage that you possibly shot yourself. Next, you've got a designer who has various kinds of art for the project (if a one person guerilla showman, this designer may well be you). That person will give you layered Photoshop artwork that contains elements of a wholly conceived production design. They'll probably also give you Illustrator art, or at the very least a font specification which you will then use to create your own vectorized type in Illustrator. Lastly, an editor on the project (this could still, in fact, be you) might have edited the cut of video in Premiere and given you the Premiere project which you can import into After Effects, allowing you to composite with the benefit of the edit decisions having already been made.

Neat, no? Adobe's efforts have made this hypothetical scenario a very tangible reality that you'll find in most broadcast and a lot of other production environments out in the "real" world. For this, we are extremely grateful, because deadline-oriented video production can be rather grueling, and it's a good thing to get as much help as you can. Adobe has been quite honorable in this department. In the following sections, you'll examine ways of working across the various Adobe file types as they relate to After Effects.

Importing layered Adobe Photoshop files

When creating a Photoshop file, you might find it very useful to take advantage of its potential as a layered structure rather than flatten it and export it as a single image. After Effects can import a Photoshop file as a layered composition with masks, paths, layer effects, adjustment layers, alpha channels, and transfer modes intact. Now, hold on a minute. What were those last few terms? Stay the course. More, as they say, shall be revealed. In any case, you import a layered Photoshop file in the steps that follow.

Note

Again, this section assumes a basic understanding of Photoshop and Illustrator on your part. These exercises shouldn't throw you off, but just in case, be prepared to spend a little time alone with Photoshop if the following parts of this chapter seem intimidating. Adobe has created excellent tutorials that ship with the software, and doing a couple of these will more than prepare you for the lessons and points that follow. Strive for a basic working knowledge. Complete Photoshop mastery is not required. That subject, such as this one, fills long and densely packed Bibles in their entirety!

STEPS: From Photoshop to After Effects

1. **Control+click/Right-click in the Project window and choose File ⇨ Import ⇨ File.**

2. **Navigate your way to the Photoshop elements we include or to your own layered Photoshop file source.**

3. **Select a Photoshop file you know contains layers and select Composition from the pull-down menu in the Import File dialog box (see Figure 2-17).**

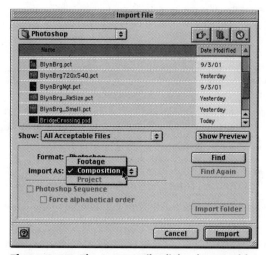

Figure 2-17: The Import File dialog box enables you to import a Photoshop file as a composition.

4. **Click Import.** After you complete this step, look at your Project window and take stock of what's just been added. A single composition and a folder full of the layers make up that composition (see Figure 2-18).

Each multi-layered Photoshop file
that is imported as a composition also
creates a folder with separated layers.

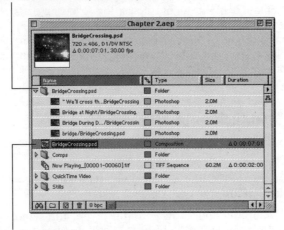

Multi-layered Photoshop files can be
imported as After Effects compositions.

Figure 2-18: The Project window displays the newly
imported layered Photoshop file.

5. **Double-click the newly imported composition to see its layers in the
Timeline window (see Figure 2-19).**

You just learned how to import the whole darned thing, layers and all. What if you
only want to import a single layer, or a composite of all the layers? Stay tuned.
Here's how:

1. **Double-click a white area in the Project window; specifically, don't click a
footage item.** This brings up the Import File dialog box again.

2. **This time, select the same Photoshop file, but choose Footage instead of
Composition.**

3. **Click Import.** Look at the next dialog box in Figure 2-20. You have the option
of importing a flattened version of the entire image (Merged Layers) or a single layer as indicated by the names you gave the various layers when creating
the file in Photoshop.

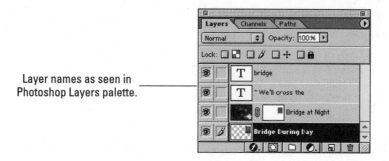

Layer names as seen in Photoshop Layers palette.

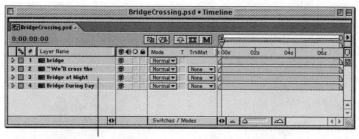

Layer names as they appear in the After Effects Timeline window.

Figure 2-19: The Timeline window displays all the layers of the newly imported Photoshop file.

Bitmaps and vectors: What's the big deal?

If you're new to motion graphic design, or design in general for that matter, you might not be familiar with these terms. Understanding them is critical before doing any heavy lifting in After Effects.

Simply put, a *bitmap image* is made up of pixels, the dimensions of which can vary. Bitmap file formats include TIFF, JPEG, and PICT, to name a few. They can be 1000 x 1000 pixels, 720 x 480 pixels, 100 x 50, and so on. Their dimensions aren't really significant unless you scale them up beyond their original values. That's when things can get a bit ugly, literally. More on this ugliness in just a moment.

Vectors, which come in the form of AI (Illustrator) or more generic EPS files, are *not* made up of pixels. In essence, they consist of mathematical descriptions. These bits of math are most easily recognized as fonts, or digital typography. Unlike bitmaps, vectors *can* be scaled up beyond 100% of their original dimensions without losing clarity. By contrast, the results are not ugly. For example, the text you see on a print ad displayed on the side of a bus contains text whose edges are still clean and aesthetically acceptable. Vectors come in many more shapes than text. Artwork prepared in Illustrator or Freehand is all vector art.

Continued

Continued

Look at the following figure. On the left is a bitmapped version of the edge of a 100 x 100 circle magnified to 1200%. On the right is a vectorized version of the edge of the same 100 x 100 circle also magnified to 1200%. Underneath them is the Illustrator file from the center picture after being opened in Microsoft Word. You don't have to believe us without proof. We meant it when we told you that mathematical descriptions are all that's contained in a vector art file. See the proof on the right of the figure.

You have important factors to consider when working with these two different groups of file formats. You can't recklessly scale Illustrator art up beyond 100% all the time. After Effects needs to recalculate the numbers contained in the file's mathematical descriptions when resampling a vector image beyond its original dimensions. If need be, you can continuously rasterize vector art when rendering compositions, but you'll greatly increase your rendering time.

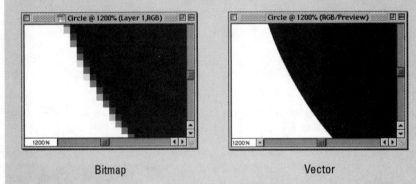

Bitmap   Vector

```
%%Title: (Circle)¶
%%CreationDate: 9/8/01 1:51 PM¶
%%BoundingBox: 220 379 320 479¶
%%HiResBoundingBox: 220 379 320 479¶
%%DocumentProcessColors: Black¶
%%DocumentSuppliedResources: procset Adobe_level2_AI5 1.2 0¶
%%+ procset AGM_Gradient 1.0 0¶
%%+ procset Adobe_ColorImage_AI6 1.3 0¶
%%+ procset Adobe_Illustrator_AI5 1.3 0¶
%%+ procset Adobe_pattern_AI5 1.0 0¶
%%+ procset Adobe_cshow 2.0 8¶
%%+ procset Adobe_shading_AI8 1.0 0¶
%AI5_FileFormat 5.0¶
%AI3_ColorUsage: Color¶
%AI7_ImageSettings: 0¶
%%RGBProcessColor: 0 0 0 ([Registration])¶
```

Figure SB 2-4: Look at the difference between vectors and bitmaps after they're both magnified. Also, if you take a look at the Illustrator file after you open it in Microsoft Word, you'll see purely mathematical descriptions.

Figure 2-20: The layer selection dialog box gives you options for importing a Photoshop file as a footage item comprised of the entire image or a single layer.

That covers importing Photoshop files. Why so many options? Going forward, you'll find that it's very convenient to work with Photoshop layers in After Effects if you're completing the dynamic media component of an imaging project, which also works in static media, such as print or the Web. Today's well-integrated marketing of products is an obvious example of this kind of workflow. An ad campaign for a major movie often uses the same artwork for a movie poster as can be seen in the 30 second broadcast spots promoting the same picture. This kind of production benefits the most from Adobe's efforts to integrate its software offerings. Imagine your relief as a broadcast designer if you're given layered Photoshop files from the design department and are told to add tasteful motion to the separate layers. A cool request indeed. You don't need to reinvent the wheel, but you do get to have the fun of putting the text and images in motion as separate entities.

Next, you apply the same principles to Illustrator and other vectorized artwork.

Importing layered Adobe Illustrator files

The basic concept at work in the Photoshop section applies here as well. Importing layered artwork has enormous benefits, as you just read. The key difference is that Photoshop images are primarily concerned with bitmaps. This used to be entirely true, but nowadays Photoshop makes use of vectorized text. Illustrator, on the other hand, is entirely vector-based. That brings us to the next major point of understanding what's involved in designing across media. What are the fundamental differences between bitmaps and vectors as still image sources? How does it affect your approach to your After Effects work? The answers lie in the manner in which you affect the scale of these different kinds of objects in your compositions.

To better understand the properties of vector art, bring some of it into After Effects.

STEPS: From Illustrator to After Effects

1. **Choose File ⇨ Import ⇨ File (Command+I/Ctrl+I).**

2. **Open a layered 720 x 540 Illustrator file.** If you don't have one, we've prepared one called *Abstract.ai* and placed it on the DVD-ROM in the *Illustrator* folder, which is located in the *Source Material* folder.

3. **As with the Photoshop import, select Composition from the pull-down menu in the Import File dialog box.**

4. **Click Import or press Return.** After the file is imported, it will reside in the Project window as a composition and a folder full of the comp's individual layers. Click the composition in the Project window to reveal its properties. The info returned indicates the comp's dimensions, which are 720 x 540. These dimensions are correct because we prepared the file for use in a D1, NTSC 720 x 486 composition, but you need to resize it in order for it to appear properly in D1 standard video. This resizing requires you to *nest* the 720 x 540 in a 720 x 486 comp.

5. **Click the New Composition button at the bottom of the Project window to create a new comp.**

6. **Give the new comp a name, select the D1, NTSC 720 x 486 preset, and then click OK.**

7. **In the Project window, click and drag the comp created by the imported Illustrator file (*Abstract.ai*) onto the 720 x 486 comp you just created.** Look at Figure 2-21 for reference. This is the first time you've *nested* a comp inside another comp, and it won't be the last. At this point, we're only introducing the concept, but the basic premise is the following: *Pre-compose,* or *nest,* compositions in other compositions so that any changes you make to the original pre-composition are globally applied in the other compositions in which they exist as an element. In this case, if you want to animate the individual layers of the *Abstract.ai* comp, you'd still want the complete animation to remain resized as a whole. That's why you want to nest it in a 720 x 486 comp.

Cross-Reference

Pre-composing and nesting is addressed in detail in Chapter 8.

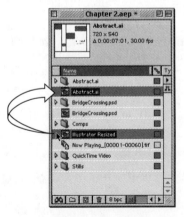

Figure 2-21: Click and drag the imported comp (720 x 540) on top of the new comp (720 x 486) in the Project window.

8. **To resize the 720 x 540 comp you just laid into the 720 x 486 comp, select its layer and press Command+Option+F/CtrAlt+F.** This command is the Shrink to Fit command.

Now that you've imported Illustrator artwork successfully into After Effects, remember that the same logic that applied to your Photoshop imports applies here. You can import both layered Illustrator and Photoshop files as compositions, separate layers, or merged layers. Just be sure to keep a vigilant eye on problems related to pixel aspect ratios. They occur regularly, and an understanding of these issues usually means you can get out of trouble more quickly than you might otherwise.

Importing Adobe Premiere projects

Now you get a look at another example of Adobe's efforts at integration. Assume that you're an After Effects artist working on movie promos at a cable network. If the network wants to create a 30-second promo to plug a movie it will be showing during primetime, it might have an editor cut together some choice scenes using Premiere as the application for editing the video. At that point in the process, the editor would give you a copy of his or her Adobe Premiere project. You would then import that project file into After Effects and add motion graphics, network logos, and other design touches that you like (or ones that a producer demands).

In the following steps, you import an Adobe Premiere project. We provide one for you on the DVD-ROM if you don't have access to one.

STEPS: From Premiere to After Effects

1. **Double-click in some white space in the Project window to invoke the Import File dialog box.**

2. **Navigate your way to an Adobe Premiere project file.** If you're in need of one, use the *Chapter 2.ppj* project file located in the *Premiere* folder located in the *Source Material* folder on the files included on the DVD-ROM.

3. **Select the file and click Import.** A Premiere project is always imported as a composition. In addition to the new comp, a folder containing the Premiere project's video clips is created.

4. **Double-click in the new composition, which now appears in the Project window.** Our example, *Chapter 2.ppj,* contains a very simple comp consisting of two video clips with a dissolve between them and a fade out at the very end. Figure 2-22 shows the project in both Premiere and After Effects after it's imported.

A Premiere project timeline

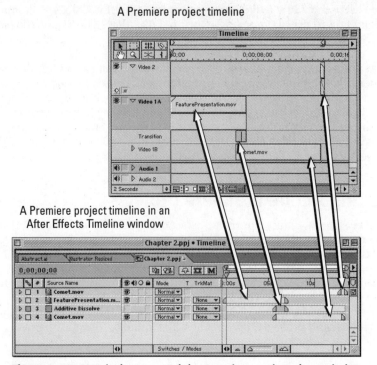

A Premiere project timeline in an
After Effects Timeline window

Figure 2-22: Here's the same Adobe Premiere project shown in its
native environment as well as in its sibling's domain of After Effects.

That's how you import an Adobe Premiere project, but you have several details
to keep in mind here. First of all, After Effects gets a scaled-back version of the
Premiere project. Specifically, no transitions, fades, or other effects are imported
along with the footage. If you take a careful look at Figure 2-22, the Additive
Dissolve between the first and second clips is simply a solid layer with the visibility
turned off. Its purpose is to serve as a placeholder that indicates the editor's decision to use that transition at that point for that length of time.

So, what's the real benefit then? There are a few, actually. First of all, the editor
using Premiere doesn't have to render anything before handing the project over to
the After Effects artist. Other video editing applications would necessitate rendering a final cut to import into After Effects, so this saves both time and disk space.
Secondly, the running time, frame rate, and composition dimensions remain consistent in translation. The stacking order and video clip lengths also remain the same.
You're basically getting a straight-cuts version of the Premiere project in which
each layer in the Timeline reflects each clip in the Premiere Timeline. Lastly, After
Effects is a *compositing* application, whereas Premiere is an *editing* application.
Premiere can play clips in real time; After Effects has to load frames into RAM in
order to give you a real-time preview, so this is really the big plus. Edit for content.
Composite after you've settled on a rough cut.

Tip Here's an interesting little tidbit of information. Did you know that you can also import PDFs into After Effects? They're interpreted as generic EPS files. This can be a big help if you want to integrate a design department's print campaign into your video design. In keeping with the theme of integration, if you're a proud owner of After Effects 5.5, now you can also import Macromedia Flash (SWF) files. Going back to the notion of a multimedia campaign, this is great if you want to incorporate the design from a preexisting Flash (SWF) animation from a Web site into your video project.

Interpreting Source Media

After Effects has to process a lot of information when bringing footage into a project. If you click an item in the Project window, After Effects' interpretation of that footage is found next to the item's thumbnail at the top of the Project window, as shown in Figure 2-23.

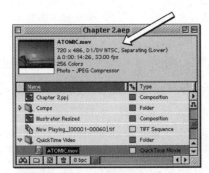

Figure 2-23: After Effects' interpretation of a footage item is visible if you click a footage item in the Project window and look at the information displayed to the right of the footage item's thumbnail.

In some sense, you should learn to think in the same manner as the application. What kind of file are you dealing with? Is it a still image, a sequence of stills, or out and out video? What pixel aspect ratio is native to the footage being imported? Just what kind of transparency information is contained in this file? If it's video, what codec was used when authoring it? How many frames are there per second? Is the video separated into two interlaced fields per frame? If so, does the upper or lower one come first? Did the video begin life as film? If so, film's frame rate is 24 frames per second (fps) and video's is 29.97. How do you overcome this discrepancy? Will you be working in 8-bit or 16-bit color space? Is there an afterlife? Those sorts of things. As soon as you start thinking in this fashion and are able to comprehend the answers to most of these questions, you'll be on your way to creating complex, maybe even beautiful, projects. By coming this far, you've already begun the process.

The following section delves deeper into the issues that stem from the preceding stream of questions. Press on. It is this knowledge you seek.

Preparing motion footage for import

You have a number of ways to prepare video for After Effects. Generally speaking, you get it from various videotape formats, such as the analog BetaCAM or entirely digital DV. You might also need to import film that has been transferred to video. In these scenarios, the video needs to be captured from its native source, maybe edited, and then imported into After Effects.

NTSC video runs at 29.97 fps, and each frame is made up of two interlaced fields. What does this mean exactly? Each of the frames involves the combination of two scans. Each scan is made up of alternating horizontal lines. The odd field contains lines 1, 3, 5, 7, and so on. The even field contains lines 2, 4, 6, 8, and so on. When viewing NTSC video on an NTSC monitor, your eye blends these two alternating scans and perceives them as one of 30 fps. Other formats, such as film, PAL video, and video prepared for playback on a computer monitor are *progressive scan* video formats. Computer monitors always display images by means of a progressive scan. This means that you're looking at an entire frame at once, not the combination of alternating fields.

Some video hardware configurations display the upper or odd field first. Others display the lower field first. The order in which these fields are displayed is critical, and at no time is this more apparent than when a video clip contains motion. Imagine a ball moving across a video clip from left to right. If the field order is incorrectly displayed, the ball will appear to stutter in its movement because it will keep jumping back to the left a little bit as it completes its move to the right. The good news is that a QuickTime file usually contains all the important information about a video clip, so when you import it into After Effects, After Effects is already clued in as to the clip's field order, frame rate, and other details. For any number of reasons though, After Effects can get these details wrong or not interpret footage at all. If this is the case, After Effects needs some input from you, and you provide it with the right interpretation of field order in the Interpret Footage dialog box shown in Figure 2-24. We explain how to correct this problem later in the section.

Field order involves only one aspect of the Interpret Footage window. In the sections that follow, you gain an understanding of all the properties you can define for a footage item by adjusting the settings in this crucial part of the interface.

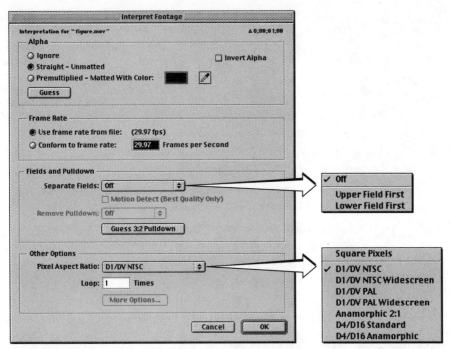

Figure 2-24: The Interpret Footage dialog box is where you can set a number of parameters that define the manner in which After Effects handles footage if it is placed in a composition.

Understanding alpha channels and transparency

After Effects processes every pixel it deals with as the composite of four channels: red, green, blue, and the oft-misunderstood alpha channel. Each of these four channels contains an 8-bit grayscale value ranging from 0 to 255. 0 is black, 255 is white, and all numbers in between are shades of gray. This is fairly easy to understand in terms of the RGB values. For example, R:250, G:20, B:20 appears to your eye as a very red pixel. The alpha channel defines transparency, not color in the way you think of red, green, and blue. An alpha channel value of 255, or white, in terms of its grayscale equivalent, indicates a completely opaque alpha channel. An alpha channel value of 0, or black on the other hand, indicates a completely transparent alpha channel.

What do these factors really serve to accomplish? The answer is clear when compositing multiple images in the same composition. If you layer an image with transparency in its alpha channel (that is, values less than 255) over another image, the underlying image will be more or less visible in those areas of the top layer in which the alpha channel has a value less than 255. To better understand this fundamental concept, check out Figure 2-25.

Figure 2-25: The first picture shows only the RGB channels of an image. The second picture shows the Alpha channel of the same image. The third picture shows all four channels laid over another image, revealing the areas where it is transparent.

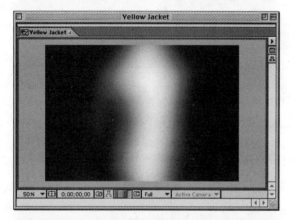

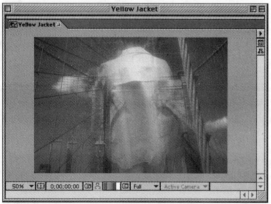

After Effects handles every bit of footage in a project as an RGBA entity. Even if you import footage without an alpha channel, After Effects adds a completely opaque alpha channel to it (completely white, if you think of it in terms of grayscale). In terms of interpretation, you discover more about this aspect of alpha channels just a bit later in the section.

 Chapter 16 covers transparency and alpha channels in much greater detail.

What's a codec?

In After Effects, imported video clips are most often QuickTime movie files. The QuickTime file type is simply a container for a series of still image frames. In order for these frames to be played back at, say, 30 fps, some compression is usually involved. Uncompressed frames of video are large and unwieldy, and only expensive and very fast high-end desktop systems can handle the high-speed throughput of these massive images. To address this problem, video software developers created codecs, a word that's short for **co**mpression/**dec**ompression.

A lot of different codecs are out there. Basically, they're a means by which video files can be made smaller than their original uncompressed format. A codec compresses video so that it takes up less space on the hard drive. When your computer reads a video file with a certain codec associated with it, it decompresses the compressed data and plays back the video. Some codecs lean toward *lossy.* That is, the compression degrades the video to the point where so much information has been lost that you notice an appreciable decrease in image quality. Other codecs line up more on the side of *lossless,* which is to say that compression is minimal by contrast, and image quality remains high. Some lossless examples native to QuickTime include MJPEG, DV, and Photo JPEG. The Sorenson codec, which has become very popular for delivering video on the Web, is an example of a lossy codec. In addition to these, there are proprietary codecs as well, proprietary meaning that they work in conjunction with specific hardware, such as a Media 100 or Avid video board.

In order for After Effects to properly handle video, it needs to have the right codecs loaded for each type of video file that's been imported into a project. For example, you can import a video file that uses the Media 100 codec, but if you don't have that codec loaded on your system, your computer won't know how to decompress the data. So, this is another consideration when thinking in terms of preparing motion footage for use in After Effects.

8 bpc color depth versus 16 bpc color depth (Production Bundle)

The Production Bundle of After Effects 5 contains a new feature as evidenced by the appearance of a small button next to the others at the bottom of the Project window, which cryptically reads 8 bpc by default. This button tells you whether your project is operating in 8- or 16-bit color. 8-bit color space allows for a range of 256 grayscale values in each channel. 16-bit color space allows for a range of 32,768 values in each channel! That's a lot of color space in case you're wondering. A couple of high-end formats can take advantage of this development. Specifically, film and HDTV are capable of using the 16-bit color space; but remember that you can turn on 16-bit color only if you've purchased the Production Bundle. You can also prepare 16-bit color images in Photoshop to import into After Effects

If you have the Production Bundle, you can convert your project to 16-bit color by Option+clicking/Alt+clicking on the 8 bpc button at the bottom of the Project window. Try it out and then drag your pointer across the Comp window while watching the numbers returned by the Info palette. The results show quite a bit more variation than the 0–255 range you've been seeing.

You have a few elements to keep in mind when operating in this much larger data framework. Obviously, render times are going to be affected because After Effects is going to be mathematically working out trillions as opposed to millions of colors. Also, not every effect has been configured to work in 16-bit color.

Cross-Reference   Topics like working in HDTV and applying effects are addressed in Chapters 8 and 28. The point here is to show you the range of options when dealing with different kinds of footage.

Setting interpretations

This section of the chapter deals with each of the settings in the Interpret Footage dialog box. Despite the native settings of a file that gets imported into After Effects, you can force changes in the way in which the file is interpreted. Sometimes, you have to adjust a file's interpretation because the imported file might come in without any information telling After Effects how to use it properly in the composition you're building.

The first property you can change deals with alpha channels. There's more to it than the fact that After Effects uses an alpha channel for every footage item in the Project window. Actually, After Effects can change its interpretation of the alpha channel so that it looks as good as possible given the image with which it forms a composite. Next on the list, the frame rate of a video clip can be directly changed. Considering interlaced video, you can also force After Effects' interpretation of the field order of a video source. Lastly, you can specify the pixel aspect ratio of any footage item. We identified these properties in the preceding parts of this chapter, but now you'll see the direct influence you can wield over the interpretation of these variables after you bring footage into a project.

Alpha channels

When you import footage with a labeled alpha channel, After Effects keeps the predefined interpretation. If the alpha channel is undefined, After Effects will ask you how you want to interpret it. At this point, you should select Guess and let After Effects try and figure it out. The Interpret Footage dialog box offers three alpha channel interpretations, as shown by the upper portion of the window in Figure 2-26. Select the *YellowJacket.pct* footage item in the Project window by clicking it. Press Command+F/Ctrl+F to bring up the Interpret Footage window for this footage item.

Figure 2-26: The upper portion of the Interpret Footage dialog box deals with After Effects' treatment of a footage item's alpha channel.

✦ **Ignore:** If selected, this simply means that After Effects will disregard the alpha channel entirely.

✦ **Straight - Unmatted:** With this type of alpha channel, there's no color smoothing at the edges. Most alpha channels are straight. If a footage item's alpha channel is misinterpreted and ignored, any transparency you intended will not exist in any composition in which you place the image.

✦ **Premultiplied - Matted With Color:** This kind of alpha channel factors in a theoretical background color, which, in turn, can affect the edges. The problem you're most likely to experience is when a premultiplied alpha channel is interpreted as straight, which can create an unsightly and undesirable halo around its edges.

If these definitions don't make complete sense to you, try each of these settings when you run into trouble. By trouble, we simply mean if your image doesn't look right. Look at Figure 2-27 to see the various interpretations as reflected by the Project window when a footage item with an alpha channel is selected.

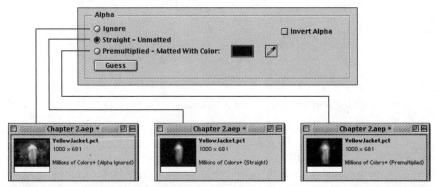

Figure 2-27: The Project window shows the various alpha channel interpretations a footage item can have.

Frame rate

Frame rates differ across formats. NTSC video is 29.97 fps, PAL is 25 fps, and film is 24 fps. When you import footage into After Effects, the file's frame rate remains unchanged. You can reset this frame rate in the Interpret Footage dialog box, as shown in Figure 2-28.

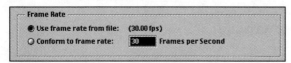

Figure 2-28: The Frame Rate portion of the Interpret Footage dialog box enables you to force a video clip's frame rate.

Bear in mind that changing the frame rate here doesn't change any of the frames of the source file; it only changes the relative speed of the movie's playback. In our example, *NASA.mov* has a native frame rate of 30 fps. You can enter 15 here instead. If you do so, your render will play the movie at half-speed in a composition that runs at 30 fps. Each frame of the movie will last for two frames in the composition. Alternatively, you can enter 60 in this field, and the movie will play twice as fast in the same composition, but you will actually see only every other frame of the original movie because the composition is set to 30 fps. Put another way, you will be seeing only half of the actual frames that comprise the original source file.

Caution   Be careful here. You can lose audio sync.

What's the point? The answer is in the output. We hypothetically asked you earlier, "What are you making?" If your final output is NTSC video, it will be important to change the native number of 30 to 29.97. More often than not, you're probably going to leave this number alone until you're consistently working across different formats. Also, once in a composition, you can time-stretch a layer of video in the Timeline so that you have two ways to come at this. If you want, however, this is a perfectly good way to time-stretch video.

Cross-Reference   Time-stretching and remapping are addressed in Chapter 12.

Fields and 3:2 Pulldown

We've already discussed the fact that After Effects can handle interlaced video. We're now concerning ourselves with exactly how it interprets the separate fields. Actually, this is a common problem faced in post-production. It's absolutely essential that After Effects properly interprets this field order, especially if you plan on doing anything at all to the clips in a composition. This extends to scaling the video, rotating it, moving it around the frame of a composition, or adding any effects. Select an interlaced video clip in the Project window and press Command+F/Ctrl+F to bring up the Interpret Footage dialog box, and let's get to the bottom of this (see Figure 2-29).

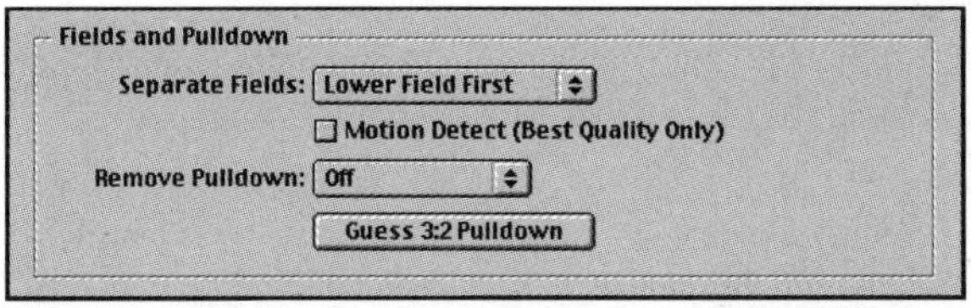

Figure 2-29: The Fields and Pulldown portion of the Interpret Footage dialog box deals with interlaced video and field rendering issues.

If you're using video hardware, such as a Media 100, Avid, or Aurora video capture board, the specific hardware is configured to capture interlaced fields in a specific order. When you import this footage, you want to make certain that the field order remains consistent between your hardware and After Effects. Fear not though. The aforementioned high-end video hardware systems actually label the QuickTime files they create. Typically, After Effects reads those labels and interprets the clips properly. In addition to video captured by proprietary hardware, there are some universal standards. For example, the overwhelmingly popular NTSC DV standard is Lower Field first. Still, if you're experiencing problems, click the footage item in question in the Project window, press Command+F/Ctrl+F, and check to make sure that After Effects has "gotten it right." If not, use the Separate Fields menu in the Interpret Footage dialog box to change the field order.

The key to understanding this field order is that After Effects combines the two fields to make one complete frame. Having pointed that out, it's not hard to imagine the problems you might encounter if After Effects combines two halves of different frames. An incorrect interpretation results in what is usually a very undesirable and unnatural looking strobe effect in your final render. Clean lines appear jagged, and you'll see "combing" as you play back the movie. How do you address these issues?

If the QuickTime movie has no labeled field order in the Project window, a specific solution addresses the issue. This solution involves opening the clip in its own Footage window.

Working in the Footage window

In the Project window are two ways to view QuickTime movies. If you double-click the clip, it opens up in a no-frills version of the QuickTime player, but if you Option+double-click/Alt+double-click the same file, the video will open up in its own Footage window (see Figure 2-30).

Figure 2-30: The Footage window enables you to check unlabeled footage to determine the field order.

Image Courtesy of ArtBeats

Viewing the clip in the footage window enables you to determine the field order, because the footage window shows *all* the fields in the frame, whereas the same clip in the Comp window does not. The Comp window only displays the field selected for that movie's field rendering preference as it has been defined in the Interpret Footage settings. Put another way, the Comp window won't indicate that there's a problem. If an interlaced clip is unlabeled in the Project window, we highly recommend the following test.

1. **Select the clip in question in the Project window.**

2. **Select Upper Field first in the Interpret Footage settings.**

3. **Option+double-click/Alt+double-click the clip in the Project window to open it in its own Footage window.**

4. **Watching an area of the clip that contains motion in the footage window, click the Next Frame button in the Time Controls palette (press the PgDn key) to advance one field at a time.**

5. **After five steps (five fields) forward, you can tell if the field ordering is correctly by whether the motion in the clip jerks backward.** If it does, change the field order in the Interpret Footage window. If the motion is smooth, the settings are correct. If need be, consult Figure 2-31 for reference.

Figure 2-31: The Time Controls palette's navigation buttons include a Next Frame button (really, next field in this case), which you use to step through the fields.

Image Courtesy of ArtBeats (Daring Men)

Removing 3:2 Pulldown from film transferred to video

Transferring film to video involves a process called 3:2 Pulldown. This process derives its name from the conversion of the 24 fps frame rate of film to the 29.97 fps frame rate of NTSC video. The end result of the transfer is that the first frame of film is spread across two video fields, the next frame of film is spread across three video fields, whereupon the next frame of film is spread across two fields, and so on.

Before you can figure out exactly how film was transferred, you must enter the right field order. You just discovered how to do that in the last section. As soon as you have the right field order, you can have After Effects sort out the specifics of the film transfer by having it guess the 3:2 Pulldown phase in the Interpret Footage dialog box. Looking at the video in a footage window, some frames appear whole and others split, hence the notations. The "S" and "W" notations in the remove pulldown menu refer to split and whole frames. These varying appearance from frame to frame is due to the fact that the film frames are spread across an alternating number of fields (3, 2, 3, 2, and so on).

1. **Select a clip that includes film transferred to video in the Project window.**

2. **Select the correct field order in the Interpret Footage settings.**

3. **Click the Guess 3:2 Pulldown button to let After Effects figure out the 3:2 Pulldown phase (see Figure 2-32).**

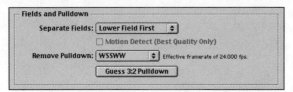

Figure 2-32: After you've clicked the Guess 3:2
Pulldown button, After Effects determines the correct
pulldown phase as indicated by the result shown here.

Note   If there is enough material, After Effects can accurately guess the 3:2 Pulldown but
might have trouble with material of which there are only a few frames. In that
case, it may be possible to extract the 3:2 info from a longer piece from the same
source if a longer piece does exist.

If you apply these steps when you work with footage comprised of film transferred
to video, you'll avoid any distortions. After Effects only applies effects to the film in
perfect sync with the film's native frame rate. Open the newly interpreted footage in
its own footage window and step through it frame by frame to see the results of the
interpretation.

Setting pixel aspect ratios

A number of video formats have their own different pixel aspect ratios. Regardless
of your final output, you should make sure that all your imported footage is set
to its native pixel aspect ratio. You can manually set this property in the bottom
portion of the Interpret Footage dialog box (see Figure 2-33).

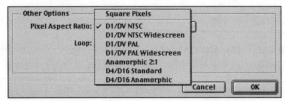

Figure 2-33: Make certain that imported footage is
set to its native pixel aspect ratio by using the menu
in the bottom portion of the Import Footage dialog box.

The following information gives specific details on the varying pixel aspect ratios
across the different video formats, all of which are offered in the pull-down menu of
the Interpret Footage dialog box. The numerical values given for the pixel aspect
ratios refer to the result of height divided by width. For example, the 1.0 value for a
pixel aspect ratio is derived from an equal width and height. A pixel aspect ratio
value that is less than 1.0 indicates a rectangular pixel, which is taller than it is

wide. Alternatively, a pixel aspect ratio value that is greater than 1.0 indicates a rectangular pixel, which is wider than it is tall.

✦ **Square Pixels:** Uses a 1.0 pixel aspect ratio. If your footage has a 640 x 480 or 648 x 486 frame size, select this setting.

✦ **D1/DV NTSC:** Uses a 0.9 pixel aspect ratio. If your footage has a 720 x 480 or 720 x 486 frame size and you want it to have a 4:3 frame aspect ratio, select this setting.

✦ **D1/DV NTSC Widescreen:** Uses a 1.2 pixel aspect ratio. If your footage has a 720 x 480 or 720 x 486 frame size and you want it to have a 16:9 frame aspect ratio, select this setting.

✦ **D1/DV PAL:** Uses a 1.0666 pixel aspect ratio. If your footage has a 720 x 576 frame size and you want it to have a 4:3 frame aspect ratio, select this setting.

✦ **D1/DV PAL Widescreen:** Uses a 1.422 pixel aspect ratio. If your footage has a 720 x 576 frame size and you want it to have a 16:9 frame aspect ratio, select this setting.

✦ **Anamorphic 2:1:** Uses a 2.0 pixel aspect ratio. If your footage was shot using an anamorphic film lens, select this setting.

✦ **D4/D16 Standard:** Uses a 0.948 pixel aspect ratio. If your footage has a 1440 x 1024 or 2880 x 2048 frame size and you want it to have a 4:3 frame aspect ratio, select this setting.

What's new in After Effects 5.5: Expanded Import Options

Over the years, Adobe has continued to expand the import capabilities of After Effects. After Effects 5.5 provides additional support for importing various kinds of files.

For example, you can now import Macromedia Flash (SWF) files to use in your compositions.

You can also import 3D files saved in the RPF (Rich Pixel Format) file format. RPF files are commonly used by 3D applications such as 3D Studio Max.

After importing these files, you can use the 3D channel effects in the Production Bundle to work with the 3D data in these file formats. Coverage, z-depth information, and alpha channel information are all included in an RPF file.

After Effects 5.5 also expands support for importing and working with MPEG files. After Effects 5.0 allowed import of MPEG-1 files from Windows. In After Effects 5.5, MPEG-1 files created on the Macintosh format can also be imported.

Also, in addition to the existing support for 16-bit Photoshop and Cineon files, 8- and 16-bit Maya IFF, QuickTime, RLA, RPF, and SGI files are now supported in After Effects 5.5.

✦ **D4/D16 Anamorphic:** Uses a 1.896 pixel aspect ratio. If your footage has a 1440 x 1024 or 2880 x 2048 frame size and you want it to have an 8:3 frame aspect ratio, select this setting.

In most cases, you want to set your composition settings to match those of the footage you're working with. To be certain you've done this correctly, open the composition containing the footage whose settings you want to match, choose Composition ➪ Composition Settings (Command+K/Ctrl+K), and select the matching pixel aspect ratio. Given that a computer monitor won't accurately reflect these exotic dimensions, a very cool feature in the Comp window will give you an accurate preview of the final output of your composition. Click the arrow at the upper-right corner of the Comp window and select Pixel Aspect Correction to get an accurate look at the final product's general appearance before rendering (see Figure 2-34).

Looping

Last but not least, there is the Looping function at the very bottom of the Interpret Footage dialog box. Use this field to enter a whole number, which defines the number of times you want a motion footage item to repeat itself, and the Project changes its reference to the running time of the movie. For example, if you enter 3 in the looping field of the Interpret Footage dialog box for a 10 second clip, the Project will reference the clip as if it was imported as a 30 second clip. When you add the same clip to a comp, its length will be 30 seconds. This can be quite useful for stock footage that is loopable. *Loopable* footage has no visible end point and can be played indefinitely for as long as you need it in a given composition. Examples include spinning logos and the like.

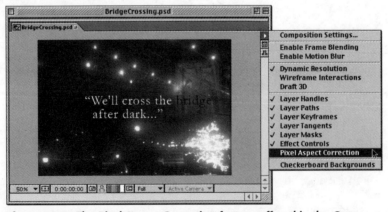

Figure 2-34: The Pixel Aspect Correction feature offered in the Comp window's option menu can be a useful timesaver if you're wondering about the final appearance of your comp, especially when using an exotic pixel aspect ratio.

Life After Importing

We hope that you now have a better handle on importing all kinds of footage into After Effects. We introduced topics in this chapter that we cover in much more detail later on, but it's important that you know how to bring any kind of element into After Effects as you build a project. Even more important, perhaps, is knowing how to change the way in which After Effects interprets those items you import if things get a bit muddled. If most of this is new to you, don't be too concerned. Some of these concepts are a little difficult to understand. The following chapters put a lot of the issues raised here into a more concrete and specific context.

✦   ✦   ✦

Moving Your Artwork

You're getting into the good stuff now. Elegantly moving elements across the screen is what After Effects is all about. This chapter centers on the Timeline window, because that's where you set keyframes, which define the motion contained in your animation. First, we describe all the various panels in the Timeline and their switches and menus. As soon as you know how to manipulate the various transform properties of a layer of the Timeline, you begin creating basic animations by adding keyframes to the layers in a composition. After you begin getting your feet wet with keyframe animations, you can try your hand at sketching a motion path for a layer, flipping it, spinning it, and some other cool techniques. The goal here is to get a layer to go where you want it to go and then do what you want it to do once there. That's the big prize.

This sounds like a wonderland for control freaks, but that's not a bad thing when it comes to making an animation actually play out the way you've visualized. We believe After Effects is a great tool for a whole bunch of reasons, and one that should begin to be clear by the end of this chapter is this: Simply knowing the basic procedures for creating animations narrows the gap between what you imagine and what you create.

Deconstructing the Timeline

First, you want to look at all the components of the Timeline window as a whole (see Figure 3-1). As the section continues, you get into more granular detail. Once you master the intricacies of the Timeline window, After Effects will really start to bend to your will.

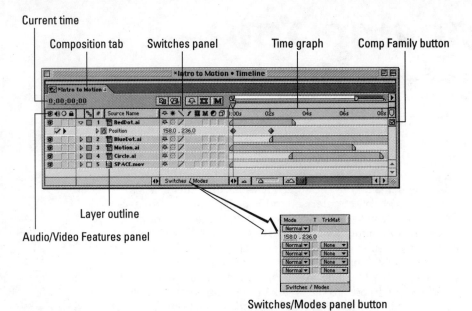

Figure 3-1: The Timeline window is literally covered with columns and functional buttons of one kind or another. Clicking the Switches/Modes panel button toggles the view between the Switches and Modes panels.

✦ **Composition tab:** This tab indicates the name of the composition whose properties you can modify using the features in the Timeline.

✦ **Current time:** This field displays the current time position of the playhead.

✦ **Audio/Video Features panel:** This panel contains switches that enable you to turn a layer's visibility or audio on or off.

✦ **Layer outline:** This column contains the composition's layer names, labels, and numbers according to the stacking order of the layers.

✦ **Time graph:** This is a graphical representation of the running time of a composition. It also shows the temporal positions of keyframes and where a layer's In and Out points are located in time. You can scale this view to include the entire running time of a composition, or you can narrow its visible timeframe down to a very small number of frames.

✦ **Comp Family button:** Pressing this button reveals the composition being modified in the Timeline up in the Comp window.

✦ **Switches panel:** This panel contains switches that affect the quality of a layer's display in the Comp window.

- ✦ **Switches/Modes panel button:** Clicking this button hides the switches panel and brings up the Modes panel in its place.

- ✦ **Modes panel:** This panel enables you to specify transfer modes and track mattes on a specific layer.

Introducing the Switching Columns

A careful look at the Timeline window reveals quite an eyeful of little icons and check boxes. These reside in panels that are located on either side of the column containing layer names. By default, the A/V Features Panel is located to the left of the layer outline column, and the Switches/Modes Panel is positioned to the right of the layer outline column. You can change the overall layout of these columns and alter the appearance of the Timeline to suit your taste by clicking and dragging the columns to the left and right, releasing them after they're in the positions you prefer. Click a switch to turn it on or off; even better, click and drag across a column of switches to toggle multiple switches. Also, you can increase or decrease a panel's width by clicking and dragging the raised vertical bar at the edges of the panel.

Seeing and hearing — The A/V panel

There are a number of different kinds of switches in the Timeline window, and the ones under the A/V panel affect individual layers. The A/V panel, shown in Figure 3-2 below, contains a very useful bunch of switches: visibility, audio, solo, locking, and the keyframe navigator.

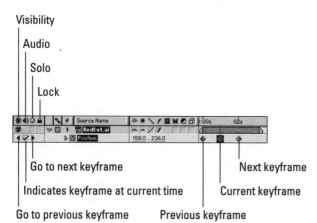

Figure 3-2: The A/V Panel contains a number of switches related to a layer's video and audio tracks.

The following list explains each of these switches in detail.

✦ **Visibility:** The visibility icon is intuitively represented as an eye. Turning this switch on and off for a layer determines whether you can see it in the Comp window. It is useful if you want to focus on certain layers by hiding the visibility of others.

✦ **Audio:** The audio icon is displayed as a speaker with sound waves emanating from it. This switch allows you to turn on or off an audio track on a given layer.

✦ **Solo:** Clicking the solo switch turns on the visibility and audio for only the layer that has the solo switch turned on.

✦ **Lock:** Clicking this switch locks a layer down. After turning this switch on, any attempt to change the layer at all is prevented. It can be quite useful after you get a layer's animation down because you won't have to fear that an errant mouse click will ruin any of your work.

✦ **Keyframe Navigator:** If a keyframe has been set for a layer, this box appears, enabling you to set more keyframes at other points in time or to see that the playhead is parked where a keyframe has already been set.

Global composition switches

There are a number of buttons at the top of the Timeline window. These switches, shown in Figure 3-3, affect a composition as a whole. They apply to all layers in a composition.

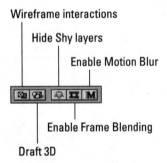

Figure 3-3: These switches affect all the layers in the Timeline window.

The following list explains each of these global switches in detail.

✦ **Wireframe Interactions:** If you're compositing in 3D, turning on this switch keeps previewing time at a minimum by showing only wireframes for the layers that make up a 3D comp.

✦ **Draft 3D:** If compositing in 3D, turning on this switch also keeps previewing time down by rendering the 3D layers at a lower resolution.

✦ **Hide Shy layers:** Turning on this switch hides from the Timeline window all the layers that have their own shy switch turned on.

✦ **Enable Frame Blending:** Turning on this switch enables Frame Blending for all motion footage items that have their own Frame Blending switch turned on.

✦ **Enable Motion Blur:** Turning on this switch enables Motion Blur for all layers that have their own Motion Blur switch turned on.

Flipping switches in the Switches panel

The items under the Switches panel are similar to the ones under the A/V panel in one respect. These switches, shown in Figure 3-4, also affect individual layers.

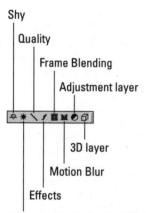

Figure 3-4: These switches affect the individual layers in the Timeline window.

The following list explains each of these switches in detail.

✦ **Shy:** Turning on this switch hides a layer's visibility in the Timeline if the Hide Shy Layers switch has been turned on.

✦ **Collapse Transformation/Continuously Rasterize:** This button is bit more complicated than the others. It's only available as an option if the layer is either a nested composition or an Illustrator file. If the layer is a nested composition, then the switch represents the collapse transformation function. If the layer is an Illustrator file, the switch represents the continuously rasterize function.

✦ **Quality:** This switch determines the image quality of the layer in the Comp window.

✦ **Effects:** This box appears if one or more effects have been applied to a layer. You can turn the visibility of the effect(s) on or off by using this switch.

✦ **Frame Blending:** Turning on this switch blends frames of a motion footage layer if the Enable Frame Blending switch is turned on.

✦ **Motion Blur:** Turning on this switch blends frames of a motion footage layer if the Enable Frame Blending switch is turned on.

✦ **Adjustment Layer:** Turning on this switch turns a layer into an Adjustment Layer. Effects applied to an adjustment layer are applied to all other layers beneath it in the stacking order.

✦ **3D layer:** Turning on this switch enables the Z dimension of a layer.

Finding the hidden panels

The following panels are optional and not visible by default. These hidden panels are probably good things because there's hardly screen space to include all of these panels unless you have dual monitors. You can display the hidden panels by Control+clicking/right-clicking on any of the Timeline window panel headings (see Figure 3-5).

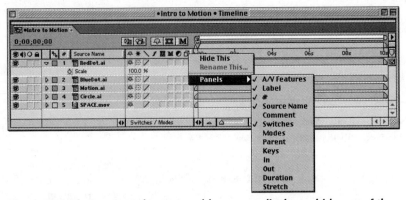

Figure 3-5: The contextual menu enables you to display or hide any of the optional panels one at a time.

The unchecked items are the panels that are presently hidden from view. Select them individually from the contextual menu to make them visible. Also, you can click the Optional Panel button to show the In, Out, Duration, and Stretch panels all at once (see Figure 3-6).

Figure 3-6: Clicking the Optional Panel button displays all of the optional panels at once.

✦ **Comment panel:** You can type your own production comments in this column.

✦ **Parent panel:** This panel contains a button and a pull-down menu, both of which allow you to specify a parent or child layer.

✦ **Keys panel:** This panel, if displayed, becomes a detached keyframe navigator panel. Remember that if it is not displayed, you can set keyframes from the usual location in the A/V features panel.

✦ **In panel:** This panel displays the In point of a layer. You can manually enter a timecode value here to change the In point if you like, but this is much more easily achieved by dragging a layer handle in a layer's time graph.

✦ **Out panel:** Like the out panel, this panel displays the Out point of a layer. You can enter a specific timecode to change the Out point of a layer.

✦ **Duration panel:** This panel displays the duration of a layer. You can change it by manually entering a timecode value.

✦ **Stretch panel:** This panel enables you to time-stretch a layer.

Knowing the time graph in depth

Do you know what time it is? Chances are you'll know exactly where you are in time, at least with regard to your After Effects composition if you understand the following aspects of the time graph (shown in Figure 3-7). A thorough grasp of these features in this part of the Timeline window will have you manipulating the layers of a composition with ease (also see the upcoming sidebar, entitled "Navigating your way in time without losing any time").

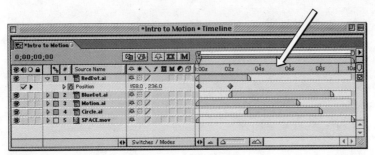

Figure 3-7: The time graph is the section of the Timeline window in which you can wield precise control over a layer's in and out points, the temporal locations of its keyframes, and whether or not a layer is time-stretched.

✦ **Viewing-area markers:** Clicking and dragging on these markers adjusts the amount of time that is visible in the time graph. Use them to zoom in on a specific area of the time graph.

✦ **Navigator view:** This depicts a miniaturized view of the entire composition so that you can see your present view of the time graph as it relates to the whole.

✦ **Work-area markers:** These markers serve as the boundaries within which After Effects renders or previews a comp. By default, they are set to the entire length of a composition, but you can click and drag them to single out a specific area of the time graph for a smaller render or preview.

✦ **Time ruler:** These tell you the exact temporal location in the time graph. Occasionally, you need to look at these milestones to know your relative position.

Three buttons are also located next to the time graph, in the upper-right corner of the Timeline window (refer to Figure 3-8 to see what each one looks like). The Window menu button displays the Timeline window menu, which offers the features shown in Figure 3-8.

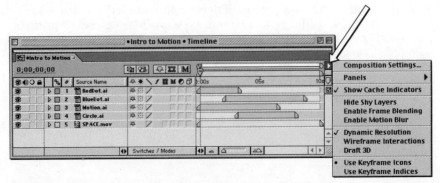

Figure 3-8: Click the Timeline window menu button to see the list of available options.

The comp marker bin button enables you to add markers to your composition as a whole. Click and drag from the button toward the middle of the time graph, releasing the mouse to add your marker after it has been properly positioned. You can move the position of these markers after you've initially placed them by clicking and dragging on them as well (see Figure 3-9). You can use up to 10 markers per composition.

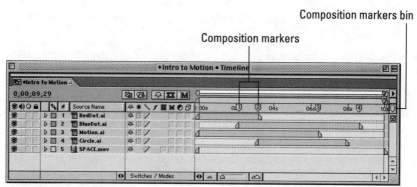

Figure 3-9: You can use composition markers in the Timeline window by clicking and dragging them from the comp marker bin.

Last of the three buttons, clicking the comp family button brings the comp at the front of the Timeline to the front of the Comp window as well.

There you go. You've just learned the function of all the switches in the Timeline. Earlier in our history of using digital tools in design work, a friend told us that if you really want to learn what a piece of software can do, push every button and see what happens. We found this to actually be a great piece of advice when learning the nuances of an application, such as After Effects. (It's also a distinctly bad bit of advice to try in front of a paying client, but we assume you know that.) Still, if you've absorbed the preceding information at all, now you can push most of the buttons in the Timeline without flying blind.

Undergoing a Transformation

After you place a layer in the Timeline, you can alter its appearance in a composition in the following three ways: You can add masks to it, you can apply effects to it, and you can alter its *transform* properties. These transform properties are the focus of this chapter. Add a footage item to a composition and twirl down the arrow to the left of its layer name in the Timeline to see the layer's main properties. As soon as these are visible, twirl down the transform properties to display each of them (see Figure 3-10).

Navigating your way in time without losing any time

Set aside a few minutes to get this right. Doing so will really pay off later on. Ultimately, you want to be able to directly control your relative view of the time graph so that you can zero in on an area of time whose scale is so enlarged that individual frames appear visible just as easily as you can see the composition as a complete piece.

Dragging the playhead moves you around the time graph with ease. Sometimes though it's a clumsy and imprecise way to get to a specific location in time. You can increase your accuracy when navigating time in a number of ways.

✦ **Click the Current Time and key in a numerical value:** Use the Command+G/ Ctrl+G keyboard shortcut if you prefer. Navigating time this way can be very efficient, but here's an important note on that: You'll make the most of this feature if you enter base 30 numbers. For instance, entering 29 takes you to 0:00:00;29. Entering either 30 or 100 takes you to 0:00:01;00. You don't have to enter any number using the SMPTE timecode conventions, which involve seven digits, two colons, and one semicolon. You could, but why bother when you can save so much time just by sticking to the numeric keypad? The Go To Time dialog box also conveniently tells you the base 30 equivalent of your numerical entry, as shown in the figure in this sidebar.

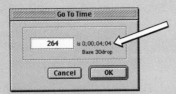

Figure SB 3-1: The Go To Time dialog box conveniently converts your numerical entry into its base 30 equivalent.

✦ **Drag the playhead while holding down the Shift key:** Using the playhead in this manner makes it snap to important locations in the Timeline. For example, the playhead will jump to the In or Out point of a layer, a comp marker, a keyframe location, and so forth. If you have something going on the Timeline, dragging the playhead through a composition while holding down the Shift key will, like a tour bus, hit all the important destinations.

These transform properties are displayed in the following order: Anchor Point, Position, Scale, Rotation, and Opacity. You experiment with each one of these in the following exercises.

Tip

The rest of this chapter is very step-intensive. Rather than just read about them, you'll become a lot more familiar with the various transform properties by altering and animating them. Regarding this particular aspect of After Effects, you learn more by doing than anything else. The steps are fairly specific at the top of the section, but by the end, the instructions become a lot more open-ended. By then, you should be leaning more on the side of creating than following directions.

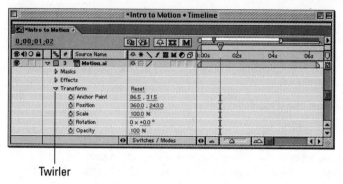

Twirler

Figure 3-10: The transform properties of a layer are listed under the transform twirler of a layer: Anchor Point, Position, Scale, Rotation, and Opacity.

To better understand what happens when you make changes to each of these properties, you'll experiment with each of them to reveal their inner workings. We should mention that we listed them in a different order than they appear under a layer in the Timeline. Our reason for this shuffling is that you can better understand changes to the anchor point after you've tried your hand at position, scale, and rotation. Before you rush through the exercises, start After Effects, open a new project, and save it with a recognizable name (such as *Chapter 3.aep*).

Changing position

The position property represents the X- and Y-coordinates of a layer as they relate to the Comp window. After Effects treats the upper-left corner of a composition as 0, 0. If a layer is in the center of a 320 x 240 comp, its X- and Y-coordinates are 160 and 120, respectively. Therefore, an increase in the x-value shifts a layer to the right and an increase in the y-value shifts a layer down. The following steps demonstrate ways to change a layer's position.

The following exercise uses footage items, which are located on the DVD-ROM in a folder called *Source Material*. Just as a reminder, you need to copy the *Source Material* folder from the DVD-ROM to your hard drive.

Feel free to import whatever items you like. We provide you with some items to get you going, but if you have your own elements, by all means, please use them. These general concepts apply regardless of whatever media you import.

Typically, we won't describe every method of completing the same action in step exercises, but we are going to do it in this chapter. We just want to make you aware of all the ways to affect changes in each property. Because you have numerous ways to complete the same action in After Effects, it pays to know what all of them are before developing your own style of working.

STEPS: Changing a Layer's Position

1. **Create a new 320 x 240 composition, give it a name, and take a footage item from the Project window and add it to the new composition.** We use *FourPoints.ai* from the *Illustrator* folder located in the *Source Materials* folder on the DVD-ROM.

2. **Select the layer in the Timeline.**

3. **Twirl down the layer's transform properties.**

Tip

After selecting the layer in the Timeline, press the P key to solo the position property. This way, you don't have to look at all of the other properties if you only want to change the values for one.

4. **Using the Selection tool, move the layer around in the Comp window by clicking and dragging it.** Be careful not to click and drag the corners of the layer because this will scale it, not move it. Watch the x- and y-values change in the position property for the layer in the Timeline as you move the layer around. Add the Shift key while moving the layer in order to limit the positional change to only one coordinate. Refer to Figure 3-11 to see what's involved in changing a layer's position.

Layer

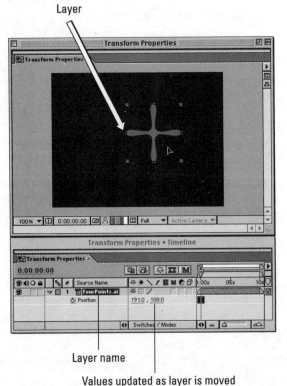

Figure 3-11: Look at what's involved in changing a layer's position.

Layer name

Values updated as layer is moved

5. **Move the layer by "scrubbing" (clicking and dragging) across the x and y fields in the position property.** You can also enter exact numerical values in these fields by clicking them and typing numbers, or you can Control+click/right-click one of the fields and choose Edit Value to bring up a separate dialog box in which you can enter specific values (see Figure 3-12).

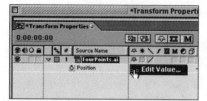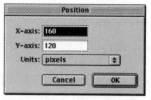

Figure 3-12: Control+click/Right-click the position property's value and choose Edit Value to bring up a separate dialog box in which you can enter specific values.

Tip

You can also enter specific values simply by clicking the numerical value in the Timeline, which then changes to a dialog box enabling you to enter the value directly.

Tip

By default, regular scrubbing changes a property value in whole numbers. Hold down the Command/Ctrl key as you scrub to increase or decrease a property's value in increments of $\frac{1}{10}$. Hold down the Shift key as you scrub to change a property's value in increments of 10.

6. **Also, you can adjust a layer's position in one-pixel increments by using the arrow keys.** Hold down the Shift key and use the arrow keys to move a layer in 10 pixel increments.

If you lose your way, a couple of things you can always do regardless of the property you're altering are as follows:

✦ Choose Edit ➪ Undo (Command+Z/Ctrl+Z) to undo your last action.

✦ Click the word Reset at the top of the list of transform properties under the layer to reset the position property to its initial state.

Note

The differing methods of changing a property's values are universal in their application. Just to remind you, they are as follows: scrubbing a field, clicking and entering exact numerical values in a field, and Control+clicking/right-clicking a field to bring up a separate dialog box. Now that you know what these different methods are, there's no need to keep repeating them.

Changing scale

By default, the scale property of a layer is set to 100%. By indicating a value of 100%, After Effects is telling you that the layer is set to the exact size of the original file's pixel dimensions. You can set this scale value above and below 100%, and you can also have a negative scale value. You can scale a layer well past the edges of a composition, and you can change scale disproportionately. Doing so changes the layer's pixel aspect ratio.

STEPS: Shrinking and Expanding Scale

1. **Using the same composition from the last exercise, make sure the layer is selected in the Timeline.**

2. **Twirl down the layer's transform properties to see the scale property or press the S key to solo the scale property.**

3. **Using the Selection tool, click and drag on a corner of the layer in the Comp window.** This changes the scale of the layer. Dragging toward the center of the layer makes it smaller. Dragging away makes it larger. To maintain the layer's aspect ratio, hold down the Shift key as you drag. As you adjust the scale of the layer, watch the scale values change in the Timeline (see Figure 3-13).

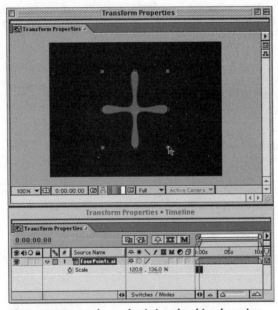

Figure 3-13: Look at what's involved in changing a layer's scale.

4. **Also, you can adjust a layer's scale in 1% increments by holding down the Option/Alt key and pressing the + (bigger) or – (smaller) keys on the numeric keypad.**

What's new in After Effects 5.5: Revealing modified properties and constraining scale

In After Effects 5.5, now you can opt to see only the modified properties of a layer in the Timeline. This saves you major screen real estate, which is always a good thing. In order to take advantage of this feature, you can press the "U" key twice, or you can select Animation ➪ Reveal Modified Properties. Not only is this great for simplifying your view of the Timeline, but also it helps you keep track of exactly what you're doing to any given layer.

Another improvement in After Effects 5.5 has to do with the Scale transform property. In the Timeline, you can scrub a layer's horizontal and vertical dimensions so that they scale uniformly, or you can click the little "chain" link icon next to the numerical scale values, which makes it disappear and enables you to change the scale of a layer disproportionately.

5. **Reset the scale of the layer to 100%.**

6. **Using the Select tool in the Comp window, click and drag one of the middle handles on either side of the layer toward the middle of the layer.** Continue dragging through the middle of the layer and release the mouse after you reach the other side. In case that's confusing, you may find it easier to flip the layer the following way: Control+click/Right-click on the Scale value field and choose Edit Value. Enter –100 in the width field of the dialog box and then click OK.

Note   If you ever need to "flip" a layer, setting its horizontal scale to –100% will invert the image.

Changing degrees of rotation

The rotation property is pretty much what you'd expect. By changing a layer's rotation property value, you can spin a layer clockwise or counter-clockwise. By default, a layer's rotation is set to the orientation of its source file's original state. The rotation property is measured in two fields, complete turns and number of degrees. We tell you a little more about this later, but a layer rotates around its anchor point.

STEPS: Changing Degrees of Rotation

1. **Using the same composition from the last exercise, make sure the layer is selected in the Timeline.**

2. **Twirl down the layer's transform properties to see the rotation property or press the R key to solo the scale property.**

3. **Using the Rotation tool, click and drag the layer, dragging in a circular motion to rotate it.** Rotate the layer multiple times. Rotate the layer in either direction. If you rotate the layer while holding down the Shift key, the layer will rotate in increments of 45 degrees. As you adjust the rotation of the layer, watch the rotation values change in the Timeline (see Figure 3-14).

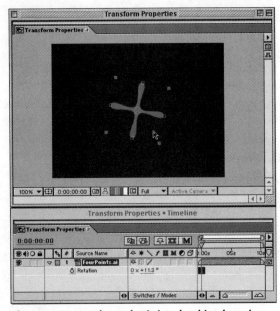

Figure 3-14: Look at what's involved in changing a layer's rotation.

4. **You can also adjust a layer's rotation in increments of one degree by pressing + (clockwise) or – (counter-clockwise) on the numeric keypad.** Add the Shift key to change the increments to 10 degrees.

Adjusting the anchor point

The anchor point property is what After Effects refers to when rotating or scaling a layer. Like position, the anchor point property is comprised of x- and y-coordinates, but these are relative to the layer, not the composition. By default, the anchor point of a layer is set to its center. If you change its value and then scale or rotate the layer, the results will be quite different than those you just witnessed in the previous exercises.

STEPS: Shifting the Anchor

1. **Using the same composition from the last exercise, make sure the layer is selected in the Timeline.**

2. **Twirl down the layer's transform properties.** (You can press the A key to solo the anchor point property, but you want access to the scale and rotation properties.)

3. **Using the Pan Behind/Anchor Point tool, click inside of the center of the layer where the x symbol is located and drag it away from the center toward another part of the layer.** After you position the anchor where you want it, release the mouse (see Figure 3-15).

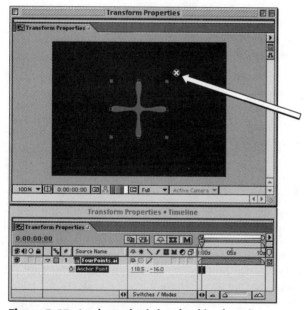

Figure 3-15: Look at what's involved in changing a layer's anchor point.

Cross-Reference

You can also set the anchor point for a layer in the Layer window. We cover this later in the chapter.

4. **Scrub the rotation and scale properties to see how repositioning the anchor point has fundamentally changed these properties.** When rotating, the layer rotates around its anchor point, not its center (see Figure 3-16). When scaling, the layer increases and decreases in size relative to its anchor point, not its center.

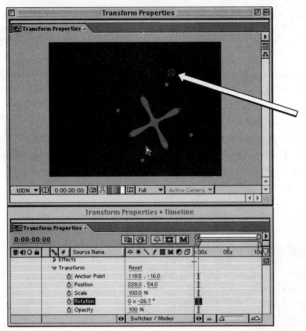

Figure 3-16: Rotate a layer after adjusting its anchor point.

Fading opacity

The opacity property defines a layer's transparency. By default, it is set to 100%. At 100%, the layer is fully opaque or completely visible. At 0%, the layer is fully transparent or invisible. Set to a level in between these extremes, both the layer and whatever is behind it are partially visible. Unlike the other properties described so far, opacity does not involve motion or space. Regarding transparency, opacity levels do not apply to the places in a layer where a mask has been placed or an alpha channel has been defined.

Cross-Reference Masks are discussed in further detail in Chapter 9. Alpha channels are discussed in Chapter 2.

STEPS: Fade In, Fade Out

1. **Using the same composition from the last exercise, make sure the layer is selected in the Timeline.**

2. **Twirl down the layer's transform properties to see the opacity property or press the T key to solo the opacity property.** (It's easier to remember T as standing for transparency.)

3. **Option+click/Alt+click the Opacity property name and hold the mouse
   button down.** A slider appears to the right of the layer's transform properties.
   As you continue holding the mouse down, move it up or down to adjust the
   opacity value, releasing the mouse after you have set the level that you want.
   As you move the slider, the changes in the layer's opacity are updated in the
   numerical next to the property name (see Figure 3-17).

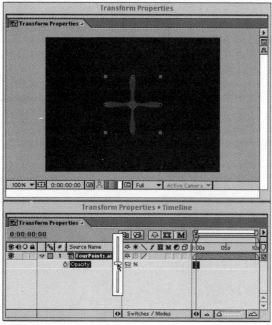

Figure 3-17: Look at what's involved in changing a
layer's opacity.

Tip   You can also invoke a slider for the scale and rotation properties by Option+click-
       ing/Alt+clicking the property names.

Note   The Info Palette reports all the changes to a layer's properties as you alter them.

Now you can identify and modify each of the transform properties of a layer. The
next section of the chapter involves animating each of these properties over time,
so that you won't regret having learned the details of these properties in the previous exercises.

Introduction to Keyframes

After Effects is software for creating dynamic media. You can use Photoshop and Illustrator to create artwork, but you need After Effects to make your images move. Keyframes enable designers to control the way their designs move over time. A keyframe in the Timeline specifies a value for a property at a specific time. A keyframe animation requires the use of at least two keyframes. The keyframes must have different values specified for the same property, and they must be placed at different points in time.

For example, you may assign an opacity keyframe at 0;00;01;00 in which you set the opacity level to 100%; then you could add another opacity keyframe at 0;00;03;00 in which you set the opacity level to 0%. Over the course of those two seconds, After Effects interpolates the opacity value in between the two keyframes, displaying intermediate opacity levels in the frames between 0;00;01;00 and 0;00;03;00. Admittedly, that's a pretty long explanation for something as simple as making After Effects perform a two-second fade out, but some essential concepts are in that description. Remember, in order to carry out a keyframe animation, you need to specify at least two keyframes for After Effects to interpolate over time.

Note   There are a number of different kinds of keyframes, and we look into those in greater detail in Chapters 5 and 6.

Working with Keyframes

You can set keyframes for any property of any layer. After you create them, you can move, copy, or delete them, and you can also change their value. The following exercise demonstrates the components of a basic two-keyframe animation.

STEPS: Moving a Layer over Time — Keyframe Basics

1. **Create a new 320 x 240 composition, give it a name, and specify a length of 10 seconds.** Add a footage item to it by dragging one from the Project window to the Timeline. We use *Motion.ai* from the *Illustrator* Folder located in the *Source Material* folder in the materials included on the DVD-ROM.

2. **Select the layer and display its transform properties.** Drag the playhead to 0;00;01;00.

3. **Using the Select tool, move the layer outside the right edge of the Comp window.** Hold down the Shift key as you move the layer in order to limit the position change to the horizontal dimension (see Figure 3-18).

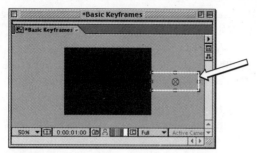

Figure 3-18: Move the layer outside the right edge of the Comp window. Constrain the move to the layer's x- coordinate by holding down the Shift key as you drag the layer.

4. **In the Timeline, click the stopwatch icon next to the Position property name (or click the Position property name and choose Animation ⇨ Add Position Keyframe).** This sets a position keyframe at the current time (see Figure 3-19).

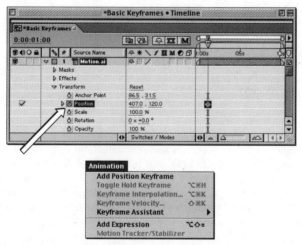

Figure 3-19: Click the stopwatch icon next to the Position property name to set a position keyframe. You can also do this by clicking the Position property name and choosing Animation ⇨ Add Position Keyframe.

5. **Select Command+G/Ctrl+G and enter 400 in the Go To Time dialog box to set the current time to 0;00;04;00.**

6. **Move the layer to the center of the Comp window.** You can click and drag the layer, but in this case, clicking the Reset transform properties button under the layer in the Timeline is actually easier because this returns the layer to the state it was in when it was added to the comp. Regarding position, resetting the position property places the layer at 160, 120. A new keyframe should appear in the Timeline (see Figure 3-20). The important point in this step is that if you change a property's value after it has been assigned a keyframe at another point in time, After Effects automatically creates another keyframe.

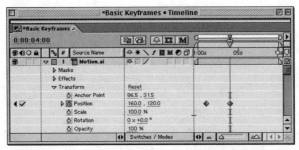

Figure 3-20: Set another keyframe by changing the current time to 0;00;04;00 and changing the position of the layer. After Effects automatically creates another keyframe because one had already been set for a different position at 0;00;01;00.

Note The appearance of these two keyframes is relevant. Looking at them closely reveals that the keyframes have some visually distinguishing characteristics. First of all, the outer halves of the icons are gray. This tells you that there are no adjacent keyframes in the direction of the half that appears gray. Secondly, they're shaped like diamonds. This shape indicates that the keyframe is using a standard method of interpolation. Other kinds of keyframes are represented by different shapes, and we address these in Chapters 5 and 6.

7. **Press 0 on the numeric keypad to preview your new animation.**

You've done it! You created a keyframe animation in which a layer crawls from off the right of the frame into the center. Granted, it doesn't seem like a big deal, but as soon as you understand these concepts and put them into action, you can take them and run. Bear in mind that most text treatments used in high-end broadcast environments are quite simple, so the animation you just made isn't merely an exercise. Tasteful, elemental text movement is some-times enough for great motion graphic design.

Cross-Reference We devote two entire chapters to text animation. See Chapters 21 and 22.

Before you move to the next exercise, finish your work on the animation from the previous steps. You keep the layer centered in the comp from 0;00;04;00 to 0;00;06;00, and then move it off the left side of the composition by 0;00;09;00.

8. **In the Timeline, click the second position keyframe at 0;00;04;00 to select it.**

9. **Choose Edit ⇨ Copy (Command+C/Ctrl+C) to copy the keyframe.**

10. **Drag the playhead to the right until the current time is 0;00;06;00.**

11. **Choose Edit ⇨ Paste (Command+V/Ctrl+V) to paste the keyframe into the current time.** This copies the keyframe located two seconds earlier. After Effects won't have a new position value to interpolate between 0;00;04;00 and 0;00;06;00, so the layer remains still during this timeframe.

12. **Drag the playhead until the current time is 0;00;09;00.**

13. **Scrub the x-value for the position property, watching the layer move to the left in the Comp window until it is no longer visible.** This sets a fourth keyframe, which completes the animation.

14. **Press 0 on the numeric keypad to preview the animation.**

In your revised animation, the layer should move onto the frame from the right, sit still in the center of the comp, and then move to the left until it is off the frame.

Tip One last detail: Try moving the second and third keyframes to different points in the Timeline. You do this by clicking and dragging the keyframes. For instance, if you move the second keyframe closer to the first (anywhere between 0;00;04;00 and 0;00;01;00), then the first part of the animation will happen faster because the change in position is taking place in less time. Experiment with moving the keyframes in the Timeline until you get a feel for the changes in speed that result in the Comp window when you preview the revised animations. This feature will prove to be very convenient as you start fine-tuning your animation techniques. See Figure 3-21 for reference.

Modifying a motion path

After you create a positional animation in a layer, After Effects displays the layer's motion path in the Comp window. You can change this path two ways. You can change the position of an existing keyframe, or you can add new keyframes. The x markers denote the keyframes of the animation, and the dots in the dotted line represent the positions for the layer at each frame in the Timeline. Figure 3-22 shows the motion path of a layer in the Comp window as well as the window's options menu. The options that you select in this menu define the appearance of the any motion path.

Figure 3-21: Move keyframes in the Timeline by clicking and dragging them.

Note   If you're having problems getting a motion path to appear as it does in Figure 3-22, make sure you clicked the Position property layer name in the Timeline. Clicking the layer shows the motion path, but clicking the Position property name enables you to see the direction handles on the keyframes.

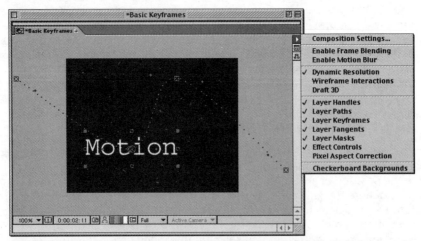

Figure 3-22: In the Timeline, select a layer that contains a positional animation to see the layer's motion path. You can also change the viewing options of a motion path by clicking the Timeline's options menu.

In the next exercise, you create another positional animation. Unlike the one you just made, this one involves a more complex motion path.

STEPS: Moving and Adding Position Keyframes

1. **Create a new 320 x 240 comp, give it a name, and specify a length of 10 seconds.** Drag a footage item from the Project window to the Timeline of your new composition. We use *Arrow.ai* from the *Illustrator* folder located in the *Source Materials* folder on the DVD-ROM.

2. **Select the layer in the Timeline and press the P key to solo the position property.**

3. **Move the layer in the Comp window to the lower-left corner of the composition.**

4. **Set a position keyframe (on the first frame of the composition, or 0;00;00;00) by clicking the stopwatch to the left of the Position property name.**

5. **Drag the playhead two seconds forward and move the layer to the upper-left corner of the composition.** This sets a second keyframe at 0;00;02;00. If you want the motion path to be straight, hold the Shift key as you drag the layer to its new position.

6. **Drag the playhead two seconds forward again, this time moving the layer to the upper-right corner of the composition.** This sets a third keyframe at 0;00;04;00.

7. **Drag the playhead two seconds forward another time, this time moving the layer to the lower-right corner of the composition.** This sets a fourth keyframe at 0;00;06;00.

8. **Select the first keyframe located at the beginning of the Timeline (0;00;00;00) and copy it by choosing Edit ⇨ Copy (Command+C/Ctrl+C).** You copy this keyframe so that you can paste it later in time.

9. **Move the playhead forward two seconds so that the current time reads 0;00;08;00 and choose Edit ⇨ Paste (Command+V/Ctrl+V).** This sets a fifth keyframe.

10. **Click the Position property layer name.** This highlights all the keyframes in the Position property line of the Timeline, and it also displays the motion path you just created for the layer up in the Comp window. The results of these steps are shown in Figure 3-23.

11. **Press 0 on the numeric keypad to preview your work.**

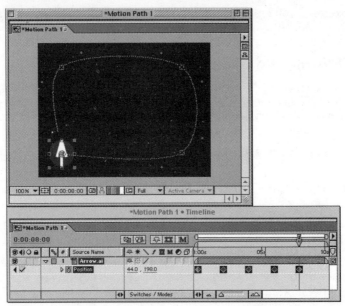

Figure 3-23: After creating the motion path in this exercise, your Timeline and Comp windows should resemble these here.

You have a basic motion path here. Still yearning for more lively motion? Continue ahead. It keeps getting better. Next, you're going to use a couple of different methods to move some of the keyframes you just made, and then you're going to add more keyframes directly to the motion path in the Comp window.

12. **If necessary, press any key to stop your preview from looping.**

13. **Select the layer in the Timeline to deselect all of the property keyframes that you selected after you completed Step 11.**

14. **In the Comp window, the x markers represent the position keyframes. Click and drag the keyframe in the upper-left corner of the Comp window and drag it toward the center of the frame.** Using this method, you can change a position keyframe's coordinates without having to be located at the keyframe's location in time.

15. **Use the right arrow of the keyframe navigator to jump to the third keyframe at 0;00;04;00.** The keyframe navigator is shown in Figure 3-24. You use it to move the current time directly from keyframe to keyframe within a given property.

Figure 3-24: Click the arrows of the keyframe navigator to jump from keyframe to keyframe within a given property. The check mark in the check box indicates that the playhead is parked on a keyframe.

16. **After you navigate to the third position keyframe, scrub the x-value of the position property to move the layer to the upper-left corner of the Comp window.** This is a different method of changing an existing keyframe than the one you learned in the last step; specifically, you're making certain that the current time marker is positioned on a keyframe and then changing the keyframe's value.

17. **Using either method, move the fourth keyframe in the comp to the upper-right corner of the Comp window.**

18. **Again, using either method, move the fifth keyframe to the center of the Comp window, next to the second keyframe.**

19. **Using the Pen Tool, position the pointer over the motion path between the fourth and fifth keyframes (see Figure 3-25).**

20. **Click this part of the motion path to add a keyframe.** Look at the Timeline to see the addition of a new keyframe between 0;00;06;00 and 0;00;08;00 (see Figure 3-25).

21. **In the Comp window, drag what is now the seventh keyframe to the lower-right corner of the composition.**

22. **Drag the sixth keyframe, the one you just added to the motion path with the Pen tool, to the center of the composition, next to the second keyframe.**

23. **In the Timeline, copy the first keyframe.**

24. **Press the End key to go to the last frame of the composition and paste the keyframe you just copied.** Your motion path should resemble Figure 3-26.

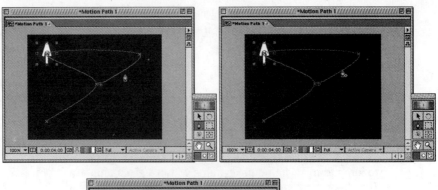

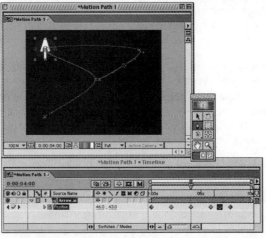

Figure 3-25: Position the Pen tool over the motion path. Click the motion path to add a new keyframe when the appearance of the Pen tool's icon changes to the Add Point tool as shown. This new keyframe lies between 0;00;06;00 and 0;00;08;00 in the Timeline.

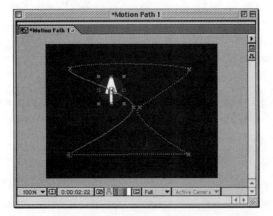

Figure 3-26: Your motion path should resemble the Comp window shown here.

25. Press 0 on your numeric keypad to preview your animation.

You'll notice speed variations in the second half of the animation. Reposition the placement of the keyframes in the Timeline to experiment with the speed between keyframes.

Note

After Effects has an excellent feature that can be a lifesaver at times. What if you have to change the speed of your animation as a whole? Put another way, what if you like your motion path but need it to take place in less time? In the Timeline, select all of the position keyframes by clicking the Position property layer name. Hold down the Option key and click and drag the last keyframe toward the beginning of the composition. All of the keyframes will scale to a smaller duration while maintaining their relative temporal distance from each other. Test the results by creating a RAM Preview and watch the speed changes.

By now, you've mastered the basics of adding and changing position keyframes to a layer in the Timeline and Comp windows. The next exercise involves using an entirely different way of creating a motion path. You can actually draw a motion path with your mouse in After Effects by using the Motion Sketch palette. Warm up your freehand drawing skills and take a pass at the steps that follow.

STEPS: Using the Motion Sketch Palette to Create a Motion Path

1. **Create a new 320 x 240 composition, give it a name, and drag a footage item from the Project window to the Timeline of your new composition.** We use *Arrow.ai* from the *Illustrator* folder located in the *Source Materials* folder on the DVD-ROM.

2. **Select the layer in the Timeline.**

3. **Choose Window ⇨ Motion Sketch to bring up the Motion Sketch palette (see Figure 3-27).**

Figure 3-27: The Motion Sketch palette

Before continuing, we should mention a few words about the features of the Motion Sketch palette. By default, Capture Speed is set to 100%, Show Wireframe is checked, and Keep Background is not. The work area you've set in the Timeline defines the Timeframe shown at the bottom of the palette. The Capture Speed percentage defines how quickly After Effects will play back your motion sketch relative to the speed at which you draw the path. Show Wireframe enables you to see only the layer's wireframe when drawing the path. Keep background shows the other layers in a comp in case you want to draw a path while seeing the placement of other layers as you draw. For this exercise, you can stick with the defaults because you're working with the only layer in the comp.

4. **Click the Start Capture button on the palette.** When you're ready, click and drag the layer in a path of your choosing, and After Effects will create position keyframes for the path you draw (see Figure 3-28). The Motion Sketch palette stops recording after you release the mouse.

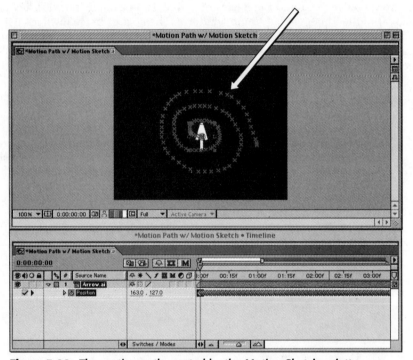

Figure 3-28: The motion path created by the Motion Sketch palette

Preview your animation and look at how the Motion Sketch palette recorded your every move. In the Timeline, pay attention to the vast number of keyframes that exist in the Position property for the layer. You're probably glad you didn't have to set all of those keyframes individually. Think of this as a tool to be used in conjunction with the techniques we just explained in the last exercise. To simplify the motion, you can select any of the keyframes and move or delete them. You can also move them in the Comp window. If you want to give a layer complex motion, think of using the Motion Sketch palette as a point of departure (also, take a look at the upcoming sidebar on The Smoother). As soon as you create a motion path this way, you can always adjust the keyframes.

Tip To delete a keyframe, select it in the Timeline and press the Delete key.

Don't stop now; you're just getting started. What if you could make the layer rotate relative to its motion path? Well, you can.

Tip Make certain the layer you just sketched a motion path for is still selected. Then choose Layer ⇨ Transform ⇨ Auto-Orient (Command+Option+O/Ctrl+Alt+O). Preview your work or drag the playhead through the Timeline to get a sense of the changes in your animation. Big timesaver, don't you think? As with the Motion Sketch palette, imagine if you had to set all those rotation keyframes yourself.

Caution If your layer isn't pointed in the right direction, adjust its rotation until it is. We had to rotate our *Arrow.ai* layer a little over 90 degrees to properly adjust the animation.

Economies of scale

Scale animations are a commonly seen animation technique across dynamic media. Using scale, you can make images disappear off into the horizon, or you can expand them until they appear to come forward right through the frame like a tidal wave. The following steps introduce you to these basic scale animations. We applied them to typography in our example.

STEPS: Scaling a Layer

1. **Create a new 320 x 240 comp, give it a name, and specify a length of 10 seconds.** Drag an Illustrator footage item (preferably type) from the Project window to the Timeline of your new composition. We use *Motion.ai* from the *Illustrator* folder located in the *Source Materials* folder on the DVD-ROM.

2. **Select the layer in the Timeline and press the S key to solo the scale property.**

3. **Click the stopwatch next to the Scale property name to set the first keyframe.**

4. **Move forward in time by a second or two (we're not going to get pushy over animating in two second increments anymore; the point of that was to get comfortable navigating to specific points in time at will).**

5. **Decrease the scale value way down to anywhere between 0 and 10%.** You can do this in either the Timeline or the Comp window. Remember that if you change the scale in the Comp window, you should hold down the Shift key if you want to maintain the layer's aspect ratio. Regardless of how you change the scale, this sets a second keyframe.

6. **Go forward in time again, click in the scale field, and enter a value of 300%.** Look at your results in the Comp window (see Figure 3-29).

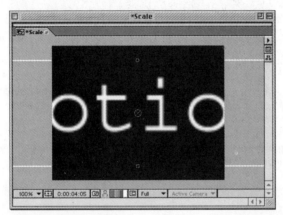

Figure 3-29: Illustrator text scaled to 300% without continuous rasterization

Smoothing a motion path

Since we've briefly touched on the Motion Sketch palette, we should also tell you a bit about its companion, The Smoother (see Figure SB 3-2). As you may have noticed, when left at its default settings, the Motion Sketch palette generates a large number of keyframes. When you're recording the movement of the mouse with the Motion Sketch palette, unless you're consistently graceful, some of the keyframes are going to give your moving object a "jerky" kind of motion. In any case, you're probably going to end up with far more keyframes than you need to complete your animation.

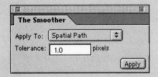

Figure SB 3-2: The Smoother palette's simple appearance belies its power.

Enter The Smoother. It gets rid of unnecessary keyframes and smoothes out the overall motion path of you layer as much or as little as you specify. For example, if you look at Figure SB 3-3, you'll see a motion path for a layer that was created using the Motion Sketch palette.

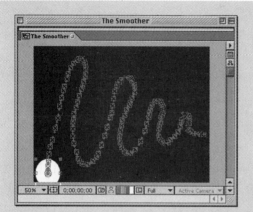

Figure SB 3-3: Here's a motion path created using the Motion Sketch palette.

After applying The Smoother to all those keyframes, you get the cleaner results shown in Figure SB 3-4.

Figure SB 3-4: Here's the same motion path greatly simplified with the aid of The Smoother.

The following steps explain how you can take advantage of this small, yet indispensable, palette.

STEPS: To Smooth a Motion Path Created with the Motion Sketch Palette:

1. **In the Timeline, click the Position property name to select all the keyframes created with the Motion Sketch palette.**

   Just so you know, you can select as few as three keyframes to take advantage of The Smoother

2. **Select Window ➪ The Smoother.**

3. In The Smoother palette, set a value of 5 in the Tolerance field.

The new keyframes that The Smoother generates will vary from the original motion path created with the Motion Sketch palette no more than the value you specify here. Higher tolerance values create smoother motion paths, but bear in mind that as you specify greater tolerance values, the shape of the original motion path will be pretty compromised. Look for the right balance.

4. In The Smoother palette, click Apply.

5. Tap 0 on the numeric keypad to see if you like what The Smoother did for you.

6. If you're happy, that's great. If not, select Edit ⇨ Undo The Smoother to reset the keyframes, enter a new Tolerance value, and click apply once again.

Preview your animation. At 300 % scale, the Illustrator type looks slightly fuzzy and distorted. At values above 100%, Illustrator artwork looks sharp only if you turn on the Continuously Rasterize switch for the layer in the switches column. Turn the switch on and preview the animation once again. This improves the image quality immensely, except it takes After Effects longer to make the preview. For more information, see "The Continuously Rasterize switch" sidebar.

The Continuously Rasterize switch

You might have noticed that we used Illustrator artwork for all of the basic animation exercises in this chapter. If you were paying even closer attention, you may have noticed that we had the high quality switch turned on in the switches column as well. Turning on the high quality switch tells After Effects to create an anti-aliased (non-pixelated, clean and soft edged) image of the Illustrator file. Illustrator artwork usually looks superb in After Effects because an Illustrator file is a vector-based image, not a bitmap image.

Because Illustrator files are mathematically derived vector-based images, you may think that you can scale them up indefinitely toward infinity. You can, but not without consequences. After Effects reads the mathematical vector information in the Illustrator file and actually converts it to a bitmap image through a process called rasterization. After Effects can only cleanly rasterize an Illustrator file up to 100% of the file's original size. If the scale of an Illustrator file is set to above 100% of its original dimensions, After Effects needs to be "told" to recalculate the vector math to produce clean lines. You tell it to do so by turning on the Continuously Rasterize switch in the switch column of a layer, as shown in Figure SB 3-5. Depending on the complexity of the Illustrator file, these recalculations can put a heavy load on your processor as well as your RAM when previewing. In general, try your best to create Illustrator files that are already properly sized for their use in a comp. Otherwise, you run the risk of losing precious render time that could easily be shortened by increasing the Illustrator file's dimensions in Illustrator and re-importing the file rather than sticking with one that was too small to begin with.

Figure SB 3-5: Turn on the Continuously Rasterize switch to cleanly size an Illustrator file past 100% scale.

By contrast, you can't rasterize a pure bitmap, because if you scale a bitmap beyond 100%, there's no mathematical data to recalculate. Scaling a bitmap past 100% merely multiplies the existing number of pixels in an image to the point of distortion. Doing so merely repeats pixels in areas of an overscaled image, which don't have any pixels defined.

Employing spins, fades, and a moving anchor

Our guess is that you probably don't want to spend any more time creating animations that focus on a single property anymore. Lucky for you, we put together an exercise that incorporates rotation and a moving anchor point.

STEPS: Spinning Around a Moving Anchor

1. **Create a new 320 x 240 composition, give it a name, specify a length of 10 seconds, and drag an Illustrator footage item (preferably type) from the Project window to the Timeline of your new composition.** We use *FourPoints.ai* from the *Illustrator* folder located in the *Source Materials* folder on the DVD-ROM.

2. **Select the layer in the Timeline and press the R key to solo the rotation property.**

3. **Hold down the Shift key and press the A and T key to add the anchor point and opacity properties to the soloed list.**

4. **Click the stopwatch next to the Rotation property name to set the first keyframe.**

5. **Press the End key to go to the last frame of the composition and enter a value of 20 in the first Rotation property field.** This means that the layer will make 30 complete turns during the course of the composition. Preview it to make sure that the layer spins over time.

6. **Press the Home key to return to the beginning of the composition.**

In the next few steps, you use the Layer window to set the anchor point keyframes. You can access any Layer window by double-clicking a layer in the Timeline. (See Figure 3-30.) We're only going to use the Layer window to work with the anchor point. Most After Effects users also use it to move an effect point or create a mask, but those topics are covered in later chapters.

7. **Move forward in time until the playhead is at least a second into the composition.**

8. **Click the stopwatch next to the anchor point property to set the initial anchor point key frame.**

9. **Move forward in time by a couple more seconds and double-click the layer in the Timeline.** This brings up the Layer window (see Figure 3-30).

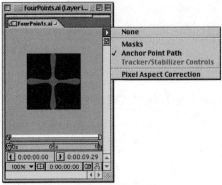

Figure 3-30: The Layer window is the preferred place for animating anchor points, effect points, and creating masks.

10. **Click the Layer window options menu located at the upper-right corner of the Layer window and select Anchor Point Path.**

11. **In the Layer window, click and drag the anchor point away from the center of the layer out to either side until it is positioned at the layer's edge.**

12. **Preview your work by scrubbing the playhead back and forth through the Timeline or pressing 0 on the numeric keypad.** The layer spins around its center until the anchor point starts its move. At that point, the rotation completely changes character because the basis for the rotation has changed.

13. **Make the anchor point animation symmetrical.** In other words, copy the second anchor point keyframe and paste it a couple of seconds further down the Timeline. Copy the first keyframe and paste it a moment or two before the end of the composition. This way, the composition begins and ends with the layer spinning around its center.

14. **Preview your work and work with it until you can adjust and move the keyframes at will.** As soon as it looks good to you, be sure to save your project if you haven't already.

Now that you've started animating across the different transform properties within the same composition, it's time to leverage that last animation you just made. In After Effects, if you make it once, you can use it again anywhere. For a finale, you're going to treat the comp you just put together as its own footage item in another comp.

Introduction to nesting compositions

Nesting, or pre-composing is a central component of working in After Effects. The basic idea behind it is fairly simple. Compositions are organized hierarchically. For example, you can nest Composition #1 into Composition #2, which, in turn, can be nested into Composition #3, and so on. A nested composition appears as a layer in its parent composition, and you can animate it the same as any layer you just animated in the previous exercises. Just to reiterate the fundamentally important lesson in this case: A composition is its own footage item in the Project window. You can use it as an element in any other composition in your After Effects project.

Cross-Reference Nesting, or pre-composing, is explained in terms of After Effects' rendering order in Chapter 4, the focus of which is the Render Pipeline.

STEPS: Using Carbon Copies

1. **Create a new 320 x 240 comp, give it a name, specify a length of 10 seconds, and drag the last comp you worked on directly from the Project window into the Timeline of your new composition.**

2. **Select the layer in the Timeline.**

3. **Choose Edit ➪ Duplicate (Command+D/Ctrl+D) to duplicate the layer.** Do this two more times. You should have four instances of the layer representing the nested comp in the Timeline (see Figure 3-31).

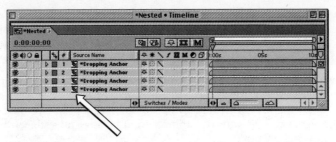

Figure 3-31: The Timeline contains four instances of the same layer, which in this case is a nested composition.

On the DVD-ROM

The design that we created with this particular composition involves moving each layer diagonally across the comp toward its opposite corner. We scaled the pre-comp layers to 40%. As the move begins, we simultaneously fade up the opacity of all the layers. We flipped two of the four layers of the composition so that the movement down the central axis is symmetrical. If you feel so inclined, we recommend that you deconstruct our project and re-create it yourself. You can either work backwards from the final output, which is a QuickTime movie called *Nested.mov*, or you can cheat a little, and look at the compositions in the *Chapter 3.aep* After Effects project.

At this point, we leave it to you, really. Animate to your heart's content. The key concept is that you now know how to create keyframe animations in all of the transform properties of any layer, whether its origin is a source file or a nested composition. Even though we cover more advanced keyframe animations in Chapters 8 and 9, a thorough mastery of these basic techniques will serve you well. Don't forget that simple motion and opacity changes can be used to great effect.

✦   ✦   ✦

Setting Your Preferences

A whole chapter on preferences? You're kidding, right? It's not nearly as bad as it sounds, and in the end, you'll thank yourself for reading it. Preferences determine everything from the workings of the interface to the appearance of actual rendered output that you create with After Effects. In other words, not understanding them may result in animations that don't come off properly.

So, put aside your misgivings about a chapter whose subject matter appears to be mundane, because it isn't. Really. Besides, skimping here will only result in all kinds of extra and unwanted pressure in a performance situation. We raise issues here that are exactly the kind you need to understand when working on a deadline. You're always likely to hit bumps on the road from project to project, but at least you'll be better prepared for them if you know a thing or two about the underlying structure of the software.

Preferences and settings can be divided into three major categories. First, we deal with preferences that affect the application as a whole. Next, we discuss settings that are specific to any given project. Lastly, we deal with settings that concern only a composition in a project. So, start the journey from the top and take a look at After Effects' general preferences.

Setting Overall Preferences

Pull up the General tab in the Preferences dialog box by choosing Edit ➪ Preferences ➪ General (Command+Option+; /Ctrl+Alt+;). A glance at the first screen tells you this involves more than simply how you'd like your fonts to appear on-screen (see Figure 4-1). Use the Next and Previous buttons to navigate through the different preferences: General, Preview, Display, Import, Output, Grids & Guides, Label Colors, Label Defaults, Cache, and Video Preview.

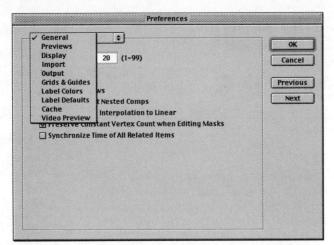

Figure 4-1: The pull-down menu in the Preferences dialog box shows all of the different preferences you can change.

When you start After Effects for the first time, After Effects creates a preferences file. This file contains all of the default settings and preferences exactly as you find them after installing the software. If you're a Mac user, you can find the *Adobe After Effects 5 Prefs* file in the preferences folder located inside the system folder. If you're a PC user, you'll need to do a search for the *Adobe After Effects 5 Prefs.txt* file (see the sidebar on directly editing the prefs file). If you ever need to reset the preferences to their original defaults, just delete this file and restart After Effects. Restarting the app creates a new preferences file once again.

The rest of this section focuses on each of the screens offered in the General Preferences menu. When it's over, you should be able to change the appearance of a motion path just as easily as you can explain the title-safe margin of the Comp window.

Setting General Preferences

Look at the General tab in the Preferences dialog box and see if you immediately understand all of the options it displays (see Figure 4-2). This ought to give you a relatively good idea of how much you already know about the application. If you're just getting started with After Effects, some of these options won't make any sense. If this is the case, make it a goal to understand the meaning of your choices in these windows. You'll really benefit from it.

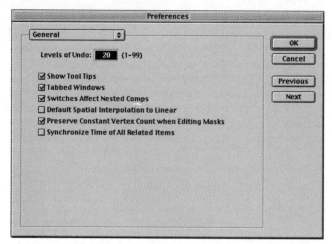

Figure 4-2: The General tab of the Preferences dialog box

Changing Levels of Undo

Working in After Effects would be impossible without the Undo function. When you're moving objects around the Comp window and setting keyframes in the Timeline, you need to be assured that you can backtrack your way to the point where you made a mistake. A lot of beginning users are surprisingly gun-shy with the software because they're afraid of making a mistake or losing something that looks good at the moment. To them we always say, save early and often, and set your Levels of Undo well above the default.

The default number of Levels of Undo is set to 20, and as the window tells you, it can be set from 1–99. Your choice here affects the amount of RAM that After Effects has at its disposal. The higher the number, the larger the RAM footprint, but we still suggest setting this number at 50 or above. These days, RAM has gotten a lot cheaper, and most people creating After Effects animations have pretty beefy workstations loaded up with at least 256MB of RAM. More often than not, they've got 512MB to 1GB's worth, on average! These numbers were unthinkable several years ago, but they're commonplace now. If you're one of the lucky souls with tons of RAM, set the Levels of Undo high. If you're a relic of the not so distant past, 20–50 makes more sense.

What for? Well, changing the current time is an undoable action, for instance. See where that's headed? Imagine that you created an elaborate motion path for a layer in a composition. At that point, you'd want to preview your work, and perhaps you'd want to do that by dragging the playhead through the Timeline to get a sense of the layer's movements. If you change the current time 20 times, you'll no longer be able to backtrack to whatever steps you went through in creating your animation. Instead, you'll have to recreate it from memory. No huge deal, but a hassle nonetheless, so set this number higher than the default.

Tool Tips

This feature is on by default, and we generally feel no consequence for leaving this switch turned on. If you're new to After Effects, definitely leave it on. You've probably seen Tool Tips at work. If you hold the mouse over any item in the tool palette or a switch in the Timeline, a Tool Tip will tell you the function of the item in question as well as a keyboard shortcut in some cases (see Figure 4-3). Tool Tips are very useful to see what everything does, and sometimes you can forget the keyboard shortcuts for tools and the like. At times like these, it's best if you leave Show Tool Tips checked.

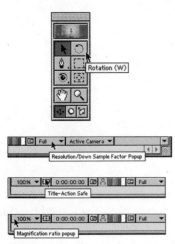

Figure 4-3: When activated, Tool Tips show you the function of a switch or tool as well as its keyboard shortcut in some cases.

Tabbed Windows

By default, if you have more than one composition open at a time, they appear as tabs in both the Comp and Timeline windows. Many moons ago, actually in After Effects 3.1 and prior versions, each individual composition appeared in its own Timeline or Comp window. You can always view them in their own separate windows by turning the Tabbed windows switch off in general preferences, but we leave this switch on because you can still view any tabbed window on its own.

For example, open a project with multiple compositions and double-click at least two of the comps in the Project window. This opens the comps up as tabbed windows in the Comp and Timeline windows. You can reorder the layout of the comps in the Comp and Timeline windows by clicking and dragging them within their respective windows, or you can drag them out of their tabbed positions so that they stand in their own windows. You can also drag them back (see Figure 4-4). So, to get the best of both worlds, we leave the default setting alone.

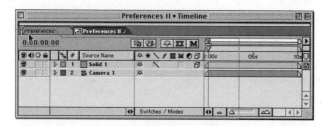

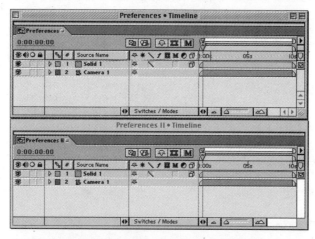

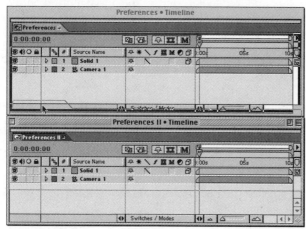

Figure 4-4: You can either reorder a comp's position in the Comp or Timeline window, or you can drag it out to its own window. You may want to do this to compare two different comps' timelines. You can also drag it back.

Switches Affect Nested Comps

By default, this option is checked. If you leave the default as is and nest compositions into other compositions, the state of the parent comp's quality and Continuously Rasterize/Collapse Transformation switches override those of any of the nested compositions. Organizationally speaking, the uppermost comp in a chain of compositions is the only one in which those switch positions matter.

Try it if you don't believe it. For example, take some Illustrator text and drop it into a composition. Leave the Illustrator text layer at low quality. Nest this new composition into another new comp and set the nested composition layer of the new comp to high quality. The Illustrator text will no longer be jagged because the switch settings travel through all of the comps that are nested in a parent comp.

Why would anyone change the default setting of this preference? The answer lies in the complexity of your compositions. For instance, say your final composition in a project consists of more than one highly detailed nested composition. If you've worked out the details and nuances of this particular nested comp in the larger framework of the parent comp, you may want to leave it in low quality resolution just to see its footprint while you work on other parts of the parent comp. This keeps your preview time at a minimum as you work out the details of the other pieces of the entire composite.

Default Spatial Interpolation to Linear

Left unchecked by default, this preference determines the initial motion path of a positional animation. When a moving layer arrives at its keyframe locations in a composition, it moves smoothly through these points using something called Auto Bezier spatial interpolation. If you change this preference, the default spatial interpolation will be linear, meaning that an object will turn a hard corner at its keyframe locations. See Figure 4-5.

If you're doing a lot of animation, this can be a big timesaver if your moves need sharp, hard-edged corners. Still, as in the case of tabbed windows, you can leave this default setting alone and change these interpolation methods very easily when you're animating, so it's not a big deal. Smooth moves are on by default, and we recommend that you not worry about this one too much.

 Cross-Reference We cover all spatial interpolation methods of animation in Chapter 7.

Preserve Constant Vertex Count when Editing Masks

This preference is checked by default. Performing a basic mask animation illustrates the ramifications of this preference pretty clearly. For the following exercise, leave the preference checked.

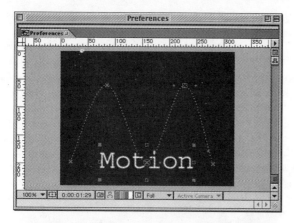

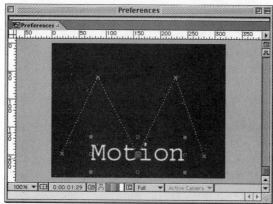

Figure 4-5: Shown on top is the default spatial interpolation (Auto Bezier). The bottom image shows the appearance of a motion path if you change this preference and put a check in the check box.

STEPS: Testing the Constant Vertex Preference

1. **Create a new 320 x 240 composition that's 10 seconds in length and give it a name.**

2. **In the new comp, create a white comp size solid layer by choosing Layer ➪ New ➪ Solid (Command+Y/Ctrl+Y).**

3. **Double-click the new solid layer to bring it up in its own Layer window.**

4. **Using the Rectangular Mask tool, create a simple rectangular mask.**

5. **In the Timeline, twirl down the Solid layer to reveal the mask's properties.** Set a Mask Shape keyframe at 0;00;00;00.

6. **Change the current time to 0;00;01;00.**

7. **In the solid layer window, use the delete point tool to delete several of the mask's points.** You are presented the error message in Figure 4-6. Click OK and move some of the remaining mask points to new positions.

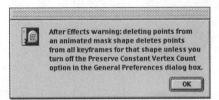

Figure 4-6: After Effects gives you the following warning if you change the number of mask points in a mask animation without changing the constant vertex preference.

8. **Return the current time to 0;00;00;00 and scrub the playhead between the two different mask shapes at 0;00;00;00 and 0;00;01;00.** The number of mask points won't change between the two points in time, and your desired animation won't occur.

We recommend changing this one so that After Effects does *not* preserve a constant vertex when it comes to editing and animating masks. Changing this preference allows After Effects to add its own points to masks that make the most sense in terms of an efficient interpolation between two defined shapes. Change the preference so that the box is unchecked and repeat the steps in the previous exercise. You won't be given any warnings, and the steps between the two shapes you define show mask points in the frames between your mask shape keyframes, which you didn't explicitly specify, but this is because After Effects is not maintaining a constant vertex. See Figure 4-7 for reference.

Cross-Reference   This preference really comes into play when performing the art of rotoscoping. We cover this in much more detail in Chapter 9.

Synchronize Time of All Related Items

This preference is unchecked by default. We strongly recommend that you change it and turn it on. After changing this one by putting a check in the check box, if you nest compositions in a project (which you will, all the time), the current time marker will stay in the same relative place when jumping from nested comp to nested comp in the tabbed comp windows of the Timeline. Trust us. You'll find this a lot more convenient than if the playhead is in a different place every time you change your view to a different nested comp in the same family of compositions.

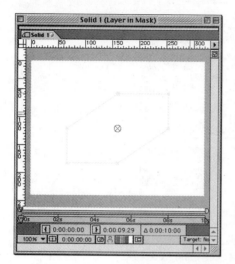
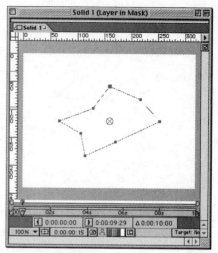
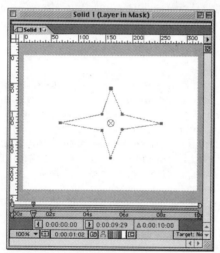

Figure 4-7: Defining a mask shape animation when the Preserve Constant Vertex preference is unchecked allows for unlimited variation in the shapes defined at the Mask Shape keyframe locations in the Timeline.

Setting Previews preferences

The Previews preferences define your visual perceptions of a composition as you work on it. How does it look as you make changes to the visuals? If you're dragging the playhead through the Timeline, where do you draw the line in terms of the resolution of the dynamically updated image in the Comp window? How much of your audio track do you hear if you preview the sound? The answers lie in the Previews preferences shown in Figure 4-8.

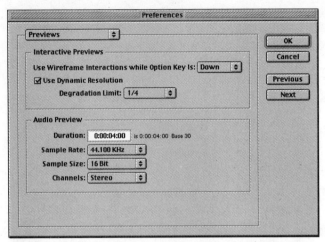

Figure 4-8: The Previews tab in the Preferences dialog box contains information that defines how a composition looks and sounds as you build it.

Interactive Previews

Previous users will recall that After Effects never used to be this way. In fact, you used to have to hold down the option key as you dragged the playhead in order to see what was happening in the Comp window. Now when you drag the playhead, an updated image automatically appears in the Comp window, even if its resolution is less than perfect. In an effort to become more of a real-time application, Adobe added dynamic preview functionality to this build of After Effects, and you can control its parameters in this Preferences dialog box.

If you leave this preference at its default setting, holding down the option key as you drag the playhead through the Timeline results in you seeing only the wire-frames of layers in a comp. If you drag the playhead through the Timeline without holding down the option key, dynamic preview viewing is enabled by default, and the Comp window will reflect the current time and keep up with you as best as it can. By this, we mean it gives you the best dynamic preview it can. If you've added effects to multiple layers of video in a sophisticated composition, then the Comp window won't immediately return a full resolution frame for every frame you drag through in the Timeline. It can't. Parking on a single frame, you have to wait a few seconds for a full resolution look at only that frame. Just as a note, you can reverse the option key function — up for a wireframe preview, down for a dynamic preview.

You can imagine that if you're rapidly moving through time, the preview will be seriously compromised if it's going to approach anything we might call dynamic or real time. Just how much you compromise that preview is determined in the second pull-down menu. By default, it's set to ¼. So no matter what you do, the preview will never fall below quarter resolution. This is about right actually; ½ is too stringent for layered comps containing high-resolution video, and ⅛ is so compromised that it's hard to get any sense of what's really happening visually. You could opt to turn dynamic previewing off altogether, but we feel that this is a nifty new addition to the After Effects workflow, which had always been a feature request amongst the faithful in previous versions of the software. So, in essence, we prefer the defaults in this case.

Audio Preview

Regarding the first audio preference, the audio preview has been set to four seconds by default. Pressing the period on your numeric keypad gives you an audio preview, the length of which you define in this Preferences dialog box. Ultimately, you set this on an as needed basis. Because an audio preview needs to be loaded into RAM, setting it to a long amount of time makes for a longer wait before you hear the preview, so your aversion to longer preload times are the basis for your choice regarding this preference. Unlike a visual preview, an audio preview plays from wherever the current time marker is, not from the beginning of the defined work area.

With regards to the second audio preference, you should set the audio preview sample rate to match the sample rate of the audio file you're working with. Otherwise, After Effects needs to spend time resampling the native file to play it back at the different sample rate. Why lose time if you don't need to? By default, the sample rate is set to 44.1 kHz, and that's because that's the native sample rate of CD audio, which constitutes most of the audio After Effects users end up putting into a Timeline. We find ourselves regularly changing this setting to 48 kHz though, because we import a good deal of video that uses this higher sample rate. DV video as well as other video acquired from various capture boards uses the higher sample rate, and you may want to change the preview sample rate accordingly.

Setting Display preferences

The Display preferences augment certain aspects of the interface as you do your work on a project. The appearance of a motion path, thumbnails in the Project window, and other visual displays of quantitative information are impacted by your choices in this group of preferences shown in Figure 4-9.

Motion Path

If you create complex or looping animation paths for a layer, you can end up with very messy Comp windows if you display the resulting motion paths. With this preference, you can specify the amount of a motion path that is shown in the Comp window. By default, this preference is set to show you the motion path for five seconds of a layer. This means two and one-half seconds in either direction of the current time in the Timeline. Figure 4-10 shows five seconds worth of a relatively simple motion path, a very complex motion path, and a circular motion path. Seeing five seconds worth of a simple animation seems sensible and convenient. The same idea seems downright awful when applied to a complicated motion path. Finally, a circular path looks simple enough at first glance, but how can you tell which keyframe symbol in the Comp window corresponds to the same keyframe in the Timeline? You can't. "You can't handle the truth!"

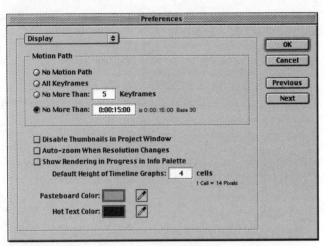

Figure 4-9: The Display tab in the Preferences dialog box contains information that defines the visual display of the quantitative information of an After Effects project.

If you adjust this preference to include a smaller timeframe, the relative motion path should be easier to interpret. So, basically, adjust this setting according to the complexity of your animations. You can set it to a chosen number of keyframes or a chosen timeframe, or you can select no motion path if you don't want your vision disturbed by the dotted lines of a motion path whatsoever. Why select no visible keyframes? If you worked out your motion path and you don't plan on altering it at all, selecting this may rid you of visual clutter. You can also opt to show all keyframes, but for all the previously listed reasons, we would recommend this only in rare cases.

Disable Thumbnail Views

Why would you ever disable thumbnail views? Well, if you're working with complicated compositions that contain other compositions involving lots of graphic elements and high-resolution video, creating those thumbnails actually costs you quite a bit of both processor time and RAM. Again, as is the suggestion with so many of these preferences, play it by ear. Adapt according to need. Thumbnails can be very useful visual guides, but so can a sensible composition-naming scheme. This option is definitely something to consider if the thumbnails are taking forever to appear in the Project window.

Auto-zoom When Resolution Changes

This preference is not selected by default. If you always want to maintain a 1:1 pixel resolution in the Comp window, then you should select it. For example, if you're viewing a 320 x 240 comp at 100% magnification and full resolution, your Comp window will directly reflect every pixel in a composition. If you select half resolution from the resolution pop-up menu in the Comp window, then you'll only see half the pixels in the comp, but it will still be displayed at 100% magnification.

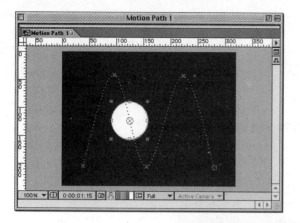

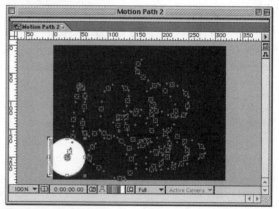

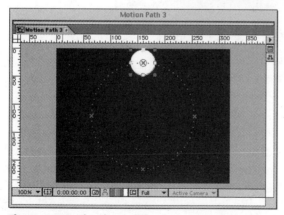

Figure 4-10: The three different motion paths for a five second timeframe all look quite different.

Try selecting this preference and noting the results. Doing so will ensure that the magnification of a comp will always match its resolution. Using the same example from the previous paragraph, selecting half resolution will drop the comp's magnification to 50%, thereby maintaining full resolution. In other words, if you select this preference, you will always be viewing the Comp window at full resolution regardless of the magnification.

Show Rendering in Progress in Info palette

We just turn this preference on to get a sense of where the bottlenecks are in a render. It keeps us from wondering why a certain comp is taking so long to preview and points us to the culprit whether it's a RAM intensive effect or something of that nature. Knowing what After Effects is "thinking" about is always better than just getting irritated by the fact that it continues to hang in certain places. Why do guesswork? As we said, we turn it on; by default though, it's turned off.

Default Height of Time Layout Graphs

When you twirl down an individual transform property, the height of the graph is determined by this preference (see Figure 4-11). You can change the default height of this graph by changing the number of cells in this preference, but you need not concern yourself with this too much because you can change the height of the graph by clicking and dragging the graph's edge up or down directly in the Timeline.

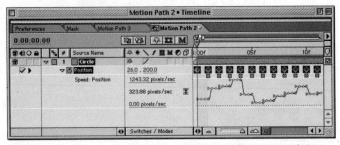

Figure 4-11: The default height for this time layout graph is set in the Display preferences.

Pasteboard and Hot Text Color

The pasteboard is the area inside the comp window, which is outside the composition's dimensions. Editable property values in the Timeline or Effects Control windows are comprised of "hot text." You can set the colors for both of these by using the color picker in this preference option.

Setting Import preferences

The Import preferences determine the default manner in which you import any media into a Project. You can influence parameters ranging from the length of still footage to the way in which After Effects handles any alpha channel. Look at the Import tab in the Preferences dialog box in Figure 4-12.

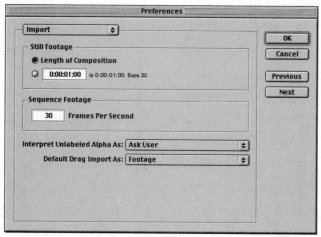

Figure 4-12: The Import tab in the Preferences dialog box determines the manner in which you import media into a Project.

Still Footage

By default, stills run for the length of the composition into which they are placed. Sometimes you may want to create a slideshow, and in a case like that, you may want to change this default setting to one second or whatever you prefer. If you change this preference, remember that you can always change the out point of the still footage layer back to the length of the composition by dragging the layer's handle directly in the Timeline.

Sequence Footage

The Sequence Footage frame rate determines the frame rate of any imported sequence of still images, in other words, a TIFF or a JPEG sequence. Simply change this preference if need be.

Alpha channels

Unless you know that you're going to bring a hundred of the same kind of alpha channels in at once, it's better to leave this option in its default Ask User mode. After Effects imports labeled alpha channels appropriately. This preference only pertains to those alpha channels that are unlabeled.

Default Drag Import

You can select either footage or composition from this pull-down menu. By default, it's left as footage. You may want to change this if you're consistently working with layered Photoshop or Illustrator files, but we tend to leave this one alone because you can change it as you import files along the way.

Setting Output preferences

The Output preferences determine the manner in which After Effects prepares its rendered files (see Figure 4-13).

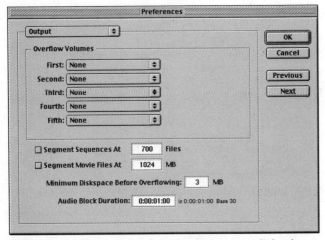

Figure 4-13: The Output tab in the Preferences dialog box determines the manner in which you save your After Effects renders.

Overflow Volumes

If applicable, you can select Overflow Volumes in this set of preferences. If you're rendering huge film files, you'll probably find yourself needing to set these preferences. After Effects spreads render files across overflow volumes after it has run out of disk space on the original volume. You may have multiple RAID arrays as part of your setup. If this is the case, you can specify each one of these as an overflow volume.

Segment options

The segment options determine the size of the segments that constitute a final render. The default sequence setting is 700 files. If you were exporting a TARGA sequence, After Effects would place the first 700 TARGA files in one folder and begin a new folder on the 701st file from the render. The default movie file segment is

1GB, meaning that if a render were to exceed 1GB in size, After Effects would continue placing the rendered output in a new file. Some systems have problems playing back files over 2GB in size, so that's why this option was engineered.

Setting Grids & Guides preferences

All of the Grids & Guides preferences deal with partitioning the available screen real estate of the Comp window into sections that serve as a visual guide for the layout of elements. They can also help you remain mindful of the fact that most NTSC screens don't display complete frames as they appear on your computer screen in After Effects. Look at the Grids & Guides Preferences in Figure 4-14.

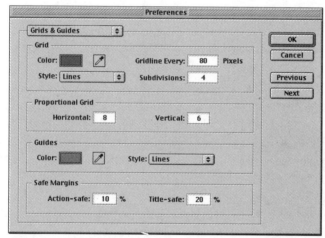

Figure 4-14: The Grids & Guides tab in the Preferences dialog box determines the manner in which you lay out your elements when building compositions in After Effects.

Grid

In these preferences, you get to determine the color of the grid lines as well as their appearance: lines, dashed lines, or dots. You can also determine the number of lines and their distance apart from one another as well as the number of subdivisions between each grid line. To see the grid in action, Command+click/Ctrl+click the Title Safe button at the base of the Comp window (see Figure 4-15).

Proportional Grid

The Proportional Grid always appears the same regardless of the composition you may be working on. Its lines are positioned relative to a composition's dimensions. To see the proportional grid in action, Option+click/Alt+click the Title Safe button at the base of the Comp window (see Figure 4-16).

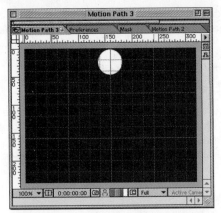

Figure 4-15: The grid appears in the Comp window according to the specs defined in the Grids & Guides preferences.

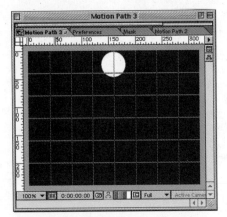

Figure 4-16: The Proportional Grid appears in the Comp window according to the specs defined in the Grids & Guides preferences.

Guides

In this part of the Preferences dialog box, you can set the color and appearance (lines or dotted lines) of guides in the Comp window. You set guides in After Effects in exactly the same way as you do in Adobe Photoshop or Illustrator. Turn rulers on by pressing Command+R/Ctrl+R and drag a guide from the ruler margin out into the Comp window, releasing it after you line it up where it needs to go. The Info palette indicates the exact location of your guide as you drag it into place.

Safe Margins

Title safe (20% in from the edge) and action safe (10% in from the edge) areas indicate those parts of a composition in a frame of NTSC video that are considered "safe" for type and motion according to industry standard. You can change the percentages of these margins in this Preferences dialog box, but we never do in the interest of making certain that our creations remain visible to all audiences. (Refer to Figure 4-17.)Typically, NTSC frames are bigger than TV sets unless they can overscan. Most TVs don't. Usually, you can only see the overscanned areas of an NTSC image on a nice expensive NTSC monitor. Click the action-title safe button in the Comp window to remind yourself of NTSC limitations while building a composition.

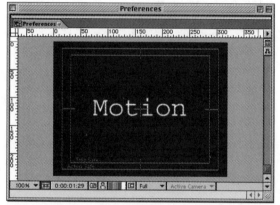

Figure 4-17: The action-safe and title-safe margins of a composition are visible when you click the Action-title safe button at the bottom of the Comp window.

Tip Look at the View menu to see the keyboard shortcuts related to grids and guides.

Setting Label Colors and Label Defaults preferences

Use the Label Colors preferences to assign specific colors to the label headings that After Effects offers as a means of visually differentiating between media types (see Figure 4-18).

Assign labels to the different media types through the use of the pull-down menus in this Preferences dialog box, as shown in Figure 4-19.

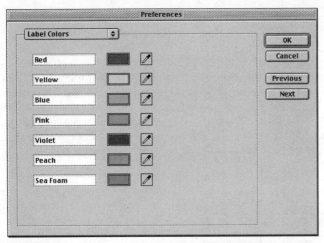

Figure 4-18: The Label Colors tab in the Preferences dialog box determines the colors and label names assigned to the label headings in After Effects.

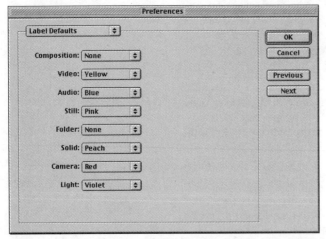

Figure 4-19: The Label Defaults tab in the Preferences dialog box determines the labels that are assigned to different media types in the Project and Timeline windows.

There are no rules on how to use these visual enhancements to the interface. The defaults tend to work for us, so we leave them as is. Look at Figure 4-20 to see how these labels appear in different parts of the After Effects interface.

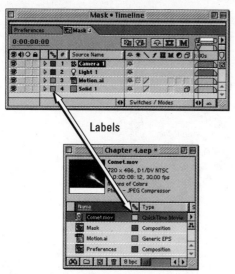

Labels

Figure 4-20: Look at the labels in the Project and Timeline windows. Note that you can sort a project's footage items by clicking the label column.

Setting Cache preferences

This preference determines how After Effects uses the RAM that's been allocated to it. You can set the percentage of RAM allocation dedicated to Image Cache, and you can also set whether or not the RAM favors speed or memory, as shown in Figure 4-21. If you select speed, this will limit the number of frames that are loaded for a RAM preview but will improve your performance when using RAM intensive effects. If you favor memory, After Effects will use its memory allocation more judiciously at the expense of your preview time. We leave this setting to the default of Favor Speed.

Setting Video Preview preferences

This preference is new in After Effects 5. Hallelujah! Now you can preview your output on an NTSC device, and this extends to FireWire compliant DV gear. This feature also works on capture cards. Rather than having to wait until a render is complete to see your work on an NTSC monitor, you can check the progress of your design in its intended output format right away, as shown in Figure 4-22. Folks, this is a big step forward. This has already become a cornerstone of our workflow, especially pressing / on the numeric keypad to preview a specific frame. The days of saying "I don't understand; I mean, all those reds and blues and thin lines looked so good on my computer monitor" are over.

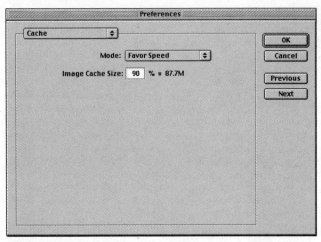

Figure 4-21: The Cache tab in the Preferences dialog box determines the manner in which After Effects employs the allocated RAM.

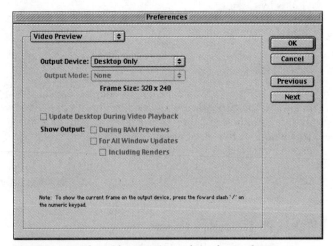

Figure 4-22: The Video Preview tab in the Preferences dialog box determines the device you use to preview your video output. You can specify an external NTSC device.

Directly editing the Preferences file

Now that we've told you how to go in and tweak the various settings in all of the dialog boxes, there's an even greater level of control for the bolder ones among you. You can open up the After Effects Preferences in a word processor such as Microsoft Word and edit them directly. To make life interesting for those of us who want more customization and control, this method actually enables some features that would otherwise remain inaccessible.

Remember, if you're a Mac user, you can find the *Adobe After Effects 5 Prefs* file in the Preferences folder located inside the system folder. If you're a PC user, you'll need to do a search for the *Adobe After Effects 5 Prefs.txt* file (make sure that "hidden" files are visible before you do your search).

Once you open up the *Prefs* file in a word-processing application, you can go hunting for things you want to customize. Amidst the 40 or so pages of confusing gibberish is a lot of intelligible English. The real power lies in modifying these passages. In Figure SB 4-1, you can see some preferences that you can't control in all the dialog boxes that we just showed you in the preceding sections.

Figure SB 4-1: Editing the *Prefs* file in a word-processing program provides the ultimate level of customization and control.

For example, in Figure SB 4-1, you can cycle the mask colors so that every time you add a mask to a layer, it will appear in a different color. By default, masks are bright yellow, and they stay that way regardless of how many you place on a layer. If you change the Cycle Label Colors entry from 00 (No) to 01 (Yes), the mask's color will change every time you create a new one.

Once you've got the 00=No to 01=Yes trick down, you can move on to other specifics. Essentially, you can do whatever you want here; just remember to save your changes before you close the document. Whatever changes you made will be apparent only when you restart After Effects.

Enjoy yourself, and if you get in trouble, you can always trash the prefs and start customizing anew.

Setting Project Settings

Project settings are largely concerned with whether or not you're working in video or film. You can pull them up by choosing File ➪ Project Settings (Command+Option+Shift+K/Ctrl+Alt+Shift+K). This dialog box displays options for timecode display and color space (see Figure 4-23). Display Style has to do with only the way a frame count is measured in the Timeline. The frames themselves don't change; you're simply using a different method of counting them. Your first option is Timecode Base with a pull-down menu offering the following choices: 24 fps, 25 fps, 30 fps, 48 fps, 50 fps, 60 fps, and 100 fps. The second option is to simply give each frame its own sequential number starting from the value you specify in the bottom field. The third option refers to film timecodes in both the 16 and 35mm formats. You can define a project's color space in this window, but you can also define it at the Project window level by Option+clicking/Alt+clicking on the 8 bits per channel/16 bits per channel button at the bottom of the Project Settings dialog box.

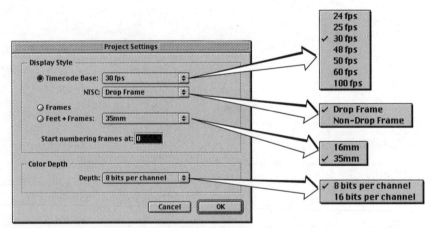

Figure 4-23: The Project Settings dialog box determines the units of temporal measurement in a project as well as its color space.

Setting Composition Settings

Chances are that you've already worked with the Composition Settings dialog box pretty extensively. Unless you always create a new composition by dragging a footage item directly onto the New Composition button at the bottom of the Project window, you'll see the composition settings window when you initially create a new composition (see Figure 4-24). After you begin working on a new composition, you can always bring back the Composition Settings window by selecting Composition ➪ Composition Settings (Command+K/Ctrl+K).

Save and Delete preset buttons

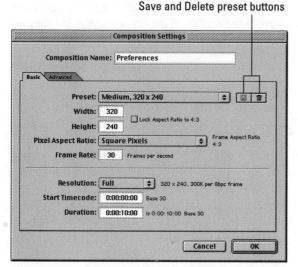

Figure 4-24: The Composition Settings dialog box determines the overall structure of your entire composition.

Setting Basic Composition settings

Remember to set your composition's settings with the final output in mind. If you're working toward creating a DV production as your final delivery medium, then set the parent composition of your project to the 720 x 480 preset offered in the Preset pull-down menu. Using the presets can save you from having to meticulously tweak each individual setting.

Setting Preset composition dimensions

Apart from selecting presets, if you find yourself consistently working in dimensions that are not defined here, you can create and save your own preset comp dimensions by using the buttons to the right of the pull-down menu. For example, you may be working to create high-end QuickTime files for a high-speed CD-ROM. These files might be authored to the following specification: 400 x 300 with square pixels at 15 fps. In this case, enter these settings and click the save button to give this preset a name. Doing this enables you to pull those settings up again without having to re-enter the information every time you create a new comp.

Setting Pixel Aspect Ratio

Despite all the choices, most of the time, you'll be selecting either square or D1 pixels in this menu option; square, 1:1 pixels for computer screen playback, and D1 pixels for either PAL or NTSC video signals. If you're outputting your work on film though, you'll need to determine which of the other choices is correct.

The latter section of Chapter 2 describes the different pixel aspect ratios in detail. Granted, these descriptions are in the context of imported footage, but they're the same regardless of whether you're tweaking comp settings or imposing pixel aspect ratios on to imported footage.

Setting Frame Rate

You can set the frame rate of your composition in this field. 24 fps is standard for film, 25 fps is standard for PAL, and 29.97 is standard for NTSC video. You can also specify other numbers, which may be appropriate for other multimedia productions. For instance, you might type in 15 for a project that will get rendered for a CD-ROM, and you might specify an even smaller number for a QuickTime movie that will get streamed over a narrowband Web connection.

29.97 fps is actually 60 fps considering that each frame is comprised of an interlaced field. See the shutter angle description in the Advanced Composition settings in the following sections for more information.

Setting Resolution

Resolution refers to the number of pixels shown in the Comp window relative to the actual number of pixels in a composition. You can set resolution in the composition settings, but you can just as easily change it by using the resolution pop-up menu in the Comp window. The equivalent keyboard shortcuts are Command+ + or –/Ctrl+ + or – (put another way, hold down the modifier key and press either the plus key or the minus key on the numeric keypad).

Setting Start Timecode and Duration

You'll probably need to change these settings fairly often if you keep adding footage to a composition and increasing its total running time. You may also want to define an exact timeframe if you're working on a tightly defined part of a larger whole. Say that you're the chief animator of the segment that runs between 30 and 45 seconds in a minute-long title sequence. In this case, you set the starting timecode at 0;00;30;00 and specify a running time of 15 seconds.

Setting Advanced Composition settings

As the name suggests, these settings aren't as intuitively understood as their basic counterparts, especially with regard to shutter angle. Read this section carefully so that you can take advantage of the appearance of any Motion Blur that you want to add to a layer in a composition. See Figure 4-25.

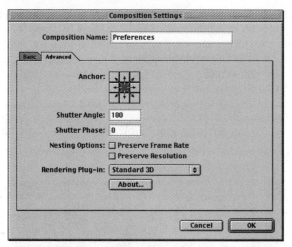

Figure 4-25: The Advanced tab in the Composition Settings dialog box determines important details that govern the appearance of work you do in a composition.

Setting a composition's Anchor

How do layers behave when you change a comp's size? This setting determines the answer to that question. For example, create a 320 x 240 composition, create a solid layer that is 160 x 120, and place the solid in the lower-right corner of the comp. Press Command+K/Ctrl+K to bring up the comp settings, click the advanced tab, and set the anchor to the lower-right corner. Return to the basic tab of the comp's settings and reset the comp's dimensions to 160 x 120. The resized comp should now have the solid layer at its center. This brief demo should explain the workings of the anchor settings, but continue to experiment with it until the mechanics become second nature. If you ever need to change a multi-layered comp's dimensions, understanding this advanced setting can minimize your headaches.

Setting Shutter Angle

Shutter Angle is actually a critical component of motion graphic design. This setting simulates the shutter speed of a real film camera. It directly affects the Motion Blur of a moving layer placed in a comp (which needs to have Motion Blur enabled for both the layer and its composition). By default, the shutter angle has been set at 180 degrees. Changing it to 360 degrees gives you the full motion blur spanning the distance covered by a moving object during the course of a frame. Put another way, imagine a moving layer covering a distance of 50 pixels per frame. A 360-degree shutter angle will display a Motion Blur for that layer which spans all of those 50 pixels; 180 degrees gives you half. The highest possible value, 720 degrees, yields the most blur. Lowering the frame rate will increase the distance the layer moves between frames, resulting in a larger relative blur.

You can test these numbers by using rulers and guides in the Comp window. Command+R/Ctrl+R displays the rulers, and clicking and dragging from within the ruler margins enables you to set guides. Mark the distance with rulers in your own example. Look at Figure 4-26 to see the different results obtained when you change these settings.

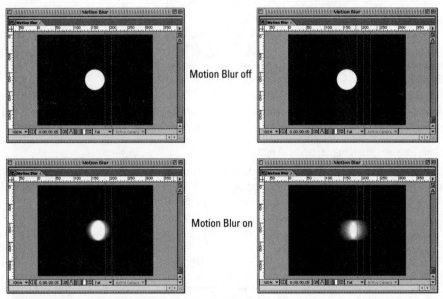

Motion Blur off

Motion Blur on

Figure 4-26: A spherical object moving from left to right in a composition set to a frame rate of 29.97 fps with a shutter angle of 180 degrees on the left and a shutter angle of 360 degrees on the right

Setting Nesting Options: Frame Rate and Resolution

This setting enables you to lock down the native frame rate and resolution of a nested composition within another composition. If you leave this setting unchecked, the parent composition's frame rate will override any frame rates of any nested compositions that may be different. To sum up, if you're nesting compositions that have frame rates different than those of the comps they are being nested into, you should check this setting for optimal playback.

What's new in After Effects 5.5: Choosing a rendering plug-in

Not so long ago, you could only get a beta of the Advanced 3D Renderer from the Adobe Web site. Now, you can choose between the Standard and the Advanced 3D Rendering options in this part of the Advanced Composition settings. So what's the big deal? It all comes down to intersecting layers. The Standard 3D Renderer doesn't handle layers whose planes cross each other, whereas the Advanced 3D Renderer renders intersecting layers while accurately reflecting their anti-aliasing, Motion Blur settings, and transfer modes. This is great, but only use it if you need to because it can dramatically increase render times depending on the sophistication of your comp.

✦   ✦   ✦

Keyframes and Rendering

Sharpening Positional Animations

Up until now, you may have had some success animating layers with keyframes. The question is, have you really been able to make your elements hit their marks with all of the subtle speed and movement changes you had envisioned in your mind's eye before you picked up the mouse? Unless you have a good grasp of the different kinds of keyframe interpolation, moving beyond creating simple-looking animations in After Effects is pretty difficult.

That's where this chapter comes in. If you're looking for that measure of control that resolves the disconnect between your motion path of choice versus the one you settle for because you're not quite sure how to make it happen, go ahead and read the pages that follow. They cover both spatial and temporal interpolation as they relate to the animated position of a layer.

To get the most out of this chapter, envision your own anima-tion. In an effort to make our point on a global level, we used the orbital motion of our planet as a point of departure. As far as space and time are concerned, you want planet Earth to be moving relatively quickly when it's close by and more slowly as it moves further away. What kind of motion path would you create? How would you affect its speed in different places? We hope to answer those questions in this chapter.

What Is Interpolation?

Words such as *interpolation* have a tendency to scare away otherwise eager designers. If you're unfamiliar with it, the concept of interpolation is simple. If you move an object from one place to another in After Effects, you tell it where the object is going and where it's coming from. After Effects does the rest by interpolating between the two positional keyframes. In other words, you don't have to build every frame from scratch.

To give you a little background on both the concept and origin of keyframes, let us say that they were invented in the early days of animation. Inside the studios of revered institutions, such as Disney and Warner Brothers, the lead animators would draw the keyframes of a cartoon. These were essentially *storyboards,* a collection of the "key" frames comprising the critical moments of the complete feature. Of course, the junior staff would have to do the grunt work of drawing all the frames in between the keyframes. After all of this work was complete, the various collections of drawings would be melded together into a final cut.

The advent of the modern digital age has changed everything once again. You may have guessed this, but After Effects handles all the frames of an animation. You specify where the keyframes go, and it deals with the rest of the details rather elegantly. In essence, you get to do more creative work while your processor, in concert with After Effects, gets to do the heavy lifting. Now that's progress.

This interpolation might not seem like such a big deal. Plenty of other animation programs have one "tweening" feature or another, but After Effects allows you to meticulously control all aspects of interpolation without the software being overly difficult. After Effects simplifies animation techniques with the help of intuitive visual aids. You can put together simple animations in no time at all. However, fabricating more realistic and sophisticated moves takes a bit more finesse. Think of *The Sorcerer's Apprentice* here. A little power can be dangerous, so sharpen your senses. In the time it takes to read a single chapter, you'll go a long way toward your quest for mastering space and time, in this application anyway.

Regarding this frequently used buzzword called interpolation, here's what you can expect to learn from this chapter:

✦ **Spatial interpolation:** Modifying a layer's path in space by adding keyframes to it and tweaking those keyframes in the Comp window.

✦ **Temporal interpolation:** Modifying a layer's speed as it moves through time by adding keyframes to it and tweaking those keyframes in the Timeline window.

✦ **Motion path and Timeline Value Graph:** Building a thorough understanding of the workings of both the motion path and the values shown in the Timeline Value Graph that correspond to a layer's position.

Cross-Reference   Just so you know, another animation method in After Effects is called *procedural animation.* As far as those techniques are concerned, you control the parameters of a computer borne animation derived from Expressions or filters, such as Particle Playground, but those topics are covered in Chapters 18 and 25.

Putting a Layer in Motion: Animating Position

The first transformation property you should learn about in detail is Position. However, if you don't have a clear idea what transform properties are at this point, take note. After Effects animates the layers of a composition in the order in which they are stacked. The top layer is processed first, the bottom last. Within each layer, the application deals first with masks and effects in that order. Finally, After Effects looks at transform properties—namely, Position, Anchor Point, Rotation, Scale, and Opacity. Translated roughly, these mean a layer's place in a comp, the location that After Effects perceives as the layer's center, its angle in the comp's layout, its size in relation to its original dimensions, and its transparency.

 Chapter 3 introduces all the transform properties and explains how to create basic animations involving each one of them.

Right now, you're only concerned with Position. More attention is paid to Anchor Point, Rotation, Scale, and Opacity a bit later. Remember that each layer in a composition contains all four of these transform properties, and each one can be animated. As soon as you discover all of the advanced ways in which you can manipulate the position of a layer in a composition, you will see that most of the same concepts will apply when you animate any of the other transformation properties.

Moving a layer through space

Every keyframe animation must contain at least two keyframes. As far as Position is concerned, you need a keyframe for a layer's place of origin and another for its destination. If you change the position of a layer without setting a keyframe, that position will remain constant for the length of the composition. In order to create a positional animation in a composition, you set a position keyframe on a layer and change the position of that layer at a different point in time. Without two keyframes of differing values, there is nothing for After Effects to interpolate.

You have several ways to set the first keyframe. You examine all of these in the following exercise.

 Regarding the pictures that complement the steps, the following exercise uses footage items, which are located on the DVD-ROM in the folder called *Source Material*. Just as a reminder: You need to copy the *Source Material* folder from the DVD-ROM to your hard drive. The following exercise deals with positional keyframe animations, and our own corresponding After Effects project is called *Chapter 5.aep* and can be found in the *Project Files/Chapter 5* folder.

Tip

Feel free to substitute your compositions with the examples on the DVD-ROM. If you prefer, just work with a single 100 x 100 solid, which we explain how to create in the following steps, and apply positional keyframes to that layer just as you would the *Planet Earth* layer referred to in the following exercises.

STEPS: Setting the First Positional Keyframe of a Layer

1. **Start After Effects and save your new project, or if you prefer, open the project called *Chapter 5.aep*.**

2. **Create a new D1 720 x 486 29.97 fps 10-second composition; otherwise, open the composition called *Positional Animation* in the *Chapter 5.aep* project.**

3. **Click the Timeline to make it the active window.**

Tip

You should know how to create a solid whether or not you use our project to complete the exercises in this chapter. Step 4 shows you how.

4. **If you aren't going to work from the project on the DVD-ROM, choose Layer ⇨ New ⇨ Solid (Command+Y/Ctrl+Y).** Specify 100 x 100 dimensions and a white color for the new solid and give it a unique name if you like. The new solid appears in the Timeline as a layer, and you can see it in the Comp window as a white square centered in the composition.

5. **Activate the layer in the Timeline by clicking the layer name.** If you're working from the DVD-ROM project, click the *Planet Earth* layer name in the Timeline to make *Planet Earth* the active layer.

6. **Click the twirler to the left of the layer.**

7. **Click the Transform twirler, and you see all of the layer's transform properties: Anchor Point, Position, Scale, Rotation, and Opacity.**

8. **Turn on the action-title safe button in the Comp window to see these action and title-safe areas clearly defined.**

9. **Move the layer to the lower-left corner of the composition, placing its edges comfortably inside the action-safe area.**

10. **Click the stopwatch to the left of the Position property to create a position keyframe for the layer 0;00;00;00.**

11. **Press the P key, and the Position property for the layer is "soloed."** See Figure 5-1 for reference.

Now it's time to add several more keyframes to the animation you've begun creating. After you do that, you look at all the ways you can modify a motion path. Before moving ahead though, review some alternatives for adding keyframes and soloing properties. You have a lot of options, and you may find some of them quite useful.

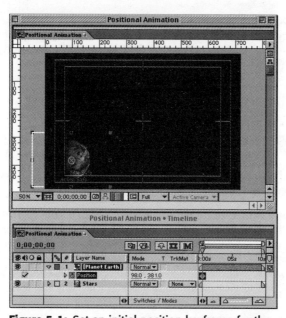

Figure 5-1: Set an initial position keyframe for the Planet Earth layer at the edges of the action safe area, and solo the Position property to focus your view.

Image courtesy of EyeWire by Getty www.gettyimages.com (Cosmic Moves)

✦ Select the position property by clicking the word Position under the transform property subheading. It should be highlighted as it is in Figure 5-1, only no keyframe should be visible in the Timeline. Then choose Animation ➪ Add Position Keyframe.

✦ Pressing Option+P/Alt+P sets a position keyframe for *all* selected layers.

You can also set Rotation, Scale, and Opacity keyframes for all selected layers by pressing Option+R/Alt+R, Option+S/Alt+S, Option+T/Alt+T, respectively.

✦ Control+click/Right-click the Position property and choose Add Keyframe.

Remember that you can solo properties by pressing the P key for Position, the A key for Anchor Point, the R key for Rotation, the S key for Scale, and the T key for Opacity (the easiest way to remember "T" is to think in terms of *transparency* rather than opacity).

Here's a very helpful tip that we use all the time: Pressing the U key on the keyboard will display all properties of the selected layer that contain keyframes. Pressing U in this case should reveal the soloed Position property.

Note   For this chapter, you'll want to see all of the keyframes that you create in the Comp window, not just a limited number defined by the default preferences. So, choose Edit ⇨ Preferences ⇨ Display (Command+Option+;/Ctrl+Alt+;) and choose *All Keyframes* from the Motion Path options.

STEPS: Adding the Second Positional Keyframe to a Layer's Animation

1. **Returning to your project from the last exercise, click in the Timeline window to make sure it's the active window.**

2. **Drag the playhead forward two seconds or press Command+G/Ctrl+G and enter a value of 200.** The Current Time should read 0;00;02;00.

3. **In the Comp window, click and drag the layer to which you've added a position keyframe until its position is in the opposite corner of the frame.** As you do this, you'll notice a series of dots extending from the initial position to the current one. Release the mouse button after you put your layer where you want. Your Comp window should look similar to Figure 5-2, and you should have a second position keyframe for your layer in the Timeline window.

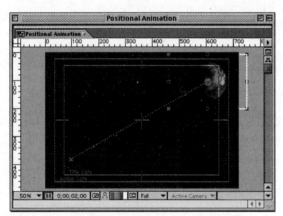

Figure 5-2: Check out the dotted lines denoting the path of Planet Earth. Each dot represents a frame in the Timeline.

Image courtesy of EyeWire by Getty www.gettyimages.com (Cosmic Moves)

4. **Preview your work with a RAM Preview by pressing 0 on the numeric keypad or by clicking the RAM Preview button, farthest to the right in the Time Controls palette.**

And so there it is. If you've been working from the DVD-ROM project, you have launched Planet Earth on a journey through space and are no doubt pondering the possibilities of wielding your newfound god-like power. Nonetheless, a couple of things are worth mentioning at this point. While there is some satisfaction at having created an animation, you've probably noticed that your motion can only be described as crude at best. You work toward improving the quality of your animation in the exercise to follow. Before going on, we should also mention that you have several other ways of creating that second keyframe.

Tip After Step 2 in the previous section, you could have clicked in the Keyframe Navigator's check box in the A/V Features panel (see Figure 5-3). Either way, you still would have to move Earth to its new location. Actually, the very act of moving Earth to its new home in the upper-right corner automatically creates a keyframe provided that you've created an initial keyframe at a different point in time. In this case, you did that at 0;00;00;00. To navigate between the keyframes of a given property, clicking the arrows on either side of the Keyframe Navigator takes you to the next keyframe in the direction of the arrow. In Figure 5-3 for example, clicking the arrow to the left of the check box takes you to the prior keyframe, which in this case, is the first one you set at 0;00;00;00.

Figure 5-3: Here's the Keyframe Navigator in the A/V Features panel. The check box indicates that a keyframe is in that property at that point in time for that layer. Clicking the arrow to the left of the check box brings you to the point in time of the previous keyframe.

So, if you revisit the existing animation, your layer moves at a constant velocity and stops on a dime in the upper-right corner of the frame. You may have found it exciting at first, but ultimately it's an empty thrill. You're going to try to create a path that mimics something more like a realistic orbit around the Comp window. As is becoming clear, After Effects gives you a lot of options in pulling this off.

Note Velocity is defined as the rate of change of position; furthermore, acceleration (or deceleration) is the rate of change of velocity, and the change can be positive or negative — that is, speeding up or slowing down. After Effects is precise and powerful enough to manipulate these parameters in addition to velocity, and this will become evident in the following exercises.

Changing a layer's positional path

You have more than a couple of ways to change a layer's path in space, and that's what you're looking into in this section. Specifically, you examine the following kinds of spatial interpolation between keyframes:

✦ Linear

✦ Bezier

✦ Auto Bezier

✦ Continuous Bezier

You start by adding a third keyframe to your layer's animation, and then you delve into all your interpolation options for that layer's motion.

STEPS: Adding the Third Positional Keyframe to a Layer's Animation

1. **Make certain that the Timeline is the active window by clicking it.**

2. **Click the Current Time in the upper-left corner of the Timeline and enter a value of 400 in the resulting dialog box.** This makes the Current Time 0;00;04;00.

3. **In the Comp window, click and drag the layer that you've been animating, adding the Shift key as you drag (in order to maintain a perfectly straight line or, in this particular instance, a consistent X-coordinate).** Position it so that it has the same x-value as it does in the first keyframe. Your Comp and Timeline windows should appear somewhat like they do in Figure 5-4.

4. **Press 0 on the numeric keypad to preview the new motion of Planet Earth.**

Notice how the layer makes a little buttonhook of a break to the left as it reaches its second keyframe. This is because After Effects' default spatial interpolation is set to Auto Bezier. That last sentence may have been a little off-putting, but fear not. More will be revealed. To that end, let's see if we can't explain these concepts of spatial interpolation in a bit more detail.

Click the second Position property keyframe in the Timeline and then choose Animation ➪ Keyframe Interpolation (Command+Option+K/Ctrl+Alt+K). Click the Spatial Interpolation drop-down menu to see your options here (see Figure 5-5).

Note   For those of you who are curious about this strange word associated with interpolation, Pierre Bezier (bez-ee-ay) was a French mathematician (1910–1999). He developed methods for manipulating the control points of parametric curves and used them for putting smooth curved lines into the designs of Renault automobiles in the early 1960s. Cars have never looked the same since, and neither has graphic design.

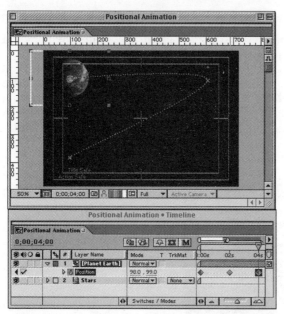

Figure 5-4: You've got a new and slightly curved motion path denoting Planet Earth's movement over time.

Image courtesy of EyeWire by Getty www.gettyimages.com (Cosmic Moves)

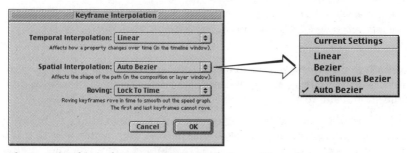

Figure 5-5: This is the Keyframe Interpolation settings dialog box.

Notice the list of options, namely Linear, no-frills Bezier, Continuous Bezier, and Auto Bezier. Auto Bezier is the default Spatial Interpolation setting. This means that as you animate the position of a layer in a comp, the object will move through its keyframes with Auto Bezier interpolation. If this seems a bit much, don't lose hope. All it means is that the object will have a smooth rather than abrupt rate of change through the keyframe. Click OK, and now experiment with changing the second keyframe so that you can see the difference between all these different kinds of movement through space.

STEPS: Understanding Spatial Interpolation Methods

After Effects provides a number of ways to alter a keyframe's interpolation. Look at all of them and decide how you prefer to work as you keep going.

1. **Click the second Position keyframe for your animated layer in the Timeline so that it becomes highlighted.** In the Comp window, look at the two gray dots above and below the x-symbol representing the second keyframe (see Figure 5-6). An Auto Bezier Position keyframe looks like this in the Comp window.

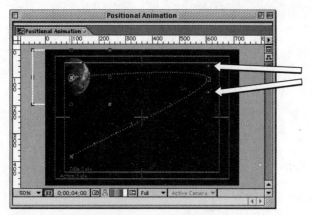

Figure 5-6: Look at the two equidistant gray dots indicating an Auto Bezier Spatial Interpolation keyframe.

Image courtesy of EyeWire by Getty www.gettyimages.com (Cosmic Moves)

2. **To confirm this, pull up the Keyframe Interpolation dialog box by choosing Animation ⇨ Keyframe Interpolation.** The spatial interpolation drop-down menu should still read Auto Bezier.

3. **Click OK and then click and drag one of the gray dots above or below the x-symbol marking the second keyframe in the Comp window so that it looks similar to Figure 5-7.** As you drag, the gray dot becomes a handle.

4. **Choose Animation ⇨ Keyframe Interpolation (Command+Option+K/Ctrl+ Alt+K).** The Spatial Interpolation menu now indicates that your keyframe is of the Continuous Bezier variety. Continuous Bezier keyframes allow for even smoother motion than Auto Bezier keyframes.

5. **Grab the handle opposite from the one you just extended and drag that one out as well as making the line of the handles perpendicular to the width of the Comp's frame (see Figure 5-8).** This is still a Continuous Bezier keyframe.

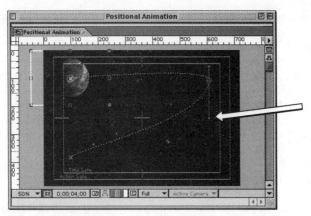

Figure 5-7: Now you see an extended handle, which means that this keyframe has crossed the threshold from Auto to Continuous Bezier.

Image courtesy of EyeWire by Getty www.gettyimages.com (Cosmic Moves)

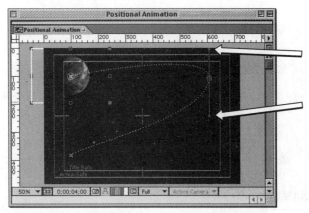

Figure 5-8: Long handles are in this Continuous keyframe variant.

Image courtesy of EyeWire by Getty www.gettyimages.com (Cosmic Moves)

6. **Press 0 on your numeric keypad and preview the layer's new motion path.**
   As you can see, you're getting close to our goal of realistic motion, but you're not all the way there yet.

7. **Press any key to end your RAM Preview after you feel you've sufficiently absorbed the nuances of your new motion path.**

Note Auto and Continuous Bezier keyframes have a couple of distinguishing character-istics worth mentioning. The handles, or control points of Auto Bezier keyframes form a line that is parallel to the line between the preceding and following keyframes. If you don't believe it, click and drag the x-symbols denoting the first and third keyframes in the Comp window to different locations. Then click the sec-ond keyframe in the Timeline and notice that the two Auto Bezier handles of the second keyframe in the Comp window are in fact parallel to an imaginary line con-necting keyframes one and three. Also, notice that if you drag the handles of a Continuous Bezier keyframe across the Comp window, the line connecting the handles remains straight despite any variation in the angle. Experiment with these two keyframes, and don't be gun-shy because you can use the Undo command (Command+Z/Ctrl+Z) as often as you need to if you lose your way.

8. **Picking up where you left off after Step 6, Command+click/Ctrl+click one of the handles of the second keyframe and drag it to a new location in the comp.** The keyframe handles are now separate (see Figure 5-9). You can manipulate them independently, and this denotes that the second keyframe has become a Bezier keyframe. Bezier keyframes allow for more control of a motion path. Make a RAM Preview of your new path if you like.

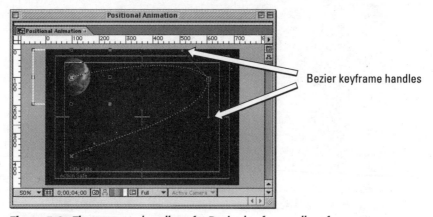

Bezier keyframe handles

Figure 5-9: The separate handles of a Bezier keyframe allow for more sophisticated manipulation when creating a motion path.

Image courtesy of EyeWire by Getty www.gettyimages.com (Cosmic Moves)

Caution The act of creating a Bezier keyframe by pressing the Command/Ctrl key and click-ing one of the handles has occasionally proven difficult for some folks. Holding down the Command/Ctrl key changes the Selection tool to the Pen tool, and if you place it over a Bezier keyframe handle, it then becomes the Convert Point tool (see Figure 5-10). If you prefer, you can also use the Convert Point tool by choosing it directly from the tools palette. Nonetheless, our advice is to get used to this short-cut simply because it allows you to create your ideal motion path more quickly. Again, don't underestimate the power of the Undo function while you're on the steep part of the learning curve.

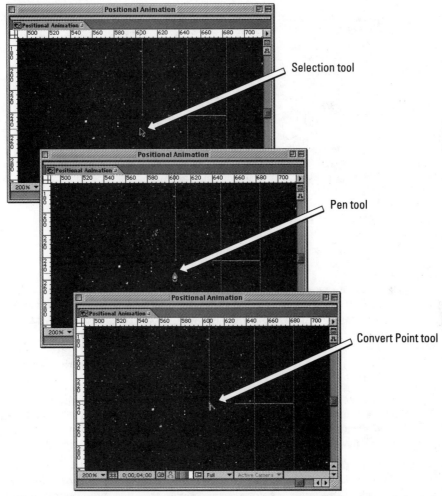

Figure 5-10: The Selection, Pen, and Convert Point tools. Both the Pen and Convert Point tools can be invoked by holding down the Command/Ctrl key when using the Selection tool.

Image courtesy of EyeWire by Getty www.gettyimages.com (Cosmic Moves)

9. **Once again, hold down the Command/Ctrl key and click directly on the x-symbol representing the second keyframe.** Notice that it has now become a Linear keyframe (see Figure 5-11). The Linear option creates the motion path of a tight corner with straight paths of entry and exit through the location of the keyframe. Preview this motion if you like.

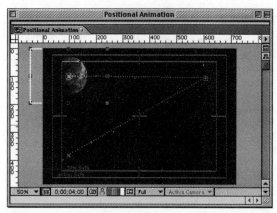

Figure 5-11: Observe the straight and, yes, linear paths of a Linear keyframe.

Image courtesy of EyeWire by Getty www.gettyimages.com (Cosmic Moves)

10. **Click the word Position in the Timeline under your animated layer in order to select all three keyframes.** Control+click/Right-click any of the keyframes in the Comp window and choose Toggle Hold Keyframe. After doing this, all you're left with are three keyframes (x-symbols) in the Comp window without any motion path between them (see Figure 5-12). Preview this, and the nature of Hold keyframes should be clear. Here one frame, gone the next.

11. **Choose Edit ⇨ Undo (Command+Z/Ctrl+Z) and return the composition to its previous state in which your animated layer had a motion path between keyframes.** Ultimately, we don't want to use Hold keyframes in this exercise, so this step returns the animation to its state following Step 9.

12. **Using the Selection tool, hold down the Command/Ctrl key (which converts the Selection tool to the Pen tool) and position the pointer over the motion path of the layer.** As you do so, the Pen tool becomes the Add Point tool (see Figure 5-13).

13. **Click the motion path now, adding another keyframe to the animation as evidenced by the changes in both the Comp and Timeline windows.** You can manipulate these new keyframes using all the methods you have just learned.

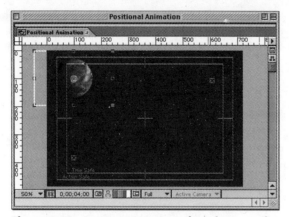

Figure 5-12: As you may expect, there is no motion path when creating Hold keyframes.

Image courtesy of EyeWire by Getty www.gettyimages.com (Cosmic Moves)

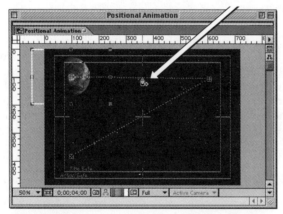

Figure 5-13: The Pen tool is converted to the Add Point tool when placed over the motion path of Planet Earth.

Image courtesy of EyeWire by Getty www.gettyimages.com (Cosmic Moves)

Well, you completed the cycle of spatial interpolation keyframes. You may want to go for a walk, clear your mind, come back, and repeat the exercise. If this is the case, don't be worried. Mastering control over space is no small matter, and neither is getting Planet Earth, or any other layer for that matter, to move along your chosen line. Just be certain that you know the different spatial interpolation methods well enough to create and modify any motion path before you move ahead.

If you're brimming with anything ranging from confidence all the way to possessing the hubris of a Greco-Roman deity, by all means, please press on. As soon as you have this aspect of animation under control, you can take Space off your to-do list and focus on Time.

Changing the Speed of a Layer

At this point, zero in on temporal interpolation instead of spatial. Temporal interpolation comes in almost identical flavors to its spatial cousin. Namely, you have the following:

✦ Linear

✦ Bezier

✦ Auto Bezier

✦ Continuous Bezier

✦ Hold

These are the same names as the options in spatial interpolation with the addition of Hold, which you actually just experimented with in the last exercise. While conceptually the same, these interpolation methods are quite different in terms of their end result in a positional animation. You can identify the different kinds of keyframe interpolation by the keyframes' appearance in the Timeline window. You'll look at all of these in detail in the exercises that follow, and when you're done, you'll have nothing less than complete control over space and time, at least when it comes to moving layers.

STEPS: Moving Keyframes in Time

Return to the project you've been working on in this chapter and try and restore it to its original three Position keyframe states. Start by clearing the decks and deleting all the positional keyframes.

1. **You can select individual keyframes and press the Delete key, or better still, you can click the word Position underneath your animated layer, which selects all the Position keyframes.**

2. **Then press the Delete key, which clears all the keyframes in a single keystroke.**

3. **If you need a reminder on rebuilding your initial animation, set keyframe #1 with your animated layer in the lower-left section of the comp at 0;00;00;00, #2 with the layer in the upper-right at 0;00;02;00 and #3 with the layer in the upper-left at 0;00;04;00.**

4. **Move the second keyframe in the Timeline by clicking and dragging it to 0;00;00;15, which is half a second or 15 frames after the first keyframe.**
You can track the position of the keyframe as you move it by watching the Info palette, which tells you the temporal location of the keyframe as you drag it back in time. Notice the difference in the number of dots in the motion path of your animated layer as you Undo (Command+Z/Ctrl+Z) and Redo (Command+Shift+Z/Ctrl+Shift+Z) the second keyframe's movement in time (see Figure 5-14). The farther apart the dots are, the faster the Earth moves through space. Remember that each dot represents one frame of the composition. Because seeing is believing, create a RAM Preview for each state as well, and notice the difference in speed. This basic demonstration of Spatial Interpolation gives you a reference point for the upcoming exercises.

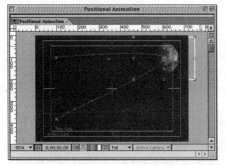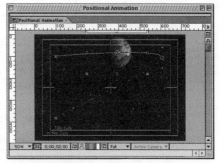

Figure 5-14: Look at the difference in the number of dots between keyframes; remember that each one represents a frame in the timeline.

Image courtesy of EyeWire by Getty www.gettyimages.com (Cosmic Moves)

Changing Temporal Interpolation with the Timeline Value Graph

Click the twirler to the left of the Position property under your animated layer. Resize your Timeline window in order to enlarge this new view and take a look around the various aspects of this part of the Interface, better known as the Timeline Value Graph (see Figure 5-15). You can also increase the size of your Timeline Value Graph by clicking its lower boundary and dragging down, releasing after you size it to your taste. This interactivity enables you to extend the border of any Timeline Value Graph as much as you like.

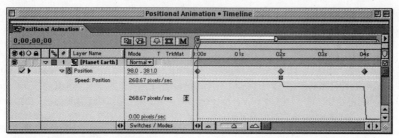

Figure 5-15: The Timeline Value Graph for the Position property of the Planet Earth layer

Select all the Position keyframes for your animated layer by clicking the property name (the word *Position*) and open up the Keyframe Interpolation dialog box again by pressing Command+Option+K/Ctrl+Alt+K. You see the default Temporal Interpolation is set to Linear. Also note your other options here, particularly the Roving keyframe menu. You examine all of these in more detail a bit later. Just so you're clear, the diamond-shaped keyframes in the Timeline are temporally linear. You create a RAM Preview after each keyframe change that you make in the following exercise just as you did in the spatial interpolation section of this chapter.

STEPS: Adjusting the Temporal Interpolation of Keyframes

1. **Drag the playhead so that the Current Time reads 0;00;06;00.**

2. **Select the first keyframe of the animated layer by clicking it.**

3. **Copy the keyframe by choosing Edit ⇨ Copy (Command+C/Ctrl+C).**

4. **Paste it into the Current Time by choosing Edit ⇨ Paste (Command+V/ Ctrl+V).** The motion path should come together at the first and last keyframes in the Comp window (see Figure 5-16).

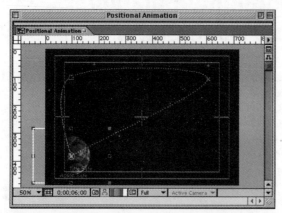

Figure 5-16: This motion path comes full circle with the addition of the fourth keyframe (which you created by copying and pasting the first keyframe).
Image courtesy of EyeWire by Getty www.gettyimages.com (Cosmic Moves)

5. **Command+click/Ctrl+click the second keyframe in the Timeline.** In much the same way that Command+clicking/Ctrl+clicking a spatial keyframe in the Comp window converts it from Linear to Auto Bezier, Command+clicking/Ctrl+clicking a temporal keyframe in the Timeline also converts it from Linear to Auto Bezier. Notice the changes in the Timeline Value Graph in the Timeline (see Figure 5-17).

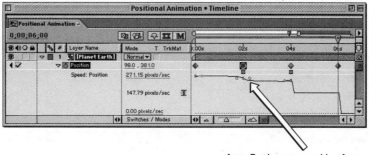

Auto Bezier temporal keyframe

Figure 5-17: Look at the changes in the Position value graph.

6. **Continue by clicking and dragging the right handle of the temporal Auto Bezier keyframe you just created in the Timeline and extend it as far as it will go.** Do the same with the left handle. Click and drag either handle up and down, releasing and beginning again until your Timeline Value Graph resembles Figure 5-18. The distance of a temporal keyframe's handle extension is called the *keyframe's influence*. Influence refers to the control that a temporal Bezier handle exerts over that keyframe's half of the time elapsed between itself and the next keyframe (see Figure 5-18).

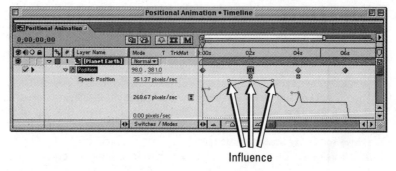

Influence

Figure 5-18: The second keyframe in the Position value graph is now a Continuous Bezier keyframe.

7. **Continue by Command+clicking/Ctrl+clicking and dragging the same handle up** *past where you can visually track it,* **let go, and view the result.**
The resulting Bezier keyframe should look similar to Figure 5-19. Notice that like its spatial Bezier counterpart, this temporal keyframe has been split into separate tangents in much the same way that you can split the handles of a spatial Continuous Bezier keyframe by Command+clicking/Ctrl+clicking on one of the handles.

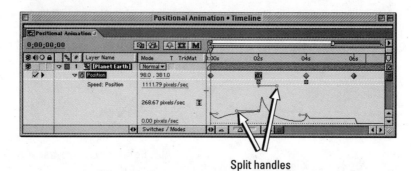

Split handles

Figure 5-19: The changes in the second keyframe in the Position value graph represent your newly created Bezier keyframe.

You might have noticed that some interesting changes take place in the Timeline Value Graph in that last step. The graph's height now represents a greater range of speed than it did previously. This is because the graph automatically resizes itself and changes the relative position of the line representing the speed of your animated layer to reflect its place within a broader range of values that were necessitated by your moving the handle off the top of the Timeline Value Graph.

Tip

If dragging the keyframe's handle off the boundary of the Timeline Value Graph is confusing to you, Undo your last speed change from Step 7 and click the small icon that's even with the Timeline Value Graph and located in the middle of the Switches/Modes panel (Figure 5-20). Turning this "dynamic Value Graph resize" switch off keeps the Timeline Value Graph within the same scale, regardless of whatever changes you make to a layer's speed. This makes it easier to visualize the relative impact of any tweaks to your temporal animation. Having turned the resize switch off, grab the same Bezier handle, and drag it over the top of the graph again. You'll no longer be able to see all of the line representing the layer's speed. We leave the resize switch on usually, but, if you like, you could turn it off to set the Timeline Value Graph's upper boundary as a "speed limit" when animating.

Fastest speed
of animation

Dynamic
resize switch

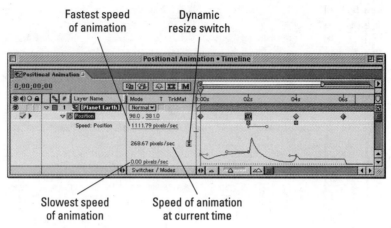

Slowest speed
of animation

Speed of animation
at current time

Figure 5-20: This switch dynamically resizes your Value Graph if left in the mode represented in this picture. Turn it off by clicking it, and the little resizing icon disappears.

Note

The maximum speed attained by your positional animation is represented by the number, in pixels per second, on the top of the Switches/Modes panel. The slowest speed of your animation is the number on the bottom. The number in the middle tells you your speed at the Current Time.

Preview your animation now and see what your last Bezier creation looks like. Spikes in the Timeline Value Graph end up mimicking a bounce-type motion. Experiment with your curves. A U-shape makes a pretty pronounced slowdown. Conversely, an upside-down U-shape makes a pretty dramatic increase in speed through a keyframe. Taking the time to experiment here will give you a good idea of how valuable the Timeline Value Graph is when creating complex speed changes. See Figure 5-21 to get a sense of some of the possible variations.

8. **In keeping with a set of examples that have their spatial parallel, click the Position property name to select all the keyframes, Control+click/ right-click them, and choose Toggle Hold keyframe (see Figure 5-22).** Make a RAM Preview and notice the partial motion/hold animation.

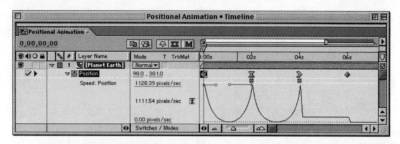

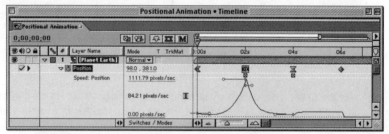

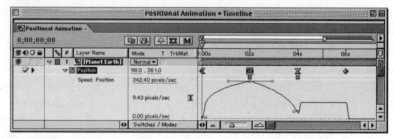

Figure 5-21: Different shapes in the Timeline Value Graph represent different kinds of speed changes resulting in different visual animations.

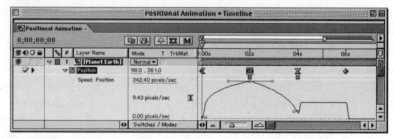

Figure 5-22: Look at the appearance of Hold keyframes in the Timeline Value Graph.

9. **Last of all, click the check boxes directly underneath the second and third keyframes (Figure 5-23) so that they're no longer checked.** This creates a pair of roving keyframes, which makes for a constant rate of speed from first frame to last. Note that Earth never deviates from the spatial path defined by the four positional keyframes in the Comp window. Make a RAM Preview and see for yourself.

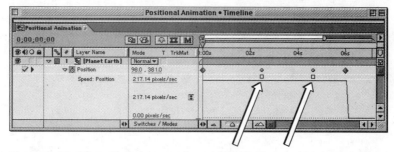

Figure 5-23: These little boxes, when unchecked, turn their respective keyframes into Roving keyframes in the Value Graph.

10. **The last feature you should try out is manipulating the Bezier handles of the first and last keyframes until you get an animation that you like.** Use Figure 5-24 as a point of departure; go where your instincts take you in making a realistic orbital path for either our lonely planet or your own animated layer.

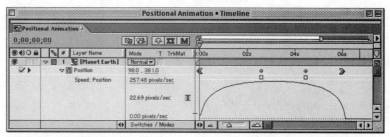

Figure 5-24: Take your cue from this visual starting point and animate your own orbit whether it's Planet Earth or your own creation.

Reviewing spatial and temporal interpolation keyframes

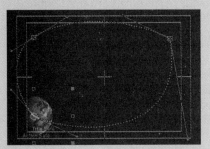

Figure SB 5-1: Review the different kinds of spatial keyframes and their appearance in the Comp window: Linear, Auto Bezier, Continuous Bezier, Bezier, and Hold.

Image courtesy of EyeWire by Getty www.gettyimages.com (Cosmic Moves)

Create a comp simply for the purpose of learning how to practice making tightly controlled motion paths. Don't stop until you can create your desired motion path at will. Rehearse this like a jazz musician learning the works of the classical composers. Charlie Parker studied the Great Works just so that he could "forget them all" in performance. In essence, you want to be fluent with these techniques so that you can improvise your way through the needs of a given project without getting hung up on the technical aspects of realizing the perfect move for an animation. And don't be gun-shy when working through this aspect of After Effects. That's the purpose of Undo.

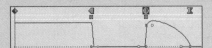

Figure SB 5-2: Review the visual differences between the temporal keyframes: Linear, Linear In/Hold Out, Auto Bezier, Continuous Bezier, or Bezier.

Do the same for the temporal keyframes. Make use of the biggest work area that your monitor(s) and resolution will allow. The larger the value graph, the greater the control you exercise over your animation.

Putting It All Together

By now, you have a fairly clear idea about how to manipulate time and space as far as the position of a layer is concerned. If you stay the course, the following chapter will help you further master control over your animations. If you are working with the DVD-ROM project files, you'll work on making Planet Earth look as though it's moving farther away as it goes behind the sun and then on making it look bigger as it comes back to where it started.

So far, you've animated only a property that has x- and y-values, in this case, Position. Similar properties include both the Anchor Point and the Effect Point, but those are covered in later chapters. While your newfound animation skills are modular in their application, Rotation, Scale, and Opacity don't contain spatial data, so they're a little bit different and, therefore, are addressed in the next chapter. Before you forge ahead, review what you covered in this chapter once more.

✦ **Spatial interpolation:** Modifying a layer's motion path and employing different keyframe interpolation methods by adjusting the Bezier handles in the Comp window.

✦ **Temporal interpolation:** Modifying a layer's speed as it moves through the time path and employing different keyframe interpolation methods by adjusting the Bezier handles in the Timeline Value Graph of a layer's property.

✦ **Motion path and Timeline Value Graph:** Building a thorough understanding of the workings of both the motion path and the values shown in the Timeline Value Graph that correspond to a layer's position.

✦　　✦　　✦

Improving Keyframe Animations

✦   ✦   ✦   ✦

In This Chapter

Using the Keyframe Assistant to improve animation

Animating multiple layers

✦   ✦   ✦   ✦

The quest continues. If you've arrived at this point fresh on the heels of the last chapter, you know how to modify positional keyframes in a number of powerful ways. Regarding keyframe interpolation, you still have a lot of ways to get more out of After Effects. Enter the handy Keyframe Assistant. Pretty soon, the phrase "Easy Ease" should make more sense to you than it might at first glance. Isn't ease, by its nature, relatively easy? Stay tuned. We put all the pieces together with you.

It's time to raise the bar a little bit higher. If you understand interpolation, the following sections will take you out of the realm of hypothetical and experimental discussions of these concepts and move you toward something you can really start to use in production. Combined with the interpolation methods we cover in Chapter 5, a mastery of these techniques should turn you into a fearless and resourceful keyframe animator.

Working with Keyframes Across All Transform Properties

Creating animations can be a frustrating endeavor. When we started using After Effects, it was very hard to resist the temptation to disregard any documentation and start trying to make everything look "right" without looking for any guidance. Only when we hit a wall would someone have to summon the courage to seek outside help or, God forbid, RTFM (a sanitized translation reads something along the lines of, "Read the *forgone* manual"). Well, whether you're initially putting your pride aside or have come to this chapter in defeat, it makes no difference. Sooner or later, if you want to incorporate professional production level motion, you just have to suffer the indignity of not knowing enough and become teachable again. It's not nearly as bad as it sounds. It's actually a blast. Go forward and have some fun while you're at it.

Animating multiple layers

Okay. Let's say that you've just been given a request by your producer to make a strong opening for a piece that showcases individual pieces of video within a larger overall composite. "I want you to tease all our home runs in a punchy opener. I need it last week." Fairly typical request. And not too hard to pull off either.

Let's get to work. You're going to leverage the scale property on the different pieces of video to create an elegant looking animated showcase. Strive to make the clips look as though they're parading past the camera, pausing for "review," and then disappearing off into the horizon. To make it all a little easier and more fluid, we're going to introduce the Keyframe Assistant.

Regarding the pictures that complement the steps, the following exercise uses footage items that are located on the DVD-ROM in the folder called *Source Material*. You can copy the *Source Material* folder from the DVD-ROM to your hard drive. The following exercise deals with positional keyframe animations, and our own corresponding After Effects project is called *Chapter 6.aep* and can be found in the *Project Files/Chapter 6* folder.

Feel free to substitute your compositions with the examples on the DVD-ROM. If you prefer, just work with a single 100 x 100 solid, which we explain how to create in the following steps, and apply keyframes to that layer just as you would any of the layers referred to in the following exercises.

STEPS: Creating the Backdrop for an Animated Video Fly-By

1. **If you're working from the *Chapter 6.aep* project, open it, then open the comp named *Scale (Clean),* and jump to Step 5. Otherwise, start After Effects and save a new project with a name of your choosing.**

2. **Import at least four video clips into the project.**

3. **Create a new composition by dragging one of the clips from inside the Project window onto the New Composition button at the bottom of the Project window.** You're probably familiar with this procedure by now. Doing this creates a composition set to the dimensions and running time of the clip that you use to create it.

You might want to rename the new composition because it will be named *Clipname Comp 1*. Renaming is generally a good idea if you don't want a million compositions on your hand whose names all end in "*Comp 1.*" Select the new comp by clicking it, pressing return, and typing a new name that better fits the comp's description.

4. **Add three or more clips to the new composition by selecting them and dragging them into the Timeline.**

5. **Select all the layers in the Timeline except the one on the bottom.** You can select all by clicking the one layer second from the bottom, holding down the Shift key, and then clicking the top layer. You leave the bottom layer to serve as the full-screen backdrop for the video fly-bys.

Tip

You have a few ways to select multiple clips, and the methods are the same regardless of the window you're working in (Project, Comp, and Timeline). Shift+ clicking items selects everything between the items you click. Command+click-ing/Ctrl+clicking items selects only those items directly clicked. Command+click-ing/Ctrl+clicking a selected item deselects it. Command+clicking/Ctrl+clicking is called *contiguous clicking*. Say that you have a list of 10 items and you want to select eight of them. Using the Shift key, you click the top and bottom items on the list to select all 10. Then you use the Command/Ctrl key to deselect the two items of the 10 you don't want.

6. **Press the P key, hold down the Shift key, and then press the S key to solo the Position and Scale properties for the selected layers (see Figure 6-1).** This prevents you from losing all your screen space to all the other transform properties you won't be concerned with in this exercise. Also, you can add to a list of soloed properties by using the Shift key. Very useful.

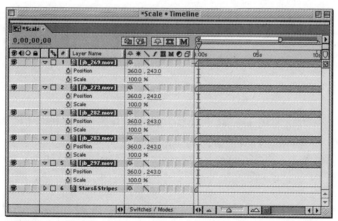

Figure 6-1: Select multiple layers and solo multiple transform properties.

7. **Click any of the selected layers' Scale values and enter a value of 10%.** This bumps all of the selected layers way down in size.

8. **In the Comp window, click and drag the scaled down layers down to the area just outside the lower-left corner of the composition's frame.** See Figure 6-2 for reference. With multiple layers selected in the Timeline, you can influence them all at once when working in the Comp window.

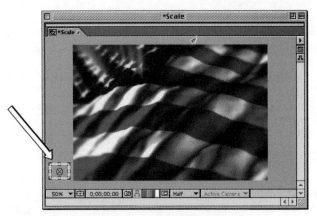

Figure 6-2: Position the multiple layers of video on the pasteboard just outside the lower-left corner of the composition.

Image courtesy of Digital Juice (Jump Backs, Vol. 7)

Alright, that's the setup. The next aspect you want to accomplish is to successively scale each layer of video up as you move it across the frame from the lower-left off to the right. Here's the catch. You want each video clip to slow down as it reaches the middle of its path across the composition.

STEPS: Creating the Basic Motion for an Animated Video Fly-By

1. **Select the layer that's second from the bottom.** Add both a Position and a Scale keyframe by clicking each stopwatch next to both of the property names under the layer. Be certain that you're doing this with a current time reading of 0;00;00;00.

2. **Click the Current Time and enter a value of 200 to jump forward two seconds.**

3. **Making certain that the layer that's second from the bottom is still selected, drag it in the Comp window out to the center of the frame.** Scale it up proportionately until it fills a large portion of the composition, but keep it well within the action-safe area. See Figure 6-3 for reference.

Figure 6-3: For the keyframe at 0;00;02;00, scale up the selected layer to 60% and position it so that it fills up a good portion of the comp while remaining well within the action-safe area.

Image courtesy of Digital Juice (Jump Backs, Vol. 7)

4. **Click the Current Time and enter a value of 400 to jump forward another two seconds to 0;00;04;00.**

5. **Scale the layer back down to 10% and drag it off to the right of the composition.** See Figure 6-4 for reference.

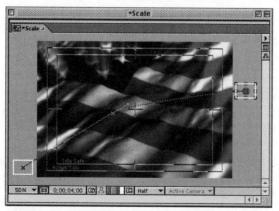

Figure 6-4: Complete the basic animation at 0;00;04;00 by scaling the layer back down to 10% and placing it outside the right edge of the comp.

Image courtesy of Digital Juice (Jump Backs, Vol. 7)

6. **Press the N key to set the end of the work area at 0;00;04;00.** By default, the beginning of the work area is set to the beginning of the comp. Shortening the work area reduces the amount of frames After Effects has to load into RAM to create a preview.

7. **Preview the Wireframe Interaction of the comp by holding down the Option/Alt key and pressing 0 on the numeric keypad.** This shows you a wireframe preview of your animation inside the work area you defined. Wireframe previews take far less time to load than regular RAM Previews, and they can be enormously helpful if you only need a rough idea as to what kind of animation you're creating. Figure 6-5 shows the Wireframe preview in progress. Wireframes reflect the boundaries of a layer in the Comp window.

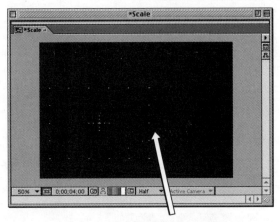

Animated layer boundary

Figure 6-5: A Wireframe preview only displays the boundaries of a layer in the Comp window.

The Wireframe preview reveals that the animation you created is in need of a little bit of help. It's almost there, but as we mentioned earlier, you need to slow down the animation as it hits its midway point. Now is the time to appeal to our friend, the trusty Keyframe Assistant.

8. **In the Timeline, click and drag across both of the keyframes located at 0;00;02;00.** This selects both of them. Make certain you did this correctly by checking to see if both keyframes are highlighted.

9. **Control+click/Right-click the selected keyframes.** This accesses a dialog box, such as the one shown in Figure 6-6.

10. **Choose Keyframe Assistant ⇨ Easy Ease.** Look at the new appearance of the keyframes at 0;00;02;00, as shown in Figure 6-6.

11. **Once again, hold down the Option/Alt key and press 0 on the numeric keypad to create a Wireframe preview.**

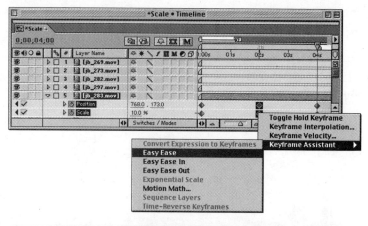

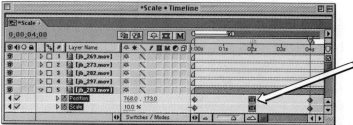

Figure 6-6: Select the two keyframes at 0;00;02;00, Ctrl+click/right-click them, and choose Keyframe Assistant ➪ Easy Ease. The keyframes in the Timeline change in appearance to indicate their conversion from linear to Bezier.

Now the motion seems to have that certain notion, doesn't it? As the layer approaches its second Position and Scale keyframes, it eases into both its enlarged size and new location. The movement no longer looks clunky or wooden. The layer moves quickly into frame before slowing down, and it begins moving quickly again after hitting its midway mark. It appears as though fruit is beginning to hang from the animation vine.

Chapter 5 focused on changing temporal keyframe interpolation, but look at how the Easy Ease function of the Keyframe Assistant has achieved such aesthetically pleasing motion without your having to get your hands dirty in the Timeline Value graph. Just for kicks, twirl down the Timeline Value graph for both the Scale and the Position properties of the animated layer (see Figure 6-7). Look at the temporal interpolation in the velocity graph. That dip in the middle is a smooth slowdown, and you didn't have to create it by manipulating influence handles either. If you've been wondering how you might consistently create animations that "ease" into place, things have probably never looked this "easy."

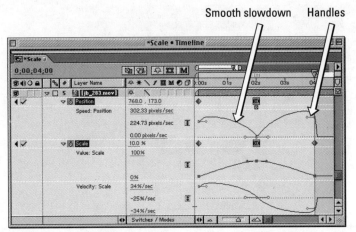

Figure 6-7: The Timeline Value graph for Position and Scale indicate the changes you brought about by using the Easy Ease function of the Keyframe Assistant.

You might want to try a real RAM Preview if you're particularly satisfied with this new addition to your keyframe toolbox. Go right ahead and see what everything really looks like. After you're happy with the ramifications of this new technique, you should finish the few remaining steps and complete the entire animation by repeating the same basic motion for the other video layers in the lower-left corner of the Comp window that are eagerly awaiting their turn to shine.

STEPS: Copying Keyframes to Complete the Animation

1. **Press the ~ key to collapse your view of the Timeline Value graph of the animated layer.**

2. **With the animated layer still selected, press the U key to solo all animated properties of the selected layer.** Once more, this displays the Position and Scale properties.

3. **Click and drag across all six keyframes of the animated layer in order to select them.**

4. **Choose Edit ➪ Copy (Command+C/Ctrl+C).** This copies all the keyframes you set for this layer.

5. **Click the Current Time and enter a value of 200 to move to 0;00;02;00.**

6. **Select the layer that's third from the bottom.**

7. **Choose Edit ➪ Paste (Command+V/Ctrl+V).** This pastes all the keyframes you set for the last layer into this layer. The only difference is that they're two seconds further down in the Timeline.

8. **Move forward another two seconds, select the next layer up from the bottom, and press Command+V/Ctrl+V to paste the keyframes into the next layer for the next two second interval in the Timeline.**

9. **Repeat Step 8 as many times as you need to until you've animated all your layers.** If you select all the layers and press the U key to solo all of their animated properties, the end result of your efforts should resemble Figure 6-8.

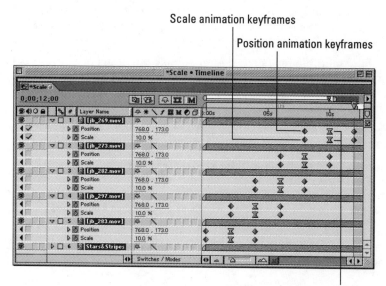

Figure 6-8: The Timeline displays the repeating animation for the video layers in the composition.

10. **First, create a Wireframe preview of your work; once you get the idea behind the animation, go ahead and create a full-fledged RAM Preview of this composition to see the end result of this cascading video composite.**

Reviewing your new techniques

If you arrived here and your animation looks good, keep up the good work and keep going. If not, try it again. Stay with it until you feel comfortable. Before charging too far ahead, you should review all the concepts covered in the previous steps.

✦ **Wireframe preview:** Hold down the Option/Alt key before pressing 0 on the numeric keypad to get a Wireframe preview instead of a RAM Preview. If you're working with a lot of large video files in a single composition, you might prefer the lightning response of a Wireframe preview to check the look of the motion in your animation.

✦ **Multiple layer/footage item selection:** Shift+click and Command+click/Ctrl+ click to select multiple items at once. This can greatly increase the speed of your workflow.

✦ **Multiple keyframe selection:** Using the mouse, drag a bounding box across the keyframes that you want to select. Not mutually exclusive from the functions described in the multiple selection technique previously, this also works with footage items and layers.

✦ **Renaming comps:** Click the comp in the Project window, press the Return key, type a new name, and press Return again. Develop good naming habits because you'll need them in a project that has more than a couple of comps.

✦ **Soloing multiple properties:** After soloing one transform property for a layer, hold down the Shift key and continue pressing the additional solo property keyboard shortcuts to add them to the list of soloed properties of a selected layer or layers.

✦ **Expand and collapse layer properties:** Press the ~ key to expand or collapse a selected layer or layers in the Timeline instead of using the twirler.

✦ **Copying and pasting multiple keyframes:** As soon as you work out an animation in terms of its keyframes, you can select all of them, cut, copy, and paste them into other layers. This saves time, and it guarantees the exact same animation across the layers into which you paste the keyframes.

✦ **Keyframe Assistant:** Bring up the Keyframe Assistant to make short work of changing any keyframe interpolation in the Timeline. We cover this in a bit more detail in the next section.

Using the Keyframe Assistant

So far, you've only used the Keyframe Assistant to create an Easy Ease keyframe. What are your other options with this self-professed assistant? How might it assist you further? Look at the following list of ways in which this feature can tighten your animations. You use almost all of these in the exercises that follow.

✦ **Easy Ease:** As you witnessed in the last exercise, using this assistant on a keyframe changes it so that animations ease both into and out of the keyframe. Its keyboard shortcut is F9.

✦ **Easy Ease In:** This assistant eases only the incoming speed of the affected keyframe. Its keyboard shortcut is Option+F9/Alt+F9.

✦ **Easy Ease Out:** This assistant eases only the outgoing speed of the affected keyframe. Its keyboard shortcut is Command+Option+F9/Ctrl+Alt+F9.

✦ **Exponential Scale:** You can only use this assistant in the Scale transform property. This assistant helps in the creation of scale animations that require exponential increases to appear realistic. For example, if you need to scale a layer from 0% to 1600%, you could use the Exponential Scale Keyframe Assistant to create the following animation: 0% at one second, 100% at two seconds, 200% at three seconds, 400% at four seconds, 800% at five seconds, 1600% at six seconds, and so on. Each increment is double the one before it.

✦ **Sequence Layers:** If you select multiple layers, you can have this assistant order the layers and position them in the Timeline so that the out-point of one layer matches the in-point of the next layer until all the layers are neatly lined up end to end.

✦ **Time-Reverse Keyframes:** This assistant can rearrange the keyframes of an animation so that they happen in reverse. This can be quite useful if you need to have an animation "retrace its steps" or "go the other way." For example, imagine that you created an animation in which a layer goes clockwise in a circular path. Applying Time-Reverse Keyframes to the keyframes of the layer's animation would reverse their order and make the motion move counterclockwise.

✦ **Convert Expression to Keyframes:** This assistant takes a Javascript expression and converts it to keyframes in the Timeline. (See the following cross-reference.)

✦ **Motion Math:** This assistant brings up the Motion Math window, which allows you to apply motion math scripts to layer properties in a composition. (See the following cross-reference.)

We cover Expressions and Motion Math in Chapters 23 and 25. For the time being, you can disregard the Convert Expression to Keyframes and Motion Math options in the Keyframe Assistant.

Making fluid-looking animations

Using Easy Ease and Exponential Scale are the first simple steps you can take towards becoming a better animator. Being able to apply more sophisticated animation techniques will definitely set you apart from other motion graphic artists who don't fully understand interpolation. The following exercises should give you a grounding in a higher level of keyframe-driven animations.

If you're going to work from your own project in the next exercise, you'll need one video clip (at least 10 seconds in length) and three Illustrator files, which are either small graphic objects or examples of typography. Also, we put a draft (QuickTime movie) of the finished product in the *Chapter 6* folder containing the After Effects project. If you like, you can look at the draft as a point of reference when completing the follow steps. Use it as a guide for what your animation should ultimately look like.

STEPS: Setting Up the Initial Linear Animation

1. If you're working from the *Chapter 6.aep* project from the DVD-ROM, double-click the **Keyframe Assistant (Clean)* composition in the Project window and go to Step 5.

2. Import a video clip and three Illustrator or general EPS files into your project.

3. **Create a new composition by dragging your newly imported video clip inside the Project window directly onto the new composition button at the bottom of the Project window.** You may want to shorten the comp's length to 10 seconds because that's all you need to do the exercise.

4. Select the new comp in the Project window, press Return, type a preferred name, and press Return again.

5. **Now that you have one layer of footage placed in the comp, lay out your three Illustrator files in an arrangement you find visually pleasing and then set the Current Time to three seconds before the end of the composition (approximately 0;00;07;00; no need to be overly specific).** If you're working with the *Chapter 6.aep* project from the DVD-ROM, use the three Illustrator files in the Project window called *Zooming.ai, Through.ai,* and *Space.ai.*

Why seven seconds? We're trying to set up the end of the composition first. We're approaching this one somewhat backwards in that we first want to create the final destination of these elements. We'll work out how they end up in their final resting places after initially setting these final positions. In other words, know where you're going and then figure out how you'll get there. If you need to, take a look at Figure 6-9 for a visual cue.

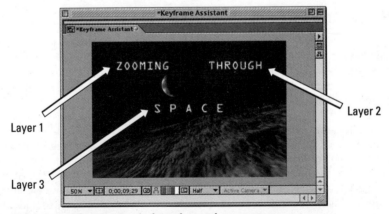

Figure 6-9: The Comp window shows the way you want your composition to end. Create this balanced closing image first and then work backwards to sort out the details of the journey towards this end.

Image courtesy of ArtBeats

Looking at Figure 6-9, say that your producer or client has told you that she likes this as a closing image for this sequence, except she wants the sequence to wind up at that neatly composed image after a dynamic, punchy animation. You might be inclined to ask, "What kind of dynamic, punchy animation?" In this hypothetical scenario, this person would respond by saying, "You know, it's gotta have that special something. I want the words to fly through space. Spin 'em and flash 'em for all I care. Make me say, 'That's cool.' Got me?"

Believe it or not, we've done work in situations such as this, and that's not a bad thing considering the range of freedom involved in such a broad request. More often than not, you'll work with a producer or a client who already has such a clear idea of what they want that any creativity on your behalf is seen as a direct assault on the purity of someone else's vision. We've been there, too.

Anyway, have a little fun with the Illustrator layers on top of the video and animate them with the aid of our new associate, the Keyframe Assistant. In the next series of steps, you animate the rotation and scale of two of the Illustrator layers, and you animate the opacity and change the Anchor point of the third Illustrator layer.

6. **Select the two layers that correspond to the two Illustrator files at the upper corners of the composition and press Option+R/Alt+R and Option+S/ Alt+S to set the Scale and Rotation keyframes for the selected layers.** If you're working with the *Chapter 6.aep* project, set the keyframes for the *Zooming.ai* and *Through.ai* layers.

7. **Set the current time relatively halfway toward the beginning of the comp (approximately 0;00;03;00).**

8. **Begin experimenting with different amounts of scale and rotation here.** Changing the values for these two properties sets keyframes because you've already set keyframes for these properties in Step 6. We use 0% scale for *Zooming.ai* and 1600% scale for *Through.ai*. We also used –10x and 10x for the number of rotations, respectively.

Note

Turn on both the High Quality and the Continuously Rasterize switches for these two Illustrator layers because we're going to be dealing with Scale values well over 100%. This makes them very sharp looking, and you needn't worry about any huge performance hit because this is a simple animation. Ordinarily, you should exercise caution when scaling vector artwork above 100%, but this instance won't bring your processor to a halt.

9. **Jump forward about one second (approximately 0;00;04;00) and set 100% scale keyframes for the two layers.**

10. **Jump forward about another second (approximately 0;00;05;00), and set additional scale keyframes for the two layers.** We inverted the values from Step 8 and used 1600% scale for *Zooming.ai* and 0% for *Through.ai* at this point in the Timeline.

11. **Jump forward about one more second (approximately 0;00;06;00) and set 100% scale keyframes for the two layers as you did in Step 9.**

12. **Set a work area that includes the timeframe of the animation you created (roughly located between 0;00;03;00 and 0;00;07;00).** We set ours by dragging the playhead to 0;00;02;15, pressing the B key to set the beginning of the work area, clicking the current time, entering **715** to jump to 0;00;07;15, and pressing the N key to set the end of the work area. See Figure 6-10 for reference.

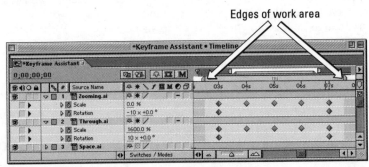

Figure 6-10: The work area defined here enables you to preview only the animation you just created in the previous steps.

13. **Deselect all layers by clicking in an empty area of the Timeline, hold down the Option/Alt key, and press 0 on the numeric keypad to see a Wireframe preview of what you set up here.** If that's insufficient as far as giving you a clear idea of what you've actually created, leave out the Option/Alt key and press 0 on the numeric keypad to create a regular RAM Preview.

Tip

A neat little trick is introduced with After Effects 5, namely, the Solo switch in the A/V Features panel, as shown in Figure 6-11. You can toggle this switch for any layer by clicking it, and you can turn it on or off for multiple layers by clicking and dragging across the solo switch column to toggle multiple switches. As far as these steps are concerned, you may want to use the solo switch as follows: Turn on the solo switch for the top two layers. (Ours are the Illustrator files, *Zooming.ai* and *Through.ai.*) Then create a RAM Preview or drag the playhead through the animation. You only see the animation of the layer or layers that have their solo switch turned on. This prevents After Effects from having to load the bottom layer into RAM. In this case, the bottom layer is a high-res video clip, so that you may find this to be a timesaver depending on the complexity of your composition.

Okay, everything's lined up for the all-important finishing touches. Now you've got to come through with the goods. As it stands presently, the spins and the scale shifts are too stiff and robotic. You need to use the Keyframe Assistant to improve the linear quality of this motion. You already tried out Easy Ease. See what happens when you use Exponential Scale and Easy Ease In. The first function you should do is improve the animation of the top layers' scale shifts between 0% and 1600% so that they increase and decrease in size in a relative, not linear fashion.

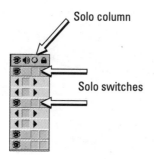

Solo column

Solo switches

Figure 6-11: Use the Solo switch in the A/V Features panel to view individual layers in the Comp window.

Note

Exponential Scale is a feature of the Production Bundle only.

STEPS: Adding Exponential Scale (PB) to the Animation

1. **Select the first two Scale keyframes of the second layer.** This is the *Through.ai* layer if you're using the *Chapter 6.aep* project, and these keyframes represent the bump from 1600% to 100% between 0;00;03;00 and 0;00;04;00.

2. **Control+click/Right-click the selected keyframes and choose Keyframe Navigator ➪ Exponential Scale.** Zoom in on this area of the Timeline and twirl down the Timeline Value graph for this layer's scale property. Your Timeline should resemble Figure 6-12. This graphically represents that the journey from 1600 to 100 is made in increments, which divide the scale number in two (1600, 800, 400, 200, 100).

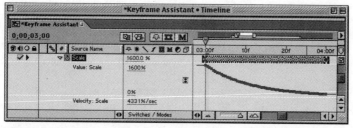

Figure 6-12: The appearance of the Scale property's Timeline Value graph after applying the Exponential Scale Keyframe Assistant

3. **Select the second and third Scale keyframes of the first layer and repeat Step 2.**

4. **Select both the last Scale keyframe from the group created by Step 2 and the next Scale keyframe roughly one second later, and then repeat Step 2 again.** Look closely at Figure 6-13 for visual cues on how to complete Steps 3 and 4.

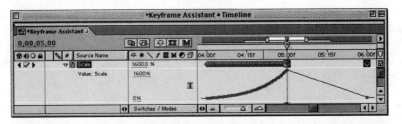

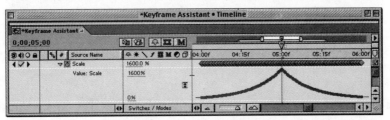

Figure 6-13: The appearance of the Scale property's Timeline Value graph before and after applying the Exponential Scale Keyframe Assistant to second half of the trio of keyframes delineating the jump between 0% to 1600% and then back to 0%

5. **Look at the results of these changes to the animation by using your preferred method of previewing (RAM Preview, Shift+RAM Preview, and Wireframe Preview, all of which can be simplified by soloing the animated layers by using the layers' solo switches).**

So you solved one problem. The scale shifts now shrink and expand exponentially, and one look at the keyframes in the Timeline should clue you in as to how much time is saved by calling on this Keyframe Assistant. Manually setting each of these keyframes would be nothing short of a major drag, so we recommend this assistant whenever it's appropriate, such as when you want to create a virtual zoom lens.

So, return to the exercise to accomplish your next goal. In the last leg of the animation, slow down the spinning Illustrator files so that they come to rest gently in their final position. Right now, they stop abruptly, and your producer/client has told you that this will not do. "Well, that's easy," you say.

STEPS: Adding Easy Ease In and Easy Ease Out to the Animation

1. **Select the second rotation keyframe for both the first and second layers, Control+click/right-click them, and then choose Keyframe Assistant ⇨ Easy Ease In.**

2. **Press 0 or Option/Alt+0 on the numeric keypad to preview the change.**

   Check it out. Pretty neat how those spinning layers slow down as though they were well choreographed. Well, in fact, they were! No sweat. Easy, indeed. Now, what about a strong finish? You've come this far, so you might as well make something you can be proud of. The final task is to fade and scale up the third Illustrator file (*Space.ai* in our *Chapter 6.aep* project). End the composition by making it a visually complete thought.

3. **Set opacity and scale keyframes for the third layer at roughly the same point in time when the first two layers stop spinning (approximately 0;00;07;00).**

4. **Double-click layer 3 to open its Layer window.**

5. **Select Anchor Point path from the list of options in the Layer window menu (which you can access by clicking the button in the upper-right corner in the Layer window).**

6. **Move the Anchor Point to the base of the layer (see Figure 6-14).**

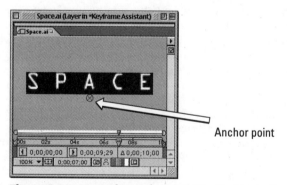

Anchor point

Figure 6-14: Move the anchor point to the base of the layer so that it scales up from the bottom, not the middle of the layer.

7. **Close the Layer window.**

8. **In the Timeline, enter values of 0% for the third layer's opacity and scale.**

9. **Jump ahead about one second and change both of those values to 100%.**
   This creates two new keyframes at approximately 0;00;08;00.

10. **Select the two keyframes you created in Step 3 and use the Keyframe Assistant to make them Easy Ease Out keyframes.**

11. **Select the two keyframes you created in Step 9 and use the Keyframe Assistant to make them Easy Ease In keyframes.**

12. **Make a RAM Preview for the entire animation by pressing 0 on the numeric keypad.**

You just finished all the tricky bits of the animation. We trust you to create more opacity keyframes to round out the piece. For example, you'll want to fade in layers one and two sometime shortly after their motion begins at around 0;00;03;00. You'll also want to find some way to fade layers one, two, and three out of view somewhere between 0;00;08;00 and the end of the composition at 0;00;10;00. See to these matters on your own, and, if you like, use the *Keyframe Assistant.mov* QuickTime file in the *Chapter 6* Project folder from the DVD-ROM as a point of reference.

So what's the sorcery behind this ballyhooed Keyframe Assistant? What is it really doing? Option/Alt+double-click any keyframe in the Timeline to see the Keyframe Velocity dialog box for a keyframe. A great deal of information is here, and you can manually change as much of it as you like. Option/Alt+double-click one of the Easy Ease keyframes and compare it to its Timeline Value graph (see Figure 6-15). The information is the same, but it's just represented differently. The *influence* is the clue that you're looking at the same math. In Chapter 5, we discussed a keyframe's influence handle in the Timeline Value graph. Just to refresh your memory, a keyframe's influence handle is at 100% if it's stretched out to the halfway point between itself and the adjacent keyframe. At 33%, or ⅓, it's stretched to ⅙ of the distance between itself and the adjacent keyframe. The influence handle shows how much influence the value of a keyframe is having over the temporal interpolation leading into it. You can specify the influence either by adjusting the handle or directly entering values in the Keyframe Velocity window. If any of this is confusing, don't worry too much. You know all the different ways you can change a keyframe's interpolation, so that you can make something "look right" even if you can't explain a keyframe's influence to your high school math teacher. If it isn't confusing, all the more reason to keep moving forward.

The Keyframe Assistant is an indispensable part of our daily use of After Effects, but it's important to point out that we don't use it for absolutely everything. A lot of designs don't benefit at all from smooth motion. Spend an hour channel surfing and carefully deconstruct the pieces that catch your eye. Good ones contain all different kinds of motion. There are no hard rules here. As always, it's just good to know what your options are, and it's even better to avoid getting stumped if you need to use tightly controlled motion in a project.

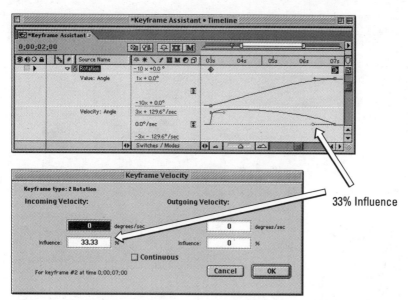

Figure 6-15: Compare an Easy Ease In keyframe's Timeline Value graph with its Keyframe Velocity window.

Sequencing layers

Sometimes you need to work with a large number of layers in a composition. You might need to create a slide show of still images, or you might be called on to create something similar to the video fly-by you made in the first exercise of this chapter. As you're already aware, layers can be comprised of any type of footage item, be it a video clip or a still, regardless of its dimensions or running time. Layers can also consist of solids, and we cover that in the following exercise. The Sequence Layers Keyframe Assistant enables you to order a number of layers in the Timeline so that they appear in succession. The Keyframe Assistant does this by placing the layers end to end, and it can even add a cross fade between layers if you like.

To quickly get an idea of what this Keyframe Assistant can do, create a new composition and drop a whole bunch of footage items into it. Put the layers in the order that you want them displayed and select them all (Command+A/Ctrl+A). Control+click/Right-click the layers, choose Keyframe Assistant ➪ Sequence Layers. Accept the defaults and click OK without worrying about the overlap settings right now. Your Timeline should now contain neatly stacked layers. See Figure 6-16 to review the entire process. The following exercise shows you all of the extra functions you can get out of this helpful aid.

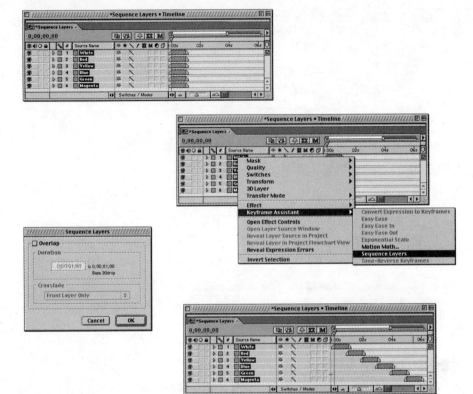

Figure 6-16: The Sequence Layers Keyframe Assistant neatly sequences layers in the Timeline. Just select the layers, apply the Sequence Layers command, and there you have it.

STEPS: Using the Sequence Layers Keyframe Assistant to Create a "Solid" Slide Show

1. **Create a new composition with the following settings: 320 x 240, square pixels, 15 fps, 10 seconds long.**

2. **Choose Layer ➪ New ➪ Solid (Command+Y/Ctrl+Y).** This displays the Solid Settings dialog box shown in Figure 6-17.

3. **Rename the Solid by entering *White* in the Name field.** Enter dimensions of 160 x 120, and if the color isn't already white, click in the color swatch, and select white from the Color Picker.

4. **Click OK.** The white solid appears in the center of the Comp window. It appears in the Timeline set to the length of the composition.

5. **Click the new solid layer in the Timeline to select it and then choose Edit ➪ Duplicate (Command+D/Ctrl+D) to duplicate the layer.**

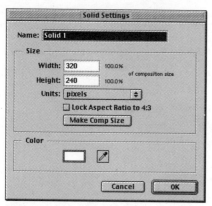

Figure 6-17: The Solid Settings dialog box enables you to pick a solid's dimensions and color.

6. **Repeat Step 5 another four times using the Command+D/Ctrl+D keyboard shortcut.** Your Timeline should now contain six layers.

7. **Click Layer 2 or press 2 on the numeric keypad to select it and then choose Layer ⇨ Solid Settings (Command+Shift+Y/Ctrl+Shift+Y).**

8. **Rename the layer *Red*, click the color swatch, and choose a red color from the Color Picker.** Click OK.

9. **Repeat Step 8 for the remaining layers, but select different names and colors for each layer to make them all different.**

10. **Position the layers in the Comp window so that you can see each individual layer clearly.** Your Comp window should resemble Figure 6-18. Don't worry about the positions of the layers. Just be certain that all of them are visible.

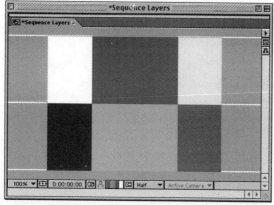

Figure 6-18: The Comp window should display all of the solid layers that you just created.

11. **In the Timeline, set the Current Time to 0;00;01;00.**

12. **Select all the layers (Command+A/Ctrl+A) and trim them to one second in length by pressing Option+]/Alt+].** Your Timeline should resemble Figure 6-19.

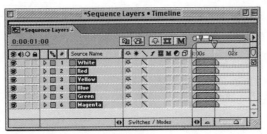

Figure 6-19: The Timeline should reflect your newly trimmed solid layers.

13. **Choose Animation ⇨ Keyframe Assistant ⇨ Sequence Layers.**

14. **Check Overlap in the Sequence Layers dialog box, specify a duration of five frames (0;00;00;05), select *Front and Back Layers* from the pull-down menu, and click OK.**

15. **In the Timeline, press the U button to display the animated properties of the selected layers.** Your Timeline should resemble Figure 6-20.

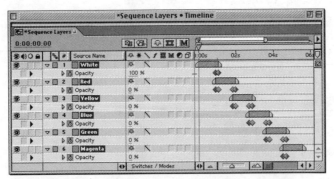

Figure 6-20: The Timeline should display the crossfades of the sequenced solid layers.

16. **Press 0 on the numeric keypad to preview the composition.**

You can see how useful this might be, regardless of whatever elements you might use with the technique. We used only solids as placeholders. The basic concept of trimming layers and sequencing them is what's important. You'll lean on this technique heavily as you move forward.

Tip

We kind of snuck in the trim function in Step 12. You can trim the In point of a selected layer by pressing Option+[/Alt+[, and you can do the same for the Out point by pressing Option+]/Alt+]. Used alone, the bracket keys simpy set the In and Out points of a layer to the Current Time in the Timeline.

Take stock of the animation skills you just acquired. With the Keyframe Assistant, you applied the Easy Ease, Exponential Scale, and Sequence Layers Assistants to several animations. Combine this information with the additional keyframe techniques covered in Chapter 5, and you've come quite a long way in improving your skills as a creator of detailed and sophisticated motion. Practice these techniques as often as you can. Simply experimenting with the Keyframe Assistant and tweaking the influence handles in the Timeline Value graph will be far more instructive now that you've debunked the technical specifics of these animation techniques in After Effects.

✦　　✦　　✦

Working the Render Queue

Why are you doing all this work in After Effects, anyway? What do you get out of it? What's the end result of taking lots of time to create a gorgeous composition? The answer is just about anything you want. You can create files in After Effects that can wind up on a Web page just as readily as they can end up in a high definition television broadcast or a film print. How so? The answer to that question lies in the process of After Effects known as *rendering*.

If you've shown up at this page after having read the previous chapters, you know a lot about previewing your work. Although certainly related, rendering is really a different feature altogether. Unlike previewing, the act of rendering your compositions creates files that are independent of After Effects and can either be used in a variety of different applications or re-imported for further use in After Effects. Some of these include different kinds of QuickTime files, Flash (SWF) files, AVI files, Photoshop files, JPEGs, TIFFs, and many more. The beauty of rendering is that After Effects can take a single composition and render it across all these different media types. After you start this process, you'll leave your machine alone to quietly churn out all of that work while you tend to other matters. Pay careful attention to these matters because rendering in After Effects is the last stop for all of your compositions before they leave your computer and enter the universe outside your studio. Sooner or later, everything you do in this application will lead you to the Render Queue.

Introducing the Concept of Rendering

Of course, a large number of After Effects users work in environments where they produce one kind of output specific to their own professional workflow. For example, an After Effects artist working at a broadcast network which exclusively uses

Avid editing equipment only exports Avid ready files from the Render Queue. When the files are ready in this scenario, an editor takes them and puts them into a larger Avid sequence that gets laid off to tape. Still, others in the After Effects community might have to adapt to a number of different environments given the shifting nature of their freelance work. In either case, learning this critical part of the After Effects production line is a good idea. The Render Queue is the part of the interface where all of this happens (see Figure 7-1).

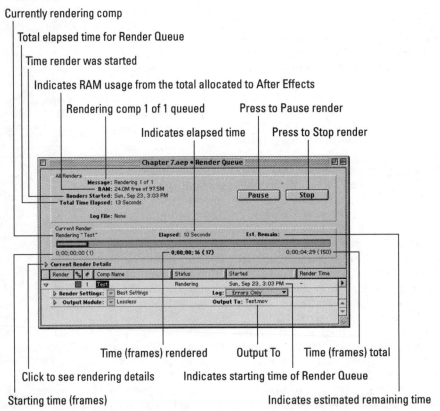

Currently rendering comp

Total elapsed time for Render Queue

Time render was started

Indicates RAM usage from the total allocated to After Effects

Rendering comp 1 of 1 queued

Indicates elapsed time

Press to Pause render

Press to Stop render

Time (frames) rendered   Output To   Time (frames) total

Click to see rendering details   Indicates starting time of Render Queue

Starting time (frames)   Indicates estimated remaining time

Figure 7-1: After a composition is ready for rendering, you send it to the Render Queue, shown here.

You can render compositions one at a time, or you can render a whole batch. The important factor to consider is that rendering completely ties up your computer. Renders need to be left alone while they create their output files, so you can either watch over them or leave them unattended, but you won't be able to do any more work on your machine until rendering is finished, paused, or stopped altogether. After Effects users usually handle this constraint in one of two ways. If they're limited to one machine, they save their rendering for lunch, nighttime, or for time otherwise spent away from the office. Another way of dealing with this issue is to take advantage of other computers across a network and make them do the number crunching while you keep creating. We look at network rendering in the last section of the chapter.

Rendering happens in two stages. First, After Effects looks at the frame of the composition being rendered and builds an image based on a number of factors. First among these, After Effects looks at the layers of the comp starting from the bottom of the stacking order, and it checks to see if there are any masks applied to those layers. From there it checks if any effects have been applied to the layers. Lastly, After Effects calculates any transformations that might have been carried out. This three-tiered progression is what is commonly known as the *Render Pipeline*. As soon as this image has been fully composited by using this process, After Effects saves that image according to the file format and compression you specified (for example, QuickTime MJPEG-A at Medium).

Cross-Reference If you ever need to carry out transformations *before* an effect is applied, you can do so with the Transform effect. We look at the issue a bit more closely with the Drop Shadow effect in Chapter 15.

Making movies

So, you put together your masterpiece—an After Effects composition that's been lovingly, agonizingly made with multiple layers of gorgeous high quality footage, clean, crisp text, carefully created masks, masterfully applied effects, the whole bit. Unless you want this creative expression of your soul to remain unseen by the world at large, it's time to make a movie. Most rendering in After Effects consists of making movies out of compositions. The following brief set of steps explains how to do it.

STEPS: Setting Up a Simple Render

1. **Select a composition in the Project window.**

2. **Choose Composition ➪ Make Movie (Command+M/Ctrl+M).**

3. **In the Output Movie To dialog box, enter a filename and location for the movie.** By default, After Effects names the file based on the composition's name. You can change it if you like, just make sure you don't ruin the three-letter extension at the end of the filename if you're working on a PC. If you do, your PC might not be able to recognize the file that gets created.

4. **Click Save.** This brings up the Render Queue with your composition all lined up and ready to go. The rest of the chapter deals with all of the options you can select in the Render Queue, so don't worry about them just yet.

Pretty simple, right? That's how easy it is to tell After Effects to make a movie from your composition. For now, fight the urge to click the Render button in the Render Queue dialog box, because it probably is better if you understand the full range of options before diving in. If you absolutely must, go ahead; just realize that the movie you make might not turn out right until you know how to manipulate the render settings. If you're just dying to make something happen, try saving a movie based on a RAM Preview. We explain how to do that in the following section.

Saving a RAM Preview

If you want instant gratification, you can save your RAM Previews as movies. Ordinarily, you use the RAM Preview function to load the frames of your composition into RAM to get a real-time playback in the Comp window, but you can also make a stand-alone movie file from the same cached frames. Remember what's involved in creating a RAM Preview? To briefly recap, After Effects looks at the defined work area, and given whatever resolution and quality settings you defined in the Timeline, it loads as many of those frames into RAM as it can. As soon as the RAM has reached its capacity or all the frames of your preview have been loaded, After Effects then displays a real-time playback of your comp. To put those cached frames into their own movie, complete the following steps:

STEPS: Saving a Rendered Version of Your RAM Preview

1. **Choose Composition ⇨ Save RAM Preview.**

2. **In the Output Movie To dialog box, enter a filename and location for the movie.** By default, After Effects calls the file by the composition's name followed by the word RAM. Again, change the name if you like, just be careful not to change the three-letter extension at the end of the filename if you're working on a PC.

3. **Click Save.** If you already created a RAM Preview when you opted to save it as a movie, the rendering begins right away. If you haven't yet created a RAM Preview, the frames must first be loaded into RAM. Either way, the render Queue swings into action without being prompted. After it's finished, After Effects emits an alert sound to tell you that the Render Queue has completed its work.

There are a couple of peculiarities with saving RAM Previews as movies. First of all, the frame size and resolution are retained from Comp to movie, but the zoom setting is not. Also, any movie created from a RAM Preview will not contain any interlaced fields. If you need to render a movie that does contain interlaced fields, then you'll need to use the Render Queue in the more conventional manner, which we explain next.

Getting the Most out of the Render Queue

You can drag and drop one or more compositions from the Project window into the Render Queue dialog box. To pull up the Render Queue dialog box, choose

Window ➪ Render Queue (Command+Option+0/Ctrl+Alt+0). You can also add compositions directly to the Render Queue by selecting one or more compositions in the Project window and then choosing Composition ➪ Add to Render Queue (Command+Shift+/ or Ctrl+Alt+/). If you want to get rid of compositions in the Render Queue, just select them and press Delete. If you want to reorder the items in the queue, click and drag them to your desired position in the line-up. When you're dragging a comp through the Render Queue, a black line indicates where the comp will be placed after you release the mouse. After you line up your comps in the Render Queue, click Render to let After Effects chew its way through all of them.

Using the buttons in the Render Queue dialog box, you can pause or stop a render in progress. Pausing a render won't allow you to go in and change any settings, but it will temporarily stop your processor from being completely occupied while it crunches algorithms on the way to making your movie. If you need to free up your machine for just a little while to check your e-mail or use some other application, pausing a render works perfectly. You can also stop a render. Stopping a render closes the file being created and requires that you give After Effects new Output File To instructions for the unrendered portion, which subsequently appears in the Render Queue as a newly added item. If you want to start the Render Queue at a later time, you can save your project and come back to it later. All Render Queue information is saved in a project file. This is convenient for a number of reasons, one of them being that you can put your project on a removable drive and take it on the road with you. If you go to any other machine with After Effects 5 installed on it, import your project, and your Render Queue will be entirely intact.

After you add the comps you want to render to the Render Queue, when you click Render and fire off the batch, the compositions are rendered by using the default render settings and output module templates. Before beginning a render, you can change these settings by selecting a different template from the pull-down menus for either the Render Settings or the Output Module options (see Figure 7-2), or you can change the individual settings within the templates by clicking the underlined template names. Clicking the template names pulls up the individual Render Settings and Output Module windows (see Figure 7-3).

Later in the chapter, we explain how to create more templates and add them to the list of options shown in Figure 7-2. If you have certain combinations of settings that you're using all the time, it makes sense to create templates for them so that you don't have to manually select all of the settings each time you need to render the same kind of movie.

After you begin rendering a batch of compositions, the Render Queue dialog box dynamically displays important information about the progress of your render. See Figure 7-4 to look at the Render Queue on active duty.

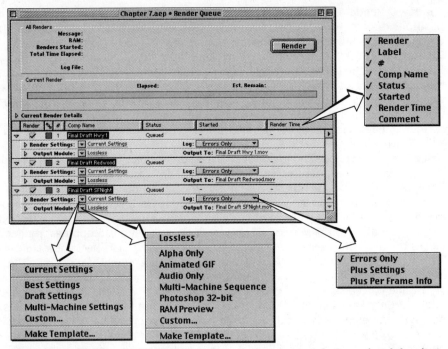

Figure 7-2: This view of the Render Queue displays its state before a batch has been "fired." You can select preset Render Settings and Output Module templates from the pull-down menus shown in each composition's render properties.

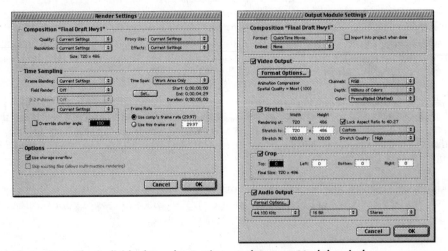

Figure 7-3: The individual Render Settings and Output Module windows

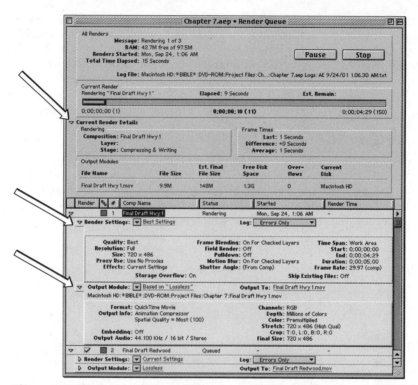

Figure 7-4: The Render Queue while a render is in progress. We opened all the twirlers to show you the most expanded view possible.

If you're rendering a batch of compositions, a log file of the render batch gets created in the same folder where the After Effects project is located at the system level. By default, After Effects writes an Error Only log. Opening and reading this file after a batch render is complete tells you exactly how long it took to complete the batch as well as other details. You can specify what kind of log you want created in the log pull-down menu in the Render Queue dialog box. If a render is aborted on account of an error, the log will explain what went wrong, and if you're at your machine when the error occurs, After Effects will bleat like a goat to tell you that something has gone awry.

Note

This note is completely useless but some of you might find it funny. We do anyway. If you want to hear the goat without waiting for a Render Queue, Open the Effect Controls window and Option+Ctrl+Shift+click/Alt+Shift+right-click the asterisk on the Effects tab.

In the next section, we discuss all the settings you can change by using the menus and fields in the Render Settings and Output Module windows. These settings directly influence a number of important elements to consider when preparing your final output. For example, you can set parameters ranging from frame size to field rendering on the Render Settings side, and codecs and alpha channels on the Output Module side.

Tweaking render settings

As soon as you add a composition to the Render Queue dialog box, click its Render Settings template name to study the resulting dialog box in detail. From here, you'll define everything about the way After Effects builds uncompressed frames from a composition before saving them to disk in your file format of choice. See Figure 7-5 to examine every rendering option over which you have control.

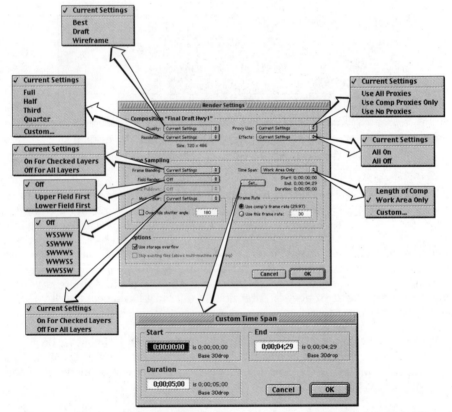

Figure 7-5: The Render Settings dialog box determines all the ways in which After Effects handles the frames of a composition.

Setting Quality and Resolution

Setting Best, Draft, or Wireframe quality is a global setting for all the layers in a composition. Regardless of how you might have set any layers in the Timeline, this switch overrides all individual layer settings and sets one quality level. Wireframe is an interesting choice if you need a very quickly generated view of the Wireframe interaction put into a movie. Draft is also useful if you need to quickly turn around a draft to see how an animation is developing in a general sense.

Concerning rendering, choosing a resolution is no different than your choice of resolution in the Comp window. Half renders half of the comp's pixels, Quarter renders one in four, and so on. Why might you do this? They render faster and give you a quick idea of how your composition looks as a whole. One interesting feature about the choices here is the Current Settings option. This maintains the resolutions of any nested comps within the overall composition. Selecting any of the other options overrides any nested comp settings.

If you choose Half resolution for a 720 x 480 comp, After Effects will render a 360 x 240 output file—¼ the size of the composition. If you choose Quarter resolution, your render will yield a 180 x 120 output file—¹⁄₁₆ the size of the composition. Rendering at Half resolution goes four times as fast as Full, and rendering at Quarter resolution goes 16 times as fast. These are pretty dramatic shifts in render speed, and they're ideal for proofing your work. Create rough drafts by using these settings to get a general sense of your composition.

If you prefer, here's how you can create a much higher quality draft. It takes a bit longer but still not as long as a full resolution render. Take the same 720 x 480 comp and place it in a 360 x 240 comp. Reduce the nested comp's scale to 50%. Render the half-sized comp at Full resolution. Following these instructions results in a far better looking output file than if you choose the half resolution method, but it all comes down to how much time you can afford to have your machine locked up during a render.

Setting Proxy Use and Effects

Proxies are placeholders you select to stand in place of any of the following examples: a dense and unwieldy nested comp, or in the world of footage items, a huge film file, or a still image made from a massive pixel scan. If you've defined proxies for any of these heavy original items, this setting determines how After Effects handles rendering with regard to these proxies. Select Use All Proxies to leave them in place, Comp Proxies Only to leave proxies which stand in place of nested comps, and No Proxies to disregard any proxies and render all of the nested comps and footage items, however heavy. Selecting Use No Proxies is the right choice for a final render. Selecting the others allows you to put together quick drafts to chart your progress.

You can opt to turn all effects on or off or maintain the current state of affairs in your comp by selecting Current Settings. This setting truly depends upon your preferred way of working with effects. Selecting All On renders every effect you've applied whether it's turned on the Timeline or a layer's Effect Controls dialog box. Selecting All Off simply renders no effects at all. Current Settings renders your comp in its present state. This choice is the right one if you stacked up five effects in the Effect Controls dialog box to test them and only left one turned on. Using All On renders all the effects that you were just testing in that case, resulting in a long render and a highly undesirable result. If you're inclined to delete effects after you realize you don't want to use them, then selecting All On has no adverse consequences. You'll begin to feel this out more clearly as you begin working more regularly with effects.

Setting Frame Blending and Motion Blur

Frame Blending takes footage and creates new frames by interpolating between the frames of the original material. This creates an especially good look if you're using footage that has been slowed down below its native frame rate, but using it causes a big performance hit when rendering because After Effects needs to blend the frames into a composited image before saving the file. Before you render a composition, you can opt to turn Frame Blending on for layers that have their Frame Blending switch checked, or you can opt to turn it off for all layers. You can also choose Current Settings. This option checks the Frame Blending switch at the comp level and renders the layers accordingly.

As is the case with effects, you need to find your own way of working with these options. Our suggestion is to turn Frame Blending on at the layer level whenever appropriate and concern yourself only with the comp level switch when previewing. When it comes time to render, you can use the Off For All Layers option to quickly render a rough draft, and you can employ the On For Checked Layers option when you're ready to do a final render. That way you don't need to worry about whether you've turned the comp level Frame Blending switch on, because you might turn it off to lower your preview times when working in the Timeline.

As far as rendering goes, Motion Blur works exactly the same way as Frame Blending. Motion Blur creates a beautiful look for certain items moving through a composition, but like its Frame Blending sibling, it can really slow down your ability to quickly put a composition together by hanging during previews. The issues surrounding the Current Settings, On For Checked Layers, and Off for All Layers switches are the same. There is one neat twist with Motion Blur though. You can override the shutter angle specified in a composition's advanced settings before rendering. If you want to, you can check the override box and set a value between 0 and 720 degrees, 720 being the most blur. The resulting amount of blur depends on the frame rate of the composition, and you can override that value in the Render settings as well.

Cross-Reference   We cover Motion Blur in detail in the Advanced Settings window of a composition's settings in Chapter 4.

Setting Field Render and 3:2 Pulldown

Use the Field Render switch to incorporate interlaced fields into your rendered output. If you're rendering for playback on progressive scan formats, such as a computer monitor or film, you don't need to turn the Field Render switch on. If you're outputting to an interlaced video format, such as NTSC video, then you want to turn this switch on. Choosing upper or lower field first depends entirely on your video hardware setup and whatever video formats have been developed to work with it. See the upcoming sidebar entitled "Determining a video board's field render order."

Use the 3:2 Pulldown switch in order to render a composition that uses NTSC video that has been transferred from film. When film is transferred to video, its images are taken apart to handle the transfer from 24 fps to 29.97 fps. Even though the footage is imported at 29.97 fps, if you interpret it with the right field render order and 3:2 pulldown phase, After Effects will enable you to work with the footage at its native film frame rate, in this case 23.976 fps (23.976 is the closest and cleanest derivative when stepping down from 29.97 to 24). After you've inter-preted the transferred footage this way, you can work in compositions set to 23.976 fps. If you want to render these compositions back to NTSC's native frame rate of 29.97 fps, use the 3:2 pulldown switch in the Render Settings dialog box. You can also use it to render a composition so that its motion looks like film motion because it changes the frames to mimic film's native frame rate of 24 fps while still made to run at the NTSC frame rate of 29.97 fps. Even though you have five pulldown phases to choose from (S stands for split and W stands for whole), most of them seem to render the same. You only need to be vigilant about this aspect of the switch if what you're creating in After Effects is going to get laid back into the video footage from which it originated.

STEPS: A Very Abbreviated Telecine/Inverse Telecine Workflow in After Effects

1. **If you're working with footage transferred from film to video, remove the 3:2 pulldown and have After Effects guess the correct phase in the Interpret Footage settings.**

2. **Place the correctly interpreted clips in a 23.976 fps comp.**

3. **Before rendering the 23.976 fps comp for video, set the field order cor-rectly according to your hardware and use a phase option from the 3:2 Pulldown switch.** If you're working this render back into existing footage, be sure to get the phase right (just match the guessed phase from the inter-pretation in Step 1).

Cross-Reference For more on 3:2 pulldown, refer to Chapter 2.

Determining a video board's field render order

Ordinarily, most video capture boards clearly indicate their field order either in their own documentation, or better still, they actually label their field order preference within the QuickTime files that they create upon capturing video. You have those rare occasions when you won't know what a system's field rendering order actually is. Because you have a 50-50 chance of getting it right, you could render a composition with a lot of motion in it twice, once with Upper Field First, and once with Lower Field first. Looking at the results should clue you in pretty quickly as to what the right setting is, but there's also a more concrete way to figure out this occasionally thorny production issue.

1. **Create a new composition, name it *Field Test*, and set it to the correct frame size and frame rate of your video hardware.** Also, specify a running time of no more than five seconds because you don't need any more than that to carry out the test.

2. **Create a new solid layer by choosing Layer ⇨ New ⇨ Solid (Command+Y/Ctrl+Y).** Specify small dimensions, for example, 100 x 100. Make sure you choose a color that stands out sharply from the Composition's background color.

3. **Move the solid to the left edge of the composition's frame.**

4. **Set a position keyframe for the layer at the beginning of the Comp.**

5. **Jump forward so that the current time is somewhere between two and five seconds later.**

6. **Reposition the solid at the right edge of the comp, which sets a new keyframe at the current time.**

7. **Add the comp to the Render Queue.**

8. **Choose Edit ⇨ Duplicate (Command+D/Ctrl+D) to make a copy of the same comp in the Render Queue.**

9. **In the render settings for the first of the two copies, choose Upper Field First from the Field Render pull-down menu.** In the Output To field, specify a clear filename for the movie, for example, *UpperField.mov*.

10. **In the render settings for the second of the two copies, choose Lower Field First from the Field Render pull-down menu.** In the Output To field, specify a clear filename for the movie, for example, *LowerField.mov*.

11. **Render the batch of two comps.**

12. **After they finish, bring the movies into your editing system and see which one of the two handles the basic animation correctly on an NTSC monitor.** One should "strobe" and look all wrong. The other moves smoothly. Note which of the two this is, and you figured out your hardware's native field-rendering order.

Keeping the correct field order when going from 720 x 486 to 720 x 480

The very popular NTSC DV 720 x 480 format has been known to present a few challenges for those who render movies for this format from After Effects. If you ever need to use NTSC D1 720 x 486 video in a 720 x 480 comp that you plan on rendering as DV (by specification, the DV format is Lower Field First), you'll need to get rid of the six extra lines from the traditional D1 format. Forcing an NTSC D1 720 x 486 video layer to fit-to-fill into a 720 x 480 composition muddies up the cleanliness of the field order, so rather than do that, just align the 720 x 486 layer so that the fields match evenly. For example, if you center 720 x 486 Lower Field First Footage into a 720 x 480 comp, three extra lines are outside the top and bottom edges of the frame. The first visible line of this 720 x 486 layer in the 720 x 480 comp is actually its fourth line, which is an upper field. If you nudge the 720 x 486 layer up one pixel, you solve this problem. You might need to test this with a couple of second long renders, which you can play back in your DV device to see whether what you're doing is working properly.

Defining the time span and frame rate

By default, when you put a composition in the Render Queue, it's set to render the work area you defined. If you changed the work area since you created the comp, then After Effects will only render that part of the comp. You can override this in two ways. You can use the pull-down menu to tell After Effects to render the entire composition and disregard the work area, or you can skip the pull-down menu and specify your own time span by clicking the Set button.

Tip   If you leave this setting at its work area default, you might run into trouble if you're not careful. If you send a comp to the Render Queue and change the work area between the times you submit the comp and the time you start the render, After Effects will render the new work area, not the one that used to be in place.

By default, a composition submitted to the Render Queue keeps its assigned frame rate. You can override it if you choose. If you do, After Effects will have to build more or less frames within the same defined running time of the movie. As is so often the case with these settings, it can be helpful to modify them in the event that you need a quickly rendered rough draft to chart your overall progress when building a composition. For example, you might want to enter 15 fps so that After Effects only renders one out of every two frames in the composition. Half the number of frames is a suitable choice if you only need a generalized view of your progress.

Tip   If you do opt to manually override the default frame rate, try and stick with numbers that factor cleanly into the composition's original frame rate. Coming from 29.97 fps or 30 fps, numbers such as 15 and 10 work well.

Using that little box at the bottom of the dialog box

The last option in the Render Settings dialog box deals with Storage Overflow and the Skip Existing Files render option. Storage Overflow refers to the action After Effects takes when it runs out of disk space while rendering a composition. If you check this box before beginning a render and disk space actually runs out as the output file is being saved, After Effects then looks to whatever Output preferences you set. The Output preferences specify any additional volumes to be used during an overflow. When a render that overflowed past a single volume has finished being rendered, the full extent of the output is saved as separate files within each volume. To view them as a complete render, you need to place the separate files comprising the complete render from end to end in your editing system to view the results of the render as a whole.

You can opt to use the Skip Existing Files option when rendering a sequence of still images across a network of multiple rendering stations. We cover Skip Existing Files at the end of the chapter where we look at issues surrounding network rendering as a whole.

Understanding Output Module Settings

Whereas render settings take care of the first part of the render process, output modules take care of the second. As soon as After Effects has composited an uncompressed image, it needs to save it as part of a movie file according to a significant number of specifications. These specifics have to do with file formats, compression in those formats, stretch and crop settings you define and, if applicable, an audio file with a defined sample rate.

Adjusting Output Module Settings

Click the Output module name of a composition in the Render Queue to pull up the Output Module Settings dialog box. As Figure 7-6 suggests, you can specify a myriad of options in this dialog box.

Choosing a format

With regard to format, After Effects can prepare files for a number of different applications. The Format menu enables you to choose which file type you want After Effects to render the composition. QuickTime movies are the most commonly used option here, and this is the default format chosen if you don't opt to select another before rendering. PC users can specify Windows video formats from this pull-down menu if they desire.

Deciding whether to embed

By default, this option is set to none. You can override it to include a link to the After Effects project in the output file, or you can opt to include both a link to and a copy of the After Effects project file used to author the output file. This can serve as a kind of insurance policy for the future. If you ever need to resuscitate a project long after you finished it, selecting this option for a final render can prove to be invaluable. For example, you might have worked on a news story or an ad campaign many months ago, and whomever you did the work for might come back and ask you to pick up the project where you left off. No problem. At least not until you realize that you deleted the After Effects project you used to render the final composition. An archived copy of the final output file complete with an embedded link to a copy of the After Effects project is a true lifesaver in this case.

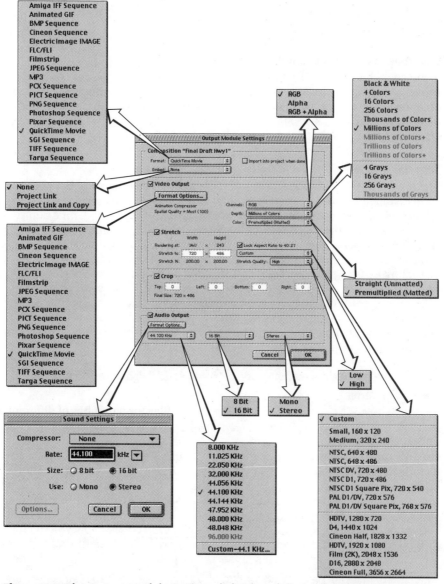

Figure 7-6: The Output Module Settings dialog box defines all the ways in which After Effects saves the composited uncompressed frames of a composition.

Tip   Just to be safe, you should always make a habit of archiving your After Effects project files because they're not prohibitively large in size.

Caution   Embedding is a relatively new feature, and it only works if you can import the output file into an application that allows you to select Edit Original. Adobe Premiere and Final Cut Pro are examples of video editing applications that have this feature. In other words, test your output file to make sure that the embedded link and its requisite copy of the After Effects project file used to author it are actually "visible" to the application you're using to work with the Output file.

Importing into project when done

If you click this check box, the output file will be placed in the Project window when the render is complete. This is a timesaver when you're pre-rendering nested compositions. A lot of times you can substitute nested comps with pre-rendered output files in the interest of keeping overall render time down for a large and complicated composition.

Selecting a format

The format options available to you are a direct consequence of the codecs you have installed on your system (see Figure 7-7). You select a format based upon the needs and requirements of your workflow. If you're working on a comp to be put on the Web, you might select a highly compressed format, such as Sorenson. Or you could go another route and select the Animation codec, which is a lossless format. After it's rendered, you might compress the output file and prepare it for streaming by using another application, such as Terran's Cleaner (formerly Media Cleaner Pro). You might need to choose a format that's native to certain video capture and editing hardware, such as MJPEG-A for the Aurora Igniter card. In any case, you make these choices in the Compression Settings window, which you access by clicking the Format button (see the sidebar entitled "Understanding compression options").

Cross-Reference   We address codecs (**co**mpression/**dec**ompression algorithms) in Chapter 2.

Choosing channels

Use this drop-down menu to decide which channels you want After Effects to include in the output file. You can choose RGB, RGB + Alpha, or simply Alpha. This choice depends on whether your composition contains an alpha channel, and it also depends on the limitations of your desired output format. More often than not, you'll accept the RGB default, but you'll also need to render alpha channels on a regular basis. Certain formats, such as the Animation codec allow you to choose RGB plus an alpha channel when rendering an output file. Other formats don't allow for this, but you can also use this pull-down menu to tell After Effects to render an output file consisting solely of an alpha channel.

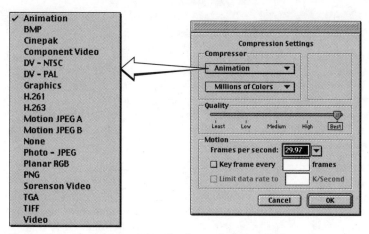

Figure 7-7: The Compression Settings window enables you to choose a codec and quality setting within that codec.

Selecting color depth

Like the Channels pull-down menu, the Depth menu is limited by the format you select for the output file. Left alone, the default setting is usually the same as the color space of your composition. If you've been working in 8-bit RGB color space, then the comp will be rendered as an 8-bit RGB output file. This is indicated by the Millions of Colors selection shown in the menu. If you specified that you want an alpha channel rendered along with the RGB channels, then the color depth menu will dynamically adjust and indicate Millions of Colors + as its selection. If you want to, you can override these settings and reduce the color space incrementally all the way back to simple black and white values.

Specifying color as it relates to an alpha channel

This pull-down menu specifies the way in which an alpha channel will be rendered in the output file. You can select either straight (unmatted) or pre-multiplied (matted).

Cross-Reference

For more information on this subject, check the section on the interpretation of alpha channels in Chapter 2.

Stretching

By default, this option is unchecked. This means that an output file is rendered at the same dimensions as its composition. You can change this by using the Stretch option to change the dimensions of the output file to the exact dimensions of your choosing. In our opinion, you should always try and set a composition's dimensions to the same size you need to render your output file. It keeps you more organized and prevents you from having to deal with nasty surprises right around the time you're finishing a project. If you need to stretch your output file and you're looking for a quick turnaround of a rough draft, you should specify Low Stretch quality. High Stretch quality settings can take forever because After Effects is so good at subpixel rendering and resampling.

Understanding compression options

Compression technology is what enables digital video folks to have a career. All digital video, that is, video digitized from any number of sources, has been compressed to some degree. Video capture boards all use a compression scheme in which an image is broken down into a collection of ones and zeros that represent pixels and their color values. The less compressed an image is, the more natural it looks to your eye. Conversely, the more compressed an image is, the more you can visibly notice artifacts, jagged edges, and other indicators of information that's "missing."

Before rendering, you choose the kind of compression you want when you select the format options for your output file. Those options are listed in the QuickTime Compression Settings window that opens after you click the Format Options button, and they're based on whatever codecs you have loaded on your system. There are *lossless* codecs, and there are *lossy* codecs. Lossless codecs retain all the data that comprises an image; they only compact or concentrate that data. The image itself isn't compromised. Lossless codecs generally produce large file sizes. Lossy codecs actually get rid of information about the image as part of their compression. Data, which constitutes color and light information, is discarded; however, depending on the severity of the compression, the discarded information might not be perceptible. Lossy codecs produce smaller files that make them easier to play back in real time. As file sizes decrease with lossy codecs, image quality begins to visibly degrade. Basically, the trade off is between image quality and file size.

If you're working with a proprietary video-editing suite, such as Avid, you'll also have proprietary codecs listed among your options in the compression settings. We include a few words on some of the generic codec options in the QuickTime Compression Settings window.

✦ **Animation:** This is the lossless format of choice. Although it produces large file sizes, it retains the highest image quality standard. If you're creating animations in After Effects, the animation codec is the default lossless format option, for good reason. All of the subtle shades of your composition will be retained in the final render. If you're going to be preparing work for use in multiple video formats, try and derive them from a lossless master version if you can.

✦ **MJPEG-A:** This is generally considered to be the best lossy codec. At high data rates, image quality is excellent, and this is the codec of choice among video hardware makers. Media100 and Aurora's video capture boards work natively with the MJPEG-A codec. At draft quality data rates though, images start to visibly degrade.

✦ **DV:** DV is actually quite a compressed format to begin with. There are several variants of DV, but the most common is sometimes called DV25 because its data rate is approximately 25 Mbits/second (approximately 3.5 Mbytes/second). The data rate alone suggests a fair amount of compression.

✦ **Sorenson:** The Sorenson codec is very lossy, but it produces excellent results with very small amounts of data. This is the codec of choice when preparing video for playback on the World Wide Web.

A good number of high-end cards support "uncompressed" capture, and a project warrants that kind of throughput if you're working with DigiBeta or film. In short, you want to use a codec that's suitable for the material. Another thing to keep in mind is what a given video board can handle as far as output is concerned. For example, some cards support MPEG-2 compression, which allows for the production of DVDs.

Cropping

By default, this option is also unchecked. After you enable it, you can increase or decrease an output file's size by adding or subtracting pixel width lines. Approaching from any of the four sides, you can enter positive or negative values in the fields. Typing positive numbers decreases the image size because that's how much you're cropping. Typing negative numbers adds pixels to an output file's dimensions.

Caution

If you're careless with this setting, you can upset the field-rendering order of a composition. Because NTSC video has an even number of fields, adding or subtracting an odd number of horizontal lines changes the interlaced field order.

Specifying audio output options

If your composition contains audio, click the Audio Output check box to enable the options. Adjust the settings so that they match your output device. For example, if you're outputting to DV, select 48.000 kHz, 16-bit, and Stereo from the three pull-down menus.

Saving Time by Creating Templates

You can create as many templates as your workflow requires. Creating templates is really quite easy after you're familiar with the variables you're selecting. You can also make changes to existing templates. The ideal is to have as many on hand as you might need. Be prepared. Also, you need only do this once, and you can access the templates without having to put a composition into the Render Queue. Additionally convenient, you can save your templates and load them into another After Effects workstation. The next couple of short exercises show you how to create new templates and set them as the defaults.

STEPS: Creating a Render Settings Template

1. **Choose Edit ➪ Templates ➪ Render Settings.** Doing this brings up the dialog box shown in Figure 7-8.

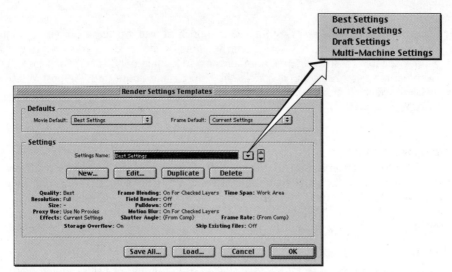

Figure 7-8: The Render Settings Templates dialog box enables you create new Render Settings templates and edit existing ones.

2. **Click New.** A Render Settings dialog box for *Untitled 1* appears.

3. **Make the selections from the pull-down menus that are the ones you use most often.**

4. **Click OK.**

5. **In the Settings Name field, type a name in place of the automatically created *Untitled 1*.** Try *Bobby's Best Settings* or something that you'll recognize.

6. **Make it the default template by selecting it from the Movie Default pull-down menu.**

If you ever need to edit your template, pull up the Render Settings dialog box, select your template from the template pull-down menu at the right edge of the Settings Name field, and click Edit to change any of the settings. If you need to create a new template that differs only slightly from any that already exist, select the closest match from the template pull-down menu and click Duplicate. From there, edit and rename the duplicated template. Finally, if you want to delete a template, select it from the template pull-down menu and click Delete.

After you finish creating the templates you need, you can save them in order to load them into other machines that have After Effects installed. Click Save All and save the *.ars* file with a name of your choosing. If you need to load Render Settings templates, click Load and navigate your way to the desired *.ars* file.

Creating templates is all pretty straightforward, but essential nonetheless. The more time you spend working in After Effects, the more you'll find ways to increase your efficiency, and this is an easy step towards getting the most from your time. The next exercise explains the same process for Output Module settings.

STEPS: Creating an Output Module Template

1. **Choose Edit ⇨ Templates ⇨ Output Module.** This brings up the dialog box in Figure 7-9.

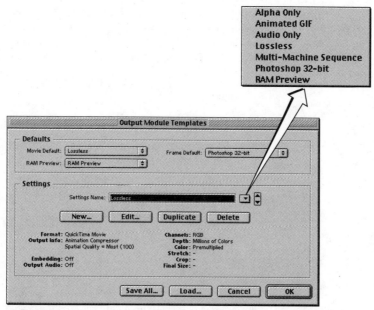

Figure 7-9: The Output Module Templates dialog box enables you create new Output Module templates and edit existing ones.

2. **Click New.** An Ouput Module window for *Untitled 1* appears.

3. **Make the selections from the pull-down menus that include the options you use most often.** This includes any format options that you select (codec and quality).

4. **Click OK.**

5. **In the Settings Name field, type a name in place of the automatically created *Untitled 1*.** Try *Greatest Movie Ever!* or something that you'll recognize.

6. **Make it the default template by selecting it from the Movie Default pull-down menu.**

What's new in After Effects 5.5: Advanced RealMedia Output

With the advent of version 5.5, After Effects is now capable of creating RealMedia files directly from the Render Queue. In case you're not familiar with preparing video for the Web, RealNetworks' RealMedia is one of the "Big Three" players in the streaming video market — the other two being Apple's QuickTime and Microsoft's Windows Media Player.

To render RealMedia files, drag a footage item or a composition to the Render Queue, and in the Output Module Settings dialog box, select RealMedia from the Format pull-down menu. For even tighter control, you can click the Format Options button in the Output Module Settings dialog box and select from various options that will help you customize your RealMedia output for a specific audience (see Figure SB 7-1).

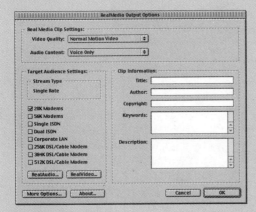 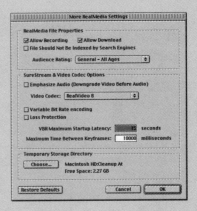

Figure SB 7-1: As you can see, there are tons of RealMedia settings that you can tweak before firing off a render.

For example, you can elect to create RealMedia files that have various data rates. You can also embed keywords, descriptions, and other information within the movies. These keywords can be accessed later by search engines on the Web. Of course, once your render is complete, you can view these creations only by using the RealPlayer software.

Tip   Set your default templates to those you use most often. That way, when you send a composition to the Render Queue, it's already set up to be rendered at your most preferred pairing of Render and Output Module settings. If you ever want to change the default without having to go through the Edit ⇨ Templates route, hold down the Command/Ctrl key as you select a new template from the drop-down menus for either the Render Settings or Output Module for a comp in the Render Queue, and your default template will be set to your selection.

You've probably been able to pick up on the fact that both of the templates share the same modular structure and work almost identically. You can create new Output modules, and you can edit, duplicate, and delete existing ones in exactly the same manner as you would Render Settings templates.

With regard to saving your output modules and sharing them across multiple machines with After Effects installed, the only difference between the two templates is that Output Module settings are saved to an *.aom* file as opposed to an *.ars* file. The process of saving and loading them is identical.

The only pull-down menus we didn't address in this section were the options concerned with rendering still frames. We cover that in the next part of this chapter.

Improving Your Render Choices

As your work in the application continues to improve, you'll begin to realize that although After Effects is a great piece of software, it's very easy to hemorrhage time as you use it in a variety of different ways. As you discover each feature of the program and increase your knowledge, you also increase your capacity to spread yourself thin and lose track of your time management. Potential bottlenecks include nesting compositions, applying effects, continuously rasterizing EPS layers, and collapsing transformations, to name only a few.

Nowhere is efficiency more critical than when you're rendering. You can learn a number of techniques towards keeping the larger investment of your time geared towards creativity. This beats the opportunity cost of remaining idle while you computer takes forever to render something it could have rendered in a fraction of the time if you only you knew a little better. In time, you'll learn that getting a design to look good is only part of a balanced equation. Granted, it is the biggest part, but design chops are best if they're complemented with a little technical know-how.

In the interest of efficiency, we've outlined a couple of timesavers that we lean upon fairly regularly. As soon as you've got these tricks up your sleeve, you're already begun a commitment to work smarter, not harder.

Increasing Efficiency

You have a couple of ground rules when working in any digital video application, and we cover these before getting into specifics about the Render Queue.

✦ **Turn off virtual memory:** This is always a good idea. The whole point of loading frames into RAM is that they can be accessed more quickly than a disk when the processor calls for them. Because Virtual Memory is simply RAM overflow written to disk, you undercut any speed advantage you might gain if it's turned on.

Tip

PC and OSX users needn't worry about this tip because those operating systems allocate RAM on a dynamic as-need basis. On the other hand, Mac users who haven't made the move to OSX should allocate their RAM somewhat carefully. Say you've installed 512MB of RAM on your After Effects workstation. If you're only using After Effects during a given session, you might be tempted to allocate somewhere close to 480MB to it and leave the remaining portion for the Mac OS. You want to leave the Mac OS more breathing room than that because it always seems to want to allocate more for itself as you keep working. In this scenario, we recommend something closer to 450MB. Of course, you might want to run other applications concurrently, and you might need to experiment with allocations to find the right combination for running several applications, such as Final Cut Pro and After Effects at the same time.

✦ **Install the latest version of QuickTime:** Because most of your work in After Effects is based upon accessing the data in QuickTime files, you want to be sure that you've got the benefit of whatever features are in the current build of this versatile software.

✦ **Defragment your hard drive:** We don't concern ourselves with this all the time, but it's a good idea to clean house once in a while. Severely fragmented disks can slow down a render because After Effects will needlessly spend time searching for empty disk blocks that are scattered far and wide across the disk's surface. When it gets bad enough, reading and writing information to disk can become prohibitively slow, and because rendering involves writing a file to disk, you can see why this may become an issue.

✦ **Check the Adobe Web site for information pertinent to After Effects:** Once in a great while, Adobe may release updates for After Effects. For example, version 4.0 had a memory leak which caused problems with Illustrator files scaled up past 100%. Adobe solved the problem by putting a patch for the memory leak on their Web site before they fully incorporated the fix in version 4.1. Stay tuned in to these kinds of developments to get the best performance out of your work in After Effects. These kinds of things tend to become a problem when you have the least amount of time to adapt.

After you take care of those system level variables, you can turn your attention to speeding up your renders from within After Effects.

✦ **Close the Comp window when rendering:** If you leave a composition open in the Comp window while it renders, After Effects updates the image as it builds the output file. Initially, you might find it kind of neat that you can see each frame of a composition as After Effects constructs its requisite ouput file one frame at a time, but this is a waste of precious processor and RAM resources. To complete a render as quickly as possible, close its Comp window tab before beginning the render. If it's too late and you've already begun rendering, press the Caps Lock key to prevent the Comp window from dynamically updating its contents

✦ **Close the Render Details twirler when rendering:** When rendering, sometimes it's pretty cool to chart a render's progress by twirling down the render details in the Render Queue dialog box. This can be a great way to watch the logic of After Effects in action while you're learning the intricacies of the Render Pipeline; sad thing is, opening this twirler diverts a large amount of resources towards giving you that detailed frame-by-frame account of what the render is crunching on at any given moment. Well, what's it there for? The answer is that it's there to help you identify where a render might be experiencing a slow-down. For example, if you see that each frame is taking between 10 and 30 seconds to render, you'd want to know what was causing such a hang-up. In that case, you'd open the Render Details twirler to see what was getting the largest share of render time. It might be a resource-intensive filter, such as Gaussian Blur or something similar. Whatever it is, the Render Details should make it clear to you. So use it as you need it. Actually, After Effects does its best to help you in this regard. If you've opened the twirler, it closes it after a few minutes to completely dedicate itself to the task of building the output file.

There's another great timesaving feature when rendering in After Effects, and not everyone knows about it. If you need to render a composition for different media types (such as for broadcast, Web, and print), you only need to set up one render in the Render Queue. The following steps explain exactly how.

STEPS: Selecting Multiple Output Modules

1. **Add a composition to the Render Queue.**

2. **Choose Composition ⇨ Add Output Module.** Repeat this step as many times as you require. The Render Queue reflects the added output modules (see Figure 7-10).

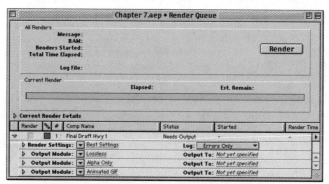

Figure 7-10: In the Render Queue, this composition indicates that multiple output modules have been assigned to it.

3. **Specify file names and locations for the various output files.** You need to do this for all the modules before you can render.

4. Click Render. Twirl down the Render Details to see After Effects build the multiple output files (see Figure 7-11).

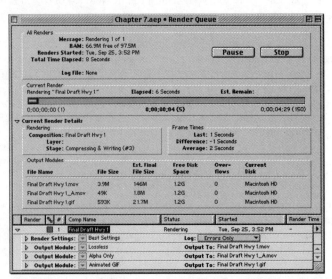

Figure 7-11: The Render details for this render indicate that multiple output files are simultaneously being saved.

Caution

Using this technique presumes that you want to maintain consistent Render Settings across the different output files. This won't work if you want different frame sizes or color depth among the renders. You can, however, change the settings in the Render Queue using the templates or accessing the settings for each output file as outlined before.

Rendering Still Frames

You can render still frames for use in different kinds of media, and you can also render them for use in Photoshop, with or without layers intact. You might recall that After Effects can import all different kinds of still image formats, and it can also import Photoshop files with layers intact. The converse is also essentially true. After Effects can export just as many different kinds of still images, and you can use those stills in print, Web, and video media. Some folks would actually rather prepare a layered Photoshop file in After Effects rather than in Photoshop. Wait. Really? Yes, in fact. Perhaps that sentence should read as this: Broadcast designers more familiar with After Effects than Photoshop would rather prepare a layered Photoshop file in After Effects rather than in Photoshop. The rest of this section is devoted to rendering stills from within After Effects.

What's new in After Effects 5.5: Post-Render Actions, Proxies, and Output Chains

After Effects 5.5 adds Post-Render Actions to the Render Queue. If you're just getting started with After Effects, these may seem a bit complicated and difficult to fathom, but as you grow more advanced with the application, you'll definitely appreciate their power. The Post-Render Action items can be found under the Output Module settings in the Render Queue.

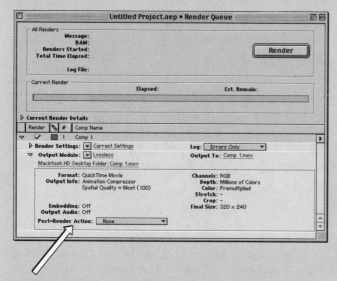

Figure SB 7-2: The Post-Render Action item menu can be found in the expanded view of the Output Module settings.

In the most basic sense, Post-Render Actions make the Render Queue a bit more interactive and user-friendly. In previous versions of After Effects, all you could really do in the Render Queue was, well, render. Now you can specify certain actions to take place *after* the rendering has been completed. For example, if you select Import and Replace Footage from the Post-Render Action menu, After Effects will import the rendered item back into the project after the render is complete and replace a specified comp, footage item, or placeholder in the Project window. Essentially, what you have now is a level of automation in the rendering process that was previously unavailable.

Beyond the Post-Render Actions, After Effects 5.5 also allows for some highly interactive ways for working with Proxies. For example, you can do the following:

✦ Create quick proxies by dragging footage or compositions from the Project window straight to the Render Queue.

Continued

Continued

✦ Select File ⇨ Create Proxy to quickly create a proxy for any item in the Project window.

✦ Make a placeholder for any item in the Render Queue by dragging the queued Output Module back into the Project window. Default settings for the proxies are set in the Render Settings by creating templates.

By combining Post-Render Actions and proxies, you can set up output chains in the following manner. Say that you want to render a composition at 30 fps and then use the render for another 15 fps composition. Here's how to create an output chain:

1. **Drag the 30 fps composition into the Render Queue.**

2. **Drag the resulting Output Module for the 30 fps comp back from the Render Queue into the Project window to create a placeholder.**

3. **You can now drag the placeholder from the Project window into a new 15 fps composition and drag this new composition into the Render Queue again and set the Render Settings to 15 fps.**

After Effects will first render the 30 fps composition, and then the resulting render will automatically replace the placeholder in the 15 fps comp, at which point you can render the 15 fps comp.

Note   Photoshop is an amazing application in its own right, and we're hardly suggesting that you bypass learning it. Photoshop didn't get to be the world's most popular image manipulation software by being anything less than superb. In fact, understanding it well enough to use it as a complement to After Effects is critical, and it's even better if your knowledge of the application goes further than that. At the very least, its retouching tools and CMYK color space capacity have no equivalents in After Effects. Still, it should be pointed out that you can indeed export a frame of a composition in After Effects as a layered Photoshop file. The point is that the versatility in working across applications goes both ways.

Rendering Still Images

Exporting stills is essentially no different than exporting movies, but the procedures vary a bit. The following exercises explain how to render different kinds of still images.

STEPS: Rendering a Single Frame as a Flattened Still Image

1. **Choose Composition ⇨ Save Frame As ⇨ File (Command+Option+S/Ctrl+Alt+S).** This opens the Output Frame To dialog box.

2. **Enter a file name and click OK.** The Render Queue is displayed with the still image placed at the top of the list. By default, the output module is set to the Frame Default defined in the Output Module Template window. You can go into the Output Module settings if you want to change the default file format, which in this case is a flattened Photoshop file. Different formats include BMPs, PNGs, PICTs and TIFFs.

3. **Click Render.**

Tip

Before Step 1, set the current time to the frame of the comp that you want to make the still from.

STEPS: Rendering a Single Frame as a Layered Photoshop File

1. **Choose Composition ⇨ Save Frame As ⇨ Photoshop Layers.**

2. **Enter a file name and click OK.**

This bypasses the Render Queue altogether and creates a Photoshop file with all layers intact. It also carries over masks, effects, transfer modes, and adjustment layers. Amazing.

Not surprisingly, After Effects can render a composition as a series of stills. This has its applications in areas as far reaching as printing film to prepping stills for use in a PowerPoint presentation.

STEPS: Rendering a Sequence of Stills

1. **Add a composition to the Render Queue.**

2. **In the Render Queue, click the comp's Output Module name.**

3. **Under Format, select any of the still image sequence options (such as TIFF sequence).**

4. **Click OK.**

5. **Click the Output To field to specify a name and click OK.** We recommend that you create a new folder for the sequence because it will drop a lot of frames into it if you've specified a time range of more than half a second (15 files from a 30 fps composition in that particular case). The file name needs to have the *[###]* part in its name to properly number the frames of the sequence, so don't change that.

6. **Click Render.**

When the render is complete, navigate your way to the export folder to look at the results. A lot of files are probably in there, but the numbering scheme will clearly indicate their order.

If you want to rotoscope a movie in Photoshop, render your comp as a filmstrip. *Rotoscoping* is that especially neat technique in which an artist paints on each of the individual frames of a movie to create a very interesting stylized look. A filmstrip is a very unusual format in which all of the frames of a composition are laid out on to one large still image file.

STEPS: Prepping a Filmstrip File

1. **Add a composition to the Render Queue.**

2. **In the Render Queue, click the comp's Output Module name.**

3. **Under Format, select Filmstrip.**

4. **Click OK.** If necessary, go into the Render Settings to set the timeframe you want to convert into a filmstrip.

5. **Click Render.**

When rendering is complete, open Photoshop and open the newly created filmstrip. When opening this file in Photoshop, it should look like Figure 7-12.

Figure 7-12: The Filmstrip file consists of each of the rendered frames laid from top to bottom in a column offset by a gray margin in which frame numbers and timecodes are visible.

Image Courtesy of Videometry

This unusually cool-looking file has a couple of distinguishing characteristics worth explaining. First, these frames are completely uncompressed and subsequently constitute a very large file. Therefore, you might want to break filmstrips into smaller chunks that won't overwhelm Photoshop's allotted RAM. Secondly, there's a gray margin in between the individual frames in which the frame number and timecode are displayed. You can paint and retouch in this area, but these parts of the file are invisible when you bring them back into After Effects or any other digital video application. Lastly, you can make changes to the RGB and alpha channels (to add an alpha, create a fourth channel in the channels palette). Just remember that you need to flatten any layers you add because a filmstrip is a flattened file by nature. If your painting is on separate layers and you don't flatten the file before saving it, your work will not be visible when you bring the filmstrip into another application.

Caution   Don't change the file's dimensions or it will become unreadable when you try and import it into a digital video application.

For kicks, edit and save the file in Photoshop and import the filmstrip back into After Effects. Unlike its column display in Photoshop, After Effects interprets the filmstrip as just another video file. Experiment with this and have some fun with it if your time allows.

That pretty much covers using After Effects as a tool to create still images. Remember that you can use these stills in as many ways as you can imagine. Web pages, printed matter, broadcast video, CD-ROM multimedia, and DVD-ROM menus could all be applications for your stills. As you become more accustomed to using After Effects, think integration. Get as much mileage from your best compositions as you possibly can.

What's new in After Effects 5.5: Performance optimizations

After Effects 5.5 supports Windows XP and introduces optimizations for Pentium 4 processors. After Effects 5.5 also supports *asynchronous* output for Photoshop, Cineon, and PICT sequence formats. In previous versions of After Effects, the frames for still sequences were first rendered and then written to disk. In After Effects 5.5, the output is speeded up by separating the way each frame is rendered and written to disk. That way, each process overlaps instead of running sequentially. As soon as one frame is rendered, the rendering for the next frame is begun. Writing to disk is handled as a separate step, thus speeding up the entire process considerably.

Authoring Flash Files

Brand new in After Effects 5 is the capability to save your composition in the popular and versatile Flash file format (SWF). Flash's inherent strength lies in the fact that it's a vector-based animation tool. Because vectors generate small files compared to bitmaps, animations created in Flash usually take up minimal amounts of file space. Of course, this is why its format has become so popular on the Web. Because Flash is a vector-based animation tool, there are restrictions on what can go from an After Effects composition into its SWF file export. To see that it can be done, first you export a composition as a Flash file. Then we explain what kinds of elements work better than others when working with this file format.

STEPS: Exporting a Composition as a Flash File

1. **Select the composition that you want to export as a Flash file either by clicking it in the Project window or bringing its tab to the front of the Comp and Timeline windows.**

2. **Choose File ⇨ Export ⇨ Macromedia Flash (SWF).**

3. **Specify a file name and a location for the export.**

4. **Click Save or OK.** This brings up the SWF Settings window shown in Figure 7-13.

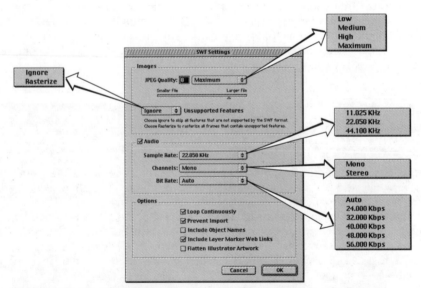

Figure 7-13: The SWF Settings window enables you to select the options, which determine image quality, audio quality, and how to handle various aspects of the composition you exported as they relate to the Flash file format (SWF).

5. Make your selections and click OK to begin the export.

Both a Flash movie file and an HTML report are created as a result of these steps.

Adjusting SWF settings for export

The choices you make with regard to the options in the SWF settings dialog box are critical in determining the final file size of the Flash file. We're assuming that you would create a Flash file for use on the Web, so we're going to approach these settings with the goal of keeping file size at a minimum while still creating a high quality Flash file. The following list should help you toward understanding each of the options in the SWF Settings window:

✦ **JPEG Quality:** Drag the slider, enter a value directly, or select a preset from the drop-down menu to select the quality of images that are not vector based. This includes any video or still images in the After Effects composition, and it also includes Illustrator files if you opt to rasterize unsupported features in the pull-down menu beneath the image quality settings.

✦ **Ignore/Rasterize Unsupported Features:** If you've created your comp with Flash in mind and have stayed within the limits of supported features, you should select Ignore to take advantage of Flash's strengths and keep your file size small. If you must include bitmap images of all the layers in the composition that contain elements that are unsupported by the Flash file format, select Rasterize, and these elements will be imported at the JPEG compression settings specified in the previous image quality setting. We recommend against doing this unless you don't mind creating a large Flash file.

✦ **Audio:** You can select the sample rate, stereo/mono setting, and bit rate of the audio file if you have audio in your composition. Once again, it all comes down to file size. We recommend that you experiment with the sample rate and stereo/mono options and settle on a quality baseline. After you do that, select Auto from the bit rate option to optimize the audio file that gets created as part of the exported Flash file. Flash audio is created using the MP3 format.

✦ **Loop Continuously:** Select this if you want the Flash animation to loop continuously as it plays back.

✦ **Prevent Import:** This option prevents users on the Web from being able to import the Flash file.

✦ **Include Object Names:** This includes layer, mask, and effect names from the After Effects composition in the Flash file.

✦ **Include Layer Marker Web Links:** You can specify Web links in layer markers for each layer in the After Effects composition.

✦ **Flatten Illustrator Artwork:** We recommend leaving this unchecked so that any layers comprised of Illustrator files scale cleanly when the resulting Flash file gets scaled.

Learning which features are supported by Flash

Okay. So what elements are supported? Which ones aren't? Think bare bones here. Most of your favorite After Effects features don't carry over, but that makes sense considering how differently you apply vector-based Web media compared to video media. Pay careful attention to these constraints if you're intent on creating small files.

✦ **Layers:** Normal is the only supported transfer mode. Track mattes, 3D layers, 3D cameras, or 3D lights are not supported, and among the switches, neither are Preserve Transparency, Adjustment Layer, Collapse Transformations, and Motion Blur. As far as Illustrator files are concerned, you can only use stroked and filled paths.

✦ **Masks:** Only the Add and Difference mask modes are supported. If you use multiple masks on a layer, they must all be set to Add or Difference. Variance in opacity and mask inversions work only if the Add mode is selected. Mask Feathering is not supported either.

✦ **Effects:** You only have one option here. Yep. One. At least it's a good one: Path Text. It can be used only once per layer, too. And within the Path Text options you can select only Fill. Also, you cannot select Composite on Original. So, it's really a very stripped-down version of Path Text that's allowed if you're going to go the Ignore route in the SWF settings.

After you create this Flash file, look at the report file in Web browser to see exactly what you've done here. Figure 7-14 shows an example of one. Experiment freely, and always keep an eye on your file size to see how different setting selections affect your output.

Note   You can use layer markers to define embedded Web links in a Flash file. We cover layer markers in Chapter 8.

Making an animated GIF

As long as we're on the subject of exporting compositions to a Web-based format, such as Flash, we may as well take a moment to tell you that you can use After Effects to create an animated GIF. In the Render Queue, select the composition's Output Module name and select Animated GIF from the Format menu. This brings up a dialog box in which you specify which 8-bit color scheme you want to use as well as how to handle transparency. This is a great option when you need to quickly put together animated Web graphics. If you have time, experiment with the results. Quite often, things can appear a little muddy and you might want to tweak your color options to know how to take full advantage of this export feature.

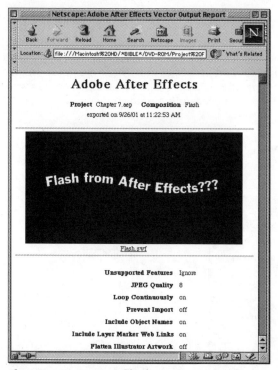

Figure 7-14: A report file that got generated along with the exported Flash file recaps the SWF settings you used for your export.

Managing a Complex Workflow: Workgroup Rendering

If you use After Effects in a networked environment, then you have a number of interesting distributed rendering options. The Production Bundle of After Effects ships with a Render Engine that can be installed on other computers in a network without having to install the entire application. At no extra cost to you, you can install the Render Engine on as many different machines as you like without regard to licensing fees or serial numbers. It should be noted that you can install the Render Engine whether or not the machine is on a network. Independent of the render engine, the Collect Files option is a great way to back up a project, give it to another After Effects artist to pick up where you left off, or to use a different machine to render the compositions lined up in a project's Render Queue.

Collect Files

When you use the Collect Files feature, After Effects makes a copy of the project file as well as copies of all of the footage files used in the project. Just as important, it creates a detailed report of the collection process. All of these elements are placed in a single folder, and the report specifies which files are missing, if any, as well as what effects and fonts are required to successfully render the compositions. Rather cool.

To use this feature, choose File ⇨ Collect Files. This brings up the dialog box shown in Figure 7-15.

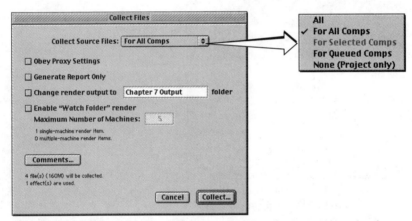

Figure 7-15: The Collect Files dialog box specifies the instructions for the ensuing file collection.

Here's how to make sense of the options in the dialog box.

- ✦ **Obey Proxy Settings:** Use this option to specify how you want the collection process to handle any proxy items that may be used in comps that are in the Render Queue.

- ✦ **Generate Report Only:** Use this option to only generate a report so that you can pre-empt any need to copy effects and fonts to the machine where you'll be taking the Collected project.

- ✦ **Change render output to:** Use this option to change the default location for output files. If you choose, After Effects creates an output folder, which it places inside the folder in which all the files are being collected.

- ✦ **Enable "Watch Folder" render:** Use this option to specify that output files be rendered to a specific Watch Folder. For more on this, take a look at the Watch Folder section of the following section.

- ✦ **Maximum Number of Machines:** Use this option to specify how many machines you want to use for distributing the rendering load.

After you're finished, the original project remains open, and any changes you make won't be reflected in the copy created by the Collect Files command.

In this dialog box, you also specify whether you want to collect all the files in the project or only those that are used by all compositions or only those that are in the Render Queue. See the pull-down menu in Figure 7-15. You can also specify None, and this simply copies the project file. Add comments if you like. They are added to the bottom of the report that's generated and when you're ready, click OK. After Effects then creates the new folder and copy and collects all the specified files into it.

Look at the new folder after the process is complete. In it you find the copy of the Project file, the generated Report, a folder called *Footage* holding all of the footage items, and an output folder if you specified that one be created.

The folder names have been placed in parentheses to tell any Render Engines that these folders are not to be searched for projects.

Watch Folder

The Watch Folder command is available only to users of the Production Bundle of After Effects. This command takes advantage of the distributed rendering capabilities we mentioned at the beginning of this section. A network only has to have one copy of the Production Bundle installed on one of its machines. The rest of the computers you want to use in this process need only have the Render Engine version of After Effects installed.

Working across multiple platforms in a mixed network can be a minefield if you aren't vigilant about file naming conventions. If you're a Mac user on a mixed network, use PC file name extensions for all the different file types so that all of them will be recognizable to their PC counterparts.

If you've used third-party plug-in effects in a composition you plan on rendering across a network, they must be installed on each machine on the network. Check each third-party plug-in's licensing agreement to see whether you can copy them across the network in this manner. In some cases, the different copies definitely won't work without separate serial registration codes for each copy.

STEPS: Using a Watch Folder Across a Network

1. **After you install the Render Engine on other networked machines, create a watch folder anywhere on the network as long as it's visible to all the machines you plan on using.**

2. **On each After Effects workstation you want to use for distributed rendering, choose File ⇨ Watch Folder and point to the Watch Folder you just created.**

3. **Set up you Render Queue with all the compositions that you want to render.** Set the Render Settings and Output modules for each one as you would normally.

4. **Use the Collect Files command to collect all the Project files into the Watch Folder on network.** Be sure to use the Watch Folder option in the Collect Files dialog box. Also enter a maximum number of machines if you want to limit the number of machines involved in the rendering process.

After the Collect Files process is complete, the distributed rendering gets under way. If you want to monitor the progress of the Render Queue, you can point a Web browser to the HTML pages that will be created and placed in the Watch folder. Pretty darn cool if you ask us. If you want to keep working this way, collect files from multiple projects and drop the resulting folders into the Watch Folder. The Render Engines start looking for more work to do after a project's render queue is completed.

Tip

You can start After Effects in Watch Folder mode simply by saving a project called *Watch This Folder.aep,* placing it in a folder you want to be a Watch Folder, and then opening the project. Going a step further, you can boot a machine so that it opens this project when it starts up. For Mac users, put the folder containing the *Watch This Folder.aep* project in your Startup Items in the system folder. For PC users, put the folder containing the *Watch This Folder.aep* project in your Startup folder.

Because multiple machines cannot simultaneously render a single movie, using the distributed rendering model to work on a still image sequence is actually more efficient. Take advantage of this workflow if you can. Not all video productions are based on still image sequences, but production houses with Targa video capture boards or other hardware setups that allow for single frame sequences as an acceptable video playback format can make use of this feature. Here's how it's done.

STEPS: Rendering Still-Frame Sequences Across a Network

Caution

Using the still-frame sequence method requires that you install a full version of After Effects on each system that you want to join in the distributed rendering. This is because the Render Engine version of After Effects isn't capable of rendering the same composition on more than one machine.

1. **After you've finished installing full versions of After Effects on all the computers consigned to the task, open the project on one of the systems and add your composition to the Render Queue.**

2. **From within the Render Queue dialog box, select one of the still-image sequences as the format in the Output Module Settings dialog box.**

3. **Select a destination folder in the Output File To field for the composition in the Render Queue and make sure that the folder is visible to all the networked After Effects machines.**

4. **While still in the Render Queue, go into the Render Settings and be certain that you've checked the Skip Existing Files option at the bottom of the dialog box.**

5. **Save the project.**

6. **Put a copy of the project file and its source footage on each of the machines that you want to handle the distributed rendering.**

7. **On each machine that you've copied the file, open and save the project, and check to make sure that the output destination is recognized as the networked folder you pointed to in Step 3.**

8. **Click Render in the Render Queue dialog box on each machine.** Together, they'll work in concert and only render each frame once because they'll skip ones that have already been saved.

This seems like a lot of work to get a few machines to render together, but it's worth it if you have a huge amount of stills to create. If you're only working on a relatively small amount of output, it's not really worth it.

Caution

This is a pretty unfortunate word of warning for the still-image sequence across a network scenario. If you used Production Bundle effects in your composition, you need to install the Production Bundle on every machine you use to render that composition. Yep. You read that correctly. Kinda defeats the purpose of building an elaborate composition with lots of fancy effects if you planned on being able to render it quickly with lots of machines. Oh well. Actually, it's still pretty cool given this rather large constraint, but if you plan on rendering this way, keep this caveat in mind when building your composition.

✦   ✦   ✦

Building Complex Compositions

In this chapter, you start to work with compositions that take advantage of most of what the application has to offer. First of all, it's time to start learning how to apply effects. Our subject is called After Effects, after all. Even though After Effects contains lots of different kinds of effects, learning how to apply them is essentially the same across the board. You also start discovering the virtues of good parenting, even if you aren't a parent. In this latest version of After Effects, the developers at Adobe added the parenting feature, and we look into what that's all about. Add to parenting the phenomenon of nesting. You may have tried it a couple of times already, but you examine nesting and pre-composing in detail during this chapter.

Doing all that requires you to start putting together more complex Timelines. After you're finished working through this chapter, your compositions will consist of multiple layers that include, among other things, video, audio, solids, and layer markers. Twirling down these layers will reveal effects. Some of these layers will be pre-composed. All of them will be part of an animation hierarchy, which you learn how to define. As you can see, this chapter begins to combine a lot of different areas of After Effects.

Introducing Effects

You can do a number of things to modify the appearance of a layer in the Comp window. As well as adding transformational animations or masks to a layer, you can unleash the big fun by adding effects, sometimes called *filters*. Effects can be a blast, but as with using filters in Photoshop, you may be prone to being a little overzealous if you're new to the program. There's no harm in that if it's done in the name of self-education, but as you become a more disciplined and advanced user of the software, you'll probably approach effects as a function of a design rather than as the basis of one.

After Effects ships with a lot of effects, and you get even more of them if you invest in the Production Bundle. Third-party developers also make tons of effects for different kinds of projects across different market segments, so you have no shortage of them; however, learning how to apply and adjust them is simple. The methods are essentially the same regardless of the effects you end up using. As with using transform properties or other core After Effects components, the elegance and joy lie in your ability to animate properties over time. In much the same way that you can animate something such as the scale of a layer, you can also animate the properties of any effect. Just keep in mind that effects can have up to 127 of these properties in some cases!

Learning how to apply effects

You can use effects to alter a layer's appearance in ways both minute and profound. Some effects are subtle and simple; others are completely off the wall. Either way, you'll start by adding a simple one to a layer to see what an effect's basic components are.

On the DVD-ROM

Regarding the pictures that complement the steps, the following exercise uses footage items that are located on the DVD-ROM in the folder called *Source Material*. Just as a reminder, you need to copy the *Source Material* folder from the DVD-ROM to your hard drive. The following exercises deal with effects, hierarchies, and nesting. Our corresponding After Effects project is called *Chapter 8.aep* and is found in the *Project Files/Chapter 8* folder.

Tip

Feel free to substitute your own footage with the examples shown in the figures.

STEPS: Adding a Fast Blur to a Layer

1. **If you haven't already, open After Effects and save a new project.**

2. **Create a new composition by dragging a footage item onto the New Composition button at the bottom of the Project window.**

3. **Rename the new comp to clearly indicate its contents.**

4. **Select the layer in the Timeline if it isn't already selected.**

5. **Choose Effect ⇨ Blur & Sharpen ⇨ Fast Blur.** You can also Control+click/right-click the layer and make the same selection. This brings up the Effect Controls window. See Figure 8-1 for reference.

6. **Move the slider to the right in the Effect Controls window.** Watch the changes in the appearance of the layer in the Comp window as you change the slider's position.

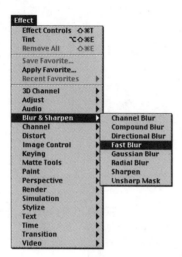

Figure 8-1: Adding an effect to a layer is as simple as selecting a layer in the Timeline and specifying an effect in the Effect menu.

That's how you add an effect. Not much to that, is there? After you finish adding the effect to the layer, you see that the Effect Controls window appears. As long as you're there, go ahead and apply another effect to the layer by choosing any one that you like from the Effect menu. All the effects for any layer are visible under the layer's tab in the Effect Controls window. You can also see any effect that's been applied to a layer by opening the layer's twirler in the Timeline. Figure 8-2 shows the Effect Controls window and the Timeline for the same layer.

If you're working in the Timeline, you can turn the visibility of all of a layer's effects off by clicking the layer's effect switch in the switches panel, or you can turn an individual effect's visibility off by clicking the switch in the A/V features panel. Look at the Timeline in Figure 8-2 for reference.

Tip

For those of you who like your effect names to be a little less generic, once you apply an effect to a layer, you can give it whatever name you want. For example, click the Fast Blur effect name in the Effect Controls window, press Return, type **Fast Blur @ 5**, and press Return again. Voilà! Your effect has been renamed. We've found that this can be a very useful way to organize multiple instances of the same effect.

You can copy and paste effects in much the same way that you can copy and paste layers or keyframes. The same goes for deleting unwanted ones.

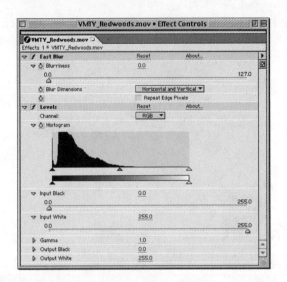

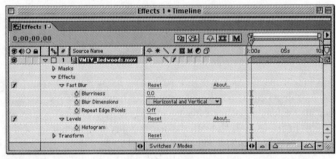

Figure 8-2: The Effect Controls window and the Timeline both reflect the fact that several effects are applied to the layer.

STEPS: Copying and Pasting Effects

1. Using the same composition from the last exercise, add another footage item to it by dragging one from the Project window to the Timeline.

2. Select the layer you applied the effects to (not the one you just added to the comp), and bring the Effect Controls window to the foreground by choosing Effect ➪ Effect Controls (Command+Shift+T/Ctrl+ Shift+T).

3. In the Effect Controls window, select one of the two effects you applied to the layer by clicking on the effect's name so that it's highlighted. If you want to, you can select more than one effect by using the multiple selection methods that work across the entire application. Shift+click to select a group, Command+click/Ctrl+click to add or subtract selections from a group.

4. Choose Edit ➪ Copy (Command+C/Ctrl+C).

5. **Select the layer that you just added to the Timeline by clicking it.**

6. **Choose Edit ➪ Paste (Command+V/Ctrl+V).**

7. **Twirl down the new layer to make sure you successfully pasted the effect.**

Here's a brief summary of how to view, add, remove, and reorder and effects:

✦ **To open the Effect Controls window or bring it to the foreground:** Select the layers for which you want to see the Effect Controls window and choose Effects ➪ Effect Controls (Command+Shift+T/Ctrl+Shift+T) or double-click an effect's name under a layer in the Timeline.

✦ **To add one or more effects to one or more layers:** Select all the layers that you want to add effects to in the Timeline and choose your desired effects from the Effects menu.

✦ **To add the last effect you added:** Choose Effects ➪ Last Effect (Command+ Option+Shift+E/Ctrl+Alt+Shift+E).

✦ **To remove one or more effects:** Select one or more of them in the Effect Controls window and press Delete.

✦ **To remove all the effects from one or more layers at once:** Choose Effect ➪ Remove All (Command+Shift+E/Ctrl+Shift+E).

✦ **To reorder the effects applied to a layer:** Click the effect name in the Effect Controls window and drag it up or down, releasing it after it's in position. The black line in the window indicates where the effect will be placed in the stacking order.

A layer's effects are processed from top to bottom in the order in which they're laid out in the Effect Controls window.

Some effects only operate in 8-bit color, and applying them to layers in a 16-bit color project will create color distortions in the application of the effect. If you apply an 8-bit effect to 16-bit color space, a warning will appear next to the effect's name in the Effect Controls window.

Keyframing effects

Each effect property that has a stopwatch next to its name indicates that it's a property that can be animated over time with keyframes. If you're familiar with keyframe animations as they relate to transform properties, you'll see that the basic premise of animating effects is essentially no different. We created a short series of steps to help you start thinking alone these lines.

If you want to follow along using our simple illustrative composition, refer to the *Effects 1* comp in the Project window of our *Chapter 8.aep* project, which can be found in the *Project Files/Chapter 8* folder.

What's new in After Effects 5.5: Effects Palette

After Effects has long set the standard for effects and plug-in architecture. There is no question that After Effects remains the one product for which there are the most third-party plug-ins in the world! Literally hundreds of these plug-ins are available for After Effects (if not thousands by now). One of the long-running gripes from After Effects users was the way effects were organized in After Effects. The effects fall under various categories under the Effects menu, and locating one (especially if you have hundreds of them as many users do) was a frustrating chore.

With After Effects 5.5, you now have the magical Effects Palette at your beck and call. For example, you can now arrange your plug-ins in various folders on the Finder level, and then in the Effects Palette, select the Finder Folders option to see the organization of your plug-ins. You can also elect to view your effects by categories or in alphabetical order. Perhaps the best option in the Effects Palette is the Contains text entry box. Just click in the box and begin typing a name. For example, typing Blur in the Contains text entry box will show you only the effects that have the word Blur in their name (see the figure in this sidebar).

Figure SB 8-1: Typing Blur in the Contains text entry box will show you only the effects that have the word Blur in their name.

The Effects Palette also allows for some very nifty ways to apply effects. For example, you can drag any effect from the palette onto a layer in the Timeline or the Comp window. You can even control the order of the effect as you apply it by dragging it relative to any other effects you've applied. Of course, you can also drag effects from the palette into the Effect Controls window of any layer. Furthermore, you can drag effects from the Timeline back into the Effects Palette. Doing so will bring up the Save dialog box and allow you to create and save your own favorite effects in the Effects Palette. Happy After Effects users are probably on their knees offering thanks to the Gods of Adobe.

STEPS: Applying the Fast Blur and Tint Effects to a Layer

1. **Create a new composition by dragging a footage item on to the New Composition button at the bottom of the Project window.**

2. **Rename the new comp to clearly indicate its contents.**

3. **Select the layer in the Timeline if it isn't already selected.**

4. **Choose Effect ⇨ Blur & Sharpen ⇨ Fast Blur.** You can also Control+click/right-click the layer and make the same selection. This brings up the Effect Controls window.

5. **Choose Effect ⇨ Image Control ⇨ Tint.** Both effects should now be visible under the layer's tab in the Effect Controls window.

6. **In the Effect Controls window, click the stopwatch next to the Blurriness property to set an initial keyframe for this effect property at the outset of the composition.**

7. **In the Effect Controls window, drag the Blurriness slider to the right until the layer in the Comp window is significantly blurred.** We set ours to about 70, but you can use any amount you like.

8. **In the Effect Controls window, click the Repeat Edge Pixels check box to clean up the strange edges you get from cranking the Blurriness up to a high value.**

9. **In the Effect Controls window, click the Map Black To color swatch for the Tint effect and use the color picker to select a color related to the color scheme of the footage item used to make the layer.** You may find it easier to use the dropper to pick this color, but we leave that to you. For our forest footage we used a dark pine green.

10. **In the Effect Controls window, click the stopwatch next to the Amount to Tint property to set an initial keyframe for this effect property.** This is the same as the one you set for Blurriness, and it will also be at the outset of the composition. At this point, your Effect Controls window should look similar to Figure 8-3.

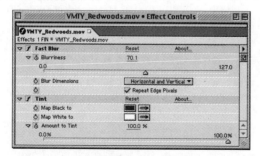

Figure 8-3: Your Effect Controls window should resemble this window, which reflects the state of affairs for this composition at its first frame.

11. **Jump forward about five seconds in the Timeline.**

12. **Set the Blurriness of the Fast Blur effect to 0.** This sets another keyframe.

13. **Set the Amount to Tint of the Tint effect to 0.** This sets another keyframe.

14. **Select the layer in the Timeline and press the U key to show only those properties which have keyframes assigned.** Your Timeline should resemble Figure 8-4.

15. **Preview your work to start experiencing the high-life of effect animation.**

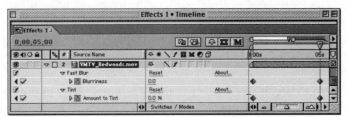

Figure 8-4: Your Timeline should display the basic effect animation you just completed.

Animating effects is a lot of fun, and if you like, make as many modifications to this basic animation as you want. For example, try animating a color change with the Tint effect. This series of steps was meant to merely whet your appetite. Somewhere in this process, you'll begin to grasp the possibilities of this simple concept when you start noticing effects in the Effect Controls window that have tons of keyframeable properties. At that point, someone may have to stop you.

Saving and applying favorites

If you added and adjusted one or more effects on a layer and want to save your work so that you can apply the same look once again, After Effects enables you to save your favorite effects so that you can use them again later on down the road. This extends to the keyframes that have been applied to the layer over time as well. The next few steps show you how it's done.

STEPS: Saving an Effect Combination as a Favorite

1. **Add multiple effects to a layer.** You can animate layers with keyframes if you like. If you're working from the composition in which you just started animating effects in the last exercise, go right to Step 2.

2. **Open the Effect Controls window for the layer.**

3. **Select one or more of the effects by using the Shift+click and Command+click/ Ctrl+click selection methods.**

4. **Choose Effect ➪ Save Favorite.**

5. **Give your favorite a filename and location.** This is a FFX file. We recommend that you collect them in one place for organizational reasons.

That's how you save one effect. How might you apply it? Read on.

STEPS: Applying a Favorite Effect

1. **Select a layer in a composition that you want to apply your favorite effect to.**

Tip   If you're working from the composition in which you just saved a favorite, you may want to add another layer and use it as the one you apply the favorite effect to for the sake of clarity. If you apply the favorite to the layer you just used to save the same favorite, the results may not be all that conclusive.

2. **Choose Effect ➪ Apply Favorite.**

3. **Navigate your way to the spot where you've begun collecting Favorites (FFX files) and select the one you want to apply.**

Tip   After Effects "remembers" the last 20 favorites saved or used, and you can apply any from that list by choosing Effect ➪ Recent Favorites ➪ MyFavorite or whichever one you want. The keyboard shortcut for applying the most recently used favorite is Command+Option+Shift+F/Ctrl+Alt+Shift+F.

Favorites are a great convenience for cutting down the number of mouse clicks in the creative process. They also keep you from having to open old projects to see how you built certain effect combinations that you want to use again. They alleviate any need for writing detailed logs on how you got a certain something to look exactly right. Okay. Enough said. Take advantage of them.

Cross-Reference   Just a word about our coverage of the introduction to effects: An entire part of this book is dedicated entirely to this subject, so if you have a lot of questions about the various skills you just acquired, you can find them addressed in Part IV of the book.

Learning the different layer property controls

You can use either the Timeline or the Effect Controls window to change effect property values. If you twirl down an effect for a layer in the Timeline, you'll see all the effect properties listed. As is the case with transform properties, you can scrub a property's numerical value, or you can directly click the number in the value field and type in a specific value, though, as you'll come to see, not all effect properties are numerical.

If most cases, we prefer to use the Effect Controls window to tweak a layer's effects. It tends to be easier, faster, and subsequently more fun. All effects use the same kinds of adjustable modular controls. These usually provide you with very specific and intuitive ways to change the values of its properties. We next provide you with a picture and a brief description of each of the different controls.

Adjusting sliders

You can drag a slider back and forth to change this type of property value for an effect (see Figure 8-5). As you move a slider around, its effect on the layer is reflected in the Comp window. You can Control+click/right-click the numerical value of a slider's property and select Edit Value to enter a specific property value as well as change the minimum and maximum values represented by the slider's range of movement. If you significantly increase the range of values, moving the slider will result in greater incremental changes to the effect. Decrease the range for tighter control. The default range of an effect's slider is almost an editorial comment about the effect by its developers in the sense that it represents the practical limits of the effect's application. Look at the following Figures 8-6 and 8-7 to see how you can effect changes in the range of a slider.

Figure 8-5: Drag the slider to change the value for this effect property.

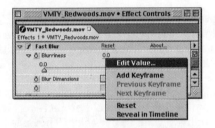

Figure 8-6: Control+click/Right-click a slider's numerical property and select Edit Value to change a slider's numerical range (as well as enter a specific property value).

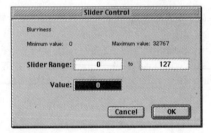

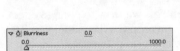

Figure 8-7: Check out the new range of values for the slider control.

Turning dials

Click inside the angle control dial shown in Figure 8-8 and drag the line stemming from its center to change this kind of property value. You can drag the line in complete circles, and this will result in changes to the integer values that indicate the number of complete turns. As with the rotation transformation property, the values of this kind of effect property are displayed in the format of complete turns plus degrees (0–360).

Figure 8-8: Click and drag within the angle control dial to change the value for this effect property.

Using color swatches

Color swatches display a color's property value. Click a color swatch to open up the color picker, which you can then use to change the color property value. You can choose different kinds of color spec conventions when using the color picker (HSB, RGB, and so on). You can also select a color property value by clicking the dropper and placing it over an area in the Comp window that contains your color of choice. After you position it over your chosen color, click it again to make this the color value for the color swatch in the Effect Controls window, as shown in Figure 8-9.

Figure 8-9: Click the color swatch to change the color value for this effect property.

Selecting pop-up options

Pop-ups define effect properties with a limited range of values. The Fast Blur effects shown previously are either horizontal, vertical, or both. You can't interpolate between these differences because the properties affect an entire dimension. In other words, you can't be a "little horizontal." However, you can make Hold keyframe animations for some pop-up properties. In our Fast Blur example, you can change the effects of a blur from horizontal to vertical at a specific moment in time. Because it would be a hold keyframe animation, the change would be instantaneous wherever you placed the keyframe in the Timeline. See Figure 8-10.

Figure 8-10: Select options in the pop-up menus to change the value of this effect property.

Understanding the effect point

Effect points are properties with an X-coordinate and a Y-coordinate. In that way, they resemble the position transform property, except that certain effects have multiple effect points. To set an effect point, click the crosshair icon in the Effect Controls window, position the crosshairs where you want the coordinate in the Comp window, and click again to set the property value, as shown in Figure 8-11. You can also set effect points in the Timeline as well as in the Layer window. You put all these methods to work in the animated effects exercise later in the chapter.

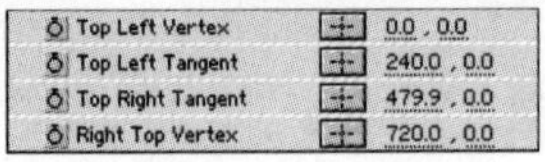

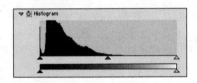

Figure 8-11: Click the crosshairs icon to set coordinates for this effect property in the Comp window.

Tweaking custom interfaces

We've shown you the Levels effect histogram previously, and this is an example of a custom effects interface. Even though this isn't a modular control such as the ones shown previously, it's still easy to manipulate and animate. The stopwatch next to the word Histogram indicates that you can set keyframes for this property, as shown in Figure 8-12. In between keyframes, After Effects interpolates the different values indicated by the slider positions. The point here is that even when you're using an effect with a slightly unusual custom interface, all the basic rules and concepts of After Effects apply.

Figure 8-12: Make adjustments to a custom interface to change the property values for this kind of effect.

Clicking options and reset buttons

Click the About button to read a description of what the effect does. Click the Reset button to reset the effect properties to their default values. Click the Options button to open any dialog boxes that contain special options pertinent to the effect. See Figure 8-13.

Figure 8-13: Click the Options button to enter special values and the Reset button to reset the effect properties to their defaults.

Using After Effects as a Video Editor of Sorts

If you're familiar with video-editing software, you know that its strength comes from its capability to play clips in real time. In the context of an edit suite, you can decide how to cut clips down and rearrange them so that they form some narrative structure that's a product of an editor's discretion. After Effects is simply not up to that task; actually, it was never designed for it, so drawing any comparisons on that level is not fair. Still, even though it's not officially recommended by anyone, there are times when you need to get some form of video editing functionality out of After Effects.

A typical After Effects workflow goes along these lines. An editor prepares some video cuts for further work in After Effects, and these cuts may be anywhere from a few seconds to many minutes long. The After Effects artist imports the cuts and begins to work on them. "Work on them" can mean adding text, applying various effects, and possibly carrying out the wishes of an art director who has supplied the artist with a series of design guidelines. These guidelines might determine which fonts will be used, what color scheme should be adhered to, and maybe some special requests. As far as these requests are concerned, the art director might supply the After Effects artist with layered Photoshop and Illustrator files that contain elements that need to be laid into the various composites.

From there, the After Effects project begins to grow and take on a life of its own. As compositions begin to emerge from the process, the artist might render some drafts for the art director and the producers to look over. They'll critique the work and request revisions, and this process of fine-tuning will go on as long as there's time to revise the compositions before they need to be delivered. As soon as everything's been signed off, the After Effects artist will fire off final draft, high resolution, best settings, production quality renders of the compositions. The resulting output will go back to the editor who initially handed off the cuts, and from there, the editor will lay the composited pieces into their niches inside of the entire whole for which they were prepared. Anything is possible, and the details vary widely from one production to another, but that's a general idea of how an After Effects project could develop.

Bear in mind that all of the details of this hypothetical world are completely open-ended. The aforementioned editor, After Effects artist, art director, and producers might total one person (you, probably) or twenty or more (a large production company, perhaps). The special needs might require that the After Effects artist work with files prepared by a 3D artist. As we said, absolutely anything is possible.

Given this general overview, any number of complex problems might arise during the After Effects part of the overall job. What if the imported video cuts need to be reworked? You may need to change the order of the clips in some of the cuts, and some clips may need to be shortened. Other bits and pieces have to be taken out altogether. And so the list of changes continues. Do you need to have the editor prepare new cuts for you to work with? Unless you're missing footage that's simply just not in the prepped video cuts, the chances are that you can make most of these adjustments within After Effects. This way, you won't be forced to ask more of the editor. More importantly, you won't have to lose more of that precious commodity called time.

The following section looks at how you can take advantage of After Effects' capabilities as an editing tool. As we mentioned at the beginning of this discussion, After Effects was not conceived as an editing solution, but some features allow for enough editing adjustments to warrant their mention here.

Trimming layers in the Timeline

Video-editing software works with multiple clips in a Timeline, and so does After Effects for that matter. You can select a number of video footage items from the Project window, and as a group, click and drag them on to either the New Composition button at the bottom of the Project window or on to an existing composition in the Project window. The order in which they're laid into the Timeline reflects the order in which you selected the clips before dragging them into a composition. If you change your mind down the line, you can reorder clips in the Timeline as easily as dragging and dropping them into new spots in the layering order. In the exercises that follow, you edit video with After Effects by trimming the In and Out points of video layers, performing slip edits, lift edits, and the like.

STEPS: Working the Bracket Keys I: Setting Ins and Outs

1. Select one or more layers in the Timeline of any composition.

2. Press the [key to set the In point of the selected layer(s) to the current time.

3. Press the] key to set the Out point of the selected layer(s) to the current time.

Tip   As soon as you set an In or an Out point for a layer, you can press the I or O keys to change the current time to the selected layer's in or Out point, respectively.

Folks who are just getting familiar with After Effects often miss a frame of two when aligning in and Out points and sometimes leave flashes and frame glitches in the layers of a composition. After you set an In and an Out point for multiple layers that comprise a composition, preview your work often, especially at the edit points, and make certain that you included the desired frames from the footage.

You can trim layers by dragging their In and Out points in the Timeline. Your only constraint is the actual limit of the media contained within the layer. In other words, you can't drag an In or an Out point past the point where there's no more video. As you drag an In or an Out point, the Info palette tells you which frame you're located on as well as the new duration of the layers so that you know the exact details of the changes that you're making.

On the DVD-ROM   If you want to follow along using our composition, refer to the *Editing* comp in the Project window of our *Chapter 8.aep* project, which can be found in the *Project Files/Chapter 8* folder.

STEPS: Working the Bracket Keys II: Speedy Trimming

1. **Select three or more video footage items from within the Project window and drag them onto the New Composition button at the bottom of the Project window.** This creates a new composition with the video layers stacked in the order that you selected them. The new composition's settings are set to the defining properties of the video clips with regard to dimensions, frame rate, pixel aspect ratio, running time, and so forth.

2. **In the Timeline, set the current time forward to 0;00;02;00.**

3. **In the Timeline, select all the layers by pressing Command+A/Ctrl+A.**

4. **Press Option+]/Alt+].** This trims the layers so that their Out points are changed to the current time.

5. **In the Timeline, set the current time to 0;00;01;00.**

6. **Press Option+[/Alt+[.** This trims the layers so that their In points are changed to the current time.

7. **In the Timeline, press Home to set the current time to 0;00;00;00.**

8. **In the Timeline, with all the layers still selected, press the [key to set the In points of all the layers to the present time (the beginning of the composition).**

9. **Control+click/Right-click the layers and choose Keyframe Assistant ⇨ Sequence Layers.**

10. **Click OK without specifying an overlap.** This places the layers end to end. Your Timeline should look similar to Figure 8-14.

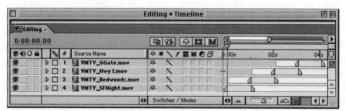

Figure 8-14: The Timeline displays layers with trimmed In and Out points laid end-to-end much like a video edit.

In essence, the steps you just completed were the same kinds of functions you carry out by using video editing software. Minus the real-time playback, you can place video layers in a Timeline, trim their In and Out points, move the edited layers by dragging them to different points in time, and place the layers end to end together to form an "edit."

The next set of steps continues to show you more technique along the lines of "editing" type functionality.

STEPS: Performing a "Slip" Edit in the Timeline

1. **Position the playhead anywhere in the Timeline, as long as it's parked on one the video layers.**

2. **Click and drag the grayed out area of the layer that extends past the layer's duration bar (the textured area between the layer's In and Out points).**
   After you click, the area of the layer outside the In and Out points becomes textured like the footage inside the trimmed area. The pointer indicates that you're "sliding" the footage underneath the existing In and Out points. As you drag, the textured area moves with the pointer in the Timeline window and dynamically updates the image, indicating that new frames are being placed in between the existing in and Out points. See Figure 8-15 for reference.

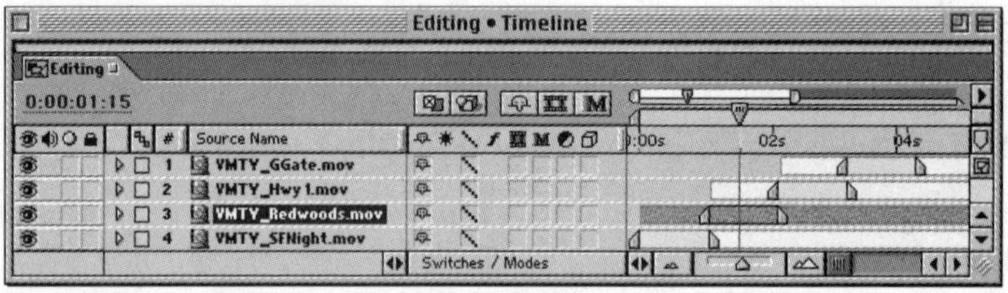

Figure 8-15: When performing a slip edit, click and drag the portion of a layer outside a layer's In and Out points.

This method maintains the In and Out points of a layer but changes the content between the In and the Out points by using an earlier (if you drag to the right) or later (if you drag to the left) portion of the video. The length of the grayed out area is the complete unedited length of the footage.

In addition to slip edits are also other editing functions, most of which you will probably use quite often. What if you need to repeat certain footage in a composition? What if you need to re-order the sequence of images in a piece of imported footage? What if you need to maintain the running time of a layer but need to put different footage in its place? The next exercise directly answers all three of those questions.

STEPS: Duplicating a Layer

1. **Select a layer by clicking it or entering its layer number on the numeric keypad.**

2. **Choose Edit ➪ Duplicate (Command+D/Ctrl+D).** This places a copy of the layer beneath the original layer in the Timeline. By copy, we mean that the duplicate has the same In and Out points.

STEPS: Splitting a Layer

1. **If you haven't already, position the playhead somewhere in between the In and Out points of a layer in the Timeline.**

2. **Make certain that this layer is selected and then choose Edit ➪ Split Layer (Command+Shift+D/Ctrl+Shift+D).** This trims the selected layer so that its Out point is trimmed to the current time. It also makes a duplicate of the layer, the In point of which is trimmed to the current time. This is essentially the same as making a "cut" in a video editing application.

STEPS: Swapping the Contents of a Layer

1. **Select a layer in the Timeline and select a footage item in the Project window.** Both items should be highlighted.

2. **Hold down the Option/Alt key and drag the selected footage item from the Project window until it's above the selected layer in the Timeline.** After it's in position, release the mouse. This enormously useful feature enables you to substitute the contents of a layer in the Timeline without changing the layer's In and Out points or its position in the stacking order. This is basically a "swap" edit.

STEPS: Trimming the Work Area

1. **Set the work area in the composition by using the B and N keys or by adjusting the work area handles at the top of the Timeline. Go to Step 2 to lift the work area. Go to Step 3 to extract it.** Be sure to set the work area to include the portions of the layers that you want to remove from the composition. If there are layers inside the work area that you want to leave in place, lock them with the lock switch.

2. **Choose Edit ➪ Lift Work Area.** This command removes all items within the work area. Items can include entire layers or portions of layers depending on the defined work area. To understand the difference between lift and extract, choose Edit ➪ Undo (Command+Z/Ctrl+Z) and go to Step 3.

3. **Choose Edit ➪ Extract Work Area.** This command removes all items within the work area and closes the gap left by the extraction. See Figure 8-16 to look at the results of lifting and extracting.

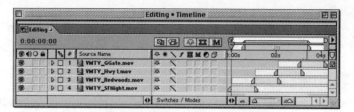

Timeline before lifting or extracting work area

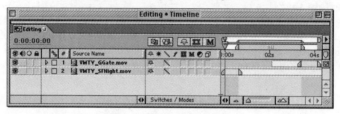

Timeline after lifting work area

Timeline after extracting work area

Figure 8-16: The Timeline before and after both a lift and an extraction of the Work Area

Tip

You can also trim a composition's length to the defined work area. Often times, your composition will be longer than the clips that are contained in it. This is usually the result of trimming down or removing layers. For example, you may have just used the Extract Work Area command and you may want to shorten the composition length to reflect its newly abbreviated layers. If so, choose Composition ➪ Trim Comp to Work Area to shorten the comp's duration in the defined work area. This feature nicely rounds out the Lift and Extract commands.

What's new in After Effects 5.5: Pasting layers at the current time

After Effects 5.5 provides a new and useful keyboard shortcut. After copying layers, press Command+Option+V/Ctrl+Alt+V to paste layers at the current time, instead of at their original In point locations.

Trimming in the Layer and Footage windows

You can also trim footage by using parts of the interface outside the Timeline. The Layer and Footage windows look very similar, but there are some critical differences. A Layer window refers only to a layer as it exists in a composition. A Footage window refers to In and Out points of a footage item as you add it to compositions throughout the scope of an entire After Effects project.

Trimming in the Layer window

Double-click a layer to open it in its own Layer window. In addition to the bracket key combinations, you can set an In or an Out point for a layer by clicking the in and out buttons by using the Layer window interface. It should seem self-evident, but remember that changing the In and Out points of a layer changes its use in the Timeline. Look at Figure 8-17 for an explanation of the Layer window features.

Set In point   Set Out point   Duration

Figure 8-17: You can edit a layer by using the controls in the Layer window interface. Double-click a layer in the Timeline to access the Layer window.

Image courtesy of Videometry

Note   You can trim a layer in the Timeline far more quickly than you can in its Layer window. The Layer window's inherent strength lies in the fact that it's the place where you have the most control when editing a mask or changing the location of a layer's Anchor Point.

Trimming in the Footage window

Editing a clip in the Footage window differs from editing layers in that you're working with the "master" clip. You make changes to the In and Out points in the Footage window only in order to perform a Ripple Insert edit and an Overlay edit. Otherwise, these In and Out points have no relevance when you add a footage item to a composition by dragging it to the Comp window or the Timeline.

Tip

Once again, this example works best on a video clip as opposed to a still.

STEPS: Editing Footage in the Footage Window

1. **In the Timeline, set the current time to the point where you want to add a clip.**

2. **Hold down the Option/Alt key and double-click a footage item in the Project window.** This opens up the footage item in its own Footage window (see Figure 8-18).

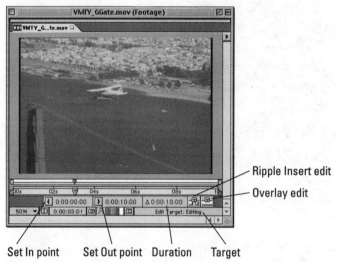

Figure 8-18: The Footage window has its own edit controls.
Image courtesy of Videometry

3. **In the Footage window, set an In point and an Out point for the clip based on the portion of it that you want to add to the Timeline.** Go to Step 4 if you want to overlay the footage. Go to Step 5 to perform a Ripple Insert edit.

4. **Click the Overlay edit button to layer the trimmed footage on top of the target composition's existing layers at the current time (Overlay).** The target indicates which composition is being affected by the edit decision in the

Footage window. If you want to see the difference between the two edit functions, choose Edit ➪ Undo (Command+Z/Ctrl+Z) and go to Step 5.

5. **Click the Ripple Insert edit button to place the trimmed footage in the target composition at the current time.** However, this will also push all of the layers after the current time ahead by the duration of the clip being inserted. Hence, the "ripple" name for this function — because using it has a ripple effect on the entire composition by changing the In and Out point times of the layers that follow the inserted layer.

As far as being handed off footage prepared for use in After Effects, all the "editing" methods you just learned give you enough flexibility to make the best of whatever hand you may have been dealt. At this point, you can slice and dice your way through video clips so as not to be constrained by the order of their content. Remember though, as we mentioned in the beginning, After Effects is not editing software, so get as much help as you can with any footage *before* you import it.

Using markers

Placing markers in After Effects is a great way to set up timing cues in much the same way that you use markers in a video editing program. For example, it wouldn't be unheard of if you were told, "Make sure the scenes change when you hear the drumbeats in the music." In that case, you could preview the audio track and add a marker on each beat, using them to visually line up your scene changes in the Timeline. You can also use layer markers in a less conventional way to specify chapter headings in QuickTime movies and Web links in Flash files, among other things. In this section, we explain both composition and layer markers.

Setting composition markers

To use composition markers, click and drag them into the Timeline from the comp marker bin located at the upper-right corner of the Timeline window. Release the mouse after you have the marker positioned where you want it. If, at any time, you want to change the marker's position, just click and drag it again, or press Shift plus the comp marker's number on the main keyboard (not the numeric keypad) to set the comp marker to the current time. The Shift plus number method also works when initially setting these markers.

To delete a composition marker, click and drag it back to the comp marker bin (upper-right corner of the Timeline). To delete one or all of them, Control+click/right-click one of them and select either Delete this marker or Delete all markers from the resulting contextual menu.

You can use up to 10 comp markers. If you drag them out from the comp marker bin, they will be numbered sequentially. If, however, you add the first comp marker by pressing Shift+8 on the main keyboard, for example, the comp marker labeled 8 will be positioned at the current time.

Setting layer markers

Use layer-time markers to provide cues for the key moments during a layer's visual or audio progression. You can also position them on a layer to serve as markers that trigger events in media types that support Web link markers.

To set a layer-time marker, select a layer in the Timeline, position the playhead where you want to set the marker, and choose Layer ⇨ Add Marker. To move it after you've added it, click and drag it to a new location. To place a comment or other information in a marker after you've set it, either double-click the marker or Control+click/right-click it and select Settings. The process is shown in Figure 8-19.

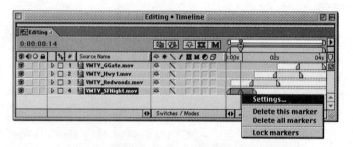

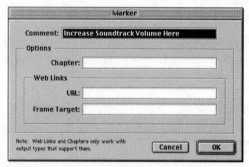

Figure 8-19: Control+click/Right-click a layer-time marker to add a comment to it.

To delete a layer-time marker, hold down the Command/Ctrl key, position the pointer over the marker, and after the pointer's icon changes to resemble a pair of scissors, click the marker to remove it. To remove all of a layer's markers, Control+click/right-click one of them and select Delete all markers.

STEPS: Setting Layer Markers on an Audio Layer

1. **Place an audio footage item as the bottom layer in a composition.** Feel free to add one from the Project window to the comp you worked on in the previous exercises. If need be, we provided you with one called *XYZ.aif*.

2. **Press . (the period key) on the numeric keypad to begin an audio preview of the comp.**

Remember that an audio preview begins from wherever the playhead is positioned, and that the length of an audio preview is defined by the Previews Preferences. You may have to change the length of the audio preview in order to hear the portion of the audio layer required to set markers for the whole composition.

3. **As you're listening to the audio preview, press * (the asterisk key) on the numeric keypad at the points in the music where you want to add a marker.** After you finish, press any key to stop the audio preview and look at the audio layer to see the positions of your newly added markers. Use them to line up footage items so that key edits and animation movements fall on audio cues.

If you like, you can use an audio footage item from the *Audio* folder we include in the *Chapter 8.aep* project.

If you select an audio layer in the Timeline, the L keystroke solos an audio layer's levels, and the LL keystroke solos an audio layer's waveform sketch. You can also use an audio layer's waveform to serve as the basis for your animation decisions, especially when the waveform provides clear information as to when beats or other significant increases in volume occur in a soundtrack.

With regard to all markers when you're working in the Timeline, if you want to line up either the playhead or a layer's In or Out point with a marker, hold down the Shift key as you drag and it will snap into place.

Using layer markers for QuickTime and Flash

Double-click any layer-time marker to bring up its settings as you were shown in Figure 8-19. You can add a Web link by typing in an address in the URL field. For example, you could specify a URL in a marker on a layer at the end of a composition and export it as a Flash (SWF) movie. As you view the end of the exported Flash movie, your Web browser opens a new window, which is directed to the URL you specified in the layer-time marker. Use the frame target field if you want to specify an exact frame within a Web site (see Table 8-1).

Note With regard to Flash movie syntax, the comment field becomes a frame label, the specified URL is added to the GetURL action, and the table below specifies how Flash handles the specified frame targets. If no frame target is specified, the frame target defaults to the current frame of the browser window.

Table 8-1
Frame Target Syntax for Flash

Syntax	Function
_blank	Loads the document into new browser window.
_parent	Loads the document into the parent frame in which the Flash movie is playing.
_self	Loads the document into the current frame.
_top	Loads the document into the top frame in the current window.
_level0	Launches another Flash movie (SWF) into level 0. A Flash movie different from the current one must be specified.
_level1	Launches another Flash movie (SWF) into level 1. A Flash movie different from the current one must be specified.

Chapter headings are supported in QuickTime movies as embedded SMIL (Synchronized Multimedia Integration Language). As far as chapter headings go, simply enter the name of the chapter number and keep your naming conventions correct (see the following Tip).

Tip For more information on building interactivity into QuickTime files and other video media types, look into Terran Interactive's Web site at www.terran.com. This site contains excellent information on codecs in general as well as providing information on their video compression software, Cleaner 5. Cleaner 5 employs EventStream technology, which makes use of embedded SMIL across QuickTime, RealMedia, and Windows Media files. Also, check the Apple site for authoring interactivity into QuickTime files using SMIL, at www.apple.com/quicktime/authoring/qtsmil.html.

Building Good Nesting Habits

As long as this chapter is dedicated to the idea of learning how to build complex compositions, it simply must include a discussion on the virtues of nesting. Your entire approach to animation changes after you begin taking advantage of this basic yet fundamental concept. If you've arrived at this section of the book having started from the beginning, you know that we've only worked on animating individual layers in a composition. We briefly introduced the concept of nesting at the end of Chapter 3, but now we're going to take a much closer look at this aspect of the software.

After Effects truly begins to reveal its power as you begin nesting entire compositions into other compositions and animating the nested compositions as individual layers. This process is regarded as nesting if you approach the idea of placing a composition into another composition as part of your initial plan for an animation. The exact same process is called pre-composing if you decide to place a group of layers into their own composition after you've already begun building your initial animation. The net result is essentially identical. The difference stems from the point in your process where you decide to group layers into their own composition. To summarize this explanation, nesting involves forward thinking, and pre-composing involves what could be thought of as some kind of retroactive crisis management. You'll see the difference more clearly as you work through the examples.

In the course of learning these concepts, you need to understand the basic workings of the render pipeline. In its most distilled form, the logic of the render pipeline can be summarized in the following way: After Effects renders a layer by first applying masks, then effects, and lastly any transformations you may have added to it. For a more visually intuitive look at this process and how it's directly applied to your own work, you'll look at the Flowchart View of your project to better understand exactly what After Effects is doing to the individual components of your compositions.

Nesting compositions

To try and explain nesting, we've created an animation that benefits a great deal from approaching it with the idea of nesting in mind to begin with. Imagine a stylized view of an atom's structure. In this example, you have a core of protons and neutrons that are rapidly being orbited by electrons. Instead of using the building blocks of matter, what if you were to substitute some form of the solar system? Instead of using a core of protons and neutrons, you would substitute the sun instead. Instead of using electrons, you would substitute one or more planets from the solar system. If this seems a little confusing, look at the following steps to gain a better understanding of these ideas. We set this up as a modular animation and use it repeatedly as a nested composition.

On the DVD-ROM This exercise is based on our compositions entitled *Nesting 1* and *Nesting 2*. You find them in the Project window of our *Chapter 8.aep* project, which you find in the *Project Files/Chapter 8* folder.

STEPS: Nesting an Atom

1. **Open the *Nesting 1* comp by double-clicking it in the Project window.** If you don't want to use our composition, create your own and make sure to include a basic transformational animation in it. You see how this is relevant in the following steps.

2. **Press 0 on the numeric keypad to see a RAM Preview of the *Nesting 1* comp to get a sense of its motion.**

3. **In the Project window, drag the *Nesting 1* comp on to the New Composition button at the bottom of the Project window.** This nests the *Nesting 1* comp inside a new composition, which is set to the dimensions and duration of *Nesting 1*. The new comp is called *Comp 1*. Rename it *Nesting 2*.

Tip Naming conventions for compositions suddenly become rather important after you begin nesting them. Always try to use names that won't leave you looking at a list of comps in the Project window wondering what the difference between *Comp 3* and *Comp 17* is.

4. **Double-click the *Nesting 2* composition in the Project window to open it up in the Timeline and Comp windows.**

5. **Drag the *Nesting 1* comp from the Project window into the *Nesting 2* Comp window.**

Tip In the Project window, drag the *Nesting 1* comp directly on to the *Nesting 2* comp icon or the Comp window of *Nesting 2*, select the nested comp layer (*Nesting 1*), and duplicate it by choosing Edit ➪ Duplicate (Command+D/Ctrl+D).

6. **Repeat Step 5 two more times so that there are four instances of the *Nesting 1* layer in the Comp window and the Timeline.**

7. **In the Comp window of *Nesting 2*, using the Action-safe border as your guide, position the four layers at the four corners of the Comp window.** No need to be too specific. *Nesting 2*'s Comp window should approximately resemble Figure 8-20.

8. **Make a RAM Preview of the *Nesting 2* comp to see what it looks like.**

Having completed those steps, your nesting journey has officially begun. Still, what's the point? Why might you do this regularly? Nesting is one of those things you'll be doing practically all the time. In the next set of steps, you're going to make changes to the nested composition, and all four instances of it in the *Nesting 2* comp will reflect the change. This ought to give you a sense of why this is so critical to becoming proficient with After Effects.

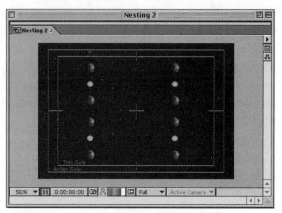

Figure 8-20: The *Nesting 2* Comp window indicates that you have duplicated the *Nesting 1* nested comp layer three times and positioned each copy of it in four different locations.

Image courtesy of EyeWire by Getty Images www.gettyimages.com

(Cosmic Moves)

STEPS: Changing the Atom in the Nested Comp

1. **Option+double-click one of the *Nesting 1* layers in the *Nesting 2* Timeline to open it up and bring its tab to the front in the Timeline and the Comp windows.**

2. **Set a scale keyframe for the Sun layer at the beginning at the composition.** You want to animate it so that its scale pulses every second or so.

3. **Move forward roughly one second in the Timeline and set another scale keyframe, raising its value so that it's noticeably larger than it was at the beginning of the comp but not so big that it obscures its orbiting planets.**

4. **Copy these keyframes at roughly the same intervals to repeat the animation until the end of the composition.**

5. **After you've got the sun's scale animation looking the way you want, click the *Nesting 2* tab in either the Comp window or the Timeline to bring it forward.**

6. **Make a RAM Preview of the *Nesting 2* comp.** You see that the work you carried out once is repeated in as many instance of the *Nesting 1* comp that you want to spread throughout the project.

7. **For kicks, place the footage item of the stars (*EVO0167N.MOV* in the *Eyewire* folder in the Project window) at the bottom of the *Nesting 2* Timeline to give this layout of animated nested comps a good-looking backdrop.**

Tip   For reference, you may want to consult our finished compositions, entitled *Nesting 1 FIN* and *Nesting 2 FIN*.

Note   Right away, you can see that nesting is essential to any reasonably sophisticated After Effects project. Imagine a bicycle that needs two identical spinning wheels. Perhaps you need to make a graphics bed for "This Week's Feature Movie" in which the only thing that changes amongst all the graphic flourishes are the actual clips from the new movie every week. You can probably imagine all sorts of other applications for nesting compositions, and now that you know how the basic concept works, you can run with it.

If you want to keep having fun with the planetary atoms, try offsetting their orbits so that they're not completely uniform. Or, if you like, nest the *Nesting 2* comp into another new composition and animate its rotation. Now that you've absorbed the general idea, there's no limit to its application. Run wild. If it's too much, your producer/client/art director will undoubtedly pull on the reigns.

Next up is the business of pre-composing layers. As we mentioned earlier, this is essentially no different than nesting except for the fact that you pre-compose layers after you've begun animating them because you've somehow managed to get stuck with a few problems. To see what this entails, move forward to the next section.

Pre-Composing layers

We've all been there. You're starting to build momentum with a project and you're about to fire off a final render when the bottom drops out. After telling you for several weeks that they love the work, your client/producer makes big changes to the comp with only a couple of days to go before delivery. All of your nesting logic no longer holds up in light of what's been requested on short notice. We prepared the following simple exercise as an attempt to explain what might happen if your needs (or a client's demands) suddenly change during the course of building a composition.

On the DVD-ROM   For this exercise, we prepared an Illustrator file with lots of text and placed it in a composition called *Why Pre-Compose???*, located in the Project window of the *Chapter 8.aep* project from the DVD-ROM.

STEPS: Animating, Pre-Composing, and Animating Again

1. **Double-click the *Why Pre-Compose???* comp in the Project window to open it up in the Timeline and Comp windows.** If you don't want to use the composition from our project, create an Illustrator file that uses a lot of text, separate each letter so that they reside in their own layers, and import the resulting file as a composition.

2. **Using opacity keyframes, fade up each layer from 0% to 100% at approxi-mately 15 frame intervals, one after the other.** The text should appear to progressively "light up," one letter at a time. This would be the extent of your original idea, but at this point, the request is made to move all of the letters off the composition in a quick move immediately following the last opacity keyframe. Another request is that the text have a white drop shadow.

3. **Select all the layers in the Timeline by choosing Edit ⇨ Select All (Command+A/Ctrl+A).**

4. **Choose Layer ⇨ Pre-compose (Command+Shift+C/Ctrl+Shift+C).** This brings up the Pre-compose dialog box. You can only select the latter option in this case (Move all attributes into the new composition). See Figure 8-21 for reference.

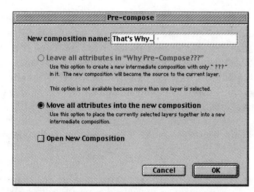

Figure 8-21: The Pre-compose dialog box only offers one option if you're pre-composing more than one layer.

5. **Give the New composition a name and click OK.** We named ours *That's Why . . .* Only the pre-comp layer will remain in the Timeline.

6. **Set the current time to a point after the last characters have been faded up.**

7. **Select the pre-comp layer and then choose Effect ⇨ Perspective ⇨ Drop Shadow.**

8. **Specify white as the color with the color picker so that the shadow isn't hid-den by the black default background color.**

9. **You can experiment with your own drop shadow choices regarding settings.** Ours were Opacity 80%, Direction –160 degrees, Distance 10, Softness 20.

10. **Set a position keyframe for the pre-comp layer.**

11. **Move the playhead forward in time.**

12. **In the Comp window, drag the pre-comp layer off the right edge of the composition.**

13. **Turn Motion blur on at both the layer and the composition level.**

14. **Press 0 on the numeric keypad to look at a RAM Preview of your animation.**

The point here is that the opacity animations in the original composition serve as an example of building a composition, which, in and of itself, would be complete when finished. Instead, a request came in and you were informed that all the letters had to move off screen together with a motion blur applied. Again, this is a simple example of a process that could be infinitely more complicated, but the essence of the point remains.

Would you want to set position keyframes and turn on the motion blur switch for all of the individual layers, or would it make more sense to pre-compose all of them and achieve the same result with far fewer keystrokes? Granted, you could set position keyframes for all the layers using the Option+P/Alt+P command in the original composition, but you don't always have that kind of flexibility. This was immediately made clear by the request to add the Drop Shadow effect. It would have been a considerable drag to set that effect for 15 layers. To sum up, in After Effects, you can take a dynamic approach to the creative process and not have to concern yourself with prearranging a nested comp hierarchy. You can always find a way to make things work out.

Tip

By the way, you can also pre-compose a single-layer. You may find that you want to add an effect to a layer containing an Illustrator or EPS file that has its Continuously Rasterize switch turned on. If this is the case, you need to pre-compose the layer in order to apply the effect. This is a function of the Render Pipeline, which we discuss in detail in Chapter 7.

Looking at the flowchart

The flowchart can help make visual sense of the pieces that make up a composition. By looking carefully at it, you can better understand how After Effects is handling all of the layers that comprise each composition, including nested compositions. To see the flowchart of a composition, bring the comp's tab to the front of the Timeline and Comp windows by clicking it, and then click the flowchart button at the upper-right corner of the Comp window. Alternatively, you can choose Composition ➪ Comp Flowchart View, and you can also view the flowchart for an entire project by choosing Window ➪ Project Flowchart View. Figure 8-22 shows the flowchart for the *Nesting 2* comp you completed during the Nesting Compositions exercises.

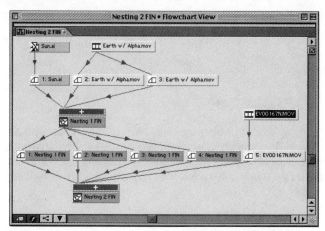

Figure 8-22: The Flowchart View visually demonstrates how After Effects handles all the components that make up a composition, whether they're layers or nested compositions.

You'll start to appreciate the Flowchart View around the same time that you start building enormous multi-layered compositions that contain numerous nested comps. It's the easiest way to stay on top of a comp project that's threatening to grow past your control. To view this window's view options, click the button at the upper-right corner of the Flowchart View.

In the Flowchart View, a plus-sign button at the top of a composition tile tells you that it's a root comp. Click the button to expand the view, and the Flowchart View shows you all the elements that went into the root comp. Click the individual layers or nested comps to reveal their places in either the Timeline or the Project window. Control+click/Right-click the icons on the left of the individual items to bring up the relevant contextual menus for those items. You can also select layers and delete them by pressing the Delete key.

You can customize your Flowchart View with the four buttons at the lower-left corner of the window. The layers switch turns the visibility of all the layers on and off. When turned on, the effects switch displays all the effects that were applied on all the various layers. The third button from the left toggles between displaying straight and angled lines. The fourth button contains a menu, which enables you to pick which way the flowchart "flows." Hold down the Option/Alt key to turn the effects switch into a slider for the justification of the items in the Flowchart View.

Also, use the Option/Alt key in conjunction with the line toggle switch to automatically clean up the items in the view. Lastly, you can Control+click/right-click the individual items (not on their icons at the upper-left) to change their label colors.

Parenting and Hierarchies

Parenting is the ultimate compliment to nesting compositions and keyframe animations. In the last section on pre-composing, you learned how to apply keyframes and effects to a large number of layers at once by placing them all into their own composition. Parenting offers a more controlled way to animate groups of layers. Besides that, it's also a lot of fun.

Understanding parenting

Parenting enables you to define layers in a composition as parent or child layers. If you make one layer a parent to another, then any transformation changes you make to the parent are also applied to the child, except for opacity; therefore, any changes to a parent layer's position, scale, rotation, or anchor point are reflected in the child layer. Changes to a parent layer's position directly change the child layer's position. Changes to a parent layer's scale also change the child layer's scale proportionately. Changes to a parent layer's rotation rotates the child layer around the parent layer's anchor point. A child layer can contain its own keyframe animation, but it will simultaneously mirror its parent layer's transformations while carrying out its own motion. This explanation may be hard to understand on paper, so you can try some transformations across parent and child layers a bit later on. Before doing that, first you should look at how to assign a hierarchical parenting structure to the layers in a composition.

Grouping layers as "parents" and "children"

In order to take advantage of After Effects' parenting feature, you need to display the Parent column in the Timeline. Control+click/Right-click one of the panels in the Timeline and select Parent from the contextual menu to add the Parent column to those columns that are already visible (see Figure 8-23).

After you add the Parent column to the other columns on display, you can assign layers in the Timeline as parent or child layers. In the Timeline, select the layers that you want to designate as the child layers to a parent layer, and either drag the pick whip from the layer's parent column on to the desired parent layer or use the pull-down menu to make the same assignment (see Figure 8-24).

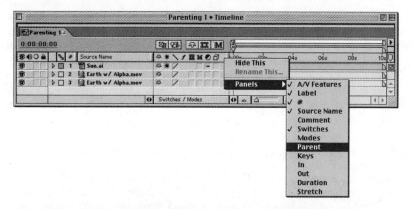

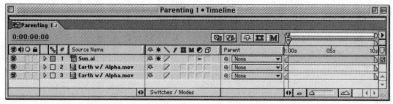

Figure 8-23: Add the Parent column to those already visible in the Timeline.

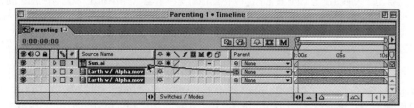

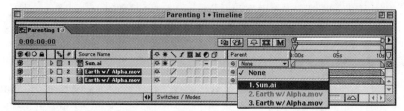

Figure 8-24: Select layers in the Timeline that you want to designate as child layers and use either the pick whip or the pull-down menus to assign their parent layer.

After you establish the hierarchical relationship, go ahead and make transformational changes to the parent layer to better understand the parenting function. As a suggestion, first try position, then scale, then rotation, then anchor point, and then rotation again. Keep in mind that you can set keyframe animations for both parent and child layers. The child layers perform their keyframe animations as they always have, but they are also synchronized with their parent layer's animations as they complete their own. To remove a parent, select None from the child layer's parent pull-down menu.

STEPS: Making a Parent of the Sun

1. **In the Project window, select the *Nesting 1* comp that you used in the Nesting exercises and then choose Edit ➪ Duplicate (Command+D/Ctrl+D).** This makes a copy of this comp in the Project window, and its default name is *Nesting 1**.

2. **Rename the copy of the comp.** You may want to do this so that it clearly has some association with parenting as opposed to nesting.

3. **Double-click the comp to open it up in the Comp and Timeline windows.**

4. **Assign the sun layer as the parent to the orbiting planet layers.** Because you already animated the scale of the sun, this pulsing animation is reflected in the child layers.

5. **If you like, create more transformational keyframe animations for the sun layer.** For example, setting a keyframe rotation for the sun layer provides you with interesting results because the planets were already orbiting the sun layer.

Going further, you can assign a chain of parent-child relationships. A layer can be a child layer to its assigned parent layer at the same time that it can also be a parent layer to a different designated child layer. Imagining this hierarchy with a puppet is easiest. In this example, the arm would be the parent layer to the hand layer, and the hand layer would be the parent to the finger layers.

Using Null Object layers

Use Null Object layers as parent layers if you want to animate a group of child layers without altering any other layers that are visible in the composition. In other words, if you want to create a group animation but there's no parent to lead the way, you can animate a null object and assign it as the parent layer. Null objects are invisible layers that have all the transform properties of regular layers except for opacity (which makes sense given that you can't really adjust the opacity of an invisible object). A Null object is visible in the Timeline as a layer and in the Comp window as a rectangular outline. To add one to a composition, choose Layer ➪ New ➪ Null Object.

✦   ✦   ✦

Broadening Animation Skills: Masks, Transparency, and Time

Making Use of Masks

Masks are one of After Effects' most powerful and versatile features. If you're completely new to them, masks are usually used like a pair of scissors to cut out the parts of an image that you want to hide from view, but you probably knew that much. Either way, you might not know that you can use masks for everything from creating motion paths to animating the appearance of an unseen hand "drawing" freehand lines over the course of an animation. In short, they have a number of applications beyond what "masking" sounds as though it should entail, and we look at all of those in this chapter.

After Effects allows up to 127 masks on each layer (!), and you can animate them to change over time. If you're working with multiple layers, you can use masks to cut out portions of layers so as to reveal what's underneath. This business of cutting holes to let underlying layers shine through can be employed in a number of ways to make beautiful compositions. If you've developed skills at drawing paths and using masks in Adobe's other graphics offerings, such as Photoshop and Illustrator, those skills can be put to good use in After Effects. This is yet another area where your skills in the Adobe domain are cumulative. Any talent you may be developing with Bezier curves will pay off nicely as well.

Another great aspect of learning After Effects' masking tools is the confidence you'll build from knowing that you can almost always find artful ways to deal with images that contain bits that you want to hide. That way, hardly any footage becomes unusable. That's really the larger goal of this chapter. Attain mastery of this part of After Effects so that you have a number of design and compositing options that you couldn't have even imagined, and couple that with easing any worries you may have about footage items needing to be free of imperfections before you can start working. You won't always be able to say, "We'll fix it in post. . . ." In fact, you should always be careful about saying that. But masks go a long way toward giving you options. So jump in.

Creating Masks

In essence, masks add an alpha channel to a layer in a composition. That's the fundamental idea behind using them in After Effects. Sometimes, you're lucky enough to work with footage items that already contain cleanly made and clearly labeled alpha channels. Other times, you're just not going to have that kind of good fortune. In some cases, you may be required to mask out something as mundane as a hair on the lens used to shoot the film footage that's the basis of your composition. We should all be so lucky. Just as likely, you may need to remove a large part of an image that is moving all the time. For example, you could be working with less than perfect footage in which a logo is on a building, and your producer has told you that it absolutely must be removed and, no, there's no time to reshoot. As the camera pans, you'll need to animate the mask that hides the logo. Still, these are some of the trickier scenarios you may find yourself in, so for the meantime, don't worry about it. Instead, put a little time into learning the basics of masking and have some fun.

Understanding mask paths

A couple of mask shapes are shrink-wrapped and immediately ready for you to use. In the Tools palette, you have both a Rectangular and an Oval Mask tool, and these enable you to throw a mask on to a layer with a couple of clicks. Then you have the Bezier mask, the shape of which is most often the result of your usage of the Pen tool. Bezier masks are as simple or as complex as you need them to be. If you have any experience with creating and modifying motion paths, then you know that there's no limit to how minutely detailed you can get with Bezier handles and paths.

As we mentioned earlier, you can apply one or more masks to a layer, and you can do so in either the Comp window or the Layer window. After you add a mask to a layer, its properties appear under the layer in the Timeline. They're color-coded in both the Timeline as well as the Comp and Layer windows. You'll create a few masks in the following sections at which point you can look more closely at their properties in all the various windows of the interface.

Drawing Rectangular and Oval masks

Take a look at the Tools palette and click the Rectangular/Oval tool button, holding the mouse down to see both tool options (see Figure 9-1). Release the mouse over the tool that you want to select. You can use these tools to get working with a mask in a hurry. In the following exercise, you can take advantage of both of these tools.

On the DVD-ROM

Regarding the pictures that complement the steps, the following exercise uses footage items that are located on the DVD-ROM in the folder called *Source Material*. Just as a reminder, you need to copy the *Source Material* folder from the DVD-ROM to your hard drive. The following exercises deal with masks. Our own corresponding After Effects project is called *Chapter 9.aep* and can be found in the *Project Files/Chapter 9* folder.

Figure 9-1: The Tools palette uses one button for both the Rectangular and Oval tools.

Tip Feel free to substitute your own footage with the examples listed in the steps and shown in the figures.

STEPS: Adding an Oval Mask to a Layer

1. **If you haven't already, start After Effects and save a new project.** You may want to call it *Masking.aep* or something related to the topic. Our project on the DVD is called *Chapter 9.aep,* and the corresponding exercise is contained in the *Mask 1 - Oval* composition.

2. **If you haven't already, import footage items and be certain that they include either video clips or still images so that you can apply masks to them.**

3. **Create a new composition and place a footage item in it.** This works best if the footage item fills up the dimensions of the Comp window.

4. **Make sure the layer in the Timeline is selected.**

5. **Double-click the Oval Mask tool.** This places an Oval Mask over the layer, and its dimensions match those of the layer. Your Comp window should resemble Figure 9-2.

Figure 9-2: The layer in the Comp window indicates that an oval mask has been added to it.

Tip   If you want to avoid jagged looking mask edges, set the quality switch for the layer to Best quality.

Simple though it may be, that exercise gets the ball rolling as far as masks go. To better understand the implications of what you just accomplished, twirl down the layer in the Timeline and then twirl down the general mask properties to look at the details of the newly added mask (see Figure 9-3). Also, you may want to click the Show Alpha Channel button in the Comp window to see how the transparency has been changed for this layer by adding the mask to it.

Tip   To solo all of a mask's properties in the Timeline, select the layer that the mask belongs to and press MM (the M key twice.) To solo only a mask's shape, simply press M once.

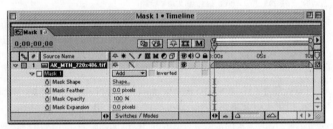

Figure 9-3: Twirl down the small triangle next to the layer name in the Timeline, and then twirl down the triangle next to the mask properties to view details about a mask.

Click the mask shape property to bring up the dialog box shown in Figure 9-4. The Mask Shape dialog box enables you to change the mask's overall dimensions by entering specific numerical values. In the next exercise, you create a rectangular mask and make some minor adjustments to it in the Layer window.

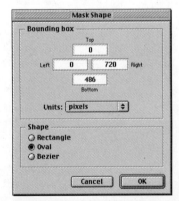 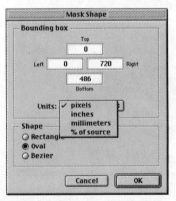

Figure 9-4: The Mask Shape dialog box enables you to enter specific dimensions for a mask's overall dimensions.

STEPS: Adding and Adjusting a Rectangular Mask

1. **Create a new comp and drop a footage item into it, preferably one that fills the comp's dimensions.** Our comp is called *Mask 2 - Rectangle*.

2. **Double-click the layer in the Timeline to open the Layer window.**

3. **In the Layer window, choose Masks from the Layer window menu located at the upper-right corner.**

If you neglect to specify Masks in this menu, you won't be able to edit any masks in the Layer window.

4. **Control+click/Right-click the image and choose New Mask.** This adds a rectangular mask, the dimensions of which match the layer. You see that the mask has six control points, one in each corner.

5. **Choose Layer ⇨ Mask ⇨ Free Transform points (Command+T/Ctrl+T).** This places free transform points over the mask. You may be accustomed to working with these in Photoshop or Illustrator. If you have room on your monitor, position the Layer window next to the Comp window to watch your changes to the Mask's dimensions in Step 6.

You can also invoke the Free Transform points by double-clicking the edges of the mask in either the Comp or Layer windows. To turn off the Free Transform points, double-click the mouse while it's positioned over the pasteboard outside the edges of the composition, or you can also press Return.

6. **Drag the Free Transform points to frame specific contents in the layer.** As you do so, the Comp window updates the results of the changes to the mask as they relate to the composition. See Figure 9-5 for reference.

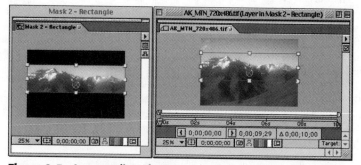

Figure 9-5: As you adjust the Free Transform points of a mask in the Layer window, the changes to the composition are updated in the Comp window.

Caution

When you're tweaking the Free Transform points, be careful not to rotate the mask. If you position the mouse just outside the edges of the corners, you may rotate the mask by mistake. We cover this later. If it happens, just Undo (Command+Z/Ctrl+Z).

Before you jump to the next section and start going wild with the Pen tool, take a moment to learn a couple more tricks with the Rectangular and Oval Mask tools.

STEPS: Using the Mask Tools with the Modifier Keys

1. **Create a new comp and drop a footage item into it, preferably one that fills the comp's dimensions.** Our comp is called *Mask 3*.

2. **Select either the Rectangular or Oval Mask tool.**

Note

Despite the fact that they create different shapes, the Rectangular and Oval Mask tools both work the same way.

3. **Click and drag across the image in the Comp window.** This adds a mask, the dimensions of which you control by dragging the mouse.

4. **Before releasing the mouse, experiment by using the Shift key and the Command/Ctrl key.** The shift key maintains square or circular proportions for the mask depending on the selected tool. The Command/Ctrl key draws the mask out from the center. Experiment by using the two modifier keys together as well. For example, if you want to create a circular mask, which is centered on the layer, select either the Rectangular or Oval Mask tool, position the mouse over the middle of the comp. Then click with the mouse and press Shift+Command/Ctrl and drag out toward any corner of the Comp window.

5. **Release the mouse after you create the mask that you want.**

Tip

Although you can create and adjust a mask directly in the Comp window, we find it easier to make adjustments to a mask in the Layer window. You're free to choose either method; our experience has shown that working with masks in the Comp window can get a bit tricky. Inadvertently clicking in the Comp window can occasionally leave you groaning in pain, because sooner or later, you'll end up moving layers rather than mask control points.

Caution

Creating a mask by double-clicking either of the Rectangular or Oval Mask tools when an existing layer's mask is selected overwrites the existing mask. To avoid this, make certain that a layer's mask is not selected in the Timeline or if you're working in the Layer window, make sure the Target menu is set to None.

Now that you know how to add masks to layers by using these methods, here's a list of features to round out the introduction to the masking tools.

✦ **To Delete a Mask:** Select it in the Timeline and press Delete. You could also select the mask from the Target menu in the Layer window and press Delete.

✦ **To Rename a Mask:** Select it in the Timeline and press Return. This highlights the mask's name at which point you can type in a new name. After you finish, press Return again.

✦ **To Change the Color of a Mask:** Click the color to the left of the mask name in the Timeline. This opens the color picker that you can use to specify the color of your choice. This can be useful if you're using multiple masks and need to differentiate between them in the Comp and Layer windows.

✦ **To View Mask Options:** After you create a mask, double-click its layer to open the Layer window. Select the mask that you want to adjust from the Target menu at the lower-right corner of the Layer window and then Control+click/ right-click inside the target mask's boundaries. You are presented with the list of options shown in Figure 9-6.

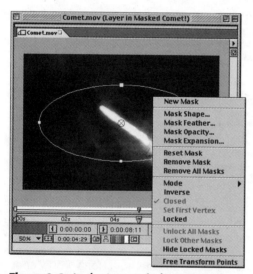

Figure 9-6: In the Layer window, Control+ click/right-click inside a target mask's boundaries to view the options for that mask.

Image courtesy of Bestshot.com, Inc. ©2001 (Celestial Backdrops)

Drawing Bezier masks with the Pen tool

Now that you worked with the cookie cutter type masks created by the Rectangular and Oval Mask tools, you should try your hand at using the Pen tool to create a more detailed mask. If you've had any experience using the Pen tool to create motion paths, the same general set of skills carries over quite nicely in the world of masks. The most important aspect of creating paths with the Pen tool is to practice until the process no longer intimidates you.

Select the Pen tool from the Tools palette and start by clicking a layer in the Comp or Layer windows. Each time you click, you set a control point for the mask, and you see that a straight line connects each of the control points. Look at Figure 9-7 to get a visual sense of this method of mask creation.

Figure 9-7: In the Layer window, click the Pen tool at various locations on the image to create a mask comprised of straight lines.
Image courtesy of Digital Juice (Jump Backs, Vol. 7)

You can also create a mask with curved lines. After you initially click a layer to add control point, continue holding the mouse down and drag it to set a curved line. Using this method, you can add a series of control points linked by curved lines. Figure 9-8 shows a mask being created by using this method. Don't worry about getting the exact shape that you want just yet. After you make a mask, you can always move its control points and modify its curves later on.

To complete the "cut out" created by any mask you added control points to, click the first control point you created to close the mask. Believe it or not, you can have open masks, and you can try using these as a complement to various effects a bit later in the chapter. For now though, you work with closed masks because only closed masks create transparency.

To briefly recap, you now know how to create masks using the three different masking tools in the Tools palette: the Rectangular and Oval Mask tools, and the Pen tool.

After you create a mask, you can edit it and make adjustments to it as you see fit. We cover all the ways you can do this in the next section, entitled "Modifying Masks."

Figure 9-8: In the Layer window, click and drag the Pen tool at various locations on the image to create a mask comprised of curved lines.

Image courtesy of Digital Juice (Jump Backs, Vol. 7)

Modifying Masks

If you've been reading this chapter from the beginning, you're now at one of those points in the learning curve where you could be a danger to yourself and others, at least as far as masks are concerned. You should now take the time to learn how to modify all the different kind of masks you know how to create, be they rectangles, ovals, Bezier creations, or paths carried over from Photoshop or Illustrator.

Selecting one or more control points

Whether you're working in the Layer or Comp window, you can select one or more individual control points by using the basic selection tool in conjunction with a couple of the modifier keys. Look at the upcoming list for a rundown of the mask selection methods.

Importing Masks from Photoshop and Illustrator

Once again, Adobe's terrific integration between their graphics products has resulted in some very cool functions that are shared across various applications. If you've created the perfect path in either Photoshop or Illustrator, there's no need to make it again from scratch. You can also use paths that you didn't necessarily create, as is the case with creating outlines from text in Illustrator. We've provided you with two small exercises to get you working between the different applications.

STEPS: Importing a Basic Mask from Illustrator or Photoshop

1. **In Photoshop or Illustrator, create a path by using the methods specific to the different applications.** The methods are fairly universal, but there are a few small differences.

2. **Select the entire path or only those control points that you want to carry over to After Effects.**

3. **Choose Edit ➪ Copy (Command+C/Ctrl+C).**

4. **Switch over to After Effects or open After Effects if it isn't running.**

5. **In After Effects, open the Layer window for the layer that you want to apply the mask to.**

6. **Choose Edit ➪ Paste (Command+V/Ctrl+V).**

That's the basic idea, which is remarkable in that it's so simple and elegant. Now, raise the stakes and copy and paste a mask created from the outlines of text in Illustrator.

STEPS: Importing a Mask Created from Type in Illustrator

1. **Create a new document in Illustrator.**

2. **Using the Text tool, place a single letter in the document.**

3. **Select another tool from the Tools palette to get out of text editing mode.**

4. **Choose Type ➪ Create Outlines (Command+Shift+O/Ctrl+Shift+O).** Your Illustrator document should now have paths outlining the edges of the letter (see Figure SB 9-1). This becomes your mask in After Effects.

5. **Choose Edit ➪ Copy (Command+C/Ctrl+C).**

6. **Switch over to After Effects or open After Effects if it isn't running.**

7. **In After Effects, open the Layer window for the layer that you want to apply the mask to.**

8. **Choose Edit ➪ Paste (Command+V/Ctrl+V).** After pasting the outline, your Layer window should look similar to Figure SB 9-2.

Figure SB 9-1: After you select Create Outlines, your Illustrator document should have paths outlining the edges of the letter.

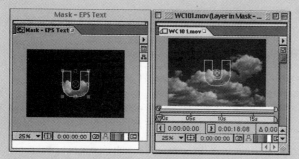

Figure SB 9-2: After you select Create Outlines, your Illustrator document should have paths outlining the edges of the letter.
Image appears courtesy of ArtBeats (Starter Kit)

Extremely cool, no? Well, those are the basics. After you start animating masks, you can begin experimenting with morphing mask shapes. At that point, knowing how to extrapolate text outlines from Illustrator will be good, because you'll be using the resulting masks as shapes for keyframes.

Cross-Reference This isn't the only way to use Illustrator text as the basis for a "knock out." In Chapter 11, we look at the After Effects phenomenon known as *Track Mattes*. Using Track Mattes alleviates the need to convert outlines to masks by enabling you to take advantage of transparency directly from the alpha channel in an Illustrator file.

✦ **To select one control point:** Click directly on the point.

✦ **To select more than one control point:** Hold down the Shift key and click as many points as you want; alternatively, you can also click and drag a marquee around one or more points. You can hold down the Shift key and perform multiple marquee selections as well.

✦ **To deselect control points:** Hold down the Shift key and click selected points to deselect them.

Tip

Control points appear filled if selected, hollow if not.

✦ **To select an entire mask:** Use either the Layer, Comp, or Timeline windows.

• **In the Layer or Comp windows:** Hold down the Option/Alt key, and click the edge of a mask. To select multiple masks, add the Shift key to the Option/Alt key, and continue clicking the edges of other masks.

• **In the Timeline window:** Select the layer that the mask belongs to and press the M key to solo the layer's mask(s). Select the mask by clicking the mask name. To select multiple masks, hold down the Shift key and click multiple mask names for a layer.

Adding, deleting, and adjusting control points

After you select one or more control points, you can move them in the Layer or Comp windows by simply dragging them. You can also change their shape by adding or removing control points. The next list reviews the ways you can change a mask's shape.

✦ **To move one or more control points:** After you select the control point(s), use the Select tool to click and drag them.

✦ **To add a control point:** Select the Add Control Point tool from the Tools palette, or press G on the keyboard until your pointer indicates that you've selected the Add Control Point tool. Position the pointer between two control points on a mask and click to add another control point.

Tip

Cycle through the Pen tool family (Pen tool, Add Control Point tool, and Delete Control Point tool) by pressing G on the keyboard until your pointer indicates that you selected the Pen tool variant that you want to use.

✦ **To remove a control point:** Select the Delete Control Point tool from the Tools palette or press G on the keyboard until your pointer indicates that you selected the Delete Control Point tool. Position the pointer over a control point and click it to remove it.

✦ **To change a control point from Bezier to linear (smooth to corner) or vice versa:** Select the Convert Control Point Tool from the Tools palette, or press G on the keyboard until your pointer indicates that you selected the Convert Control Point tool. Position the pointer over a control point and click it to convert it. Alternatively, you can use the basic Select tool and hold down the Command/Ctrl key to momentarily invoke the Convert Control Point tool.

✦ **To change the shape of a segment of a mask:** In addition to moving one or more control points, you can also click and drag a mask segment between two control points. The control points stay put, but the line between them changes according to how much you move the mouse. Of course, you can also adjust the directional Bezier handles that jut out from a curve control point. We cover that in more detail just a bit later in this section.

Replacing, resetting, and deleting masks

Some common actions you may take with the masks are replacing, resetting, or deleting one or more masks. The following list acquaints you with each of these actions as well as how to achieve the desired effect.

✦ **To replace a mask:** In the Layer window, select the mask that you want to replace from the Target menu. Draw a new mask, and this overwrites the existing mask.

Caution

If you've selected a specific mask from the Target menu, drawing a new mask shape will always replace the existing mask. Be sure that's what you want to do. If you want to create a new mask, set the Target to None before drawing a new shape.

✦ **To reset a mask:** Control+click/Right-click the mask in the Layer or Comp window and select Reset Mask. This sets the present mask to the dimensions of the layer.

✦ **To delete one or more masks:** Control+click/Right-click the mask in the Layer or Comp window and select Remove Mask or Remove All Masks.

Try putting these principles to work with the following exercise.

STEPS: Selecting and Moving Control Points

1. **Open the composition called** *Adjust this Mask* **from the** *Chapter 9.aep* **project on the DVD-ROM.** If you don't want to work with our comp, you can just as easily create your own. If you opt to work with your own, place a simple mask at the top of the layer that's highest in the stacking order (if you're using more than one layer).

2. **Double-click the masked layer in the Timeline to open the Layer window.**

3. **From the Target menu, choose the mask called** *Yes, Adjust this Mask!*
   If you're working with your own comp, choose the mask you created.

4. **Add the rings of Saturn to the area included in the mask.** Add control points
   and move them to accommodate the area of the image that needs to be
   included in the mask. If necessary, adjust the Bezier handles of the control
   points. If you get stuck with the Bezier handles, read the next section and
   practice your Bezier curves techniques. As soon as you feel more in control,
   give it another shot. Look at Figure 9-9 for reference.

Figure 9-9: Add control points to the mask
and adjust its Bezier curves to include
Saturn's rings.

Image courtesy of Bestshot.com, Inc. ©2001 (Celestial Backdrops)

Tip

Try making the adjustments by adding only two more control points to the mask.

Tweaking Bezier curves

Bezier curves are a wonderfully precise tool for specifying paths, and they can also
be incredibly vexing if you're not familiar with their mechanics and idiosyncrasies.
Bezier curves seem to improve through attrition. Just keep working at them until
they start to look the way you want them to appear. A few techniques should keep
this phase of your development as quick and painless as possible, and we cover

these next. You actually have a lot of ways to control this aspect of After Effects, but we distilled our collective wisdom down to a quick primer consisting of a few key points.

✦ **Don't worry about whether a mask is perfect as you're initially creating it.** Put your points down with the Pen tool and fix them later. Look at the rough sketch of the heart shape we created by using straight lines in Figure 9-10. Always try and use as few points as possible. Curves are easier to manipulate that way.

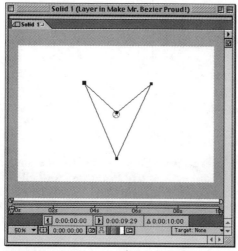

Figure 9-10: Begin work on a mask by initially laying down a rough sketch.

✦ **After you have the rough mask sketched out, use the Convert Control Point tool (or the Select tool with the Command/Ctrl key which temporarily converts it to the Convert Control Point tool) and click directly on the points you want to convert from hard corners to smooth points.** See Figure 9-11 to view the next stage of this mask's development.

If you inadvertently convert all the control points to smooth points, the entire mask was selected when you used the Convert Control Point tool. After creating a mask, deselect it first and then go in and select one or more specific points with the Select tool. In this case, we selected the two uppermost control points and converted them to smooth points.

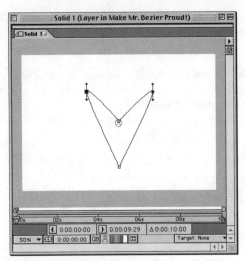

Figure 9-11: The mask indicates that the two continuous Bezier handles on the upper control points have been modified.

✦ **As soon as your sketch is closer to the desired shape, break any continuous Bezier handles by using the Convert Control Point tool and clicking and dragging the end of a single handle.** See Figure 9-12 to see the results of breaking the apart the control point handles.

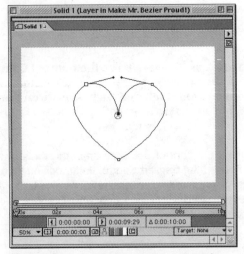

Figure 9-12: Break the continuous Bezier handles for more control if necessary.

✦ **If necessary, use the Select tool to change the position of a control point by clicking and dragging it.** You can also drag multiple control points if need be. Press the Shift key as you drag to keep the control point(s) on the same vertical or horizontal plane. See Figure 9-13.

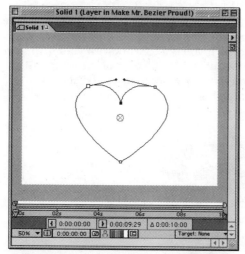

Figure 9-13: You can move control points to further change a mask's shape. In this case, only one was moved.

Now that you have some info on the various ways of manipulating paths, practice creating different shapes to get the hang of it. If you're ready for some tricky ones, attack the following exercise with reckless abandon!

Tip

Because it's not covered in the previous example, we should explain how to create a control point with a curved line on one side of it and a straight line on the other. Here's how: Break the smooth point handles and drag either broken handle all the way into the control point, releasing the mouse after it's positioned over the center of the control point.

Cross-Reference

In Chapter 5, we cover methods of adjusting Bezier curves as they relate to motion paths. The fundamental concepts of creating curves and straight lines are essentially the same when you're creating a mask. Masks don't have a temporal component unless they're animated over time, whereas motion paths always have a temporal component because they always refer to a layer animating over time. Nonetheless, when you are using the Pen tool to create Bezier curves, remember that all the following tricks work the same way as far as their mechanics are concerned: Command+click/Ctrl+click the control points to toggle between linear and curved lines, and Command+click/Ctrl+click a Bezier handle to break a smooth point.

Tip

Adobe's HTML Help file is a good resource here. Choose Help ⇨ After Effects Help and look at the sections entitled "Applying Bezier interpolation graphically," "Adjusting direction handles to create curves and corners," and "Retracting and extending Bezier direction handles."

STEPS: Masking Multiple Sections of a Layer

1. **Open the composition called *Cut Out the Objects* from the *Chapter 9.aep* project on the DVD-ROM.** If you don't want to work with our comp, you can just as easily create your own. If you opt to work with your own, create several basic masks, which "cut out" various pieces of the layer that's highest in the stacking order (if you're using more than one layer). If you're going to create your own composition, it should look similar to Figure 9-14.

Figure 9-14: The initial state of the composition in this exercise reveals three roughly sketched masks.

Image courtesy of Bestshot.com, Inc. ©2001 (Retravision)

2. **Double-click the masked layer in the Timeline to open the Layer window.**

3. **From the Target menu, select any of the three masks (their names are *Pot*, *Jar* and *Spoon*).** If you're working with your own comp, select one of the masks you created.

4. **Work on each of these masks until you have tight boundaries on each of the objects in the layer.**

Adjusting mask properties besides shape

If you read the chapter from the beginning, you know quite a bit about the Mask Shape property by now. Try scrubbing the other mask property values to get a sense of how each one influences the end result in the Comp window. All of these properties can be animated, as is indicated by the stopwatches next to the property names. The following list describes each of these mask properties in detail.

✦ **Mask Shape:** Reflects the composite of the mask's dimensions and represents all points that comprise the boundaries of the mask. Directly clicking the word Shape in the Timeline only enables you to change the dimensions of the mask's bounding box, not its actual shape.

✦ **Mask Feather:** Defines the amount of softness that's applied to a mask's edge. Great for getting rid of hard and unforgiving edges if that's what you need. Control+click/Right-click the numerical value and choose Edit Value to enable the option of entering different values for horizontal and vertical feathering.

✦ **Mask Opacity:** Defines the opacity of the mask, not the section of the layer showing through the mask. 100% opaque means that the mask is fully solid and not "see-through." 0% opaque means that the mask is transparent and completely "see-through." At first glance, this appears as though it doesn't make sense, but it does. A fully opaque mask results in a fully transparent "hole" in the image. If you still find this concept a bit challenging, click the Show Alpha Channel button in the Comp window and then scrub the mask opacity slider around.

✦ **Mask Expansion:** Negative or positive, defines the amount by which a mask expands or retracts beyond its dimensions.

Putting Masks in Motion

You've got the hard stuff down, and it's time for the investment to yield a return. Now you get to put these masks in motion to reap the full reward for surgically tweaking those Bezier curves. As you probably ascertained by now, After Effects enables you to accomplish tasks in so many different ways, and mask animations are no different. Numerous kinds of animations are derived from masks, and you take a look at them in the following sections. These include animating masks with the Free Transform points, interpolating between highly different mask shapes, animating multiple masks on a single layer, and panning a layer behind a mask. Get to it.

Animating a mask with the Free Transform points

One of the most commonly used methods of mask animation involves changing the dimensions of a mask's bounding box over time. It's really easy and very useful. It works especially well with text files created in Illustrator, but you can use it to "uncover" anything on a layer as quickly or slowly as your tastes require. Run through the following steps to get started with animating masks.

Look at our composition entitled *Anim. Mask 1 Transform* in the *Chapter 9.aep* project. Use it as a reference for completing this exercise. Figure 9-15 shows our mask before and after its animation across the Illustrator text layer.

Figure 9-15: The before and after states of the rectangular mask as it animates across an Illustrator text layer over time

Image courtesy of Bestshot.com, Inc. ©2001 (Cinematix)

STEPS: Unleashing the Animated Mask!

1. Create a new composition 10 seconds or less in duration.

2. Drag an Illustrator text file footage item into the Timeline with its In point set to the first frame.

3. In the Timeline, double-click the Illustrator text layer to open up its Layer window.

4. Using the Rectangular Mask tool, click and drag a bounding box across the layer that includes the text. Don't frame it too tightly. Leave yourself some extra room at the top. The reason for this will become clear towards the end of the exercise.

5. In the Timeline, go forward in time a few seconds.

6. Make sure that the Illustrator text layer is selected, and press M to solo the layer's Mask Shape property.

7. Click the stopwatch to the left of the Mask Shape property name to set a Mask Shape keyframe.

8. Drag the playhead back a couple of seconds.

9. In the Timeline, double-click the Illustrator text layer to open up its Layer window once again.

10. In the Layer window, select the mask you created from the Target menu.

11. Press Command+T/Ctrl+T to put Free Transform points on the mask.

12. **Click and drag the lower-middle Free Transform point on the bounding box until the text is no longer framed by the mask.** You should have a little breathing room at the top of the mask if you followed Step 4 carefully. This creates a new Mask Shape keyframe.

13. **Press 0 on the numeric keypad to see a RAM Preview of your animation.**

As the mask uncovers the underlying text, the animation may look a bit crude at the edges. Increase the Mask Feather to soften the edges of the animation, just be careful with the settings. If you go too high, the feather will spill over the edges of the mask and may reveal more than you want. If you absolutely must have a high feather setting, adjust the boundaries of the mask to compensate for the feather setting's overspill.

You can select segments of masks (as opposed to entire masks) and place Free Transform points on them. Only those points comprising the segments change positions as you change the dimensions of the Free Transform points bounding box.

When you place Free Transform points on a mask, the resulting bounding box has its own anchor point. Change its position if you want to rotate the mask around an Anchor point besides the center of the bounding box. Bear in mind that if you animate a mask shape by using this rotation method, the interpolation won't mirror the rotation. The mask travels straight to its new position without following an arc. The proper way to mask a layer if you want that kind of interpolation is to use a Track Matte. Track Mattes are covered in Chapter 11.

Creating more mask animations

Earlier in the chapter, we explain the process of importing a mask from Illustrator in a sidebar entitled "Importing Masks from Photoshop and Illustrator." Complete the steps in the following exercise to "morph" between masks shapes created from text outlines in Illustrator. Also, think about the general concept of interpolating between mask shapes and then experiment with as many different masks as you can create in order to learn how After Effects handles the interpolation between different kinds of shapes. During the course of your experimentation, you may want to change the Preserve Constant Vertex Count When Editing Masks preference in the General preferences, which you can see by choosing Edit ➪ Preferences ➪ General (Command+Option+;/Ctrl+Alt+;).

STEPS: Changing Shapes

1. **Create a new composition.**

2. **Drag a video footage item into the Timeline from the Project window or create a comp-sized white solid and use that as the base layer for the comp.** Either way, set the layer's in point to the first frame of the comp.

3. **In Illustrator, convert a letter of text to outline and copy the path.** Refer to the "Importing Masks from Photoshop and Illustrator" sidebar, earlier in this chapter, if you need help with this.

4. **In After Effects, double-click the layer in the Timeline to open the Layer window.**

5. **Paste the path to create the first mask shape.**

6. **In the Timeline, select the layer, press the M key to solo the Mask Shape property, and click the stopwatch to the left of the property name to set a Mask Shape keyframe.**

7. **Drag the playhead forward a couple of seconds.**

8. **Go back to Illustrator and repeat Step 3, but only use a different letter.**

9. **Repeat Step 4.**

10. **In the Layer window, select the mask you created in Step 5 from the Target menu.**

11. **Paste the path to create the second mask shape.** This creates a new Mask Shape keyframe.

Failing to create a second mask shape creates a new second mask for the layer.

12. **Press 0 on the numeric keypad to see a RAM Preview of your animation.**

Look at our composition entitled *Anim. Mask 2A - Text Outlines* in the *Chapter 9.aep* project. Use it as a reference for completing this exercise. We use the letters U and M. Figure 9-16 shows our mask before, during, and after its interpolation between shapes.

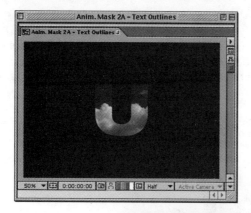

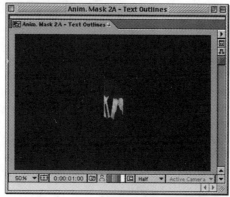

Figure 9-16: The before, during, and after states of the mask shape as it interpolates between the different text outlines

Image courtesy of ArtBeats (Starter Kit)

Caution

Some mask shapes derived from Illustrator text actually involve multiple masks. This is true for letters that contain closed "white space" such as O, D, P, R, B, and so forth. Pasting these paths as masks in After Effects can be tricky because you can't interpolate from two mask shapes to one (O to S, for example). In other words, morphing isn't quite as easy as it sounds on a conceptual level. Nonetheless, you have workarounds for this, and we include the O to S example in the *Chapter 9.aep* project in a composition entitled, oddly enough, *O to S*. The secret lies in keyframing the Mask Expansion property for the mask that is only relevant in one of the two shapes. In our example, the inner ring of the O has no place in the S mask.

Tip   If you need clues on how to handle the steps between multiple mask shapes, use Illustrator's Blend tool (see Figure 9-17).

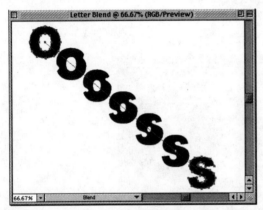

Figure 9-17: Illustrator's Blend tool can provide useful clues on how to approach the task of interpolating between multiple masks in After Effects. This is a blend from O to S.

In terms of understanding more basic mask animations, try this easy rotoscoping exercise. The concept of rotoscoping, which we introduced at the beginning of the chapter, deals with masking a subject that moves over time. Rotoscoping can be tricky work, especially if you're cutting out a person that's moving all over the place. In those cases, the people who usually do that kind of work make it their main occupation, and they also use a tool better suited to the task, such as Commotion. You're not going to try and match that level of cutout right now, and masking complex moving figures is something you should try only after your Bezier curves are always lining up exactly the way that you want. In any case, the basic premise is still the same.

Cross-Reference   This business of "knocking people out" is usually easiest if done with the keying effects, which we cover in Chapter 19.

STEPS: Completing a Basic Rotoscope

1. **Create a new composition.**

2. **Drag a footage item into the Timeline from the Project window.** Make sure that you're using a video clip containing a moving object.

3. **Using any of the masking tools, place a mask around the object that you want to cut out in the Layer or Comp window.** Make any adjustments to the mask that you feel are necessary.

4. **In the Timeline, select the layer, and press the M key to solo the layer's Mask Shape property.**

5. **Click the stopwatch to set an initial mask Shape keyframe.**

6. **Watch the development of the composition, using the Page Down (sometimes labeled PgDn) key to step through the progression of the video layer's motion one frame at a time.**

You only need to set as many additional keyframes as the motion of the object in a clip requires. If the object you're cutting out maintains a constant rate of speed and the same size area as it moves, you'll only need to set two mask shape keyframes. If it changes all the time, you'll obviously need to set more than a pair of keyframes. You may even need to create more than one mask.

7. **At the critical points in the clip's motion, set additional mask shape keyframes and make adjustments to the mask's shape in the layer window.**

Make sure that you select the right mask from the Target menu in the Layer window.

8. **As you work through this process, drag the playhead through the critical keyframes to dynamically preview the contents of the Comp window and measure the accuracy of your shifting mask shapes.**

Figure 9-18 compares the Mask in the Layer and Comp windows.

Look at our composition entitled *Anim. Mask 2B - Easy Roto* in the *Chapter 9.aep* project. Use it as a reference for completing this exercise. We cut out the comet as it moves across a colorful background and placed it over a "quieter" background of stars.

Animating multiple masks

You may remember us telling you that you can have up to 127 masks on a single layer. Well, it's true. Each mask you add to a layer appears under the mask heading of that layer's general properties in the Timeline, and we generally find it useful to rename masks after it starts to become difficult to differentiate between *Mask 3* and *Mask 11*.

More than renaming them, multiple masks on a single layer enable you to select different mask modes for each mask. As is the case with layers, the masks of a layer are processed by After Effects from the top down. This is especially relevant when discussing mask modes. By default, closed mask shapes are set to Add by default. Figure 9-19 shows the stacking order and selected mask modes for multiple masks on a layer.

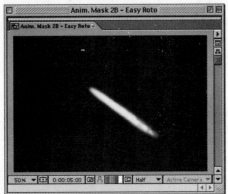

Figure 9-18: Look at the layer in its Layer
window and check its masked appearance
in the Comp window.

Image courtesy of Bestshot.com, Inc. ©2001 (Celestial Backdrops)
and EyeWire by Getty Images www.gettyimages.com (Cosmic Moves)

To better understand mask modes, create two overlapping masks and place them
on a layer. Leave the top mask's mode at its default setting of Add. Experiment with
the second mask's mode, and their functions should become fairly evident.

Tip   Once again, Adobe's HTML Help file can be a helpful resource. Consult the section on "Using Mask Modes" for some useful tips.

On the
DVD-ROM   Look at our composition entitled *Anim. Masks 3 - Mult.* in the *Chapter 9.aep* project. Use it as a point of departure if you need help getting started with these concepts. We use four copies of the same mask and move them around the Comp
window to let you adjust their interactions.

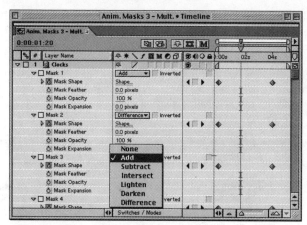

Figure 9-19: This composition's Timeline window shows multiple masks on a single layer.

Panning behind a mask

You can use the Pan Behind tool to change the portion of a layer that's showing through a mask. To get a sense of how this works, imagine a piece of paper with a hole cut out of it and then imagine placing it over a photograph. If you were to move the photograph underneath the piece of paper, the visible part of the photograph would change. That's pretty much how a Pan Behind works.

Pan Behind animations actually involve two different interpolations. First, After Effects animates the position of the layer, and then it also animates the mask to hold it in place as the layer moves beneath it in the Comp window.

STEPS: Animating a Pan Behind

1. **Create a new composition.**

2. **Drag a video or still footage item into the Timeline from the Project window.**

3. **Using any of the masking tools, place a mask on the layer by using either the Layer or Comp window.** Make any adjustments to the mask you feel are necessary.

4. **In the Timeline, set keyframes for both the layer's position and the mask's shape.**

5. **Drag the playhead forward a couple of seconds.**

6. **Using the Pan Behind tool, click inside the mask and drag the layer in the Comp window to a new position.** This creates new position and mask shape keyframes.

7. **Press 0 on the numeric keypad to see a RAM Preview of your work.**

Tip

To really see what After Effects is doing, open the Layer window and watch the mask travel across the image. In the Comp window, the mask animation equals the positional changes to the layer thereby making it appear still.

On the DVD-ROM

Look at our composition entitled *Pan Behind* in the *Chapter 9.aep* project. Use it as a reference for completing this exercise. We use the Pan Behind technique to follow the ridge of a mountain range through a small mask.

NEW IN AE 5.5: SMI: Smart Mask Interpolation (PB)

With the addition of SMI to the Production Bundle of After Effects 5.5, the challenge of animating masks and morphing from one complex shape to another is considerably easier. Just look at the difference between the journey from the letter S to the letter T before and after applying SMI in Figure SB 9-3 below.

Figure SB 9-3: Look at the interpolation betwwen the different mask shapes before (top) and after (bottom) applying SMI. Going from S to T never looked this good.

So, how do you take advantage of this new feature? Applying Smart Mask interpolation is easy. Tweaking it requires a bit more patience. To get started, all you need to do is select the two Mask Shape keyframes that comprise your mask animation and then choose Animation ➪ Keyframe Assistant ➪ Smart Mask Interpolation. The SMI palette will appear. Click the little arrow in the palette's upper-right corner and select Show Options. The SMI palette will look like it does in Figure SB 9-4.

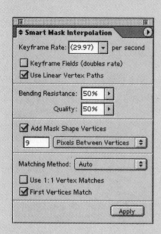

Figure SB 9-4: The SMI palette, shown here with all of its options visible

At this point, if you click the Apply button on the SMI palette, you'll end up with a keyframe on every frame between the two Mask Shape keyframes you initially selected. Before this happens, the Info palette will inform you of SMI's progress as it crunches the math involved in the interpolation. Preview your results to see if you like them. If you step through the individual frames of the new animation, the first thing you'll notice is that SMI adds a lot more vertices, or control points, to your masks than you first started with. The issue becomes how to make use of SMI to create the smooth kind of animation you're looking for. If you find the results to be less than perfect, Undo (Command+Z/Ctrl+Z) back to the step before you applied SMI, tweak the SMI options, and click Apply again.

Adjusting the SMI Palette's Options

The following list will give you a few clues as to what the various options do to the interpolation process, and the Tool Tips for the SMI palette are also instructive.

✦ **Keyframe Rate:** The number you select here determines the number of keyframes that will be generated between the two you initially selected. The default setting of Auto will match the frame rate of the composition.

- **Keyframe Fields (doubles rate):** Just like it says, checking this box doubles the number of keyframes generated. You'll need to do this if you want to match the motion of other graphic elements in a composition intended for interlaced output. For example, if you're designing for NTSC video, you select 29.97 fps as your keyframe rate, and you also click this check box.

Continued

Continued

- • **Use Linear Vertex Paths:** Selecting this option generates an interpolation built on the shortest possible distance between the various mask vertices. If you want SMI to generate more fluid and curved interpolations, leave this box unchecked.

✦ **Bending Resistance:** Would you like your interpolation to bend or stretch? Set to 0, your interpolation will bend. Set to 100, your interpolation will stretch. Now, if someone would explain the difference between bending and stretching, this might be a bit more clear. . . .

✦ **Quality:** The higher the Quality, the more creative license you grant SMI. Set to 0, SMI will get from one mask shape to the other as economically as possible. Set to 100, you may be surprised by the outcome, because SMI won't be bound by any constraints when thinking up ways to match vertices. You need to experiment with both the Bending Resistance and Quality sliders to see what works best on a case-by-case basis. Just remember that higher quality settings require longer processing times. Keep your eyes peeled on the Info palette, and if you run into trouble, press the Esc key to bail out.

✦ **Add Mask Shape Vertices:** If you opt to add mask shape vertices, which by the way, you'll almost always want to do if you want to get the best results, then the following three options make up the different ways you can do so. Adding many vertices can greatly increase the amunt of time SMI needs to generate all the necessary keyframes of the interpolation.

  - • **Pixels Between Vertices:** Adds a vertex at a regular interval of pixels, the number of which you define.

  - • **Total Vertices:** Alternatively, you can set a fixed total number of vertices from the beginning.

  - • **Percentage Of Outline:** With this option, you can add a vertex at any percentage point of the total length of the mask that you want, including decimal point increments.

✦ **Matching Method:** You can choose from the three options in the pull-down menu, but Auto tends to work just fine unless you have some interesting experiments in mind.

✦ **Use 1:1 Vertex Matches:** If you have the same number of vertices between mask shapes, try selecting this option to see what SMI can do. Otherwise, there's not much point.

✦ **First Vertices Match:** Buried here at the end of this list is a very useful tip. If you're becoming frustrated about the various ways SMI can create interpolations between two masks, one quick way to get good results is to select this option. For example, in Figure SB 9-3, we set the first vertex of the S in the middle of its upper curve, and we also set the first vertex of the T at its central uppermost point. By making these first vertices consistent and selecting the First Vertices Match option, you give the SMI process a guideline that keeps the animation from going way out of bounds. If you ever need to change the first vertex of a mask, Control+click/right-click on it in the Mask controls of the Layer window and select Set First Vertex.

Using a mask as a motion path (and vice versa)

One of the most interesting features about using the Pen tool to create a mask, at least in contrast to the other closed oval and rectangle shapes, is that a mask doesn't need to be closed. In other words, it can just be a path or line; its ends don't need to be joined.

Going further, you can create a mask from the motion path of a layer, and you can also use a mask to directly create a motion path. You can also add this technique to your path skills that you've been using across the Adobe graphics applications. An Illustrator path can become a mask just as easily as it can become a positional motion path in After Effects. You see how all this works in the following steps.

STEPS: Converting a Motion Path to a Mask

1. **Create a new composition.**

2. **Drag a video footage item into the Timeline from the Project window or create a comp-sized white solid and use that as the base layer for the comp.** Either way, set the layer's in point to the first frame of the comp.

3. **Set a series of position keyframes for a layer.** To best illustrate the example, define a fairly complex motion path complete with curved lines. See Figure 9-20 for reference.

4. **Select the layer in the Timeline and press the P key to solo the position property.**

5. **Click the Position property name to select all of the layer's position keyframes.**

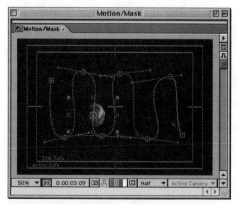

Figure 9-20: Make a complex motion path complete with curved lines.

Image courtesy of EyeWire by Getty Images

www.gettyimages.com (Cosmic Moves)

6. **Choose Edit ⇨ Copy (Command+C/Ctrl+C).**

7. **Double-click the layer in the Timeline to open its layer window.**

8. **In the Layer window, Control+click/right-click the layer and choose New Mask.**

9. **Select the new mask you just created from the Target menu at the lower-right corner of the Layer window.**

10. **Choose Edit ⇨ Paste (Command+V/Ctrl+V).** The motion path should now define the mask of the layer. The same process works in reverse. The next set of steps explains that process. See Figure 9-21.

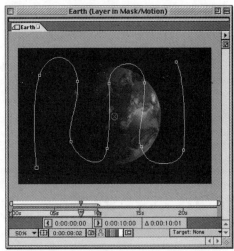

Figure 9-21: Behold the alchemy of After Effects. The motion path is now the mask.

Image courtesy of EyeWire by Getty Images

www.gettyimages.com(Cosmic Moves)

STEPS: Converting a Mask to a Motion Path

1. **Using the Pen tool in either the Layer or Comp window, create a mask for a layer.** It can be open or closed. If you want, you can use the mask you created in the last set of steps.

2. **In the Layer window, select the new mask that you just created from the Target menu at the lower-right corner.**

3. **Choose Edit ⇨ Copy (Command+C/Ctrl+C).**

4. **In the Timeline, select the layer whose motion path you want to define.**

5. **Set a position keyframe for the layer by clicking the stopwatch next to the property name.**

6. **Choose Edit ➪ Paste (Command+V/Ctrl+V).** The mask should now serve as the layer's positional motion path.

You must complete Step 6 to paste a mask as a motion path.

This technique also works with other properties involving positional coordinates, such as Anchor and Effect Point. As soon as you're familiar with this technique, you can speed up or slow down any part of the layer's motion by dragging keyframes in the Timeline. Between paths in Photoshop and Illustrator and masks and motion paths in After Effects, you should be able to get as much mileage as you possibly can from any line art to which you have access.

Take a minute to think about the applications for this method of copying and pasting line art. For example, you can use a perfectly circular mask as the basis for a perfectly circular motion path.

Using Masks with Effects

After Effects includes some effects that require you to define a layer's mask as the basis for the effect. To further explain this concept, take a look at the Stroke and Fill effects from the Render grouping in the Effects menu.

To add an effect to a layer that contains a mask, select the layer in the Timeline, and then choose your desired effect from the Effect menu. That's all there is to it. Try it out by first choosing Effect ➪ Render ➪ Stroke.

In the Effect Controls window, tweak the various settings to change the width of the stroke, its color, opacity, brush hardness, and so forth. The pull-down menu at the top of the effect controls enables you to specify which mask you want to use for the effect, or you can override this setting and select the check box which allows you to stroke all of the masks for the layer. The Start and End properties give you the opportunity to animate a "write-on" effect for the stroke over time. The Stroke effect can be used on either an open or closed mask.

Unlike Stroke, the Fill effect can only be applied to a closed mask. This effect is far less feature-heavy. You can animate the color, feather settings, and opacity, as well as specify whether you want the fill to be applied to the inverse selection of the mask. The point isn't how sexy the effect may or may not be. What's important is that you know how to take full advantage of all the options at your disposal as far as masks are concerned. Also, remember that you can apply these effects to animated masks. In other words, mask shape and effect property animations can run concurrently.

Using masks as the basis for other effects

Tip   Other effects, such as Audio Waveform or Path Text, also use mask shapes as the basis for their effect animation.

On the DVD-ROM   Look at our composition entitled *Mask Path Effect* in the *Chapter 9.aep* project. Use it as a reference if you like. We applied the Audio Waveform effect to an animated mask on a layer (see Figure 9-22).

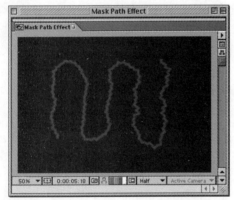

Figure 9-22: You can use masks as the basis for various effects. In this case, we applied the Audio Waveform effect to this mask.

✦   ✦   ✦

Creating Mattes: Creative Hole-Punching

If you look at this book as a linear progression of ideas, you'll notice that we approach the process of learning After Effects along certain lines. First, of course, is the interface. Then comes the means by which you can bring artwork into the application. As soon as you know how to bring elements in, you learn how to make them move. After discussing some animation techniques, we turn our attention to getting finished movies out of the program. After we cover rendering, we dive into the numerous divisions within the general topic of transparency.

Transparency is an essential component of After Effects, but it's also a bit more difficult to understand than the aspects of the software we've covered up until now. The reason for this is that you can't see which part of a layer is transparent unless something is visible behind it. Basically, until these chapters on masks and mattes, we try to keep the subject on those matters that you can see clearly. But you can only go for so long before you have to tangle with transparency, especially because it's such a fundamental concept within the realm of compositing.

Compositing is defined as working with multiple images simultaneously. So, as you probably figured out, without transparency, your compositing options are fairly limited. Unless you plan on always combining patchworks of small, fully opaque images when creating a composition, if you want to take advantage of all that After Effects offers, it's time to devote your attention to understanding the different kinds of transparency

Understanding Transparency

The convergence of numerous technologies has led to a fair amount of confusion, at least as far as what the official names are for the different parts of this process. Plenty of analog broadcast professionals, whose personal history predates the appearance of After Effects in post-production, typically call the transparent area of an image a "key." Post-production artists from the film world use "mattes" when making optical composites. So what is it? A key, a matte? Keep going. More will be revealed.

After Effects processes every layer as the composite of its red, green, blue, and alpha channel values. For those of you that are only just tuning in, an alpha channel isn't visible; rather, it defines what part of an image is visible, that is, the transparency of an image. As is the case with red, green, and blue channels in 8-bit color space, an alpha channel is comprised of 256 grayscale values. A value of 0, or black, is transparent. Whatever is behind it shows through completely. A value of 255, or white, is opaque. Whatever is behind it is completely obscured from view. You can always check the alpha channel of footage in After Effects by pressing the Show only ALPHA channel button in any of the Footage, Layer, or Comp windows.

Say that you have video of an object that you want to lift or cut out from its background. If you're supremely lucky, and you will be from time to time, the footage will come with a clearly labeled alpha channel that already takes care of the problem. If this isn't the case, you may decide that you want to mask the object, and this can be relatively easy if the object holds still, but a lot harder if you have to animate your mask or rotoscope the object as it moves through the unwanted background.

If you worked with masks in the last chapter, you know that you can use masks to cut holes in layers, and that the holes are really opaque alpha channel values in those layers. In addition to prepared preexisting alpha channels and masks, you can also define transparency in After Effects with the use of a Track Matte. In After Effects, a *Track Matte* is a separate layer that defines which part of the layer underneath it will show through. Last but not least, you can key out a background based upon its color. Greenscreen or bluescreen footage is made transparent if you key out the green or blue color of the image with a keying filter. Any of these methods lifts the object out of its background and enables you to use the layer and its transparency as part of a larger overall composite.

Working with Track Mattes

Track Mattes can be derived from either the alpha channel or luminance values of any layer. One layer acts as a Track Matte for another. Two kinds of Track Mattes are in After Effects, the Luma Matte and the Alpha Matte. Technically speaking, you can say that there are four kinds because you can invert either matte type to create either an Alpha Inverted Matte or a Luma Inverted Matte as well.

Using a layer's alpha channel as a Track Matte

Alpha mattes are based on an alpha channel, and, as we mentioned, you won't always have the benefit of an alpha channel at your disposal. However, if you're constantly working with Illustrator files, you will usually have an alpha channel to play with. Rather than discuss it much further, you should just complete the next exercise to better understand how you may actually use this type of Track Matte.

Regarding the pictures that complement the steps, the following exercise use footage items that are located on the DVD-ROM in the folder called *Source Material*. Just as a reminder, you need to copy the *Source Material* folder from the DVD-ROM to your hard drive. The following exercises deal with Track Mattes. You can find our own corresponding After Effects project called *Chapter 10.aep* in the *Project Files/Chapter 10* folder.

Feel free to substitute your own footage with the examples listed in the steps or shown in the figures.

STEPS: Making an Alpha Matte

1. **If you haven't already, start After Effects and save a new project.** You may want to call it *Mattes.aep* or something related to the topic. Our project on the DVD is called *Chapter 10.aep,* and the corresponding exercise is contained in the *Alpha Matte* composition.

2. **If you haven't already, import footage items and be certain that they include either video clips or still images so that you use them when working with Track Mattes.**

3. **Create a new composition and place a footage item in it.** This works best if the footage item fills up the dimensions of the Comp window.

4. **By dragging it into the timeline, add an Illustrator file comprised of text to the composition.** As far as the stacking order is concerned, make sure that it's positioned above the footage that you added to the comp in Step 3 (see Figure 10-1). Our example uses the *AlphaTime.ai* file from the DVD-ROM.

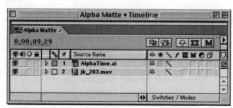

Figure 10-1: In the Timeline, make sure that the Illustrator text is positioned above the footage that you added to the comp.

5. **Click the Switches/Modes button at the bottom of the switches column to change the column view to Modes (see Figure 10-2).**

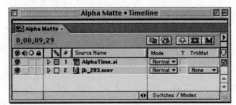

Figure 10-2: In the Timeline, click the Switches/Modes button at the bottom of the switches column to change the column view to Modes.

6. **Using the Track Mode pop-up menu, choose *Alpha Matte "YourIllustrator-File.ai"* from the list of options (see Figure 10-3).** We use *AlphaTime.ai* as the Alpha Matte.

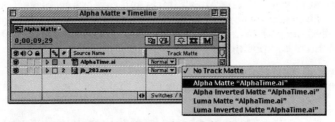

Figure 10-3: In the Timeline, select *Alpha Matte "YourIllustratorFile.ai"* from the list of options in the Track Mode pop-up menu.

7. **Click the Switches/Modes button at the bottom of the modes column to change back to Switches view.**

8. **Turn on the Best quality switch for the Illustrator text layer so that it has clean edges.** Your Comp and Timeline windows should resemble Figure 10-4.

That's the Track Matte trick, in essence anyway. In that exercise, you used an Illustrator file's alpha channel as the Track Matte for viewing the footage beneath it. Here are the basic conditions for working with Track Mattes as far as the Timeline window is concerned. These hold up whether you're working with either Alpha Mattes or Luma Mattes.

✦ Place the Track Matte layer directly above the layer you want to appear through it.

✦ Select the Track Matte type from the layer you want to see through the Track Matte, not the layer you want to use as the Track Matte.

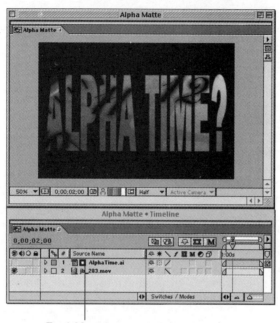

Track Matte icon

Figure 10-4: In the Comp window, the video footage should appear through the shapes of the Illustrator text. In the Timeline, turn on the Best quality switch for the Illustrator text layer so that it has clean edges.

Image courtesy of Digital Juice (Jump Backs, Vol. 7)

If you consistently meet these two conditions, then your Track Mattes should always work. From the last exercise, look at the Timeline to recognize the telltale signs, which indicate that a Track Matte has been set up. First, a Track Matte icon is next to the layer icon; second, the visibility icon for the Track Matte layer is turned off, and the same icon for the layer showing through the Track Matte appears filled.

Using a layer's luminance as a Track Matte

Luma Mattes are based on the luminance values of a layer. You want to use a Luma Matte in those cases where you have nice high-contrast imagery but don't have an alpha channel. For example, take a look at a picture frame we created in Figure 10-5.

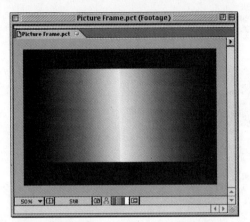

Figure 10-5: We created this TIFF file in Photoshop in order to use it as a picture frame in After Effects. Click the Show only ALPHA channel button to confirm the absence of any defined alpha channel.

To use an image such as this as a Track Matte in After Effects, you can circumvent the need for an alpha channel altogether by putting it to work as a Luma Matte. Follow the steps in the next exercise and give it a try.

STEPS: Making a Luma Matte

1. **Create a new composition and place a footage item in it.** This works best if the footage item fills up the dimensions of the Comp window.

2. **Add a high contrast, picture frame-type still image to the composition.** As far as the stacking order is concerned, make sure that it's positioned above the footage you added to the comp in Step 1. Our example uses the *Picture Frame.pct* file on the DVD-ROM.

3. **Using the Track Mode pop-up menu, choose *Luma Matte "YourPicture-FrameFile"* from the list of options.** We use *Picture Frame.pct* as the Luma Matte. This process, in terms of both the Timeline and Comp windows, is reflected in Figure 10-6.

As you can see, Luma Mattes are a nifty workaround if you're given artwork without any specifically defined transparency. You should always be able to create whatever basic transparency you may need on your own.

Why may you be doing anything like this? Well, layering video on top of a graphics "bed" is very common. For example, you can layer some additional footage underneath your matted video (see Figure 10-7). As soon as you begin thinking this way, the sky's the limit. Depending on the complexity of your project, you may want to pre-compose both the Track Matte as well as the layer that fills it. By placing them in their own comp, you won't have to worry about disturbing the layering order of your matte arrangement.

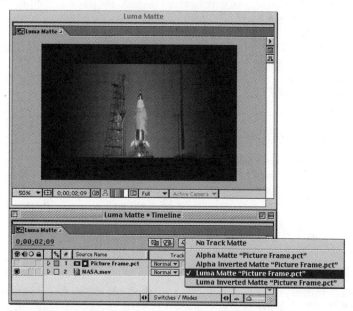

Figure 10-6: In the Timeline, select the high contrast image of Layer 1 as the Luma Matte for Layer 2. The Comp window now displays the images in Layer 2 through the higher luminance values of Layer 1.

Image courtesy of ArtBeats (NASA — The Early Years)

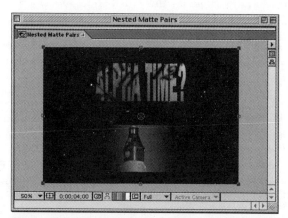

Figure 10-7: Layer additional footage beneath your matted video to create any number of design options.

Images courtesy of ArtBeats (NASA — The Early Years), Digital Juice (Jump Backs, Vol. 7), and EyeWire by Getty Images www.gettyimages.com (Cosmic Moves)

Inverting mattes

We don't want to overly complicate something that's fairly simple and elegant, but you probably noticed the other options in the Track Matte pop-up menu. The Inverted Matte options are there for you, so one way or another, you can get the look you need. For example, imagine that the still image we used as a picture frame for our Luma Matte in Figure 10-5 is inverted. Do you go back to Photoshop to fix the problem, or do you just choose Luma Inverted Matte from the Track Matte pop-up menu? The net result makes no difference, so use the Inverted Matte options in the interest of saving time (see Figure 10-8).

Creating traveling mattes

A traveling Track Matte involves animating either the matte layer or the layer used to fill the matte. For instance, you can animate the transform properties of the Alpha Matte layer from the first exercise and move the letters across the Comp window. Alternatively, you can animate the video that's visible behind the Illustrator letters comprising the Alpha Matte. Either way, you're in the travelling matte domain. Complete the next set of steps to see what this looks like.

STEPS: Animating an Alpha Matte

1. **In the Project window, click the comp you worked on in the first exercise, and choose Edit ⇨ Duplicate (Command+D/Ctrl+D).** This creates a copy of the comp in the Project window. Rename it *Traveling Alpha Matte* or something related to the exercise so that you can tell it apart from its copy.

2. **In the Comp Window, drag the Track Matte layer out of view past the left edge of the composition.** You may want to hold down the Shift key to keep the movement strictly horizontal.

3. **In the Timeline, set a position keyframe for the Track Matte layer.**

4. **In the Timeline, drag the playhead forward a few seconds.**

5. **In the Comp Window, drag the Track Matte Layer into position in the center of the composition.** This sets another position keyframe. Again, you may want to hold down the Shift key.

That's a traveling matte, folks. If you like, give the animation some production touches. For instance, enable Motion Blur for the layer and turn it on at the composition level. Also, using the Time Graph for the position property of the Track Matte layer, set the interpolation of the position keyframes so that the Track Matte comes screaming in from the side yet still somehow manages to gently come to rest in its final position. These are suggestions only. By all means, turn it out as nicely as you like. Refer to Figure 10-9 if you want to make your Track Matte travel as we suggest.

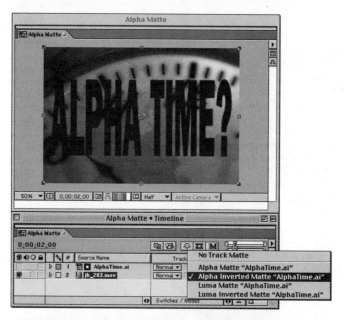

Figure 10-8: The Inverted Matte options are fairly self-explanatory.
Images courtesy of ArtBeats (NASA — The Early Years) and Digital Juice
(Jump Backs, Vol.7)

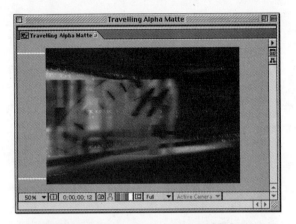

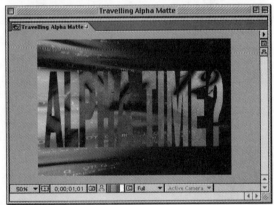

Figure 10-9: If you like, bring the Alpha Matte in from the side at high velocity, but change its motion so that it gently comes to rest at the end of the animation.

Image courtesy of Digital Juice (Jump Backs, Vol. 7)

If you're inclined to animate the fill layer, either by itself or in addition to the matte layer, go right ahead. You see this effect in movie titles fairly often. In fact, moving the fill layer is very similar to panning a layer behind a mask, a technique we cover in Chapter 9.

What's new in AE 5.5: Safely splitting mattes

As part of the bumper crop of terrific new developments in After Effects 5.5, when you either duplicate or split the two layers that comprise your matte, the matte stays intact. In the not-so-old days, when you duplicated or split a matte, you needed to rearrange the new layers to set up the matte again. Never again!

Working with Stock Footage Mattes

If you've used After Effects for some time, you've probably worked with a fair amount of high quality stock footage. If you're relatively new to the application, you may not have been exposed to that much of it yet. Either way, sooner or later, you're going to end up working with moving images that were professionally prepared by unseen artists who have sold the results of their efforts to a stock footage company. If you're working under time and budget constraints (who isn't?), professional stock footage can often be the path of least resistance. Completing a sharp-looking motion graphics project is hard enough without having to handle major production issues. Your schedule may not allow you the flexibility to shoot everything in-house. After Effects' strength is generally used to composite existing elements. Spending a modest sum on the right royalty-free footage CDs can often provide you with exactly what you need to do a job well without needlessly hemorrhaging time or money on nailing the right shot before you ever open After Effects. If you have a week to put together a promotional piece and you need crisp film or video that contains rich colors and high contrast, this is sometimes the only way to go.

Typically, stock "houses" provide mattes with some of their footage. The industry standard for preparing CD-ROMs full of stock footage is to compress the video files using Photo-JPEG compression set to dimensions of 720 x 486 pixels running at 30 frames per second. Over time, this has been worked out as the best way to provide the highest image quality while using the least amount of disk space and allowing for the most flexibility between the various editing and compositing applications throughout the field. One immediate limitation of this industry standard is that Photo-JPEG compression doesn't allow for alpha channels, so stock footage companies prepare mattes as separate files for certain kinds of footage.

You've probably seen stock footage CD-ROMs containing elements, such as fire, smoke, water, and the like. Those CD-ROMs are usually divided into a folder of the original clips and another folder full of the matching mattes. Figure 10-10 displays both the original footage of a flame shot in a studio and its corresponding matte, in case you need to composite the flame with other images. As we said, Photo-JPEG compression does not feature an alpha channel, so you need to use these additional mattes as Luma Mattes in After Effects.

Because you already know how to use a separate file as a Track Matte, you can immediately begin working with these two files in an After Effects composition. Still, you may run into some problems if the grayscale levels of the matte don't quite line up with the whole of the composite you're creating. Sometimes, the contrast of a matte file is less than ideal, especially when you're working with a bright background behind the matted footage. In this case, you want to change its levels to increase its contrast, and you can do this by using the Levels effect. If you use Photoshop at all, you're probably familiar with making adjustments to the Histogram of the Levels filter. In any case, complete the next exercise to see how this is done in After Effects.

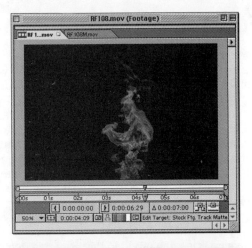

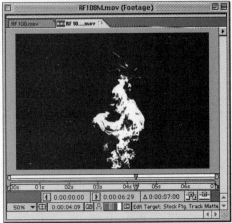

Figure 10-10: One image is professionally prepared footage of a flame. The other is its corresponding matte. Both are provided on the stock footage CD-ROM.

Image courtesy of ArtBeats (Starter Kit)

In the *Chapter 10.aep* project, we provide you with footage of a flame as well as its matte. Feel free to use your own stock footage/matte pairing if you have one. Just be sure that the matte has a fair amount of varying intermediate grayscale values so that changes to its levels will be visible.

STEPS: Tweaking a Matte's Contrast with Levels

1. **In the Project window, create a new composition set to the dimensions of the stock footage by selecting both the clip and its matte and dragging them onto the New Composition button at the bottom of the Project window.** We used the files named *RF 108.mov* and *RF 108M.mov*. Rename your comp so that you can easily recall its contents.

2. **In the Timeline, set up the Luma Matte by placing the matte layer above the full color video layer and selecting Luma Matte from the track matte options for the full color video layer.**

3. **Place a bright layer behind the matted footage.** This is third in the layering order of the Timeline. It can be a video, still, or a solid layer; it's your choice. Just make sure it's not dark.

4. **Select the Track Matte layer and then choose Effect ⇨ Adjust ⇨ Levels.**

5. **In the Effect Controls window, drag the sliders furthest to the left and right of the Histogram while keeping a close eye on the results in the Comp window.** See Figure 10-11 for reference. The slider on the left defines the point at which the original dark values become completely black. The slider on the right defines the point at which the original bright values become completely white.

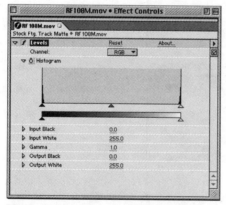

Figure 10-11: The Levels Histogram visually displays information about the range of brightness values in an image.

Note

This particular histogram is unusual because it indicates very little variance in the image. Histograms are typically far richer in detail.

6. **Look at a RAM Preview of your work and continue making adjustments as necessary.**

This technique can be a handy eleventh hour fix. It can also help you to rest assured that the money you spent on the CD-ROM was, in fact, worth it. The point is that the Track Matte technique isn't some binding limitation. After you've set up a Track Matte, you can still make changes to the hole that's been created by the matte. Before moving on to the Preserve Transparency function, look at Figure 10-12 to see the difference between mattes that have a sharp variance in their levels.

Figure 10-12: Making a change to a matte's levels can be the difference between a lackluster muddy look and an effective "popping" appearance.

Image courtesy of ArtBeats (Starter Kit)

Using the Preserve Transparency Switch

You have to turn your thinking upside down to take advantage of the Preserve Transparency switch. So far in this chapter, you've been placing layers above video images and having them serve as Track Mattes. The Preserve Transparency switch functions somewhat similarly, but in order for it to work, your approach to the layering order needs to be reversed. The switch itself is in the center of the Modes panel where you've been setting up Track Mattes. Its only distinguishing characteristic in the interface is the capital letter T over its column in the Modes panel. Whether you're turning the switch on or off, the top of the Modes panel indicates that you're altering this aspect of a layer (see Figure10-13).

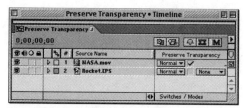

Figure 10-13: After Effects tells you when you're clicking the Preserve Transparency switch.

The key to understanding how it works is if you turn Preserve Transparency on for a layer, then the transparency of all the layers beneath it define what is actually visible. There's really no difference between what you can accomplish with a Track Matte versus what you can do with the Preserve Transparency switch. The critical difference is that a Track Matte can only work for the layer directly beneath it, whereas the Preserve Transparency function works through all of the layers underneath it in a composition. If you're predisposed to getting all your elements into a single comp, then the Preserve Transparency feature is for you. If nesting and pre-composing do not put you off, then you're probably more inclined to use Track Mattes. Our suggestion is that you become completely comfortable with pre-composing.

✦   ✦   ✦

Mixing It Up with Transfer Modes

Sometimes After Effects can create beautiful images without your ever having to add a single keyframe or effect. It's entirely possible for you to get gorgeous results simply by applying different transfer modes to the layers of a composition. Throughout the preceding chapters, we consistently discuss the fact that you can use After Effects to create simple and elegant looking pictures without going overboard on all of the application's features. Transfer modes are no exception to this wisdom.

In Photoshop, they're called *blending modes,* and in the After Effects manual, they're referred to as *layer modes.* Strangely enough, everyone in the After Effects community seems to refer to them as *transfer modes.* Whatever you want to call them, transfer modes enable you to combine the pixels of different layers to form results you might never have imagined possible. Unlike masks, effects, or transform properties, you can't apply keyframes to transfer modes. Every layer in the Timeline employs a certain transfer mode, and that's final. If you want to, you can split layers to use different transfer modes on the same footage, and we show you how to do that later in the chapter.

This aspect of After Effects is quite different from the concepts you've been looking at so far. Transfer modes are completely separate from any animation technique you've been learning up until this point. Every layer uses a transfer mode, and by default, any footage item added to a composition begins life as a layer set to the Normal transfer mode in the Timeline. The Normal setting leaves a layer's color unchanged. All of the others result in changes ranging from subtle to what could only be termed as obscene. You'll see what we mean as you make your way through the chapter.

Using the Different Layer Modes

If you apply a transfer mode to a layer, it affects all the layers beneath it. At least, that's the basic description of how they work. There's a lot more to it than that, but you can use that as a point of departure. The best approach you can take toward learning the different transfer modes is to try each one. In the section that follows, we describe all of them so that you aren't shooting blind. You should still try them all; it's just that having a basic understanding of the math behind the modes will keep you from just guessing how After Effects is coming up with the resulting images.

On the DVD-ROM

Regarding the pictures that complement the steps, the following exercise uses footage items that are located on the DVD-ROM in the folder called *Source Material*. Just as a reminder, you need to copy the *Source Material* folder from the DVD-ROM to your hard drive. The following exercises deal with transfer modes. You can find our corresponding After Effects project, called *Chapter 11.aep* in the *Project Files/Chapter 11* folder.

Tip

Feel free to substitute your own footage with the examples that may be listed in the steps and shown in the figures.

STEPS: Selecting a Transfer Mode for a Layer

1. **If you haven't already, start After Effects and save a new project.** You may want to call it *Transfer Modes.aep* or something related to the topic. In our project, *Chapter 11.aep,* we based this exercise on the composition entitled *Transfer Modes 1,* which you can find in *Chapter 11.aep*'s Project window.

2. **Create a new composition and place two footage items in it.** This works best if the footage items fill up the dimensions of the Comp window. Look at Figure 11-1 to see the Timeline for our composition called *Transfer Modes 1.*

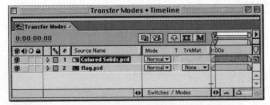

Figure 11-1: Create a composition with two layers in it. Change the Switches/Modes panel to Modes view by clicking the bottom of the column or pressing F4.

3. In the Modes column of the Timeline, select a new transfer mode for Layer 1. Look at Figure 11-2 for reference. You may want to look at all of them to get a sense of each one's function. Remember that changing a layer's transfer mode affects the layers beneath it. Making changes to the transfer mode of Layer 2 won't have any effect.

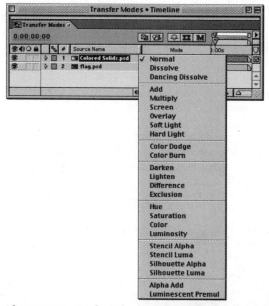

Figure 11-2: Look at the list of options you have after selecting a new transfer mode for a layer.

That's how you do it. As you can see, there isn't too much rocket science involved yet. To get a sense of what's really happening here, keep going.

Understanding the result in the Comp window

Now that you know how to change a layer's transfer mode in addition to having some foggy idea that the resulting image is based on the layers underneath, we'll try to explain this transfer modes business a bit further. Like anything else that's digital, you can break it down into math. When you specify an alternate transfer mode for a layer, After Effects does a little number crunching.

First, it looks at the pixel values of the layer with the new transfer mode. Then it looks at the corresponding pixels of the composite of the layers beneath it. After Effects then proceeds to apply a mathematical function defined by the chosen transfer mode on the two different pixel values. For instance, using Add will take the RGB pixel values from the layer for which you selected the Add transfer mode and add them to the RGB pixel values of the composite of the underlying layers. The image shown in the Comp window is the result of the mathematical addition.

Note   By "composite of the layers beneath it," we mean that you can have multiple layers of differing opacities beneath the one for which you specified an alternate transfer mode. In the example we use for most of this chapter's figures, we include only one layer at 100% opacity.

Note   After Effects still processes a layer's masks, effects, and transformational properties before it applies any transfer mode math.

In order to provide a visual reference for the functions of the various transfer modes, we blend the same two images so that you can more readily understand what each of the modes actually does. Figures 11-3 and 11-4 show the two images we've placed as separate layers in a composition to demonstrate the effect of applying the different transfer modes (see also Color Plates 11-1 and 11-2).

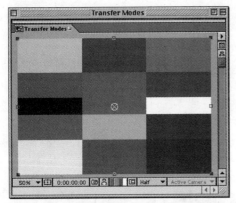

Figure 11-3: We created this still image by exporting a single frame from a composition we made out of different colored solids. In addition to providing black, white, and gray solids, we made certain to include fully and partially saturated areas of color.

Figure 11-4: This image is an exported frame from a QuickTime movie of a stylized American flag.

Image courtesy of Digital Juice (Jump Backs, Vol. 7)

In a good number of cases, the layering order doesn't matter because the math involved in the selected transfer mode equally affects the color values of the pixels in both images. As far as the following transfer mode descriptions are concerned, we created a simple composition with the colored solids image layered above the American flag. We try to make the process of understanding the impact of the various transfer modes a bit easier by using the Stars and Stripes. We're guessing that most of you know what the flag's colors should look like, and this is useful for understanding exactly what the different transfer modes are doing to the layers to which you apply them.

Note Dissolve, Dancing Dissolve, Alpha Add, Luminescent Premultiply, and the Stencil transfer modes are a bit different from the others, so we put them in their own section later on in the chapter.

Using Add

True to its name, selecting the Add mode for a layer adds that layer's color values to those of the layer beneath it. In 8-bit color space, values clip at 255. In other words, if the sum of the added pixels is greater than 255, the value stays at 255. This will almost always result in a brighter looking image because higher RGB values are closer to white. If a pixel being added is already white, it stays white. At R 255, G 255, B 255, it can't get any whiter. If a pixel being added is black, then the sum of the addition value remains unchanged because you can't bring about change by adding the number 0 (black) to anything. Look at Figure 11-5 to see the results of adding our two layers (see also Color Plate 11-3).

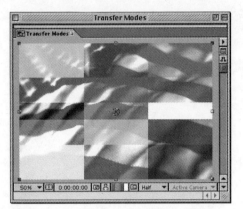

Figure 11-5: The Comp window reflects the result of applying the Add transfer mode to the top layer of colored solids. Notice that the black area of the top layer leaves the corresponding area of the second layer unchanged.

Image courtesy of Digital Juice (Jump Backs, Vol. 7)

Using Multiply

Calling this transfer mode Multiply is a bit misleading. It should really be called, "Multiply the two pixel color values and then divide the product by the white color value. In 8-bit color, that's 255. In 16-bit color, that's 32768." Somehow, that doesn't quite have the same ring as Multiply though, does it? Anyway, using it will always result in a darker image.

Plugging some numbers into the formula should make this clear. Take the 8-bit color space example of 100 x 200. The product of that multiplication is 20,000. 20,000 divided by 255 equals approximately 78. So, you can see that using this transfer mode darkens the result. If either of the two pixels has a black color value of R 0, G 0, and B 0, multiplying any number by zero results in 0, so the result will be black. If either of the two pixels has a white color value of R 255, G 255, B 255, multiplying and then dividing any number by 255 results in no change.

In essence, what this means is that if either of the images contains any areas that are black, the resulting composite in those areas will be black. Conversely, if either of the images contains any areas that are white, the resulting composite in those areas will create what is basically a Luma Matte based on whichever of the two images contained the white color values. See Figure 11-6 and Color Plate 11-3.

Tip Think of Multiply as taking two images and printing them on top of each other. Areas that are dark in both images would appear even darker when adding dark inks on top of each other, right?

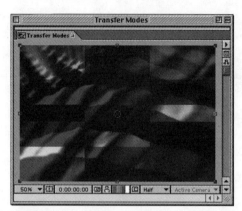

Figure 11-6: The Comp window reflects the result of applying the Multiply transfer mode to the top layer of colored solids. Notice that the white area of the top layer leaves the corresponding area of the second layer unchanged.

Image courtesy of Digital Juice (Jump Backs, Vol. 7)

Using Screen

Screen is, in effect, the opposite of Multiply. Screen always results in a brighter image. Screen uses the same mathematical procedure as Multiply. In 8-bit color space, that's x times y divided by 255; however, unlike Multiply, it starts out with numbers that are the inversions of the original color values of their layers. So, to modify that equation, it's really (255 minus x) times (255 minus y) divided by 255. See Figure 11-7 and Color Plate 11-3.

 Tip Think of Screen as using two different slide projectors that would each project its slide on to the same projection *screen*. Unlike printing the composite of two images together, the result in this case is one of additive light, not ink. In fact, the results are very similar to using the Add transfer mode, but you'll see the difference between the two if you adjust the opacity of the top layer. Screen is less severe because the composite won't top out at the maximum value as often as Add.

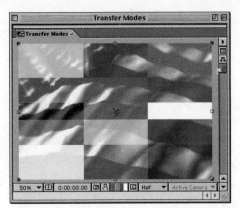

Figure 11-7: The Comp window reflects the result of applying the Screen transfer mode to the top layer of colored solids. Notice that the white area of the top layer leaves the corresponding area of the second layer unchanged. To see the difference between Screen and Add, adjust the opacity of the top layer when applying the different modes.

Image courtesy of Digital Juice (Jump Backs, Vol. 7)

Tip   When comparing Multiply and Screen, remembering that Multiply drops out white and Screen drops out black is helpful. For example, if you have footage that was shot against a black background and you want to create an instant matte by dropping out the black, use the Screen transfer mode.

Using Overlay

The Overlay transfer mode is a hybrid of the ones we've described this far. While blending the colors between the two images, it also lightens the areas of the top image that are above 50% luminance and simultaneously darkens the areas of the top image that are below 50% luminance. Also, all of the transfer modes we describe until now have the same result regardless of the stacking order of the layers; however, Overlay behaves differently. Those areas that are lightened or darkened are contingent upon the luminance of the top layer. In essence, you could say that Overlay makes the peaks higher and the valleys lower. Using it increases the contrast between the two images, if possible. See Figure 11-8 and Color Plate 11-3.

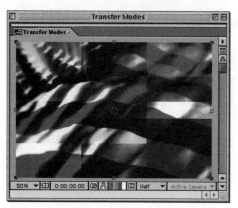

Figure 11-8: The Comp window reflects the result of applying the Overlay transfer mode to the top layer of colored solids. Notice that the colors of the two layers are blended and the contrast of the two images is increased.

Image courtesy of Digital Juice (Jump Backs, Vol. 7)

Using Soft Light

Like Add or Screen, this transfer mode's effect is well explained by its name, Soft Light. It's really a more muted version of Overlay. Lighter areas on top result in a lighter composite, and darker areas on top result in a darker composite. The mixture of colors is less intense than Overlay, and the overall effect is, indeed, like shining a soft light through the top layer. See Figure 11-9 and Color Plate 11-3.

Using Hard Light

While Soft Light is Overlay's understated counterpart, Hard Light goes well beyond Overlay and tends toward oversaturation when mixing colors. Whereas Soft Light is subtle, Hard Light is extremely harsh. In Figure 11-10 (see also Color Plate 11-3), you can see that wherever you have a fully saturated color in the top layer, it's kept completely in the final composite. The name Soft Light is accurate, but the name Hard Light would be more appropriate if it were changed to Hard Light with HyperEvil Saturation.

Tip You can think of Overlay, Hard Light, and Soft Light as a grouping whose common ground is to increase the contrast of the images that are blended together. Also, the stacking order of the layers is critical when using any of these modes, whereas it's unimportant when using Add, Screen, and Multiply.

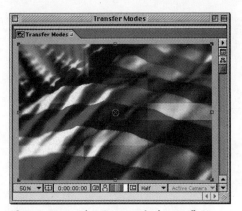

Figure 11-9: The Comp window reflects the result of applying the Soft Light transfer mode to the top layer of colored solids. Like Overlay, the colors of the two layers are blended and the contrast of the two images is increased, just not as much.

Image courtesy of Digital Juice (Jump Backs, Vol. 7)

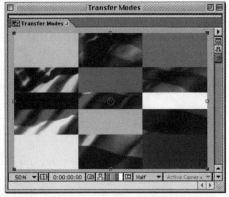

Figure 11-10: The Comp window reflects the result of applying the Hard Light transfer mode to the top layer of colored solids. Like Overlay, the colors of the two layers are blended and the contrast of the two images is increased, only a whole lot more.

Image courtesy of Digital Juice (Jump Backs, Vol. 7)

Using Color Dodge and Color Burn

When using Color Dodge, any black areas in the top layer appear to become transparent. Color Burn is the opposite in that white areas in the top layer appear to become transparent. In Color Dodge, areas of extreme brightness in the top layer cause ugly distortions, and you may have to lower the top layer's opacity to keep this effect at bay (see Figure 11-11 and Color Plate 11-3). For example, you can see that wherever you have a fully saturated color in the top layer, it's kept completely in the final composite. Similarly, Color Burn causes the same problem in dark areas of the top layer. If you apply Color Dodge or Color Burn to layers that include heavily saturated colors, distortion again becomes an issue (see Figure 11-12 and Color Plate 11-3). We tend to use these transfer modes on source material that's washed out and lacking in any sharp color contrast. As we suggest at the beginning of the chapter, experimentation is key.

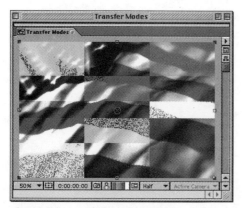

Figure 11-11: The Comp window reflects the result of applying the Color Dodge transfer mode to the top layer of colored solids.

Image courtesy of Digital Juice (Jump Backs, Vol. 7)

Using Darken and Lighten

The names of these transfer modes are initially misleading. You would think that they might have something to do with luminance, and in an indirect way they do, but Darken and Lighten refer to color values, not brightness values. When applying Darken, After Effects compares the two images and displays the darker of the two Red values, the darker of the two Green values, and the darker of the two Blue values. (See Figure 11-13 and Color Plate 11-3.) Lighten, as you might have guessed, displays the lighter of those values. This can lead to some truly unusual results because the higher or lower numbers can differ between color channels. (See Figure 11-14 and Color Plate 11-3.) For example, if you apply Darken, the top layer might retain its lower Red value in a certain area but pick up the bottom layer's Green and Blue values because they were higher than those of the top layer. White on the top layer is disregarded by Darken as is black by Lighten.

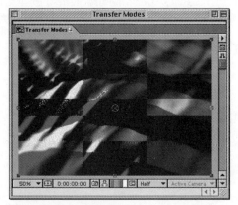

Figure 11-12: The Comp window reflects the result of applying the Color Burn transfer mode to the top layer of colored solids.

Image courtesy of Digital Juice (Jump Backs, Vol. 7)

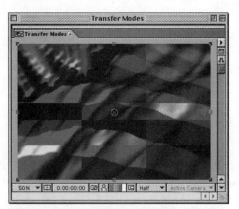

Figure 11-13: The Comp window reflects the result of applying the Darken transfer mode to the top layer of colored solids.

Image courtesy of Digital Juice (Jump Backs, Vol. 7)

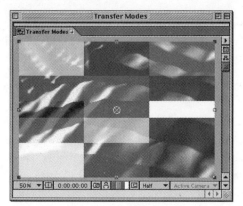

Figure 11-14: The Comp window reflects the result of applying the Lighten transfer mode to the top layer of colored solids.

Image courtesy of Digital Juice (Jump Backs, Vol. 7)

Using Difference and Exclusion

Difference is pretty cool. It's sort of the opposite of Add, but not quite. With Difference, the two color values are subtracted from one another, but there's a major catch. Add cuts off any sum at 255 regardless of the true numerical value of the addition. Difference does not cut off any subtraction at 0; instead, it completes the math and displays the absolute value of the subtraction. For example, if the top layer has a Red value of 100 and the other has a Red value of 200, the subtraction would be 100 minus 200 equals –100. The absolute value of –100 is 100, and that is what After Effects displays in the Comp window. The stacking order doesn't make a difference because if you reversed the order of the subtraction, 200 minus 100 equals 100. Same difference, as it were. So you can't count on this transfer mode to consistently darken or lighten a composite; with varying and divergent images, Difference always comes up with an unusual result. (See Figure 11-15 and Color Plate 11-3.)

If you think about that logic for a minute, you can come up with a couple of interesting scenarios. Suppose that you think two images are identical but aren't quite sure. You can easily check to see if this is the case by layering them both into a single comp and applying the Difference transfer mode. Any difference should be immediately apparent. Going further, you can try to plan production around using this transfer mode. If you lock down a camera and shoot a background and then get further shots after you introduce new elements to the foreground, those new elements will be all that is different between the first and later shots.

Tip

Blending any areas of black won't result in any change to the second layer since subtracting 0 leaves the second layer's values unchanged. Blending areas of white results in inverting the second layer. Look at Figure 11-15 for reference.

Cross-Reference

A similar method of keying involves using the Color Difference Key filter, and we cover that in Chapter 19.

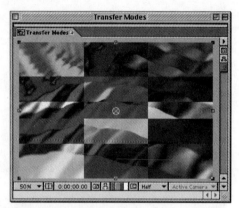

Figure 11-15: The Comp window reflects the result of applying the Difference transfer mode to the top layer of colored solids.

Image courtesy of Digital Juice (Jump Backs, Vol. 7)

The Exclusion transfer mode is really an extension of the Difference transfer mode, except that the resulting subtractions between the two layers' color values are softened. Look at the variation between Figures 11-15 and 11-16 (also see Color Plate 11-3) to visually understand how these two transfer modes yield different results. Ultimately, we think of Exclusion as the less useful sibling of Difference, because it tends to be muddy where Difference is dramatic.

Using Hue, Saturation, Color, and Luminosity

These four transfer modes can be grouped together because they operate in the same HSL color framework. All of the transfer modes you looked at so far deal with RGB color values. Instead of Red, Green, and Blue, these modes are based on Hue, Saturation, and Luminance. You can view the same color in each of these separate colorspaces simply by picking a color with one of the color pickers and switching between color pickers to see how the same color is quantified in the different colorspace. Figures 11-17 and 11-18 (refer also to Color Plate 11-3) show the same color in the two different colorspaces so that you can understand their equivalent values.

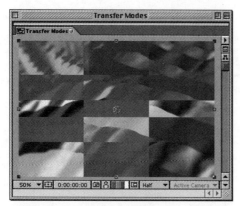

Figure 11-16: The Comp window reflects the result of applying the Exclusion transfer mode to the top layer of colored solids.
Image courtesy of Digital Juice (Jump Backs, Vol. 7)

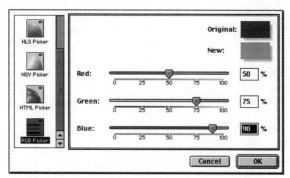

Figure 11-17: The RGB color picker doesn't allow for any control over brightness.

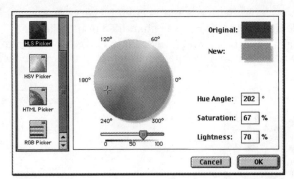

Figure 11-18: The HLS color picker is a more precise tool for selecting color.

Using the Hue transfer mode combines the hue of the top layer with the saturation and luminance values of the bottom layer (see Figure 11-19 and Color Plate 11-3).

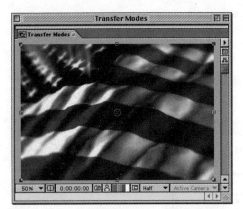

Figure 11-19: The Comp window reflects the result of applying the Hue transfer mode to the top layer of colored solids.

Image courtesy of Digital Juice (Jump Backs, Vol. 7)

Using the Saturation transfer mode combines the saturation of the top layer with the hue and luminance of the bottom layer (see Figure 11-20 and Color Plate 11-3).

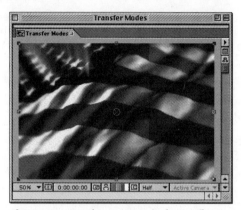

Figure 11-20: The Comp window reflects the result of applying the Saturation transfer mode to the top layer of colored solids.

Image courtesy of Digital Juice (Jump Backs, Vol. 7)

Using the Color transfer mode combines the hue and saturation of the top layer with the luminance of the bottom layer (see Figure 11-21 and Color Plate 11-3).

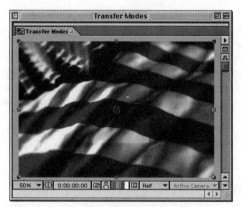

Figure 11-21: The Comp window reflects the result of applying the Color transfer mode to the top layer of colored solids.

Image courtesy of Digital Juice (Jump Backs, Vol. 7)

Exactly opposite to using the Color transfer mode, using the Luminosity transfer mode combines the luminance of the top layer with the hue and saturation of the bottom layer (see Figure 11-22 and Color Plate 11-3).

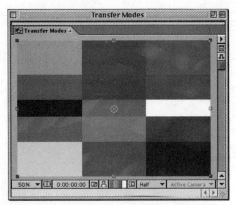

Figure 11-22: The Comp window reflects the result of applying the Luminosity transfer mode to the top layer of colored solids.
Image courtesy of Digital Juice (Jump Backs, Vol. 7)

Although these four transfer modes are united by their common color space, some are more immediately useful than others. Both Hue and Color can serve as a means to drench everything in a color of your choice. If that's something you want to do, create a colored solid, place it at the top of the layer stacking order, and then apply Hue or Color. Hue gives the overall composite a flat, tinted look, and Color preserves the luminance of the underlying layer and gives a more lively, tinted look. As always, experiment freely and don't forget to vary the opacity of the layer to which you applied the transfer mode.

Beyond Math: Designing with Transfer Modes

Unlike some heavy-duty effects, transfer modes render quickly. When you begin the creative process for a project, try applying the different transfer modes on the footage to see if anything looks good. Doing this can often point you toward some design options that you probably weren't considering. Drop footage into comps. Alter the layers' transfer modes and opacity levels. Play with different stacking orders for the layers in the Timeline. Throw clay on the wheel and start molding. Now that you know what each transfer mode does, you won't be playing with tools you don't understand. Keep an open mind and try everything you can. Experiment freely. Having said that, there are a few studio techniques we like to use when it comes to transfer modes.

What's new in After Effects 5.5: New transfer modes and keyboard shortcuts

After Effects 5.5 includes five new transfer modes: Vivid Light, Pin Light, Linear Light, Linear Burn, and Linear Dodge. Even better than that, you can sample all the different transfer modes quickly by selecting a layer in the Timeline and pressing Shift+ + (plus sign) or Shift+ − (minus sign) to quickly cycle through them.

Making instant Track Mattes

We mentioned this before, but it's worth repeating. Multiply drops out white, and Screen drops out black. Knowing that, you can apply the Screen transfer mode to a footage shot against a black background if you don't have a corresponding matte to go with it. The same thing goes for using Multiply on footage shot against a white background. Try it out yourself.

On the DVD-ROM, we include footage of a flame shot against a black background. If you layer it on top of any other footage in the Timeline, you can get an instant matte just by applying either the Screen mode or the Add transfer mode (see Figure 11-23).

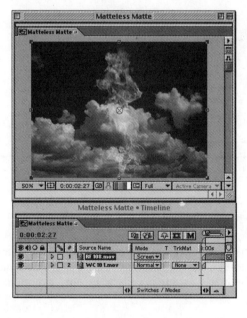

Figure 11-23: Once you put a layer on top of any other footage in the Timeline, you can get an instant matte just by applying the Screen mode or the Add transfer mode to it.
Image courtesy of ArtBeats (Starter Kit)

Animating by splitting layers

You can't use keyframes to change a layer's transfer mode. If you want to do that, you have to split the layer. This technique can get you out of a tight spot in a couple of situations. To use multiple transfer modes on the same layer, complete the following exercise.

STEPS: Splitting Layers

1. **Place two footage items in a new composition.**

2. **In the Timeline, drag the playhead forwards a couple of seconds.**

3. **Make sure that the top layer is selected and choose Edit ⇨ Split Layer (Command+Shift+D/Ctrl+Shift+D).** This splits the top layer into two trimmed layers.

4. **Repeat Steps 2 and 3 several times.** Make sure that you select the correct layer before splitting it.

Now you can specify different transfer modes for each of the split layers. To take it one step further, you can cross-fade between the split layers. Your Timeline should resemble Figure 11-24.

Cross-Reference
Using the Compound Arithmetic effect enables you to animate across the different visual looks created by the various transfer modes, which we cover it in Chapter 14.

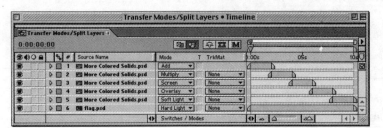

Figure 11-24: The Timeline window contains split layers that each have a different transfer mode applied.

Working with the Stencil Transfer Modes

The Stencil transfer modes are a lot like Track Mattes, which we cover in Chapter 10. There are some key differences though, the biggest one being that a track matte can only display one layer through the matte, whereas a stencil transfer mode can display all of the layers that are visible underneath it. Complete the following exercise to get a taste of the stencil modes.

STEPS: Using a Layer's Alpha Channel as a Stencil

1. **Create a new composition.** Name it as you see fit.

2. **Add at least two comp-sized footage items from the Project window to the Timeline of the new composition.**

3. **Using transfer modes, blend the layers together.**

4. **Add a third layer to the top of the stacking order in the comp, making sure that it contains an alpha channel.** Once again, we use text created in Illustrator.

5. **Specify the Stencil Alpha transfer mode for the layer you just added.** Your Comp and Timeline windows should resemble Figure 11-25.

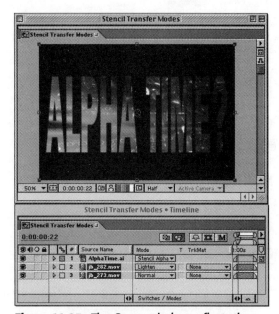

Figure 11-25: The Comp window reflects the result of applying the Stencil Alpha transfer mode to the top layer of Illustrator text. The underlying blended layers show through its alpha channel.
Image courtesy of Digital Juice (Jump Backs, Vol. 7)

Note   In Step 5, if you specify Silhouette Alpha as your transfer mode, your results resemble Figure 11-26. A silhouette is merely an inverted stencil.

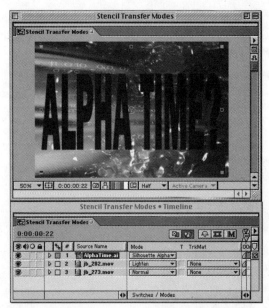

Figure 11-26: The Comp window reflects the result of applying the Silhouette Alpha transfer mode to the top layer of Illustrator text. The underlying blended layers show through the inversion of its alpha channel.

Image courtesy of Digital Juice (Jump Backs, Vol. 7)

Using a layer's luminance as a stencil

If you want to use a layer's luminance as a stencil, select the Stencil Luma transfer mode for the layer that you want to act as a stencil. In Figure 11-27, we created an image with varying luminance values to illustrate this concept.

Instead of using the alpha channel of Illustrator text as a stencil, we used the luminance of the image from Figure 11-27. We replaced the Illustrator text with this image in the same comp from the last exercise, and then we applied the Stencil Luma and Silhouette Luma transfer modes to it. See Figures 11-28 and 11-29 for reference.

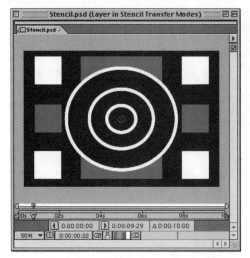

Figure 11-27: We created this image by using white, gray, and black solids. We also applied the Stroke effect to three circular masks on a black solid in the foreground. The luminance of this image acts as a stencil in Figures 11-28 and 11-29.

"I've never been too sure about these . . ."

There are a few remaining transfer modes that leave a lot of people guessing as to just exactly what function they serve. In some cases, they even leave us guessing. Anyway, we've included a few words about the transfer modes we haven't mentioned.

Dissolve and Dancing Dissolve

These transfer modes take any transparent areas of the layer they're applied to and create a very clunky-looking dithered effect. The Dancing variant animates the dither by randomizing it in each frame. To this day, we're still not sure why this is included among the transfer modes. We've been told that it has something to do with Web design and exporting animated GIFs. If that's your thing, then you can tell us what it's all about!

Alpha Add

This transfer mode takes visible edges of separate alpha channels within a composite and makes them seamless.

Luminescent Premultiply

This transfer mode takes a premultiplied alpha channel and increases its brightness. This can be useful if you created an alpha channel for a clip based on its luminance values. The resulting alpha channel from that process can sometimes darken the overall clip, and this transfer mode can restore the brightness that was lost. In order to use it properly, you need to interpret the alpha channel as Straight in the alpha interpretation.

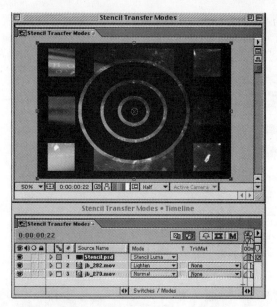

Figure 11-28: In this picture, we used the image from Figure 11-27 and applied the Stencil Luma transfer mode to it. The underlying blended layers are the same ones from the Stencil Alpha exercise.
Image courtesy of Digital Juice
(Jump Backs, Vol. 7)

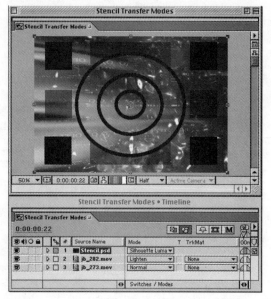

Figure 11-29: In this picture, we used the image from Figure 11-27 and applied the Silhouette Luma transfer mode to it. The underlying blended layers are the same ones from the Stencil Alpha exercise.
Image courtesy of Digital Juice
(Jump Backs, Vol. 7)

You can add as many layers below the Stencil/Silhouette layer as you want. Creating Track Mattes is essentially no different than using these transfer modes; however, if you'd rather keep all of your elements in a single composition, you can avoid using Track Mattes and use these transfer modes instead. As we mentioned earlier, you shouldn't be prejudiced against nesting and pre-composing because these are critical components of After Effects.

✦　　✦　　✦

Manipulating Time: Relativity in After Effects

Have you ever wanted to control time? Who hasn't, really? There are probably a few critical moments in your life that you'd try to approach differently if you could roll back time and live them out again. What about that date that went sour? Remember the time you found out that you could have asked for a bigger raise? We're sure the list goes on. Well, once again, that miraculous wonder known to all of us as After Effects continues to reveal its power, and lucky for you, you've reached the chapter that shows you how to control time!

Please forgive the false advertising. Any regrets in your life should be taken up with a shrink or your chosen spiritual adviser. Nonetheless, controlling time is still a very cool feature of the application. After Effects allows you to control time either by time-stretching or time-remapping a layer. *Time-stretching* enables you to change a layer's speed by a fixed amount. You can use it to make a 2-second clip play out over 10 seconds or only 1 second. Time-remapping is a more sophisticated method of changing a layer's speed, enabling you to vary a layer's playback speed with keyframes. Keyframing time? Yep, it's pretty amazing.

Why might you need this kind of control? Occasionally, you may be working with an audio track that runs longer than the video you have to match it. Other times, you may want to create a speed-shifting effect. You've probably seen commercials where sprinting runners suddenly seem to go from full speed into super slow motion. Depending on the quality of the footage you have to play with, time-stretching and time-remapping can provide you with some beautiful results.

Time-Stretching a Layer

Time-stretching in After Effects is basically the same concept as when a video editor performs a "fit-to-fill" edit. If you need a layer to be slower or faster or if you want it to play in reverse, you can make it happen with the time-stretch function. This goes for a video layer, an audio layer, or a layer that contains both video and audio. You need to be aware of a couple of aspects about this feature. First of all, any keyframes associated with the layer will also be stretched in proportion to the amount you stretch the clip. (More to the point, the *interval* between the keyframes will be stretched, rather than the keyframes themselves.) Secondly, stretching a clip copies or skips that clip's frames depending on whether you've sped it up or slowed it down. This can sometimes produce less than perfect results.

Complete the following steps to see how you actually time-stretch a layer. From there, you can look at any problems that arise from the speed shift.

Regarding the pictures that complement the steps, the following exercise uses footage items that are located on the DVD-ROM in the folder called *Source Material*. Just as a reminder, you need to copy the *Source Material* folder from the DVD-ROM to your hard drive. The following exercises deal with time-stretching and time-remapping. Our own corresponding After Effects project is called *Chapter 12.aep* and can be found in the *Project Files/Chapter 12* folder.

Feel free to substitute your own footage with the examples listed in the steps and shown in the figures.

STEPS: Time-Stretching a Layer

1. **If you haven't already, start After Effects and save a new project.** You may want to call it *TimeStretching.aep* or something related to the topic. If you're using our project called *Chapter 12.aep,* refer to the *Time-Stretch* composition after completing this exercise.

2. **If you haven't already, import video footage into the project.**

3. **Create a new composition and place a clip of video footage into it.** This works best if the footage has an obvious temporal progression, such as an explosion or something of that nature. We use stock footage of smoke. The point is that you want to be able to visually determine whether the clip is moving forward or backward in time without difficulty. You may also want to make the comp quite a bit longer than the running time of the clip that you add to it. This gives you some leeway if you want to stretch the clip by a factor much greater than 100%.

4. **Make sure that the layer in the Timeline is selected.**

5. **Choose Layer ⇨ Time Stretch.** The resulting dialog box is shown in Figure 12-1.

6. **Enter a new Stretch Factor or Duration for the layer.**

7. **Press 0 on the numeric keypad to make a RAM Preview of the newly stretched clip.**

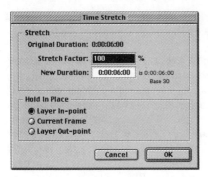

Figure 12-1: The Time Stretch dialog box enables you to specify a percentage by which you want to stretch a layer or a new duration for it. You can also select the reference point that will be used as the basis for the stretch.

 Tip

You can enter negative values if you want the clip to play backwards.

 Tip

Control+click/Right-click the top of any of the panels in the Timeline and add the Stretch Panel if you like. This enables you to bring up the Time Stretch dialog box as easily as clicking the Stretch Factor visible for each layer in the panel. See Figure 12-2 for reference.

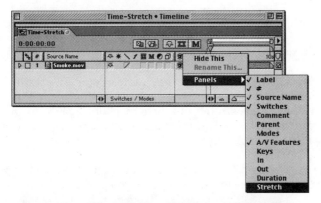

Figure 12-2: You can add the Stretch panel to the panels in the Timeline. Clicking the Stretch Factor value for a layer brings up the Time Stretch dialog box shown in Figure 12-1.

That's how you time-stretch a layer. Experiment with video and audio clips to see the results. Here are a couple of details to keep in mind regarding this feature:

✦ **When time-stretching a layer by a factor greater than 100%:** After Effects copies frames from the clips and plays them accordingly. For example, if you time-stretch a layer by a factor of 200%, each frame of a layer is displayed twice. If you use factors that aren't clean multiples of the original (that is 200%, 300%, 400%, and so on), After Effects will inconsistently copy frames and yield somewhat unpredictable results. In other words, if you time-stretch a layer by 150%, After Effects will display half of the clip's frames twice. The question is, which frames get doubled up and which ones don't? To work around this problem, use clean multiples of the clip's original duration, if possible.

Doubling up of frames becomes a major issue only if you really slow down a clip (that is, 200% or more). You can also potentially solve this problem by turning on Frame Blending for a time-stretched layer, and we discuss that a bit later in this section.

✦ **When time-stretching a layer by a factor less than 100%:** After Effects skips frames of a layer if it's time-stretched to play in less time than its original source material. The more you shorten a clip's duration by time-stretching, the fewer of the original clip's frames you display.

We should mention once more that you can time-stretch a layer with a negative factor. In those cases, a factor of 0 to −100% skips frames. A factor of −100% or higher negative values copies frames.

✦ **When time-stretching a layer that contains keyframes:** After Effects will also time-stretch those keyframes (see Figure 12-3). If you don't want the keyframes included in your time-stretch, cut them by choosing Edit ⇨ Cut (Command+X/Ctrl+X), time-stretch your layer, and then paste them in again by choosing Edit ⇨ Paste (Command+V/Ctrl+V).

Make a note of where the keyframes were located relative to the layer before you cut them. This way, you know where to paste them after you time-stretch the layer.

Alternatively, you could time-stretch your layer, pre-compose it, and then apply keyframes to the nested composition containing your time-stretched layer. This method keeps the time-stretched layer independent of any keyframe animations you may apply to it. If you do not follow this tip and your keyframes get inadvertently time-stretched with your layer, you can always realign your keyframes proportionately by selecting all of them and Option/Alt+dragging the first or last of the keyframes to restore them to their original temporal positions.

Figure 12-3: This layer's transformational animations get time-stretched along with the layer.

✦ **When time-stretching a layer that contains audio:** After Effects time-stretches the audio. If you want to avoid time-stretching your audio along with the video, you have a simple workaround. First, duplicate the layer before applying the time-stretch. On the original layer, turn off the audio switch in the A/V Features panel and complete the desired time-stretch. On the duplicate layer, turn off the video switch in the A/V Features panel.

Going backwards

You have two ways to get a layer to play in reverse. In the Time Stretch dialog box, you could enter a Stretch Factor of –100%, but this method is less than ideal, because it usually hides almost the entire layer before the first visible frame in the Timeline. This happens because if you accept the default in the Time Stretch dialog box and hold the layer's In point at its current location, that In point becomes the end of the layer when it's reversed. Instead, we prefer the following handy keyboard shortcut: Command+Option+R/Ctrl+Alt+R. Try it out on a layer. If you do it right, your layer should look similar to Figure 12-4.

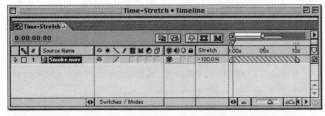

Figure 12-4: When you reverse a layer, After Effects gives you a "heads-up" by putting red stripes through it to indicate that it's going to play backwards in the comp.

Seems straightforward enough, right? Nonetheless, there are a few details worth pointing out. As is always the case with time-stretching, all keyframes will be stretched as well. Additionally, if you step through the frames of the layer in its own Layer window, the beginning of the clip in the Layer window will correspond to the end of the layer in the Timeline. If this sounds too weird to be true, try opening the Layer window for a reversed layer by double-clicking it in the Timeline. Look at Figure 12-5 for reference. Wacky, eh? We like this sort of thing, but if it bugs you, feel free to pre-compose it so that it appears to playback in a linear fashion between both the Layer and Comp windows.

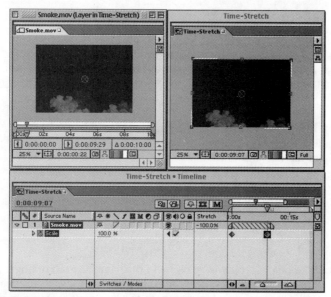

Figure 12-5: When you step through a reversed layer in its own Layer window, the beginning of the layer in the Layer window refers to the end of the clip in the Timeline and Comp windows.

Image courtesy of ArtBeats (Starter Kit)

Tip   If you ever want to reverse a layer's animations as opposed to the visual content of its video frames, you can use the Time-Reverse Keyframes Keyframe Assistant (say that 10 times quickly). Select any number of keyframes across one or more properties, Control+click/right-click them in the Timeline and then choose Keyframe Assistant ⇨ Time-Reverse Keyframes. In other words, if you have an animation exactly right except for the fact that the rotation goes the wrong way, you can time-reverse only the rotation keyframes.

Using the time-stretching keyboard shortcuts

Along with time-stretching, you have a couple of keyboard shortcuts you can add to your layer-trimming arsenal. If you want to time-stretch a layer to a specific point in time, press Command+Shift+, (comma) /Ctrl+Shift+, (comma) to stretch the In point to the current time or press Command+Option+, (comma) /Ctrl+Alt+, (comma) to the stretch Out point to the current time.

Alternatively, you can add the In and Out panels to your Timeline interface by Control+clicking/right-clicking one of the panels and selecting them. After adding these panels, your Timeline should resemble Figure 12-6. In addition to the keyboard shortcuts you just learned, you can also stretch a layer's In or Out point to the current time by Command+clicking/Ctrl+clicking the values in these panels.

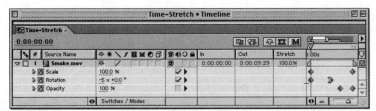

Figure 12-6: Command+click/Ctrl+click the values in the In and Out panels of the Timeline to stretch the In or Out point of a layer to the current time.

Frame Blending

As we mentioned earlier, if you time-stretch a layer, After Effects will either skip or copy frames of the layer to make up for the change in speed. If this produces clunky-looking playback, you can opt to turn on Frame Blending for a layer. For example, if you time-stretch a layer by a factor of 200%, by default After Effects will play each frame of the clip twice to double the clip's playing time. If you turn on Frame Blending for that layer, instead of copying the frames, After Effects will create new frames that are interpolations of the existing frames to make it look as though frames really do exist for the newly specified duration. This is true for clips that are either sped up or slowed down. Turning on Frame Blending for a layer whose frame rate matches its composition won't make any appreciable difference because a frame exists for every frame in the composition.

Note For what we hope is a fairly obvious reason, Frame Blending doesn't do anything to a still image.

Going back to our 200% stretch example, real frames from the source clip only really exist for every other frame that is displayed. If Frame Blending is turned on and the layer is set to Draft quality, After Effects blends the two nearest frames to create a step between. If Frame Blending is turned on and the layer is set to Best quality, After Effects blends up to 11 frames (instead of the two nearest frames, it looks at the five before and after the current time in the clip). In either case but especially at Best quality, After Effects needs to do some serious "thinking," or number crunching to render the new frames in between the existing ones in the clip. You should be careful about turning it on because your previews and your renders will take a noticeable performance hit. Experiment with this technique by stepping through the frames of a composition with the Page Up (sometimes labeled PgUp) and Page Down (sometimes labeled PgDn) keys to see what kinds of results it produces. Try it for clips that are both slowed down and sped up. Figure 12-7 shows a Timeline with Frame Blending turned on at both the Layer and the Comp level.

Caution　　Turning on Frame Blending for a layer whose frame rate matches its composition's frame rate will still result in the performance hit we mentioned, even though you won't see any difference in the clip. Be prudent when turning this feature on. Use it only if it's appropriate.

Note　　We should also point out that Frame Blending can be used on a layer whose native frame rate differs from the composition into which it's placed. Say that you put a 15 fps clip into a 30 fps comp. If you enable Frame Blending for the layer, After Effects will create steps in between. In other words, a layer doesn't necessarily need to be time-stretched in order for you to take advantage of Frame Blending.

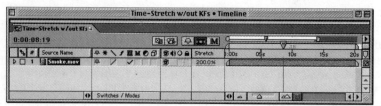

Figure 12-7: In order to see After Effects create new frames for a time-stretched clip, turn on Frame Blending at both the Layer and Comp level.

Understanding Time-Remapping

If you thought time-stretching was fun, wait until you get your head around time-remapping. Time-remapping enables you to speed up, slow down, or stop a clip altogether by using keyframes. Remember when Superman flew around the Earth so fast that it slowly came to a halt and started spinning backwards? Well, it's kind of like that in terms of the kinds of things you can do with video clips. Complete the following short series of steps to see how to enable and manipulate time-remapping for a layer.

Note Unlike time-stretching, time-remapping doesn't affect existing animation keyframes.

STEPS: Time-Remapping a Layer

1. **Create a new composition and place a video clip footage item into it.** Once again, this works best if the footage has an obvious temporal progression. For this exercise, we use the same stock footage of smoke, only this time we burned timecode on it. The point is that you want to be able to visually determine whether the clip is moving forwards or backwards in time with ease. Make the comp a good bit longer than the running time of the clip you add to it. That way you can stretch the clip without worrying about running out of room in the Timeline. You can always trim your comp's length after you're finished.

2. **In the Timeline, with the layer selected, choose Layer ➪ Enable Time Remapping (Command+Option+T/Ctrl+Alt+T).**

3. **Press the U key to display any properties containing keyframes.** This solos the time-remapping keyframes for the layer. See Figure 12-8 for reference.

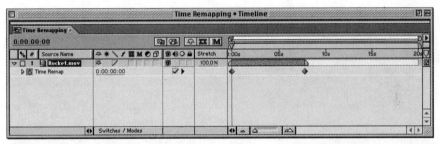

Figure 12-8: Enabling time-remapping for a layer adds the Time Remap property to that layer in the Timeline. By default, two keyframes are created for the first and last frames of the clip, respectively.

 Tip Pressing RR solos the Time Remap property of a clip if the property has been enabled.

That's how you set up time-remapping. Now the real fun begins. The two keyframes visible in Figure 12-8 represent the first and last frames of the clip. The grayed out area to the right of the layer in the Timeline indicates that you can extend the clip's Out point wherever you like. Experiment with moving the two existing keyframes to different locations in the Timeline. For example, if you move the last keyframe to the left by a couple of seconds, you'll make the entire clip play faster by those two seconds. That would essentially be time-stretching the layer by a factor of less than 100%. What sets time-remapping apart is that you can set multiple keyframes that increase and decrease a layer's speed by various degrees throughout the same clip.

Using the keyframe navigator, add multiple keyframes to the Time Remap property. Shift their position in the Timeline and preview the results.

After you add multiple keyframes to the Time Remap property and reposition them in the Timeline, you can view their velocity on the corresponding Time Graph. Look at Figure 12-9 for reference. When you move Time Remap keyframes, you speed up or slow down the portions of the clip between those keyframes. The Time Remap value at the upper-left corner of the Time Graph tells you which frame of the original clip is visible at the current time. In this example, the range of the graph is defined by the first and last frame of the clip as indicated by the values at the top and the bottom of the Time Graph. If you look at the velocity graph, positive values indicate forward playback, and negative values denote reverse playback. Lines below the dotted line indicate reverse playback. The range shown in the margin of the velocity graph indicates the maximum and minimum playback speeds of the clip (+100% is normal playback).

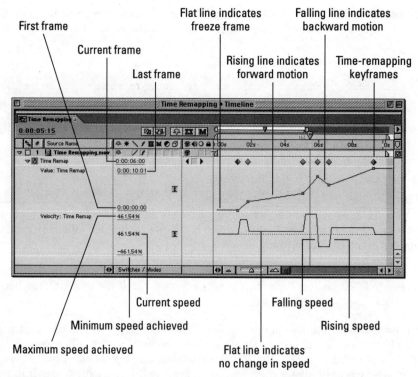

Figure 12-9: After you add multiple keyframes to the Time Remap property and reposition them in the Timeline, look at their velocity on the corresponding Time Graph.

Using the Layer window to see two timelines

Double-click the layer in the Timeline to view the Layer window for the time-remapped layer (see Figure 12-10). You probably notice some unusual things about this Layer window right away. Most importantly, there are two Timelines. The one on the bottom shows the layer as it exists in the Comp. The one on top represents the original clip. To help you understand what's really happening in this part of the interface, the timecode burn in the lower-right corner of the image matches the time of the top timeline. Preview the layer's playback by hitting the spacebar, and you'll see the playheads of the two timelines move around disproportionately in relation to the shifts you specified by moving around the time-remapping keyframes. Very cool indeed.

Figure 12-10: The Layer window for a time-remapped layer contains two Timelines. The top one refers to the original clip. The bottom one refers to the time-remapped layer as it exists in the composition. For easier comprehension, the timecode burned into the image matches the time value of the top Timeline.

Image courtesy of ArtBeats (Starter Kit)

Setting time-remapping keyframes

Everything you know about temporal keyframe interpolation can be applied here. You can set and manipulate Hold, Bezier, Continuous Bezier, and Linear keyframes at will in the Time Graph. To that end, you can use the Keyframe Assistant to create Easy Ease keyframes as well. Using the Pen tool, you can add keyframes and convert their control points in the Time Graph. You can also tweak the Bezier handles in either graph to change a keyframe's speed and extend its influence. Just remember that if you drastically slow a clip down, you may want to enable Frame Blending to keep the playback from losing its fluidity. Experiment with these different velocity adjustments using as many different kinds of footage as you can get your hands on. For example, try speeding up and slowing down the spinning of a planet, the flight of a hummingbird, the punches in a boxing match, and so on. The Time graph gives you clues as to the relative playback speed of a video layer so that you can set your keyframes accordingly.

Preparing footage for time-remapping

In order to truly take advantage of this marvelous feature, you'd be well advised to shoot film at unusually high frame rates. You can't do this with video cameras because their frame rate is fixed (NTSC is 29.97 fps, and PAL is 25 fps). If you're working in film media and know you want to slow down your footage while maintaining a high degree of detail, plan your shoot with the DP well in advance so that he or she is aware of the need for an unusually high frame rate. This will affect their choice of film stock and factor into their lighting decisions. The point here is that if you really need to slow down the footage when time-remapping, you'll still have enough frames to play with so that your playback won't be compromised. If you look at dramatic shifts in speed during some scenes in a movie such as *The Matrix,* you can be sure that some of those cameras captured as many as 300 frames a second.

✦   ✦   ✦

Using Effects: The Big Fun

◆   ◆   ◆   ◆

◆   ◆   ◆   ◆

Photoshop in Motion: Color Correction and Selective Blurring

In the world of Adobe graphics software, After Effects completes an amazing triad of tremendous applications. Illustrator is a superb piece of software that enables you to use vectors as a means of illustration. Photoshop is the ultimate image editor. Enter After Effects, which completes the equation, taking the strengths of both of those applications and putting them in motion for whatever media you can imagine. After Effects has sometimes been called Photoshop at 30 frames per second. It's really an interesting hybrid of Photoshop *and* Illustrator at however many frames per second you desire.

You really don't need to know Photoshop or Illustrator at the doctorate level before commencing any meaningful work in After Effects. Of course, knowledge doesn't hurt, but there are a number of people who have bypassed Adobe's excellent still image creation tools and jumped directly into After Effects' realm of motion without missing a step. Our opinion is that a working knowledge of these applications is all that's needed to start making After Effects compositions that have some real punch.

This chapter contains a good deal of information about using After Effects as the animated equivalent of skills you may or may not have acquired when editing images in Photoshop.

If you're a Photoshop junkie, you should find it interesting to see how you can use After Effects to do what are typically thought of as Photoshop tasks, such as color correction. If you arrived here and don't really have any chops with Photoshop-type skills, don't worry. Either way, we explain how you can use After Effects to handle features, like sharpening an image or desaturating its color.

Applying the Adjust Effects to Footage

The first group of effects we look at is the Adjust series of effects (see Figure 13-1). At this point, some of you may be excited by the prospect of applying effects to your footage and ending up with your very own *Close Encounters of the Third Kind* after only a day's work and a night's render. You should know that After Effects is primarily about taking footage and improving its visual quality in subtle and elegant ways. A surprisingly large amount of the best work in After Effects consists of correcting color, sharpening contrast, tweaking levels, and the like. If you're looking for pyrotechnics, we cover a lot of those kinds of effects in the chapters that follow, but don't lose sight of the basics. If you can take ordinary footage and turn it into richly colored broadcast quality visuals, you'll begin to see that a lot of effects, while they may be a blast to use, are really "gravy" in some sense.

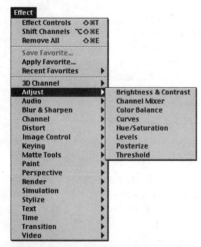

Figure 13-1: The Adjust group of effects forms the core of After Effects' strengths as a post-production tool.

Cross-Reference   Chapter 8 describes working with effects in general. If you aren't familiar with applying effects or working in the Effect Controls window, take the time to read (or re-read) the beginning of Chapter 8.

Just as a prefatory explanation, we want to mention that our discussion of effects is a biased and opinionated description of only those effects we think are helpful when working on an After Effects project. There are a number of filters that we rarely, if ever, use, and while we discuss all of them, some get scant coverage simply because we don't really see the need to explain something in great detail for which we feel you have no real use.

As far as the following explanations of effects are concerned, we created an After Effects project that includes a composition for each effect we cover in the chapter. Just as a reminder, you need to copy the *Source Material* folder from the DVD-ROM to your hard drive. Additionally, the exercises that follow cover some of these effects in detail. Our own corresponding After Effects project is called *Chapter 13.aep* and can be found in the *Project Files/Chapter 13* folder. Feel free to substitute your own footage with the examples shown in the figures and exercises.

The Online Help (choose Help ➪ After Effects Help) is an HTML document that goes well beyond the printed User's Guide in explaining After Effects in detail. In addition to containing all the information included in the User's Guide, the Online Help contains a lot of very useful basic information on all of the effects that ship with After Efffects. Refer to it as often as you need to; our purpose in writing about these effects is to supplement that information rather than repeat it.

Using the Brightness and Contrast effect

In essence, this filter is a quick and dirty fix. We don't like to use it, period. It's a clumsy tool that doesn't have any means by which you can adjust an image's highlights, midtones, or shadows. Using it, you can make an entire image brighter or darker, more contrasted or less contrasted. If that's all you need, then go ahead and use it. Chances are, you're going to need far more control when manipulating an image, and thankfully there are several filters that give you that control. For those sorts of adjustments, we rely upon Levels and Curves, in the tradition of Photoshop.

Using the Channel Mixer effect

We don't use this filter that often, but it is a fairly interesting effect that has its place. After you apply it to a layer in the Timeline, the resulting Effect Controls window visually assaults you with a large number of sliders. Each of these sliders controls how much of the information in the first channel of the pairings (*Red*-Red. *Red*-Green. *Red*-Blue, and so on) is derived from the second channel of the pairings (Red-*Red*. Red-*Green*. Red-*Blue,* and so on). By default, the filter leaves a layer unchanged by telling it to get 100% of its red influence from the information in the red channel, 100% of its green influence from the information in the green channel, and 100% of its blue influence from the information in the blue channel. You can change this so that any of the color channels can become a mixture of the information in the other channels. For example, you could set it so that the red channel is made up of any combination of the other channels besides red. You can also select the Monochrome option to create a grayscale image based on the various channels' input.

The most immediately useful application of this filter is to create stylized tinting effects. Complete the following steps to see how to employ this technique. Once again, we remind you that you should push every button and experiment with all of the sliders to see what works and what doesn't. You can also keyframe these properties so that they subtly ease in over time.

STEPS: Adding a Stylized Tint to Footage

1. **If you haven't already, open After Effects and save a new project.**
   Remember, you can use our project called *Chapter 13.aep* if you like.

2. **Create a new composition by dragging a footage item on to the New Composition button at the bottom of the Project Window.**

Save time when editing effects

At this point, we should review some basic effect editing techniques that are helpful time-savers.

✦ After you apply an effect, you often benefit from resizing the Effect Controls window so that you have greater control over the increments of any adjustments you make when moving a slider left or right (see Figure SB 13-1).

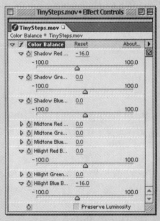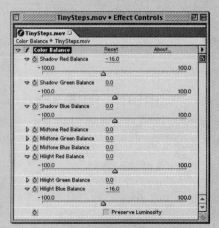

Figures SB 13-1: Resizing the Effect Controls window gives you more control over the increments of a slider.

✦ If you need to pull up the Effect Controls window, don't forget your keyboard short-cuts either. Use F3 or Command+Shift+T/Ctrl+Shift+T to bring this window to the foreground at will. You can also set an effect's properties underneath the layer's Effects twirler in the Timeline.

✦ Contextual clicking (Control+click/right-click) a value in the Effect Controls window enables you to take advantage of some useful features, such as Reset Value (see Figure SB 13-2). It's a lot better than using the Reset function at the top of the Effect Controls window because you can reset individual values, especially if you only want to reset one value within an effect for which you've correctly set 20 other values. Also, remember that every effect property with a stopwatch can be animated.

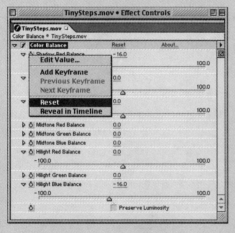

Figure SB 13-2: Contextual clicking (Control+click/right-click) in the Effect Controls window enables certain powerful options, not the least of which is the ability to reset individual effect properties.

✦ Sometimes the quality setting of a layer impacts the result of an effect pretty drasti-cally. For example, Fast Blur behaves very differently when it's applied to a layer in Draft Quality as opposed to when it's applied to the same layer at Best quality. See for yourself if you like, or you can wait until we cover these filters later on in the chapter.

✦ The most important effects timesaver of all is the ability to save Favorites. Whenever and wherever you can, use this feature to save and apply groupings of effects as well as any keyframes that may be associated with them. If you need a refresher on this aspect of effects, repeat the favorites exercise in Chapter 8.

3. **Rename the new comp to clearly indicate its contents.** Our composition is called *Channel Mixer* and includes some film footage transferred to video, entitled *TinySteps.mov*.

4. **Select the layer in the Timeline if it isn't already selected.**

5. **Choose Effect ⇨ Adjust ⇨ Channel Mixer.**

6. **Single out the channel that contains the best grayscale image by clicking each of the single channel selection buttons at the bottom of the Comp window.** For our image, the most richly detailed channel is red.

7. **Armed with this information, change the values of the effect properties so that the green and blue channels get 100% of their influence from the red channel.** If that sounds confusing, look at Figure 13-2 for reference.

Typically, when it comes to video, most of the detail in an image usually resides in the green channel. This isn't mere trivia, especially if you need to pull grayscale images from video sources on a regular basis.

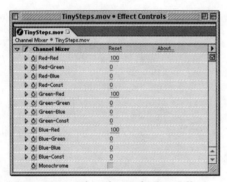

Figure 13-2: The Channel Mixer effect properties are adjusted so that the Comp window contains a grayscale image based solely on the information in the red channel.

Image courtesy of Director of Photography, Axel Baumann

8. **Tweak the remaining sliders to experiment with stylized color treatments.** For example, if you additionally adjust only one color channel's properties, you can create a single color tint. If you work across two additional colors, you can create a tint based on two colors (that is, Red-Blue set to 60 and Blue-Green set to –80). You can also make psychedelic distortions if that's what your shot needs.

Using the Color Balance effect

This filter breaks each color channel's input into shadows, midtones, and high-lights. These terms refer to an image's darker, medium, and lighter areas. If you want to maintain the luminance values of the original image, select Preserve Luminosity. If you look at the same color correction tool in Photoshop, it appears as it does in Figure 13-3. The equivalent effect in After Effects appears in the Effect Controls window as shown in Figure 13-4.

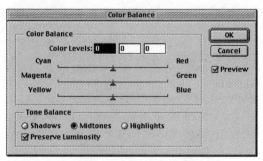

Figure 13-3: Compare the Color Balance adjustment window in Photoshop with its counterpart in After Effects.

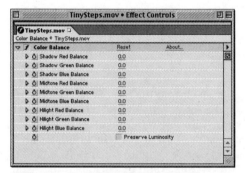

Figure 13-4: Compare the Color Balance effect in the Effect Controls window in After Effects with its counterpart in Photoshop.

The changes to the interface between applications are necessitated by the need to make the effect properties keyframeable, but the filter is identical to its corresponding function in Photoshop. It's pretty useful to know that the absence of red, green, and blue indicates the presence of cyan, magenta, and yellow, respectively. In other words, you can increase the levels of cyan, magenta, and yellow in an image's darker, medium, and lighter areas by pushing this effect's sliders to the left. Ultimately, while less precise, this filter is no different than using Levels or Curves. It's just a different way of manipulating the same data. Experiment with it, but we recommend that you first learn Levels and Curves, at which point you can return to it to see if it holds any extra value for you.

Using the Curves effect

On our way through this section, you may have noticed that we are hyping this effect quite a bit. The reason for this is that the Curves filter gives you complete control over any specific range of an image's pixels. Furthermore, you can import Photoshop curves into After Effects. So, how does this work, and why do we refer to it as one of the better color correction methods. Apply it to a layer so that you can see the Curves graph in the Effect Controls window (see Figure 13-5).

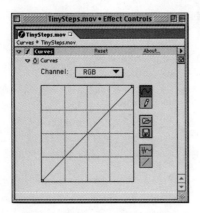

Figure 13-5: The initial appearance of the Curves effect

The bottom of the graph represents 100% black, and the top of the graph represents 100% white. The line running from the lower-left corner to the upper-right corner represents the distribution of color values within the pixels of an image. The pop-up menu in the Effect Controls enables you to alter the graph for all of the RGB channels together, or you can influence each channel separately, including the alpha channel. You can add control points to this graph by clicking directly on the line. If you click the center of the line and drag the newly added control point up towards the upper-left corner, you'll increase the color values of the layer's midtones. Conversely, if you drag the control point toward the lower-right corner, you'll decrease those values (see Figure 13-6). Adding a control point to the center of the line and moving it works well for basic adjustments, but check out some more specific controls by using Curves.

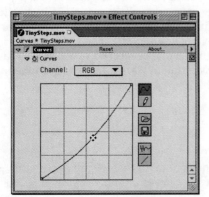

Figure 13-6: With the Curves effect, you can have a broad impact on the middle range of an image by adding a control point in the middle of the graph and dragging it up or down.

You can click the line to add up to 15 control points. That's all good and fine, but if you want to zero in on specific parts of an image, here's a solid and reliable technique:

✦ Isolate the part of the image that you want to adjust by "framing" it with control points. For example, say that you want to brighten the lighter parts of an image. Set two control points on the curve that are just a bit outside of the range that you want to focus on, and then set two more points at the boundaries of the range you want to work on. This sounds a little confusing, but it's easier to see than to explain. Look at Figures 13-7 and 13-8 to better understand this concept of manipulating curves.

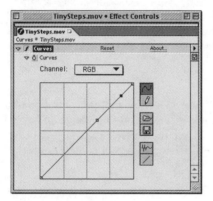

Figure 13-7: Set two control points on the curve that are just a bit outside of the range that you want to focus on.

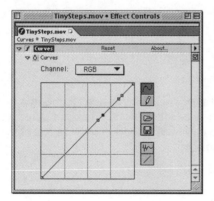

Figure 13-8: Set two more points at the boundaries of the range that you want to work on. We're focusing on the brighter part of an image in this example.

✦ Now you want to set another control point in the middle of your selected range and drag it up or down to influence the range of pixels you defined with your control points. Look at Figure 13-9 to see what this looks like. If you hadn't framed off that range of pixels, then influencing that section of the curve would have had a greater impact on the rest of the image because the entire line bends to move smoothly through all of the curve's control points. Figure 13-10 displays the result of attempting to influence the same range of pixels without having "framed" your range with additional control points. This will prove to be the most important trait about this effect as you begin experimenting with it to see what it can do for you. In essence, how can you influence the part of an image you need to change without adversely affecting the rest of the pixels in the image? The answer is by experimenting with additional control points. Practice this a lot. Mastering it will give you real control. Combined with the Levels effect, Curves is an excellent color correction tool.

Tip

If you really want to know what's up with the Curves effect, apply it to a grayscale image, especially a gradient of some kind. You can create a gradient with Photoshop, or you can use the Ramp filter from the Render group of Effects. Watching how the Curves filter clamps blacks and whites and increases or decreases intermediate color values is an invaluable way to truly figure out what the Curves filter is all about.

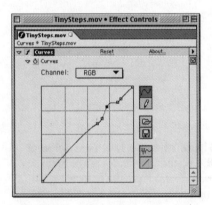

Figure 13-9: Set another control point in the middle of your selected range and drag it up or down to influence the range of pixels that you defined with your control points.

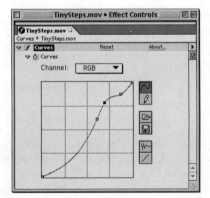

Figure 13-10: If you don't frame your range with additional control points, changes to a curve will broadly impact the rest of the image.

✦ You can clip white and black values by dragging the ends of the line in toward the middle of the graph. Look at Figure 13-11 to better understand this particular concept.

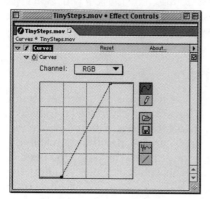

Figure 13-11: You can clip white and black values by dragging the ends of the line in toward the middle of the graph.

While you can animate the Curves effect, the resulting interpolation can cause some noisy bumps along the way. By noise, we mean stray pixels that are loudly offset from their neighbors that muddy an otherwise clear image. For that reason, we recommend against animating Curves. Setting them only once for an image is best, or at least once per edited clip within a series of clips, which you can separate as different layers in a composition.

✦ You can remove a point from the graph by dragging it off of the graph.

✦ You can smooth out a curved line with the smooth button.

✦ You can save your curves as an *.acv* file with the save button, and you can load curves from either Photoshop or After Effects with the load button.

✦ If you click the Pencil tool, you can draw what's called an arbitrary map to define an image's color interpretation. Experiment with it if by drawing in the graph if you like. You may get some interesting and severely blown out results. We hardly ever use this method, though. If you play with it a bit, you will begin to grasp the mechanics of the graph. For example, if you set the line to run from the upper-left corner to the lower-right corner, you'll completely invert an image.

✦ Click the Bezier control point button above the pencil button, and the Curves line now has nine evenly spaced control points on it. If you want to get rid of these, click either the reset button at the top of the Effect Controls window or straighten the line by clicking the linear graph button beneath the smooth curve button.

Tip

We remind you that you can use Curves on individual color channels as well as the alpha channel. In the *Chapter 13.aep* project on the DVD-ROM, we created a Curves-Alpha composition to very simply demonstrate an adjustment to an alpha channel's curves when the alpha is derived from a crude mask. If your alpha channel has a wide range of grayscale values, adjustments to its curve can make for some pretty interesting stylized transparency.

Using the Hue/Saturation effect

Some folks love the Hue/Saturation effect because it carries over almost identically from Photoshop. Others don't like it so much because its interface is pretty confusing. You can divide the use of this effect into two categories. Either you can make adjustments to the HSL balance of a layer, or you can colorize (read, tint) it. By default, the colorize options are disabled; in order to turn them on, you need to select the Colorize check box in the Effect Controls window. When you initially apply this effect to a layer, it appears as shown in Figure 13-12. More often than not, you'll use this filter like you would use Levels or Curves by generally applying it once to an image that needs overall color correction.

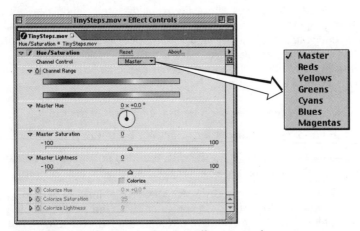

Figure 13-12: The Hue/Saturation Effect Controls are pretty confusing at first.

Cross-Reference

We discuss the difference between RGB and HSL colorspace in Chapter 11, which focuses on transfer modes. The four transfer modes, Hue, Saturation, Color, and Luminosity, all operate in HSL colorspace. A particular color is not different between the two colorspaces. The difference between different colorspaces is best defined when you look at how the same color is created from different colorspaces. A specific color is arrived at quite differently when it's derived from a combination of red, green, and blue as opposed to when it's derived from a combination of a specific hue value and saturation and brightness levels.

Adjusting HSL values within the Channel Range property

Putting aside colorization for the moment, when it comes to tweaking the HSL balance features, the important factor to remember here is that you can animate this effect's properties despite the fact that the only visible stopwatch in the Effect Controls appears to exist for the Channel Range property. If you fuss with the color bars representing the Channel Range, nothing happens. Clicking, dragging, and contextual clicking all leave those color bars unchanged. So what are they there for?

The Channel Range property is defined by the subdivisions of hue, saturation, and lightness. The top color bar represents the range of input values for the hues within an image, and the bottom color bar represents the output values. In other words, if a hue in an image looks like it does in the top bar, it will appear in the Comp window as it does in the color bar directly beneath it in the Effect Controls window.

You can shift the position of the bottom color bar by changing the position of the hue dial (hues are measured on a 360 degree scale). You can also change a layer's saturation and lightness percentages with their corresponding sliders. If you set a Channel Range keyframe, any changes to these three values will be animated over time. This is understandably confusing because there aren't any stopwatches next to any of these properties. Just know that the channel range property includes those three subdivisions. For example, if you want to change a layer's HSL values over time, click the channel range stopwatch to set an initial keyframe, change the current time, and then adjust the hue, saturation and lightness values. This will set another channel range keyframe, and all of the specified changes will take place during the time between the keyframes. The effect would no doubt be improved if you could animate the individual HSL values, but as it stands, it's still a pretty neat tool.

By default, the Master Hue is visible in the Effect Controls. You can use the Channel Control pop-up window at the top of the Hue/Saturation Effect Controls to specify parts of an image other than the Master Hue; specifically, you can define color ranges for reds, yellows, greens, cyans, blues, and magentas. For example, if you wanted to change the color of an actor's red shoes within a piece of footage, you could specify Reds in the Channel Control pop-up, and then animate a hue shift within the reds so that those colors change over time. Of course, that may be more difficult than it sounds because you'll be changing all of the red values within the entire image, but you could duplicate the layer and mask the shoes and apply the effect to only the masked layer. That's the start of a brainstorm, anyway (see the Hue/Saturation comp in the *Chapter 13.aep* project on the DVD-ROM).

To change the hue within the narrower color ranges besides the Master Hue in the Channel Control pop-up, select, say Reds, for example (see Figure 13-13). The smaller rectangular sliders define the color range for reds, and the triangular sliders determine the "fall off" for variations within the various red hues. The "fall off" accounts for feathered gradations that run along the red hue's outer boundaries within its defined range.

Caution

In other words, if you push the "fall off" in too close to the rectangular sliders, you run the risk of incurring noisy pixelated distortions at the outer limits of the red hue in the original image.

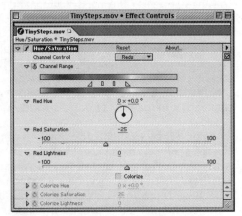

Figure 13-13: The Hue/Saturation Effect Controls appear with additional slider controls if you select anything other than Master from the Channel Control pop-up menu.

By default, the color range is 30 degrees, and each "fall off" margin equals 30 degrees. This allows for feathered colors wherever red colors in the original image don't fall exactly within the center of the specified red color range. You can move all of these sliders as you choose. As we told you a moment ago, you can use this filter to change the color of objects within an image. Just don't forget that images are comprised of a mixture of colors, and if you change the hue of reds in an image, you change the hue for ALL reds, whether or not they're plainly visible.

Colorizing a layer with the Hue/Saturation effect

As we stated at the beginning of this effect's description, you can tint an image by selecting the Colorize option at the bottom of the effect's controls (see Figure 13-14). After you do this, you can specify the hue of the tint as well as its saturation and luminance. If you need a quick tint, this feature works just fine. Unlike the Tint filter in the Image Control group of effects, this effect preserves an image's original luminance values, whereas the Tint filter maps the black and white values of an image to two colors of your choice. Selecting Colorize turns off the effect's other features.

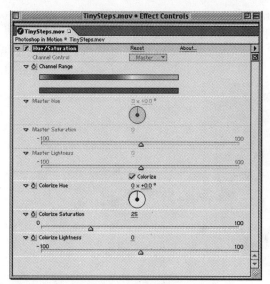

Figure 13-14: The Hue/Saturation Effect Controls change in appearance once again if you select the Colorize option.

Using the Levels effect

Along with Curves, Levels is our other favorite among the color correction tools. If you apply it to a layer in the Timeline, its appearance in the resulting Effect Controls window is marked by the presence of the Histogram (see Figure 13-15 and Color Plate 13-1). The Histogram is a very cool visual representation of data. The horizontal length of the graph represents the brightness values of an image starting from the left at 0, or black, and going towards the right to 255, or white. This effect works in 16-bit color, in which case white would be 32768(!). The shapes within the graph represent the distribution of a layer's pixels within the brightness range. For example, a large "mound" in the middle indicates a lot of gray intermediate values; for that matter, large concentrations at the outer limits of the graph indicate the presence of a lot of very dark and very light values. To sum up the Histogram, the X-axis represents brightness, and the Y-axis represents the pixels of an image.

By default, when you initially apply the Levels effect, you're looking at a combination of the red, green, and blue channels. As is the case with Curves, you can view the levels for the individual channels as well as the alpha channel with the pop-up menu located at the top of the Effect Controls window. In our example in Figure 13-15 (again, also see Color Plate 13-1), it appears as though the brightest pixels top out in the neighborhood of 210, and the black letterbox that frames the image isn't really black. Instead, it's a muddy mix of the color channels in the 20 range, and the Histogram reflects this brightness distribution.

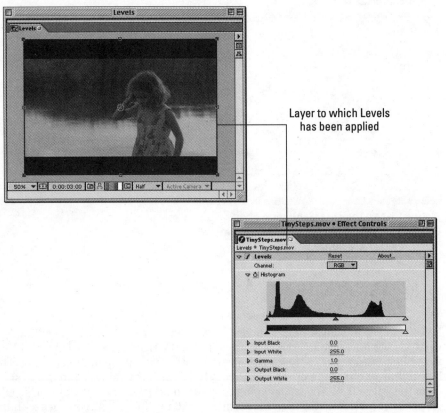

Layer to which Levels
has been applied

Figure 13-15: The Levels Histogram indicates how an image's pixels are distributed along the range of brightness values from black (left) to white (right).
Image courtesy of Axel Baumann, Director of Photography

You can confirm this pixel data with the Info palette by dragging your pointer over the various parts of the image. The Info palette tells you the exact color values for the pixels underneath the pointer. Clearly, this image is in need of a little help as far as color correction is concerned. Ideally, you want the brightest parts of the image, such as the reflection of the sun on the water, to be closer to white, and you definitely want the black letterbox to be completely black. These adjustments will improve the overall highlights and contrast of the footage. The following steps show you how to manipulate this powerful and extremely useful filter.

STEPS: Tweaking the Levels Effect

1. **Once you set up a composition, select a layer in the Timeline that needs color correction.** If you want to use our example, open the Levels comp in the *Chapter 13.aep* project on the DVD-ROM.

2. **Choose Effect ⇨ Adjust ⇨ Levels.**

3. **In the Effect Controls Window, move the slider at the right side of the Histogram so that it's positioned at the edge of the brightest part of the image.** This slider represents the Input White value. All pixels in the image that equal or exceed the Input White level are displayed as complete white. In our example, we set the Input White level to the brightest part of the image, and this very noticeably brightens the reflection of the sun on the water as well as increasing the brightness of the specular highlights on the girl's hair.

4. **Move the slider at the left side of the Histogram so that it's positioned at the edge of the darkest part of the image.** Tweaking levels improves with experience. In our example, the large spike in the darker portion of the graph represents the black letterbox that frames the image. To make certain that this is truly black, we positioned the Input Black slider just to the right of this concentration of pixels in the graph. We did this even though there are other black values before it in the graph where we could have placed the slider.

Tip

As we stated earlier, you can also use the numbers returned by the Info palette to help you set the Input Black level. Drag your pointer over a part of the image you know should be black and then manually enter the average of the RGB values returned by the Info palette into the Input Black field in the Levels Effect Controls.

5. **Move the middle slider to adjust the mid-range of an image.** This is called the Gamma property. As soon as we make our black and white adjustments to an image, we adjust this slider so that the image looks like it has the right degree of color balance. You can usually adjust the gamma by feel; in our case, we moved it to the left to increase the brightness of the middle range because it was so heavily influenced by the darker grass at the water's edge. The result of these changes in the Levels on our footage is shown in Figure 13-16 (see also Color Plate 13-2).

That's basically how we use the Levels effect. You can also adjust the values for the output displayed in the Comp window if you know you need to clamp these values. For example, setting the Output White to 230 guarantees that no pixel anywhere in the image will be higher than 230. The same logic applies to Output Black. We rarely use these parts of the filter though.

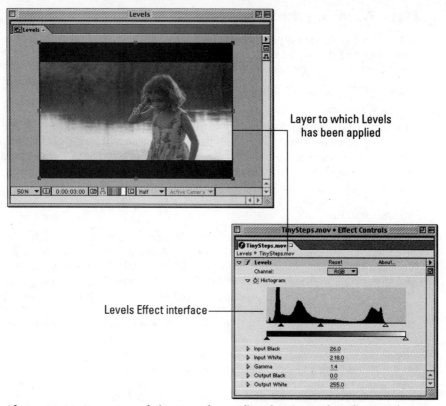

Layer to which Levels
has been applied

Levels Effect interface

Figure 13-16: You can vastly improve the quality of an image by adjusting the Input White, Input Black, and Gamma properties of the Levels effect.

Image courtesy of Axel Baumann, Director of Photography

As is the case with all of the color correction tools, you can animate all these values over time, and you may find a need to do this if there's a long lighting change in a shot, for example. Most of the time, we tweak a layer's levels only once for overall color correction. We almost always apply Levels to every clip that we captured for use in After Effects. Even if we don't tweak them, it's always good to confirm whether or not we captured footage correctly. As was the case with the footage in our example, however, it definitely needed some adjustment.

Note   If you step through the frames of a clip with the Levels Effect Controls open, the graph will change for each frame. Of course this makes sense, but we mention it in case your footage should get brighter or darker as it plays out in the Timeline. You may make the perfect color correction for a certain frame of a clip, only to realize that the remaining frames are differently white balanced. Our advice is to familiarize yourself with the entire contents of a layer before making global changes with the Levels effect.

Using the Posterize and Threshold effects

We group these two effects together because they share a certain handicap. One of After Effects' greatest assets, among many, is its capability to render images at the subpixel level. What does this mean? Subpixel rendering is better exemplified than explained, and if you apply either the Posterize or Threshold effects to a layer, you'll see what an effect looks like if it isn't programmed to display subpixel clarity.

Note A fairly good analogy for subpixel rendering is when you perform calculations to four decimal places, for example, when the result is actually a number to one decimal place. It makes the result more accurate.

For example, apply the Threshold effect to a layer in the Timeline that includes some video footage, and the results will appear rather clunky. Threshold simply takes the information of a pixel and changes it to either black or white. All pixels lighter than the value specified in the slider are converted to white, and all pixels beneath the threshold are converted to black. By default, it's set to 127, which is half the distance between black and white in 8-bit color. You can adjust this value to change the point at which pixels meet their simplistic black or white fate. While you can create some interesting stylized effects with this filter, it's clumsy and crude, to say the least. It's very "blocky" looking because no subpixel gradation is between the wholly black or white pixels created by applying this effect (see Figure 13-17).

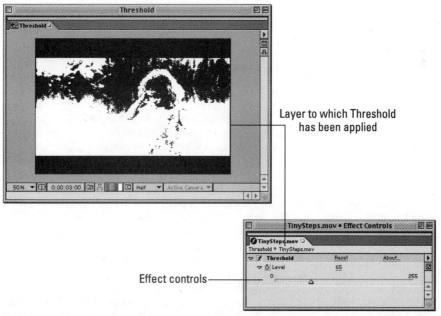

Figure 13-17: The Threshold effect is a rather clunky way to simplify an image into strictly black or white pixels.

Image courtesy of Axel Baumann, Director of Photography

If you apply Posterize to a layer in the Timeline that includes video footage of some sort, the results suffer from the same sort of handicap (see Figure 13-18). By default, Posterize is set to seven. What does seven mean, in this case? The answer is that it reduces the grayscale image comprising each color channel into seven separate values: black and white plus five intermediate shades of gray. The resulting image in the Comp window is a very compromised image. You can reduce the slider's value to two, which is basically the same as applying the threshold command to each individual color channel.

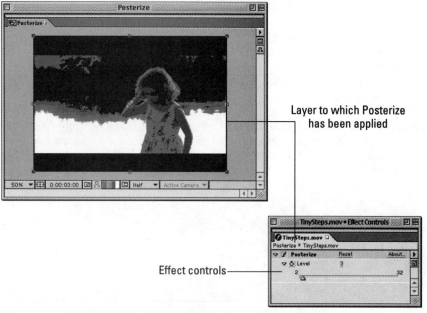

Layer to which Posterize
has been applied

Effect controls

Figure 13-18: The Posterize effect reduces the range of values in each color channel by the amount specified in its Effect Controls window.

Image courtesy of Axel Baumann, Director of Photography

In any case, we've never really found much use for these filters beyond creating certain stylistic effects. Nonetheless, Adobe specialist Alan Hamill disagrees and loves using them for creating "funky '70s-style" video graphics, and he's got a point. If you ever need to create a distinctly "retro" feel, these filters are a great place to start.

Wrapping up the Adjust effects

You want some real advice, some sort of decoder ring, some shred of something you can hang on to in this challenging and ever-changing world of post-production? Here goes: For good color correction results, you should apply the Levels filter to a layer, make adjustments there if necessary, and then you should add Curves if you need to augment more details. That's typically all you're going to need when it comes to solid color correction technique. Nonetheless, all of the Adjust effects

What's new in After Effects 5.5: The Levels (Individual Controls) effect

At first glance, it doesn't seem as though much value was added with the new Levels (Individual Controls) filter, shown in Figure SB 13-3. Upon further review, it becomes clear that this is a welcome addition to the Adjust group of effects. Now you can set keyframes for the levels within the individual red, green, and blue channels. Along the same lines, you can create expressions that take advantage of these more specific effect properties. For more info on expressions, see Chapter 25.

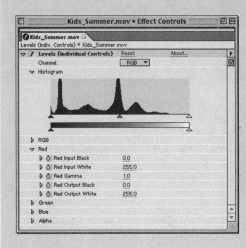

Figure SB 13-3: As its name suggests, the Levels (Individual Controls) effect offers tighter control over the levels of each individual channel.

render very quickly. No matter which one of these you use, there's no real performance hit as far as your render time goes.

Adding Basic Text

The basic focus of this chapter is on mimicking some of Photoshop's better features. In addition to making color correction adjustments to footage, you'll want to quickly add some basic text filters to your growing arsenal of effects.

Cross-Reference   We get into very elaborate text effects later in Chapters 21 and 22. The Basic Text filter doesn't involve too much blood, sweat, and tears on your part.

STEPS: Applying Basic Text to a Solid Layer

1. **Create a composition and add at least one layer of footage to it.**

2. **Choose Layer ➪ New ➪ Solid (Command+Y/Ctrl+Y).**

What's new in After Effects 5.5: The Color Stabilize effect (PB only)

If you've managed to procure the Production Bundle of After Effects 5.5, you'll find that the Color Stabilize filter is a great addition to the Adjust group of effects. You might be a whiz at manipulating levels and curves, but what good is your expertise if you're working with film that has varying levels of exposure within the same clip? If that's the particular bind you're in, the Color Stabilize effect will come in very handy.

After you apply the Color Stabilize effect to a layer comprised of a video clip, find a single frame of footage (called the "pivot" frame) that you've determined to be properly exposed. Once you've defined that frame, you can tell the Color Stabilizer to balance the remainder of the clip based on brightness (in which you only define a black point), levels (in which you define a black point and a white point), or curves (black, white, and mid-point). The Color Stabilizer effect looks at the rest of the frames within the clip and makes adjustments according to the levels that you set at the pivot frame.

The Color Stabilize effect is truly versatile. Firstly, you can animate the position of any of the reference points if your footage contains a lot of motion. If necessary, you may find it useful to use the Motion Tracker (see Chapter 27) to set precise keyframes for the position of the effect points. Secondly, you can control the size of the area that gets sampled at the reference points to account for grainy, "noisy" footage.

3. **In the Solid Settings dialog box, make the solid Comp Size and name it "Text" or something similar.** Don't worry about its color.

4. **Making sure that the new solid is selected in the Timeline, choose Effect ⇨ Text ⇨ Basic Text.**

5. **In the resulting Options dialog box, enter the text of your choice.** You can also specify other options for the layout of the text. See Figure 13-19 for reference.

Note   Your choice of fonts is limited by how many fonts you loaded onto your system.

6. **After you enter the text and options that you want, click OK.** Your text now appears in the Comp window. To make it appear as smooth as possible, set the solid layer to Best quality.

7. **Pull up the Effect Controls window for the solid layer by pressing F3 (see Figure 13-20).**

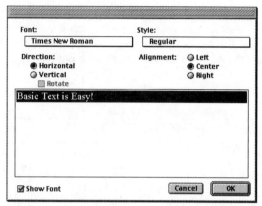

Figure 13-19: The Basic Text Options enable you to specify a font, style, direction, and alignment.

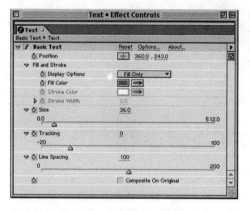

Figure 13-20: The Basic Text Effect Controls contain a fairly powerful range of properties for such a simple effect.

8. **Edit the effect properties so that the text appears the way you want it.** For example, change its position, specify a size for your chosen font, pick a fill color, change the tracking values (that's the space between letters, in case you don't know), and so on. You can even specify separate stroke and fill colors as well as a stroke point width.

If it's Basic Text you need, well then, that's what you get! Make a note of which properties can be animated by looking for stopwatches in the Effect Controls (see Figure 13-21). You can create some stylish-looking effects by animating the font size or tracking values.

Caution   One note about position: If you want to move your text around the Comp window with a motion blur, animate the position property of the solid layer, *not* the Basic Text effect's position property. Additionally, turn on Motion Blur for the solid layer as well as the comp.

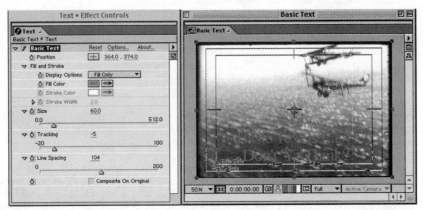

Figure 13-21: The Basic Text filter is a quick and easy solution for adding text to a composition.

Image courtesy of ArtBeats (Daring Men)

Applying the Blur and Sharpen Effects to Footage

You use the Blur and Sharpen group of filters in order to soften images ranging from noisy, pixelated source footage to text that contains edges that are unrelentingly harsh. They're indispensable design tools, and they also provide you with options when you have to work with footage that is otherwise less than perfect. If you are forging your way through the book in a linear fashion, you have already used the Fast Blur effect. Needless to say, one look at the Blur and Sharpen group of filters should tell you that there's more than one way to make an image fuzzy (see Figure 13-22).

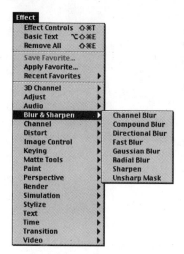

Figure 13-22: The Blur and Sharpen group of effects offers you multiple ways to soften an image.

Using Channel Blur

Adding Channel Blur to a layer gives you control over the blur in each color channel as well as the alpha channel (see Figure 13-23). As compared with Fast Blur or Gaussian Blur, which blurs the combined RGB channels, this effect has a lot more flexibility. Seasoned veterans from the world of After Effects really appreciate it on account of the alpha channel option. Experiment with the sliders to gauge the effect of this filter and be sure to experiment with the horizontal and vertical controls.

Because the alpha channel is the option most people get excited about, try applying this effect to some Illustrator text in a composition. The results can be surprising. If you look at Figure 13-24, you'll notice that blurring the alpha channel adds a stylish edge to the letters.

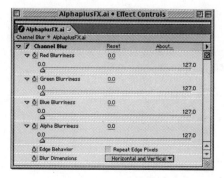

Figure 13-23: The Channel Blur Effect Controls give you control over the blur in each color channel as well as the alpha channel.

Figure 13-24: Slightly blurring the alpha channel of Illustrator text adds an interesting-looking outline to the letters.

Image courtesy of Axel Baumann, Director of Photography

Tip

If you ever need to make film footage look dated, you can slow it down a little and add a blur to the red channel. If you work at it, this can make your footage look as though it were shot on a Super8 film camera sometime in the '60s.

Using Compound Blur

The Compound Blur effect is an interesting one. If you want to take full advantage of it, you should use another layer as the displacement map for the effect. When you apply this effect to a layer, your Effect Controls appear as they do in Figure 13-25. The critical element of this effect is the Blur Layer pop-up menu. By default, the effect uses the same layer it's applied to as the Blur Layer. Compound Blur blurs a layer according to the luminance values of the selected Blur Layer.

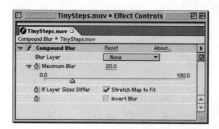

Figure 13-25: The Compound Blur Effect Controls is fairly unremarkable except for the Blur Layer pop-up menu.

In our example in Figure 13-26, we apply the Compound Blur effect to our layer of the girl at the water's edge by using the luminance of stock footage of smoke as the specified blur layer. When you use another layer as the displacement map for this effect, you'll probably want to hide it. You can do this either by turning off the displacement map layer's visibility switch or by placing it underneath the visible layers at the top of the stacking order.

Tip   You can create gradients in Photoshop, or you can apply the Ramp filter from the Render group of effects on to a solid layer to serve as a displacement map for the Compound Blur filter (see Figure 13-27). The term *displacement map* refers to any grayscale image that's used as the basis for certain kinds of distortion effects. The confusion is furthered by the fact that a Displacement Map filter is in the Distort group of effects. Stay tuned. More will be revealed.

Tip   You can animate the displacement map, which acts as the blur layer, and you can also animate the blur amount in the Compound Blur Effect Controls. With a little work, you can create some interesting focus shift animations. This is a popular technique that's visible in a lot of ads these days. A person in the foreground will be in focus, and then that person will dramatically disappear behind a blur while someone in the background suddenly jumps into focus. Of course, this is often achieved by shifting focus in camera, but you can easily pull it off in post-production by using the Compound Blur filter in conjunction with an animated displacement map.

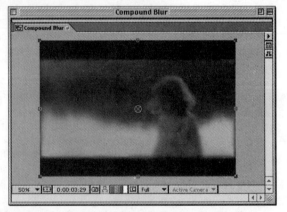

Figure 13-26: In this group of images, the first is the layer before we apply the Compound Blur, the second is the layer we're going to use as the Blur Layer, and the third is the original layer with the effect applied to it.

Images courtesy of ArtBeats (Starter Kit) and Axel Baumann, Director of Photography

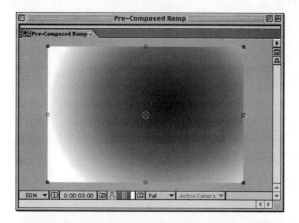

Figure 13-27: In this example, we use a solid with the Ramp filter applied to it as the Blur Layer. We set it up the ramp so that the girl's face is in focus.

Image courtesy of Axel Baumann, Director of Photography

Using Directional Blur

The Directional Blur filter is easy enough to understand with two properties, direction and amount. You can specify the direction by manipulating the radial dial. We provide you with two sets of pictures that can probably do a better job of explaining this filter than we can. Figure 13-28 shows a solid layer in a composition with both the Basic Text and Directional Blur filters applied to it. For the blur amount, we specified a value of ten, and we left the direction at its default. Figure 13-29 simply shows the difference made to the text when we changed the direction of the blur to 45 degrees. That's really all there is to it. You can set keyframes for either of its properties.

Figure 13-28: Some text with a little blur applied to it

Image courtesy of Axel Baumann, Director of Photography

Using Fast Blur and Gaussian Blur

These two blurs are the most commonly used blurs in the whole bunch. Typically, most post-production folks use them at very low levels to get rid of stray pixel noise in footage or to soften the hard edges of text. Using Illustrator text without any blur applied can often produce unsightly flickering edges. Applying a Gaussian Blur within the 0.1 to –0.3 range fixes this problem without visibly compromising the image quality. Of these two filters, the results of applying Fast Blur at draft quality differ considerably from the results when applying it at Best quality. Gaussian Blur produces the same results at either quality setting. Furthermore, Gaussian Blur takes a *lot* longer to render than Fast Blur, especially when applied at higher settings.

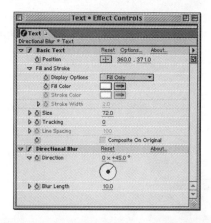

Figure 13-29: The same text with the direction of the blur changed to 45 degrees

Image courtesy of Axel Baumann, Director of Photography

Note

The term *Gaussian* is derived from the name of the famous German mathmetician Karl Friedrich Gauss (1777–1855). We say "famous," because he's pictured on the 10 Mark bill in Germany. He made vast contributions to mathematics and astronomy, and his work in quantifying bell curves ultimately gave rise to the Gaussian Blur in graphics software.

We put together a taste test for you in the following figures. Figure 13-30 is the original image. Figure 13-31 shows a Fast Blur setting of 30 applied to the layer set to draft quality. Figure 13-32 shows a Fast Blur setting of 30 applied to the same layer set to Best quality. Figure 13-33 shows a Gaussian Blur setting of 30 applied to the same layer. What's the difference between Figures 13-32 and 13-33? We don't see any, do you? If you need to keep your render times to a minimum, we recommend that you use Fast Blur because hardly any appreciable difference is between the two.

Tip   Fast Blur is especially cool because it has a Repeat Pixels option. Turning this on keeps you from getting strange buildups of pixels at the edge of an image when you really crank up the blur setting. This is especially useful when it comes to the alpha channel so that your transparency doesn't get overly distorted.

Tip   Both filters enable you to limit a blur to either the horizontal or vertical dimension. While you can't animate this property gradually, you can animate it with hold keyframes.

Figure 13-30: The original image before applying any blur filters

Image courtesy of Axel Baumann, Director of Photography

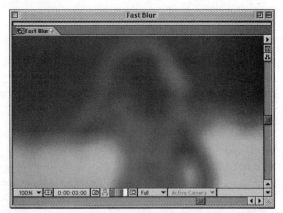

Figure 13-31: The same footage with a Fast Blur setting of 30 applied to the layer set to draft quality

Image courtesy of Axel Baumann, Director of Photography

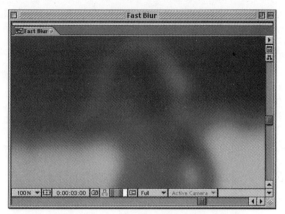

Figure 13-32: The same footage with a Fast Blur setting of 30 applied to the same layer set to Best quality

Image courtesy of Axel Baumann, Director of Photography

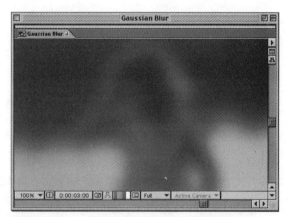

Figure 13-33: The same footage with a Gaussian Blur setting of 30 applied to the same layer

Image courtesy of Axel Baumann, Director of Photography

Using Radial Blur

The Radial Blur filter is a little on the "noisy" side, but it is pretty interesting. Its properties are visible in a fairly unconventional looking Effect Controls window that appears in Figure 13-34. You can specify either a Radial or Zoom type blur, and the blur amount increases as you move out from the effect's control point. You can move the effect control point in the Comp window or by dragging in the blur map inside the Effect Controls window. You can also set the anti-aliasing quality of the blur when it's applied to a layer that's set to Best quality. At draft quality, this setting has no effect. We rarely use this effect, but on those rare occasions when we do, we also apply the Fast Blur filter to the layer to clean up the stray pixels that result from the initial application of Radial Blur.

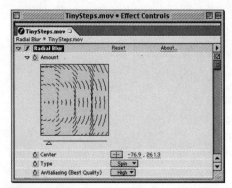

Figure 13-34: The Radial Blur properties in this Effect Controls window are a little unusual.

Using Sharpen and Unsharp Mask

Unlike the blur filters, these two perform the opposite of a blur because they increase the contrast of neighboring pixels. These filters appear to sharpen the image quality of the layer that they're applied to, but the resulting noise is a bit overwhelming. Sharpen increases the brightness and color contrast of neighboring pixels, and Unsharp Mask does the same thing where it senses "edges," or dramatic shifts in color and brightness.

These filters are carried over from Photoshop, and they work well with still images, but they produce pretty uninspiring results when applied to moving images. Still, they can produce an interesting visually stylized effect if your output medium doesn't suffer too much from adding noise; for example, if you're creating movies that will end up as streaming media, then Unsharp Mask creates some cool looking edges. Generally though, we avoid these filters.

✦   ✦   ✦

Color Plate 11-1: We created this still image by exporting a single frame from a composition we made out of different colored solids. In addition to providing black, white, and gray solids, we made certain to include fully and partially saturated areas of color.

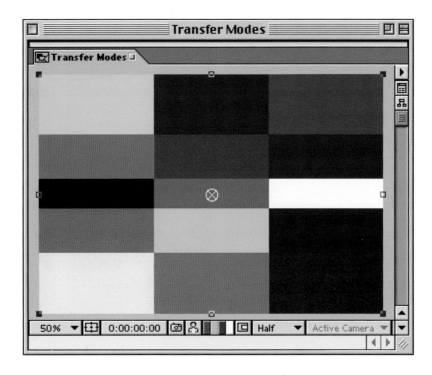

Color Plate 11-2: This image is an exported frame from a QuickTime movie of a stylized American flag. *Image courtesy of Digital Juice (Jump Backs, Vol. 7)*

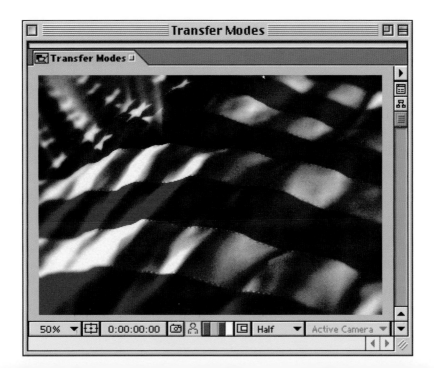

Color Plate 11-3: The Comp window reflects the result of applying the different transfer modes to the top layer of colored solids. *Image courtesy of Digital Juice (Jump Backs, Vol. 7)*

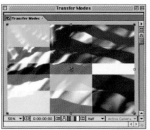 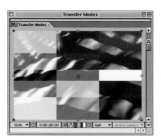 

Add   **Multiply**   **Screen**   **Overlay**

  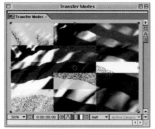 

Soft Light   **Hard Light**   **Color Dodge**   **Color Burn**

 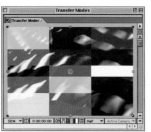 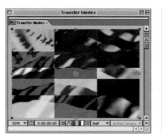 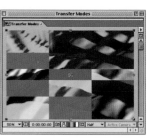

Darken   **Lighten**   **Difference**   **Exclusion**

  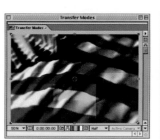 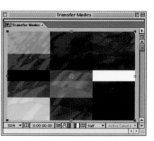

Hue   **Saturation**   **Color**   **Luminosity**

Color Plate 13-1: The Levels Histogram indicates how an image's pixels are distributed along the range of brightness values from black (left) to white (right). *Image courtesy of Axel Baumann, Director of Photography*

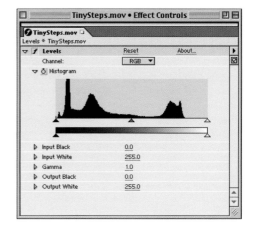

Color Plate 13-2: You can vastly improve the quality of an image by adjusting the Input White, Input Black, and Gamma properties of the Levels effect. *Image courtesy of Axel Baumann, Director of Photography*

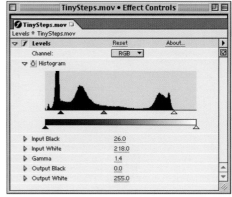

Color Plate 14-1: The cabs in the footage were looking a bit more orange than yellow, but after doing a little tweaking with the Color Change filter, the cabs are now a decidedly bright yellow. *Image courtesy of Sekani (Corbis NY Vistas, Vol. 213)*

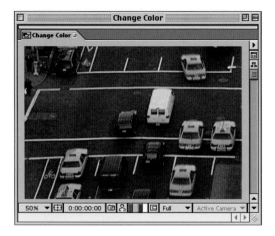

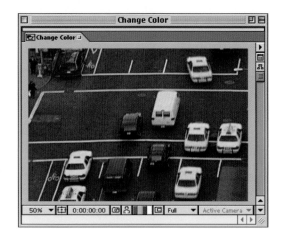

Color Plate 14-2: The Colorama Effect Controls are pretty intimidating at first glance.

Color Plate 14-3: Initially applying the Colorama effect produces some pretty dramatic results. *Image courtesy of Sekani (Nature Splendor)*

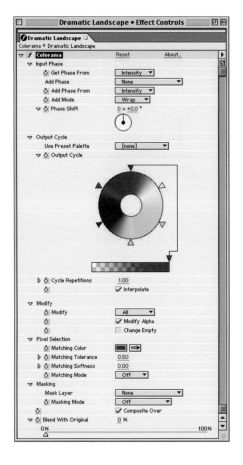

Color Plate 14-4: Adjust the position of the new triangles to change the levels as necessary. *Image courtesy of Sekani (Nature Splendor)*

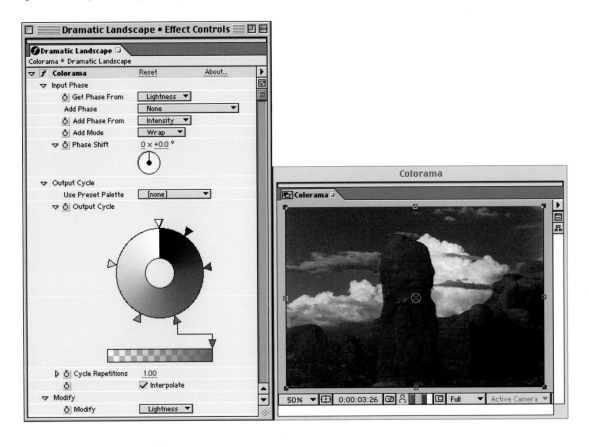

Color Plate 14-5: Using a displacement map with Colorama can create some interesting results. *Image courtesy of Sekani (Nature Splendor)*

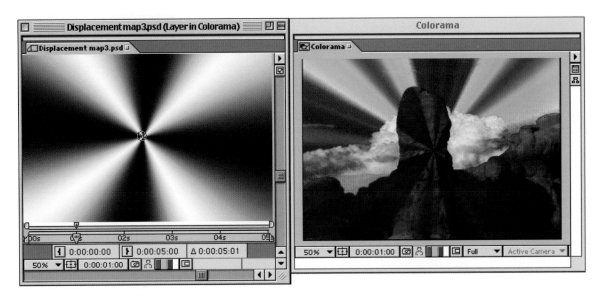

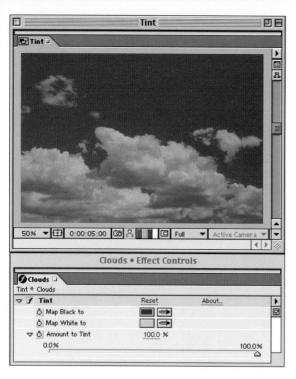

Color Plate 14-6: The Tint effect enables you to map the black and white values of a layer to colors you choose with the Color Picker. *Image courtesy of ArtBeats (Starter Kit)*

Color Plate 15-1: You can achieve transparency with the PS+Lens Flare effect by pre-composing the layer and adding the Shift Channels and Remove Color Matting effects to the pre-composed layer. *Image courtesy of EyeWire/Getty Images www.gettyimages.com (Cosmic Moves)*

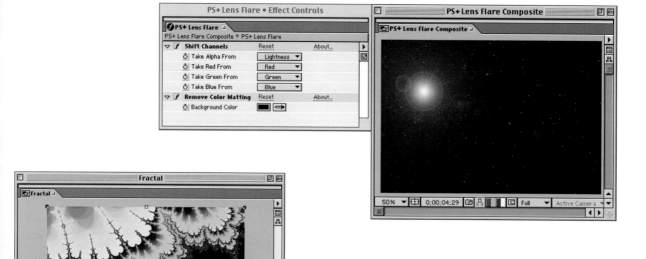

Color Plate 15-2: Magnify the Fractal in the Effect Controls to zero in on its incredibly minute details.

Color Plate 18-1: Using a Layer Map (left) composed of Blue and Red colors, we can make the particles enlarge when they pass under the magnifying glass.

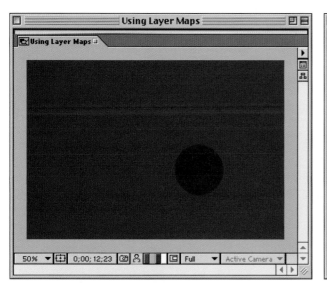 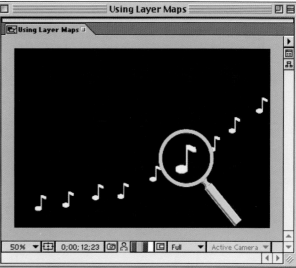

Color Plate 19-1: The Color Difference Key Effect Controls window is shown here.

Color Plate 22-1: NYC traffic, before and after a multiplied Glow. *Image courtesy of Sekani (Corbis NY Vistas, Vol. 213)*

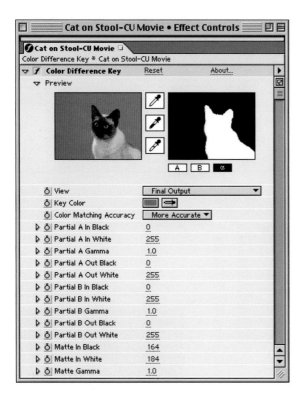

Color Plate 24-1: The Custom Views provide very useful visual cues toward understanding 3D space in After Effects.

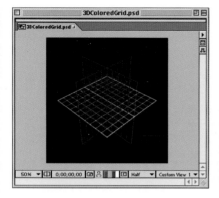
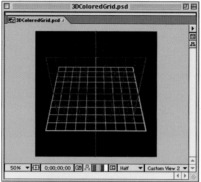
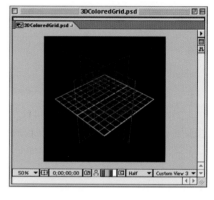

Color Plate 24-2: Spot lights can be tightly controlled, and Point lights are great for throwing shadows out of perforated objects. Parallel and Ambient lights are more general in their application.

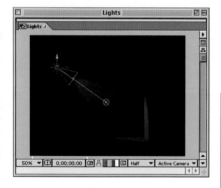

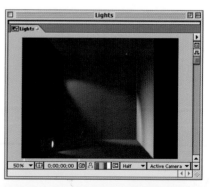

Changing Channels and Colors

✦ ✦ ✦ ✦

In This Chapter

Adding to your color correction skills

Manipulating color channels

Replacing color with precision

✦ ✦ ✦ ✦

If you are having some success with color correcting your footage, this chapter will give you even more options in this department. Some of the Channel and Image Control filters produce beautiful stylized results, and others among them include more practical color tools that enable you to do things such as change individual colors within layers. Of course, as is always the case, some of these effects are infinitely more useful than others. As has become our method of explaining filters, we give serious weight to our favorites and spend a little less time on those we hardly ever use.

A good number of After Effects filters are carried forward from older versions of the software so that your older projects don't become obsolete if you open them in the latest, greatest build of the application. Of course, any new version also brings new effects, and in the realm of the Channel and Image Control effects, we are blessed with Colorama, a pretty stunning tool that was available before only as a third-party filter from Atomic Power. Colorama contains a staggering number of properties, but we zero in on the most important ones.

If you combine the information in this chapter and Chapter 13, you'll have a pretty good handle on how to make your video footage bend to your whim before you add any overtly special effects. Having options is always nice. If you want, you can make it look like film that's been given a range of different treatments. Just the same, you may want to go for a blown-out video look. Anyway, enough chatter about all the possibilities. Jump forward, check out the filters, and then go out and change our perceptions of color forever.

Cross-Reference Chapter 8 describes working with effects in general. If you aren't familiar with applying effects or working in the Effect Controls window, take the time to read (or re-read) the beginning of Chapter 8.

Applying the Channel Effects to Footage

The Channel Effects (see Figure 14-1) contain their share of winners and losers. We let you make the final judgment as to exactly which is which, but we hope to heavily influence your judgment. In an effort to establish an early bias on your part, we may as well tell you that we've used the Invert filter in almost every project we've ever worked on, but we want you to keep an open mind. Having said that, most of the remaining filters in this group can be pretty useful; on occasion, they're indispensable. Go ahead and get to the bottom of them.

On the DVD-ROM As far as the following explanations of effects are concerned, we created an After Effects project that includes a composition for each effect we cover in the chapter. Just as a reminder, you need to copy the *Source Material* folder from the DVD-ROM to your hard drive. Additionally, the exercises that follow cover some of these effects in detail. Our own corresponding After Effects project is called *Chapter 14.aep* and can be found in the *Project Files/Chapter 14* folder. Feel free to substitute your own footage with the examples shown in the figures and exercises.

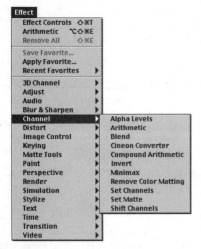

Figure 14-1: The Channel group of effects as they appear in the Effect menu

Using the Arithmetic effect

Arithmetic predates the addition of transfer modes to the world of After Effects. In the days before you could assign anything such as "Screen" to a layer, you were relegated to choosing between the Arithmetic and Compound Arithmetic effects for anything approximating the look you get from applying the different transfer modes. The Arithmetic filter is a bit on the strange side. If you apply the Arithmetic filter to a layer, the layer gets blended with itself in ways that you define. The Arithmetic Effect Controls are shown in Figure 14-2.

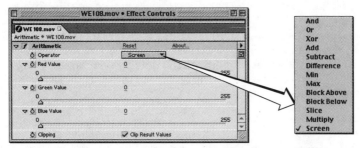

Figure 14-2: The Arithmetic Effect Controls window where you select the manner in which the layer gets blended with itself from the pop-up menu

In the Arithmetic Effect controls, you define the mathematical operation, or arithmetic, to be performed on the color channels according to the values you set with the sliders. Experiment with the different kinds of arithmetic. You may recognize some of the language used to define the blending options from your experience with transfer modes. Others may not make immediate sense. For example, Slice is a threshold operation. With Slice, numbers above the value specified by the sliders appear as white in their respective channels. Conversely, channel values less than their requisite slider amounts appear as black. The rest of them pretty much follow along the lines of their descriptive names. You can get some pretty psychedelic color distortions if you work at it. If you leave the default Clip Result Values switch on, the color channel values won't go past their range. Having said all this, we also feel obliged to tell you that we never use this effect.

Cross-Reference If all this talk about transfer modes has left you utterly perplexed, they are the exclusive subject of Chapter 11.

Using the Blend effect

As opposed to Arithmetic, Blend is a very friendly and useful filter. On a stylistic level, Blend offers a great way to add a textural appearance to a layer simply by borrowing it from another element in your project. On a more functional and utilitarian level, this effect is critical when you're crossfading layers that contain transparency.

Cross-Reference The Online Help (choose Help ➪ After Effects Help) is an HTML document that goes well beyond the printed User's Guide in explaining After Effects in detail. In addition to containing all of the information included in the User's Guide, the Online Help contains a lot of very useful basic information on all the effects that ship with After Efffects. Refer to it as often as you need to; our purpose in writing about these effects is to supplement that information rather than repeat it.

Using Blend as a design enhancement

We're going to look at blending as a design tool first. Suppose that you have some pretty line art that you've made in Illustrator or Freehand. For our example, we have an illustration of a friendly-looking crescent moon (see Figure 14-3). It's fine, except that it suffers from being a little on the flat side. How do you solve this problem? When you're working on an After Effects project, having some video or still images on hand that contain interesting and subtle textures is always a good idea. Figure 14-4 shows an example of some video that could provide you with some versatile design options. You've probably connected the dots by now. You're going to learn how to use the Blend effect to place the texture of the video in Figure 14-4 onto the line art of the moon shown in Figure 14-3.

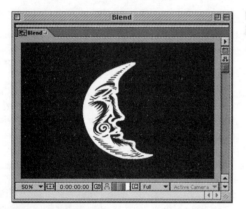

Figure 14-3: An example of an illustration composed of line art

Image courtesy of Creatas (Scratchworks 1)

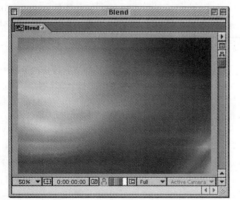

Figure 14-4: This video clip is soft and unobtrusive enough to serve as a texture for other elements in an After Effects project.

Image Courtesy of Digital Juice (Jump Backs, Vol. 7)

On the DVD-ROM

For reference, you may want to consult the composition named *Blend* in the *Chapter 14.aep* project.

STEPS: Using the Blend Effect as a Design Tool

1. **Place the two elements in a new composition.**

2. **Hide the video layer by turning off its visibility switch.**

3. **Select the line art layer.** Single color EPS illustrations created in Illustrator or Freehand work well in this case.

4. **Choose Effect ➪ Channel ➪ Blend.** The Blend Effect Controls window appears, and it should resemble Figure 14-5.

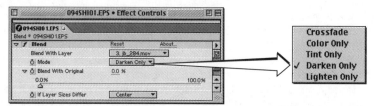

Figure 14-5: The Blend Effect Controls enable you to select the Blend With layer, the blending mode, and a slider for the blending amount.

5. **In the Effect Controls window, specify the textural video as the Blend With layer.** If you want to, you can also use a still image.

6. **Experiment with the blending mode and amount until you get a satisfying result.** We used Darken at 30%, the results of which are shown in Figure 14-6.

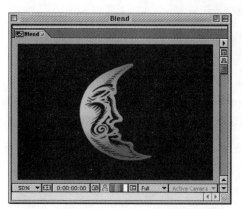

Figure 14-6: The video layer is now visible as the texture of the Crescent Moon EPS illustration. We also added a layer of stars for the background. *Images courtesy of Creatas (Scratchworks 1) and EyeWire by Getty Images www.gettyimages. com (Cosmic Moves)*

7. **Make a RAM Preview of your work by pressing 0 on the numeric keypad.** If you used a still image in Step 5, there's no need to create a RAM Preview; in that case, what you see is what you get.

Using Blend to maintain transparency during a crossfade

While the last set of steps acquainted you with the Blend filter as a design possibility, as we mentioned earlier, you can also solve a specific problem with this effect. When you crossfade two layers in After Effects, you won't experience any problems unless there are other layers visible behind the two layers being crossfaded.

Note   By *crossfade*, we mean fading out the opacity of one layer while bringing up the opacity of another.

On the DVD-ROM   The following figures explain this concept pretty clearly, but if you want a closer look at the mechanics of a crossfade blend as compared to crossfading opacity, look at the *Blend 2* composition in the *Chapter 14.aep* project on the DVD-ROM.

For Figure 14-7, we layered separate instances of the crescent moon directly on top of each other. We also gave them crossfading opacity animations lasting one second. While one fades from 100% to 0%, the other does the opposite, fading from 0% to 100%. At the halfway point of the animation, both of the layers are at 50% opacity. Seems okay, no? Well, look closely. The layer containing the lined texture is peeking through from behind the two crossfading moons. What do you do now?

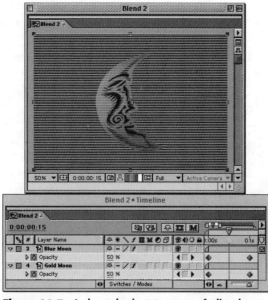

Figure 14-7: A closer look at two crossfading layers in the foreground reveals that any additional layers behind them are visible.

Image courtesy of Creatas (Scratchworks 1)

Figure 14-8 displays how the Blend effect solves this problem. First, we applied it to one of the two moon layers and selected Crossfade as the blend mode in the Effect Controls. Then we set a second long Blend With Original keyframe animation in which the property changes from 100% to 0%. In this case, the layer containing the lined texture is fully obscured behind the crossfading moons. Just to prove the point, we singled out the alpha channels of the two different crossfades in Figure 14-9.

Note The second layer doesn't even need its visibility switch turned on in order for the effect to work properly.

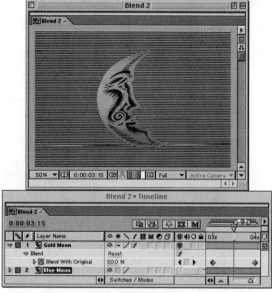

Figure 14-8: Using the Blend effect in Crossfade mode solves the transparency problem raised by the standard opacity crossfade.

Image courtesy of Creatas (Scratchworks 1)

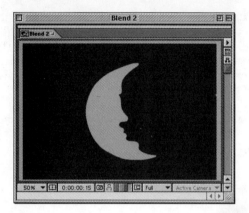

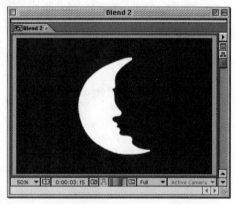

Figure 14-9: Compare the alpha channels of layers with transparency during an opacity crossfade versus using the Blend effect used with the Crossfade mode.
Image courtesy of Creatas (Scratchworks 1)

Using the Compound Arithmetic effect

As we told you when describing its Arithmetic cousin, Compound Arithmetic was developed prior to the addition of transfer modes as a layer option in the Timeline window. The addition of the word Compound refers to the fact that, unlike its Arithmetic counterpart, Compound Arithmetic works between two layers. If you look at its properties in the Effect Controls window in Figure 14-10, you can set up a transfer mode type of interaction between the layer that you apply it to and the one you specify as the Second Source. The Second Source layer needs to be in the same composition, but its visibility can be turned off. This is pretty straightforward and easy to understand. Still, we have a couple of interesting details to point out about this filter.

Unlike transfer modes, with Compound Arithmetic, you can do the following:

✦ Apply it to the alpha channels of two images.

✦ Use the Blend With Original slider. Transfer modes are permanent, non-keyframeable properties that cannot be changed for the duration of a layer. By tweaking Blend With Original, you aren't locked in.

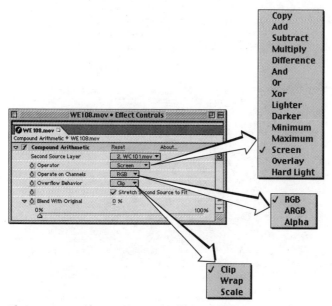

Figure 14-10: The Compound Arithmetic Effect Controls offer more options than transfer modes.

Using the Invert effect

The Invert filter is a lifesaver. Simple and easy to use, its utility cannot be underestimated, especially if you're working with a lot of EPS text and line art created in Illustrator. Practically everyone we know has to work with these elements, and you'll probably benefit a great deal from learning this effect. Its Effect Controls are very simple (see Figure 14-11).

The most common use for this filter is when you bring text or line art into a composition and it's black when you want it to be white or vice versa. Slap on the Invert filter, and you're in business (see Figure 14-12). It definitely beats having to spend time changing the color of your elements in Illustrator.

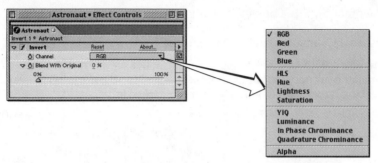

Figure 14-11: The Invert Effect Controls are quite straightforward.

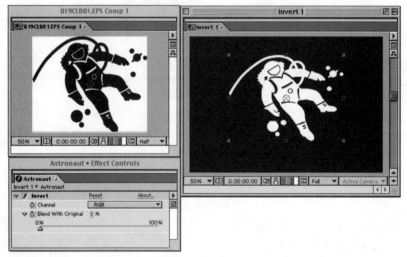

Figure 14-12: Use the Invert filter to flip-flop EPS art that is the wrong color in your composition.

Image courtesy of Creatas (Silhouettes 1)

Another great aspect of this simple little tool lies in the Channel pop-up menu. You can get some interesting stylized effects by inverting video footage by using these different settings. You often see this effect used to heighten the stakes at critical moments in various promos and trailers. The footage slows down at a critical moment, and then a negative of the image will be visible for a brief time before appearing normal again. Think horror movie trailers or murder mysteries. All it requires is quick keyframe animations by using the Blend With Original effect property.

There are two related compositions in the *Chapter 14.aep* project on the DVD-ROM; *Invert 1* is for line art, and *Invert 2* is for more traditional footage.

Using the Minimax effect

Minimax is a fun filter (see Figure 14-13). It creates a stylized effect that may or may not be appropriate for your project. If you look at the footage before and after you apply the effect with a radius of three in Figures 14-14 and 14-15, you'll begin to get a sense of this effect's mechanics.

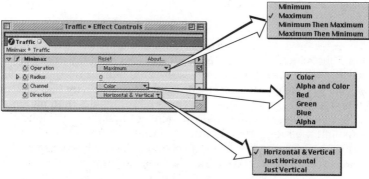

Figure 14-13: The Minimax Effect Controls contain a number of important pop-up menus.

Figure 14-14: A shot of traffic before applying *Minimax*

Image courtesy of Creatas

Figure 14-15: After applying Minimax set to Maximum with a radius of three, the traffic takes on an elegant and stylized appearance.

Image courtesy of Creatas

The name Minimax is derived from the words minimum and maximum. You set the radius, and After Effects looks at the footage and replaces all of the pixels inside that defined radius with the one pixel that contains the minimum or maximum channel value depending on your selections in the pop-up menus. Going by that logic, it's not hard to understand that maximum produces brighter results than minimum. You can specify the channels that the effect influences, including the alpha channel, and you can also limit the radius to either the horizontal or vertical dimensions if you like. Selecting the alpha channel from the channel pop-up menu can create unexpectedly interesting results. Have a little fun and experiment with this one.

Caution

This Minimax effect compromises the quality of an image because it reduces the information within it. Be prepared to lose detail and amplify noise if you apply it to grainy footage.

Using the Remove Color Matting effect

The Remove Color Matting is an easy and useful filter built for one purpose. We discussed creating mattes in Chapter 10, but this aspect of post-production can cause problems depending on the background that the matted footage was shot against. For example, look at the video clip of the flame in Figure 14-16. Then look at its matte in Figure 14-17.

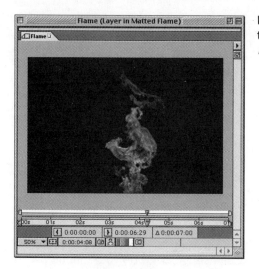

Figure 14-16: The original clip of the flame

Image courtesy of ArtBeats (Starter Kit)

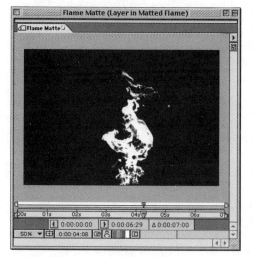

Figure 14-17: The matching matte for clip of the flame

Image courtesy of ArtBeats (Starter Kit)

The resulting Track Matte looks great when it's composited with dark elements, but an interesting problem arises when you use the same Track Matte with lighter elements. Look at the edges of the Track Matte when it's composited against a white background in Figure 14-18.

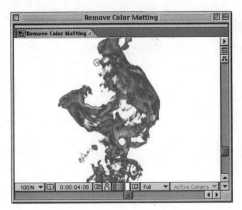

Figure 14-18: The Track Matte contains some unsightly black edges when it's composited against a white background.

Image courtesy of ArtBeats (Starter Kit)

Because the flame was shot on a black background, its matte has been pre-multiplied with black. This just looks wrong, pure and simple. How do you "unmultiply" the black? The Remove Color Matting filter was designed to address exactly this problem. First, apply the effect to the pre-composed Track Matte. Then, use the dropper in the Remove Color Matting Effect Controls to sample the pre-multiplied color by selecting it and then clicking the background of the original footage, as shown in Figure 14-19. Those ugly black highlights at the edges disappear, and your problem is solved (see Figure 14-20).

Figure 14-19: Use the dropper in the Remove Color Matting Effect Controls to sample the background of the original footage of the flame.

Image courtesy of ArtBeats (Starter Kit)

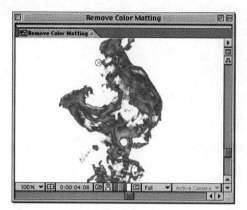

Figure 14-20: Those ugly black highlights at the edges disappear, and your problem is solved.

Image courtesy of ArtBeats (Starter Kit)

Using the Set Channels effect

The Set Channels filter enables you to take information from other layers and use it as either the red, green, blue, or alpha channel of the layer to which you apply the effect. The Set Channels Effect controls are shown in Figure 14-21.

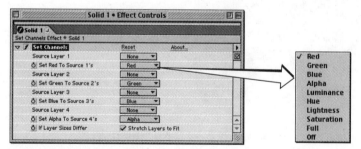

Figure 14-21: The Set Channels Effect Controls enable you to define the channels of a layer based upon information from other layers.

There isn't an awful lot to say about this effect. It's kind of fun to play with, but it isn't that great because you can mix the channels of different layers by using a number of the different effects we cover in this chapter. Nonetheless, one clear advantage with this effect is the alpha channel option. If you need to, you can create an alpha channel based on the luminance or lightness of a layer in a couple of easy steps. If it weren't for this particular function, this filter wouldn't really add much value.

STEPS: Creating an Alpha Channel from the Luminance of a Layer with the Set Channels Effect

1. **Place two sharply contrasting video clips into a new composition.** Look at the examples in Figures 14-22 and 14-23 for reference.

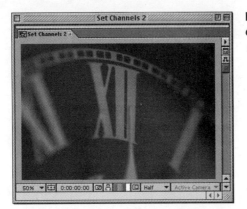

Figure 14-22: This footage of a clock contains a lot of dark pixel values.

Image courtesy of ArtBeats (Bundle Pack)

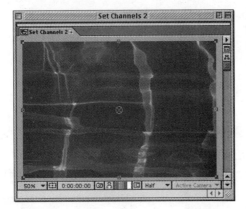

Figure 14-23: This footage of rippling water contains lighter pixel values by contrast.

Image courtesy of ArtBeats (Bundle Pack)

2. **In the Timeline, turn off the visibility of the lighter layer.**

3. **Select the darker layer and apply the Set Channels effect to it (choose Effect ⇨ Channel ⇨ Set Channels).**

4. **In the Effect Controls window, select the darker clip as the option for the Source Layer 4 pop-up menu, and Luminance as the option in the Set Alpha to Source 4's pop-up menu.** The results of your efforts should resemble Figure 14-24.

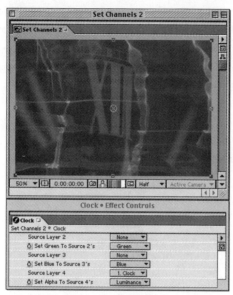

Figure 14-24: Because the alpha channel is based on its luminance, the darker parts of the clock footage reveal the water layer.

Images courtesy of ArtBeats (Bundle Pack)

Using the Set Matte effect

Simply put, the Set Matte effect is a leftover from older versions of After Effects. Before you could apply Luma or Alpha Mattes or select the Stencil and Silhouette transfer modes, this filter was the only way to create the same kinds of effects. It still exists as an option so that you can open older projects in newer versions of the software without generating errors. Because its presence in the list of Channel effects is to provide backwards compatibility, there's really no need to cover it in detail.

Cross-Reference If you aren't clear as to what Track Mattes and transfer modes are, Chapters 10 and 11 cover them, respectively, in detail.

Using the Shift Channels effect

The Shift Channels filter is a simpler version of the Set Channels effect. One look at the Shift Channels Effect Controls tells you pretty much all that you need to know about this effect (see Figure 14-25). Like the Set Channels effect, you can use this filter to create an alpha channel from the luminance of the same layer. Another cool thing about it is that you can use it to create a sharp looking black and white image.

If you need to make a crisp black and white image from color footage, figure out which channel has the best looking grayscale image by viewing the individual channels by using the buttons at the bottom of the Comp or Layer windows. For example, say that you determined that the red channel contains the cleanest grayscale image. You can then use the Shift Channels filter pop-up menus to Take Red From Red, Take Green From Red, and Take Blue From Red. This is almost always an improvement over desaturating the combined RGB channels with other filters.

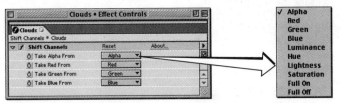

Figure 14-25: The Shift Channels Effect Controls enable you to define the channels of a layer based upon information from other channels in the same layer.

Applying the Image Control Effects to Footage

Now that you can change channels at will, the Image Control effects contain some more color correction and color replacement tools that complete the set of effects we inherited from Photoshop (see Figure 14-26). We looked at those in the last chapter, and you should familiarize yourself with those effects as well as the ones we're about to investigate.

Caution

No discussion of color would be complete without mentioning that NTSC video colorspace is distinctly different from the colorspace you work with when using After Effects on your computer. The NTSC video colorspace is known as YUV (sometimes YcrCb), and your computer monitor uses the colorspace we call RGB. Some RGB values can't exist in the YUV realm. Typically, "hot" colors, such as over-saturated reds will exceed their range in YUV colorspace and get clamped when they're carried over. So why are you going to all the trouble to learn these color correction tools? More often than not, if you're doing post-production work with After Effects in a broadcast environment, an online video editor will make a final pass of any work you've prepared for air. With an analog tool, such as a processing amplifier (a "proc amp," in professional lingo), they can cool off any hot color values so that your work doesn't appear distorted and no one gets yelled at, at least not over "illegal" colors.

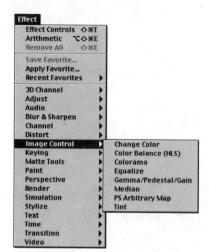

Figure 14-26: The Image Control effects round out the color correction skills that you acquired when learning the Adjust group of filters.

Using the Change Color effect

The Change Color filter is a great one. Have you ever wanted to change the color of a loudly colored sweater without changing anything else about a clip? Well, we have. While we don't want to get into what that says about us, you'll benefit from knowing how this is done. Sometimes a broadcast design campaign is partially predicated on a range of colors, and you might have a clip that is perfect except for the fact that a few facets in it don't fit the color scheme that's required. We laid out some steps to show you how to apply this effect.

Caution

In order for this effect to work smoothly, you really need to apply it to footage that contains sharply contrasting levels and distinctly clear colors. If your footage lacks contrast and the colors are muddy and not clearly offset from each other, your results are going to be pretty shoddy. As is the case with all of these filters, you need to experiment with them to get the hang of when they're really going to pack a punch. Also, at this point, you probably have a better sense of the inherent danger of uttering, "We'll fix it in post!" Some clips are a lot easier to work with than others, even when you have the benefit of a great filter such as Change Color.

On the DVD-ROM

For reference, you may want to check out the Change Color composition we made for this exercise. We took a clip of New York City traffic and made the yellow cabs a brighter yellow. We also used this comp for the figures that complement the following steps.

STEPS: Changing Color Within a Clip

1. **With the previous warning fresh in your mind, take a choice clip and place it in a new composition.**

2. **In the Timeline, select the layer and apply the Levels effect (choose Effect ⇨ Adjust ⇨ Levels).** Take a look at the Histogram and, if necessary, make any adjustments that will improve the overall contrast of the image.

3. **Now apply the Change Color effect to the layer (choose Effect ⇨ Image Control ⇨ Change Color).**

4. **Click the dropper in the Change Color Effect Controls, place it over a portion of the image whose color that you want to change, and click it again to set the color (see Figure 14-27).**

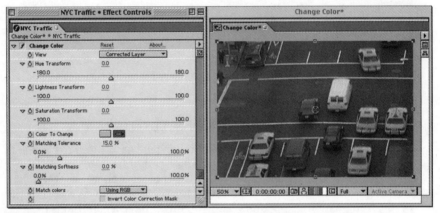

Figure 14-27: Use the dropper in the Change Color Effect Controls to select the color that you want to change within the layer.

Image courtesy of Sekani (Corbis NY Vistas, Vol. 213)

5. **In the Change Color Effect Controls, select Color Correction Mask from the View property pop-up menu.** Your Comp window should display a grayscale map revealing the parts of the image that match the color you selected with the dropper. See Figure 14-28 for reference.

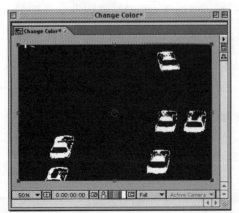

Figure 14-28: Selecting Color Correction Mask from the Change Color Effect Controls displays a grayscale map in the Comp window that reveals the parts of the image that match the color you selected with the dropper.

Image courtesy of Sekani (Corbis NY Vistas, Vol. 213)

6. **In the Effect Controls window, make adjustments to the Matching Tolerance and Matching Softness sliders while keeping an eye on the results in the Comp window.** Work at it until you've really isolated the parts of the image that include your selected color (see Figure 14-29).

Tip   The Match Colors pop-up menu in the Effect Controls offers you three different colorspace options. If you're having problems nailing down your particular color, this pop-up menu can be invaluable. For example, selecting Hue from the list will select all pixels with the same hue regardless of their saturation or lightness values. This selection will almost always select more pixels than a specific RGB value, but that may just be what you need.

Tip   As you work your way through isolating and tightening your selection, you may find it useful to jump back and forth between the Color Corrected Mask and the Corrected Layer in the View pop-up menu to gauge your progress.

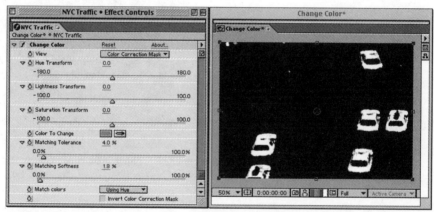

Figure 14-29: Improve your Color Correction Mask by adjusting the Matching Tolerance and Matching Softness sliders as well as the Match Colors pop-up menu.
Image courtesy of Sekani (Corbis NY Vistas, Vol. 213)

7. **After you lock off the parts of the image you're going to change, start moving the Hue Transform, Lightness Transform, and Saturation Transform sliders to change the color of the areas within the Color Correction Mask.** As soon as you settle on the HSL blend that you want, your work is done. In our example, we took the muted orange color of what should be yellow cabs on the streets of NYC and turned them into a bright yellow. See the before and after comparison in Figure 14-30 and in Color Plate 14-1, and if you can, look at the *Color Change* composition in the *Chapter 14.aep* project on the DVD-ROM.

Figure 14-30: The cabs in the footage were looking a bit more orange than yellow, but after a little tweaking with the Color Change filter, the cabs are now a decidedly bright yellow.
Image courtesy of Sekani (Corbis NY Vistas, Vol. 213)

Caution   Make sure that you're viewing the Corrected Layer in the View pop-up menu to see your color change.

That's how it's done. If you're hungry for more, we created an additional composition on the DVD-ROM called *Change Color 2* that gives you the opportunity to experiment with the Change Color effect on a number of color gradients that we created in Photoshop.

Using the Color Balance (HLS) effect

If you understand the mechanics of the Hue/Saturation filter in the Adjust group of effects, then nothing about the Color Balance (HLS) filter will provide you with any extra functionality. This filter is more intuitively designed in the sense that there are stopwatches for the Hue, Lightness, and Saturation properties in its Effect Controls window (see Figure 14-31). Other than that, the Hue/Saturation filter actually offers more control after you get past the idiosyncrasies of its own particular Effect Controls window. As you may have guessed, it's another leftover from an earlier era in After Effects.

 We cover the Hue/Saturation filter in the Adjust group of effects in Chapter 13.

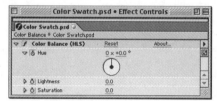

Figure 14-31: The Color Balance (HLS) Effect Controls can't be any more self-explanatory.

Using the Colorama effect

What can we possibly say about the Colorama filter? Just look at its Effect Controls in Figure 14-32 (see also Color Plate 14-2). Dude! This is an extremely powerful tool. The Online Help offers almost five pages of information on all of the properties within this masterpiece of an effect. Back when it was available only as a third-party filter from Atomic Power, its documentation spanned 20 pages! There's so much we could say, but we distill its potential uses to three gems. If you're turned on by the possibilities and have some time to play, you can go beyond our exercises and spend a week with it on your own. It's that sophisticated.

Figure 14-32: The Colorama Effect Controls are pretty intimidating at first glance.

STEPS: Animating Colorama's Phase Shift Property

1. **Add a bit of footage to a new composition.** A movie with a broad range of colors will provide the most dramatic results.

2. **In the Timeline, select the layer and add the Colorama effect (choose Effect ⇨ Image Control ⇨ Colorama).** The immediate results of doing this look pretty vibrant and psychedelic. See Figure 14-33 and Color Plate 14-3 for reference if you don't believe your eyes.

Figure 14-33: Initially applying the Colorama effect produces some pretty dramatic results.

Image courtesy of Sekani (Nature Splendor)

3. **In the Effect Controls, twirl down the Input Phase property and click the Phase Shift property stopwatch to set a Phase Shift keyframe.**

4. **Go forward in time a few seconds by dragging the playhead.**

5. **Change the value of the Input Phase property by twirling its radial dial or directly entering values in the numerical fields above the dials.** This sets another Input Phase keyframe.

6. **Look at a RAM Preview of your work by pressing 0 on the numeric keypad.**

Wow. So what would you use that for? According to the Colorama documentation, this filter was initially developed to re-create the effect of color cycling that you used to see in old animated weather maps on TV. This is pretty stylized stuff, to say the least. To get a clue as to what's really happening when you animate the Input Phase of the Colorama filter, take another look at the Effect Controls.

The Output Cycle property helps make sense of the process if you're confused. When you initially apply the effect, Colorama converts the layer to a grayscale image and maps the color values from the Output Cycle on to it. Pure black in the grayscale image is remapped as red, and so is pure white, but all the grayscale variations in between are mapped to the range of colors visible in the Output Cycle circle. You can change these colors manually, or use a different Preset Palette from the pop-up menu under the Output Cycle property (see Figure 14-34).

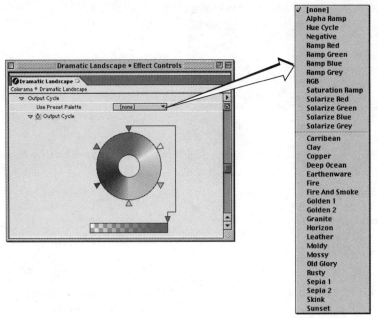

Figure 14-34: The Preset Palette changes the default color values of the Output Cycle property.

As soon as you figure out the logic of the Output Cycle, you can modify its properties. To change the colors on the wheel without using one of the presets, you have a few options. You can place as many as 64 triangles on the Output Cycle wheel, and you can modify each one's properties. Here are some handy tricks:

✦ **To add an Output Cycle triangle:** Click the area inside the Output Cycle color wheel where you want the new triangle to be located. This brings up the Color Picker, which you use to define the color of the new triangle. After you pick your desired color, click OK. If the triangle isn't located exactly where you want it, you can drag it to change its position.

✦ **To copy an Output Cycle triangle:** Hold down the Command/Ctrl key and click and drag an existing triangle. This creates an identical triangle that you can place at a new location.

✦ **To modify an existing Output Cycle triangle:** Double-click one of the triangles to change its color. Drag them to new locations if you want, and you can also hold down the Shift key as you do so to snap them into locations at 45-degree increments on the Output Cycle wheel.

✦ **To delete an Output Cycle triangle:** Drag it outside of the Effect Controls window.

In Chapter 13, we extol the virtues of the Levels and Curves effects. When combined, they're pretty unbeatable, but Colorama takes color correction to another level. The Levels effect has three control points and the Curves effect can have up to 15, but get this: Colorama can have up to 64! Here's how you can get started on your journey to color correction knighthood.

STEPS: Using Colorama as a Levels Control

1. **Apply the Colorama effect to a layer in a composition.**

2. **In the Effect Controls window, select Lightness from the Get Phase From pop-up menu in the Input Phase properties.**

3. **Select Ramp Gray from the Use Preset Palette pop-up menu in the Output Cycle properties.**

4. **Select Lightness from the Modify pop-up menu in the Modify properties.** The white to black progression in the Output Cycle wheel represents the unedited levels of the layer.

5. **Add Output Cycle triangles to the Output Cycle wheel to set the Levels control points for the layer.**

6. **Move the newly added triangles to change the levels.** If you practice this a little bit, you should be able to figure out exactly what's happening here. In case you want to check your work, we outline the process in Figures 14-35, 14-36, and 14-37 (which is also shown in Color Plate 14-4).

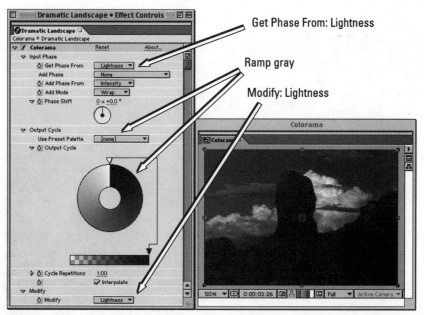

Figure 14-35: Your Effect Controls and Comp windows should resemble these after completing Steps 1–4.

Image courtesy of Sekani (Nature Splendor)

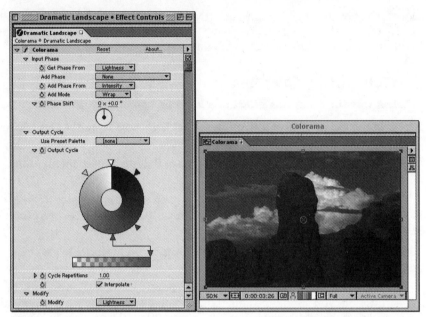

Figure 14-36: Add as many triangles as you need to tweak specific level ranges within the layer.

Image courtesy of Sekani (Nature Splendor)

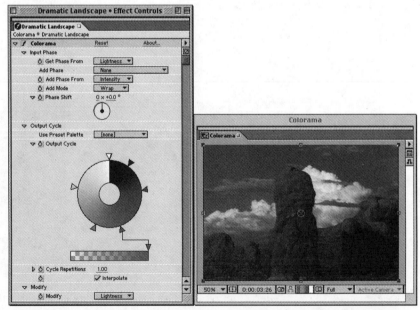

Figure 14-37: Adjust the position of the new triangles to change the levels as necessary.

Image courtesy of Sekani (Nature Splendor)

We have one more offering for your expanding bag of Colorama tricks. We introduce you to the idea of a displacement map when we cover the Compound Blur filter in the last chapter, and this concept is going to keep reappearing throughout the Effects section of the book. As if Colorama weren't sophisticated enough, you can use another layer as a displacement map for its color remapping capability.

STEPS: Using Colorama with a Displacement Map

1. **Apply the Colorama effect to a layer in a composition.**

2. **In the Effect Controls window, select Hue from the Get Phase From pop-up menu in the Input Phase properties.**

3. **Select Hue Cycle from the Use Preset Palette pop-up menu in the Output Cycle properties.**

4. **Select Hue from the Modify pop-up menu in the Modify properties.** This time we're focusing on the hue values of the layer.

5. **Add a layer to the composition that serves as a displacement map.** In our example, we add a black and white gradient we created in Photoshop. Look at the Colorama composition in the *Chapter 14.aep* project on the DVD-ROM if you need a reference for what we're talking about here.

6. **In the Timeline, turn off the visibility for the newly added displacement map layer.**

7. **In the Effect Controls window, select the displacement map layer from the Add Phase pop-up menu in the Input Phase properties.** Look at Figure 14-38 and Color Plate 14-5 for reference.

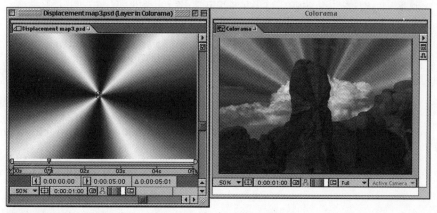

Figure 14-38: Using a displacement map with Colorama can create some interesting results.

Image courtesy of Sekani (Nature Splendor)

We usually summarize a filter by discussing its limitations, but in this case, we're quite comfortable in saying that there's no telling where you might wind up with this one. It's honestly hard to imagine all of the applications you may find for Colorama because it has so many properties that you can adjust. At first glance it seems as though it would only be appropriate for certain kinds of highly stylized treatments, but as we showed you with its ability to tweak levels, there's a lot more to it. Go wild, gang!

Tip   Don't forget to complement our limited introduction to Colorama with the information contained in the Online Help (choose Help ➪ After Effects Help). You can get a lot more functionality from it. We've only started you down the path.

Using the Equalize effect

As we've mentioned throughout our chapters, if you see something that you like in film or television, you should do your best to approximate the same effect. That's generally the best way to learn After Effects, and the Equalize filter was the first bit of help we got when trying to make footage look like older and slightly washed out film. Its Effect Controls are simple enough (see Figure 14-39).

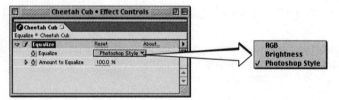

Figure 14-39: The Equalize Effect Controls are refreshingly simple.

The Equalize filter takes the pixels of an image and adjusts them so that their brightness values are more evenly distributed. You can get that older film look by selecting Brightness from the Equalize pop-up menu (see Figure 14-40). You can also control the Equalize amount with the slider at the bottom of the Effect Controls. The drawback seems to be that your image quality is somewhat reduced while pixel noise gets a bit amplified. You can offset this by adding a little blur on top of the effect, or better still, it works very well with the Median filter, which we cover just a bit later in the chapter.

Figure 14-40: Selecting Brightness from the Equalize pop-up menu can make your footage look like older, washed-out film.

Image courtesy of Sekani (Funny and Furry 1)

Using the Gamma/Pedestal/Gain effect

This filter is an older channel-based Levels control. From the top, we should say that we're not huge proponents of it because you can use so many other powerful effects to improve the image quality of a movie. Its biggest limitation is the absence of any visual aid, such as a Histogram in its Effect Controls (see Figure 14-41).

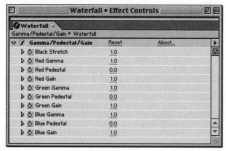

Figure 14-41: The Gamma/Pedestal/Gain Effect Controls lack any visual aid, such as a Histogram.

Having said that, if you absolutely must, you can set the levels for each channel with this effect. Comparing it to the Levels effect, the Pedestal property is equivalent to the Input Black property, and the Gain property is equivalent to the Input White property. As always, the Gamma property refers to the middle range.

Using the Median effect

The Median filter makes your footage look as though it has been painted by hand. Pretty nifty, if that's what you're looking for. Its Effect Controls contain only two properties: a radius slider and an alpha channel option. This effect reduces the amount of pixel information in a layer because it looks at pixels from within the specified radius, figures out what each one's median color value is, and replaces all of them with that value. A picture does a better job than words in this case. Look at Figure 14-42 to see what a Radius value of 6 does.

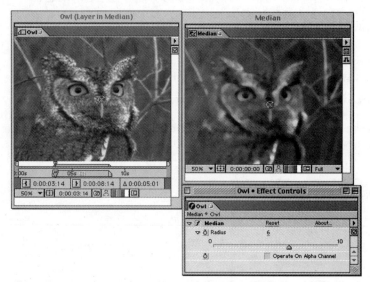

Figure 14-42: The Median effect reduces the pixel information in a layer while adding a pretty hand-painted look.

Image courtesy of Sekani (Funny and Furry 1)

Using the PS Arbitrary Map effect

Photoshop lovers unite! You can map the color values of a clip by using your very own color map created from within Photoshop. Click the Options at the top of the Effect Controls and import your Color Map (ACT) or Curves (ACV) files in the resulting dialog box.

With the addition of Colorama to version 5 of After Effects, getting really excited about this effect is hard. Furthermore, the Online Help tells you that it's only included for users of earlier versions of After Effects who created projects using the older Arbitrary Map effect. Furthermore, it goes on to suggest that you use the Curves filter for new work. Beyond that, we don't have much to add.

In the interest of being comprehensive, we included a composition on the DVD-ROM that uses this effect. If you're curious, it's called *PS Arbitrary Map*.

Using the Tint effect

This filter is a quick and easy way to turn your movie into a duotone creation, but beyond that, it's pretty limited. In the Effect Controls, you can select the colors that you want to use to tint the black and white values of a layer. We prefer to use the Colorize option in the Hue/Saturation effect, because it keeps the brightness (read, black) detail of a movie intact. See Figure 14-43 and Color Plate 14-6.

Figure 14-43: The Tint effect enables you to map the black and white values of a layer to colors you choose with the Color Picker.

Image courtesy of ArtBeats (Starter Kit)

✦   ✦   ✦

Simulating Natural Physics: Perspective, Light, and Sound

As we continue through our coverage of all the various groups of effects in After Effects, we should point out that we spend more time on the filters we deem to be more useful than others. If you've read the two chapters prior to this one, you're probably aware of this practice already. It's worth repeating, because we're going to keep distilling the vast number of effects down to the true all-stars.

Speaking of all-stars, we're about to drop a few on you. While the Perspective group of effects may not have tons of properties with millions of parameters, they do contain some incredibly useful favorites. In some cases, the Render group of effects actually alleviates the need to create elements in other applications. Lastly, we'll take a look at the Simulation group of effects, which is largely made up of what used to be called Evolution.

If you read the last chapter, you probably remember the tremendous complexity of the Colorama filter. Colorama began life as only one of an entire set of effects called Evolution from Atomic Power Corporation. All of these have been acquired by Adobe and worked into the Standard Version of After Effects. These can create some genuinely remarkable looking treatments, not the least of which is the ability to smash a layer into bits as though it were a glass wall! Go check 'em out.

Getting Perspective

The Perspective group of effects (see Figure 15-1) adds some rudimentary depth to your elements. Since the third dimension has been added to After Effects' capabilities as a compositing tool, the perspective effects suddenly seem pretty dated. Nonetheless, you can get some elegant looking effects from using these filters.

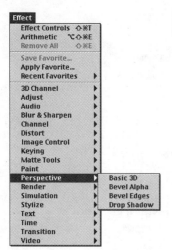

Figure 15-1: The Perspective group of effects as they appear in the Effect menu

Chapter 8 describes working with effects in general. If you aren't familiar with applying effects or working in the Effect Controls window, take the time to read (or re-read) the beginning of Chapter 8.

The Online Help (choose Help ➪ After Effects Help) is an HTML document that goes well beyond the printed User's Guide in explaining After Effects in detail. In addition to containing all the information included in the User's Guide, the Online Help contains a lot of very useful basic information on all of the effects that ship with After Efffects. Refer to it as often as you need to; our purpose in writing about these effects is to supplement that information rather than repeat it.

As far as the following explanations of effects are concerned, we created an After Effects project that includes a composition for each effect we cover in the chapter. Just as a reminder, you need to copy the *Source Material* folder from the DVD-ROM to your hard drive. Additionally, the exercises that follow cover some of these effects in detail. Our own corresponding After Effects project is called *Chapter 15.aep* and can be found in the *Project Files/Chapter 15* folder. Feel free to substitute your own footage with the examples shown in the figures and exercises.

Using Basic 3D

The Basic 3D effect used to be pretty important. We won't bore you with all the details, but prior to After Effects 5, there was no third dimension to be found anywhere in the software, so this filter used to be the only way to make objects move in 3D. These days, the Online Help recommends that you no longer use it except to support projects you created using previous versions of the application. Instead, it's now recommended that you turn on the 3D switch for the layer that you want to animate in 3D. This enables you to play with the layer's basic transform properties that now include a Z dimension, among other properties otherwise unavailable unless you turn on a layer's 3D switch. We cover After Effects' new 3D capabilities in Chapter 24.

Okay. Since we've said that, we still put together a composition on the DVD-ROM called *Good Ol' Basic 3D*. There are some inherent problems with this effect. For example, it doesn't work with motion blur and to make matters worse, moving its anchor point doesn't affect its movement in the third dimension. Coupled with the fact that so many broadcast design jobs demand 3D elements, the inherent limitations of the Basic 3D filter resulted in Adobe's effort to develop a true 3D component for the software.

Using the Bevel effects

The Bevel effects, Bevel Alpha and Bevel Edges, may appear to be similar, but short of having the word "bevel" in common, we'd like to tell you that we're big fans of Bevel Alpha, yet find almost no use for Bevel Edges. The two sets of Effect Controls are practically identical (see Figure 15-2), yet they produce dramatically different results.

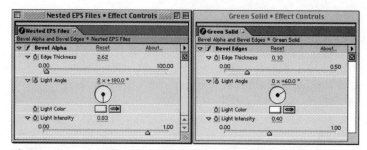

Figure 15-2: The Effect Controls for the Bevel Alpha and Bevel Edges effects are practically identical.

The Bevel Alpha effect works beautifully with Illustrator text or other EPS files that have clean alpha channels. Look at Figures 15-3 and 15-4 to see text and line art before and after we added a bevel to the alpha channel.

Figure 15-3: Text and line art before we apply the Bevel Alpha effect

Image Courtesy of Creatas and Eyewire by Getty Images
www.gettyimages.com

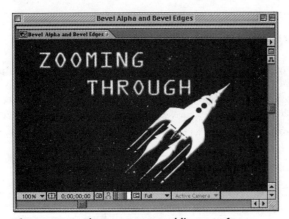

Figure 15-4: The same text and line art after we apply the Bevel Alpha effect and tweak it a bit

Image Courtesy of Creatas and Eyewire by Getty Images
www.gettyimages.com

There are no hard and fast rules with the Bevel Alpha effect. Just be careful with the Edge Thickness property. Kicking it up too high can distort the three-dimensional embossed appearance that works so well at lower levels. Pick a color for the light that matches your design, adjust its brightness according to taste, and animate the light angle if you want it to look as though your text is reflecting a light that's moving behind the virtual camera angle view of the Comp window. Used in conjunction with the Drop Shadow effect, you can get some very sexy looking results.

We almost never use Bevel Edges unless we need a crude sort of "frame" to place behind an image. Unlike Bevel Alpha, the Bevel Edges effect works inward from the edges of a layer's dimensions, regardless of whatever transparency may exist within the layer itself. Look at Figure 15-5 to see the kind of image this effect creates after you apply it to a solid layer.

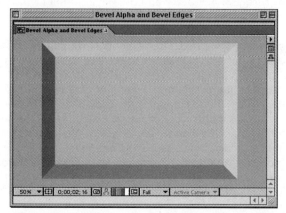

Figure 15-5: Applying the Bevel Edges effect to a solid gives it the appearance of a picture frame of sorts.

Using the Drop Shadow effect

The Drop Shadow filter is a real workhorse, not unlike Invert in the sense that it's a joy to use, simple to apply and tweak, and it creates aesthetically pleasing results. Look at Figure 15-6 to see what we mean.

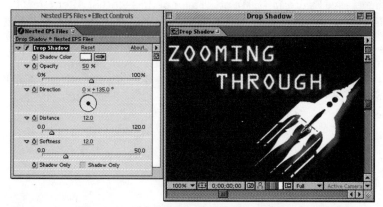

Figure 15-6: The Drop Shadow can be hard, soft, offset at a great distance, or so close that it can be thought of as alternative glow effect.
Image Courtesy of Creatas

True to its name, the effect adds a drop shadow that you can adjust to suit your needs. All of its properties are pretty self-explanatory. Tweak and animate the color, opacity, softness, distance, and angle of the shadow as you see fit. You can add it each time you want to add another virtual light source. Like the Bevel Alpha effect, the Drop Shadow effect is based on a layer's alpha channel, and as we mentioned earlier, these two filters work very well together, especially if you synchronize the animations of the Drop Shadow Direction property and the Bevel Alpha Light Angle property.

Caution

We need to tell you one important thing about this effect. Strange and unnatural looking things start to happen when you play with the scale or the rotation of a layer after you've applied the Drop Shadow effect to it. This has to do with the Render Pipeline. You can address the problem in a number of ways. The issue stems from the point at which After Effects computes the Drop Shadow. Because you know that things are processed in the order of Masks, Effects, and Transform properties, the problem comes from the normal procedure of After Effects performing transformations *after* an effect, in this case the Drop Shadow, is applied. One way to reorder this process is to add the Transform filter (from the Distort group of effects) to the layer in question. Another method involves nesting or pre-composing the layer. Lastly, an adjustment layer can also solve the problem.

On the DVD-ROM

We created two extra comps, one of which displays the combined effect of applying the Bevel Alpha and Drop Shadow effects simultaneously, the other of which demonstrates issues arising from scaling and rotating layers with the Drop Shadow applied.

Throwing Light and Visualizing Sound

As we told you at the beginning of the chapter, the Render group of effects can yield original elements (see Figure 15-7). We make a lot of the fact that After Effects is a great aggregator. In other words, elements from Photoshop, Illustrator, as well as QuickTime movies exported from editing suites usually make up the basis of an After Effects project. Some of the Render effects enable you to create original art with the application without having had to do any prep work elsewhere. Well, maybe that isn't entirely true because the first two are predicated on an audio file, but that's still a pretty slim prerequisite.

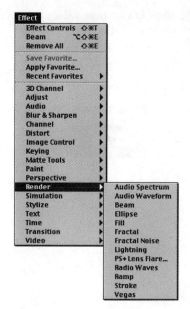

Figure 15-7: The Render group of effects enables you to create original elements from within After Effects.

Applying the Audio Spectrum and Audio Waveform effects

If you're a fan of MP3 player software that gives you cool-looking visual feedback as you play your tunes, then you'll love this. If that last sentence doesn't mean anything to you, hang on a minute because you'll probably like this effect too. All you need is a composition containing an audio file and a solid layer. If you want to get truly interesting results, you can work static or animated masks into the process, but we'll hold off on that for the moment.

STEPS: "Seeing" Sound

1. **Create a new composition containing an audio file.** A high-quality WAV or AIFF file will do nicely. If you need one, we provide you with an example in our *Chapter 15.aep* project on the DVD-ROM.

2. **Add a solid layer to the comp by pressing Command/Ctrl+Y.** The color doesn't matter; just make sure that it's comp-sized. Give it any name you like.

3. **Apply the Audio Spectrum effect to the solid layer by clicking the layer and choosing Effect ➪ Render ➪ Audio Spectrum.**

To really see what's going on with this effect, you want to set the layer switch to Best quality. Draft quality looks pretty awful.

4. **In the rather vast Audio Spectrum Effect Controls window, select the layer comprised of the audio file as your option for the Audio Layer pop-up menu.** See Figure 15-8 for reference.

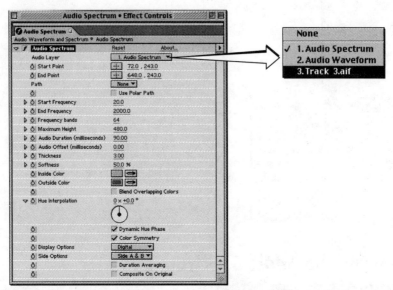

Figure 15-8: Select the layer comprised of the audio file as your option for the Audio Layer pop-up menu.

Your Comp window is probably not looking that hot yet, but now that you've set up the basic framework, take a look at the various effect properties and see how we can get something slick out of the Audio Spectrum effect. Set up your work area so that your Effect Controls and your Comp window are side by side. This way, you can immediately see the impact of your adjustments to the effect properties.

✦ **Narrow the frequency range that the effect is derived from by adjusting the Start and End Frequency sliders.** Typically, we find that we like to lower both of these. We want the Start Frequency property to use everything it can from the bass side. We almost always bring the End Frequency way down from its default, which appears to be set more for dogs than people. In our example, we set our range between 1 and 460.

✦ **Adjust the Maximum Height property to suit the amount of "activity" in the audio file.** The default setting can sometimes produce rather inert-looking results that don't amply show how dramatic this effect can actually be.

✦ **Set Start and End Points or select Polar Path to position the visualized Audio Spectrum in the Comp window.** By default, when you apply this effect to a solid layer, the area behind the pixels created by the effect is transparent. Click the alpha channel button if you want to confirm this or just place a layer behind the Audio Spectrum layer.

✦ **Experiment with the remaining properties to suit your aesthetic needs.** First of all, the three Display Options of Digital, Analog Lines, or Analog Dots create rather different looks. The color options allow for highlights, and the number of visible frequency bands along with their thickness and softness settings are also important considerations. If you poke around a bit more, you'll find that cranking the radial dial for the Hue Interpolation property introduces the entire color spectrum into the effect. If you opt to Blend Overlapping Colors, you can end up with animated colored toothpaste. You can also offset the time of the animation from the actual real-time spectrum spikes of the audio file. As always, as soon as you nail down the basic mechanics of a filter such as this, experimentation is key.

With this filter, it's important to remember to select the correct audio layer and to set a useful frequency range and height. After you have a "fat" spectrum to work with, you can do whatever you want to the design-type effect properties. For reference, compare the Audio Spectrum Effect Controls in Figure 15-9 with the resulting Comp window shown in Figure 15-10. Figures 15-11, 15-12, and 15-13 show you just a couple of results you can get with this effect. Go see what you can cook up and remember that you can always create keyframe animations with the properties in the Effect Controls that have a stopwatch next to their names.

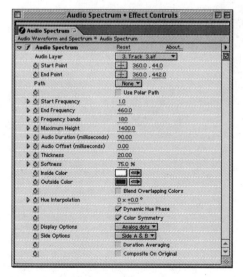

Figure 15-9: The Audio Spectrum effect properties specified here result in the Comp window shown in Figure 15-10.

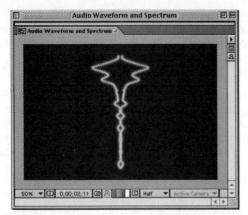

Figure 15-10: The Audio Spectrum settings shown in Figure 15-9 created these results.

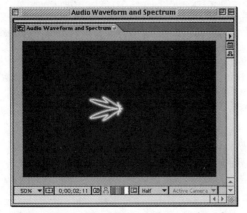

Figure 15-11: The same settings with only minor adjustments to the Polar Path and Display properties produce a very different look.

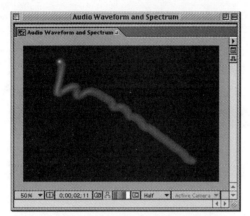

Figure 15-12: Select Blend Overlapping Colors to turn the same layer into something that looks like paint squeezed from a tube.

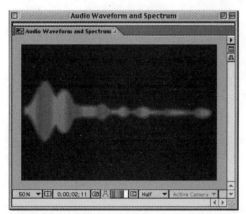

Figure 15-13: Crank the Hue Interpolation dial to introduce the color spectrum into the effect.

The Audio Waveform effect is very similar to its Audio Spectrum counterpart. The only difference is that the effect is derived from the waveform of the audio layer as opposed to the parts of the audio spectrum that you selected. You also have fewer properties to influence, but the general gist is the same.

As far as this pair of effects is concerned, the big fun happens when you introduce masks into the equation. To avail yourself to all the possibilities of this combo, here are a few guidelines:

✦ Create a mask on the same solid layer you used to apply the Audio Spectrum or Audio Waveform effect.

✦ Set the Mask Mode to None.

✦ The mask can be static or animated, open or closed.

✦ Select the mask from the Path option in the Effect Controls.

Cross-Reference

If you need a refresher, we cover masks in Chapter 9.

You can see the results of using a square mask with the Audio Spectrum effect, and an open mask with the Audio Waveform effect in Figures 15-14 and 15-15.

Note

One last word on these two filters: Seeing the effect react to the sound as you hear it is fun, but the audio layer doesn't need to be turned on in order for the effects to work.

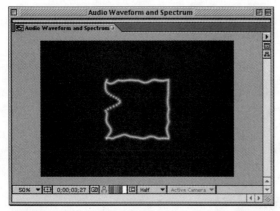

Figure 15-14: The result of using a square mask as the path for the Audio Spectrum effect

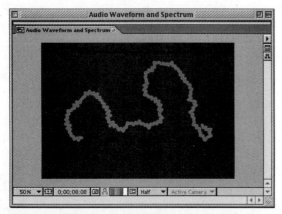

Figure 15-15: The result of using an open mask as the path for the Audio Waveform effect

Using the Beam effect

The Beam effect involves throwing simulated light around a composition. With this one, you can simulate a shooting laser beam, or if you prefer, you can create the illusion of a sharply focused spotlight scanning across a composition. Being fairly ardent fans of science fiction set in space (big surprise, right?), we're going to show you how to shoot laser beams across the sky.

STEPS: Blasting a Hole in the Sky

1. **Create a new composition.**

2. **In your new composition, create a new solid by pressing Command/Ctrl+Y.** The color doesn't matter; just make sure it's comp-sized.

3. **In the Timeline, make sure the new solid layer is selected and apply the Beam effect to it (choose Effect ➪ Render ➪ Beam).** At first glance, this effect looks pretty lame. Set the solid layer to Best quality.

4. **Using either the Effect Controls or the Effect Points visible in the Comp window, set the Start Point well outside the lower-left corner of the comp and set the End Point at the center of the comp.**

 Note   If you want to work with the Effect Points in the Comp window, make sure that the effect is selected in the Effect Controls window.

5. **In the Effect Controls window, set the starting thickness somewhere in the range of 50.**

6. **Set a keyframe for the Time property by clicking its stopwatch and drag the slider back to 0%.**

7. **In the Timeline, go forward about a second.**

8. **In the Effect Controls window, set the value of the Time property to 100%.**

9. **Press 0 on the numeric keypad to see a RAM Preview of this shooting laser beam.** If you want to, you can tweak some of its properties to change the beam's length, color, or thickness. By default, the 3D Perspective switch is turned on, and you want to leave it this way because we're shooting the beam into infinity.

10. **As soon as you're satisfied with the look of your beam, duplicate the layer so that you can set up the same effect on the right side of the comp.**

11. **Select the duplicated layer and press F3 to bring up its Effect Controls.**

12. **Change the x-value of the Start Point's coordinates so that they're located outside the lower-right corner of the comp.**

13. **Press 0 on the numeric keypad to make another RAM Preview.** Your laser beam effect should be symmetrical. (See Figure 15-16 for reference.)

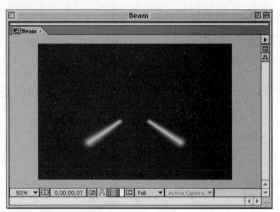

Figure 15-16: Two laser beams shoot through the far reaches of outer space.

Image of stars courtesy of EyeWire by Getty Images
www.gettyimages.com(Cosmic Moves)

Note   The layers that you applied the Beam effect to are transparent except for the beams themselves, so you can composite anything you want behind them.

Note   To "keep shooting" and repeat the effect at will, trim the layers at the point in time when the beams reach the center of the comp and duplicate them (Command/ Ctrl+D). Move the duplicates in the Timeline to create multiple "shots."

Using the Stroke, Fill, Ellipse, and Ramp effects

We cover Stroke and Fill when we cover the subject of masks in Chapter 9. These effects need masks to work properly, and other than that, there isn't much else to tell you. The Stroke effect can be animated over time, and this can create some interesting looking "write-on" effects if you like. The critical detail to remember about these two is that you really need to master the art of mask animation to fully leverage them.

The Ellipse effect is as straightforward as it sounds. Need a quick circle, oval, or ellipse? Slap this effect on a solid layer, tweak its properties, and you've got an ellipse with a clean alpha channel. End of story.

The Ramp effect really shows its value when it's used as a displacement map for other effects. You may remember that we used it as the displacement map for the Compound Blur effect that we discussed in Chapter 13. In and of itself, it doesn't produce much of an effect that you'd really want to see on its own. You can select the colors to ramp between, and you can add noise. More often than not, a clean grayscale ramp serves as a perfect displacement map, so there isn't much to add to the discussion. Figures 15-17 and 15-18 show the Ramp Effect Controls as well as the resulting images in the Comp window.

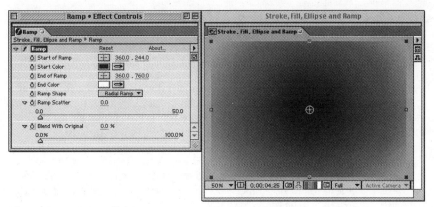

Figure 15-17: A Radial Ramp

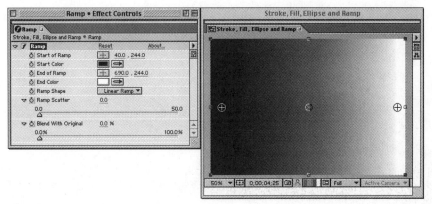

Figure 15-18: A Linear Ramp

What's new in After Effects 5.5: The 4-Color Gradient effect

After Effects 5.5's new 4-Color Gradient effect is basically an improvement over the old reliable Ramp filter. Instead of the two effect points that you can control using the Ramp effect, the 4-Color Gradient offers control over the position and color of four effect points. In addition to these parameters, you have control over how much the four colors blend together (the Blend property) as well as whether there's any noise in the gradient (the Jitter property). The 4-Color Gradient filter is perfect for making sophisticated displacement maps that are based on color, as opposed to luminance.

Using the PS+Lens Flare effect

The PS+Lens Flare effect is taken directly from Photoshop (see Figure 15-19). It creates the illusion that the Comp window is a virtual camera pointed at a light source. Unlike some of the other members of the Render group of effects, such as Beam or Ellipse, the PS+Lens Flare is composited with the layer that it's applied to, so there's no transparency behind the pixels created by the effect. This sort of stinks in terms of its ease of use, but there are a few good things about it. Complete the following steps to learn the workaround for this filter's handicap.

Note   If you've picked up version 5.5 of After Effects, you'll notice that this effect has been slightly improved. First of all, it's native to After Effects, so it's no longer the Photoshop cousin called PS+Lens Flare. Secondly, it's a lot faster than it used to be.

Figure 15-19: The PS+Lens Flare effect applied to a black solid

STEPS: Adding Transparency to the PS+Lens Flare Effect

1. **Create a new composition.**

2. **In your new composition, create a new solid by pressing Command/Ctrl+Y.** Make sure that it's black and comp-sized and click OK.

3. **In the Timeline, make sure the the new solid layer is selected and apply the PS+Lens Flare effect to it (choose Effect ➪ Render ➪ PS+Lens Flare).** Accept the effect's defaults for now. The layer's quality setting doesn't matter with this effect.

4. **Add a layer of footage to the composition and place it underneath the "flared" layer in the stacking order.** Because no transparency is in the top layer, the new footage you just added is hidden. The next few steps solve this problem.

5. **Select the solid with the PS+Lens Flare effect and press Command/Ctrl+Shift+C to pre-compose the solid layer.** In the Pre-Compose dialog box, give the pre-comp a name and opt to move all attributes into the new composition. You know that you did this correctly if the effect travels with the solid into the new comp.

6. **Select the newly pre-composed layer and apply the Shift Channels effect to it.** In the Effect Controls, select Lightness from the Take Alpha From pop-up menu. At this point, the PS+Lens Flare effect is visible in front of the background layer you added in Step 4. The only problem is that the effect appears "muted." Because the PS+Lens Flare effect is pre-multiplied with black, you need to remove the black matting from the edges of the lens flare in the image in exactly the same manner the black edges were removed from the matted flame in the last chapter.

7. **With the pre-composed layer still selected in the Timeline, apply the Remove Color Matting effect to it.** Because the Remove Color Matting effect is set to black by default, the improvement to the image quality in the comp is immediate. (See Figure 15-20 and Color Plate 15-1 for reference.)

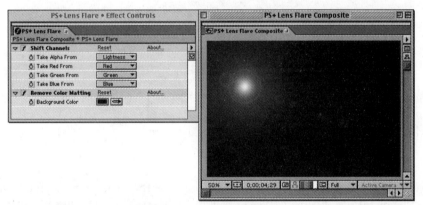

Figure 15-20: You can achieve transparency with the PS+Lens Flare effect by pre-composing the layer and adding the Shift Channels and Remove Color Matting effects to the pre-composed layer.

Image courtesy of EyeWire by Getty Images www.gettyimages.com (Cosmic Moves)

Tip   You can copy the position keyframes created by using the Motion Sketch keyframe assistant to animate the position property of the PS+Lens Flare effect to create a traveling light beam.

Tip   If you want to see how to create a "glinted" highlight on a layer of text created in Illustrator, use the Preserve Transparency switch on the lens flare layer and place it above the layer containing the Illustrator text. Animate the position of the effect so that it travels over the letters. For reference, take a look at the composition called *PS+Lens Flare Glint* in the *Chapter 15.aep* project on the DVD-ROM.

Using the Fractal effect

The Fractal effect is a newcomer. Apply it to a solid layer, and its default settings result in the creation shown in Figure 15-21. Fractals are gorgeous products of infinitely repeating math, and they're certainly quite pretty. The Online Help devotes two pages to describing the various properties of this filter, so we don't plan on adding too much to the information that's already contained in there. The only comment we feel we must make about this effect is that there's really no useful place for it in terms of designing for broadcast media. This, despite the fact that one of us likes the Grateful Dead! Of course, you may find this to be untrue in your own work (especially if you're doing Woodstock-type documentary pieces), and if that's the case, more power to you!

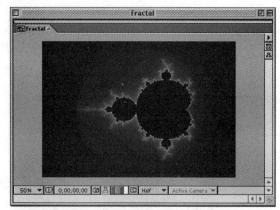

Figure 15-21: This Comp window reflects the default Fractal effect setting.

If you open the Fractal Effect Controls, some of the tools from the Tools palette take on Fractal specific functions. For example, the Zoom tool enables you to increase the magnification of the fractal while maintaining the same Comp window resolution. If you increase the magnification of the selected pattern in the Effect Controls, you can zero in on some beautiful details of the fractal. Figure 15-22 includes an example (see also Color Plate 15-2).

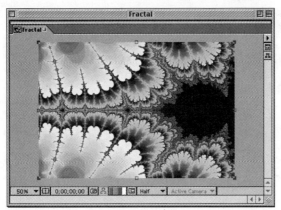

Figure 15-22: Magnify the Fractal in the Effect Controls to zero in on its incredibly minute details.

Note

All of the remaining effects contained in this chapter used to be the set of plug-ins known as Evolution from the Atomic Power Corporation. A casual glance at an Effect Controls window containing one of these effects gives you some idea as to the complexity of these filters, as well as the sophisticated nature of the plug-in architecture of the application in general. These aren't going to be easily explained along the lines of filters, such as Invert or Drop Shadow. The Online Help contains reams of information about these effects, and we highly recommend that you consult this material in your efforts to attain mastery of these new additions to the lineup. Because there's really no need for us to repeat what's contained in the documentation, we've taken the liberty of covering these effects by illustrating only one use for each one. Back when they were available as third-party offerings, the documentation on these filters ran in excess of 200 pages! Their chief architect, an incomparable After Effects master known as Brian Maffitt, created a number of video tapes explaining their various uses, so there's obviously a great deal to be learned about these effects. Our intent is to get you up and running, and if you want to explore them in much greater detail, you should take the time to read the Online Help in its entirety and really experiment with them. The DVD-ROM also includes at least one comp for each of these effects.

Using the Radio Waves effect

When you initially apply Radio Waves to a solid layer, the effect creates pulsing circles that emanate from its effect point. If you want to composite this over video, you can get a stylized look that looks like old newsreel footage (see Figure 15-23). Better yet, you can use this effect to create interesting displacement maps that nicely complement some of their siblings in the Simulation group of effects.

Figure 15-23: The Radio Waves filter is capable of producing a stylized effect that's appropriate for an old newsreel look required by a project.

Image courtesy of Bestshot.com, Inc. ©2001 (RetraVision)

STEPS: Making a Versatile Radio Wave

1. **Create a new composition.**

2. **In your new composition, create a new solid by pressing Command/Ctrl+Y.** The color doesn't matter; just make sure it's comp-sized.

3. **In the Timeline, make sure the new solid layer is selected and apply the Radio Waves effect to it (choose Effect ⇨ Render ⇨ Radio Waves).** To see the full extent of the effect, set the solid layer to Best quality. You have three distinctly different ways to use this effect, which are indicated by the Wave Type property pop-up menu, whose options are Polygon, Image Contours, and Mask. We're going to stick with the default setting of a 64-sided Polygon, which, for all intents and purposes, is a circle. When you experiment with this effect, know that the Image Contours mode works on the visible "edges" in an image, and the Mask mode applies the effect to the mask of your choice on the solid layer. Because we're working in Polygon mode, the Image Contours and Mask properties are grayed out and unavailable for use in the Effect Controls.

4. **In the Timeline, drag the playhead forward by a few seconds to see the results this filter produces over time.**

5. **In the Effect Controls, twirl down the Wave Motion properties.** Make adustments to the Frequency and Lifespan properties to make your own pattern of concentric rings.

6. **Twirl down the Stroke Properties and experiment with the Profile, Start Width, and End Width properties to improve your pattern.** The profile types are amply explained in the Online Help, and so are all the other properties for that matter.

7. **Because we're going to be using this comp as a displacement map, set the Stroke's Color property to white for maximum contrast.** The results of our own tinkering are shown in Figure 15-24 for reference.

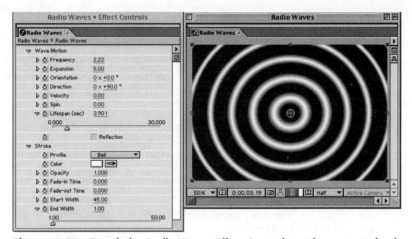

Figure 15-24: Tweak the Radio Waves Effect Controls as shown to make the composition on the right.

Here are some ideas for further experimentation:

✦ **Animate the Producer Point.** The shapes will emanate from a moving origin.

✦ **Try Image Contours mode on some footage.** For best results, experiment with the Threshold property. If your image contains noise, crank up the Pre-Blur setting to make the delineations of any edges of the image clearer so that the effect won't be applied in areas where you don't want it.

✦ **Try Mask mode on a solid layer.** Put an animated mask on the solid and select it from the Mask property pull-down menu. The emanating shapes change with the mask animation.

✦ **Animate the Spin and Orientation properties under the Wave Motion twirler.**

This effect could never be faulted for a lack of options. Don't stop there . . .

Using the Vegas effect

The Vegas filter places lines of scrolling marquee lights on the contours of an image or, if you prefer, a mask. As its name suggests, Vegas can make your Illustrator text look as though it was taken directly off the sign of a Las Vegas hotel. This is all good fun, but you can use it over logos and other shapes to create very slick looking treatments that hardly seem as trivial or restrictive as casino lights. Of course, you're going to have to do most of that investigative work on your own, but we hope this intro sets you on the path.

STEPS: Putting Vegas Highlights on Illustrator Text

1. **Create a new composition.**

2. **Place a layer of some Illustrator text or EPS artwork in it.**

3. **In the Timeline, make sure the the new solid layer is selected and apply the Vegas effect to it (choose Effect ➪ Render ➪ Vegas).** To see all the details of the effect, set the solid layer to Best quality. Similar to its Radio Waves sibling, there are a couple of different ways to use this filter, and they're enabled by the Stroke property pop-up menu, the options of which are Image Contours and Mask/Path. We're going to keep the default and go with Image Contours on top of the Illustrator text.

4. **In the Effect Controls, twirl down the Image Contours properties and select the layer that you added in Step 2 as the option for the Input Layer.** If your text is black to begin with, you may want to select the Invert Input option.

5. **Twirl down the Rendering properties and select Transparent from the Blend Mode property pop-up menu.**

6. **Twirl down the Segments properties and make adjustments to the number of segments and their length.**

7. **In the Segments properties, create a keyframe animation for the Rotation property over time.** This step makes the lights travel. The results of our own tinkering are shown in Figure 15-25.

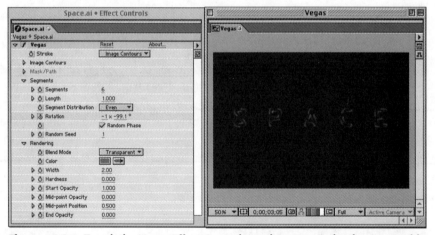

Figure 15-25: Tweak the Vegas Effect Controls as shown to make the composition on the right.

You can add the Vegas effect to a layer containing a QuickTime movie or a still image and the traveling lights move around any contrasting edges. Like Radio Waves, the success of this effect depends on the Threshold and Pre-Blur settings in the Image Contours properties. Once again, consult the Online Help to learn exactly what each property is responsible for.

Tip

If you want to scale the learning curve quickly, try taking a corporate type of logo, preferably a layered Illustrator file and see what kinds of stylized treatments you can create with Vegas. If you're strapped for logos, use Illustrator to approximate something such as the symbol for the Olympics, import it into After Effects, and then apply Vegas to it. As a final clue, try applying the effect to two versions of a logo. One should contain all of the line art, and the other should separate each line or shape into a separate layer.

Cross-Reference

A bit later, we look at two offerings from the Render group of effects. We cover Fractal Noise in conjunction with the Displacement Map effect in Chapter 17, and we also look at Lightning in that chapter.

Simulating Natural Physics and Breaking Stuff

The Simulation group of effects adds to our continuing coverage of what used to be the Evolution set of plug-ins. The only one in the bunch that's not an evolution of Evolution is Particle Playground, which is such a useful and complicated effect that it gets its very own chapter. All of these effects were created with a recognizably similar sensibility. You may have recognized this when working with the Vegas and Radio Waves effects. They also contain 3D controls of one kind or another since they were developed before After Effects became a 3D application. So, stay alert and press on with our introduction to this sophisticated bunch of effects (see Figure 15-26).

Cross-Reference

Chapter 18 is devoted entirely to Particle Playground, a truly amazing effect.

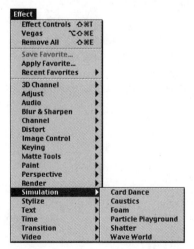

Figure 15-26: The Simulation group of effects is primarily composed of what used to be the Evolution set of plug-ins.

Note

The Card Dance, Card Wipe, Caustics, Foam, and Wave World effects are available from the Adobe Web site only after you've registered your copy of After Effects. After you've installed your copy, go to the After Effects Web site to complete the registration/download process at www.adobe.com/products/aftereffects.

Using the Card Dance effect

The Card Dance effect enables you to break a layer up into rows and columns. You can then animate the resulting tiles, or "cards," in 3D space (see Figure 15-27). Furthermore, you can use a displacement map as the basis for the animation (see Figure 15-28). The effect also contains camera controls that make the Comp window appear as though it's a camera moving around the animation in 3D.

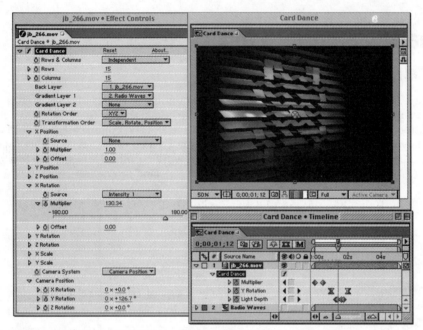

Figure 15-27: The Card Dance effect enables you to break a layer up into rows and columns and animate the resulting tiles as well as a virtual camera in 3D space.

Image courtesy of Digital Juice (Jump Backs, Vol.7)

Using the Caustics effect

The Caustics effect simulates the appearance of a surface (your source layer) reflecting light based on the motion of virtual water moving above it (see Figure 15-29). You can use a displacement map to drive the animation of the water. Used in conjunction with displacement maps made with either Radio Waves or Wave World, you can attain some very natural-looking water effects.

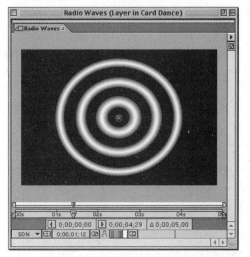

Figure 15-28: We used our Radio Waves comp as the displacement map for rotating the tiles on their X-axis. If a tile is located over white pixels from the animated radio waves, they react accordingly.

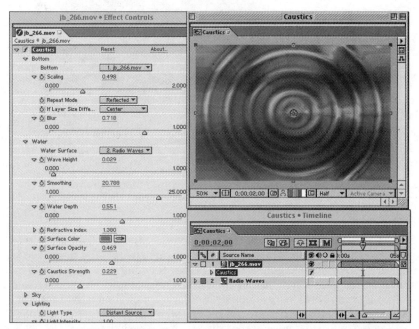

Figure 15-29: The Caustics effect takes the layer it's applied to and places it under virtual water, which you can influence with a displacement map. In this case, we used our versatile Radio Waves animation once again.

Image courtesy of Digital Juice (Jump Backs, Vol.7)

Using the Foam effect

The Foam filter is a particle-based effect that simulates bubbles moving through liquid (see Figure 15-30). You'll never guess. Yep, you can control the parameters of the foaming bubbles with a displacement map, called a "Flow Map" when used with the Foam effect. We made a separate comp out of simple black and white solids and used it as our flow map (see Figure 15-31).

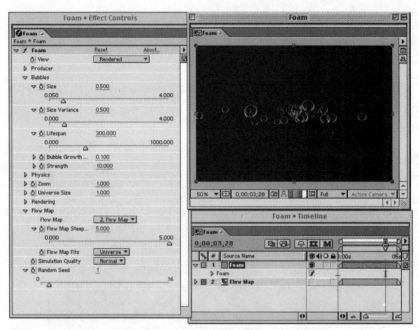

Figure 15-30: The Foam effect generates bubbles, which emanate from a control point and move within a flow map if you specify one.

The beauty of this effect stems from the filter's versatility, which allows you to define exactly what the "bubbles" are with your own artwork. You may have initially wondered just how you were going to incorporate teeming masses of bubbles into your project, but it goes much further than that. For example, you could place a layer into your comp containing an illustration or a QuickTime movie and specify that as the "bubble," which is randomly generated by the effect. For example, think of leaves floating in a stream or cockroaches racing across the floor.

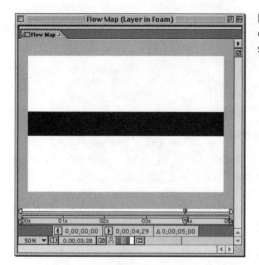

Figure 15-31: We made a separate comp out of simple black and white solids and used it as our flow map.

Using the Shatter effect

The Shatter effect enables you to turn a layer into exploding fragments in 3D space (see Figure 15-32). You can add dimensional depth to the fragments with the extrusion controls, and you can also directly control the location and the forces of the explosion. Furthermore, you can define whether the fragments come at the camera or go backwards towards the horizon, and as if that weren't enough, you can control the forces of gravity that pull on the fragments after they become dislodged from the exploding layer. In essence, you can blow stuff up any which way your mind can imagine.

You have a large number of preset shapes that you can choose for the types of fragments created by the explosion, but as with Foam, you can create your own Custom Shatter Map to determine the shape of the exploding particles. Like Card Dance, you have extensive 3D camera controls that enable you to view the explosion from any distance or angle from the layer to which you apply the effect.

Displacement maps, called Gradient Maps in the world of Shatter, are a bit tricky, and we're going to let you figure them out with the Online Help. For example, you can use them on extruded masks containing letter shapes for pretty fancy 3D text treatments.

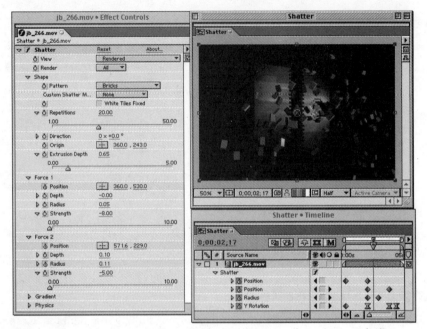

Figure 15-32: The Shatter effect enables you to turn a layer into exploding fragments.

Image courtesy of Digital Juice (Jump Backs, Vol.7)

Using the Wave World effect

The Wave World effect simulates ripples on the surface of water (see Figures 15-33 and 15-34). This effect's sole purpose is to create a displacement map for use with the other simulation effects. The Wireframe Preview viewing option enables you to clearly visualize the height of the waves, the point at which they create white and black pixels, as well as the topography of the ground beneath the virtual water. If you pre-compose your Wave World compositions, they will also work beautifully as the water surface for the Caustics effect.

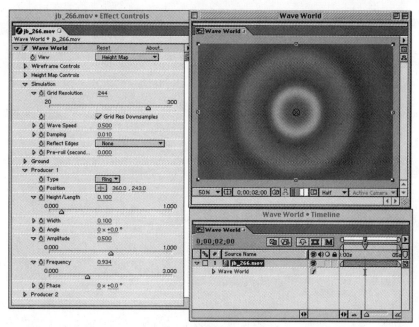

Figure 15-33: The Wave World effect simulates ripples on the surface of water.

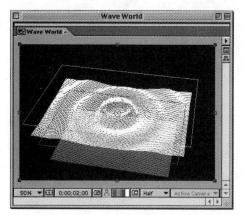

Figure 15-34: Viewing the Wave World effect in Wireframe Preview mode gives you a detailed 3D look at exactly what kind of waves are controlling the white and black values in the height map.

What's new in After Effects 5.5: The Cell Pattern effect

New in After Effects 5.5, the Cell Pattern effect creates organic-looking patterns like the one shown in Figure SB 15-1. The filter offers a choice of 12 shapes. Because you have control over a number of effect properties, you can animate the movement, size, and contrast of the cellular textures. The Cell Pattern effect also provides you with a great way to make displacement maps that work exceedingly well with effects such as Shatter, Caustics, Card Dance, Card Wipe, and Displacement Map.

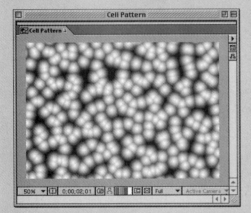

Figure SB 15-1: You can use these organic patterns by themselves or as displacement maps.

✦ ✦ ✦

Designing with Style

This chapter is largely concerned with the effects from the Stylize category. If you want your footage to appear as though each frame is an oil painting, you can learn how to do that here. If you want to animate text directly on to the screen as though an unseen pen was writing it, you can learn how to do that as well. Ever wondered if you could create that "hidden identity" look that you see in parts of real-life cop shows where the suspect's face has been obscured by big blurry pixels? Well, get to it. It's in here.

The Time filters are also included in this chapter. These are a tad difficult to explain without showing you, but one effect, Echo, can take footage or an object and create a tracer effect from its motion. For example, if you want to visibly "step-through" the motion of a karate chop shot at a high frame rate, you can look into the nuances of the Echo filter.

The Transition effects provide you with ways to move from one layer to another in the timeline if a crossfade just won't do, and the Video filters deal with certain aspects of production geared toward preparing your output in a broadcast setting. You may not realize that a good deal of color that you can use in After Effects is actually impossible to display in broadcast video. If you already knew this, you may not have known that After Effects contains a filter that lets you clean up your color choices for broadcast.

There's a lot in here. Keep shooting for the big fun.

Going for That Certain Look

The Stylize group of effects (see Figure 16-1) is aptly named, because they generally result in a look that's pretty rooted in the style created by the effect itself. Unlike a set of effects such as you can find in the Adjust group, these are less universal. Either they're appropriate for your project or not.

A good number of them have been lifted out of Photoshop, and some of these are more successful than others when applied to the world of motion, but we'll let you be the final judge.

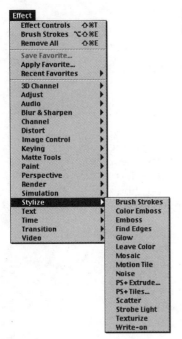

Figure 16-1: The Stylize group of effects as they appear in the Effect menu

Chapter 8 describes working with effects in general. If you aren't familiar with applying effects or working in the Effect Controls window, take the time to read (or re-read) the beginning of Chapter 8.

As far as the following explanations of effects are concerned, we created an After Effects project that includes a composition for each effect we cover in the chapter. Just as a reminder, you need to copy the *Source Material* folder from the DVD-ROM to your hard drive. Additionally, the exercises that follow cover some of these effects in detail. Our own corresponding After Effects project is called *Chapter 16.aep* and can be found in the *Project Files/Chapter 16* folder.

Using the Brush Strokes effect

This effect adds a painted look to your footage. When using the Brush Strokes effect, you can set the direction of the strokes by using the Stroke Angle property. However, the strokes are automatically given a slightly random scatter to achieve a more "natural" feel. Bear in mind when using this effect that you will be painting on the alpha channel of your image as well as the color channels. So, if you have masked a portion of your footage, the Brush Strokes effect will paint over the edges of your mask. See Figure 16-2.

Figure 16-2: Use the Brush Stroke effect to achieve that "painterly" look.
Image courtesy of ArtBeats (Starter Kit)

The Online Help (choose Help ➪ After Effects Help) is an HTML document that goes well beyond the printed User's Guide in explaining After Effects in detail. In addition to containing all the information included in the User's Guide, the Online Help contains a lot of very useful basic information on all of the effects that ship with After Effects. The Online help is particularly good because it tends to explain the purpose of each and every setting in an effect. Refer to it as often as you need to; our purpose in writing about these effects is to supplement that information rather than repeat it.

Using the Color Emboss effect

The Color Emboss effect works exactly like the Emboss effect (see the next section), without altering the original colors of your image. In the regular Emboss effect, the colors of the original layer are ignored, whereas the Color Emboss effect almost seems to lay over a duplicate of the layer at a slight offset from the original.

Using the Emboss effect

The Emboss effect sharpens the edges of items seen in the footage and suppresses their colors. This effect also highlights the edges of the object from the angle of your choice. Using the Direction property, you can set the direction from which the light source for the highlight is cast. The Relief property controls the height of the embossing. See Figure 16-3.

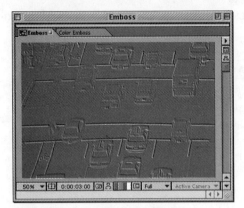

Figure 16-3: The Emboss effect
Image courtesy of Sekani (Corbis NY Vistas, Vol. 213)

Using the Find Edges effect

Using the Find Edges effect works best on footage that has clear outlines and edges. This filter emphasizes the edges and often makes the footage look like photo negatives of the original.

The Invert setting reverses the image. When the Invert option is used, the edges show up as bright lines over a dark background (this is ideal for creating the cheesy Elvis painting on black velvet effect you may have seen when traveling the streets of Las Vegas). When the Invert option is turned off, the edges of the objects in the image appear as dark lines over a light background.

Using the Leave Color effect

The Leave Color effect is an absolute blast! This filter removes all colors from a layer, except the one specified by you. For example, in a scene of New York City traffic, you can choose to see only the color of the yellow cabs, and the rest of the scene will appear black and white (assuming there are no other yellow objects around). You may have seen commercials on TV where a brightly colored orange rolls across a black and white landscape. You can create your own version of this effect by using the Leave Color effect.

Use the Color to Leave setting to select the color that you want to leave untouched. In this case, you can select the eye dropper from the Color to Leave setting and choose the yellow color of the cabs. Use the Amount to Decolor slider to reduce the saturation amount of the remaining colors.

Using the Mosaic effect

The Mosaic effect enables you to turn a layer into solid color rectangles. There's no doubt you've seen it on television, especially on very popular cop shows. You can use this filter to create the "hidden identity" effect that the producers slap onto the faces of the suspects in these real-life dramas. (See Figure 16-4.) You can also use this effect to simulate a very pixilated look for a piece of footage. For best results, make sure that the layer is set to Best quality.

Figure 16-4: Protect the identity of furry creatures by using the Mosaic effect.
Image courtesy of Sekani (Funny and Furry 1)

When using this effect, use the Horizontal/Vertical Blocks options to set the number of mosaic sections in each direction. You may have to use this option to reduce the size of the blocks. The Sharp Colors option allows you to give each mosaic tile the color of the pixel in the center of the original layer.

Tip

An item to remember here is that if the Horizontal/Vertical Block setting is set to the inherent resolution of the footage, you won't see any change. For example, if the Horizontal/Vertical Block setting is set to 720 and 486 for a 720 x 486 image, the image will remain at its full resolution. You can set keyframes at this setting and then animate the block settings to lower numbers in order to create an animation that takes the footage from full resolution down to a pixilated look. You can also reverse the effect to create the illusion that you're increasing the clarity of an image. You've probably seen this when a piece of surveillance video gets enhanced to reveal a perpetrator in a spy movie.

STEPS: Using the Mosaic Effect to Protect the Identity of Furry Animals

1. **Make a new comp by choosing Composition ⇨ New Composition.**

2. **Drag the footage from your project window to the Timeline window.**
   As you can see, we use footage of the cheetah cub.

3. **Choose Layer ⇨ New ⇨ Adjustment Layer.**

4. **Select the Adjustment Layer in the Timeline and choose Effects ⇨ Stylize ⇨ Mosaic.**

5. **Double-click the Adjustment Layer in the timeline so that it opens in the Layer window.**

6. **Double-click the Oval Mask tool in the tools palette. This will add an oval Mask in the window.** Resize this mask as needed.

7. **Select the Adjustment layer and press F3 to call up the Effects window for the layer.**

8. **Adjust the Horizontal and the Vertical Block setting to 20.**

9. **Select the Adjustment Layer in the Timeline and press the F key to open its Mask feather settings in the Timeline.** Change the Mask Feather settings to 50 for vertical and the same for horizontal.

Voilá! The identity of this furry creature is now protected, and he is considered innocent until proven guilty in a court of law.

Using the Motion Tile effect

This effect re-creates the source image as a tile or tiles in the output image. The reason this effect is called Motion Tile is because, when shifting the location of the tiles, it uses the Motion Blur setting (if enabled) to accentuate any movement of the tiles. Using the Tile Center control, you can change the position of the main tile. See Figure 16-5.

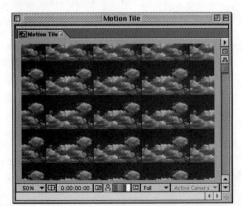

Figure 16-5: The Motion Tile effect with the settings for Tile Width and Tile Height set at 25

Image courtesy of ArtBeats (Starter Kit)

What's new in After Effects 5.5: The Roughen Edges effect

The Roughen Edges effect is a worthy addition to the Stylize group of effects. This one lets you have fun with the edges of an alpha channel, so it's perfect for applying to a layer of text (like we've done in Figure SB 16-1). You can animate it to make an object look as though it's organically falling apart, or you can give the object's edges a more controlled and tattered look. There are eight different edge types to choose from, and you can completely randomize their appearance if you like.

Figure SB 16-1: If you want to give your text a grungy feel, use the new Roughen Edges effect.

Using the Noise effect

Using the Noise effect, you can randomly alter the color values of pixels throughout your footage. The Amount of Noise setting specifies the amount of noise that you want in your image. At 0%, this setting adds no noise, whereas at 100%, the image may not be recognizable at all. The Noise effect is commonly used to add film noise to video and other footage. See Figure 16-6.

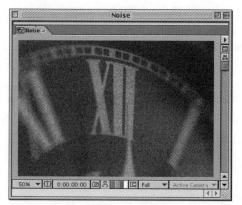

Figure 16-6: Use the Noise effect to give an arty film look to your footage. We use an Amount of Noise setting of 40% to exaggerate the effect here.
Image courtesy of ArtBeats (Bundle Pack)

Using the PS+Extrude effect

The PS+Extrude filter gives a 3D texture to a layer. This effect is kind of a holdover from the early days of Photoshop, and we have trouble imagining a good use for this effect unless you're trying to re-create a bit of forgotten glory from the 1980s. But, hey, it's not our place to guess. See Figure 16-7.

Figure 16-7: The PS+Extrude effect applied to a layer. My! Life is just like a box of chocolates — so many effects, so little time.

Image courtesy of Creatas

STEPS: Using the Extrude Filter to Travel Back to the 1980s

1. **Select a layer in the Timeline and choose Effect ➪ Stylize ➪ PS+Extrude.**

2. **A dialog box appears for you to choose your settings.** Choose a 3D type:

   Selecting Blocks creates objects with a square front face and four side faces.

   Selecting Pyramids creates objects with four triangular sides that end at a point.

3. **In the Size text box, enter a value to determine the length of any side of the object's base.** You can enter any value from 2 to 255 pixels.

4. **In the Depth text box, enter any value to indicate how far the tallest object appears to extend from the screen.** You can use any value from zero to 255.

5. **Next, in the same dialog box, choose a depth option:**

   Select Random to give each block (or pyramid) a random depth.

   Select Level-based to make each object's depth correspond to its brightness. Brights protrude more than darks.

6. **You should select Mask Incomplete Blocks if you want to hide any object extending beyond the selection.**

7. **Click OK.** And there you have it! A cheesy effect from the early days of Photoshop.

Using the PS+Tiles effect

Using the PS+Tiles effect, you can break up an image into a series of tiles, off-setting the layer from its original position. See Figure 16-8.

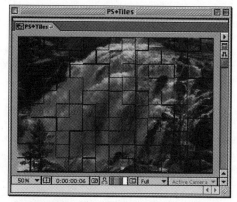

Figure 16-8: The PS+Tiles effect applied to a layer

Image courtesy of ArtBeats (Starter Kit)

You can choose one of the following to fill the area between the tiles:

✦ The background color

✦ The foreground color

✦ A reverse version of the image

✦ An unaltered version of the image, which puts the tiled version on top of the original and reveals part of the original image underneath the tiled edges

Using the Strobe Light effect

Using the Strobe Light effect, you can add a flashing, strobe-like effect to your layer. This effect adds an arithmetic operation on the layer of your choice at periodic or random intervals. For example, for every second, the layer can be made to be completely white for one-half second. You can also choose to invert a layer's colors at random intervals.

The Strobe Duration setting allows you to choose the duration for which the Strobe effect lasts. The Strobe Period setting sets the time between the strobe events. For example, if the Strobe Duration is set to one second and the Strobe Period is set to two seconds, the image layer will show the Strobe effect for one second and then be without the effect for two seconds.

Using the Random Strobe Probability, you can set the probability that any given frame of the footage layer may have the effect. This gives the appearance of randomness in your final output.

Using the Texturize effect

Using the Texturize effect on a layer enables you to give the layer the appearance of having the texture of another layer of your choice. Using this effect, you can make a layer appear to have the texture of bricks, stone, or marble. You can also control the depth of your texture and the light source to make the texture more believable.

To use this effect, you need two layers in your Timeline. Select the first one and apply Effect ⇨ Stylize ⇨ Texturize to it. In the Texture Layer pop-up menu, select the layer from which you want to borrow the texture. You may want to increase the Texture Contrast to add depth to your texture. See Figure 16-9.

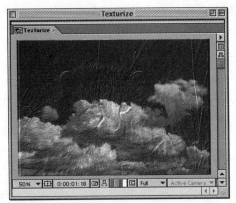

Figure 16-9: The Texturize effect enables you to add the texture of one layer to another. In this case, the sky layer gets its texture from the cheetah cub layer. We increased the Texture Contrast setting to exaggerate the effect.
Images courtesy of ArtBeats (Starter Kit) and Sekani (Funny and Furry 1)

Using the Write-on effect

Simply speaking, the Write-on effect creates animated strokes on a layer. You can use this filter to create the effect of writing on a layer. You can tweak the many settings in this effect to animate the brush size, color, hardness, and the opacity of strokes. One of the most interesting ways of working with the Write-on effect is to use it in combination with the Motion Sketch feature of After Effects. Have a look.

STEPS: Animating a Writing Effect by using Motion Sketch and Write-on

1. **Create a new composition and add a solid to it by choosing Layer ⇨ New ⇨ Solid.** Make the size of this solid just 50 x 50 pixels and name it *Dummy Solid*. This solid will simply be used as a placeholder of sorts for our exercise. Later we can easily rid ourselves of this solid.

2. **Select the *Dummy Solid* layer in the Timeline and choose Window ⇨ Motion Sketch.**

3. **Click the Start Capture button in the Motion Sketch window.** Your pointer turns into a crosshair.

4. **With the crosshair positioned over the Comp window, write out any shape or text you want.**

5. **Now, make a new solid by choosing Layer ⇨ New ⇨ Solid.** Make the size of this solid to the comp size and name it *Write On Solid*.

6. **Select the *Write On Solid* layer in the timeline and apply the Write-on effect to it by choosing Effect ⇨ Stylize@@Write-on.**

7. **Solo the Position property of the *Dummy Solid* layer by selecting that layer and pressing the P key.**

8. **Click the Position property name in the *Dummy Solid* layer to select all the Position keyframes.**

9. **Choose Edit ⇨ Copy.**

10. **Display the Brush Position property of the Write-on effect in the Timeline by Control+clicking/right-clicking it in the Effect Controls and selecting Reveal in Timeline.**

11. **In the Timeline, select the I beam of the Brush Position property for the *Write On Solid* and choose Edit ⇨ Paste.** Your position keyframes from the *Dummy* solid are now pasted into the *Write On Solid*.

12. **Preview your comp, and you see the Write-on effect animate.**

13. **Adjust the Brush Size and Brush Spacing properties to your liking.**
    See Figure 16-10.

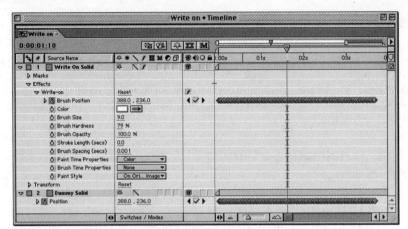

Figure 16-10: Copy the keyframes from the Position property of the *Dummy Solid* to the Brush Size property of the Write-on effect in the *Write On Solid* to make the Write-on effect animate to your liking.

Tip   If you don't use a tablet for a mouse, you may find it more gratifying to use the data from mask shapes made out of text outlines in Illustrator. If you're unclear on this, look at the chapter on masks (Chapter 9). Just copy any mask and paste it into the Brush Position property. After you do that, you can adjust the keyframes to suit the speed that you desire for the animation.

Filtering Time

The two Time effects, Echo and Posterize Time, enable you to take a layer and distort its temporal normalcy. Echo enables you to incorporate a layer's past frames (real or virtual) into your comp. Posterize Time alters the frame rate of a layer's playback. One is quite pretty, the other very practical. They're both quite a bit more complicated than they may seem at first glance, so put on your propeller hat and tune in.

Using the Echo effect

This effect can be used to create visual echoes and streaking effects based on the original image. A word of caution here: If you apply this effect, it's only visible in the Comp window and not the Layer window. Also, you only see an echo when there is motion in the layer.

There is something else that's also very tricky about the Echo effect that you should keep in mind. Applying the Echo effect to a layer negates any masks or other effects applied to that layer. To avoid this problem, pre-compose the layer and apply the other effects and masks in the nested comp. Then in the main comp, add the Echo effect. We show you this process in the next series of steps.

STEPS: Create a Rocket Trail Using the Echo Effect

1. **Drag the source footage from the Project window into the Comp window.** In our case, we're using the *080CLB01.EPS* still, which is just an EPS file of a rocket ship, courtesy of the good people at Creatas.

2. **In the Timeline, select the layer and choose Effect ⇨ Channel ⇨ Invert.** This makes our black EPS file white and makes it visible in the Comp window. You may not need to do this if your layer looks right to begin with.

3. **Select the source footage layer in the Timeline window and create a motion path using position keyframes.** We also scaled down the rocket a bit to make it fit better in the Comp window.

4. **Remember that we must pre-comp this layer for us to be able to use the Echo effect.** Select the source footage layer in the Timeline window and choose Layer ⇨ Pre-compose.

5. **Enter a name for the pre-composed composition in the Pre-compose dialog box, choose Move All Attributes into the New Composition, and then click OK.** We choose *Rocket Precomp* as the name for our pre-comp.

6. **Select the layer of the pre-composed composition in the Timeline window and choose Effect ⇨ Time ⇨ Echo.**

7. **In the Effect Controls window, apply these values to the Echo effect:**

   - Echo Time: –0.23
   - Number of Echoes: 10
   - Starting Intensity: 1.00
   - Decay: 0.38
   - Echo Operator: Add

8. **Press the spacebar to preview the trail effect, make a RAM Preview for a quicker preview, or render the composition to view the entire effect in real time.** See Figure 16-11.

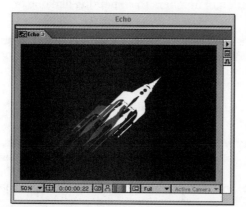

Figure 16-11: Adding the Echo effect requires pre-composing.

Images courtesy of Creatas

Using the Posterize Time effect

The Posterize Time effect sets and locks a layer to the specific frame rate of your choice. While this effect might not seem like it has much use for you, it is one of those very practical filters that addresses a specific production problem that arises when a comp is comprised of layers that run at different frame rates. For example, elements created at varying frame rates can all be made to run at 30 fps.

As was the case when you applied the Echo effect to a layer, that layer's masks and any previously applied effects are ignored. To posterize the time of a masked layer, or a layer that has other effects added to it, create the mask in another composition or pre-compose the layer with other effects before applying the Posterize Time effect.

 Caution   Be forewarned: Animating the value of the Frame Rate slider can give unpredictable and unwanted results.

A very handy use of the Posterize Time filter that we've used over the years is to slow down certain effects that otherwise move too fast to be of any good use. We explain this in the next exercise.

STEPS: Using Posterize Time with Random Numbers

1. **Make a new comp by choosing Composition ⇨ New Composition.**

2. **Make a new solid by using the Command/Ctrl+Y keyboard shortcut.** Make sure that it's comp-sized.

3. **Select the solid layer and choose Effect ⇨ Text ⇨ Numbers.** Accept the defaults and click OK.

4. **In the Numbers Effect Controls window, check the Random Values box under the Format settings.** If you play the comp now, you'll see that the numbers change every frame. This may not be what you want. What if you want to slow down the regeneration of numbers to something like one or five times every second?

5. **In the Timeline, select the solid layer with the Numbers effect applied to it and then choose Layer ⇨ Pre-Compose.** In the Pre-compose dialog box, select the Move all attributes into the new composition setting. Name your pre-comp *Numbers Precomp*.

6. **Select the *Numbers Precomp* layer and add the Posterize Time effect to it by choosing Effect ⇨ Time ⇨ Posterize Time.**

7. **At this point, you have unlimited control over the regeneration of the numbers.** In the Effect Controls window, change the Frame Rate in the Posterize Time filter. The frame rate you select determines the rate at which the numbers change in your comp. For example, a setting of 1 fps changes the number just once every second.

What's new in After Effects 5.5: The Time Difference effect

The Time Difference effect calculates the difference between the pixel values of two layers over time.

Making the Transition

Transitions are used to take you from one layer to another. A simple cross-dissolve definitely counts as one kind of transition, but there are others that are a bit more sophisticated. Other kinds of transitions include wipes, such as the Iris or Linear wipe.

To use any of these effects as transitions between one layer and another, in the Timeline, place the transition layer on top of the layer that you want to transition into and then apply the effect to the transition layer. All of the transitions are located in the Effect ⇨ Transition menu (see Figure 16-12).

They all operate in the same fashion, which is the following: set keyframe values for the Transition Completion property to animate the change from the transition layer (0%) to the layer or layers beneath (100%).

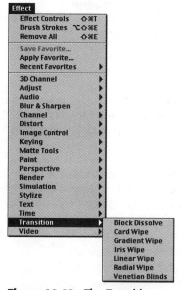

Figure 16-12: The Transition group of effects as they appear in the Effect menu

Displacing time with luminance

The Time Displacement effect (PB only) is a great filter that often produces unexpectedly beautiful images. First, you need to create a displacement map (it can be animated if you like), place it in a new comp, and turn off its visibility. Add a clip to the comp and apply the Time Displacement effect to it (select Effect ⇨ Time ⇨ Time Displacement). Select the displacement map layer as the Time Displacement Layer in the Effect Controls, and watch what unfolds. Wherever there are brighter luminance values in the displacement map, the clip will display pixels that are at the same position, but further ahead in time. For darker pixel values in the displacement map, the clip will display pixels that are at the same position, but further back in time. With the right piece of footage and a carefully animated displacement map, you can occasionally get visually stunning results.

Using the Block Dissolve transition effect

This transition effect makes a layer disappear in shapes of random blocks. The width and height of the blocks can be animated.

STEPS: Using the Block Dissolve Effect

1. **Place two layers in a new composition.**

2. **Select the top layer and choose Effect ⇨ Transition ⇨ Block Dissolve.**

3. **In the Block Dissolve Effect Controls, animate the Transition Completion values from 0% to 100% over whatever span of time that you require to see the transition from the top layer to the bottom layer.**

Using the Card Wipe effect

The Card Wipe effect was acquired by Adobe from Atomic Power's Evolution set of plug-ins. The Atomic Power filters are sophisticated, deep, and full of controls. They are never to be mistaken for the "one-trick pony" type of effects that you'll occasionally find in After Effects.

The Card Wipe effect simulates a group of cards displaying an image and then flipping over to display another image. This effect was created to simulate the signs you sometimes see at stadium games. You know, when a large group of people holds signs over their heads and then flips them over to show another picture or group of words? The Card Wipe effect is built from the same code used to create the Card Dance filter, which we cover in the last chapter.

So it should come as no surprise that the Card Wipe effect provides a ridiculous amount of control over the number of rows and columns of cards, the flip direction, and the transition direction. You can also use a gradient layer to determine the flip order. Moreover, you can control the randomness and jitter of the cards to make the effect appear more realistic, as though actual people were holding up the cards. To boot, you have the same lighting and camera controls as you do in Card Dance.

As you learned with the Block Dissolve, to create an animated transition, animate the Transition Completion value from 0% to 100%. Note that the Card Wipe effect does not come with the After Effects general release. You can, however, download it for free from the Adobe Web site, in exchange for registering your copy of After Effects. A great deal, if we may say so!

Using the Gradient Wipe transition effect

In the world of wipes, the Gradient Wipe holds a very special place. The Gradient Wipe effect creates a transition that is based on the luminance values of a second layer, which is called the gradient layer (another name for a displacement map). Gradients are commonly created as still images consisting of dark and light areas. When used with the Gradient Wipe, dark areas of the gradient layer become transparent first, followed by areas of lighter luminance values.

For example, a simple grayscale gradient that ramps from a dark top to a light bottom produces a top-to-bottom wipe. Bear in mind that the gradient layer does not have to be a still image. You can use any layer, such as a composition or video footage to serve as a gradient layer for creating unusual wipe effects.

There are many ways to have fun with the Gradient Wipe filter. You can animate the Ramp effect or the Fractal Noise effect to create a transition in all kinds of directions that contains all sorts of patterns. You can also create gradients in either Adobe Photoshop or Adobe Illustrator.

The Gradient Layer pop-up menu is used to specify the layer to be used as the basis for the animation of the transition. Note that the gradient layer must be in the same composition as the layer to which you apply the Gradient Wipe effect.

See Chapter 13 for more on using the Ramp effect in After Effects.

Figure 16-13 shows the Gradient image and the Gradient transition it creates.

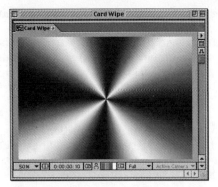 

Figure 16-13: The Gradient image (left) creates the Gradient transition seen on the right.

Images courtesy of ArtBeats (Starter Kit) and Sekani (Corbis NY Vistas, Vol. 213)

STEPS: Using the Gradient Wipe

1. **Place two layers in a new composition.**

2. **In the Timeline, select the top layer and choose Effect ⇨ Transition ⇨ Gradient Wipe.**

3. **Add a gradient layer from the Project window to the Timeline.** In our case, we're using *Displacement map3.psd*. You can turn off the visibility of the gradient layer if you like.

4. **Open the Effect Controls window for the top layer and select the *Displacement map3.psd* as your gradient by using the Gradient Layer pop-up menu.**

5. **Animate the Transition Completion values from 0% to 100% over whatever span of time that you prefer.**

6. **Press 0 on the numeric keypad to view a RAM Preview of the results.**

Using the Iris Wipe transition effect

The Iris Wipe effect creates a transition that is essentially a round wipe that reveals the underlying layer. You can specify anywhere from six to 32 points when tweaking the Iris effect. See Figure 16-14.

Using the Linear Wipe transition effect

Simply put, the Linear Wipe effect performs a basic linear wipe in the direction of your choice. The Wipe Angle option sets the direction in which the wipe travels. For example, at 90 degrees, the wipe travels from left to right. See Figure 16-15.

Figure 16-14: The Iris Wipe effect
Images courtesy of ArtBeats (Starter Kit) and Sekani (Corbis NY Vistas, Vol. 213)

Figure 16-15: The basic Linear Wipe effect
Images courtesy of ArtBeats (Starter Kit) and Sekani (Corbis NY Vistas, Vol. 213)

Using the Radial Wipe transition effect

The Radial Wipe Effect reveals the underlying footage layer using a wipe that essentially circles around a point of your choice. The Start Angle setting sets the angle at which the transition begins. At a setting of zero degrees, the wipe starts at the top of the layer. At 180 degrees, the wipe begins at the bottom of the layer. You can also choose whether the wipe moves clockwise or counterclockwise or alternates between the two. See Figure 16-16.

Figure 16-16: The Radial Wipe in progress
*Images courtesy of ArtBeats (Starter Kit) and Sekani
(Corbis NY Vistas, Vol. 213)*

Using the Venetian Blinds transition effect

The Venetian Blinds effect reveals the underlying layer using strips. You can select the size and the direction of the strips. Figure 16-17 shows the Venetian Blinds effect transition.

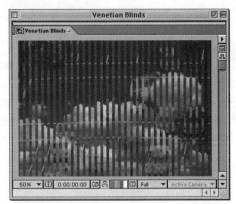

Figure 16-17: The Venetian Blinds Wipe in action
*Images courtesy of ArtBeats (Starter Kit) and Sekani
(Corbis NY Vistas, Vol. 213)*

Prepping for Broadcast

Preparing footage for broadcast is something of a necessity for many After Effects users. If you are preparing your After Effects creations for eventual airing at a TV or a cable station, you need to know about the difference between the world of computers and the world of video.

Computers, and hence the graphics programs they use, work in the RGB color space. In RGB, the colors are made up of Red, Green, and Blue; subsequently, the luminance, or black and white values of the pixels, is embedded into those colors. Video, on the other hand, generally works in the YUV color space where the brightness information is stored separately.

One of the problems that occurs when going from computer graphics to video is that brightness and color values that seem fine on computers can exceed the "legal" limits of broadcast video.

In general, you should follow these rules when preparing artwork in After Effects for use in broadcast video:

✦ Avoid using highly saturated colors when preparing graphics in After Effects for use in broadcast video.

✦ Always render a test of your movie and play it back on an NTSC monitor to check that colors do not bleed or the brightness does not exceed the video limits. If you do extensive work for broadcast, consider getting a waveform monitor and vectorscope. A waveform monitor allows you to check the brightness levels of video, while the vectorscope does the same for the colors.

✦ Avoid pure black and white values. If you are working in After Effects, you should remember that the value for black should not exceed 16 and the whites should not exceed 235. In other words, the range 16–235 should not be exceeded in either side.

The following filters may be of some use to you if your work in After Effects involves preparing material for broadcast video.

Using the Broadcast Colors effect

To apply the Broadcast Colors effect, select your layer in the Timeline and choose Effects ⇨ Video ⇨ Broadcast Colors. You can also place your entire comp into a new comp and then apply this effect to the nested comp.

Using this effect changes the pixel color values of your layer so that the image can be accurately presented in a broadcast situation. Using the Broadcast Colors effect, you can reduce both the luminance and the saturation to a "safe" level.

Bear in mind that reducing saturation requires greater amplitude changes than reducing luminance to achieve similar results.

Unfortunately, you may find that the Broadcast Colors filter may be of limited use to you because it often adds noise and artifacts. A common use for this filter is to simply use it to identify the problem areas of your comp. You can then use the Change Color filter to reduce the saturation of the offending colors to an acceptable level. Of course, for ideal results, you should always attempt to use a waveform monitor as well as a vectorscope.

You may find it helpful if we take a minute to explain some of the settings in the Broadcast Colors filter at this point.

✦ Signal Amplitude for video is measured in IRE units. A setting of 120 IRE units is generally accepted as the maximum possible amplitude that is acceptable for transmission. To be on the safe-and-conservative side, stick with the default maximum value of 110 IREs.

✦ The Key Out Unsafe and Key Out Safe settings are given to make it convenient for you to determine which portions of the layer will be affected by the Broadcast Colors effect at your current settings.

✦ An "unsafe" or "illegal" level means that some sections of your final rendered movie exceed the safe level. When viewed on a television, these areas probably won't look the way you may have intended.

Using the Reduce Interlace Flicker effect

This filter helps with another issue that comes into play when creating graphics for use in Broadcast video. Thin lines in your artwork often appear to flicker when played on a TV monitor. The obvious proof that this is a cruel joke on an unsuspecting novice lies in the fact that you'll never see this flicker on your computer monitor. That's because TV uses interlaced scanning in which a single frame of video is drawn as two alternating fields. Thin lines in graphics often fall between these scan lines and appear to flicker like mad. Computers work in a progressive scan mode in which an entire frame is drawn at once, so they don't suffer from this problem.

Adding the Reduce Interlace Flicker can help you reduce the flicker. However, you should know two items of importance. First, avoid line art that is as thin as one point or thinner. Second, this filter does nothing more than add a vertical blur to your image. You may as well use one of the blurs at a very low setting (a Gaussian or Fast Blur setting of 0.4 works rather well) to achieve the same results.

To use this filter, select the layer or the final comp and choose Effect ⇨ Video ⇨ Reduce Interlace Flicker.

Using the Timecode effect

In our opinion, this is a highly underused filter. When you apply the Timecode filter to a layer, you can display running timecode on your footage.

Using the Display Format setting, you can select whether timecode is displayed in the SMPTE format of HH:MM:SS:FF or in frame numbers, as is the custom for many people working in film.

A very common use of this effect is to add timecode to Layers or Comps which you may be preparing as a rough draft render. For example, say that you have an 18-minute comp laid out in After Effects and you are going to be doing a draft render to check your timing and make notes. You may want to add the Timecode effect to the final comp so that your draft render contains a running time reference, which you can use to make time-specific notes for any changes or adjustments.

Another very handy use of this effect is the ability to embed timecode. If you choose to embed the timecode into a movie and render it, when you import this rendered movie back into After Effects and apply the Timecode effect again, you can view the embedded timecode. See Figure 16-18.

Figure 16-18: The Timecode effect applied to a clip
Image courtesy of ArtBeats (Starter Kit)

Unfortunately, you cannot read timecode for clips that are exported out of Media 100, Avid, or other such editing systems.

Embedding timecode also has a few limitations that you should observe:

✦ Use a lossless compressor (Animation or None) when rendering out the movie.

✦ You cannot rotate or scale an embedded timecode layer. Yeah, I know . . . but that's how it is.

✦ Don't crop the lower edge of an embedded timecode layer or cover it with another layer in the Comp window layout.

✦   ✦   ✦

Warping and Morphing Matter

✦ ✦ ✦ ✦

In This Chapter

Achieving distortion
with the standard
version of After
Effects

Using the Production
Bundle for advanced
distortion

✦ ✦ ✦ ✦

What can we say about distortion? You can probably imagine what this group of effects is capable of doing to the pixels of an image. They're great for turning pretty faces into comic masterpieces, but they're also capable of transforming your elements into rubbery objects that lend a certain fluidity to your compositions. Sometimes this group of filters can lift you out of a creative rut by creating unexpectedly beautiful results. In any case, it's in your best interests to keep learning the contents of your toolbox.

The Standard Version of After Effects contains some excellent Distort effects that go beyond rubbery stretching and actually provide you with some real functionality. The Production Bundle of After Effects comes with Distort filters that are marvels of programming, but some of them can really hang up your computer because they take so long to render. Nonetheless, a few of them are extremely cool. You'll see what we mean in the pages that follow.

If you're looking for high-quality morphing tools that approximate the look and feel of shape-shifting liquid metal from the effects sequences in *Terminator 2,* you may want to lower your expectations. As always, keep an open mind, and you'll find that some *Alice in Wonderland* distortions are indeed possible. If you have some time to experiment, you should try most of these with a full-sized layer of video, as well as Illustrator text and line art. The results can vary greatly depending on the type of layer to which you apply these effects, so after you know how the filters work, you should take time to play and experiment with them on disparate elements.

Warping on a Budget

The Distort group of effects (see Figure 17-1) that comes with the Standard Version of After Effects is a loose amalgam of winners and losers. As far as our experience is concerned, some are perennial workhorses, and others lie dormant and are rarely, if ever, invoked. You'll never guess, but the ones in the latter category have been lifted from Photoshop and offer only a limited set of functions for moving images. Some from the A-list include Offset and Transform. Take a look and remember to set your layers to Best quality to see what the effect is really doing.

Cross-Reference   Chapter 8 describes working with effects in general. If you aren't familiar with applying effects or working in the Effect Controls window, take the time to read (or re-read) the beginning of Chapter 8.

Cross-Reference   The Online Help (choose Help ➪ After Effects Help) is an HTML document that goes well beyond the printed User's Guide in explaining After Effects in detail. In addition to containing all of the information included in the User's Guide, the Online Help contains a lot of very useful basic information on all the effects that ship with After Efffects. Refer to it as often as you need to; our purpose in writing about these effects is to supplement that information rather than repeat it.

Figure 17-1: The entire Distort group of effects as they appear in the Effect Menu

On the DVD-ROM As far as the following explanations of effects are concerned, we created an After Effects project that includes a composition for each effect that we cover in the chapter. Just as a reminder, you need to copy the *Source Material* folder from the DVD-ROM to your hard drive. Additionally, the exercises that follow cover some of these effects in detail. Our own corresponding After Effects project is called *Chapter 17.aep* and can be found in the *Project Files/Chapter 17* folder.

Tip Feel free to substitute your own footage with the examples shown in the figures and exercises.

Using the Mirror effect

The Mirror Effect reflects a layer according to the settings that you define for the two properties in its Effect Controls. When you initially apply the Mirror filter to a layer, the default settings are less than inspiring. The Reflection Center is swung all the way out to the right edge of the center of the layer so that you can't see any appreciable difference to the layer's appearance in the Comp window. To quickly fix this, bring the Reflection Center in toward the middle of the layer, and the mechanics of this effect start to become clear. You can do this either by dragging the effect point or scrubbing the x-value for the Reflection Center property in the Effect Controls. After you bring this point in to the middle, you can see that the layer is reflected across a line perpendicular to the layer. The angle of this perpendicular line is represented by the value of 0 degrees for the Reflection Angle property in the Effect Controls. If you spin the Reflection Angle radial dial, you'll notice that the reflection axis is changed accordingly.

Caution If you apply this effect to a layer of text imported from Illustrator, you may run into trouble because the effect will only work within the constraints of the layer's pixel dimensions. Because Illustrator text layers are cropped to the boundaries of their letters, the Mirror effect is pretty inert. To solve this problem, you may find it helpful to pre-compose the layer of text and set the pre-comp's dimensions to the size of the parent comp so that you have as much real estate as you need when making reflections.

After you apply Mirror to a comp-sized layer, you see that you can get some interesting looks out of what you may have thought were fairly mundane elements. Figure 17-2 shows a comp comprised of a single layer that's a QuickTime movie of clouds. Figure 17-3 shows the same comp with the Mirror effect applied to it. The Reflection Center of the Mirror filter has been set to the center of the layer. Now comes the big fun. You can apply the Mirror filter to a layer more than once. Figure 17-4 shows the same comp with the Mirror filter applied six times. In each case, the settings were modified in order to create a symmetrical reflection pattern. Going further still, if you apply the Transform effect and place it highest in the stacking order of effects in a layer's Effect Controls, you can get some beautiful distortions, the look of which can be dramatically altered with minor tweaks to the Transform filter properties. You read more on Transform a bit later.

Figure 17-2: The basic layer of clouds
Image courtesy of ArtBeats (Starter Kit)

Figure 17-3: The same layer after we apply the
Mirror effect and move its Reflection Center into
the middle of the layer
Image courtesy of ArtBeats (Starter Kit)

Using the Offset effect

The Offset filter is way cool. Basically, it enables you to turn a layer into an infinite
continual loop. Before we get into a lengthy discussion regarding the nature of infinity, let's start by asking, "Have you ever wished that a layer would keep repeating
itself after you move it outside the Comp window?" If so, Offset can be a big help.
The next set of steps will show you how to make an animation with the Offset effect.

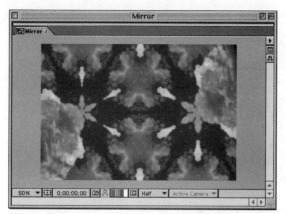

Figure 17-4: After applying and tweaking the Mirror effect six times, we get a beautiful pattern that's quite a departure from the original source.
Image courtesy of ArtBeats (Starter Kit)

STEPS: Looping a Background with the Offset Effect

1. **Create a new composition.**

2. **Place a comp-sized still image or movie into the new comp.** We use an exported frame from our *Radio Waves* composition in Chapter 15.

3. **In the Timeline, select the layer and apply the Offset effect to it by choosing Effect ⇨ Distort ⇨ Offset.**

4. **In the Effect Controls, click the stopwatch next to the Shift Center To property to set an initial keyframe for the effect.**

5. **In the Timeline, double-click the layer to open it in the Layer window.**

6. **Open the Layer window menu by clicking the arrow in the upper-right corner and select Offset from the list of options.** This enables you to animate the effect point. See Figure 17-5 for reference.

7. **In the Layer window, drag the playhead forward a few seconds.**

8. **Using the magnification ratio pop-up menu at the lower-left corner of the window, select one of the smallest options.** We selected 3.1%.

9. **Drag the effect point down a good ways.** The motion path for the effect point is now visible.

10. **To make the looping animation interesting, use the Bezier handles on the effect point keyframes to create a curved motion path.** See Figure 17-6 for reference.

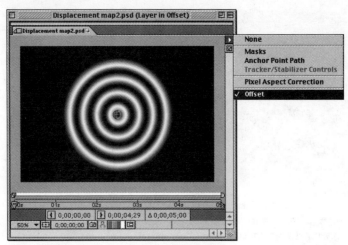

Figure 17-5: Open the Layer window menu by clicking the arrow
in the upper-right corner and select Offset from the list of options.

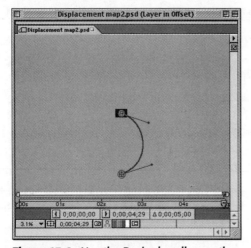

Figure 17-6: Use the Bezier handles on the
effect point keyframes to create a curved
motion path.

11. **Close the Layer window.**

12. **Press 0 on the numeric keypad to see a RAM Preview of your animation.**

If you want to adjust the speed or motion path of the animation, open the Layer
window again and make adjustments to the motion path of the effect point. So
there you go. Now you can create looping animations from a still image source.

Using the Polar Coordinates effect

Polar Coordinates is a pretty odd effect. It only has two properties: Type of Conversion and Interpolation. The Type of Conversion pop-up menu offers either Polar to Rectangular or Rectangular to Polar distortion, and the Interpolation property is a percentage slider. Figures 17-7 and 17-8 display what happens when we apply the Rectangular to Polar flavor of this effect to a grid we made in Photoshop. Because we're usually working with rectangular elements, we generally use the Rectangular to Polar option. It can create interesting results when used on a large amount of text, but we don't use this filter a great deal.

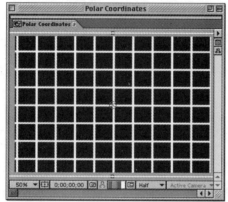

Figure 17-7: A grid we made in Photoshop

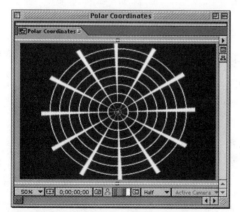

Figure 17-8: The same grid with the Polar Coordinates effect applied to it. The settings are Rectangular to Polar at 100% interpolation.

Using the Photoshop Distortion effects

As we mentioned earlier, we're not huge fans of these Photoshop filters. They lack any real controls, and they don't fit cleanly into the world of motion graphics. Another strike against them is that their anti-aliasing is pretty poor after you start cranking up the levels of distortion. Most of the other Distort effects enable you to select from a list of anti-aliasing options that do a great job of keeping artifacts out of the comp when you really start to stretch or twist an image. Also, when you apply these effects to motion footage, the render times can get steep without there being a worthy payoff for the lost time. Still, if you're a big fan of these effects in Photoshop, you get to keep them in your list of options.

PS+Pinch

The PS+Pinch effect seems pretty cool until you realize that you can't control its center point. (See Figure 17-9.) It's always stuck in the middle of the layer it's applied to, so that really doesn't help you much if you want to do anything other than vary the amount of the distortion.

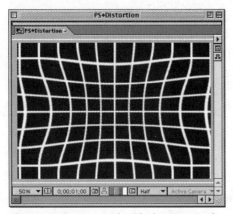

Figure 17-9: Our grid with the PS+Pinch effect applied

What's new in After Effects 5.5: Enabling the Photoshop filters

In After Effects version 5.5, the Photoshop filters PS+Extrude, PS+Ripple, PS+Pinch, PS+Spherize, PS+Tiles, PS+Twirl, PS+Wave, and PS+ZigZag still exist, but if you want to enable them, you have to make a minor modification to your Plug-ins folder. Navigate your way to the Plug-ins folder, which is in the same folder as the After Effects 5.5 application. Once inside the Plug-ins folder, open the Standard folder and remove the parentheses from around the word Photoshop. Quit and restart After Effects, and you'll have access to the filters once again.

PS+Ripple

PS+Ripple creates waves of distortion on a layer, but the waves themselves don't contain any dynamic and continually pulsing wave generation. You can only control the amount of distortion and whether it's small, medium, or large. Compared with Wave World, Caustics, and Wave Warp, there really isn't much to say about this one. See Figure 17-10.

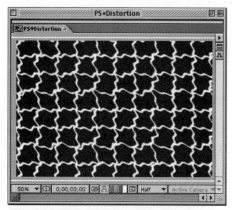

Figure 17-10: The same grid with the PS+Ripple effect applied

PS+Spherize

Considering that you have a Spherize filter with more control already available to you, there is no reason to bother with the PS+Spherize effect. We look at the Spherize filter just a bit later in the chapter. See Figure 17-11.

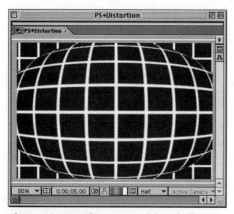

Figure 17-11: The same grid with the PS+Spherize effect applied

PS+Twirl

Like its Photoshop counterparts, you can't control the center point or the radius of the PS+Twirl effect. If you have access to the regular Twirl effect, you may as well forget this one. See Figure 17-12.

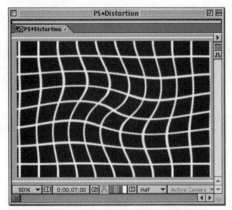

Figure 17-12: The same grid with the PS+Twirl effect applied

PS+Wave

The PS+Wave effect is definitely a cut above the rest of the Photoshop Distortion tools. You can choose from Sine, Triangle, and Square wave types, and each one creates pretty different results. (See Figure 17-13.) Still, imagining any specific use for it is pretty hard, except for the fact that it is good for creating abstract designs.

Figure 17-13: The same grid with the PS+Wave effect applied

PS+ZigZag

PS+ZigZag takes a layer and turns it into the surface of a virtual water ripple. (See Figure 17-14.) You're definitely hamstrung by the fact that you can't control the center point of the ripple. Also, you can't create an animation with a consistent wave height. Our advice to you is to forgo PS+ZigZag and put some time into learning the multiple effect properties of Radio Waves, Caustics, and Wave World.

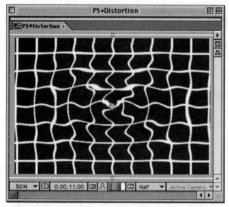

Figure 17-14: The same grid with the PS+ZigZag effect applied

Using the Smear effect

The Smear effect is poorly represented by its name. We could make a joke about a smear campaign, but we're going to leave politics to those who are better qualified. This filter is very powerful, and you can precisely control the distortion created by it. In order to take advantage of it however, you need to apply masks to the layer that you want to distort. If your masking skills aren't up to snuff yet, you should go back and read the chapter on masks (Chapter 9) before getting too excited about the possibilities of using Smear in your work.

Now that you know that masks are a precondition for a good smear, go ahead and complete the following steps.

STEPS: Learning the Mechanics of the Smear Effect

1. **Create a new composition.**

2. **Place a comp-sized still image or movie into the new comp.** We use the grid we made for some of the earlier figures in the chapter. If you want to use it, it's named *grid2.psd,* and you can find it in the Project window of the *Chapter17.aep* project on the DVD-ROM.

3. **In the Timeline, select the layer and apply the Smear effect to it by choosing Effect ⇨ Distort ⇨ Offset.** This won't accomplish anything initially because you need masks to make something of this effect.

4. **Double-click the layer to open it in the Layer window.**

5. **In the Layer window, use the masking tools to place two masks on the layer.** Make one large and rectangular and make the other small and circular. After you're finished, close the Layer window. You may find it helpful to rename the masks in the Timeline. If so, select the layer and press M to solo the new masks. Click a mask's name, press Return, and rename the mask.

6. **In the Timeline, select the layer and set the mask modes for each mask to None.** Then Press F3 to open the Effect Controls window.

7. **In the Smear effect controls, specify the large rectangular mask as the Boundary Mask and the small circular mask as the Source Mask.** With the Smear effect selected in the Effect Controls, your Comp window should resemble Figure 17-15.

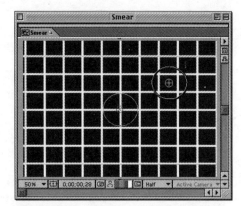

Figure 17-15: The Comp window displays the two masks as well as the effect point and offset source mask of the Smear effect.

8. **In the Comp window, move the effect point off to a corner.**

9. **In the Effect Controls, crank the Percent slider up to 100%.** Your Comp window should resemble Figure 17-16.

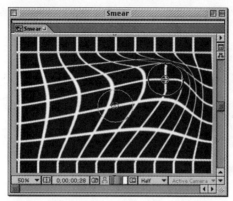

Figure 17-16: The same comp with the
Smear fully cranked

Now that you've set up the Smear effect, you should know that you can also do the
following:

✦ **Adjust the Mask Scale or Mask Rotation.**

✦ **Adjust the Elasticity.** Bear in mind that as you move from Stiff to Super Fluid,
render time goes through the roof. It's rarely worth the wait. Unless your distortion is so severe that you're experiencing problems with the anti-aliasing,
you shouldn't go more than a couple of settings above Stiff.

✦ **Set the Interpolation.** If you want to ease into the distortion by keyframing an
animation for the Percentage property, Easy Ease keyframes won't do the job.
Instead, you need to change the Interpolation Method setting from Linear to
Smooth.

For extra credit, see if you can make the cheetah cub "wink" as he growls.
Figure 17-17 explains what we mean by this. The Smear comp in the *Chapter
17.aep* project also contains this Smear animation. Just turn the visibility on for the
Cheetah Cub layer.

Using the Spherize effect

The Spherize effect is far better than its Photoshop counterpart because you can
move the effect point around the layer at will, and you can also dynamically control
the radius of the spherical distortion. It's a great filter for certain kinds of stylized
text treatments, especially if you want to make characters appear as though they're
being read with an unseen magnifying glass. Add Spherize to your growing bag of
tricks by completing the next exercise.

Figure 17-17: With the help of a Smear animation, we made the cheetah cub "wink" as he growls.

Image courtesy of Sekani (Funny and Furry 1)

STEPS: Sending a Wave under a Layer of Text with the Spherize Effect

1. **Create a new composition and call it "Text Pre-Comp."**

2. **Drag a layer of Illustrator text into the Timeline.** Set the layer to Best quality. If necessary, scale the layer up and turn on the Continuously Rasterize switch if you need to scale the layer up past 100%.

3. **In the Project window, drag the *Text Pre-Comp* composition on to the New Composition button at the bottom of the Project window.** This will make a new comp containing *Text Pre-Comp.*

4. **In the Timeline of the new composition, select the *Text Pre-Comp* layer and apply the Spherize effect to it by choosing Effect ⇨ Distort ⇨ Spherize.** Initially, nothing happens because the default Radius setting is 0.

5. **In the Effect Controls, raise the Radius level until you get a distortion level you like.**

6. **In the Comp window, if necessary, adjust the vertical position of the effect point so that the letters look as though an unseen force is pushing them up.**

7. **Move the effect point off the left side of the comp until no distortion is apparent.**

8. **In the Effect Controls, set a keyframe for the Center of Sphere property by clicking its stopwatch.**

9. **In the Timeline, drag the playhead forward a few seconds.**

10. **In the Comp window, drag the effect point across the length of the comp while holding down the Shift key to limit the movement to the horizontal plane.** This sets another keyframe. If the effect point isn't visible, click the word Spherize in the Effect Controls to select the effect.

And there you have it: a cool text treatment using the Spherize filter (see Figure 17-18).

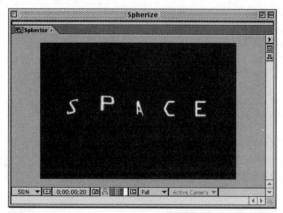

Figure 17-18: A layer of pre-composed Illustrator text with the Spherize effect applied to it

Using the Transform effect

As we pointed out with the Drop Shadow effect in the last chapter, the Transform filter allows you to circumvent the order in which After Effects processes pixels when rendering a composition. Given that After Effects "thinks" its way up from the bottom of the Timeline's stack of layers in the order of masks, effects, and transformations, this effect enables you to carry out a layer's transformation before any other effects are applied to a layer.

Caution   When adding the Transform filter to a layer, make certain that it's positioned properly in the Effect Controls stacking order. For example, if your Drop Shadow is scaling out of proportion to the layer's size, you can use the Transform filter to solve your problem, but it needs to be above the Drop Shadow effect in the Effect Controls window for the layer. Rearranging the order of effects is as easy as dragging and dropping them as you would layers in the Timeline.

Warping with Precision

The "high end" distortion tools require studious patience in some cases. These Production Bundle filters usually involve meticulous controls and long render times, so be forewarned. These filters can also be a lot of fun, but you'll want to know what they can do before you promise any clients a quick turnaround. Again, make sure your layers are set to Best quality so that you can properly gauge the true distortion of these effects.

Using the Bezier Warp effect (PB)

Look at the Bezier Warp Effect Controls in Figure 17-19. Yikes! The numerous tangents and vertexes are fairly intimidating at first sight, but they merely represent the various effect points that you can see in the Comp window.

	Grid2.psd • Effect Controls		
Grid2.psd			
Bezier Warp * Grid2.psd			
▽ ƒ **Bezier Warp**	Reset	About...	
○ Top Left Vertex	0.0 , 0.0		
○ Top Left Tangent	256.0 , 0.0		
○ Top Right Tangent	511.9 , 0.0		
○ Right Top Vertex	768.0 , 0.0		
○ Right Top Tangent	768.0 , 170.6		
○ Right Bottom Tangent	768.0 , 341.3		
○ Bottom Right Vertex	768.0 , 512.0		
○ Bottom Right Tangent	511.9 , 512.0		
○ Bottom Left Tangent	256.0 , 512.0		
○ Left Bottom Vertex	0.0 , 512.0		
○ Left Bottom Tangent	0.0 , 341.3		
○ Left Top Tangent	0.0 , 170.6		
○ Elasticity	Stiff ▼		

Figure 17-19: The Bezier Warp Effect Controls contain a confusing-looking set of properties.

If you adjust these effect points by dragging them around the composition, the mechanics of this filter become evident. The vertex properties represent the corners of the layer, and the tangents represent each vertex's Bezier handles. You're already familiar with Bezier controls from working with masks. In this case, the vertexes and tangents define the extent of rubbery distortion that gets applied to the layer. Each tangent and vertex can be keyframed over time, and you can use this effect for a whole range of tasks. For example, you can wrap text around cylindrical or spherical objects. Figure 17-20 gives a clear example of how you might use Bezier Warp.

Tip It can become progressively difficult to keep track of all the effect properties during a complex warp animation. If you get lost, click the crosshair icon in the Effect Controls to reveal the position of an effect property in the Comp window.

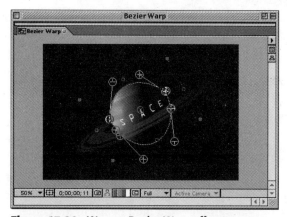

Figure 17-20: We use Bezier Warp effect to wrap the word "Space" around the planet.

Image courtesy of EyeWire by Getty Images www.gettyimages.com

(Cosmic Moves)

Using the Bulge effect (PB)

The Bulge effect takes the strengths of the Spherize effect and improves upon them. Instead of being bound by the limits of a spherical shape, this filter has independent horizontal and vertical radius controls. You can also take advantage of the Bulge Height property to make the distortion of a layer look as though it's bursting outward or caving inward. See Figure 17-21.

Tip If your distortion suffers from artifacted edges, change the anti-aliasing quality level from low to high. Additionally, you may want to check the Pin All Edges check box to keep the edges of the image from being included in the distortion.

Horizontal and Vertical Radius controls

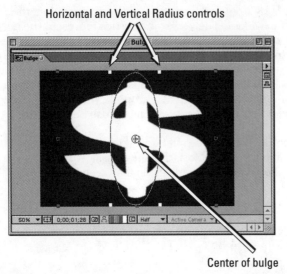

Center of bulge

Figure 17-21: The Bulge effect offers more control than the Spherize effect.

Image courtesy of Creatas

Using the Corner Pin effect (PB)

The Corner Pin effect enables you to take the four corners of a layer and place them wherever you want. The resulting distortion creates the illusion of 3D perspective. You see it used in television ads when a graphic that didn't exist in the actual footage is placed over a billboard or a wall. See Figure 17-22 for an example.

Figure 17-22: We use the Corner Pin to position a layer of text over footage so that it appears to have 3D perspective.

Image courtesy of Creatas

Using the Displacement Map effect (PB)

The Displacement Map effect is an extraordinarily powerful tool. You already know a good deal about the concept of a displacement map from working with some of the Render and Simulation effects, such as Caustics and Card Dance. The premise hasn't changed. The Displacement Map filter takes the pixel values from any layer in the Timeline you select and, in turn, uses those values as the basis for distorting the layer to which you apply the effect. You can specify whether the pixel values come from a layer's luminance or its RGB+A channels.

To see how this works, first you're going to create an animation to serve as the layer for the displacement map. Then you distort a layer of text based on the luminance of the displacement map layer.

STEPS: Preparing an Animated Displacement Map Layer

1. **Create a new composition.** Name it "Animated Displacement Map."

2. **Create a new solid in the comp by pressing Command+Y/Ctrl+Y.** The color of the layer doesn't matter; just make sure that it's comp-sized.

3. **In the Timeline, select the new solid and apply the Ramp effect to it by choosing Effect ➪ Rende ➪ Ramp.**

4. **In the Effect Controls, set keyframes for the Start and End of Ramp properties.**

5. **Drag the playhead forward in time by about a second.**

6. **In the Comp window, change the positions of the Start and End of Ramp effect points.**

7. **Repeat Steps 5 and 6 until you reach the end of your comp's duration.** Try to randomize the nature of your animated Ramp as best you can.

Okay. You have an animated displacement map. Now you want to use it as the basis for the Displacement Map effect. The next set of steps shows you how this is done.

STEPS: Applying the Displacement Map Effect

1. **Create a new composition.**

2. **Drag the *Animated Displacement Map* comp from the Project window into the Timeline.** Turn off its visibility switch after you add it to the comp.

3. **Drag a layer of text from the Project window into the Timeline.**

4. **If it isn't already selected, click the text layer and apply the Displacement Map effect to it by choosing Effect ➪ Distort ➪ Displacement Map.**

5. **In the Effect Controls, select Animated Displacement Map as the option in the Displacement Map Layer pop-up menu.** The remaining settings can be left at their defaults for the time being. Because the Ramp is a grayscale image, using the Red or Green channels as the basis for the pixel values won't compromise the effect. For future reference, you can change the options in the Use for Horizontal and Use for Vertical Displacement pop-up menus to Lightness. In this example, it won't make a difference.

6. **Drag the playhead through the Timeline to preview the distortion created by the effect.** If the distortion is too subtle, crank up the Max. Horizontal and Max. Vertical Displacement values. Wherever there are pixels in the Displacement Map Layer that contain any brightness, the layer of text will be distorted. The amount of the distortion is amplified by the Max. Horizontal and Max. Vertical Displacement values you specify.

Pretty nifty, yes? The layer of text is dynamically distorted by the changing luminance values of another layer (see Figures 17-23 and 17-24 for reference). That's how it works. At this point, you're probably wondering about the ramifications of all this. You can use any layer as a displacement map layer so long as you've placed it in the comp in which you use this effect.

Tip   If you animate a layer in a comp and then try to use that same layer as a displacement map, always remember to pre-compose it.

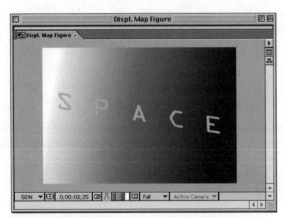

Figure 17-23: A frame from our Displacement Map composition with the visibility of the animated displacement map pre-comp turned on. The distortion of the text is based on the luminance of the displacement map layer.

For a Displacement Map finale, we're going to introduce you to the Fractal Noise filter. The Fractal Noise effect is capable of creating highly sophisticated displacement maps that seamlessly animate. This one's another bit of the Evolution inheritance, and that means it has loads of effect controls.

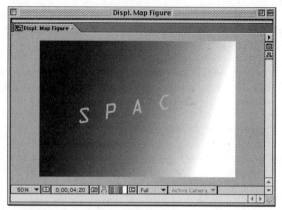

Figure 17-24: Another frame from the same comp

STEPS: Using Fractal Noise for a Displacement Map (PB)

1. **Create a new composition. Name it *Fractal Noise Displacement Map*.**

2. **Create a new solid in the comp by pressing Command+Y/Ctrl+Y.** The color of the layer doesn't matter; just make sure that it's comp-sized.

3. **In the Timeline, select the new solid and apply the Fractal Noise effect to it by choosing Effect ⇨ Render@@Fractal Noise.** Your Comp window should resemble Figure 17-25.

4. **In the Fractal Noise Effect Controls, set keyframe animations for either the Evolution property or the Transform Subproperties.**

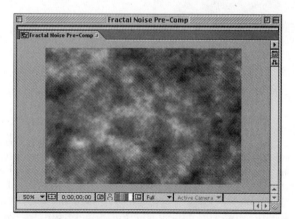

Figure 17-25: Fractal Noise creates infinite variations of seamless noise, which makes for great displacement maps.

That's all? Yep. Preview this new comp, and you see that these basic keyframe animations generate random noise. Very cool. Import this new comp into the one containing your displacement map effect, turn off its visibility, and specify it as the Displacement Map Layer in the Effect Controls for the layer of text. If you cranked up your Max. Horizontal and Max. Vertical Displacement values, you may want to turn them down, because the distortion caused by this new layer is going to be pretty heavy. Enjoy your new heights of distortion through displacement.

Tip To attain a real measure of "Displacement Power," take time to play with the Fractal Noise filter and learn its intricacies. To that end, the Online Help is particularly useful.

Using the Mesh Warp effect (PB)

The Mesh Warp places a grid over a layer. (See Figure 17-26.) The grid contains as many rows and columns as you require. You can control the shape of the grid by altering the points at which the gridlines connect. Each of these intersecting control points also contains Bezier handles, which operate in the same manner as the Bezier handles of a mask. To animate the effect, you only have to set keyframes for the Grid Values property. Any changes to the layout of the grid over time will be smoothly interpolated.

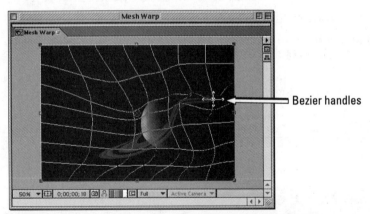

Figure 17-26: The Mesh Warp effect enables you to use the intersecting points of a grid as the control points for a layer's distortion.
Image courtesy of EyeWire by Getty Images www.gettyimages.com (Cosmic Moves)

In short, this is a powerful filter that creates very fluid and rubbery distortions, but it takes an annoyingly long time to render. Furthermore, any time you make changes to the grid in the Comp window, the grid disappears and you have to wait for the changes to finish rendering before the grid is visible again. Of course, you can lower the resolution of your comp, but then it's hard to tell if there are any anti-aliasing problems. All in all, working with this effect becomes pretty frustrating. If you're going to have success with this one, you'll need a fast processor, and we mean fast by today's standards, which we all know were hard to imagine as little as a year ago.

Using the Optics Compensation effect (PB)

Ah yes. This effect is a new addition to After Effects, and it's definitely a new favorite of ours. Why, you ask? Because now you can make the jump to light speed, that's why! Before we get into that, this effect enables you to rid footage of any optical distortions. Sometimes, footage is shot with a concave or a convex lens, and this filter can offset the in-camera distortion created by these alternative lens types.

For example, Figure 17-27 shows a piece of footage shot with a fisheye lens. Figure 17-28 shows the same footage with the Optics Compensation effect applied to it. Conversely, you can take normal looking footage and give it a distorted appearance.

Figure 17-27: A bit of footage shot with a fisheye lens
Image courtesy of Sekani (Corbis NY Vistas, Vol. 213)

Figure 17-28: The same footage with the Optics Compensation effect applied
Image courtesy of Sekani (Corbis NY Vistas, Vol. 213)

The Effect Controls for the Optics Compensation filter are easy to manipulate. The two most important ones are the Field of View slider and the Reverse Lens Distortion check box. If you need to correct distorted footage, experiment with these two properties until curved lines in the footage appear to be straight.

So what's the point of this? Say that you need to add graphics to footage shot with a fisheye lens. In that case, you need to distort the graphics to match the footage; otherwise, they will look incorrect. The fisheye view of New York City in Figure 17-28 required the following Optics Compensation settings in order to offset its distortion: Field of View set to 78 and Reverse Lens Distortion checked. Any graphics that you need to add to the footage need to be pre-composed first, and then you apply the opposite Optics Compensation settings to this pre-composed layer: in this case, Field of View set to 78 and Reverse Lens Distortion UNchecked. You could then remove the Optics Compensation effect from the footage while keeping it applied to the pre-composed layer of graphics.

You can also have some big fun with this effect. The next set of steps explains how.

STEPS: Making the Jump to Light Speed

1. **Create a new composition.**

2. **Drag a layer of footage from the Project window into the Timeline.** For best results, use a starfield. We used the QuickTime movie named *EVOO167N.MOV*, kindly provided by EyeWire.

3. **Making sure the layer is selected in the Timeline, apply the Optics Compensation effect to the layer by choosing Effect ⇨ Distort ⇨ Optics Compensation.**

4. **In the Effect Controls, click the Reverse Lens Distortion check box and set a keyframe for the Field of View property.**

5. **In the Timeline, drag the playhead forward a few seconds.**

6. **In the Effect Controls, scrub the Field of View value up until the distortion completes the jump to light speed.** This sets the second keyframe. The Comp window clues you in as to exactly what the right value is. See Figure 17-29 for reference.

7. **Press 0 on the numeric keypad to see a RAM Preview of your animation.**

Using the Reshape effect (PB)

Reshape is built on the same principles (and code) as Smear. The only difference between the two sets of Effect Controls is that Reshape has two more properties than its Standard Version sibling: a Destination Mask pop-up menu as well as some extra control provided by correspondence points. See Figure 17-30.

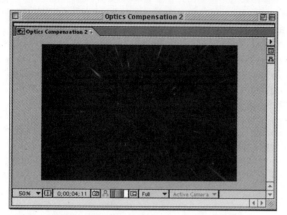

Figure 17-29: Using the Optics Compensation effect at extreme values enables you to make the jump to light speed!

Image courtesy of EyeWire by Getty Images www.gettyimages.com (Cosmic Moves)

Boundary mask   Source mask   Destination mask

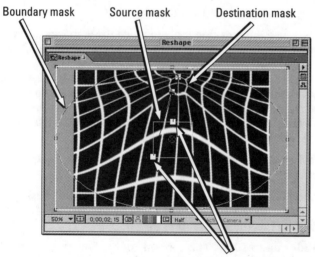

Correspondence points

Figure 17-30: The Reshape Effect Controls closely resemble those of Smear, except for the fact that they also include a destination mask as well as correspondence points.

With Smear, you need to work with two masks on a layer. With Reshape, you need three. The third mask serves as the Destination Mask, which is where the filter justly earns its name. When you set the Percent slider up to 100%, the pixels inside the Source Mask stretch to completely fill the area inside the Destination Mask, thereby reshaping the Source Mask by using the pixels within the limits of the Boundary Mask. You can further control the progression from one shape to another by using correspondence points.

The following set of steps should illuminate Reshape's mechanics and illustrate its additional features when compared with Smear.

STEPS: Tweaking the Reshape Effect

1. **Create a new composition.**

2. **Place a comp-sized still image or movie into the new comp.** Once again, we use the grid.

3. **In the Timeline, select the layer, and apply the Reshape effect to it by choosing Effect ⇨ Distort ⇨ Reshape.** As was the case with Smear, nothing happens initially.

4. **Double-click the layer to open it in the Layer window.**

5. **In the Layer window, use the masking tools to place three masks on the layer.** Make one large and rectangular, make the second a medium-size square, and make the last one small and circular. Make certain that the second and third masks are within the boundaries of the larger rectanglular mask. After you finish, close the Layer window. Rename the masks in the Timeline so that you don't get confused trying to remember which one is which. Select the layer and press the M key to solo the new masks. One at a time, click a mask's name, press Return, and rename it.

6. **In the Timeline, select the layer and set the mask modes for each mask to None.** Then press F3 to open the Effect Controls window.

7. **In the Reshape Effect Controls, specify the large, rectangular mask as the Boundary Mask, the medium-sized, square mask as the Source Mask, and the small, circular mask as the Destination Mask.**

8. **Set the Percent slider up to 100%.** The contents of the Source Mask stretch over and fill the Destination Mask.

In addition to the basic distortion provided by the effect, you can add correspondence points to the Source and Destination Masks. To add a pair of correspondence points, position your mouse over the edges of either mask, hold down the

Option/Alt key so that your pointer becomes the Add Point tool, and click. Doing this adds a pair of new correspondence points. Position your mouse over one of the new points, and your pointer changes its appearance indicating that you can move the correspondence point. Correspondence points define how the Source Mask manifests itself in the area of the Destination Mask. You can add as many of these as you need.

Using the Ripple effect (PB)

The Ripple effect is what PS+ZigZag should be. The waves dynamically ripple from the center point over time. Furthermore, you can adjust the center point and the radius of the effect. As if that weren't enough, you can also set the Wave Speed, Height, Width, as well as the Ripple Phase. (See Figure 17-31.) That's probably why it's in the Production Bundle.

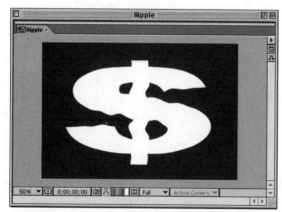

Figure 17-31: The Ripple effect dynamically generates waves, and you can also move its center point and adjust its radius.
Image courtesy of Creatas

Using the Twirl effect (PB)

Again, we have a filter that reflects what its Photoshop counterpart should be. Unlike PS+Twirl, the Twirl effect has an adjustable radius and center point, and its anti-aliasing capabilities are far superior as well. See Figure 17-32.

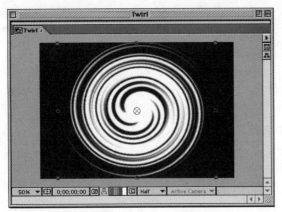

Figure 17-32: Unlike PS+Twirl, the Twirl effect has an adjustable radius and center point.

Image courtesy of Creatas

Using the Wave Warp effect (PB)

The Wave Warp effect creates dynamically rippling waves that run along the axis defined by the angle of the Direction property. (See Figure 17-33.) Best of all, you can pin the edges so that all the pixels stay within the boundaries of the layer and nothing peeks through from behind. This is what PS+Wave should have been.

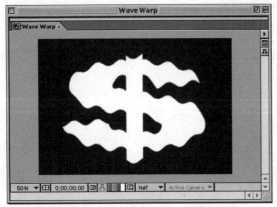

Figure 17-33: The Wave Warp effect dynamically generates waves by default.

Image courtesy of Creatas

✦   ✦   ✦

Particle Playground

Particle Playground is simply amazing. It's a tremen-
dously powerful animation tool that appears to be hidden among the Simulation effects as though it were just
another filter, but nothing could be further from the truth. In
fact, it's almost an entirely separate application unto itself.

You may be familiar with third party effects that perform some
kind of particle generation, but this is definitely a cut above.
It was introduced in version 4.0 of After Effects, and to a large
extent, widely misunderstood. Simply applying it to a layer in
the Timeline suddenly transformed your layer into a bubbling
fountain of little red squares. Unless folks were inclined to
investigate further, some of them left it where they found it.
Their loss, to be sure.

Compared to other filters, Particle Playground definitely
requires a little more concentration on your part. It contains a
staggering amount of effect properties, and if you aren't clear
on what you're doing, you may be put off by render times that
can become exceedingly long. To keep the creative process at
the forefront of your work, we've given you some pointers on
how to keep these times to a minimum. The big fun continues
with Particle Playground. Onward!

What Is Particle Playground?

You can use the Particle Playground filter to generate particles
or text, or you can use it in conjunction with elements of your
own. Particle Playground is a procedural animation tool as
opposed to a purely keyframe driven one (see the sidebar entitled "What is procedural animation?"). Particle Playground animates with the Cannon, a grid, or a layer map. Don't lose heart.
All this is explained in the sections that follow.

What is procedural animation?

So far, the kind of animation we have been showing you in After Effects is of the keyframe-able variety. In animations such as this, a keyframe is set for the value of a given property at a specific point in time. When another value is set for the same property later in time, the interpolation between these two keyframes produces the desired effect. *Procedural animation* is another type of animation where the initial states of layers and objects are set. Then the objects and properties animate along carefully programmed, but open-ended, algorithms. You have ways to influence this type of animation, and even keyframes to be set, but in its nature, procedural animation is far better suited for animated natural phenomena, such as snow, rain, wind and other such manifestations of Mother Nature.

On the DVD-ROM

To explain Particle Playground in detail, we created an After Effects project that includes a composition for each series of steps that we cover in the chapter. Just as a reminder, you need to copy the *Source Material* folder from the DVD-ROM to your hard drive. Additionally, the exercises that follow cover some of these effects in detail. Our own corresponding After Effects project is called *Chapter 18.aep* and can be found in the *Project Files/Chapter 18* folder.

Understanding the Particle Playground effect

At first glance, the depth of controls and the unfamiliarity of the properties in the Particle Playground effect may seem a little daunting. However, breaking this effect down into its basic components is easy. As soon as you understand the overall sections of this effect, you can handle the individual settings and controls with ease.

Particle Playground can be roughly understood as consisting of five separate sections (see also Figure 18-1):

✦ **Particle generators:** The particle generators section of the Particle Playground controls the parameters of the four different particle generators. Cannon, Grid, Particle Exploder, and Layer Exploder each provide different ways to generate a stream of particles.

✦ **Layer Map section:** The Layer Map section allows you to substitute layers and elements of your composition in place of the default particles that are generated by the effect. For example, you can first spend some time generating a stream of nondescript particles to simulate a snow fall. Then using the Layer Map section, you can substitute a snow flake you created in Adobe Illustrator for the particles.

Bear in mind that when you use a layer as a Layer Map, Particle Playground ignores any property that you may have tweaked or keyframe animation that you may have created for the layer within that composition. For example, if you scale down the layer in the comp, the Particle Playground will ignore the scale change and use the layer at the original 100% of its size. You can fix this a few different ways: either scale the element down in a pre-composition or scale it down in the original application, assuming that you made the element in another application.

✦ **Particle behavior influences:** This section allows you to set properties that influence particle behavior. For example, you can change the setting of Gravity under this section to alter the way the particles behave. You can also set Repel properties or contain the particles within a Wall, defined by a mask of your choosing.

✦ **Particle property influences:** Here, you can determine the influences for particle properties. For example, you can use color ramps or "maps" to alter the motion, angular momentum, and other properties of the particles as they pass over these colored maps. The visibility switch of these colored maps don't have to be on. Note that the list of property names under the Ephemeral and Persistent Property sections is identical. The difference is between the nature of the two types of properties. Ephemeral properties revert back to normal after passing through areas of influence defined in a color map. The Persistent properties persist in their change even after they leave the area of influence. For example, if you use a blue and red color map and set the Ephemeral property for the particle to rotate under the influence of blue, then after the particle leaves the blue area, it rotates back to normal. However, if the same effect is created under the Persistent properties section, then the effect persists even after the particle has left the blue colored area.

✦ **Options:** You can click the Options button to open a dialog box where you can enter any text that you want. Then you can choose to replace your particles with the text you entered.

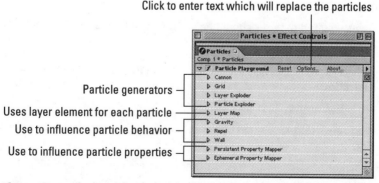

Figure **18-1:** The Particle Playground can be roughly divided into five sections by function.

Using the Cannon

When you create a solid and apply the Particle Playground effect to it, the Cannon is on by default. If you want to use another method of particle creation, you must first turn off the Cannon. By default, the Cannon creates particles as if they are coming out of a cannon-like opening. You can adjust the settings of the Cannon to get a wide variety of results with it.

On the DVD-ROM

In order to explain Particle Playground in detail, we created an After Effects project that includes a composition for each series of steps that we cover in the chapter. The After Effects project is called *Chapter 18.aep*, and can be found in the *Project Files/Chapter 18* folder. For the next series of steps, you should look at the composition called *Cannon*.

STEPS: Using the Cannon to Launch Text

1. **Make a new comp by choosing Composition ➪ New Composition.**

2. **Create a new solid by pressing Command/Ctrl+Y.** Make the solid the size of the composition by clicking the Comp Size button in the New Solid dialog box. Call this solid *Cannon Solid.*

3. **Select the solid and choose Effect ➪ Simulation ➪ Particle Playground to apply the effect.** By default, the particles appear red and spout upwards, but we change this.

4. **Click the twirler (triangle) next to the word Cannon and set the following settings under the Cannon property:**

   • Position: 10.0, 244.0

   • Particles per second: 10

   • Direction: 90

   • Velocity: 400

Note

At this point, your red particles should be going from left to right across the screen.

5. **In the Effect Controls window for the Particle Playground, click the Options section.**

6. **Click the Edit Cannon Text button.**

7. **Next, type some text in the text box.** In the text box you can set the following options:

   • Using Font/Style, select the font and style for your Cannon text.

   • Under Order, set the order in which characters come out of the Cannon. If your Cannon is pointing to the right (which it is because in Step 4 you set the Direction to 90 degrees), your text has to come out last letter first to be in a readable order of any kind. So, set this setting to Right to Left.

- For the Loop Text setting, check it to continuously create text. Leaving this option unchecked creates only one instance of the text from the Cannon.

8. **Click OK to accept your selections.**

9. **Back in the settings for Cannon under Particle Playground, click the underlined Font Size value and enter a value of 24 to enlarge the font size.** Note that before you entered any text into the text box, this setting reads Particle Radius.

10. **Change the color of the text by clicking the Color dropper and selecting the color of your choice.**

11. **If you notice that your text is spreading out into an unreadable stream, change the Direction Random Spread setting to 5.** This prevents a variance of the stream of particles to five degrees as opposed to the original setting of 90 degrees.

There you have it. Your Cannon now sprays a legible text message from left to right, as shown in Figure 18-2.

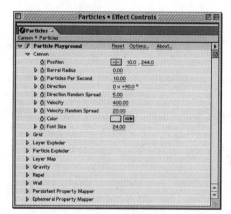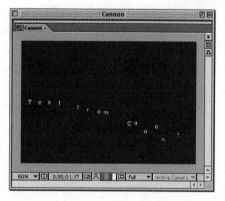

Figure 18-2: The Cannon is set to send out a stream of text. The Particle Playground settings are shown on the left.

STEPS: Turning Text Off

1. **In the Effect Controls window for Particle Playground, click the underlined Options setting.**

2. **Click the Edit Cannon Text button and delete all text from the text box.**

3. **Click OK and then click OK again to close the Options dialog box.**

Understanding the Cannon settings

The Cannon section of Particle Playground has numerous settings that you need to understand if you're going to have any real success with it. These settings are explained here.

✦ **Position:** This setting sets the X- and Y-coordinates for the particle generator.

✦ **Barrel Radius:** This sets the size of the Cannon's barrel radius. Note that negative values create a round barrel, and positive value creates a square barrel. For example, if you want to create a small barrel, such as the end of a hose, enter a small value. To simulate a large barrel, such as leaves falling from trees (which should have a fairly wide barrel), set a large value.

✦ **Particles Per Second:** Here you can set how often particles are created. Setting this to zero produces no particles. You can keyframe this value to create certain effects. For example, if you want your text Cannon to stop generating particles at a given point in time, you can start out by setting a higher number and then keyframe the value down to zero to stop producing the particles.

✦ **Direction:** This dial sets the angle at which particles are generated or "shot."

✦ **Direction Random Spread:** Sets the value for how much each particle's direction varies randomly from the Direction setting. For example, setting this value to 20 sets the range for a 90-degree Direction setting between 80 degrees and 100 degrees, or plus or minus 10 degress to put it another way.

✦ **Velocity:** This sets the initial speed of particles (in pixels per second) as they exit from the Cannon.

✦ **Velocity Random Spread:** Again, this setting sets the value of how much each particle's speed varies randomly from the Velocity setting. For example, if you set the Velocity to 40 and the Velocity Random Speed to 10, the Particles will exit at velocities between 30 and 50 pixels per second.

✦ **Color:** Use this to set the color of the particles or the text. Bear in mind that this setting is inactive if you are using another layer to replace the particles.

✦ **Particle Radius/Font Size:** Use this setting to set the radius of particles. When you enter text under the Options settings, this setting changes to read Font Size. You can then set the Font Size of the text.

Cross-Reference

The Online Help (choose Help ➪ After Effects Help) is an HTML document that goes well beyond the printed User's Guide in explaining After Effects in detail. In addition to containing all of the information included in the User's Guide, the Online Help contains a lot of very useful basic information on all of the effects that ship with After Efffects. The Online help is particularly good because it tends to explain the purpose of each and every setting in an effect. Refer to it as often as you need to; our purpose in writing about these effects is to supplement that information rather than repeat it.

Using the Grid

Using Particle Playground, you can create a Grid of either particles or text. A little later on, we show you how to replace these particles with a layer of your choice.

Making a grid simply results in an orderly layout of particles across your Comp window. Unlike the Cannon, the Grid particles start off without any Velocity. Hence, they tend to fall downward after being created because the Gravity is on by default. You can influence the Grid by using Gravity, Repel, and Wall properties.

The Grid effect also generates particles for every frame of the comp. This is usually undesirable, and you can avoid that by keyframing the Particle Radius/Font Size value to zero after generating one frame, or you can animate the values of the Particles Across or Particles Down properties down to zero.

Next, you use Particle Playground to create a basic text grid.

In order to explain Particle Playground in detail, we created an After Effects project that includes a composition for each series of steps that we cover in the chapter. The After Effects project is called *Chapter 18.aep*, and can be found in the *Project Files/Chapter 18* folder. For the next series of steps, you should look at the composition called *Grid*.

STEPS: Making a Grid of Text

1. **Make a new comp by choosing Composition ⇨ New Composition.**

2. **Create a new solid by pressing Command/Ctrl+Y.** Make the solid the size of the composition by clicking the Comp Size button in the New Solid dialog box. Call this solid *Grid Solid*.

3. **Select the solid and choose Effect ⇨ Simulation ⇨ Particle Playground to apply the effect.** By default, the particles appear red and spout upwards, but we change this.

4. **Click the twirler (triangle) next to the word Cannon and set the Particles per Second setting to 0.** This is important because to generate particles any other way, we first have to disable the Cannon. You do this by setting the Particles per Second setting to 0.

5. **Next, under the Grid properties, set the Width to 720 and the Height to 486.** That is the size of your comp.

6. **Set both the Particles Down and the Particles Across settings to 10.** This creates a Grid of 10 x 10 particles.

7. **Click the twirler next to the Gravity setting and set the Force to 0.** This prevents the particles from falling downwards, which they do by default.

   The Grid function in Particle Playground creates new particles at every frame. This is definitely not what we want. We just want a single grid of particles in this case. The next few steps ensure that.

8. **Set your current time to 0:00:00:00 or press the Home key to return to the first frame of your comp.**

9. **Under the Grid settings, turn the Particle Radius setting to 18.** Set a keyframe for this by Control+clicking/right-clicking on the Particle Radius setting in the Effects Control window and choosing Set Keyframe.

10. **In the Timeline, move one frame forward by pressing Command/Ctrl+right arrow key.**

11. **Set the Particle Radius to 0.** Set a keyframe for this by Control+clicking/right-clicking the Particle Radius setting in the Effects Control window and choosing Set Keyframe. Verify your keyframes by selecting the solid layer in the timeline and pressing the U key. This will solo all of the layer's properties that contain animations. You should see two keyframes for your Particle Radius setting.

    At this point you should have an even grid of 10 x 10 particles across your screen. The next step is to replace these particles with text.

12. **In the Effect Controls window for Particle Playground, click the underlined Options setting and then click Edit Grid Text button.**

13. **Next, type some text in the text box.** In the text box you can also set the following options:

    • Using Font/Style, select the font and style for your Grid text.

    • For the Alignment setting, select the Use Grid option.

    • Make sure the Loop Text setting is checked.

14. **Click OK to accept your selections.**

Change the color of the text to your liking. You can also change the Font Size under the Grid settings. You should now have an orderly grid comprised of the text that you entered. See Figure 18-3.

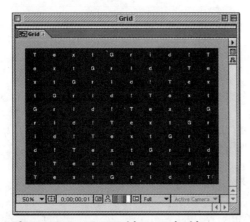

Figure 18-3: A text Grid created with Particle Playground

Understanding the Grid settings

Under the Grid settings, you can change values to create various grid effects. The settings found under the Grid property are explained here:

✦ **Position:** This setting determines the X- and Y-coordinates of the center of the grid.

✦ **Width/Height:** Sets the horizontal and vertical dimensions of the grid in pixels.

✦ **Particles Across/Particles Down:** Sets the number of particles to be created horizontally and vertically across the grid. Keyframe this setting down to 0 if you don't want any more particles to be generated.

If ever you notice that Width/Height and Particles Across/Particles Down settings are not available, the Use Grid option has been deactivated in the Edit Grid Text dialog box. Check this option back on to get the settings controls back.

✦ **Color:** Use this to change the color of the text or the particles.

✦ **Particle Radius/Font Size:** Use this setting to set the radius of particles. When you enter text under the Options settings, this setting changes to read Font Size. You can then set the Font Size of the text.

Using the Layer and the Particle Exploders

The Exploders do what they sound like they do. The Layer Exploder explodes a layer into new particles, and the Particle Exploder explodes particles into more new particles. Now, you may be wondering exactly what we mean by "explodes particles into more particles." Think of a fireworks display, and it should be easier to visualize.

The general principles of exploding layers and particles

Before we get to exploding layers and particles, you should be aware of a few general principles:

✦ In Particle Playground, a layer is exploded once for each frame. This results in a steady stream of particles for the duration of your composition. In order to start or stop a layer from continuing to explode, you have to keyframe the Radius of New Particles setting with keyframes. Set this to 0 when you don't want any more particles to be generated.

✦ When particles are exploded into newer ones, they keep the position, velocity, scale, and rotation attributes of the original particles.

✦ After the layers or the particles are exploded, you can use the Gravity, Repel, Wall, and Property Mappers options to influence their movement.

✦ You can use the exploding effect in conjunction with smoke, fire, and other effects to create some very realistic explosions. Try animating the colors to make the fireworks more realistic.

Next, let's blow up a layer, shall we?

 On the DVD-ROM In order to explain Particle Playground in detail, we created an After Effects project that includes a composition for each series of steps that we cover in the chapter. The After Effects project is called *Chapter 18.aep*, and is found in the *Project Files/Chapter 18* folder. For the next series of steps, you should look at the composition called *Layer Exploder*.

STEPS: Exploding a Layer

1. **Create a new comp, call it** *Layer Exploder,* **and place any layer that you want into it.** We are using the image of a dollar sign. Make sure that you are at the beginning of the comp be pressing the Home key.

2. **Select the layer and choose Effect ⇨ Simulation ⇨ Particle Playground.**

3. **First, turn off the Cannon.** Click the twirler next to the word Cannon and set the Particles per Second setting to 0. This is important because to generate particles any other way, we first have to disable the Cannon by turning the Particles per Second setting to 0.

4. **Twirl down the the Layer Exploder settings.** Select the layer that you want to explode by using the Explode Layer pull-down menu. In our example, we select the Dollar Sign layer.

5. **Under the Layer Exploder settings, set a keyframe by Control+clicking/ right-clicking the Radius of New Particle setting in the Effects Control window and choosing Set Keyframe.** Our explosion starts out at a radius of 2, but you can modify this if you like.

6. **In the Timeline, move forward one frame by pressing Command/Ctrl+right arrow key.**

7. **Set the Radius of New Particle to 0.** This sets the second keyframe. Verify your keyframes by selecting your exploding layer in the Timeline and pressing the U key. This will solo all of the layer's properties that contain animations. You should see two keyframes for your Radius of New Particle setting.

8. **In the Layer Exploder settings, set the Velocity Dispersion setting to 120.** This makes the explosion happen faster. For a slow explosion use a lower setting.

If you play down your comp, your layer should explode and fall to the bottom. If you want to keep Gravity out of the equation, twirl the Gravity setting triangle in the Particle Playground Effects Control window and set the Gravity force to 0. This will make your layer appear to explode in outer space. See Figure 18-4.

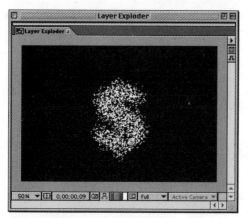

Figure 18-4: An exploding layer

On the DVD-ROM

For explaining the Particle Playground in detail, we created an After Effects project that includes a composition for each series of steps that we cover in the chapter. The After Effects project is called *Chapter 18.aep* and can be found in the *Project Files/Chapter 18* folder. For the next series of steps, you should look at the composition called *Particle Exploder*.

STEPS: Exploding Particles

1. **Make a new comp by choosing Composition ⇨ New Composition.**

2. **Create a new solid by pressing Command/Ctrl+Y.** Make the solid the size of the composition by clicking the Comp Size button in the New Solid dialog box. Call this solid *Particle Exploder Solid.*

3. **Select the solid and choose Effect ⇨ Simulation ⇨ Particle Playground to apply the effect.** By default, the particles appear red and spout upwards, but we can change this.

4. **Click the twirler next to the Cannon category and set the Particles per Second setting to 1.** This produces just one particle per second.

5. **Under Cannon, set the Position value to 354, 454.** If your comp is sized at 720 x 486 pixels, this new Position value will bring the producer point of the Cannon to the lower portion of the comp.

6. **Click the Options in the Effect Controls window and then click the Edit Cannon Text button.** Enter any text that you want and change the default font if you like.

7. **Click OK and then click OK again in the remaining dialog box.**

8. **Back under the Cannon settings, change the Font Size to something large, such as 64.** You can also change the color of the font if you like.

9. **Next, twirl down the Particle Exploder settings and set the following values:**

- Radius of New Particles: 2

- Velocity Dispersion: 120

- Affects Particles From pop-up menu to: All

- Older/Younger Than: 2 (If you want the particles to explode later, set a higher value.)

10. **Play your comp or create a RAM Preview, and you see the Cannon shoot out letters that explode as they travel upwards.** See Figure 18-5.

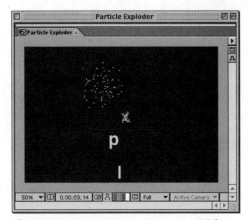

Figure 18-5: Here we use text as particles, and they explode as they travel upward.

Understanding the Exploder settings

Here's a review all the properties under the Exploder settings:

✦ **Explode Layer:** You find this setting under Layer Exploder only. Here you get to choose the layer that you want to explode. All layers currently in your comp appear under this menu.

✦ **Radius of New Particles:** Enter a value here for the radius of the particles that results from the explosion. This value has to be smaller than the radius of the original particles, because these explode into smaller bits of their former selves rather than larger ones.

✦ **Velocity Dispersion:** Here you can enter a value (in pixels per second) for the exploding particles. A high value creates a more dispersed explosion. Smaller values maintain less distance between the exploding particles.

Replacing the particles with layers

Here's one of the best, most fun features of Particle Playground. Even though the Cannon, Grid, and Exploders create useless little red squares that fly about when left at their default settings, you can use the Layer Map feature to replace the default particles with any layer of your choice. From here, you can imagine the endless possibilities. For example, you can create a snowfall-like effect with the particles streaming down from the top of your composition and then replace the default particles with an image of a snowflake you created in Adobe Illustrator. This provides you with a realistic snowfall effect in which each particle contains the snowflake image.

Next up, we show you how to replace the default particles with elements and layers of your choice. First, we set up the overall particle animation with the Cannon, and then we substitute the default particles coming from the Cannon with some line art.

In order to explain Particle Playground in detail, we created an After Effects project that includes a composition for each series of steps that we cover in the chapter. The After Effects project is called *Chapter 18.aep* and can be found in the *Project Files/Chapter 18* folder. For the next series of steps, you should look at the composition called *Replacing Particles*.

STEPS: Replacing the Default Particles with a Musical Note

1. **Make a new comp by choosing Composition ➪ New Composition.**

2. **Create a new solid by pressing Command/Ctrl+Y.** Make the solid the size of the composition by clicking the Comp Size button in the New Solid dialog box. Call this solid *Cannon Solid.*

3. **Select the solid and choose Effect ➪ Simulation ➪ Particle Playground to apply the effect.** By default, the particles appear red and spout upwards, but we can change this.

4. **Click the twirler (triangle) next to the word Cannon and set the following settings for the following Cannon properties:**

   - Position: 20.0, 424.0

   - Particles per Second: 5

   - Direction: 90

   - Velocity: 400

5. **Turn down the Gravity setting by setting the Force value to –174.** This makes the particles fly up and out of the Comp window. At this point your red particles should be going from left to right across the screen and then upwards and out. That's all fine and good. Now we replace the particles with a layer comprised of an Illustrator file.

6. **Add an Illustrator element to the comp by dragging it in from the Project Window.** We used the *Musical Note1.ai* file from the folder laveled *Elements* in our *Chapter 18.aep* project.

7. **After the layer is in the Timeline window, click the layer's eye icon to turn off its visibilty.**

8. **Next, in the Effect Controls window under Particle Playground, expand the Layer Map property by clicking its twirler.**

9. **For Use Layer, select the Illustrator element layer from the menu.** We used *Musical Note1.ai*. The Use Layer menu shows all layers presently in the current composition.

10. **Play your comp or create a RAM Preview by pressing the 0 key on the numeric keypad.** Your particles should now be replaced by whatever line art you used, in our case the musical note. They stream off to the right and then up and out of the screen. See Figure 18-6.

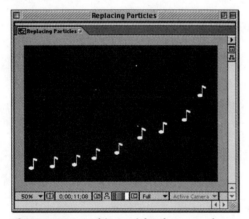

Figure 18-6: In this Particle Playground animation, we replaced the default particles with an image of a musical note. Imagine the possibilities!

Using a series of frames to replace the particles

Okay. So replacing the particles with an image is fun and can be used in all kinds of ways. But you'll soon notice a problem; all the new particles look the same. If you completed the previous exercise, you'll see that all the notes are exactly the same because only one image is used to replace the default particles.

What if you wanted the particles to be replaced with notes that looked different and random?

Well, Particle Playground has yet another trick up its sleeve that can help you achieve that. If you replace a particle with a QuickTime movie or some other sequence of images, you can choose to specify which frame each particle will use as its source. For example, if you have a short movie with four different frames of musical notes, you can use this movie as a Layer Map and opt to select random frames. This replaces the default particles with the four different notes that make up each frame of the movie. Particle Playground includes Time Offset settings that help you determine how you want to use the movie frames to replace the particles. We use this fabulous feature of Particle Playground in the next series of steps.

When replacing particles with a layer by using the Layer Map option, Particle Playground ignores any keyframes or other transformational changes you may have made to the selected layer. In other words, Particle Playground always uses the layer in its original state. If you need to scale your layer or add any effects to it, you must pre-compose the layer and make any and all changes in the pre-composition.

In order to explain Particle Playground in detail, we created an After Effects project that includes a composition for each series of steps that we cover in the chapter. The After Effects project is called *Chapter 18.aep* and can be found in the *Project Files/Chapter 18* folder. For the next series of steps, you should look at the composition called *Replacing Particles-Movie Frames*.

STEPS: Replacing the Particles with a Series of Frames

1. **Make a new comp by choosing Composition ⇨ New Composition.**

2. **Create a new solid by pressing Command/Ctrl+Y.** Make the solid the size of the composition by clicking on the Comp Size button in the New Solid dialog box. Call this solid *Cannon Solid.*

3. **Select the solid and choose Effect ⇨ Simulation ⇨ Particle Playground to apply the effect.** By default, the particles appear red and spout upwards, but we can change this.

4. **Click the twirler (triangle) next to the word Cannon and set the following settings for the following Cannon properties:**

    - Position: 20.0, 424.0

    - Particles per Second: 5

    - Direction: 90

    - Velocity: 400

5. **Turn down the Gravity setting by setting the Force value to –174.** This makes the particles fly up and out of the Comp window. At this point, your red particles should be going from left to right across the screen, and then upward and out. That's all fine and good. Now replace the particles with a layer comprised of a QuickTime movie.

6. **Add the layer *Four Musical Notes.mov* to the comp by dragging it in from the Elements folder in the Project window.** Note that *Four Musical Notes.mov* is a tiny 8-frame QuickTime movie that has four images of musical notes, each with a duration of two frames. Something else for you to keep in mind is that this movie also contains an alpha channel, which allows for a clean use of just the musical note image so that none of the background from the movie is seen in the final creation.

7. **As soon as the layer is in the Timeline window, click the layer's eye icon to turn off its visibilty.**

8. **Next, in the Effect Controls window under Particle Playground, expand the Layer Map property by clicking its twirler.**

9. **For Use Layer, select the *Four Musical Notes.mov* from the menu.** The Use Layer menu shows all layers presently in the current composition.

10. **Under the Layer Map settings, set the Time Offset Type to Absolute Random.**

11. **Under the Layer Map settings, set the Random Time Max to 60.** At this point, the Layer Map randomly utilizes the four musical note images within the *Four Musical Notes.mov* QuickTime movie to create a varied effect.

12. **Play your comp or create a RAM Preview by pressing the 0 key on the numeric keypad.** Your particles should be replaced by four different musical notes that stream off to the right and then up and out of the screen. See Figure 18-7.

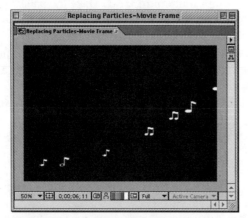

Figure 18-7: In this Particle Playground animation, the default particles are replaced by four separate images of a musical note. Each of the notes are separate frames of a four-frame QuickTime movie that we selected as our Layer Map.

Understanding the layer map options

When you use a movie as a layer map, you have a few options you can tweak to get the results that you desire. You can use the Time Offset setting to specify how you want to utilize the individual frames of a movie.

Below are some explanations of the options that you find under the Time Offset setting:

✦ **Relative:** Selecting this option begins playing the movie layer at the frame based on the Time Offset that you have selected. This offset is relative to the Playground layer's current time. When you select the Relative setting, by default, the Time Offset is set to 0, which means that the frames from your source layer movie (which replaces the particles) move in sync with the Playground layer's current frame.

✦ **Absolute:** Selecting the Absolute setting shows a frame from the movie based on the Time Offset setting. This setting is ideal if you want to show the same frame of the movie for the entire life span of the particle, instead of going through the different frames of the movie.

✦ **Relative Random:** This setting begins playing the movie layer from a frame that is selected at random, within the range between the Playgound layer's current frame and the Random Time Max you set. Specifying a Random Time Max setting of 1 will select a frame one second after the current time of the layer.

✦ **Absolute Random:** Selecting Absolute Random uses a frame from the movie at random by using a time between 0 and the value you set in the Random Time Max setting. This is the option you want to use if you want each particle to be represented by a completely different frame of the movie.

Using Gravity

When setting up a stream of particles in Particle Playground, you can use the settings found under Gravity to influence the overall behavior of the particles. To adjust any of the Gravity settings, click the twirler next to the Gravity property. The various properties are explained here:

✦ **Force:** This setting sets the force of gravity. Entering larger positive values increases the force of gravity. Entering a negative value inverts the force. Much like real world physics, particles tend to accelerate towards the direction of the gravity.

✦ **Force Random Spread:** This setting adjusts a range of randomness for the Force. When this setting is at zero, all the particles tend to fall at the same rate. Increasing the Force Random Spread can create randomness in gravity, and this is particularly useful for elements, such as falling snowflakes.

✦ **Direction:** Sets the angle of Gravity. This setting defaults to 180 degrees, which is how the force of gravity works in the real world physics.

✦ **Affects:** Selects a smaller portion of the particles to which the Gravity applies. The rest of the particles remain free from the effects of Gravity. For example, using the Particles from the pull-down menu under the Affects settings, you can choose to affect only those particles created from the Cannon, Grid, or Particle Exploder.

Repelling and attracting particles

You can influence the overall behavior of the particles by adjusting whether or not they repel or attract nearby particles. You can adjust the following settings under Repel and Attract.

✦ **Force:** Sets the repel force. A positive value repels the particles from one another, like bouncing molecules. Entering a negative value attracts them to each other, like you might find with sticky snow flakes.

✦ **Force Radius:** This property sets the radius in pixels within which particles are repelled from one another. As another particle enters this radius, it will be repelled or attracted.

✦ **Repeller:** Sets which particles act as repellers or attacters to another set of particles that you can set by using the Affects setting (see the next section).

✦ **Affects:** Here you can select a subset of a particles to which you want to apply the repel or attract qualities.

Using walls to contain particles

When creating particles in Particle Playground, you can also create "walls" that constrict particles within them. Masks that you create on the Particle Playground define the walls that you create.

Next, we complete a series of steps to create a mask that we then go on to use as a wall to contain particles.

In order to explain Particle Playground in detail, we created an After Effects project that includes a composition for each series of steps that we cover in the chapter. The After Effects project is called *Chapter 18.aep,* which you can find in the *Project Files/Chapter 18* folder. For the next series of steps you should look at the composition called *Using Walls.*

STEPS: Constricting Particles Within Walls

1. **Start out by setting up a Particle Playground composition made up of a Cannon shooting off some particles.** Make a new comp by choosing Composition ➪ New Composition.

2. **Create a new solid by using the Command/Ctrl+Y shortcut.** Make the solid the size of the composition by clicking the Comp Size button in the New Solid dialog box. Call this solid *Wall Solid*.

3. **In the Timeline window, select Wall Solid and choose Effect ⇨ Simulation ⇨ Particle Playground to apply the effect.** As usual, the particles appear red and spout upwards, but we can change this.

4. **Click the triangle next to the word Cannon and set the following settings under the Cannon property:**

   - Position: 358, –18.0
   - Barrel Radius: 325
   - Particles per Second: 20
   - Direction: 180

   At this point, your red particles should be falling from the top of the comp in a wide area across the composition.

5. **Next, replace the particles with large text.** In the Effect Controls window for Particle Playground, click the Options button.

6. **Click the Edit Cannon Text button.**

7. **Next, type some text in the text box.** Using Font/Style, select whatever font and style that you want for your Cannon text.

8. **Click OK to accept your selections.**

9. **Back in the Cannon settings, click the underlined Font Size value and enter a value of 48 to enlarge the font size.** Note that before you enter any text into the text box, this setting reads Particle Radius.

10. **Change the color of the text by clicking the Color dropper and selecting the color of your choice.**

    Okay. It's finally time to create a wall and contain the text within it.

11. **In the Timeline, double-click the *Wall Solid* layer.** This opens it in the Layer window.

12. **Select the Pen tool from the Tools Palette and create a closed mask on the *Wall Solid* layer in the Layer window.** A quick way to create a closed mask is to click around a few locations on the layer and then double-click the last point. This closes the mask. Note that if the Tools Palette is not visible, choose Windows ⇨ Tools (Command/Ctrl+1).

13. **In the Particle Playground Effect Controls window for the *Wall Solid* layer, expand the Wall property by clicking its twirler.** From the Boundary pop-up menu, choose the mask that you created. Any and all masks you may have created are listed under this menu.

At this point, your particles will be bouncing off the mask as they hit it. Particles that are born within the mask itself will be bouncing off from the inside. Using the many controls offered under the Wall settings, you can create a bunch of cool and interesting effects.

Tip   To turn off the Wall control, expand the Wall property under the Particle Playground effect and select None from the Boundary pop-up menu.

Using layer maps to influence particle behavior

If you take a look at the Particle Playground Effect Controls window, we're all the way down the list to Ephemeral and Persistent Properties. To understand these, we first have to explain what layer maps are and how these Persistent and Ephemeral properties use them.

Here is how the principle of layer maps works in Particle Playground. You can create layer maps that consist of RGB values and use each color (Red, Green, or Blue) to influence various aspects of the particles. For example, you can create a simple still image that has a blue circle in the center and red all around it. By using the Property mappers, you can tell the Particle Playground to enlarge the size of the particles as they hit the blue area of the image and turn slightly as they hit the red part of the image. When you take advantage of this feature, you can create very subtle yet realistic kinds of motion based on real world physics.

We show you how in the next series of steps.

On the DVD-ROM   In order to explain Particle Playground in detail, we created an After Effects project that includes a composition for each series of steps that we cover in the chapter. The After Effects project is called *Chapter 18.aep,* which is found in the *Project Files/Chapter 18* folder. For the next series of steps, you should look at the composition called *Layer Maps.*

STEPS: Magnifying Particles with a Layer Map

First, we create a stream of particles that we can work with. Then we replace the particles with musical notes. Last but not least, we use a layer map to have some fun with them.

1. **Make a new comp by choosing Composition ⇨ New Composition.**

2. **Create a new solid by pressing Command/Ctrl+Y.** Make the solid the size of the composition by clicking the Comp Size button in the New Solid dialog box. Call this solid *Particles.*

3. **Select the solid and choose Effect ⇨ Simulation ⇨ Particle Playground to apply the effect.** Guess what? The particles appear red and spout upwards, but we can change this.

4. **Click the twirler next to the word Cannon and set the following settings under the Cannon property:**

- Position: 20.0, 424.0
- Particles per Second: 5
- Direction: 90
- Velocity: 400

5. **Turn down the Gravity setting and set the Force value to –174.** This makes the particles fly up and out of the Comp window. At this point, your red particles should be going from left to right across the screen, and then upwards and out. Now replace the particles with a layer of our choice.

6. **Add the layer *Musical Note1.ai* to the comp by dragging it in from the Elements folder in the Project Window.**

7. **After you place the layer is in the Timeline window, click the layer's eye icon to turn off its visibility.**

8. **Next, in the Effect Controls window, expand the Layer Map property by clicking its twirler.**

9. **For Use Layer, select a the *Musical Note1.ai* from the pop-up menu.** The Use Layer menu shows all layers presently in the current composition.

    Play down your comp or create a RAM Preview by pressing the 0 key on the numeric keypad. Your particles, which should now be musical notes, will stream off to the right, and then up and off the screen.

10. **Next, drag the *Magnifying_Glass.eps* layer from the Project window into the composition and set its position to 524.0, 351.0.** You can set the position by selecting the layer in the timeline, pressing the P key to solo the position property, and then entering the numeric values previously listed.

11. **Drag the still labelled *Layer Map.pict* into the composition.** You see that this image consists of a red background and a small blue circle aligned to fall within the area of the Magnifying Glass. Turn off its visibility by clicking the eyeball icon for the layer, because the layer map doesn't need to be visible in the composition.

12. **Click the Ephemeral Property Mapper twirler and under the Use Layer As Map pop-up menu, select the *Layer Map.pict* image.**

13. **In the Map Blue to pop-up menu, select the Scale property.** This tells Particle Playground to affect the scale of the particles based on any blue color present in the layer map.

14. **Set the Min setting to 1 and the Max setting to 2 under the Map Blue to properties.**

As you play down this comp, you see that as the musical notes hit the blue area (which are not visible), they become twice as large. They go back to their original size after they hit the red area. See Figure 18-8 and Color Plate 18-1.

Cool, no? You can experiment with other properties to affect the musical notes by choosing them in the vast array of choices available under the Map Blue to pop-up menu. You can also play with the Map Red to pop-up menu in the same way.

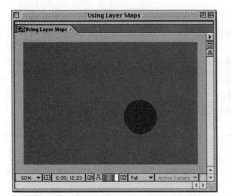

Figure 18-8: Using a Layer Map (left) composed of Blue and Red colors, we can make the particles enlarge when they pass under the magnifying glass.

Understanding Persistent and Ephemeral properties

You may have noticed that the settings under the Persistent and Ephemeral Property Mappers appear to be the same. They generally are, except for some minor differences. The important issue is to learn the difference between the two types of Mappers.

✦ **Persistent Property Mappers:** A *persistent* change in Particle Playground is one which retains the change made to it for the lifespan of the particle. It persists, hence the name. For example, if you are using a layer map to change the rotation of the particle, the particle will retain its altered rotation after it leaves the influence of the property map.

✦ **Ephemeral Property Mappers:** An *ephemeral* change in Particle Playground is one in which the particle reverts back to its original state after it leaves the influence of the property map. For example, in the previous exercise, we used a red and blue map to change the size of the musical note. When the particle leaves the influence of the map, it reverts back to the original size. These are flaky changes, if you will.

Understanding the layer map options

When using either the Persistent or Ephemeral property Mappers, you can use the Mappers pop-up menus to affect a large number of the particles' properties. We list these here:

✦ **None:** Makes no change to any particle property.

✦ **Red:** This setting duplicates the value of the particle's red channel within a range of 0.0–1.0.

✦ **Green:** This setting duplicates the value of the particle's green channel within a range of 0.0–1.0.

✦ **Blue:** Duplicates the value of the particle's blue channel within a range of 0.0–1.0.

✦ **Kinetic Friction:** Selecting this setting copies the amount of resisting force against a moving object. For example if you want create the effect of a particle braking down to a stop, increase this value.

✦ **Static Friction:** This setting copies the amount of inertia that holds a stationary particle in its place. If you set this to zero, a particle will move if Gravity is present. If you increase this value, then a stationary particle needs other forces acting on it in order to move.

✦ **Angle:** Copies the direction in which the particle points. This angle is in degrees and is relative to the particle's original angle. Viewing the angle of a particle is easier if it is a text character rather than a tiny dot.

✦ **Angular Velocity:** This setting copies the velocity of particle rotation in degrees per second. In effect, this setting controls how fast a particle rotates around its own axis.

✦ **Torque:** Copies the force of particle rotation.

✦ **Scale:** This setting is ideal for stretching a particle proportionally, both along the X-axis and the Y-axis, which is what you may find yourself doing most of the time. A value of 1.0 scales the particle to its 100% size. A value of 2.0 scales it 200%.

✦ **X Scale/Y Scale:** Use these settings to stretch a particle horizontally or vertically.

✦ **X/Y:** This setting copies the position of a particle along the X- or Y-axis in the frame. A value of zero sets a position at the left of the frame (for X) or at the top of the frame (for Y).

✦ **X Speed/Y Speed:** Affects the horizontal speed (X-axis velocity) or vertical speed (Y-axis velocity) of a particle in pixels per second.

✦ **Gradient Force:** This setting affects the force adjustment based on areas of a layer map on both the X and Y planes of motion.

✦ **Gradient Velocity:** Copies the velocity adjustment based on areas of a layer map on both the X and Y planes of motion.

✦ **X Force:** Copies the coercion along the X-axis of motion. Positive values push a particle to the right, negative to the left.

✦ **Y Force:** Copies the coercion along the Y-axis of motion. Positive values push a particle down, negative values push it up.

✦ **Opacity:** This setting copies the transparency of a particle. A setting of zero is invisible, and 1 is 100% solid. Change this value to fade particles in or out.

✦ **Mass:** Copies the particle mass, which interacts with all properties that adjust force, such as Gravity, Static Friction, Kinetic Friction, Torque, and Angular Velocity. One way to think about it is that it takes greater force to move particles with a larger mass.

✦ **Lifespan:** Copies the elapsed length of time a particle will exist, in seconds. When the time runs out, the particle is removed from the layer.

✦ **Character:** This setting applies only if you're using text characters as particles. Using it copies the value that corresponds to an ASCII text character, making it replace the current particle. You can specify which text characters appear by painting or drawing shades of gray on the layer map that correspond to the ASCII characters that you want. A value of zero produces no character.

✦ **Font Size:** This setting applies only if you are using text. Using it copies the point size of characters. You can increase this value to make the font larger.

✦ **Time Offset:** This setting only applies if you are using a movie with multiple frames. This setting copies the Time Offset value used by the layer map property.

Speeding up rendering in Particle Playground

Rendering with Particle Playground can easily turn into the most time-intensive rendering you'll ever do. The math for Particle Playground is extremely involved, and a large number of particles can easily bring your render to a standstill.

Here are some suggestions to help you manage your rendering times when using Particle Playground:

✦ The first and foremost issue that you can have with Particle Playground is that the Grid and the Layer Exploder generate particles on every frame, which, unless controlled carefully will generate way too many particles. In doing so, the effect and its render time can become painfully slow. This fact eludes most first-time Particle Playground users, and they often throw their hands up and never return to this great effect.

The trick to avoiding a continual generation of particles is to animate any of the following properties down to zero: Layer Exploder, Radius of New Particles, Grid Radius, Particle Radius, and Font Size. For example, at the first frame of the Grid particle generation, you can set the particle amount or size to your liking. But if you set the size of the particles down to zero on the second frame of your comp, the Grid will no longer produce particles on every frame.

✦ While using Particle Playground, you should keep an eye on your Info palette. Choose Window ➪ Info to bring up the Info palette. You can see the number of particles that you are generating. According to Adobe, if a Particle Playground implementation contains more than 10,000 particles, it can slow your render down to a crawl. We've experienced major render hits way below the 10,000 figure, so be careful.

✦ When using Particle Playground, you should be aware that the particle positions can extend beyond the bounds of the layer to which you applied the Particle Playground effect. You can control particles that are on the edge of a layer or even ones that you can't see. Once again, the Info pallette indicates how many particles are being tracked. You may want to consider making property maps that are much larger than the size of your comp.

✦ If you are rendering for video, you may need to field-render the Particle Playground effect. In order to do so, you must select Enable Field Rendering in the Particle Playground Options dialog box.

✦ Particle Playground works with Motion Blur. This is super for creating even more "realism" in your effect, but the render times increase even more because the motion blur needs to be calculated for each particle.

✦ ✦ ✦

Keying and Knockouts

Keying is fairly easy to understand, at least on a conceptual level. We're guessing that 99 percent of the folks who use After Effects know what's going on when they see the weatherman on the evening news. For the remaining one percent of you, here goes: Al Roker and his fellow tradesmen do their thing standing in front of a blue or green wall. The colored wall gets knocked, or *keyed* out, and the weather map is placed in the resulting transparent area. As the weatherman gives his report, he looks at the composited result in a TV monitor so that he can see where he's pointing. Even though we're all very used to it, the technology is still pretty cool.

Not content to leave this trick solely to the people who make a living telling us the likelihood of an afternoon shower, creative film and television producers have used this technology in a variety of different ways. The popular kids TV show "Blue's Clues" seen on the Nickelodeon Channel is produced using this method, and so was a great deal of *Star Wars*. In case you didn't know, the Millennium Falcon was a small model shot in front of a bluescreen. More recently, *The Matrix* employed greenscreen keying to great effect in its "bullet time" sequences.

Learning what goes into creating a clean key could be the subject of an entire book. In your mind's eye, it's not hard to imagine separating a weatherman from a bright green wall, but on a technical level, it's actually a highly sophisticated process that involves far more variables than you might have initially imagined. The act of creating a noiseless alpha channel is hard enough. Layering another element into the transparent area while making sure that the moving footage in the foreground looks as though it belongs there makes it even more difficult. This chapter examines how After Effects can help you handle this meticulous process.

Finding the Key

When it comes to keying, nothing can replace solid production methods. In other words, a successful key is largely dependent on the quality of the footage before it goes into post-production. You really don't want to be left holding the bag if the footage that needs to be keyed was poorly prepared. If you're lucky, you'll receive footage that has been properly lit against a consistently colored and highly contrasting background. Even then, skin tones, hair, and refracted light from the surfaces on the set can be especially vexing, even more so if the shoot involves glass or smoke. As always, be wary of uttering, "We can fix it in post." Nowhere is this more clear than when the issue at hand is a high-grade key.

You can use a few different filters in After Effects to create an effective key, or alpha channel, and we look at all of them in detail.

On the DVD-ROM In order to explain keying in greater detail, we created an After Effects project that includes a composition for each series of steps that we cover in the chapter. Just as a reminder, you need to copy the *Source Material* folder from the DVD-ROM to your hard drive. Our own corresponding After Effects project is called *Chapter 19.aep* and can be found in the *Project Files/Chapter 19* folder.

Navigating bluescreens, greenscreens, and spill

As we already mentioned, the idea of keying is simple. It involves removing a colored background from a foreground subject. Many people know it as *bluescreening*, because blue happens to be one of the most common colors placed behind these shots. Many other production facilities call it *greenscreening*, because they tend to use a green color for the background.

Bear in mind that there's more to it than taking any old blue or green paint to create your background. For the keying process, production technicians use standard shades of blue and green that you can sometimes find at large photo supply stores. Whether you choose blue or green depends on the context of the shoot. If the final composite is going to involve natural scenery, then green is the sensible choice, because it will make any leftover green spill a lot less obvious. *Spill* is the term given to any light that gets reflected from the surfaces on the set. If you shoot an actor against a greenscreen, you can't completely avoid some green spill onto his skin or hair. On the other hand, for something such as a metallic-looking newsroom, a blue background may be ideal because the blue spill won't be as noticeable. Generally speaking, use a bluescreen if you know that the final composite is going to end up in the blue and purple color range. Alternatively, use a greenscreen if you know that the final background is going to wind up in the yellow and green range.

Before we go any further, we want to add to our growing number of caveats. Professional keying is usually the responsibility of an entire crew that's entirely devoted to this one special task. In essence, you don't want to make any promises to clients without a clear idea of what you're getting into. Keying is not like adding a blur to some text or feathering the edges of a mask. This is tricky stuff.

So, we told you that solid production techniques on the set of the shoot are an absolute must. Another important facet we should mention is that you want to select the highest quality tape format that you can afford in order to shoot your material. In most cases a format such as BetaCam SP or Digital BetaCam is ideal. DV, and especially miniDV formats should be avoided, if at all possible. You can always count on the DV formats to contain nasty jagged edges, so they never provide a very clean final key.

If you find yourself in charge of both production *and* post-production, you'll find that it's worth every bit of your time to carefully plan, budget, light, and shoot your bluescreen shots well. Using After Effects to try and get a good key from badly shot footage has been known to turn grown men and women into wailing infants.

Working with the keying filters

Here's a simple fact you should know: If you want to do some decent keying in After Effects, you need to get the Production Bundle, pure and simple. Only in the Production Bundle will you find the proper tools to pull a good enough key for your video. Going one step further, if your work entails a lot of keying on a regular basis, you should get the keying plug-in from Ultimatte or Primatte. You'll find that either of these solutions pulls exceptional keys from all different kinds of professionally shot video. Both of these companies make the finest keying tools available, and any professional broadcast house that has heavy-duty keying requirements works with the Ultimatte or the Primatte plug-in for After Effects. There are also numerous other third-party spill and matte tools that can greatly enhance your keying work.

One more point before we explore the keying filters in After Effects: In order to obtain a proper key, you almost always have to work with more than one filter. For example, you may use the Color Difference Key filter to obtain the proper key first. You might then apply the Spill Suppressor to get rid of some of the color spill on your subject. At that point, if you still have a halo around your matted subject, you can use the Matte Choker to eliminate it. Having said all that, dive into the keying options that are available to you in After Effects.

Using the Color Difference Key (PB only)

If you're keying with the benefit of the Production Bundle of After Effects, you'll find yourself reaching for the Color Difference Key most of the time. However, you need to be aware that the first time you apply this effect to a piece of footage and take a look at the Effect Controls window, you may feel a little overwhelmed by the number of sliders and controls that you have at your disposal. Before you start to feel a little dizzy, take heart. For the moment, you can ignore more than half of these settings. To get started, the number of controls that you need to understand and manipulate is surprisingly small. After you begin to get the hang of it, you can go on to explore the rest of the seemingly endless effect properties.

The Color Difference Key is by far the most sophisticated keying tool that After Effects has to offer (see Figure 19-1 and Color Plate 19-1). Before you go through the steps of using the Color Difference Key, you should know that this filter works a bit differently than most of the effects you may have applied to a layer. In essence, the Color Difference Key creates a couple of different mattes and ultimately combines the difference between them to make a final matte.

Black eye dropper ⎯⎯⎯⎯⎯⎯⎯⎯⎯ ⎯⎯ Thumbnail eye dropper

Clean original image ⎯⎯⎯⎯⎯⎯ ⎯⎯ White eye dropper

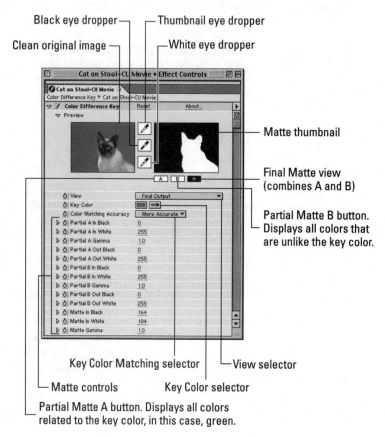

Matte thumbnail

Final Matte view
(combines A and B)

Partial Matte B button.
Displays all colors that
are unlike the key color.

Key Color Matching selector ⎯⎯⎯⎯⎯ ⎯⎯ View selector

⎯⎯ Matte controls   Key Color selector

Partial Matte A button. Displays all colors
related to the key color, in this case, green.

Figure 19-1: The Color Difference Key Effect Controls window

On the DVD-ROM

In order to explain the Keying effects in detail, we created an After Effects project that includes a composition for each series of steps that we cover in the chapter. The After Effects project is called *Chapter 19.aep* and can be found in the *Project Files/Chapter 19* folder. For the next series of steps, you should look at the composition we named *Color Difference*.

STEPS: Applying the Color Difference Key

1. Make a new comp and drag the *Cat on Stool-CU Movie* layer into it.

2. **Select the *Cat on Stool-CU Movie* layer and then choose Effect ➪ Keying ➪ Color Difference Key.** In the resulting Effect Controls window, the cat movie is shown in two different views. The first one is the original source, while the second one allows you to select a view.

3. **In the Effect Controls window for the Color Difference Key, choose Matte Corrected from the View menu.**

4. **First, you want to tell After Effects which color to key out.** In the Effect Controls window, click the Key Color eye dropper and then click in the Comp window on the green background behind the cat. You can select this green color from either the Comp window or from the thumbnail for the cat movie in the Project window. Also, be sure to set the Color Matching Accuracy to More Accurate.

5. **Next, select the black eye dropper and then click inside the matte thumbnail (in the Effect Controls) on the area that you want to make transparent or invisible (see Figure 19-2).**

Figure 19-2: Select the black eye dropper (the middle of the three eye droppers) and click inside the thumbnail to select the portion that you want to be transparent or invisible. In this case, click outside the cat on the green background.

6. **Select the white eye dropper and then click inside the matte thumbnail on the area that you want to keep opaque or visible.** This could be anywhere on the cat itself. The idea here is to create the sharpest matte of as possible. The closer you get to pure black and white values, the better. See Figure 19-3.

Figure 19-3: Select the white eye dropper (the bottom of the three eye droppers) and click inside the thumbnail to select the portion that you want to be opaque or fully visible. In this case, click the cat.

7. **If you aren't satisfied with the resulting transparency values, you can repeat Steps 5 and 6 for one or both of the partial mattes.** To do this, click the Partial Matte B button or the Partial Matte A button to select a partial matte and then repeat Steps 5 and 6. Note that the Partial Matte A button displays a matte based on all colors related to your key color, which in this case is green. The Partial Matte B button displays a matte based on all colors besides the green color. The Alpha Matte view (the small button to the left of the A and the B buttons) shows the final matte, which is a combined view of the A and the B matte.

8. **To keep refining the process, you can use some of the sliders to fine-tune your key.**

   Here's how the sliders work:

   - The black sliders change the transparency levels of each matte. When you use the black eye dropper, in effect, you're adjusting the black sliders.

   - The white slider bars change the opaque or solid levels of each matte. When you use the White dropper, in effect, you're adjusting the white sliders.

   - Gamma sliders control how accurately the transparency values follow a linear curve. Remember, the term Gamma refers to mid-levels.

9. **Finally, choose Final Output from the View menu.** The Comp window displays the final output for your key. Be sure to leave this setting on Final Output. After Effects requires that for proper rendering of the final key.

At this point, what you probably have is still a pretty crude key. But remember what we said earlier: A good key rarely results from just using one filter. In order to remove the spill of the green light from the background, you can use the Spill Supressor filter, and if a halo or a color outline is around the cat, you can use the Matte Choker filter. Both of these effects are explained a bit later in this chapter.

A super quick way to achieve a relatively decent key with the Color Difference Key filter is to select the key color, change your view to alpha matte (the combination of A and B) and adjust the bottom three sliders: Matte in Black, Matte in White, and Matte Gamma. If you have any remaining issues, adjust the Partial A and B sliders for the In White and In Black settings.

Using the Color Key

The Color Key filter eliminates all the pixels that are similar to a specified color that you choose. Keep in mind that when you select a color, that color is eliminated for the entire layer. For example, when selecting a blue background, you may also end up eliminating the blue color of someone's shirt. You can use the Tolerance slider to control the range of colors and avoid eliminating a broad range of blue shades from the layer.

In order to explain the Keying effects in detail, we created an After Effects project that includes a composition for each series of steps that we cover in the chapter. The After Effects project is called *Chapter 19.aep* and can be found in the *Project Files/Chapter 19* folder. For the next series of steps, you should look at the composition we named *Color Key*.

STEPS: Using the Color Key

1. **Make a new comp and drag the *Cat on Stool-LS Movie* layer into it.**

2. **Select the layer and choose Effect ⇨ Keying ⇨ Color Key.**

3. **In the Effect Controls window, set a key color by clicking the eye dropper and then clicking the color in the Comp window that you want to key out.**

4. **Use the Color Tolerance slider to specify the range of color to key out.** Setting lower values keys out a narrower range of colors nearest to the color you selected. Higher values key out a wider range of color.

5. **Use the Edge Thin slider to adjust the width of the keyed area's border.** You will notice that adjusting this slider will either "eat" into the cat or expand the area around it. In this particular case, you may want to leave the Edge Thin setting at 0.

6. **Finally, adjust the Edge Feather slider to soften the edges between the foreground and the background.** This removes some "jaggies" you may have around your final key.

Using the Color Range Key (PB only)

The Color Range effect is best used if your bluescreen or greenscreen is unevenly lit or if it contains otherwise varying shades of blue or green color. In most cases, you'll find it pretty difficult to light a bluescreen or greenscreen evenly. Often times, productions use colored screens that are lit from the back so that the screens glow and produce a very even color. In any case, working with the Color Range filter enables you to key out a range or colors in the LAB, the YUV, or the RGB color space. See Figure 19-4.

LAB stands for Luminance, Color A, and, Color B. The LAB color space attempts to replicate the entire spectrum of colors visible to the human eye.

In order to explain the Keying effects in detail, we created an After Effects project that includes a composition for each series of steps that we cover in the chapter. The After Effects project is called *Chapter 19.aep* and can be found in the *Project Files/Chapter 19* folder. For the next series of steps, you should look at the composition we named *Color Range Key*.

Preview of matte

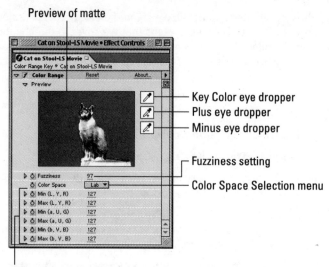

Key Color eye dropper

Plus eye dropper

Minus eye dropper

Fuzziness setting

Color Space Selection menu

Color space adjustment controls

Figure 19-4: Unlike many of the other color key filters, the Color Range Key provides only a preview of the matte for your footage.

STEPS: Applying the Color Range Key

1. **In the Timeline, select the layer that you want to make transparent in the time layout window and then choose Effect ⇨ Keying ⇨ Color Range.** In our case, we're using the *Cat on Stool-LS movie* as an example.

2. **In the Effect Controls window, choose RGB from the Color Space pop-up menu.** Sometimes, changing the color space can help if you're having trouble isolating your subject.

3. **Next, select the top eye dropper and then click in the matte thumbnail to select the area that you want to make transparent.** The area that you select should be the background you want to eliminate.

4. **Next, select a range of colors to be keyed out.** To do so, select the Plus eye dropper and then click other areas in the matte thumbnail to add other colors or shades to the range of colors that you want keyed out for transparency. After Step 3, you may have areas of green left in the greenscreen area. Using the Plus eye dropper, you can click the green areas that remain. Remember to do all this clicking in the matte preview area in the Effects Control window.

5. **If necessary, select colors and shades that you want to eliminate from the keyed out colors.** To do so select the Minus eye dropper and then click areas in the matte thumbnail. The shades and colors that you click are eliminated from the colors to be keyed out.

6. **Adjust the Fuzziness slider to soften the edges between transparent and opaque sections of your composite.**

7. **Finally, use the slider bars underneath the Color Space pop-up menu to finesse the color range that you selected earlier when using the Plus and Minus eye droppers.**

Before you go insane reading the highly cryptic slider settings, here's something to calm your nerves. The slider names attempt to cover all the possibilities for the three different color space options. In short, the first slider, Min (L, Y, R), controls the L (or luminance) setting if you select the Lab color space. Otherwise, it controls the Y setting if you select the YUV color space. Lastly, if you select the RGB color space, then this slider controls the R (Red) setting of the overall RGB mix.

Here's how all the sliders work:

✦ **L, Y, R slider:** These control the first component of the specified color space: L for Lab, Y if the choice is YUV, and R if the selection is RGB.

✦ **a, U, G slider:** These sliders control the second component. They control a if your selection is Lab, U if your selection is YUV, and G if your selection is RGB.

✦ **b, V, B slider:** The final two sliders control the third component. You know what this is by now. This slider controls the b component if your color space choice is Lab, V if your choice is YUV, and B, if your selection is RGB.

Each of these sliders represents values between 0 and 255. By setting a Min value, you tell After Effects to set the beginning of the color range at that point. To make adjustments, drag the Min slider bars to set the beginning of the color range. Then drag the Max slider bars to set the end of the color range. In the example of the *Cat on Stool-LS Movie* layer, you probably only need to work with the Min (a, U, G) and the Max (a, U, G) sliders. The reason for that is that we're working in the RGB color space, and the only item that we want to work with is the Green channel so that we can eliminate the green background.

For the rest of the exercise, you're on your own. If you stop at this stage, you will notice that your key will still be somewhat less than perfect. Go ahead and choose Effect ➪ Key ➪ Spill Suppressor and Effect ➪ Matte ➪ Matte Choker to make a better knockout. In our *Color Range Key* comp on the DVD-ROM, you see that we used these filters to clean up our key. For the final composite, we got a helping hand from the greenish background in the QuickTime movie of falling money that we used to place behind our financially savvy Siamese cat. If you can, select (or create) footage for the composite that blends well with your greenscreen footage. That way, any green color left over from the greenscreen background won't stand out.

What if you have to use a different color scheme for your background, such as red or yellow, for example? Then the trick is to apply the Change Color filter (from the

Image Control group of effects) to the greenscreen footage. You can select the green color for the Color to Change option and further refine the color to match any background you may have. While working with the Change Color filter, set the Matching Softness to a very high percentage and then alter the Hue Transform quality to match the green behind the cat to something closer to the shades that comprise the footage from your background layer. After you make the initial adjustments, you can turn the Matching Softness back down so that the clip appears somewhat normal again. Now when you apply the keying filters, the final composite won't contain any jarring green spill that might clash with the color scheme of your background layer.

Using the Difference Matte effect (PB only)

The Difference Matte filter is easy to understand. This effect compares two layers; one is the source layer, and the other is a Difference Layer. It then keys out the pixels that match between the two layers. So, for example, if you shoot an object in front of a wall and then take a shot of the same wall without the object, you could use the Difference Matte filter to eliminate the wall altogether. Makes sense, right? The pixel values that comprise the wall are what the two shots have in common. If you are planning to use this effect, be sure to use a static (read *locked down*) camera on a tripod to capture both shots. Also, you should know that the Difference Layer shot doesn't have to be a movie. It can be a still shot as well. The beauty of this feature is that you can make a Difference Layer by creating a still image in After Effects *or* Photoshop.

We should warn anyone who is excitedly jumping up and down after reading the description for the Difference Matte that this particular keying effect sounds great on paper, but in real-life situations, it can be a tricky and unreliable way to work. After you apply this effect, the edges tend to look pretty lame. More often than not, the edges are jaggy and lack proper anti-aliasing.

In order to explain the Keying effects in detail, we created an After Effects project that includes a composition for each series of steps that we cover in the chapter. The After Effects project is called *Chapter 19.aep* and can be found in the *Project Files/Chapter 19* folder. For the next series of steps, you should look at the composition we named *Difference Matte*.

STEPS: Applying the Difference Matte

1. **In the Timeline window, select a layer to which you want to apply the Difference Matte effect.** In our case we used the *Cat on Stool-LS Movie* as our layer. This movie simply shows a cat sitting on a stool in front of a green-screen.

2. **Choose Layer ⇨ New ⇨ Solid.** Name it *Difference Layer Solid*. Make it the size of the comp, and for the color, click the Color eye dropper and select the green from the *Cat on Stool-LS Movie* layer. You may also want to create a red solid layer to place behind the cat layer. The red layer serves as a gauge by which you can judge the cleanliness of your key.

3. **In the Timeline, turn off the the visibility of the *Difference Layer Solid* layer by clicking its Video switch (the eyeball).**

4. **Select the original source layer, in our case, the *Cat on Stool-LS Movie* layer, and then choose Effect ⇨ Keying ⇨ Difference Matte.**

5. **In the Effect Controls window for the Difference Matte effect, choose Final Output or Matte Only from the View pop-up menu.** The Matte Only view is best used to check for holes and artifacts in your matte.

6. **In the Difference Layer menu, choose your background layer.** This could be a special still frame you may have created, but in this case, select is the *Difference Layer Solid* layer. Figure 19-5 shows where in the window to select the Difference Layer.

7. **Ideally, your Difference Layer should be the same size as your main video layer.** If not you can select from the following options found under the If Layer Sizes Differ menu:

   • **Center:** This option locates the Difference Layer in the center of the source layer. If the Difference Layer happens to be smaller than the source layer, the rest of the layer is filled up with black.

   • **Stretch to Fit:** This option stretches or shrinks the Difference Layer to the size of the source layer. Some distortion may appear in your background layer when using this option.

8. **Next, drag the Matching Tolerance slider to set the amount of transparency.** Lower numbers result in less transparency, whereas higher numbers give you more of it.

9. **Use the Matching Softness slider to soften the edges between the transparent and opaque areas.**

10. **Choose Final Output from the View pop-up menu and check to see how well you pulled your key.**

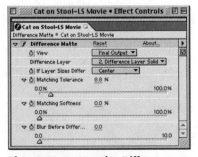

Figure 19-5: Use the Difference Layer pop-up menu to select the layer that After Effects uses to compare with the original footage to create the final key.

If you take a look at the *Difference Matte* comp that we give you, you may notice that the cat key doesn't look 100 percent clean, even after a few adjustments. This is to be expected. We simply used a flat solid colored layer as the Difference Layer, and besides, don't forget the first rule of keying in After Effects: You always need more than one filter. Go ahead and choose Effects ➪ Matte Tools ➪ Matte Choker and Effects ➪ Keying ➪ Spill Suppressor to add these effects to the layer and adjust these additional filter settings to pull a cleaner key.

Using the Extract effect (PB only)

Extract is an interesting keying effect. When using this filter, you can create transparency by keying out, or *extracting,* a specific range of brightness. Subsequently, the Extract effect works best if you shot your footage against a black or a white background. Extract is often used to eliminate shadows from footage.

When applied, the Extract effect displays a Histogram in the Effects Control window. You get to select the channel that the Histogram represents. From left to right, the Histogram displays the distribution of pixels in an image from their darkest possible values (0) to their lightest (255). Using the handles on the Histogram or the sliders underneath (these aren't mutually exclusive — changing one changes the other), you can specify the range of pixels that are made transparent.

An ideal use for the Extract key is for stills and movies that contain a black border or background. For example, if an art director has given you a flattened Photoshop file of a doll that has a black background behind it, you can use the Extract effect to get rid of the black areas.

In order to explain the Keying effects in detail, we created an After Effects project that includes a composition for each series of steps that we cover in the chapter. The After Effects project is called *Chapter 19.aep* and can be found in the *Project Files/Chapter 19* folder. For the next series of steps, you should look at the composition we named *Extract.*

STEPS: Applying the Extract Filter

1. **Select the layer you want to add transparency to and then choose Effect ➪ Keying ➪ Extract.** In our case, we use a still file that contains black and white sections. You may want to create a contrasting solid to use as a background layer so that you can monitor the progress of your key.

2. **If your plan is to key out bright or dark areas, choose Luminance from the Channel pop-up menu.** In our case, we use a black and white image, so Luminance is what we select.

3. **Finally, you can control the levels at which the filter generates transparency by dragging the upper-right and the upper-left selection handles of the Histogram.** Note that moving the handles is the same as using the sliders in the Effect Controls window.

4. **To adjust the softness of your key, drag the lower-left or the lower-right handles of the Histogram.** Alternatively, you can also use the White Softness and Black Softness sliders.

Figure 19-6 shows the adjustments possible with the Histogram display in the Extract effect.

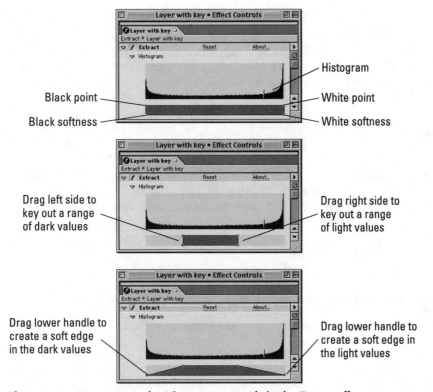

Figure 19-6: You can use the Histogram controls in the Extract effect to create an accurate key based on luminance values.

Using the Inner Outer effect (PB only)

The Inner Outer Key effect relies on masks you create for separating foreground objects from their background. The masks can be fairly rough. In other words, they don't have to follow the contours of the layers precisely.

STEPS: Applying the Inner Outer Effect

1. Select the layer that you want to add transparency to and then choose Effect ⇨ Keying ⇨ Inner Outer.

2. **Next you want to isolate your foreground.** In order to do so, draw a single, closed mask around the foreground subject's outline. After you finish masking the layer, set the mask mode to None. If you need a refresher on creating masks, review Chapter 9.

3. **Using the Foreground menu in the Inner Outer Key's Effect Controls window, select the mask that you just drew.** Leave the Background menu set to None.

4. **Adjust the Single Mask Highlight Radius to control the size of the border around the mask.**

5. **In most cases, the Inner Outer Key filter works best with subjects that have simple outlines; however, if necessary, you can create additional masks to clean up other areas of your layer.** Using the Cleanup Foreground and Cleanup Background options, you can select these additional paths and increase or decrease the opacity along these paths. Cleanup Foreground paths increase the opacity along a path, and Cleanup Background paths decrease the opacity along that path. You can also use the Brush Radius and Brush Pressure settings to adjust the size and density of each path's stroke.

6. **Use the Edge Thin setting to control how much of the matte's border is influenced by the key.** Positive values move the edge away from the transparent areas, whereas negative values move the edge closer to the transparent areas.

7. **If need be, increase the Edge Feather values to soften edges of the foreground subject.**

Using the Linear Color Key effect (PB only)

The Linear Color Key filter is perhaps the simplest of the color keys offered by After Effects. See Figure 19-7.

Applying this effect allows you to create a key based on the hue or chroma information of a layer. When applied, you get to see two thumbnails in the Linear Color Key Effect Controls. The one on the left represents the source, and the one on the right shows the view that you select from the View menu.

STEPS: Applying a Linear Color Key

1. Select a layer in the Timeline window and then choose Effect ➪ Keying ➪ Linear Color Key.

2. In the Effect Controls window, select the Key Colors option from the Key Operation pop-up menu.

3. **Select a color space from the Match Colors pop-up menu.** In most cases, you use the RGB setting; however, if you have trouble separating the foreground subject, try using another selection from the Match Colors menu.

Clean original image (before view)

Thumbnail eye dropper

Plus eye dropper

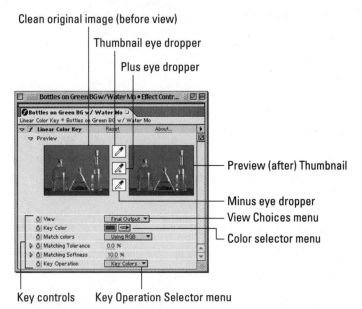

Preview (after) Thumbnail

Minus eye dropper

View Choices menu

Color selector menu

Key controls   Key Operation Selector menu

Figure 19-7: The Linear Color Key effects and the controls

4. **From the View pop-up menu, select the Final Output option.** This view appears in the right thumbnail area in the effects control window as well as in the Comp window. By the way, the Source Only setting displays only the original source image, without any key applied. And the Matte Only setting displays only the alpha channel matte.

5. **Next, select a key color.** The key color is always the color you want After Effects to make transparent or invisible. To select a key color, select the Key Color eye dropper, and then click the green or blue background area. Note that you can achieve the same results by using the top eye dropper and selecting a color.

Tip

If you hold down the Option/Alt key, you can move the dropper over different areas in the Comp window or the thumbnail area, and the transparency in the Comp window will dynamically preview as you move it over differently colored areas. After you nail it, click to select the key color.

6. **By setting the Matching Tolerance, we tell After Effects the range of colors that we want to add or subtract from the color that we want to eliminate.** First, select the Add Color eye dropper (+) and then click a color in the left thumbnail in the Effect Controls window. This adds the selected color to the key color range. This also increases the Matching Tolerance value and the level of transparency in your composite.

7. **Next, select the Subtract Color eye dropper, and click a color in the left thumbnail.** This subtracts the selected color from the key color range. This decreases the Matching Tolerance value and the level of transparency in your composite. Note that you can also drag the matching tolerance slider to achieve the same results.

8. **The last step is to drag the Matching Softness slider bar to soften the Matching Tolerance.** This sets the level of softness between the transparent areas and the opaque or solid areas. Because you see these edges the most, if any artifacts are in your key, taking the time to set the Matching Softness correctly is important.

Make sure that you select Final Output from the View menu to be sure that the filter has done its job to your satisfaction.

Using the Luma Key effect

This keying effect works by keying out specified luminance values. As you may have gathered throughout this book, luminance is just another fancy word for brightness. In effect, the Luma Key filter creates transparency based on the bright or dark areas of a layer. This effect is ideal for images where there are sharply contrasting brightness values. For example, if you have a still of black text over a white background, you can key out the white background with this effect. Then you can layer your black text over any other background. See Figure 19-8.

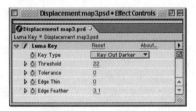

Figure 19-8: To key out the black part of an image, select Key Out Darker from the Key Type menu. To key out the white part of an image, select Key Out Brighter from the Key Type menu.

On the DVD-ROM

In order to explain the Keying effects in detail, we created an After Effects project that includes a composition for each series of steps that we cover in the chapter. The After Effects project is called *Chapter 19.aep* and can be found in the *Project Files/Chapter 19* folder. For the next series of steps, look at the composition we named *Luma Key*.

STEPS: Applying the Luma Key Effect

1. **In the Timeline, select the layer that you want to create a matte from and then choose Effect ⇨ Keying ⇨ Luma Key.**

2. **In the Effect Controls window, select a Key Type to specify which part of the brightness range to be keyed out.**

3. Next, you can adjust the following settings as needed:

- **Threshold slider:** Sets the brightness value which you want the matte to be based on.

- **Tolerance slider:** Use this to set the range of values to be keyed out. Lower values key out a smaller range of values. On the other hand, higher values key out a wider range of values.

- **Edge Thin slider:** Use this to adjust the width of the keyed area's border. Positive values make the matte expand, and negative values shrink the matte.

- **Edge Feather slider:** Controls the softness of the matte's edge. Higher values create a softer edge. Keep in mind that softer edges have a tendency to increase render times.

Using the Spill Suppressor effect (PB only)

The Spill Suppressor filter removes any spill generated by the background that has managed to work its way on to your foreground subject. In almost every keying situation, the blue or green color of the background screen will spill onto the foreground subject's clothes or face. Spill Suppressor to the rescue! See Figure 19-9.

It may very well be that the Spill Suppressor is used for just about every keying composite you create. The Spill Suppressor filter is especially needed when your foreground elements are dark due to the lighting requirements for the shot.

This effect should be used with care because not only does it take out the spill color, but it also affects the overall color balance of the foreground image.

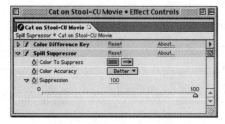

Figure 19-9: The Spill Suppressor filter eliminates color spills on your subjects. These spills are created from the reflected color of your background color screen. Note that it is almost always used in combination with another key effect, such as the Color Difference Key, as seen here.

In order to explain the Keying effects in detail, we created an After Effects project that includes a composition for each series of steps that we cover in the chapter. The After Effects project is called *Chapter 19.aep* and can be found in the *Project Files/Chapter 19* folder. For the next series of steps, you should look at the composition we named *Spill Suppressor.*

STEPS: Applying the Spill Suppressor Effect

1. **Select the layer that you want to apply the Spill Suppressor effect to and choose Effect ➪ Keying ➪ Spill Suppressor.** In our case, we use our trusty cat movie once again.

2. **In the Effect Controls, use the dropper to select the color that you want to suppress.** If you have already applied a key effect, select the Color to Suppress eye dropper and then click the screen color in the key filter's Key Color swatch. If you haven't applied a keying filter, you can simply click the Color to Suppress swatch and then select a color from the Color Picker.

3. **In the Color Accuracy pop-up menu, select Faster if you are supressing blue, green, or red.** Opt for the Better choice in this menu if you are suppressing other colors. When the Better selection is made, After Effects more carefully analyzes colors for a better key. Selecting this option definitely increases your render time, so use it wisely.

4. **To determine the final level of suppression, drag the Suppression slider until the color you want eliminated has been removed to your satisfaction.**

Working with the Matte Tools effects (PB only)

The Production Bundle of After Effects contains two very useful matte tools that make keying a lot less difficult. These are the Simple Choker and the Matte Choker filters, and they are found in the Effects ➪ Matte menu. In essence, both of these tools enable you to really polish your matte. The Simple Choker "chokes" the edge of your matte, and you can tweak its properties to move the edge in an inwardly or outwardly direction. By now, you may have noticed that edges are a persistent issue when pulling keys.

Working with the Simple Choker effect (PB only)

This filter is ideal for eliminating the slight rimmed affect of color that gets left around the edge of your keyed subjects. The only issue you should be aware of is that you often lose detail in areas that include tricky items, such as wispy hair. This is really obvious if you take the key you have created with the cat on the stool and apply the Simple Choker to the layer. Even though you eliminate a whole lot of colored lining around the cat, you also lose the cat's whiskers. We see this in the next exercise. See Figure 19-10.

On the
DVD-ROM

In order to explain the Keying effects in detail, we created an After Effects project that includes a composition for each series of steps that we cover in the chapter. The After Effects project is called *Chapter 19.aep* and can be found in the *Project Files/Chapter 19* folder. For the next series of steps, you should look at the composition we named *Simple Choker*.

The Simple Choker "chokes" the outline of the matte in or out to clean the edges.

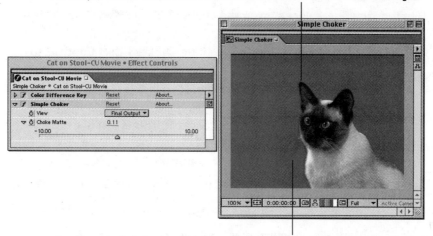

Details such as the cat's whiskers are hard to maintain when using the choker.

Figure 19-10: Applying the Simple Choker effect contracts or expands your matte. This is especially helpful if you need to eliminate the colored edges around your keyed subjects. In this case, the cat has a cleaner edge, but he has also lost his whiskers.

STEPS: Applying the Simple Choker Effect

1. **In the Timeline, select a layer whose edges you need to clean up and then choose Effects ⇨ Matte ⇨ Simple Choker.** You almost always apply the Simple Choker to the layer that contains your foreground subject. In our *Simple Choker* comp on the DVD-ROM, we applied a key effect to the cat first and then added the Simple Choker effect to it.

2. **Move the Choke Matte slider to set the choke amount.** A positive value cuts into the matte and makes it thinner. A negative value makes your matte fatter or expands it.

Using the Matte Choker effect (PB only)

The Matte Choker filter is a strange bird, but when it works, it works well. The Matte Choker repeats a series of choking and spreading operations on your matte, and you can use it to fill holes that interfere with an otherwise perfectly clean knockout. Using it involves the repetition of the choke and spread operation. As soon as you master this aspect of the filter, the matte needs to be choked again in order to preserve its original shape.

STEPS: Applying the Matte Choker Effect

1. **In the Timeline, select a layer and choose Effect ⇨ Matte Tools ⇨ Matte Choker.**

2. **Tweak the first three sliders in the Matte Choker Effect Controls to control the spread of your matte.**

   - Geometric Softness blurs the edge of your matte.

   - Choke adjusts the amount of choke. Negative numbers spread your matte and positive values choke it. This is just like the Simple Choker, explained previously.

   - Gray Level Softness adjusts the contrast of the matte.

3. **The next three sliders (sliders 4–6) enable you to control the choke of the matte.** These sliders choke your matte in a manner that complements the spread that you created after you tweaked the first three sliders.

4. **The Iterations slider determines how many times After Effects repeats the spread and choke sequence you just set.** You may find it necessary to repeat the process a few times for a clean final key.

Tip

If you want to add a tool to enhance your keys, look into purchasing the Composite Wizard set of tools from Puffin Design. This is a third-party set of plug-ins that helps you achieve a better key. With the Composite Wizard, you can correct color, blur edge borders, and clean up matting artifacts to improve the overall compositing of your layers.

As you can see, you have no magic bullet when it comes to these filters. Take time to experiment with them before you rush into a production environment that hasn't already gone to lengths to work out a lot of these issues before your arrival. If it's at all possible, set up test shots to see if what a producer or a client wants is actually something that can be achieved. And remember that third party filters can be a big help if your budget will allow.

✦   ✦   ✦

Vector Painting

Vector painting is the answer to many prayers uttered from within the After Effects community. Over the years, many dedicated users of After Effects have wished and even begged for a painting tool within After Effects. Certain effects, such as Write-on or Stroke, enable you to create a painted look, but they're pretty limited and can hardly be thought of as real painting tools.

The Vector Paint effect while available only as part of the Production Bundle, represents a revolution within After Effects. This effect enables you to paint vector-based cel animations directly within the Comp window. You can paint on a new solid that you create in After Effects, or on any pre-existing layer, such as a still or a movie.

The Vector Paint effect is completely nondestructive. Basically, that means that any amount of painting or erasing on a layer never actually alters the original layer. In other words, practically any action can be undone or modified at any point. The Vector Paint effect records all strokes as you make them and these strokes can be recalled and retimed at any point. You can even select individual strokes and modify or delete them. The Vector Paint effect also supports the Wacom style tablets that are popular with computer artists. Wacom tablets have pressure sensitive features, and these are fully supported.

So where were we all without it? Before the advent of Vector Painting, you had to create vector-based "flip-book" style cel animations in Illustrator or Freehand and then import them as EPS sequences or compositions in which each layer contained the separate frames. There's no need to suffer this indignity any longer. Save time with this new feature, and have a blast while you're at it.

Understanding Vector Painting

The Vector Paint effect can be used for matte touch-ups, animated signatures, character animations, and even full scenes of paintings in the Comp window. It's a versatile and advanced system for painting. This effect deviates slightly from the norm in After Effects in that the controls for this effect appear in the Effect Controls window as well as within a custom toolbar that appears in the Comp window. Figure 20-1 shows the Vector Paint Effect Controls as they appear in the After Effects interface.

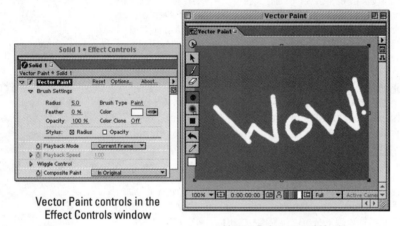

Vector Paint controls in the
Effect Controls window

Vector Paint controls in the
Comp window

Figure 20-1: The Vector Paint effect properties are spread across the Effect Controls window as well as in a custom toolbar in the Comp window.

Note   The Vector Paint effect must be selected in the Effect Controls window in order for its controls to appear in the Comp window.

On the DVD-ROM   In order to better explain the Vector Paint effect, we created an After Effects project that includes a composition for each series of steps that we cover in the chapter. Just as a reminder, you need to copy the *Source Material* folder from the DVD-ROM to your hard drive. Our own corresponding After Effects project is called *Chapter 20.aep* and can be found in the *Project Files/Chapter 20* folder. For the next series of steps, you should look at the composition called *Paint Comp.*

STEPS: Working with the Vector Paint Effect

1. **Choose Composition ⇨ New Composition to create a new comp.**

2. **Create a New Solid.** Choose Layer ⇨ New ⇨ Solid and set the Solid size to the size of your comp by clicking the Make Comp Size button in the Solid Settings dialog box. You can select any color you like.

3. **Apply the Vector Paint effect to the solid by selecting the solid layer and choosing Effect ⇨ Paint ⇨ Vector Paint.**

4. **In order for you to begin painting, make sure that you selected the Vector Paint effect in the Effect Controls window by clicking the effect name (it will then be highlighted).** Doing this displays the custom toolbar on the left side of the Comp window.

5. **In the Effect Controls window, you can select the type, size, feather, opacity, and the color of the brush; however, for the moment, you can leave all the settings as they are.** Instead, hold down the Command/Ctrl key and drag your pointer in the Comp window. Drag in or out to change the radius of the brush, and after you finish with that, release the Command/Ctrl key and drag inwards to set the feather setting.

6. **Next, select Animate Strokes from the Playback Mode pop-up menu.** Selecting this option plays back the strokes as they are drawn.

Note

In the Effect Controls window, the *Composite Paint* pop-up's default setting is the In Original option. This composites the paint stroke on the solid layer. Leave this setting as is. Later in this chapter, we explore all the other settings in this menu.

7. **Control+click/Right-click anywhere in the Comp window to bring up the Vector Paint Contextual menus.** Choose Options ⇨ Shift-Paint Record Strokes ⇨ In Realtime. This option sets the effect to record your painting strokes so that they play back in real time.

8. **Press the Home key to make sure your playhead is located at the first frame of your comp.**

9. **Hold down the Shift key and begin writing something such as "Hello World!"** Release the Shift key after you're done. You'll notice that the writing disappears after you release the Shift key. The reason for this is that the current time is set to 00:00 and the strokes haven't begun animating yet. See Figure 20-2.

10. **To playback what you wrote, press the spacebar, or you can press 0 on the numeric keypad to see a RAM Preview of the animation.**

That's really all there is to it. Do some more exploring on your own. Change the various effect properties and alter the brush style to produce different kinds of writing. In the rest of the chapter, we walk you through the details of all the other options that the Vector Paint effect offers. This tool should satisfy any of your painting or cel animation needs in After Effects.

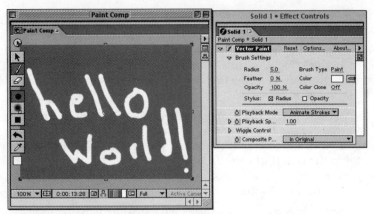

Figure 20-2: We created this "Hello World!" animation after modifying only a few of the default settings in the Vector Paint effect.

Understanding the Paint tools

The Vector Paint effect brings up a custom toolbar. This toolbar appears on the left side of the Comp window and only when the Vector Paint effect is selected in the Effect Controls window. The top of the custom toolbar contains a disclosure triangle. Clicking this triangle brings up a contextual menu for some choices that affect the Vector Paint effect. The bottom of the tool lineup consists of a color swatch that enables you to change the color of your brush.

The remaining tools are explained in Table 20-1.

	Table 20-1 Vector Paint Tools	
Icon	*Name*	*Description*
▲	Selection tool	Enables you to make selections. For example, you can click a stroke to select it.
🖌	Brush	Brings up the brush that you can use to paint.
▱	Eraser	The Eraser is used to erase through your paint strokes.

Icon	Name	Description
	Brush styles	Solid, Air, and Square are the three styles of brushes available to you. Click one to select your brush style.
	Undo	Enables you to undo your moves. This tool is grayed out if it's unavailable.
	Eye dropper	You cannot move or delete effects from a locked bin.

Tip

Press V to toggle between the Erase or Brush tool and the Selection tool. Holding down C temporarily switches you to the Eye dropper tool. Also, pressing the Esc key cancels the last color selection or the last stroke you made.

Understanding brush types and brush settings

The Vector Paint tools have three main Brush Options. These are the Solid, Air, and Square brushes. To select one of these, click and select it in the custom toolbar. Bear in mind that these three options describe the shape and behavior of the paintbrush as well as the Eraser tool. Also, when using the Air brush, you cannot set a feather setting.

Understanding how these brush options work will help you control the look and style of your painting. For example, by increasing the feather settings, the Solid setting can resemble the Air option. However, the two behave very differently. The Solid brush doesn't build up opacity, whereas the Air brush does. For example, if the strokes cross over each other, using the Air brush will result in an increase in opacity.

Details of the Brush Settings are explained here.

Understanding the Brush Settings in the Effect Controls window

Under the Brush Settings area of the Effect Controls window, you will find numerous options to control the behavior of the brush you may be using. These options are explained here:

✦ **Radius:** This setting controls the size of the brush or the eraser.

✦ **Feather:** Controls the softness of the edges of the brush or the eraser.

Note

The Feather setting does not affect the air brush option.

✦ **Opacity:** Use this setting to control the transparency of your Paint tool or the eraser.

✦ **Brush Type:** Indicates the brush type you selected.

✦ **Color:** Enables you to select the color for your strokes. You can either click the color swatch and select another color or use the eyedropper to click on any color of your choice. Note that you can also select individual strokes and change their color. To do so, simply select the stroke by clicking it with the Selection tool (the arrow at the top of the Vector Paint tools on the side of the Comp window), and then use the color swatch to select another color.

✦ **Color Clone:** When the Color Clone option is activated, the brush acts like a combination of an eyedropper and a brush. The color of the stroke is set by the color of the pixels at the location where the stroke begins. When you start another stroke at another location, the color at that location is used for that stroke.

Learning to select strokes

Each stroke in the Vector Paint effect can be individually selected and altered. Selecting a stroke is simple; just click one with the Selection tool to select it.

You may often find that you need to make all kinds of varied selections on your paint strokes. You may want to select a few strokes and delete them or modify their color, or any other settings for that matter. You can also rotate and move any strokes you selected. In that case, you need to Control+click/right-click on the Comp window when the Vector Paint effect is active. In the contextual menu that appears, you find the options listed and explained in the following section. Be aware that some of these options are linked to the current position of the playhead in the Timeline window.

The following stroke selection options are available to you in the contextual menu for the Select option:

✦ **All:** Selects all strokes on a layer. Alternatively, you can use the Command/Ctrl+A keyboard shortcut.

✦ **None:** Deselects any strokes that are currently selected.

✦ **Visible:** Selects all strokes that are visible at the current time. Alternatively, you can use the Shift+W keyboard shortcut to select all visible strokes.

✦ **Current Time:** Selects all strokes that are drawn at the current location in time. The Shift+T keyboard shortcut also does the same.

✦ **Last Painted:** This option selects the last painted or erase stroke. If you paint a group of strokes while pressing the Shift key as we did in the exercise earlier in the chapter, this command will select that entire group of strokes. You can also use the Shift+L keyboard shortcut to select the last painted stroke(s).

✦ **Similar With:** Used after one or more strokes have been selected, this selects additional strokes that have similar Brush Setting properties.

✦ **Inverse:** Inverts the current stroke selection. In other words, previously selected strokes are deselected, while previously unselected strokes are selected.

Tip

After selecting your strokes, you can rotate them by pressing the plus or minus keys on the numeric keypad. You can also use the arrow keys to move the strokes up, down, or to the right and left.

Understanding the Composite Paint options

The Composite Paint options are located in the Composite Paint pop-up menu located in the Effect Controls window for the Vector Paint effect. These options control how your paint and erase strokes interact with the layer you're drawing on. These options allow you to carefully control how and where you want your paint and erase strokes to appear. For example, you can paint on top of the layer, or you can alter the mattes or alpha channels of a layer.

You can use the Composite Paint options to accomplish various kinds of results. We have listed each option, and we show you the final results in a series of figures that follow. But before you proceed, we want to explain what you're actually seeing.

Figure 20-3 lays out the foundation for our explanation of the Composite Paint options. In this figure, we show you the original image, a paint stroke, and an erase stroke. As you read explanations for each option, you are able to see the results of each compositing mode given the same layer, paint stroke, and erase stroke.

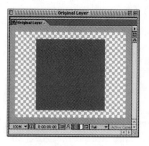  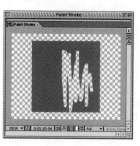

Original layer   Paint stroke   Erase stroke

Figure 20-3: In this picture, we have the original layer, a paint stroke, and an erase stroke.

✦ **Only:** When the Composite Paint option is set to Only, the layer does not appear in the comp. Only the paint strokes are shown in this mode. Erasing only removes the paint and not the original image. Figure 20-4 shows the results of selecting the Only mode.

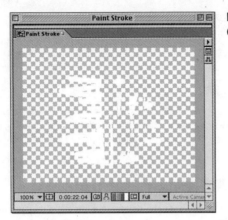

Figure 20-4: The results of selecting the Only mode

✦ **In Original:** In this mode, the paint strokes are applied to the original layer, which is visible. Any erase strokes erase the paint strokes as well as the original layer. Figure 20-5 shows the In Original mode.

Figure 20-5: The results of selecting the In Original mode

✦ **Over Original:** The paint strokes occur in a layer above the original layer. The erase strokes affect the paint strokes but not the original layer. Figure 20-6 shows the results of the Over Original mode.

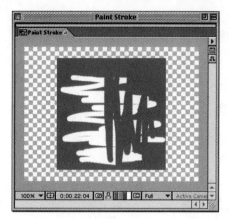

Figure 20-6: The results of selecting the Over Original mode

✦ **Under Original:** The paint strokes in this case occur on a layer under the original layer. The original layer is never affected. Any erase strokes affect the paint strokes but leave the original layer untouched. Figure 20-7 displays the Under Original mode.

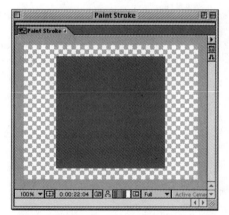

Figure 20-7: The results of selecting the Under Original mode

✦ **Track Original Matte:** Any strokes applied in this mode only affect the alpha channel of the original layer. The RGB color channels of the original layer are turned off. Erase strokes only affect the paint strokes but not the original layer. With this option, you can paint inside the alpha channel of an image file that you want to composite over another layer. For example, if there are any artifacts in the alpha channel, you can use this mode to erase them. Figure 20-8 shows the Track Original Matte mode.

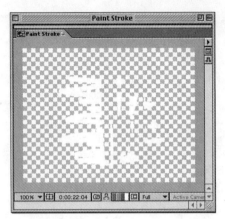

Figure 20-8: The results of selecting the Track Original Matte mode

✦ **Track Original Matte Visible:** This mode is exactly like the Track Original Matte, except that the RGB color channels for the original layer are left on and visible. Any erase strokes just affect the paint strokes and not the original layer. See Figure 20-9 for the Track Original Matte Visible mode.

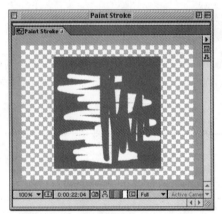

Figure 20-9: Track Original Matte Visible has the same principle as the Track Original Matte (see previous mode), except the RGB color channels remain visible.

✦ **As Matte:** In this case, the paint strokes operate in the layer's alpha channel and reveal the layer through the strokes. The erase strokes affect the paint strokes only. See Figure 20-10 for a view of the As Matte mode.

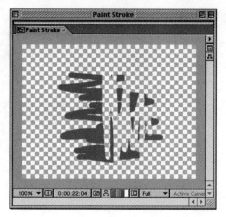

Figure 20-10: The results of selecting the As Matte mode

✦ **As Inverse Matte:** Paint strokes in this mode result in blocking out the original layer. The paint strokes only affect the alpha channel of the original layer, resulting in the creation of an inverse matte. Erase strokes affect the paint strokes only. See Figure 20-11 for the final results of this mode.

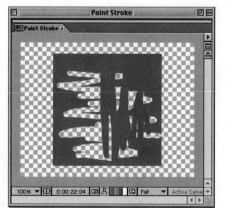

Figure 20-11: As Inverse Matte creates a combination

✦ **In Original Alpha Only:** In this mode, you can paint on the alpha channel of the original layer. Using paint strokes adds areas of transparency, and using erase strokes blocks areas of transparency. As a reference, you can think of this mode as the In Original mode (described earlier), except that the image's alpha channel is affected. Figure 20-12 shows the In Original Alpha Only mode.

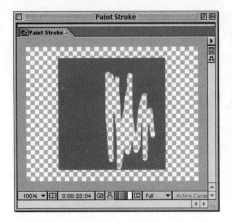 

In Original Alpha Only mode
seen in RGB

In Original Alpha Only mode
seen in Alpha channel

Figure 20-12: The results of selecting the In Original Alpha Only mode

✦ **Under Original Alpha Only:** In this mode, the alpha channel of the original image is left untouched. Instead, imagine that the paint and the erase strokes are made on a virtual layer behind the original layer. Figure 20-13 shows the results of this mode.

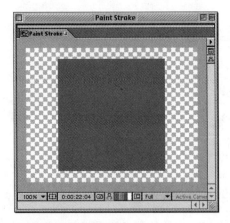 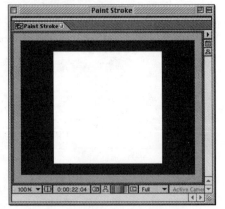

Under Original Alpha Only mode
seen in RGB

Under Original Alpha Only mode
seen in Alpha channel

Figure 20-13: The results of selecting the Under Original Alpha Only mode

Working with Playback modes

The Playback Mode pop-up menu enables you to determine how your strokes ani-
mate in the final comp (see Figure 20-14). When you are drawing the strokes, the
Vector Paint effect records the start and end time for each stroke. The Playback
Mode determines when the stroke will start and how long it will stay onscreen.
Using the Playback Speed slider can modify the speed of each stroke.

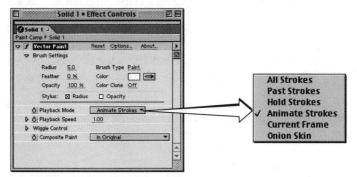

Figure 20-14: The Playback modes

You can use the *Paint Comp* you made in the last exercise to experiment with the
Playback modes. You can also use the *Paint Comp* we include in the *Chapter 20.aep*
project. To view each mode, change the *Playback Mode* in the pop-up menu of the
Vector Paint Effect Controls and then play back the comp to view the results. You can
find the *Chapter 20.aep* project in the *Project Files/Chapter 20* folder.

Understanding the Playback Mode setting

There are six modes that control the playback of your paint strokes:

✦ **All Strokes:** This mode displays all strokes, all the time. Any and all strokes
   appear for the entire duration of the image layer on which they are drawn.

✦ **Past Strokes:** Strokes in this mode appear from the frame on which they were
   drawn until the layer's Out point. As strokes are added, they appear over one
   another until you reach the Out point of the layer in the comp.

✦ **Hold Strokes:** This mode displays the strokes from the time they were drawn
   to the time when the next stroke is drawn. Imagine this mode as being like a
   hold keyframe, where the strokes appear in a slide-show-like fashion without
   any drawing.

✦ **Animate Strokes:** This mode begins drawing the stroke at the current time and animates as it was drawn.

✦ **Current Frame:** This is the default mode for the Vector Paint effect. This mode displays the stroke only at the frame it was drawn. This is the old-school cel animation technique.

✦ **Onion Skin:** The Onion Skin playback mode displays the strokes drawn on the current frame as well as the strokes drawn on the surrounding frames. The additional surrounding frames are displayed in a different color and at a reduced transparency than the current stroke. This mode is ideal for animations because you can see the previous and following frames as reference points. By tweaking the Onion Skin options in the Vector Paint Preferences dialog box, you can set how many previous and following strokes are displayed (provided you're using the Onion Skin mode).

To open the Vector Paint Preferences dialog box, control+click/right-click anywhere on the Comp window while the Vector Paint effect is selected in the Effect Controls window and choose Options. Figure 20-15 shows the dialog box for setting the preferences.

Figure 20-15: The Onion Skinning options in the Vector Paint Preferences dialog box

The Onion Skinning options are explained here:

✦ **Frames Backward/Frames Forward:** Use this setting to select the number of frames that you want displayed around your current frame.

✦ **Color Backward/Color Forward:** Sets the color of the the backward and forward strokes.

✦ **Skin Opacity:** Enables you to control the transparency of the surrounding strokes.

Working with the Re-timer

The Re-timer is an option within the Vector Paint effect that enables you to change the timing of your strokes. Even though this sounds similar to adjusting the Playback Speed slider, re-timing is significantly different.

You can select individual strokes and re-time them, whereas the Playback Speed property affects all the strokes on a layer. The Re-timer only affects playback when you select the Animate Strokes option in the Playback Mode pop-up menu. Here's an important detail to remember: Using the Re-timer does not change the start time of the strokes. It just affects the duration of each stroke. Here's another important detail: Increasing the percentage of the Re-timer speeds up the animation. For example, setting a value of 400% for re-timing will speed up the stroke animation by four times.

STEPS: Re-timing Your Strokes

1. **Select the strokes that you want to re-time by clicking them with the Vector Paint Selection tool.**

2. **Control+click/Right-click anywhere on the Comp window while the Vector Paint effect is selected in the Effect Controls window and choose Re-timer from the contextual menu.**

3. **In the Set Value dialog box, enter a percentage for the Relative Duration and click OK.**

Caution

Re-timing cannot be undone with the Command/Ctrl+Z keyboard shortcut. However, you can reverse the Re-timing effect by entering the inverse value of the change that you made earlier.

Working with the Shift-Paint Record option

In order to understand the Shift-Paint Record option, first review how Vector Paint deals with strokes ordinarily. When you create strokes, these strokes are linked to the point in time when they were created. After you make a stroke, you can draw more strokes at the same current time, or you can add strokes at another time by moving the playhead in the Timeline. You can change this default with the options in the Playback Mode pop-up menu in the Vector Paint effect, which appears in the Effect Controls window.

The Shift-Paint Record option allows you to modify how the strokes are associated with time (Adobe calls this the *QuickPaint Mode*). In this mode, you can create fast and uninterrupted recordings of your strokes without any delays for redraw.

To access the Shift-Paint Record options, Control+click/right-click anywhere on the comp while the Vector Paint effect is selected and then select one of the four options available under the Shift-Paint Records menu.

The options available are described here:

✦ **To Current Frame:** When the Current Frame is selected, all strokes start at the current time. In other words, the location of the playhead determines the start location of your stroke. This is similar to the general painting mode, except that when you use the Shift key, there are no redraw delays.

✦ **To Sequential Frames:** All stroke start times are offset by one frame. For example, if your current time is set to 0:00:01:00 and you draw two strokes, the first stroke draws at 0:00:01:00, the next one at 0:00:01:01, and so on.

✦ **In Realtime:** In this mode, the strokes are recorded and played back in real time, including any pauses you took between strokes.

✦ **Continuously:** This option is similar to the In Realtime option, except that no pauses are recorded.

Caution   You may have guessed this, but you have to hold down the Shift key while using the Shift-Paint Records options; otherwise, none of the nifty features we describe here will work.

Working with the Wiggle Control options

The Wiggle Control options affect the wiggle behavior of your strokes. Wiggles are described by Adobe as the spline-based morphing of your strokes. Well said, don't you think? By setting the wiggling amounts and behavior, you can seriously affect the style of your animation. This is a fairly common animation style, and when employed with care, it can bring your animations to life.

To enable the wiggling options, first open the twirler next to the Wiggle Control property in the Effect Controls window. You can turn on wiggling by checking the Enable Wiggling check box and then select from the options underneath.

Figure 20-16 shows the wiggling options in the Vector Paint effect.

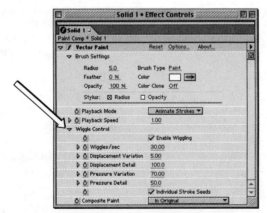

Figure 20-16: The wiggling options for the Vector Paint strokes

The settings for the Wiggle Control are as follows:

✦ **Enable Wiggling:** You need to click the Enable Wiggling check box for any wiggle settings to be activated. Otherwise, wiggling is disabled.

✦ **Wiggles/Sec:** This setting determines the wiggles per second in your composition. High values produce more rapid wiggling.

✦ **Displacement Variation:** The Displacement Variation setting controls how far the stroke moves from its original position. At high settings, the stroke moves much farther from its original location.

✦ **Displacement Detail:** This setting controls the amount by which the shape of the original stroke is altered. Higher values greatly distort the original stroke, while lower values produce a milder distortion.

Before we get into Pressure Variations and Pressure Detail settings, remember that these two settings are active only if you have already selected the Stylus Radius or the Stylus Opacity options.

✦ **Pressure Variation:** Changing this value sets the amount by which the Radius and the Opacity of the stroke varies when wiggling.

✦ **Pressure Detail:** This setting determines how close together the pressure variations appear on a stroke when wiggling.

✦ **Individual Stroke Seeds:** If you have this option checked, it creates a different random wiggle seed for each stroke on your layer. This allows for a much more randomized look. It provides a good way to avoid strokes wiggling in a similar manner.

Working with the Interface Options

The Interface Options affect the way you view your work while using the Vector Paint effect. You find these settings under the Vector Paint contextual menu. To access them, Control+click/right-click anywhere in the Comp window while the Vector Paint effect is selected and choose the Options submenu. Keep in mind that these options affect all views of your work and are saved from session to session. By default, all three options are on.

The Interface settings are explained here:

✦ **Better Preview While Drawing:** Selecting this option draws an anti-aliased preview of your stroke.

✦ **Show Actual Brush Size:** This option allows the pointer in After Effects to change its shape and size to represent the brush style and size that you have selected. Otherwise, just the regular old pointer appears.

✦ **Show Toolbar:** If this option is checked, the custom Vector Paint toolbar appears in the Comp window.

Make no mistake: Vector Paint is a great addition to the application. After Effects has always been revered as a terrific piece of compositing software, but it has always lacked the capability to create drawing-type animations from within its interface. In order to pull off real cel animations, you had to do a lot of tedious prep work in Illustrator or Freehand. With Vector Painting, you can get great results in a fraction of the time, and because time is what we're always trying to save, we think this is real progress.

✦   ✦   ✦

Aiming Higher: Advanced Techniques

◆ ◆ ◆ ◆

◆ ◆ ◆ ◆

Working with Text Within After Effects

By now, you've probably attained a degree of proficiency with After Effects, and that's a wonderful thing. If you don't already know, a lot of projects in the real world of freelance contracts involve text treatments. Elegant and creative use of text is one of the most important components of broadcast ads, movie titles, movie trailers, network IDs, and the like. Once again, it's worth repeating that a good way to approach a topic like this is to think of TV spots or movie titles that you like and see if you can re-create them yourself.

Instead of leaving you to sort this out yourself, we lay out a few techniques that ought to help speed you along in your pursuit of sexy titles. After Effects includes three text filters, and these are all very useful. Depending on your needs, you may find it necessary to branch out into the realm of Illustrator, which is pretty much an essential component of any project that requires slick-looking typography. You needn't worry about having to master Illustrator; of course, if you have, that's a good thing, but as far as this subject is concerned, you only need to know how to leverage its text functions. To that end, we'll help you out in the next chapter.

Depending on the kind of environment you work in, elements involving text are often the responsibility of an art director. Whether you or someone else is calling the shots, knowing how to control certain aspects of this part of a project is very useful. Changing the amount of space between letters or lines of text is a base-level skill that's required for most paying gigs. Words such as tracking, kerning, leading, and baseline might not mean anything to you now, but hopefully they will by the time we finish introducing you the concept of putting type in motion with After Effects.

Working with Text Filters in After Effects

After Effects includes three filters that enable you to add text to a composition (see Figure 21-1). Basic Text and Numbers are simple and dependable, and the Path Text effect is an amazing tool that's hidden behind its modest sounding name. Any discussion of text merits a discussion on fonts. If you're a seasoned veteran, you're probably no stranger to font-related production issues. If you don't know what fonts are, or if you know what they are but you don't know how to work with them, look at the sidebar entitled "Managing fonts" in Chapter 22. Without any further ado, hit the next few sections and start moving type with these effects.

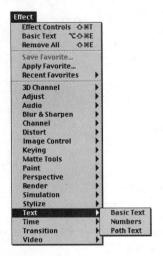

Figure 21-1: The three text filters in After Effects offer tons of creative possibilities.

Using Basic Text

Basic Text is an all-purpose, utilitarian text generator. It's great if you're looking for a quick fix. On the other hand, it's fairly limited in terms of how much you can control it, but if all you need is a simple layer of text that doesn't have to change that much, it's perfect.

Cross-Reference Chapter 8 describes working with effects in general. If you aren't familiar with applying effects or working in the Effect Controls window, take the time to read (or re-read) the beginning of Chapter 8.

Cross-Reference The Online Help (choose Help ➪ After Effects Help) is an HTML document that goes well beyond the printed User's Guide in explaining After Effects in detail. In addition to containing all of the information included in the User's Guide, the Online Help contains a lot of very useful basic information on all of the effects that ship with After Effects. Refer to it as often as you need to; our purpose in writing about these effects is to supplement that information rather than repeat it.

As far as the following explanations of text effects and text treatments is concerned, we created an After Effects project that includes a composition for each one of these we cover in the chapter. Just as a reminder, you need to copy the *Source Material* folder from the DVD-ROM to your hard drive. Additionally, the exercises that follow cover some of these effects in detail. Our own corresponding After Effects project is called *Chapter 21.aep* and can be found in the *Project Files/Chapter 21* folder.

Feel free to substitute your own footage with the examples shown in the figures and exercises.

STEPS: Using Basic Text

1. **Create a new composition by pressing Command/Ctrl+N.**

2. **Create a solid by pressing Command/Ctrl+Y.** The color doesn't matter; just make sure it's comp-sized. Go ahead and name it *Text Layer* while you're at it.

3. **Making sure the solid layer is selected in the Timeline, choose Effect ⇨ Text ⇨ Basic Text.** The dialog box shown in Figure 21-2 appears.

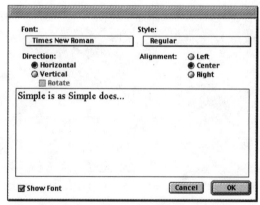

Figure 21-2: The Basic Text dialog box offers a choice of Font, Style, Direction, Alignment, and a text preview.

4. **In the dialog box, type some text.** You can take advantage of all your options now or later; it's up to you. By options, we mean Font, Style, Direction, and Alignment.

5. **Click OK.** Your text will appear in the Comp window, and the Effect Controls for the Text Layer should now be similar to those in Figure 21-3. You may notice that the initial appearance of the text is a bit on the cruddy side; fear not, a quick fix is available.

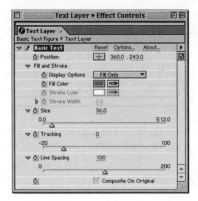

Figure 21-3: The Basic Text Effect Controls are pretty limited as far as the world of text and motion graphics is concerned.

6. **In the Timeline, set the Text Layer to Best quality.** You can do this either by clicking its quality switch or by pressing Command/Ctrl+U. This turns the jagged text into a clean-looking bit of type. The comparison between the two quality settings is shown in Figure 21-4.

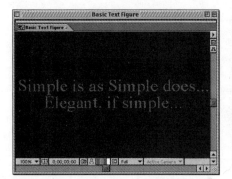 

Figure 21-4: The difference between Draft and Best quality is fairly evident.

Okay, great. The odds are pretty good that the default settings are not going to be what you really want here. Apply a few tweaks to the effect properties, and you'll be set to go.

✦ **Position:** This is the effect point of this filter.

✦ **Options:** Click the word Options at the top of the Effect Controls window in order to change the font, the font's style, whether it's justified to the left, right, or center, as well as whether the text runs horizontally or vertically.

✦ **Fill and Stroke:** Stroke refers to the width of the lines that form the outlines of the characters, and Fill refers to the color used to fill these outlines.

✦ **Size:** This property sets the font's size. This property is a fun one to animate, and it works nicely with Motion Blur enabled. In older versions of After Effects, animating this property was considered a no-no because the results usually looked pretty horrible and lacked any fluidity, but, thankfully, this has been fixed.

✦ **Tracking:** This property affects the overall spacing between letters. By overall, we mean all of the text. Kerning refers to the space in between individual letters, and Basic Text offers no control over this property. This is the big reason why most text treatments can't be sufficiently handled by this filter, because most high-end (read *client-driven*) text treatments need tight control over this property.

✦ **Line Spacing:** This is usually called *leading* by real typographers, and it refers to the space between lines of text.

✦ **Color:** You can choose a color either by clicking the color swatch or by using the dropper.

The default red color is not "broadcast safe."

✦ **Composite on Original:** Clicking this check box places the text on top of the layer to which you applied the effect. We almost never use this, because the area outside the text is transparent by default. This offers more control if you need to reposition the layer without affecting the rest of the comp.

That's Basic Text, folks. Before we move on to generating streams of numbers, we want to unload a few parting words on this tool. If you use it with a font that doesn't have glaring kerning problems, you can get good results. Only experimentation and experience will give you a good idea of which fonts in your library fit the bill here. Lastly, this effect is great for basic animations involving more than one line of text because you can influence the Line Spacing property.

If you want to spend a little more time looking into your options with this filter, look at the *Basic Text* comp in the *Chapter 21.aep* project for reference.

Using the Numbers filter

The Numbers effect generates your choice of specific or random numerical values. Unless you've been living under a rock for the last couple of decades, designs involving ever-changing strings of numbers flashing on the screen are pretty popular. This filter is a big timesaver if you need to create that kind of look (see Figure 21-5).

Figure 21-5: The Numbers filter can provide a quick turnaround if you need to create a "sci-fi" feel.
Image courtesy of EyeWire by Getty Images
www.gettyimages.com (Cosmic Moves)

STEPS: Using the Numbers Filter

1. **Create a new composition by pressing Command/Ctrl+N.**

2. **Create a solid by pressing Command/Ctrl+Y.** The color doesn't matter; just make sure it's comp-sized. Name it *Numbers Layer.*

3. **Making sure the solid layer is selected in the Timeline, choose Effect ➪ Text ➪ Numbers.** The resulting dialog box resembles something approximating the Basic Text dialog box with fewer features, the best of which enables you to preview the appearance of whatever font you select from the pop-up menu.

4. **Select a font and a style and click OK.** The numbers appear in the Comp window, and the Effect Controls for the *Numbers Layer* look something like Figure 21-6.

5. **In the Timeline, set the *Numbers Layer* to Best quality.** You can do this either by clicking its quality switch or by pressing Command/Ctrl+U. This turns your jagged-looking numbers into smooth characters.

If you preview what you've put together so far, nothing happens. The Effect Controls will need a few adjustments before you get the sci-fi feel that this filter creates. The following effect properties are different from those offered in the Basic Text Effect Controls. To start with, there are several under the Format heading:

✦ **Type:** This pop-up determines the kind of numbers this filter generates. A surprisingly large number of options are here. You can generate timecode, dates, hexadecimal numbers, numbers with zeroes in front, and regular old numbers if need be. To test the variations within each of the pop-up choices, move the Value/Offset/Random Max slider around to see what the filter does for each different type.

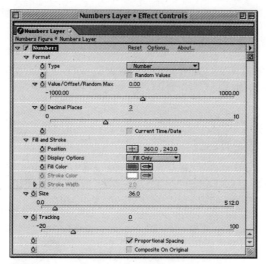

Figure 21-6: The Numbers Effect Controls contain a number of the same properties as Basic Text with a few key differences.

✦ **Random Values:** Clicking this check box generates random values within the type of numbers you selected. The numbers generated stay within the range defined in the Value/Offset/Random Max property. For example, if you choose Numbers from the Type pop-up and set the Value/Offset/Random Max property to 500, the Numbers filter will generate a random number between 0 and 500 for every frame. Setting the Value/Offset/Random Max property to –500 will set the range between 0 and –500.

✦ **Value/Offset/Random Max:** This is the multipurpose property for this effect. If you're working with numbers, this property is shown in the Comp window. If you're working with dates and you clicked the Current Time/Date check box, this property displays a value that's offset from the current date. If you're working with random numbers, this property places a ceiling on the values that the effect generates. Its range is from –30,000 to 30,000.

✦ **Decimal Places:** If the 30,000 range seems limited, don't worry. You can have up to 10 decimal places. If you click the Random Values check box, set the Value/Offset/Random Max to 0.9 and mask the zero and the decimal point, you can have a randomizing 10 digit number if need be.

✦ **Current Time/Date:** In order for this option to work, you need to have selected one of the date or time formats from the Type pop-up. If the Value/Offset/ Random Max is set to 0, then the numbers will show the current time or date. The number specified in the Value/Offset/Random Max determines the offset from this value.

One last but important detail: The Proportional Spacing check box enables you to force whatever font you selected into acting like monospaced font. This is a big help if you don't want the characters changing position in the Comp window. If you need to change your font, click the word Options at the top of the Effect Controls window.

If you want to spend a little more time looking into your options with this filter, look at the *Numbers* comp in the *Chapter 21.aep* project for reference.

Using the Path Text effect

Path Text is the Big Kahuna among the three text filters in After Effects. You can do an awful lot with it, and we give you a few ideas; however, with a filter that's this cool, you can take it much further with your own creative license.

If you need to create a lot of text (think *film credits,* or entire paragraphs chock-full of words) or if you need tight control over each character, you'll need to use Illustrator to create it and then import it into After Effects. We cover this when we deal with using Illustrator text a bit later in the chapter. Still, entering multiple lines of text in the Options dialog box is impossible, and this is new in After Effects 5.

You have five different ways to approach this all-purpose text tool. Using the Path Text effect, you can place characters on a Bezier path, a circular path, a looping path, a simple line, or best of all, on a mask of your own making, regardless of whether it's static or animated.

The next set of steps serves as an introduction to the filter. After you finish it, you find some explanations of its numerous properties as well as a couple more exercises that should further explain this plug-in.

STEPS: Using Path Text with the Bezier Option

1. **Create a new comp by pressing Command/Ctrl+N.**

2. **Create a solid by pressing Command/Ctrl+Y.** The color doesn't matter; just make sure it's comp-sized. Name it *Path Text Layer.*

3. **Be sure that the solid layer is selected in the Timeline and choose Effect ⇨ Text ⇨ Path Text.** The resulting dialog box resembles something approximating the Basic Text dialog box with fewer features, the best of which enables you to preview the appearance of whatever font you select from the pop-up menu.

4. **Just type the text you want and choose whatever font and style you want to use.** After you finish, click OK. The Effect Controls window opens. A resized version of this window appears in Figure 21-7.

5. **In the Timeline, set the *Path Text Layer* to Best quality.** You can do this either by clicking its quality switch or by pressing Command/Ctrl+U. Again, this considerably improves the appearance of your text in the Comp window. Your Comp window will not only display the text you typed in Step 4, but it will also reveal some odd-looking control points (see Figure 21-8 for reference).

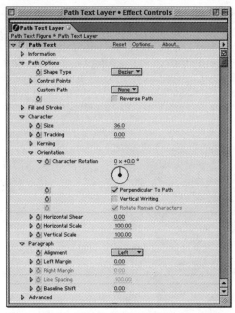

Figure 21-7: The Path Text Effect Controls contain a great deal of control.

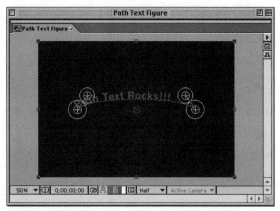

Figure 21-8: The Comp window displays the default control points of the Path Text effect when you initially apply it to a layer.

6. **In the Effect Controls window, open the Character twirler and then open the Size twirler.** Move the Size slider to increase the size of the letters as much as you want. If you need to change your text or its font, click the word Options at the top of the Path Text Effect Controls.

7. **Open the Path Options twirler and then open the Control Points twirler.**

8. **In the Comp window, set the position of the control points by dragging them across the layer.** Make whatever path you like. As you do this, you'll notice the coordinates for the control points update in the Effect Controls window. This should be pretty straightforward. Essentially, you get some nice Bezier controls that you can manipulate to make whatever two-point path you want (see Figure 21-9 for reference); what's more, you can animate them over time.

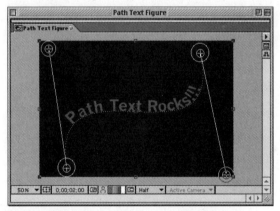

Figure 21-9: Manipulate the control points to create whatever two-point Bezier path you like. You can animate any one or all of them.

9. **In the Effect Controls window, open the Paragraph twirler and then twirl down the Left Margin property so that you have access to its slider.**

10. **Move the Left Margin slider until the text disappears off the right side of the comp.** Because the Alignment property is set to Left by default, this slider works this way. We rarely see fit to change this, but you may find otherwise.

11. **Click the stopwatch next to the Left Margin property to set an initial keyframe.**

12. **Press Command/Ctrl+G and enter a time that puts you a couple of seconds ahead of the current time.** For example, if you're at frame one, type **200** to go to 0:00:02:00 and click OK. When entering values in the Go To Time dialog box, you don't need to worry about placing colons into your string of numbers.

13. **Move the Left Margin slider until the text is centered in the Comp window.** This sets a second keyframe.

14. **In the Timeline, making sure the *Path Text Layer* is selected, press U to display any properties containing keyframes.** This will solo the Left Margin effect property.

15. **Click the words Left Margin under the layer to select all of the keyframes you set for that property and then press F9 to change the keyframes from linear to Easy Ease.**

16. **Press 0 on the numeric keypad to see a RAM Preview of the *Path Text* animation.** Your text should come on from the right side of the path and come gently to rest in the middle of your comp.

That concludes your introduction to Path Text. That's really only the very beginning of the range of options you have with this effect.

Making sense of all the Path Text properties

Going back to the Path Text Effect Controls window, twirl down the Path Options group of properties. Clicking the Shape Type pop-up menu displays the different approaches you can take with this filter.

You already tried out Bezier. To see Circle, Loop, and Line in action, we take you through each one after you set up the testing grounds. Start with a new comp by following Steps 1 through 6 from the last exercise, and then you can experiment with the different shapes and the vast number of properties as we explain them.

Using the different shape types

Because of its four different shape types as well as its ability to use your masks as paths, Path Text can almost be thought of as five separate filters. Take a look at each of the shape types you haven't experimented with yet.

✦ **Circle:** In the Path Text Effect Controls, if you select Circle from the Shape Type pop-up, only two control points remain in the Comp window (see Figure 21-10 for reference). A quick look at the Control Points properties reveals that these are the Circle Center and the Circle Point. The Circle Point defines the radius of the circular path as well as the position of the Left Margin. Moving the Left Margin slider sends the text round and round the circle; if it's set to zero, the text will be flush with the Circle Point. Again, we happily remind you that all of these properties can be animated over time.

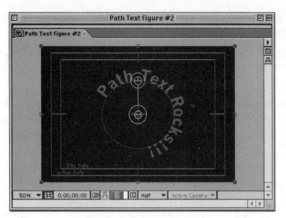

Figure 21-10: Selecting Circle from the Shape Types pop-up menu places the text on a circular path. The Circle Center and Circle Point properties, both of which are visible in the Comp window, determine the center and radius of the circle.

On the DVD-ROM

Path Text works with Motion Blur, and you can create some interesting animations by enabling Motion Blur and then keyframing the Circle Point. For reference, take a look at the *Circular Path Text* comp in the *Chapter 21.aep* project on the DVD-ROM.

✦ **Loop:** The Loop option from the Shape Type pop-up menu works in the same manner as Circle, but there's an important difference. Move the Left Margin slider around, and this difference should be quite clear (see Figure 21-11). As you move it deep into negative territory, the text launches off the circle on the tangent defined by the Circle Point. As you move the Left Margin slider deep into positive territory, the same thing happens going in the other direction. In the slider's mid-range, you'll see that the text stays on the circular path for one whole orbit. Experiment with different Circle Point positions to adjust the tangent on which the text enters and leaves the circular path.

 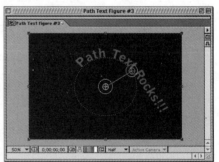

Figure 21-11: Selecting Loop from the Shape Types pop-up menu also places the text on a circular path. Animating the margin sends the text around the circular path for one orbit, and the direction that the text enters and leaves the orbit is determined by the position of the Circle Point.

✦ **Line:** Selecting the Line option from the Shape Types pop-up menu creates a simple line for the text to sit on (see Figure 21-12). You can move either control point, or you can hold down the Option/Alt key and drag within the outer range of either one of the control points to move both of them at the same time.

Why, you might ask, would you use the Line option in Path Text instead of using Basic Text? Because, we would graciously reply, you can control the kerning of the characters with the Path Text effect. Kerning, you ask? Hang on; we get there a little bit later in this section.

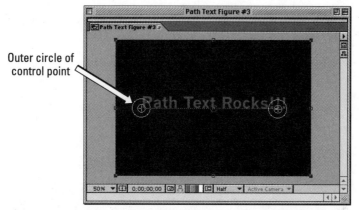

Outer circle of control point

Figure 21-12: Selecting Line from the Shape Types pop-up menu places the text on a linear path. Hold down the Option/Alt key and drag within the outer circle of either one of the control points to move both of them at the same time.

Tweaking the Path Text effect properties

We're bypassing the Fill and Stroke group of properties because we cover those in Basic Text, but the Character properties really set Path Text apart from the rest.

Within the Character properties, Size and Tracking operate exactly as they do in Basic Text, but the rest of these options add another dimension of control (see Figure 21-13).

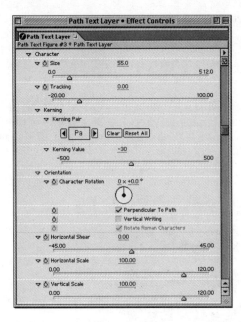

Figure 21-13: The Character group of properties makes Path Text a legitimate player among typographers.

The following list describes these options in detail:

✦ **Kerning:** We've mentioned this property in passing a couple of times. It refers to the space between individual letters. Use the Kerning Pair arrow keys to pick which pair of letters you want to influence and then move the Kerning Value slider to change the distance between the selected pair of letters. As you jump from one pair to another, you'll notice that the Kerning Value changes. These are preset values that are specific to each font. While you can't keyframe this property, it's still a great feature. Most designers usually want to change the kerning of a given string of text for their own aesthetic purposes. You can almost always improve the initial appearance of text because the default kerning values leave something to be desired. If you're not sure about this, look at Figure 21-14 to get an idea as to why having this kind of control is a good thing.

✦ **Orientation:** This radial dial rotates the letters. By default, the text rotates around the position of the path. To make the letters rotate from their center, you need to change the Baseline Shift setting so that the middle of the text is positioned over the path (the Baseline Shift property is in the Paragraph group of effect properties). See Figure 21-15.

Figure 21-14: Kerning changes, like the adjustment shown here between "T" and "e," provide you with a subtlety of control that can greatly improve the quality of your designs

✦ **Perpendicular to Path:** This property is found directly underneath the Orientation setting. Turning this check box off results in disabling the letters' automatic orientation. See Figure 21-16 for reference.

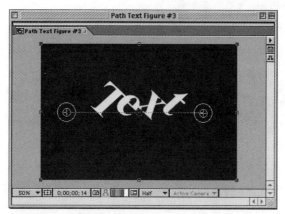

Figure 21-15: The Orientation property can be a lot of fun to animate. The Baseline Shift setting defines the basis of the rotation.

✦ **Horizontal Shear:** This slider skews the letters. It can be pretty useful if you need to create a realistic-looking distortion for a line of text entering the comp at high speed (see Figure 21-17 for reference).

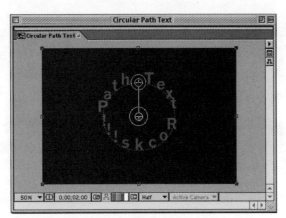

Figure 21-16: Turning off Perpendicular to Path disables the letters' automatic orientation.

Figure 21-17: In addition to enabling Motion Blur, tweaking the Horizontal Shear property can help you create realistic-looking distortions for high-speed text animations.

✦ **Horizontal Scale:** The Horizontal Scale property works in relation to the specified Alignment setting (which can be found in the Paragraph group of properties). In other words, the text scales from the margin. Figure 21-18 shows text horizontally scaling up from the left margin.

✦ **Vertical Scale:** The Vertical Scale property scales up from the position of the path (see Figure 21-19). As is the case with Orientation, if you want to scale letters from their center, you need to lower the Baseline Shift setting.

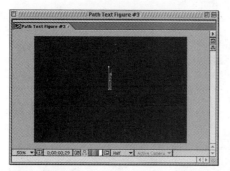 

Figure 21-18: Horizontal Scale animations are fun because you can create a text message from what initially seem to be indecipherable shapes.

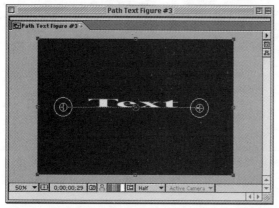

Figure 21-19: Vertical Scale uses the path as its origin. Lower the Baseline Shift to scale letters from their center.

Caution

Keep in mind that unsightly distortions can result from scale settings above 100%.

The Paragraph group of properties determines how the text relates to the path you defined. Line Spacing works in the same way as it does in Basic Text.

✦ **Alignment:** Left and Right are easy to understand, but what about Center and Force? Setting the Alignment to Center enables you to control both the Left Margin and Right Margin sliders. If both of them are set to zero, then the text will be placed in the middle of the path. Setting the Alignment to Force disables Tracking and evenly distributes the characters along the path. Increasing either of the margins "crowds" the characters in the direction of the opposite margin.

✦ **Margin:** The margin controls are simple enough to understand, and most Path Text animations involve bringing text on and off screen by animating the margin, but there is an interesting way to use these controls that may not be immediately apparent. Selecting Force for your Alignment enables you to create tracking animations with the margin controls, and this results in the text spreading out from a central point. See Figure 21-20 to get an idea as to how this works.

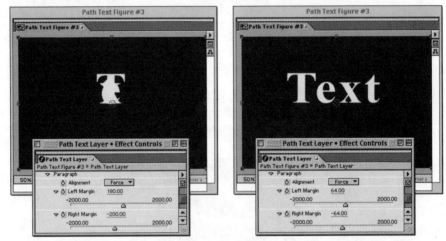

Figure 21-20: Selecting Force for your Alignment enables you to create tracking animations with the margin controls, and this results in the text spreading out from a central point.

✦ **Baseline Shift:** As we mentioned, the Baseline Shift setting controls the distance between the text and the path, but it also defines the point from which the text scales and rotates.

The Advanced group of properties includes an interesting variety of creative options. Taking full advantage of them, you can make the characters appear as though they're being typed on the screen, or you can gently fade them up. Additionally, you can make your text wobble as though invisible forces are knocking it around.

✦ **Visible Characters:** This property determines the number of characters that are visible on the path. For example, if you have six characters on your path, values between zero and six will hide some or all of the characters. Animating this value from zero to six reveals the letters in order. Animating this value from zero to negative six reveals the letters in reverse order.

✦ **Fade Time:** Setting this value above its default of 0% will fade the letters up as you increase the number of visible characters (see Figure 21-21). Leaving it at zero will make the letters "pop" on as though they're being typed. This is strictly a matter of aesthetics, but having this kind of control is great. Fade Time is relative to the space between whole numbers in the Visible Characters setting. For example, if Fade Time is set to 50%, the third letter will fade up in the time it takes to get from a Visible Characters setting of 2.25 to 2.75.

✦ **Mode:** Set to Difference, letters appear black in the space where they overlap. Left at its default, the text remains visible regardless of any overlapping characters.

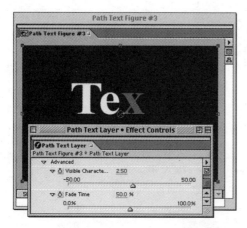

Figure 21-21: Setting the Fade Time value above its default of 0% will fade the letters up as you increase the number of Visible Characters.

✦ **Jitter Settings:** The Jitter settings generate random animations within the specified baseline, kerning, rotation and scale properties of the text. Positive values create smooth interpolations between the random values, and negative values generate linear, hence more severe interpolations between the random values. The various sliders enable you to set a maximum range for the randomness. You have a lot of leeway here. With Motion Blur enabled for the layer, the jitters can look pretty interesting (see Figure 21-22 for reference).

Granted, Path Text has a large number of properties, but the possibilities make the investment of learning all of their peculiarities more than worthwhile.

Figure 21-22: The random animations created by the Jitter Settings offer even more creative options for your text treatments.

Using masks with Path Text

Want to make your text animations really hum? You can use your own masks in conjunction with the Path Text effect, and this gives you access to the highest degree of control offered by the filter (see Figure 21-23). Much like the Audio Spectrum filter, Path Text works with either animated or static masks.

Figure 21-23: Use your own masks to get the most out of Path Text.

Image courtesy of EyeWire by Getty Images

www.gettyimages.com (Cosmic Moves)

The trick is the following: Add a mask to the same solid layer to which you applied the Path Text effect. It doesn't matter if it's open or closed. If it is closed and you're compositing on the original, make sure that you set the mask mode to None so that nothing actually gets masked. Remember, you're only concerned with the path, not the actual mask. In the Path Text Effect Controls, instead of selecting a Shape Type from the Path Options, select your mask from the Custom Path pop-up menu. Your text may appear upside down or be trapped inside the mask, but if this is the case, don't worry. That's what the Reverse Path check box is for. Check it, and the text runs along the other side of your mask.

In a nutshell, that's how it's done. If you're confused and you want the benefit of a few steps, complete the following exercise.

STEPS: Using Path Text with Your Own Mask

1. **Create a new composition by pressing Command/Ctrl+N.**

2. **Create a solid by pressing Command/Ctrl+Y.** The color doesn't matter; just make sure it's comp-sized. Name it *Path Text/Mask Layer.*

3. **In the Timeline, double-click the new solid to open it in its Layer window.**

4. **Select one of the masking tools from the Tools palette.**

5. **In the Layer window, create a mask.** After you finish, close the window.

6. **Making sure that the *Path Text/Mask Layer* is selected in the Timeline, choose Effect ⇨ Text ⇨ Path Text.** In the following dialog box, type whatever text you want.

7. **In the Effect Controls window, open the Path Options twirler and select the mask that you created from the Custom Path pop-up menu.** If the letters are trapped inside your shape or are otherwise unsightly, experiment with the Reverse Path option to see if this helps (see Figure 21-24 for reference).

Figure 21-24: The Reverse Path option can put your text on the preferred side of a mask.

Image courtesy of EyeWire by Getty Images www.gettyimages.com (Cosmic Moves)

8. **Animate the mask and effect properties to taste.**

✦   ✦   ✦

Working with Text Outside After Effects

The text filters in After Effects provide you with some excellent ways to creatively use typography in your projects. Even so, these plug-ins will often fall way short of your demands. For example, Basic Text or Path Text may prove to be a little unwieldy if you have to manage 50 lines of credits. Going further, what if you were required to animate the individual letters that comprise a line of text? What if you needed to use different fonts in the same text treatment? As your work in After Effects becomes more complex, you're more than likely going to face projects in which the limitations of the text filters will force you to look elsewhere for a solution.

Here's the good news: Look no further than Illustrator. Not only can you create beautiful vectorized text with it, but you can also separate portions of an Illustrator file into different layers, each of which you can discretely control in After Effects. Again, we want to reassure you that you don't need to master this program in order to gain a tremendous amount of power from its text features. Of course, if you're already an Illustrator master from a Web or print background, you probably know a good deal of this material. If you aren't, fear not. Its interface is a successful extension of Adobe's overall integration of its graphic design software, so the transition between the two work environments is pretty seamless.

For that matter, Photoshop is also an excellent tool when it comes to working with text. There are a number of interesting effects in Photoshop that carry over to After Effects as well. For example, if you're a big fan of Photoshop 6.0's Bevel and Emboss or Outer Glow effects, you can use these in After Effects, too. The trick is that these effects are somewhat hidden, but we show you how to uncover them. So, keep going and continue your work in the world of text in motion, only this time, we'll show you how to use some After Effects with some of Adobe's other graphic design tools.

Working with Illustrator Text

Illustrator's great for a whole bunch of things you can animate in After Effects, not just text. As a motion graphic designer, it's not uncommon to be given a Zip disk full of elements that you have to put in motion. Sometimes, these include corporate logos and other line art that a design team has already slaved over. The real value in working with Illustrator art is that you never have to worry about scale. You can always increase the size of an Illustrator file without losing any image quality, and this is undeniably a good thing. Moreover, Illustrator contains great path tools that are more powerful than the masking tools contained in After Effects. If you read Chapter 9 on masks, you'll remember that you can convert Illustrator text into outlines that can be used as masks in After Effects. This is true for any shape in Illustrator, and that's always something to keep in mind.

In any case, we're going to show you a little bit about how to use this application for generating text that you can then bring into After Effects. We start by setting the stage for an exchange between the two applications. Don't forget that Illustrator works with square pixels, and if you're doing broadcast design, you'll be working with rectangular, or D1 pixels. D1 pixels are slightly taller than they are wide, so in order for your type to appear in your After Effects project in exactly the same way that it appears in Illustrator, you need to set the dimensions of your Illustrator file to 720 x 540. This preempts any trouble you may have going from one environment to the other. The next few steps explain how to set up your Illustrator file properly.

As of this writing, our advice is informed by working between Illustrator 9.0 and After Effects 5.5. As you're most likely aware, Illustrator 10 has been released, and it's being hyped for its effectiveness when working in OSX. The basic concepts we cover in this chapter are relevant regardless of what version of Illustrator you may be using.

As far as the following explanations of text are concerned, we created an After Effects project that includes a composition for each set of steps that we cover in the chapter. Just as a reminder, you need to copy the *Source Material* folder from the DVD-ROM to your hard drive. The After Effects project that corresponds to this chapter is called *Chapter 22.aep* and can be found in the *Project Files/Chapter 22* folder.

STEPS: Setting Up Illustrator for D1 Broadcast Design

1. **Open up Illustrator by double-clicking its icon.**

2. **Choose File ➪ New (Command/Ctrl+N) to set up a new document.**

3. **Set the Color mode to RGB and make the Artboard Size 720 pixels wide by 540 pixels high.** After you're done, click OK.

Note Set the Units to pixels by choosing Edit ⇨ Preferences ⇨ Units & Undo and choosing pixels as the default units from the pop-up menus for General and Stroke.

4. **Choose Object ⇨ Crop Marks ⇨ Make.** Doing this ensures that your artwork gets imported into After Effects set to the dimensions of the artboard.

Note If you don't set crop marks, any artwork you import will be cropped at its edges. This may not seem like a big deal, but some effects won't work properly if you don't leave any space beyond the edges of your line art.

5. **Choose View ⇨ Hide Page Tiling.** This turns off the dotted lines that indicate which part of the page is visible if it's printed. Because printing doesn't concern us at all, turning it off is much easier so that you don't get distracted by it.

6. **Choose View ⇨ Show Rulers (Command/Ctrl+R).**

7. **Click in the upper-left corner of the window and drag the crosshairs to the upper-left corner of the artboard.** Before you set any guides, you want to make sure that the origin defined by the rulers (0,0) corresponds to the upper-left corner of the artboard. See Figure 22-1 for reference.

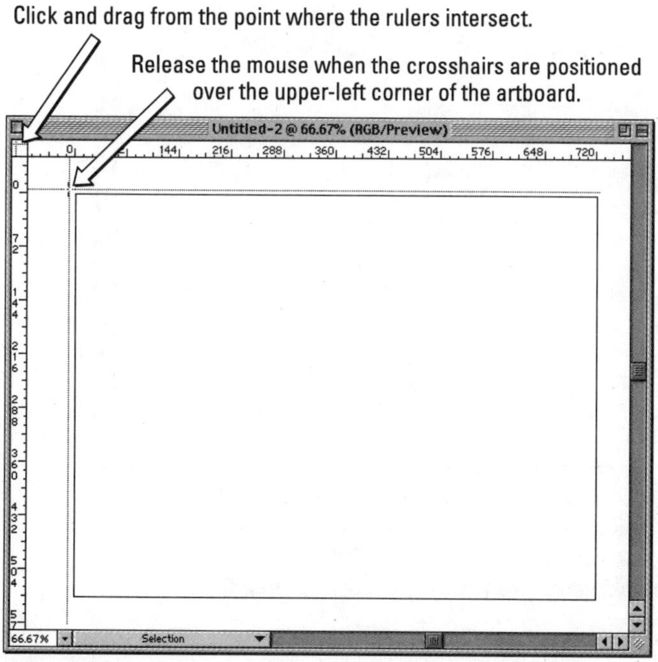

Click and drag from the point where the rulers intersect.

Release the mouse when the crosshairs are positioned over the upper-left corner of the artboard.

Figure 22-1: Set the ruler origin (the point that the rulers indicate is 0,0) to match the upper-left corner of the artboard of your Illustrator document.

8. **Now that you have set the origin, use the rulers to set guides for the title-safe boundaries.** Title-safe is generally regarded as 10% in from the edges, so you want to set vertical guides at 72 and 648 and horizontal guides at 54 and 486. To set a guide, click inside either ruler and drag toward the center, releasing the mouse after you positioned the guide. If you want to move the guides after you've initially set them, make sure that they aren't locked. You can see whether or not they are locked by choosing View ➪ Guides ➪ Lock Guides. A check mark indicates whether they're locked or not. Moving a guide is as simple as clicking and dragging it. Additionally, you may want to set guides for the halfway marks, which are 360 horizontally and 270 vertically. After you finish with this step, your workspace should resemble Figure 22-2.

Tip   When you're repositioning a guide, the Info palette tells you exactly where it's positioned so that you can release it at exactly the right place.

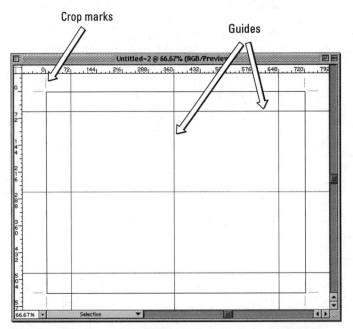

Figure 22-2: Set guides by clicking in the rulers and dragging them out toward the artboard. Use the rulers to position them initially, and if you want to reposition them, make sure that they are unlocked before you try to click and drag them to new positions.

9. **Save this template where you save any other files that you regularly call upon and name it something, such as *D1_Template.ai*.** Whenever you want to create any Illustrator art for After Effects, open this file and use the Save As function to give it a label appropriate to your project.

Managing fonts

This sidebar is really a plug for Adobe's font management software, which becomes more and more indispensable as your After Effects workload increases. If you're already an experienced designer, chances are you've been using these applications for quite some time.

What's a font?

A *font* is a file that contains all the vector shapes that form the characters of a typeset. In addition to the math for the shapes themselves, a font includes information on how each potential pairing of letters will be kerned (spaced apart). Fonts come in a few different formats, such as TrueType, Type 1 (PostScript), and so on; and are often grouped by family if there are lots of derivatives within each grouping (condensed, small caps, and so on).

How do I load them?

If it's clear that you're going to be doing a lot of video design, you'll definitely want to make the investment in Adobe's ATM Deluxe (TM stands for *Type Manager*) as well as ATR (TR stands for *Type Reunion*). If you don't have these applications and you want to add a new font to your Mac, you need to add it directly to the *Fonts* folder located within the *System* folder. After a while, this can become fairly annoying because this folder can grow past the point where it's easy to manage, to say nothing of the fact that activating these additions requires a reboot. In our opinion, you should make the investment in the previously mentioned programs, because ATM enables you to activate fonts without having to restart the machine, and ATR gives you a visual preview of the typefaces from the font menus within the various Adobe applications.

Fonts and good housekeeping

Develop good organizational habits. Most designers have libraries of CDs containing fonts, and you only want to load them when you need them. Otherwise, the list of fonts in ATM can swell to the point of confusion.

Well done! Now you've got a template that you can use over and over again to prepare any vector-based graphic elements for use in After Effects.

Putting your template to use

Now that you have created a handy template, you may as well start getting some mileage from it. For the next exercise, you're going to place some text on the artboard that you just created.

STEPS: Preparing Text in Illustrator

1. **Open the the template that you just created in the last exercise by double-clicking it.**

2. **Choose File ⇨ Save As and save the file with a new name (say, *TextForAE_v1.ai*), accepting the defaults in any remaining dialog boxes.**

3. **Make sure that the Character and Paragraph palettes are visible.** If they aren't, choose Type ⇨ Character (Command/Ctrl+T) and Type ⇨ Paragraph (Command/Ctrl+M).

4. **Using the Character palette, select a font and a point size.**

5. **From the Tools palette, select the Text tool.**

6. **Click in the area that you want to place the text and a blinking cursor appears.**

7. **Type out whatever text you want to bring into After Effects.** Press Return if you want to start a new line. After you finish, click the Selection tool from the Tools palette.

Tip   If you want to change your font, its size, or both, click and drag over your text with the Text tool to select any or all of your text, and then select a new font or size by using the Character palette.

8. **Place the text anywhere you want by selecting the Selection tool (the black arrow from the Tools palette) and dragging the text to position it on the artboard.** Look at Figure 22-3 for reference.

Okay. You have text positioned on the artboard. In and of itself, that's pretty cool, but what other bells and whistles does Illustrator offer in terms of type? What else can you do with the text now that you've laid it out?

✦ **Character palette:** This palette contains various numerical fields (illustrated in Figure 22-3). You can change the values of these fields by using either their pop-up menus or by entering numerical values directly into them.

- **Font and Point size:** These are easy enough to understand; however, sometimes the point size increments offered by the pop-up menu are pretty vast. If you need a size that's in between those offered, just type in your own number.

- **Tracking:** The Tracking control is responsible for the average overall spacing between characters. Use the Text tool to select any text that you want to space farther apart or closer together, and then change the Tracking value. By default, it's set to zero. Remember, tracking is an overall setting whereas kerning is a granular setting which affects the distance between individual pairs of letters.

- **Kerning:** The Kerning setting controls the amount of space between a pair of letters. By default, this is set to Auto, which means that the kerning pairs are determined by the information contained in the font file. Often times, the default values generate a text layout that could be improved with a little work on your part. You can override these default values by placing the blinking cursor of the Text tool in between a pair of letters, holding down the Option/Alt key, and using the left and right arrow keys to increase or decrease the size of any kerning pair. Kerning distances are measures in thousandths of an *em* (an old measurement referring to the width of the letter M). By default, each tap of an arrow key increases or decreases the distance between the letters by $^{20}/_{1000}$ of an *em.* You can change this default value by going into Illustrator's preferences (Edit ⇨ Preferences ⇨ Type & Auto Tracing) if you like. Hardcore typo-graphers generally lower this value to 10 or less for extra-tight control.

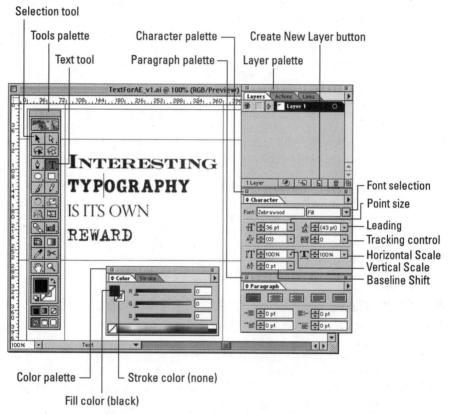

Figure 22-3: We use Illustrator to generate four lines of text using a different font for each line. To display the different palettes, choose them from the Window menu.

- **Horizontal Scale, Vertical Scale, and Baseline Shift:** We generally leave these alone because you can control these aspects of your type after you bring it into After Effects.

✦ **Layer palette:** This palette enables you to separate your Illustrator art into layers, each of which can be individually animated in After Effects. To create a new layer, click the new layer button at the bottom of the palette. The more you separate your Illustrator file into layers, the more options you have when it comes to animating them. Do it on an "as need" basis. In other words, you don't want to separate all your individual letters into layers unless your design calls for it because, in truth, that can become a little tedious.

✦ **Paragraph palette:** This palette gives you control over exactly how your text is laid out. Justify left, center, right, the works. The options in this palette are particularly useful if you plan on using a large amount of text.

✦ **Color palette:** This palette enables you to control the color of the Stroke and Fill. Typically, we like to create our text to our liking, and then we select its fill color as the last detail we do before bringing it into After Effects. The reason for this is that we generally use white text, and white is invisible in Illustrator unless you choose Outline as your view mode from the View menu. For example, after you have picked your font, typed out what you need, and positioned it on the template, select all of the text with the selection tool, choose None (the white box with the diagonal red line running through it) as the Stroke Color and White as the Fill color.

✦ **Saving your Illustrator file:** This is the last piece of the puzzle. Make sure that you save the file so that it's compatible with whatever version of Illustrator is loaded on to the machine you'll be using to render the After Effects project. As a safeguard, you may want to save two versions of the file in case there are any font-related problems. After you save your initial file, one by one, select your layers of text and convert them to outlines by choosing Type ➪ Create Outlines (Command/Ctrl+Shift+O), and then save the file under a modified name that reflects the fact that the text has been converted to outlines. If you're going to be working on a different machine than the one you created your Illustrator text on, make sure that you carry copies of the fonts so that you can load them on to other machines in case you need to make changes to the actual text.

Importing Illustrator text as a composition

Now that you've taken the time to see how Illustrator adds to your use of text in After Effects, it's time to reap the benefits. First of all, you want to create a layered Illustrator file, which you import into After Effects as a composition. After you do that, you need to resize the comp to handle the D1 aspect ratio. Also, if you ever need to make changes to an Illustrator file after you start working with it in After Effects, you can invoke the Edit Original command to make the changes without having to reload the file. Complete the next exercise to see how the two applications interact.

STEPS: Using Illustrator Text in After Effects

1. **Open up the D1 template that you made in Illustrator.**

2. **Use the Text tool to place some text on the artboard.**

3. **Create a new layer by using the button at the bottom of the Layers palette.**

4. **Use the Text tool to place some new text on the artboard.**

5. **Repeat Steps 3 and 4 until you create the text treatment that you want.** Use the Selection tool (the black arrow in the Tools palette) to position the text elements where you want them.

6. **Double-click a layer in the Layers palette to open its Layer Options dialog box.** Rename the layer to reflect the text that's included in it and click OK.

7. **Repeat Step 6 for as many layers as you created in your Illustrator file.** Your artboard should resemble something like Figure 22-4.

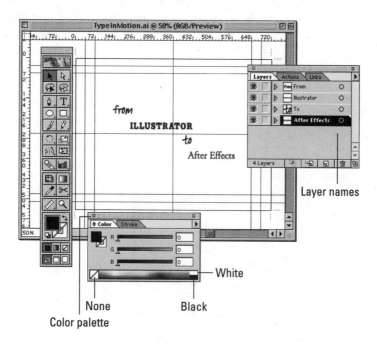

Figure 22-4: Separate your text into layers and name them so that you'll know what each layer is comprised of after you bring the Illustrator file into After Effects.

8. **Change the Fill color of each text layer to white.** Use the Selection tool to select a layer and then click the white color swatch at the lower-right corner of the Color palette. After you change the color of all the layers to white, you won't be able to see them. If you want to make sure everything is still there, choose View ⇨ Outline (Command/Ctrl+Y) to see the outlines of the artwork.

Note We're going to all this trouble because we want the text to be white in After Effects. If it's too much trouble, you can always apply the Invert effect later on.

9. **Choose File ⇨ Save As and save the file under a new name.** Close the window, but don't quit Illustrator.

10. **Open After Effects and save a new project under whatever name you like.**

11. **Create a new D1 composition (NTSC D1, 720 x 486, D1 Pixel Aspect Ratio) and place a footage item in it.** Of course, you can also drag a D1 footage item from the Project window directly on to the New Composition button.

12. **Choose File ⇨ Import ⇨ File (Command/Ctrl+I).**

13. **In the Import File dialog box, navigate your way to the Illustrator file you just saved in Step 9 and make sure you import it as a comp (see Figure 22-5 for reference).** After it's imported, the Project window will contain both a comp and a folder full of the individual layers

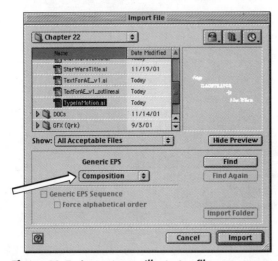

Figure 22-5: Import your Illustrator file as a comp.

14. **Drag the newly imported comp from the Project window into the comp you created in Step 11 and set it to Best quality.** You may notice that its borders exceed the edges of the D1 comp (remember, it's 720 x 540 square pixels). See Figure 22-6 for reference.

Note You always want to set any layers comprised of Illustrator elements to Best quality. The default appearance is very "blocky" because it lacks any anti-aliasing.

15. **Select the Illustrator comp layer and press Command/Ctrl+Option/Alt+F.** This makes the layer "Fit to Fill" the area of the comp. Doing this ensures that your Illustrator comp appears on a broadcast monitor exactly as it did when you were working on the file in Illustrator.

16. **Hold down the Option/Alt key and double-click the Illustrator comp in the Timeline to open its own Comp and Timeline windows.** Animate each of the individual layers to your heart's content. Apply masks and effects at will. With the file shown in the figures (also included on the DVD-ROM), we applied the Bevel Alpha, Drop Shadow, and Fast Blur effects.

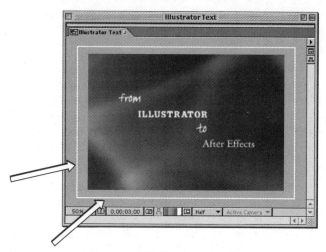

Figure 22-6: When you initially place the Illustrator comp into your D1 comp, its upper and lower boundaries extend beyond the edges (remember, it's 720 x 540 square pixels).
Image courtesy of Digital Juice (Jump Backs, Vol. 7)

Caution If you need to scale your Illustrator layer beyond 100%, you'll want to turn on its Continuously Rasterize layer switch. However, if you want to do this as well as apply masks and effects, you'll have to pre-compose the layers. As a general rule, try and create the text in Illustrator so that you don't need to scale it beyond 100%. This won't always be possible, but if you make it a standard operating procedure, you'll find that you save time working this way.

17. **If you want to make changes to the original Illustrator file, just select one of the Illustrator comp's layers from its folder inside the Project window and choose Edit ⇨ Edit Original (Command/Ctrl+E).** This opens the file in Illustrator. Make any changes that you want, save them, and return to After Effects, which incorporates all the changes that you just made.

As you become increasingly comfortable with the idea of toggling between the two applications, you'll find that it's a very quick and convenient way to work.

Having some more fun with Illustrator text

Sometimes you may need to create text in Illustrator with an unusual effect or treatment in mind. In some of these cases, you may not need to use any template, and you just have to feel it out as you go. For this section, we outline how you can re-create the opening *Star Wars* text treatment with the Corner Pin effect. This is something of a standard in the world of After Effects training, but it's still a lot of fun.

Chapter 8 describes working with effects in general. If you aren't familiar with applying effects or working in the Effect Controls window, take the time to read (or re-read) the beginning of Chapter 8.

The Online Help (choose Help ⇨ After Effects Help) is an HTML document that goes well beyond the printed User's Guide in explaining After Effects in detail. In addition to containing all of the information included in the User's Guide, the Online Help contains a lot of very useful basic information on all of the effects that ship with After Efffects. The Online help is particularly good because it tends to explain the purpose of each and every setting in an effect. Refer to it as often as you need to; our purpose in writing about these effects is to supplement that information rather than repeat it.

For this exercise, we created an 800 x 1200 Illustrator file and filled it with yellow, 32 pt Helvetica text. We placed it in a 750 x 400 comp and slowly animated its vertical position so that all of the text passes through the comp over the course of thirty seconds.

STEPS: Creating the "Star Wars" Text Scroll

1. **In Illustrator, create a new document and set its dimensions to 800 x 1200 pixels.**

2. **Choose Object ⇨ Crop Marks ⇨ Make.**

3. **Using the Text tool, fill the artboard with yellow 32 pt Helvetica type.** Keep it safely in from the edges of the artboard.

4. **Save the file and import it into After Effects.** Because it's only one layer, you can import it as footage as opposed to a comp.

5. **Create a new 30 second 750 x 400 square pixel composition and call it** *Star Wars Text Pre-Comp.*

6. **Bring the Illustrator layer into the comp and position it so that its top edge is even with the bottom of the comp.** Don't forget to set it to Best quality.

7. **With the layer selected in the Timeline, type P to solo the Position property and click its stopwatch to set an initial keyframe at the first frame of the comp.**

8. **Press the End key to go to the last frame of the comp and move the Illustrator layer up so that its bottom edge is even with the top of the comp.** Hold down the Shift key as you reposition the text so that only its vertical position changes. Drag the Playhead through the layer to confirm that you created an animation in which the text slowly scrolls upwards. See Figure 22-7 for reference.

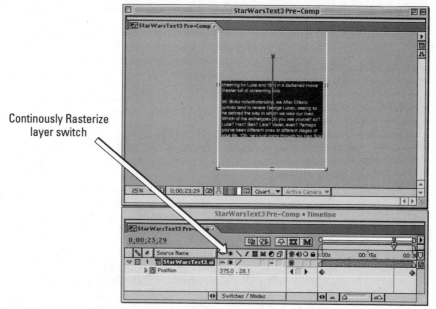

Continuously Rasterize
layer switch

Figure 22-7: Create a basic positional animation for the scrolling Illustrator text.
You may want to turn its Continuously Rasterize layer switch on.

9. **Create a new 30 second D1 (NTSC DV 720 x 486 D1 Pixel Aspect Ratio)
   comp and call it *Star Wars Text Scroll*.** For extra punch, you may want to
   add a starfield to the comp, and if you do, add the EyeWire clip called
   EV00167.MOV.

10. **Drag the *Star Wars Text Pre-Comp* from the Project window into the
    Timeline of the *Star Wars Text Scroll* comp.** Again, make sure it's set to
    Best quality.

11. **Drag the playhead about 15 seconds into the comp so that the scolling text
    is fully visible.**

12. **In the Timeline, make sure the *Star Wars Text Pre-Comp* layer is selected
    and then choose Effect ⇨ Distort ⇨ Corner Pin.**

13. **Press Command/Ctrl+R to turn the rulers on in the Comp window.**

14. **Set a horizontal guide at a point a little above the center of the comp and
    set another roughly halfway below it.** To set a guide, click inside the ruler
    and drag in toward the center of the comp. Release the mouse button after
    you have it positioned.

Tip

You may need to reduce your magnification to 25% to see as much real estate as
you need to set these guides.

15. **Make sure that Snap to Guides is turned on in the View menu.**

16. **Position the Corner Pin effect points, as shown in Figure 22-8.** They snap to the guides, and this ensures that the distortion created by the Corner Pin effect won't be off kilter. After you initially set them, adjust the horizontal positions of the effect points so that the text appears balanced in the comp. They "stick" to the guides as you move them.

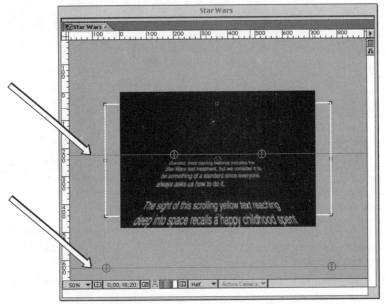

Figure 22-8: The guides help you position the Corner Pin effect points on the same horizontal axes.

Image courtesy of EyeWire by Getty Images www.gettyimages.com (Cosmic Moves)

17. **Press 0 on the numeric keypad to create a RAM Preview of your animation.** After viewing it, you may want to adjust the effect points or the speed of the text as it scrolls. To check the true appearance of the text, set the Comp window's magnification to 100% at Full resolution. If the text appears a little fuzzy, you may want to go into the *Star Wars Text Pre-Comp* and turn on the Illustrator layer's Continuously Rasterize switch. You may also want to hide the rulers and guides to get a clearer picture of your work area.

There you go. You can now add the ability to send InterGalactic facsimiles to your "temping" resume. May the Force be with you.

Working with Photoshop Text

Not to be outdone, text in Photoshop is pretty nifty as well. Version 6.0 of Photoshop adds a hefty set of new features to its predecessors, and some of these include features such as layer sets and new effects, most of which carry over nicely into After Effects.

We're taking the approach that you're going to do most of your text work in After Effects using its own native text effects in concert with Illustrator's numerous strengths in this area. Still, you may be a Photoshop wizard, or you may be given preexisting Photoshop text elements that a client is paying you to animate. If either of these situations happens to be the case, you have no need for concern. As long as you have access to a layered Photoshop file, you can always make changes to text layers.

STEPS: Importing a Layered Photoshop File into After Effects

1. **In After Effects, choose File ⇨ Import ⇨ File (Command/Ctrl+I).** Import the Photoshop file on the DVD-ROM called *PS_Text.psd* as a comp. Much like Illustrator, it comes in as both a comp as well as a folder full of the individual layers.

As was the case with the Illustrator file that you were working with in the previous exercises, you want to take the same approach when using Photoshop to create graphics for D1 NTSC video. Specifically, you want to set up your Image Size to be 720 x 540 pixels to counter the distortion created when working with the different D1 pixel aspect ratio when preparing video in After Effects. In much the same way you set guides in Illustrator, you'll probably find it very useful to set horizontal guides at 54 and 486 and vertical guides at 72 and 648 so that you know where your title-safe margins are.

Of course, you always have the option to import single layers, but we're concerned with all the value-added features you get from importing these sophisticated files as sets of layers in their own composition.

2. **Create a new D1 composition (NTSC D1, 720 x 486, D1 Pixel Aspect Ratio) and name it *Photoshop Text*.**

3. **Drag the comp you just imported from the Project window to the Timeline of the *Photoshop Text* comp that you just created and set it to Best quality.** See Figure 22-9 for reference. Because the Photoshop file was created at 720 x 540 square pixels, its boundaries will exceed the edges of the *Photoshop Text* comp.

4. **In the Timeline, select the layer and press Command/Ctrl+Option/Alt+F.** This makes the layer "Fit to Fill" the area of the comp, and in turn, takes care of the distortion created by working with the D1 pixel aspect ratio.

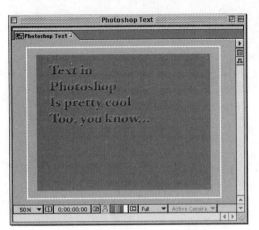

Figure 22-9: The layer exceeds the edges of the comp because the Photoshop file used to create it was 720 x 540 square pixels.

That was easy enough. So what's the big deal? Well, if you hold down the Option/Alt key and double-click the layer in the Timeline, it'll open the layered Photoshop comp in its own Timeline and Comp windows, and you might notice some pretty interesting details about some of the layers. For example, select the layers in the Timeline and press E to solo any effects. Also, click the Switches/Modes toggle button to view the transfer modes. See Figure 22-10 for reference.

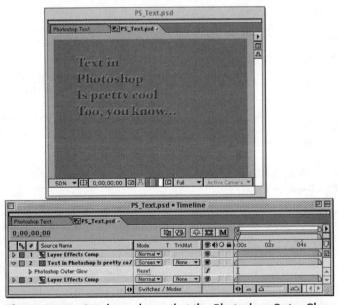

Figure 22-10: One layer shows that the Photoshop Outer Glow effect has been applied, and its transfer mode is set to Screen.

What's the Photoshop Outer Glow effect? Who set the layer to Screen? The top layer, a pre-comp called *Layer Effects Comp,* includes the text. The second layer contains the Photoshop Outer Glow effect. The third layer, another pre-comp called *Layer Effects Comp,* includes the textured background. If you Option/Alt+double-click these two pre-comps, you'll get some more interesting results along these lines. See Figures 22-11 and 22-12 for reference.

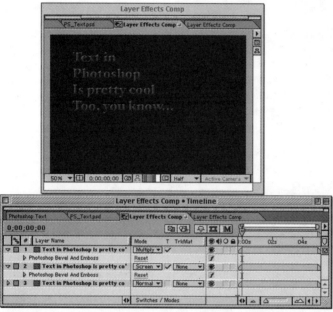

Figure 22-11: The Photoshop Bevel and Emboss effect is spread over two layers. The top layer creates the dark shadow, and the second layer creates the highlight. The bottom layer contains the text layer without any effects applied.

Going further, select a layer that has one of these strange effects applied and press F3 to open its Effect Controls window. For example, if you take a look at the Photoshop Outer Glow Effect Controls, you'll see that this is an effect just like any other you learned to use in After Effects (see Figure 22-13). Well, almost.

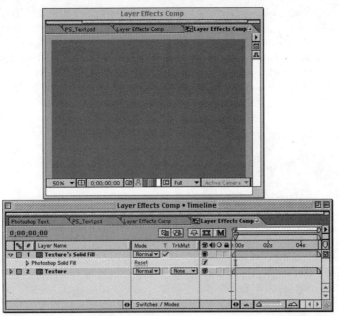

Figure 22-12: The top layer contains the Photoshop Solid Fill effect, which is really the Color Overlay effect when working in Photoshop. The bottom layer contains the background texture.

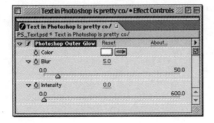

Figure 22-13: The Effect Controls window displays the Photoshop Outer Glow effect properties. Weird, huh?

Saving Photoshop effects for use in After Effects

So what do you do with these undocumented effects? We can think of at least two things. First, save them as favorites and you can use them whenever you want without having to import Photoshop files. Second, you have to know how to use them; otherwise, they won't provide much added value.

Okay, regarding the first item of business, select the effect by clicking its name in the Effect Controls window and then choose Effect ⇨ Save Favorite. Save these in the folder where you usually save your favorites, and then you'll be able to call it up whenever you like.

Tip

Typically, we keep our *Favorites* folder in the After Effects 5.0 *Application* folder and label it *FFX*. Wherever you put it, keep it handy. This folder is definitely something you want to bring with you if you're going to be working at another workstation besides your own. For example, if you've created a bunch of timesaving favorites (FFX files) such as color correction combos that might include Levels and Hue/Saturation, you won't want to be without them.

Actually using Photoshop effects in After Effects

So now that you have access to these filters, what can you do with them? You can't just slap them on to a layer, but then again they're not overly complicated. The trick is to duplicate the layer that you want to apply them to and then apply the effect to one of the duplicated layers. Sometimes it's the top layer, sometimes it's the bottom layer; it depends on the effect. We give you a demonstration, and you can sort out the rest with your own experimentation.

Note

For the following exercise, you need to save the Photoshop Outer Glow effect as a favorite before you can apply it.

STEPS: Using the Photoshop Outer Glow Effect

1. **Create a new comp.**

2. **Create a new solid.** Make sure it's comp-sized and name it *Text Layer*. Don't worry about the color.

3. **In the Timeline, select the solid layer and apply the Basic Text effect to it by choosing Effect ➪ Text ➪ Basic Text.**

4. **In the resulting Options dialog box, pick a font and type size and type some text.** After you finish, click OK and set the layer to Best quality.

5. **In the Basic Text Effect Controls, set the font size and color so that you can clearly see what's happening.**

6. **In the Timeline, select the layer and press Command/Ctrl+D to duplicate it.**

7. **Select the bottom of the two layers and then choose Effect ➪ Apply Favorite.** In the following Open dialog box, navigate your way to your favorites folder and select the FFX file that you saved for the Photoshop Outer Glow effect. Select it and click Open, and the effect will be added to the Effect Controls window for the layer.

On the DVD-ROM

We created favorites for all of the Photoshop filters that work in After Effects in the folder called *FFX*. Feel free to add them to your own collection.

8. **In the Effect Controls, set the Color, Blur, and Intensity for the Photoshop Outer Glow effect.** See Figure 22-14 for reference.

Figure 22-14: In order to work properly, the Photoshop effects require just a little extra work on your part.

Note   The Photoshop Bevel and Emboss effect works on two duplicate layers above the base layer. One is used for the shadow, and the other is used for the highlight. See Figure 22-11 for pointers.

The Photoshop Outer Glow filter is a great effect that you can animate to create a pulsing glow on just about any layer that you want. Having said that, what's the extra value behind the Glow effect that's found in the Stylize filters that come with the Production Bundle of After Effects? The After Effects Glow filter is actually quite a powerful tool that can be used on much more than text.

Using the Glow effect in After Effects (PB only)

The key to the Glow effect is to persist. Keep at it until you start getting results. Naturally, the first thing to do with any effect is to apply it to a layer and look for immediately gratifying results. We admit that's how we started with After Effects. Still, as you may have learned by now, a lot of the power of some effects lies in tweaking an intimidating number of their effect controls before you start to get any gratifying results. Glow is a particularly good example of exactly such an effect.

Understanding the Glow effect properties

The Glow filter contains a large number of effect properties, and understanding them is key to getting a lot of mileage from it. In fact, if you master it, Glow is one of the winners that you'll be using a lot of the time. See Figure 22-15 to see all of its properties.

Note The Glow effect is available only to owners of the Production Bundle of After Effects.

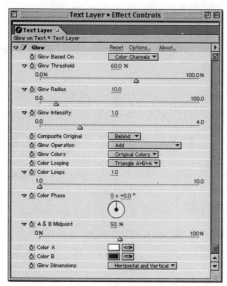

Figure 22-15: The Glow effect properties are initially a bit difficult to understand.

The following list describes the various properties of the Glow filter in more detail.

✦ **Glow Based On:** This pop-up menu lets you choose whether the glow is based on the color channels or the alpha channels in the effected layer. The Alpha Channel option works very well with text and other layers that contain transparency. Selecting the Alpha Channel option automatically sets the Glow Colors setting to A & B Colors (see following text). The Color Channels option is the correct choice when you apply it to a layer of video and you want the glow to add a stylized accent.

✦ **Glow Threshold:** This slider determines which pixels the glow is applied to according to their luminance. The higher the threshold value, the fewer pixels are affected. The lower the value, the more the entire layer is affected.

✦ **Glow Radius:** This sensitive property does what you might guess: It sets the radius of the glow emanating from the affected pixels.

✦ **Glow Intensity:** This property controls the luminance of the glowing pixels.

✦ **Composite Original:** This pop-up menu determines whether the glow is applied on top of or below the affected layer. It only concerns layers with transparency because adding a glow under a fully opaque layer of video won't exactly achieve much in the way of an effect.

✦ **Glow Operation:** This pop-up menu enables you to choose the transfer mode of the glow.

✦ **Glow Colors:** This pop-up menu enables you to choose the color that the glow is made from. The Original Colors option uses the colors from the layer. The A & B Colors option uses the colors specified in the Color A and Color B effect properties (see following text). The Arbitrary Map options button enables you to select a custom arbitrary map from Photoshop as your color scheme for the glow.

Note   None of the following options are relevant unless you select a Glow Colors option other than Original Colors.

✦ **Color Looping:** This pop-up menu enables you to choose how the A & B colors are arranged in the glow.

✦ **Color Loops:** This slider determines the number of times the glow repeats the A & B colors within the glow.

✦ **Color Phase:** This radial dial controls the cycling of the Color Loops.

✦ **A & B Midpoint:** This slider controls the transition from Color A to Color B in the Color Looping.

✦ **Color A:** This color swatch, complete with a dropper, enables you to choose a custom color for half of the glow color cycle.

✦ **Color B:** Same as Color A, except that it applies to the other half of the glow color cycle.

✦ **Glow Dimensions:** This pop-up menu enables you to specify whether or not the effect works vertically, horizontally, or in both directions.

Using Glow with text

We can start out by applying the Glow effect to a layer of text. You can see that it goes way beyond the power of the Photoshop Outer Glow effect, but you may not always need that kind of power or complexity. In any case, you have options. Complete the next exercise to start putting this filter to work.

STEPS: Applying the Glow Effect to Text

1. **Create a new five-second comp; you may want to call it** *Glow Text*.

2. **Create a new solid.** Make sure that it's comp-sized and name it *Text Layer*. Don't worry about the color.

3. **In the Timeline, select the solid layer and apply the Basic Text effect to it by choosing Effect ➪ Text ➪ Basic Text.**

4. **In the resulting Options dialog box, pick a font and type size and type some text.** After you finish, click OK and set the layer to Best quality.

5. **In the Basic Text Effect Controls, set the font size and color so that you can clearly see what's happening.** As you make adjustments to these properties, the changes will be immediately visible in the Comp window.

6. **With the layer still selected in the Timeline, choose Effect ⇨ Stylize ⇨ Glow.** Okay. So there may be a subtle glow around the letters that's based on their color (see Figure 22-16). Big deal. As we've been hinting all along, hang on. There's a lot more to it.

Figure 22-16: The initial appearance of the Glow effect is nothing to write home about.

7. **In the Effect Controls window, set the Glow to be based on the Alpha Channel (which, in turn, sets the Glow Colors setting to A & B Colors).**

8. **Set Color B to match the color of the Basic Text by clicking the Color B dropper on the color swatch located under the Stroke and Fill setting for the Basic Text effect.**

Tip

You may need to expand the size of your Effect Controls window to complete Step 8.

9. **Set the Composite Original pop-up menu to On Top.**

10. **If necessary, adjust the Glow Threshold, Radius, and Intensity sliders until the glow creates a nice highlight around the letters.** The one slider that you will most likely have to crank up is the Glow Radius setting.

11. **Set the Color Loops slider to 4.**

12. **Click the Color Phase stopwatch to set an initial keyframe for this property at the first frame of the composition.**

13. **Press the End key to go to the last frame of the comp and enter a value of 5 for the number of complete Color Phase revolutions.** See Figure 22-17 if you need a visual reference.

14. **Press 0 on the numeric keypad to see a RAM Preview of the comp, or if you prefer, you can render out the entire comp as a QuickTime movie.**

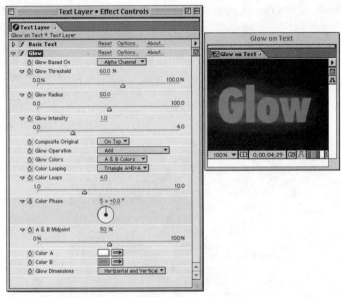

Figure 22-17: Create a pulsing Glow animation for your text by animating the Color Phase property.

Check out the animated radiating Glow effect on your layer of text. Now that we've introduced you to this filter, go ahead and tweak the other effect controls to see what they do. Refer to the descriptions of the effect properties in the last section if you need reminders as to what each property controls.

Using Glow with video

Next up is applying the Glow effect onto a layer of video. Because you have control over the transfer mode of the effect, you can create very interesting stylized effects with this one. See Figure 22-18 and Color Plate 22-1.

Figure 22-18: NYC traffic, before and after a multiplied Glow

Image courtesy of Sekani (NY Vistas)

STEPS: Applying the Glow Effect to Video

1. **Take a QuickTime movie from the Project window and drag it on top of the New Composition button (at the bottom of the Project window).** You may want to rename this comp *Glow on Video*.

2. **With the movie layer selected in the Timeline, choose Effect ⇨ Stylize ⇨ Glow.**

3. **In the Glow Effect Controls, stick with the default of the Glow Based on Color Channels and experiment with the following four properties: Glow Threshold, Radius, Intensity, and most importantly, the Glow Operation transfer mode.**

Tip

You may find it useful to apply and tweak the Levels filter on the layer of video before adding Glow to the mix. The more contrast you have in your video layer, the more precision you get from the Glow Threshold slider.

Not bad for a filter with a simple name like Glow, eh? Take a look at what's on TV and see how many times you notice one kind of glow or another. Glow is very common in footage and graphic elements. Experiment with this one, and you'll find that it'll end up in a lot of your work.

Using Text as the Basis for Effects

As kind of a parting thought for the chapter, understand that text treatments aren't limited by the text that you can generate with the text filters or even Illustrator and Photoshop for that matter. Who needs fonts when you can paste the data from mask paths into positional effect properties? We realize that the last sentence may seem a bit heady, but hang on. All we mean by that is that a lot of neat effects rely upon animating the position of an effect point. If you are making your way through all the chapters of the book, you may remember the Write-on effect. Lightning works in a very similar fashion as well. Stroke is yet another. Complete the following exercise to see only one alternative to text generated from fonts, and use it as a springboard for your own unconventional approaches to writing messages in the medium of video.

On the DVD-ROM

This is a complex composition. Look at the composition called *Fonts?* in the *Chapter 22.aep* project to see how we carried it out. Also, look at the QuickTime draft movie of the final result called *WhoNeedsFonts.mov*, which is also on the DVD-ROM.

STEPS: Fonts? Who Needs Fonts?

1. **In Illustrator, open up a new document.**

2. **Using the Pencil tool, write a message.** This is easier with a pressure tablet, but you can do it with a regular mouse as well. Click and drag when you want to write, release the mouse so that you can reposition it, and start writing again when you want to make new letters. See Figure 22-19 for reference.

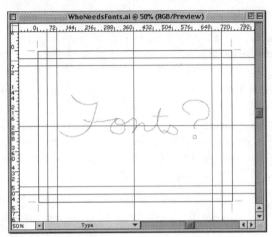

Figure 22-19: Use the Pencil tool in Illustrator to write a message.

3. **Select the entire message by using the Selection tool to drag a marquee around all your scribblings.**

4. **Choose Edit ➪ Copy (Command/Ctrl+C).**

5. **In After Effects, create a new 10-second comp.**

6. **Create a new comp-sized black solid and name it *Lightning*.**

7. **In the Timeline, double-click the solid to open it up in its own Layer window.**

8. **Making sure that Masks is selected from the Layer window menu, choose Edit ➪ Paste (Command/Ctrl+V).** This pastes all of the paths from Illustrator on to the solid (depending on what you did in Illustrator, you may only have one path; we happened to use 5). See Figure 22-20 for reference.

9. **In the Timeline, select the solid layer and press the M key to solo the masks that you just pasted on to the layer.** If any of them are closed, set their Mask Modes to None. Finally, set the layer's transfer mode to Lighten. The Lightning effect is applied to the original image, so it doesn't create transparency outside of its wiggling bolt. We need to use transfer modes if we want to see anything underneath it, and because we're going to add layers beneath the Lightning layer later on, we need to change the transfer mode.

10. **With the layer still selected, choose Effect ➪ Render ➪ Lightning.**

11. **In the Comp window, move the Start Point for the Lightning effect off the lower-left corner of the screen.**

12. **In the Effect Controls window, set a keyframe for the End Point by clicking its stopwatch.**

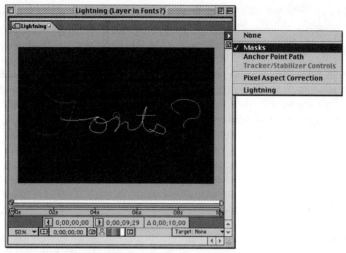

Figure 22-20: Paste the paths from Illustrator on to the solid layer in the Layer window (make sure that Masks is selected from the Layer window menu).

Image courtesy of Digital Juice (Jump Backs, Vol. 7)

13. **Open up the Layer window for the solid once again and use the Target pop-up menu to select the first mask.** This selects all of its control points.

14. **Choose Edit ▷ Copy (Command/Ctrl+C).**

15. **In the Timeline, select the Lightning solid and press U to solo any keyframed properties for the layer.** This solos the Lightning effect's End Point property.

16. **Making sure that the playhead is located on the first frame, select the keyframe for the Lightning effect's End Point and then choose Edit ▷ Paste (Command/Ctrl+V).** This pastes the spatial data of the path into the End Point position property over time. Notice that the first and last keyframes are linear, and the keyframes in between are roving keyframes.

Caution

Be sure that you select the Lightning Effect's End Point keyframe before pasting; otherwise, you'll paste another copy of the mask on to the layer.

17. **Press Page Down to move forward one frame in the Timeline.**

18. **Repeat Steps 13 and 14, this time setting the target mask as the second mask.**

19. **In the Timeline, click the Lightning Effect's End Point property name to select it and then choose Edit ▷ Paste (Command/Ctrl+V).** This pastes the second mask's path into End Point position property again. Press Page Down to move forward one frame and repeat the process for as many masks as you have.

What's new in After Effects 5.5: Copy and paste keyframes onto multiple layers

In older versions of After Effects, keyframes that were copied could be pasted only onto a single layer. In After Effects 5.5, you now can copy keyframes and simultaneously paste them onto multiple layers. After selecting and copying keyframes, simply select multiple layers and paste the keyframes, and they'll appear on all the layers you've selected.

 Caution   Be sure that you select the Lightning Effect's End Point property name before pasting; otherwise, you'll paste another copy of the mask on to the layer.

20. **After you finish pasting the masks into the Lightning Effect's End Point position property, take a moment to preview the animation and see if it's happening along a timeframe you like.** If not, you can reposition groups of keyframes so that the animation takes place according to your own time cues. The important element is to get the mask data into the Lightning Effect's End Point property first. Additionally, you may want to adjust the Lightning effect's other properties. These have to do with taste. How many branches, if any, do you want? What kind of thickness and color do you want for the traveling bolt? Take a minute to tweak these properties so that the Lightning looks the way you want.

21. **After you get the Lightning animation moving at the speed that you want, save the project.**

22. **Press the Home key to move the playhead back to the first frame of the comp.**

23. **Create a new comp-sized solid layer, color it light gray, and name it *Write-On*.** Now you'll apply the Write-on effect to it.

24. **With the *Write-On* layer selected in the Timeline, choose Effect ⇨ Stylize ⇨ Write-on.**

25. **In the Effect Controls for the newly applied Write-on effect, make whatever adjustments that you want to the effect properties later, just make sure that the Paint Style pop-up is set to On Transparent.**

26. **While you're still in the Write-on Effect Controls, set an initial keyframe for the Brush Position property.**

27. **In the Timeline, click the Lightning effect End Point property name under the Lightning layer to select all of its keyframes and then choose Edit ⇨ Copy (Command/Ctrl+C).**

28. **With the *Write-On* layer selected in the Timeline, press U to solo its animated properties.**

29. Select the keyframe for the Write-on effect's Brush Position property, and then choose Edit ➪ Paste (Command/Ctrl+V). This pastes the same positional keyframes from the Lightning effect's End Point into the Write-on effect's Brush Position. See Figure 22-21.

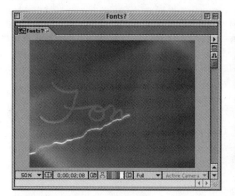 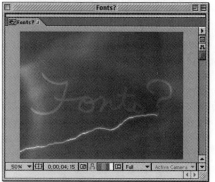

Figure 22-21: Use Lightning and Write-on to spell out an unconventional approach to text.

At this point, you should preview your animation and check to see if it looks like your message is being written out in a way that you prefer. We find it convenient to add Hold keyframes to the Brush Position animation at each point in time that we want the brush to be "picked up" from the page. Look at the comp on the DVD-ROM for clues.

Lastly, we add a few aesthetic details, all of which you can check out on the DVD-ROM as well. For example, we changed the transfer mode of the *Write-On* layer to Soft Light and added the Bevel Alpha effect to it as well. For kicks, we added a layer of textural video at the bottom of the stack and changed its color with Colorama. Not content to leave it there, we added the Displacement Map effect to the *Write-On* layer after it was finished being "written out" and used the luminance values from the layer of textural video as the basis for the displacement. Break this composition apart and then start to experiment on your own. We only made this text treatment to act as a point of departure for you to try your own unconventional approaches to the prospect of designing with text.

As you can see, there is a lot of fun to be had when you look into all the creative options you have when designing with text in After Effects. Take full advantage of the text filters, Illustrator, Photoshop, masks, and any interesting fonts that you can get your hands on. Throw 3D into the mix (which we do in a couple of chapters), and you will truly have very few limits as to what you can achieve when it comes to using After Effects to deliver a message of text to your audience.

What's new in After Effects 5.5: The Advanced Lightning effect (PB only)

As though the Lightning effect wasn't enough fun, the folks at Adobe have added the Advanced Lightning effect to the Production Bundle of After Effects 5.5. You can use this filter in conjunction with the alpha channels of a layer for even greater control. For example, you could keep the lightning within a mask shape that you've drawn (as you see in Figure SB 22-1), or just as easily, you could keep the lightning bolt from crossing through the shape of an alpha channel. In addition to the Alpha Obstacle property, there are numerous other ones from which you can choose to sculpt the perfect bolt of lightning.

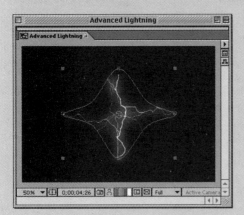

Figure SB 22-1: Harness the reach of Advanced Lightning!

✦   ✦   ✦

Putting Math in Motion: Using Motion Math Scripts

Contrary to what you may think the first time you open the Motion Math window, remember that this feature was added to After Effects to save you time. When they initially look at it, most people are thrown off by the fact that it's lacking in terms of a sexy graphical user interface (GUI). Before fleeing in disgust, you might want to take a deep breath and stay the course.

Here's why: What if you had to simulate gravity with keyframes? Imagine dropping a ball from the top of the Comp window. Now imagine setting keyframes so that it bounces realistically until gravity completely takes over and it comes to a rest at the bottom edge of the comp. This animation would be fairly time-consuming and would require a good bit of testing and tweaking (that is, *time*) on your part.

Motion Math exists for exactly such a scenario. By using custom scripts, Motion Math creates realistic keyframe animations that simulate various natural phenomena. As soon as you get past its crude-looking interface, using it becomes a real joy. Plus, it's an open standard. Anyone can write Motion Math scripts, and many do. Browse the Web and you'll find an entire community of After Effects users that write and post their Motion Math scripts.

So, cast your fears aside and jump in. It's not as tough as it looks.

Getting to Know the Motion Math Window

To begin using Motion Math, you need to select a layer in the Timeline and then choose Animation ➪ Keyframe Assistant ➪ Motion Math. The Motion Math window shown in Figure 23-1 appears. In the past, you may have approached this window once or twice on your own and upon laying eyes on its complexity, promptly closed it. We're here to tell you that the Motion Math window is your friend. As soon as you grasp how little you need to work within the Motion Math window to get fabulous results, you'll always be looking for an excuse to come back to using it.

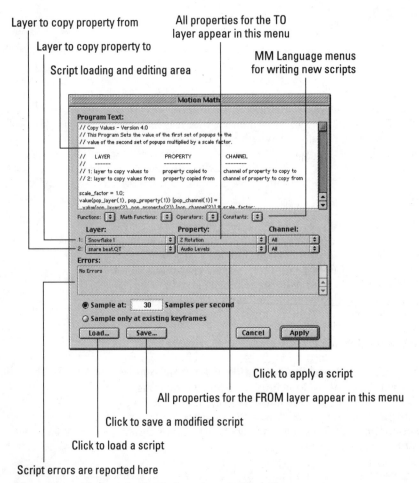

Figure 23-1: The much-dreaded Motion Math window

Figure 23-1 shows the various components of the Motion Math window, and the following section explains the purpose of each of these components. Here's some good news: You only need to know how to do a couple of small functions to take advantage of this complex looking interface. First, you want to be able to scan the contents of a Motion Math script so that you know what it does. Second, you should learn how to use the two menus labeled "1" and "2." That's it. Not too tall an order. As far as the menus are concerned, all you need to grasp is the fact that the "2" menu is a "FROM" menu, while the "1" menu is a "TO" menu. This means that by using the FROM menu, you can apply any property of any layer to any property of any layer that you select from the TO menu. Any layers, their transform properties, and effects all appear in both of these menus.

Explaining the Motion Math window interface

Motion Math has an interface all of its own. It takes a bit of getting used to, but once you get the hang of it, there is nothing difficult about it.

Here we explain the components of the Motion Math window:

✦ **Script area:** The script loading and editing area is where you can either write scripts or view and edit any script that you may have loaded. More often than not, you will simply be loading and using the scripts provided with your copy of After Effects. Keep in mind that many Motion Math scripts are available for free on the World Wide Web. The only portion of a script that you need to pay attention to in this section are any remarks that follow the // symbols. These are comments, and they tell you what the script is designed to do and how the layer menus should be set to achieve the desired results. True, fancy math symbols and formulas follow, but you can ignore these for the most part. Of course, if you're a programmer, you'll probably seize the logic of the scripting language and start whipping up your own home brew.

✦ **Language menus:** The language menus are provided to you so that you can write your own scripts. Each menu provides access to the functions, operators, and constants that you need to write a Motion Math script. As you select any element from these menus, the element is typed in automatically in the script area. Unless you're familiar with basic C or C++ programming, you will rarely interact with these. Feel free to ignore these menus altogether.

✦ **Layer menus 1 and 2:** As we said earlier, for most users of After Effects, the layer menus are all you need to focus on. Just remember that Layer 2 is the FROM menu and Layer 1 is the TO menu. Hence, you can select the layer that you want to extrapolate a property FROM in the Layer 2 menu, while any layer that you want to apply that property TO should be selected in the Layer 1 menu. For example, say that you have two files in your comp; one is an audio file, and the other is an image file. If you want to apply the audio amplitude of the audio file to affect the scale of the image file, select the audio file in menu 2 and the image file in menu 1.

Note   Some Motion Math scripts affect only one layer and do not require that you select another layer. In that case, use the layer 1 menu to select your layer. Remember that if you get confused, you can always read the part of the script that has the comment lines after the // symbols. The comments in every script tell you how to set your layer menus. Any and all layers in your comp will appear in both these menus. By default, the layer that you select before calling up the Motion Math window will appear in both of these menus, but you can go in and change that.

✦ **Property menus 1 and 2:** As you select layers using the 1 and 2 Layer menus, any and all of their properties will be available to you in the property menus. Hence, after first selecting the order of layers in the 1 and 2 Layer menus, you can then select the properties you want affected in Property menus 1 and 2. For example, following the previous audio file and the image file example, you need to select the amplitude of the audio file in menu 2 and the scale property of the image file in menu 1. Any properties that are not available are grayed out in the property menus.

✦ **Channel menus 1 and 2:** Many properties in After Effects have one channel while others have two or three. For example, the amplitude of an audio file is a single channel property, while the scale of an image file has both an x and a y component. Hence, you can select whether you want both channels or a single channel to be affected by the Motion Math script.

✦ **Errors display:** Any errors that may occur while running the scripts appear here. Unless you're writing your own scripts or modifying existing ones, you can ignore this section.

✦ **Load:** Click here to load the Motion Math script of your choice. All default scripts provided by Adobe are kept in the After Effects application folder under the *Motion Math Scripts* folder. Just so you know, the Motion Math scripts are no more than text documents and can be kept anywhere.

✦ **Save:** Click to save a script that you write or modify.

✦ **Apply:** Another important button. After you make your menu choices, click this button to apply the script you selected.

Don't be afraid of the "Math"

If you're like most After Effects users, you probably opened the Motion Math window once or twice and got scared away by the possibility of lots of math hiding in the visually unappealing text heavy interface. It may very well be that you were simply scared away by the word *math*. Maybe you hated math in high school and had bad flashbacks when confronted with the Motion Math window. Fear not. You really don't need to know any math in order to take advantage of this fabulous feature. (Note to Adobe: Rename "Motion Math" to "Motion Fun," or "Motion Metamorphosis" or even "Motion Depravity." Just get "Math" out of there!) An additional item we should point out to the "Motion Math challenged" out there is that in order to use Motion Math, you only need to master a few details of the Motion Math window. You can simply ignore most of the ugly looking equations and function menus outright. You'll see what we mean in the rest of the chapter.

Getting Your Feet Wet with Motion Math

Prepare to use our first Motion Math script. This first exercise provides you with an idea of how simple it is to use Motion Math and, more importantly, the fabulous results you can get with it.

In the next series of steps, we work with two layers. The bottom layer is a layer of text that reads "Elementary, my dear Watson!" The top layer is a magnifying glass. We will animate the magnifying glass over the text. The trick is to simulate a magnified look for the text as the glass moves over it. First, we animate the magnifying glass across the text. Then we apply the Bulge effect to the text layer. Finally, we use the Motion Math script called *toeffect.mm* to tie the motion of the magnifying glass to the center of the Bulge effect so that the two move in concert.

Okay. Enough talk. On to some Motion Math!

To better explain the mysteries of Motion Math, we created an After Effects project that includes a composition for each series of steps that we cover in the chapter. Just as a reminder, you need to copy the *Source Material* folder from the DVD-ROM to your hard drive. Our own corresponding After Effects project is called *Chapter 23.aep* and is found in the *Project Files/Chapter 23* folder. For the next series of steps, look at the composition called *MM-Apply To*.

STEPS: Using the Apply to Effect Point Script

1. **Choose Composition ➭ New Compostion and create a new comp.**

2. **Create a New Solid.** Choose Layer ➭ New ➭ Solid and set the Solid size to the size of your comp by clicking the Make Comp Size button in the Solid Settings dialog box. You can select any color you like.

3. **With the solid layer selected in the Timeline, apply the Basic Text effect to it by choosing Effect ➭ Text ➭ Basic Text.** In the resulting Options dialog box, type **"Elementary, my Dear Watson!"** If you prefer, you can use the *"Elementary" text.pict* we have provided in the *Chapter23.aep* project.

4. **Drag the *Magnifying_Glass.eps* footage item into the Timeline and place it above the text layer.**

5. **Double-click the Magnifying glass layer in the Timeline to open it in the Layer window.** Click the small arrow in the upper-right corner of the Layer window and select Anchor Point Path. The anchor point of the layer is indicated by the small circle with the cross in the center of the window. Click the circle with the cross in the Layer window and move it to the center of the round section of the magnifying glass. This is important because we want the bulge to follow the center of the round portion of the magnifying glass.

6. **Create a positional animation for the Magnifying Glass across the text by setting two position keyframes.**

7. **Next, select the text layer and choose Effect ⇨ Distort ⇨ Bulge to apply the effect.**

8. **Change the Horizontal and Vertical Radius of the Bulge effect to match the size of the round portion of the Magnifying Glass.** We used a radius of 64 for both the Horizontal and Vertical Radius properties. The location of the Bulge Center is not important at the moment. We use Motion Math to fix that.

9. **Now it's time for Motion Math.** Select any of the layers in the Timeline and choose Animation ⇨ Assistant ⇨ Motion Math. The Motion Math window pops open.

10. **Click the Load button.** Locate the *toeffect.mm* Motion Math script. Adobe provides this script, which is located in the *Motion Math Scripts* folder in the After Effects application folder. Locate and select the script and click the Open button. The *toeffect.mm* script is loaded in your Motion Math window. If you read the top portion of the script, it tells you that this script is meant to translate the position attributes of one layer to the effect point attribute of another. Here we want to tie the position of the magnifying glass to the bulge center.

11. **Using the second of the two Layer menus (2), select the Magnifying glass layer.** Using the second of the two Property menus (2), select the Position of the layer.

12. **Using the first of the two Layer menus (1), select the Text layer.** Using the first of the two Property menus (1), select Bulge/Bulge center.

13. **Click the Apply button.** The Motion Math script runs and creates corresponding keyframes for the bulge center to follow the position of the magnifying glass.

To make sure that the script achieves the desired effect, we display the correct settings for the Motion Math window in Figure 23-2.

Hopefully, this exercise gives you some idea of the power of Motion Math. For example, you can add a slight lens flare to the magnifying glass layer and then have the location of the flare move around in relation to the magnifying glass to give the glass a realistic look.

Understanding the Motion Math scripts

Motion Math scripts are nothing more than text documents written with the SimpleText utility. These scripts can be readily edited, although you should only edit the portions that are marked for you to do so.

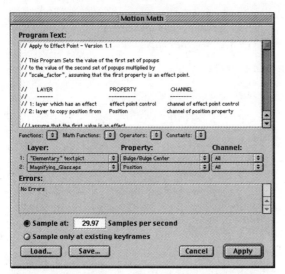

Figure 23-2: These are the correct window settings for the *toeffect.mm* script. This script is now set up to translate the position of the magnifying glass to the center of the bulge.

Figure 23-3 presents the anatomy of a simple Motion Math script.

Caution   Comments in Motion Math scripts often tell you what the key variables are, such as a scale factor that you can edit directly. However, beware that when editing the scale factor indicated by 1.0, for example, you must maintain consistency regarding any decimal points. Entering 2 instead of 2.0 where the 1.0 is located will return an error when the script is run.

Adobe provides you with numerous useful Motion Math scripts, all of which are available to you when you install After Effects. These scripts are placed in the Motion Math Scripts folder, which is located in the After Effects application folder. To load these scripts, you need to be in the Motion Math window and click the Load button. At that point, you need to navigate to the correct folder, select the script and click the Open button. The script that you select is then loaded into the Motion Math window.

If you surf the Web, you will find many free and useful Motion Math scripts. After Effects users write and freely exchange them.

Indicates how to set popup 1

" / / " indicates a line of comments that do not run in the script

Name and version of the script   Describes what the script does

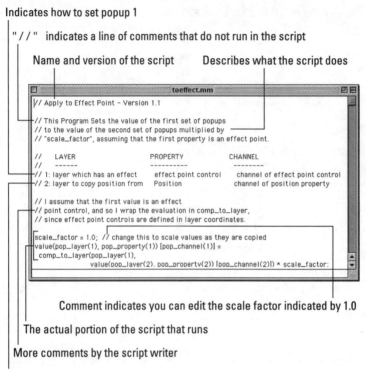

```
toeffect.mm

// Apply to Effect Point - Version 1.1

// This Program Sets the value of the first set of popups
// to the value of the second set of popups multiplied by
// "scale_factor", assuming that the first property is an effect point.

//    LAYER                PROPERTY              CHANNEL
//    -----                --------              -------
// 1: layer which has an effect    effect point control    channel of effect point control
// 2: layer to copy position from   Position               channel of position property

// I assume that the first value is an effect
// point control, and so I wrap the evaluation in comp_to_layer,
// since effect point controls are defined in layer coordinates.

scale_factor = 1.0;  // change this to scale values as they are copied
value(pop_layer(1), pop_property(1)) [pop_channel(1)] =
comp_to_layer(pop_layer(1),
              value(pop_layer(2), pop_property(2)) [pop_channel(2)]) * scale_factor;
```

Comment indicates you can edit the scale factor indicated by 1.0

The actual portion of the script that runs

More comments by the script writer

Indicates how to set popup 2

Figure 23-3: Look at the anatomy of a Motion Math script. Notice how tiny the actual math portion is. The rest of the script consists of comment lines.

Before we dive into more step exercises that use Motion Math scripts, check out the list of Adobe Motion Math scripts and their functions:

✦ **frmeffect.mm (Apply from Effect Point):** This script copies the values of an effect point from one layer, multiplies them by a scale factor, and then automatically creates position keyframes in a second layer by using the derived values. What that means is that it's a great way to copy the effect point, for example the center of a lens flare, to create position keyframes for a second layer.

✦ **toeffect.mm (Apply to Effect Point):** This script is a somewhat inverted version of the *frmeffect.mm* script. It copies the horizontal/vertical or both position values of one layer, multiplies them by a scale factor, and then creates specified effect keyframes in a second layer by using the newly derived values. In the last step exercise, we used this script to tie the position of a moving layer to the center of a bulge effect. You can also use this script to create motion keyframes for a small dummy solid by using the Motion Sketch Keyframe Assistant. Using Motion Math, you can then tie the motion of the solid to any effect point that you choose, such as a producer point for a particle effect, for example.

Tip

Both the *frmeffect.mm* and the *toeffect.mm* scripts are a bit outdated in the sense that you can now simply highlight the position keyframes of any layer, choose Edit ⇨ Copy and then select the animation channel of any effect point by choosing Edit ⇨ Paste. This way you can cut the position keyframes of any layer and apply them to any effect point and vice versa. We used this same process in the last step exercise of Chapter 22 when we copied and pasted the position keyframes between different effect points. In earlier versions of After Effects, the *frmeffect.mm* and the *toeffect.mm* scripts were the only way of accomplishing this result.

✦ **blink.mm (Blink):** Very simply, this script makes your layer blink by cycling through some pre-programmed opacity percentages. This provides a very cool and elegant way to simulate blinking lights, neon signs, and so on. This is one of those scripts that only needs a single layer. Select your layer, choose Animation ⇨ Keyframe Assistant ⇨ Motion Math, and then load the *blink.mm* script. Simply click Apply, and that's all. Your layer blinks away.

On the DVD-ROM

To see an example of the *blink.mm* script, take a look at the *MM-Blink* comp in the *Chapter 23.aep* project. You find this project in the *Project Files/Chapter 23* folder. As a reminder, you need to copy the *Source Material* folder from the DVD-ROM to your hard drive.

✦ **cmpaud.mm (Comp Audio):** You can use this script to translate the amplitude of the combined audio of all layers in a comp and apply it to an effect point. You can set the scale factor by which you want to multiply the resulting amplitude. Bear in mind that this script combines the audio for all layers in a comp. If you want to work off of a single layer of audio in a comp full of audio layers, use the *layeraud.mm* script, described in the next section.

On the DVD-ROM

To see an example of the *cmpaud.mm* script, view the *MM-Comp Audio* comp in the *Chapter 23.aep* project. This project can be found in the *Project Files/Chapter 23* folder. As a reminder, you need to copy the *Source Material* folder from the DVD-ROM to your hard drive.

✦ **copyvalu.mm (Copy Values):** This is the default script after the Motion Math window first opens. This script copies the selected property value from one layer, multiplies it by a scale factor, and applies the new derived values to a second layer.

✦ **dbspring.mm (Double Spring):** This script enables you to simulate the motion of two objects attached to either end of a spring. To make this script work out well, start out by creating a motion for one of the layers. This initial motion is used as the velocity for the layers involved.

✦ **gravity.mm (Gravity):** This script applies both a gravitational and frictional force to a layer of your choice. Sounds simple, but it's a lot of fun! The key factor is that this script requires an initial velocity to get going. So, first apply two position keyframes to your layer, just one frame apart. The farther you set the position of the layer between these two keyframes, the more initial velocity the layer has. Then apply the gravity script to this layer and watch the ensuing fun.

On the DVD-ROM

To see an example of the *gravity.mm* script, view the *MM-Gravity* comp in the *Chapter 23.aep* project. You can find this project in the *Project Files/Chapter 23* folder. As a reminder, you need to copy the *Source Material* folder from the DVD-ROM to your hard drive.

✦ **layeraud.mm (Layer Audio):** Using this script, you can translate the amplitude of the audio of a single layer and apply it to a property of your choice in another layer. Also, you can edit a scale factor. This is necessary because the amplitude may not be strong enough to translate to any meaningful values. Using the scale factor, you can amplify the final effect and still retain its relative relationship to the audio.

✦ **pointat.mm (Point At):** This script enables you to create rotation keyframes for one layer while keeping the top of its Y-axis continually pointing at the anchor point of another layer. This script works even if both the layers are moving.

✦ **cornpin.mm (Relative Corner to Absolute Corner):** The *cornpin.mm* script sets the motion path of the layer on the position of the corner-pin keyframes instead of on the anchor point. To put it another way, this Motion Math script makes the motion paths of the corner pins relative to the composition.

✦ **scaleall.mm (Scale All Layers):** This is a handy script if you want to scale both the size and the position of all the layers in a comp by the same amount.

✦ **scaleby.mm (Scale Layers by Comp Size):** This script is needed if you have changed the size of the comp midstream and need to resize your layers proportionally. It scales all layers and appropriately changes their positions as well.

✦ **span.mm (Span):** Working with three layers, you can attach each end of the third layer to the anchor point of two layers that are in motion. This script creates position, rotation, and scale keyframes for the third layer.

✦ **spring.mm (Spring):** Creates the effect of two layers attached to one another by a spring that runs between them. You need to create a positional animation for the first layer before you apply this script because it creates position keyframes for one of the two layers.

✦ **stereops.mm (Stereo Positioning):** This script takes the audio levels from popup 1 and sets them to the x-position coordinates of the layer in popup 2.

✦ **parallax.mm (Copy Relative Values):** This script multiples the relative values of a property in one layer by a scale factor and applies them to a second layer. You can use this script to simulate a parallax effect, visible through the window of a moving car or train when objects in the distance seem to move less than ones that are closer.

On the DVD-ROM

To see an example of the *parallax.mm* script, take a look at the *MM-Parallax* comp in the *Chapter 23.aep* project. You can find this project in the *Project Files/Chapter 23* folder. As a reminder, you need to copy the *Source Material* folder from the DVD-ROM to your hard drive.

✦ **layer audio remap.mm (Layer audio to time remap):** This script sets the value of popup 1 to the audio level of popup 2, scaled to lie within the range specified in the min and max settings.

Tip

The Motion Math scripts are nothing more than text documents created in SimpleText. By opening them, you can read the first few lines of comments to learn what the scripts are intended to do.

Modifying Motion Math Scripts

More often than not, you will use the Motion Math scripts exactly as they were written; however, there will be times when you'll need to modify or edit these scripts just a bit. This kind of operator input is minimal and is often required to properly tweak the final results. Most of the time, the number that you'll be editing is the scale factor of your Motion Math script. Keep in mind that any variable you can edit in the Motion Math script is indicated by both a // symbol and a comment by the writer of the script as to when and how to change that variable.

For example, in the *blink.mm* Motion Math script, you see the following lines:

```
blink_speed = 1; // blinks per second
low_opacity = 10.0; // low opacity value
high_opacity = 90.0; // high opacity value
```

What these lines are telling you is that if you change the `blink speed = 1;` line to `blink_speed = 3;` you will get three blinks per second. Similarly, you can modify the values of the low opacity and the high opacity by changing the numbers in front of them.

Caution

Again, we must warn you that before you modify any values in a Motion Math script, be aware that you must follow the number format used in the script. For example, if the value indicated is "10.0", then you must respect the format and enter values, such as "1.0", "5.5", and so on. If the numbering format indicated is "1", then you must use a similar format, such as "2" or "3" and so on. Using a "10" where "10.0" is indicated (or vice versa) will return an error, and your script won't run.

In the next series of steps, we work through a Motion Math script and edit it slightly to achieve our desired results.

To better explain the mysteries of Motion Math, we created an After Effects project that includes a composition for each series of steps that we cover in the chapter. Just as a reminder, you need to copy the *Source Material* folder from the DVD-ROM to your hard drive. Our own corresponding After Effects project is called *Chapter 23.aep* and is found in the *Project Files/Chapter 23* folder. For the next series of steps, you should look at the composition called *MM-Layer Audio*.

STEPS: Modifying the *layeraud.mm* (Layer Audio) Script

1. **Choose Composition ⇨ New Compostion and create a new comp.**

2. **Drag the following two items from the Project window into the Timeline window; the *snare beat.mov* is an audio file that consists of a drum beat, and the *Snowflake1.ai* is an Illustrator file of a snowflake.**

3. **Select any one of the layers and then choose Animation ⇨ Keyframe Assistant ⇨ Motion Math.** The Motion Math window is presented to you.

4. **By default, After Effects loads the *copyvalu.mm* script into the Motion Math window; however, we need to load the *layeraud.mm* script.** Click the load button and navigate to your Motion Math Scripts folder, which is located in the After Effects application folder. Locate the *layeraud.mm* script and click Open. The script loads into the Motion Math window. FYI: The *layeraud.mm* script translates the amplitude of audio from a layer into any other property for a layer.

5. **In your following pop-up menus, select the *snare beat.mov* layer in the popup 2 menu.** This is the bottom pop-up menu. For the Property popup for 2, select Audio Levels. (In fact, this is the only property available to you for an audio layer.) Recall that the popup 2 menu is the FROM menu, meaning we want to copy the Audio Levels property FROM the *snare beat.mov* layer and affect the layer that we select in the popup 1 menu.

6. **Next, select the *Snowflake1.ai* layer in the popup 1 menu, which is located just above the popup 2 menu.** For the Property menu for this layer, click it and select Scale. You see that you have many other properties to choose from. What we've just done is to tell Motion Math to use the Audio Levels of the drum beat to affect the scale changes in the snowflake layer.

7. **Now it's time to slightly edit this script.** Notice that the first two lines of the script set the maximum and the minimum value change that will occur.

```
max = 1000; // change this to the maximum value
min = 50; // change this to the minimum value
```

Edit the max setting to 10000 and the min to 0 from 50. By editing these minimum and maximum values, we modify the range of the scale changes in the snowflake. It then allows for much larger scale values than the ones we would get had we used the script in its unedited state.

Figure 23-4 shows the state of the Motion Math window as it should appear after Step 7.

Popup menu 1

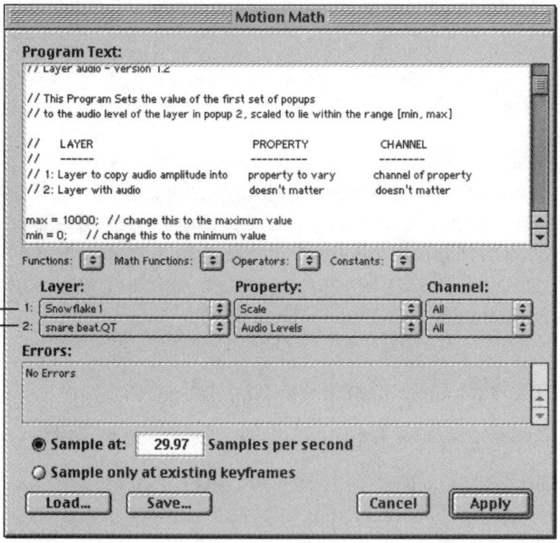

Popup menu 2

Figure 23-4: Here we are preparing to apply the *layeraud.mm* script after making some modifications to the values in it. Note the state of the pop-up menus at the bottom.

8. **Click the Apply button.** The script runs and creates scale keyframes for the snowflake layer.

9. **Play down your comp, and you see that the snowflake layer grows very large and then very small in response to the audio levels of the drum beat.** If these scale changes are not to your satisfaction, you can modify the numbers for the min and the max values and reapply the Motion Math script. Keep doing this until you like what you see.

Working with Scripts That Require Input

Certain Motion Math scripts require some input before they can be run successfully. For example, the *gravity.mm* script requires that you create an initial velocity for a layer. This initial velocity is then used as a basis for creating the effect of gravity on that layer. It all sounds fancier than it really is. All you need to do is to create motion for the layer. By setting two different keyframes for the layer's position, you create the required initial motion for the layer, at which point you can apply the gravity script. This script uses the speed of the layer between the two position keyframes as the initial velocity, and then it creates the effect of gravity for the layer. Another notable feature of the *gravity.mm* script is that this script only requires a single layer.

In the next few steps, we show you exactly how this works.

To better explain Motion Math, we created an After Effects project that includes a composition for each series of steps that we cover in the chapter. Just as a reminder, you need to copy the *Source Material* folder from the DVD-ROM to your hard drive. Our own corresponding After Effects project is called *Chapter 23.aep* and is found in the *Project Files/Chapter 23* folder. For the next series of steps, you should look at the composition called *MM-Gravity*.

STEPS: Working with the Gravity Script

1. **Choose Composition ⇨ New Compostion and create a new comp.**

2. **Next, create a New Solid.** Choose Layer ⇨ New ⇨ Solid and set the Solid size to the size of your comp by clicking the Make Comp Size button in the Solid Settings dialog box. You can select any color you like.

3. **Drag the *Eight_Ball.eps* footage item from the Project window into the Comp window, placing it in the upper-right side of the comp.** This is an Illustrator file of a billiard ball. If your background for the comp is black, you may have trouble seeing the outline of the ball. If this is a problem, choose Composition ⇨ Background Color and change the background to gray.

4. **Press the Home key to make sure you are at the first frame of the comp.** Set a position keyframe for the eight ball so that at 0:00:00:00, the ball is at the upper-right corner of the comp. You can quickly set a position keyframe by selecting the layer and using the Option/Alt+P keyboard shortcut.

5. **Move forward one frame by pressing Command/Ctrl+Right Arrow.**

6. **Now, move the eight ball to the lower-left corner of the comp.** A second position keyframe automatically is set. Play the comp and make sure this is the case. The eight ball should move from the top-right corner of the comp to the lower-left corner of the comp in one frame. What you just did by setting these two position keyframes is provide an initial velocity that the Motion Math script will put to use.

7. **Time for some more Motion Math — Select the eight ball layer and choose Animation ⇨ Keyframe Assistant ⇨ Motion Math.** The Motion Math window is presented to you.

8. **By default, After Effects loads the *copyvalu.mm* script into the Motion Math window.** However, we need to load the *gravity.mm* script. Click the Load button and navigate to your Motion Math Scripts folder, which is located in the After Effects application folder. Locate the *gravity.mm* script and click Open. The script loads into the Motion Math window.

9. **Read the comments at the top of the *gravity.mm* script, and you realize how easy it is to put it to work.** All you need to do is select the eight ball layer in the top popup 1 menu. None of the other pop-up menus matter. So, click the Layer popup 1 menu and select the eightball layer. Leave all other settings as they are, for now.

10. **Click the Apply button.** The script runs, and after it's finished, you can play down your comp. You will notice that your eight ball shoots off to the lower-left and continues to bounce around as if it's under the influence of gravity. Fun, no? Check out Figure 23-5.

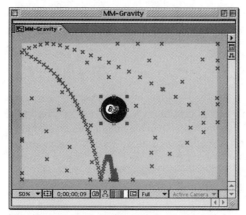

Figure 23-5: The eight ball bounces around the comp after we set an initial velocity and apply the *gravity.mm* Motion Math script to it.

 Tip

Notice that the *gravity.mm* script contains the following lines:

```
damping = 0.95; // Damping force (0 = infinite friction,
1 = none)
grav = 0.9; // magnitude of gravity force
grav_dir = {0,1,0}; // direction of gravity
```

By changing any of these values, you can control the damping, gravity force, and the gravity direction that the script produces.

Understanding the Blink Script

The Blink script is another example of a script that requires only a single layer. Like the others we've looked at so far, you can edit it to make changes to the properties of the blinking behavior. See Figure 23-6.

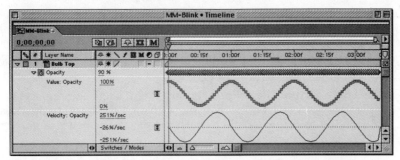

Figure 23-6: Applying the *blink.mm* Motion Math script to the *Bulb Top/Light Bulb.eps* layer uses a smooth cosine curve for the opacity values of the layer, resulting in a blinking lightbulb.

This script, when applied, makes your layer blink by varying the opacity of the layer using values derived from a smooth cosine curve.

To better explain the mysteries of Motion Math, we created an After Effects project that includes a composition for each series of steps that we cover in the chapter. Just as a reminder, you need to copy the *Source Material* folder from the DVD-ROM to your hard drive. Our own corresponding After Effects project is called *Chapter 23.aep* and is found in the *Project Files/Chapter 23* folder. For the next series of steps, have a look at the composition called *MM-Blink*.

STEPS: Using the Blink Script

1. **Choose Composition ➪ New Compostion and create a new comp.**

2. **Drag the *Bulb Base/Light Bulb.eps* and the *Bulb Top/Light Bulb.eps* layers from the Project window into the Comp window.** Arrange them so that they form a lightbulb. *Clue:* Base goes at the bottom, and Top goes at the top.

3. **Select the *Bulb Top/Light Bulb.eps* layer and then choose Animation ➪ Keyframe Assistant ➪ Motion Math.** The Motion Math window is presented to you.

4. **By default, After Effects loads the *copyvalu.mm* script into the Motion Math window.** We need to load the *blink.mm* script. Click the Load button and navigate to your *Motion Math Scripts* folder, which is located in the After Effects application folder. Locate the *blink.mm* script and click Open. The script loads into the Motion Math window.

5. **Using this script is easy; just select the layer that you want to blink in the popup 1, which is the top pop-up menu of the two menus.** In this case, you simply have to select the *Bulb Top/Light Bulb.eps* layer in the popup 1 menu.

6. **At this point, you can simply click the Apply button, and after the script has finished running, your bulb top blinks in a nice smooth fashion.** However, you may also notice the following lines in the script while it's loaded in the Motion Math window:

```
blink_speed = 1; // blinks per second
low_opacity = 10.0; // low opacity value
high_opacity = 90.0; // high opacity value
```

If you want the bulb to blink more than once a second (for example, how about three times a second?), change `blink speed = 1;` to `blink speed = 3;`. Also, you may notice that because the low opacity is set to a value of `10.0`, the bulb never goes completely out. By changing `low opacity = 10.0;` to `low opacity = 0.0;`, you can make the bulb go to 100 percent darkness. Furthermore, if you want the bulb to light up to 100 percent brightness, change `high opacity = 90.0;` to `high opacity = 100.0;`.

Understanding the Parallax Script

The next series of steps use a fabulous Motion Math script called *parallax.mm*. This script takes a set of values from one layer's properties, multiplies it by a scale factor and then applies the derived values to another layer's properties. What does all that mean? Well, there are times when you need to figure out relative values for a layer. For example, say that one layer is fading up or down, and you need another layer to fade in and out half as fast or twice as slow. In short, you need to calculate values relative to some other values. For accomplishing such tasks, this script is of great value.

In the next exercise, we show you how you can simply create a neat parallax type effect by applying this script and editing the scale factor. To understand the parallax effect, imagine that you're in a moving train and looking out the window. The telephone poles and the trees nearest to the train move by really quickly, a bit farther away the river moves by a bit more slowly, while the mountains on the horizon seem to move very slowly.

You can achieve the same kind of varying motion using the *parallax.mm* script.

On the DVD-ROM For the next series of steps, look at the composition called *MM-Parallex-Final*. This comp is found in the After Effects project called *Chapter 23.aep* and is found in the *Project Files/Chapter 23* folder. We also laid out the layers for you in a comp called *MM-Parallex-Clean*. In this comp, the layers are laid out for you without any animation. We suggest starting with the *MM-Parallex-Clean* comp and following along with the steps.

STEPS: Using the Parallax Script

1. **Choose Composition ⇨ New Compostion and create a new comp.** Alternatively, you can use the *MM-Parallax-Clean* comp. This comp has all the layers already laid out for you without any animation.

2. **In this comp, you need to lay out the following layers: Land and Sky, Large Cloud, Mesa, Mountains, Small Cloud, and Tree.**

Note These layers are found in the *Western_Scene.eps* folder, located in the *Chapter 23.aep* project.

3. **Lay out these layers in the comp to create a vista.** To help make things easier, follow these guidelines: The Tree layer should be closest, while the Land and Sky should be at the very back. The rest of the layers should be laid out in the order of their proximity. Under the Tree layer, you should have Mesa, then Small Cloud, Large Cloud, and then Mountains.

4. **In order for us to create relative values, we first have to create one set of values from which we derive the relative ones.** Create a motion for the Tree layer. Set a position keyframe at 0:0000:00 so that the tree is off to the left side of the comp. Set another position keyframe at 0:00:05:00 so that the tree is off to the right side of the comp. Play the comp and check to make sure that in five seconds, your tree enters the comp from the left side and goes off the right side. Okay, now we have created our first set of values. Now use Motion Math to derive the relative values and apply them to the rest of the layers.

5. **Select the tree layer and choose Animation ⇨ Keyframe Assistant ⇨ Motion Math.** The Motion Math window is presented to you.

6. **By default, After Effects loads the *copyvalu.mm* script into the Motion Math window.** We need to load the *parallax.mm* script. Click the Load button and navigate to your Motion Math Scripts folder, which is located in the After Effects application folder. Locate the *parallax.mm* script and click Open. The script loads into the Motion Math window.

7. **Next up, we have to set the pop-up menus.** In the Layer popup 1, select the Mesa layer. For the Property popup 1, select Position. For the Layer popup 2, select the Tree layer, and for the property popup 2, select Position. Remember that popup 2 is the FROM menu, while popup 1 is the TO menu. In short, we are telling the *parallax.mm* script to take the Position values from the Tree layer and apply them to the Mesa layer.

8. **Now, scroll down into the text of the Motion Math script until you see the following line of code:**

```
scale_factor = 1.0; // > 1 means scale up, < 1 means scale
down
```

What this line specifies is the scale factor, which is currently set to 1.0. What this means is that if you click the Apply button right now, the Mesa layer is going to move just as fast as the Tree layer. That isn't what we want, so we need to edit the scale factor.

9. **Edit the scale factor so that it changes from** `scale factor = 1.0;` **to** `scale_factor = 0.50;`.

Figure 23-7 shows the final state of the Motion Math window before you apply the *parallax.mm* script.

Edit the scale factor here

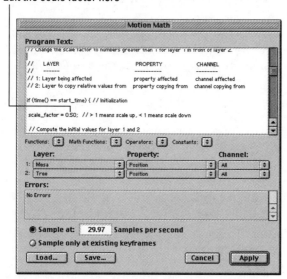

Figure 23-7: The state of the Motion Math window. We are using the motion of the Tree to create new motion values for the Mesa, only at half the speed.

10. **Now click the Apply button and the script runs and creates position keyframes for the Mesa layer.**

11. **Play down your comp and you see that the Mesa layer is moving relative to the Tree layer, but half as fast.**

12. **Select the Tree layer again and choose Animation ⇨ Keyframe Assistant ⇨ Motion Math.** The Motion Math window is presented to you. The *parallax.mm* script is still loaded.

13. **Now, we have to set the pop-up menus.** In the Layer popup 1 menu, select the Mountain layer. In the Property popup 1 menu, select Position. In the Layer popup 2 menu, select the Tree layer, and in the Property popup 2 menu, select Position. Popup 2 is the FROM menu, while popup 1 is the TO menu. We are telling the *parallax.mm* script to take the Position values from the Tree layer and apply them to the Mountain layer.

14. **We need to edit our scale factor at this stage.** Change the scale factor from `scale factor = 0.50;` to `scale factor = 0.25;`. What we just did is to tell the Mountain layer to move at a quarter of the speed that the Tree is moving. This makes sense; objects that are farther away appear to move more slowly.

15. **Click the Apply button.** The script runs and creates position keyframes for the Mountain layer. Return to your comp, play it down, and you see that now the Tree, Mesa, and Mountain layers are moving, but they do so relative to one another.

16. **Next we have to set up the two clouds to move properly.** Once again, select the Tree layer and choose Animation ⇨ Keyframe Assistant ⇨ Motion Math. The Motion Math window is presented to you. The *parallax.mm* script is still loaded.

17. **In the Layer popup 1 menu, select the Large Cloud layer.** In the Property popup 1 menu, select Position. In the Layer popup 2 menu, select the Tree layer, and in the Property popup 2 menu, select Position. Popup 2 is the FROM menu, while popup 1 is the TO menu. We are telling the *parallax.mm* script to take the Position values from the Tree layer and apply them to the Large Cloud layer.

18. **Make sure that the scale factor is set to** `scale factor = 0.25;`. We are telling the Large Cloud layer to move at quarter of the speed that the Tree is moving.

19. **Click the Apply button.** The script runs and creates position keyframes for the Large Cloud layer. Return to your comp, play it down, and you see that the Tree, Mesa, Mountain, and Large Cloud layers are all moving, each relative to one another.

We leave the very last stage of this exercise to you. You still have the Small Cloud layer left to move. Apply the *parallax.mm* script again, taking care to select the Small Cloud layer in the popup 1 menu and edit the scale factor to 0.10. At the end of these steps, you'll have a Western scene as if seen from the window of a moving train.

Without Motion Math, life in After Effects would be dull indeed.

The key here is to experiment with all of these scripts. Remember to carefully read all the comments, and then see what you can do. If you start working with Motion Math on a regular basis, you'll be able to say "Yes!" more often when clients ask you if you can animate their logo every which way but loose.

Make a point of hitting the Web in search of additions to your Motion Math Scripts library. Who knows? If you're feeling inspired, you may start to write them yourself.

✦   ✦   ✦

Adding the Third Dimension to Your Design

◆ ◆ ◆ ◆

In This Chapter

Using 3D on 2D objects

Using cameras

Adding lights

Working with Null objects

◆ ◆ ◆ ◆

After Effects has long been thought of as one of the best 2D compositing tools around. As far as software-only solutions are concerned, it can't be beat. To be sure, you can get faster results from a proprietary hardware system such as those offered by Quantel, but prices for those setups are measured in hundreds of thousands of dollars! The cost of going to a high-end post-shop and renting a few hours on one of these machines can equal that of a fully functional desktop video setup. That's one of the reasons After Effects is so revered, and rightfully so.

FACT: If you've got some talent, you can make clients happy with a reasonably fast off-the-shelf computer, a video-editing application such as Final Cut Pro or Premiere, and the Production Bundle of After Effects. Obviously, barriers to entering the field become a lot less prohibitive if you can create high-quality broadcast designs with a PC or a Mac. Free from the constraints of incredibly expensive gear, the market has certainly become a bit more populated and competitive. The venerable economist Adam "Invisible Hand" Smith would argue that's a good thing, and we would agree with him. Furthermore, if Adobe continues its commitment to developing and improving future builds of After Effects, the state of affairs will continue to improve. Of course, this sometimes results in dramatic changes to the software, because the pace of change in the market for motion graphic design in video and film is literally mind-blowing. A recent example of a revolutionary change is the addition of features like 16-bit color or 3D.

Yes, that's right. After Effects, that champion of a 2D workhorse, has rather suddenly become a 3D program. This isn't to say that it compares or competes with Maya, Lightwave, or ElectricImage, but it's still pretty cool. The biggest beef that designers tend to have about Adobe's implementation of 3D in

After Effects centers around the fact that it applies 3D to 2D objects. A typical question sounds something like, "What's the big deal with 3D if you're moving objects that don't have any depth?" While this is a legitimate question, the integration of this peculiar brand of 3D is surprisingly powerful. Sadly, After Effects is no longer the intuitively simple thing it once was, but neither are desktop graphics, or the world for that matter. This richly featured 3D capability includes such wonders as cameras, lights, and shadows, to name a few. Hang in there with this stuff. Even if you're a pro with other 3D applications, it's a little tricky at first, but it grows on you.

Introducing 3D

So, to get started using the new 3D capabilities of After Effects, make a new comp, place a layer of footage in it, and turn on that layer's 3D switch (it's in the switches column, and it looks like a cube). If you keep your eyes fixed on the Comp window, you might say, "Big deal. Nothing happens. So what? So much for 3D."

Fair enough. Indeed, nothing seems to happen, but actually, you've paved the way for a lot of interesting things to take place. First of all, look at the difference in the amount of transformational properties you can adjust in the Timeline (see Figure 24-1). You also have a new subheading full of Material Options properties. We cover those later. For now, you should focus on understanding the additional Transform properties.

Welcome to Z-space

First of all, the position and anchor point properties now include a third coordinate. This is the Z-coordinate, or the depth coordinate if you're new to 3D. X and Y are measured from the upper-left corner of the composition, and the Z-coordinate measures the distance from the virtual "camera" of the Comp window. A negative z-value positions the layer closer to you, whereas a positive z-value places it further away.

Instead of one rotation property, you now have four. Z-Rotation behaves like the rotation property you used to have in 2D space. Changes to the X- and Y-Rotation rotate the layer around its X- and Y-axes. Scrub each of these values, and it should be pretty clear how the different rotational properties work. As though that weren't enough, you also have the Orientation property. The three Orientation fields operate identically to the Rotation properties in that they control X-, Y-, and Z-Rotation, but their values can only be set within a range of 360 degrees. In other words, you can't keyframe multiple revolutions for these properties. Clarifying the difference between Orientation and Rotation should become easier as you make your way through the next several sections of the chapter.

The key to getting the most out of 3D space lies in taking advantage of all the different views of your composition. As soon as you turn on a layer's 3D switch, you can switch your view so that you're looking at it from any angle you like. After you become comfortable with the multiple 3D views, you'll start to get appreciable results for your efforts.

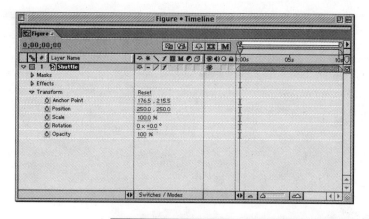

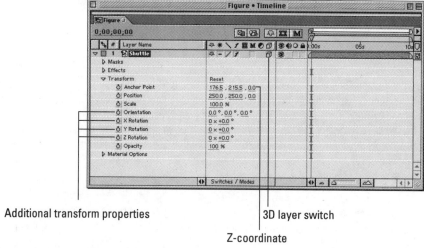

Additional transform properties   3D layer switch

Z-coordinate

Figure 24-1: If you turn on a layer's 3D switch, you'll see quite a few changes to its list of Transform properties.

Adjusting a 3D layer's Position and Rotation

You can change a layer's Position, Rotation, or Orientation by scrubbing its various property values in the Timeline, but moving a 3D layer in the Comp window is easier and more intuitive. You probably noticed that the layer's Anchor Point looks different, and if so, your observations are absolutely correct. Now that it's a 3D layer, its anchor point has three colored arrows sticking out of it. The red arrow represents the X-axis, the green arrow represents the Y-axis, and the blue arrow represents the Z-axis. Because you're looking at the layer head-on, the blue arrow looks more like a blue splotch. It becomes easier to see when you change your view of the comp, but we aren't going to do that just yet. When you move a 3D layer in the Comp window, you can drag it either on its axes or directly on the layer itself.

Working in 3D

The Wireframe Interactions and Draft 3D buttons at the top of the Timeline window (see Figure SB 24-1) have the potential to be a little confusing.

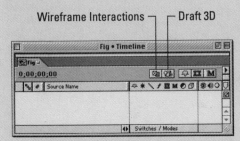

Figure SB 24-1: The Wireframe Interactions and Draft 3D buttons are located at the top of the Timeline Window.

If you enable Wireframe Interactions, whenever you move a layer, you won't get a dynamic preview in the Comp window. Instead, you'll only see the layer's wireframe. If you're in the process of building a deeply layered and sophisticated animation, the act of dragging layers around can be excruciatingly slow as your processor grinds out the math necessary to render the image. Basically, you should turn this switch on if positioning elements becomes too laborious.

If you turn on the Draft 3D switch, all lights and any shadows they might create will not be rendered. This is a great feature if you start to add a lot of these elements to your comp. We find that you want to leave this switch on when laying out your lights and cameras at first, but as you continue working, you'll definitely want to turn it off after you have a good idea what things look like. Rendering a single frame of a complex 3D animation with lots of shadows and camera moves can take up to 30 seconds. Moving a light a few pixels in any direction can really slow your creative process down to a complete standstill, so take comfort in knowing that Draft 3D mode exists, and use it on an as needed basis.

Using the Selection tool, place your pointer over the layer's Anchor Point. As you move it over each of these colored arrows, the pointer indicates which axis you'll be moving the layer on should you decide to click and drag at that moment (see Figure 24-2). Go ahead and drag the layer, doing so along a different axis each time. Moving it along its Z-axis might not produce a very visible result, and if you want to see a pronounced change to the layer's Z-coordinate, hold down the Shift key as you drag, and the layer moves in increments of 10 pixels.

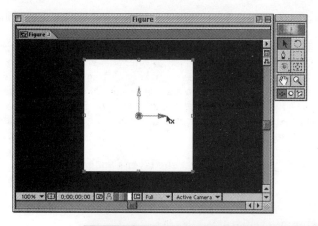

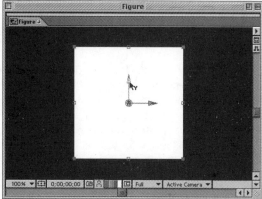

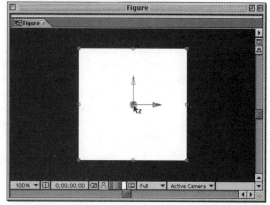

Figure 24-2: Use the Selection tool in the Comp window to move a 3D layer along any axis that you want.

Caution   In the 2D way of thinking, holding down the Shift key as you drag a layer constrains its positional change to either the horizontal or vertical plane; however, when you drag a 3D layer along one of its axes, adding the Shift key changes the layer's position in units of 10 pixels as opposed to one. This is a pretty different way of thinking, so take note of it. Here's one way to keep it straight in your mind's eye: As soon as you drag a 3D layer along an axis, its positional change is already limited to the axis you're moving it on, so in this instance, the Shift key behaves differently. 2D and 3D are different headspaces, and we admit that it takes a little while to get used to combining them.

Using the Rotate tool, position your pointer over the layer's anchor point once again. Using the same method as you did with the Selection tool, move the pointer over each of these colored arrows, and it will indicate which axis you'll be rotating the layer around if you decide to click and drag at that moment (see Figure 24-3). Practice rotating the layer around each axis.

Note   In this case, adding the Shift key limits the rotational change to multiples of 45 degrees.

Actually, in this particular instance, you're changing the Orientation values of the layer, not the Rotation values. When working in 3D, the Rotate tool has a hidden mode, which you can enable by Option/Alt+clicking it in the Tools palette. Its icon in the Tools palette now resembles one of those things you have to stick inside a 45 rpm single record to play it properly on a phonograph (see Figure 24-4). In short, when the Rotate tool looks like the 2D rotate tool, it changes a 3D layer's Orientation. When it looks like a three-headed snake, then it changes a 3D layer's Rotation values. What's the difference? While they appear to do the same thing, Rotation can be keyframed for multiple revolutions, whereas Orientation is measured only in terms of 360 relative degrees.

At this point, we should mention that you don't need to be positioned over a layer's axes (the three colored arrows) to change its Position, Orientation, or Rotation. For example, if you position the selection tool over a 3D layer and start dragging it around the Comp window, you'll change its X- and Y-coordinates as though it were a 2D layer. If you click and drag on a layer with either one of the rotation tools, the layer will rotate in all three dimensions simultaneously. You can also reposition the Anchor Point of a layer as you would in 2D space. Simply select the Pan Behind tool from the Tools palette, position the tool over the little circle in the middle of the layer, and click and drag it wherever you want.

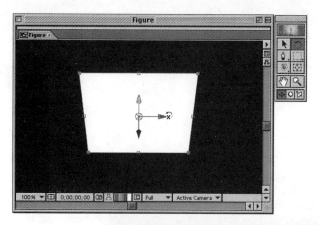

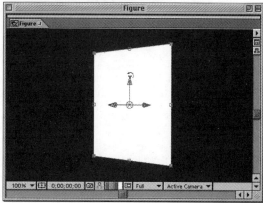

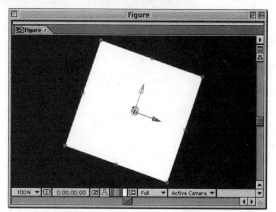

Figure 24-3: Use the Rotate tool in the Comp window to rotate a 3D layer along any axis that you choose.

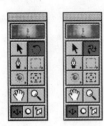

Figure 24-4: The Rotate tool has two modes for rotating a 3D layer. In its original state, the Rotate tool modifies a layer's Orientation (left). Option/Alt+click it to see it in its secondary state, which you can use to change a layer's Rotation (right).

This all seems simple enough, but pay close attention to the following: The kind of change you make to a layer's Position, Anchor Point, Orientation, or Rotation is entirely dependent upon your view of the composition as well as the axis mode you choose from the Tools palette. So far, you've only been moving a layer while viewing it head-on. Depending on how you change your View, dragging a layer in the Comp window can get pretty interesting. We discuss views and axis modes in the following two sections.

Using the different views

As we mentioned earlier, your 3D work starts to fall in line after you begin to master the multiple views and axis modes. After you turn on a layer's 3D switch, click the Comp window pop-up menu to see all the different angles from which you can view your composition (see Figure 24-5).

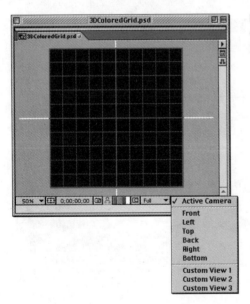

Figure 24-5: The pop-up menu in the Comp window provides a list of all the 3D views under your control.

In the next set of steps, you begin putting the various 3D views to work.

On the DVD-ROM

In order to better explain 3D, we created an After Effects project that includes a composition for each set of steps that we cover in the chapter. Just as a reminder, you need to copy the *Source Material* folder from the DVD-ROM to your hard drive. The After Effects project that corresponds to this chapter is called *Chapter 24.aep* and can be found in the *Project Files/Chapter 24* folder. For the following exercise, we refer to a Photoshop file we created that's called *3DColoredGrid.psd*.

STEPS: Working with Views

1. **Double-click in the Project window.** This brings up the Import File dialog box.

2. **Navigate your way to the file named *3DColoredGrid.psd* and import it as a Comp.**

3. **Double-click the newly imported composition to open it up in its own Comp and Timeline windows.**

4. **Turn on the 3D switch for all three layers.**

5. **Select the Green and Blue layers and press the R key to solo their Rotation properties.**

6. **Set the Green layer's X-Rotation to 90 degrees.**

7. **Set the Blue layer's Y-Rotation to 90 degrees.** Notice that you're changing the rotational values for these two layers until you're viewing them edge-on, at which point they seem to disappear.

8. **In the Comp window, use the View pop-up to cycle through the different 3D views (Front, Left, Top, Back, Right, and Bottom, as well as Custom View 1, Custom View 2, and Custom View 3).** See Figure 24-6 and Color Plate 24-1.

9. **After you've familiarized yourself with all the views, select Custom View 1.**

Note

The Active Camera view is a somewhat misleading name at this point. If you haven't added a camera to your 3D comp, it refers to the frontal view. The Active Camera view is the one that gets rendered if you add a comp to the Render Queue. Actually, you can't render out any of the alternative views. In order to render custom viewing angles, you need to add cameras to a comp. We explain that process toward the end of the chapter.

10. **Select the Orbit Camera tool from the Tools palette and click and drag anywhere in the Comp window (see Figure 24-7).** The Orbit Camera tool enables you to reposition your view of the three layers.

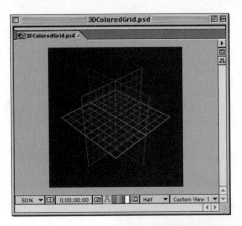

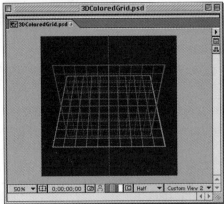

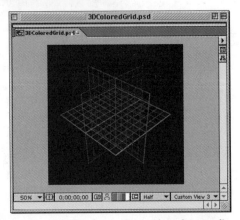

Figure 24-6: The Custom Views provide very useful visual cues toward understanding 3D space in After Effects.

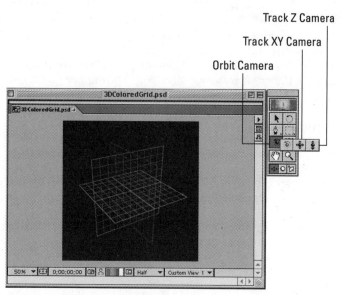

Figure 24-7: The Orbit Camera tool enables you to reposition your view of the three layers.

11. **Select the Track XY Camera tool from the Tools palette and click and drag anywhere in the Comp window.** Notice how this particular tool is limited to the X- and Y-axes relative to the camera angle.

12. **Select the Track Z Camera tool from the Tools palette and click and drag anywhere in the Comp window.** Notice how this camera tool is limited to movement on the Z-axis relative to the camera angle.

The Custom Views "remember" their points of view in a given comp. For example, whatever you did to alter Custom View 1 in Steps 10–12 are retained whenever you return to Custom View 1. Hence, the name, Custom View.

You can cycle through the Orbit, Track XY, and Track Z Camera tools by repeatedly pressing the C key.

Before we move on to axis modes, you should learn how to personalize your various views. F10, F11, and F12 can all be customized to display the view you want. The default settings for these keys are the following: F10 displays your comp from the front, F11 displays it from Custom View 1, and F12 displays the view from the currently Active Camera. Despite these initial assignments, you can associate any view that you want with these keys. If you want to change them, hold down the Shift key and press F10, F11, or F12 to reassign any one of them. In addition to these three keyboard shortcuts, the Esc key toggles your view between the current one and the last one.

Understanding the axis modes

Before you start keyframing objects in 3D space, try to understand the different axis modes. For the entire book up until now, these important looking buttons at the bottom of the Tools palette have remained gray and inactive thus far. Now that you're working in 3D, they demand your attention. They appear from left to right in the following order: Local Axis, World Axis, and View Axis.

So what exactly are these elegantly designed little icons trying to tell you? It's pretty simple, actually. The axis modes become relevant when you select a layer in the Comp window and change any of its Transform options besides Opacity. The Local Axis mode displays the axes of a layer relative to its own Orientation. The World Axis mode displays the axes of a layer relative to the world of the composition. The View Axis mode displays the axes of a layer relative to the current view.

This might sound confusing, and if so, try it out with a layer in the Comp window. First of all, skew its Orientation by dragging it a little by using the Rotate tool. Change your view to one of the custom views, and then click each of the three axis modes while keeping an eye on the layer's Anchor point (see Figure 24-8 for reference). Change a layer's position on a given axis in each of the three different modes, and you'll notice that you get different results relative to your selected axis mode.

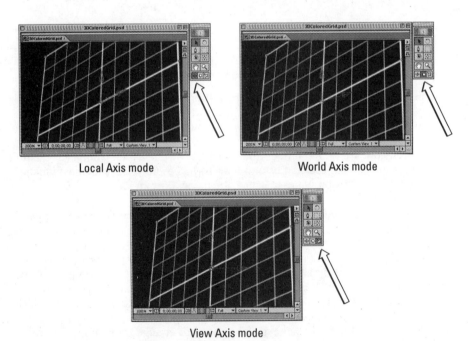

Local Axis mode   World Axis mode

View Axis mode

Figure 24-8: The axis modes set the axes of a layer relative to itself, the "world" of the comp, or the point of view from the current viewing angle. If you make changes to a layer in the Comp window, those changes occur relative to whatever axis mode you selected.

What's new in After Effects 5.5: The Grid effect

Now that After Effects 5.5 includes the Grid effect, you don't have to create grid-type graphics in Illustrator anymore. The new Grid effect generates high-quality grid textures with ease, and it's an excellent enhancement to the designer's toolbox, especially if you're looking for a quick and easy way to give a project that certain kind of "technical" feel. The large number of effect properties gives you complete control over the appearance of the grid. For starters, you can animate the dimensions of the grid's cells, the thickness of its lines, as well as its color, opacity, and transfer mode.

We decided to mention it here because we had to use Illustrator to create the grid that's shown in the figures of the first part of this chapter. If we'd had the Grid effect at our fingertips, life would have been just a little bit easier.

Note A word about Z-scale: What could changing the Z-scale of a layer accomplish if that layer has no depth? The answer lies in parenting. For example, if you make parent-child relationships between layers with different Z-coordinates, increasing the parent's Z-scale will space the parent and child layers farther apart in Z-space. If you don't believe it, try it yourself. It's definitely weird, but it actually makes sense.

Note You've probably noticed that a comp can contain 2D and 3D layers. If you turn on a layer's 3D switch and leave the other layers alone, they still behave like they used to in 2D space. No matter what your viewing angle is, 2D layers occupy the same part of the screen. The truly interesting aspect about this is the rendering order. 2D layers are rendered from the bottom of the stacking order to the top, according to their visibility. 3D layers are rendered from the layer that's farthest away from the camera to the one that's closest. If you mix these two different modes of dimensionality, you can get tripped up. For example, any 2D layer that's placed on top of any 3D layer in the stacking order of the Timeline will obscure the 3D layer. In short, if you plan on mixing these two worlds, keep the 3D layers on top of the 2D layers in the stacking order; otherwise, you won't be able to see them.

Note Regarding 3D layers and "real" 3D software versus 3D in After Effects, realize that Adobe's first crack at integrating 3D is more successful than it might initially appear. For example, if you create a polygon out of solid layers, it behaves like a polygon in other 3D apps. The only real difference is that there are no preset polygons to choose from. You have to make them yourself. Also, you can't extrude a 3D layer, not even a little. Other than these two points, 3D in After Effects is remarkably cool. If you want a point of reference, take a look at the comp called *3DBox* in the *Chapter 24.aep* project on the DVD-ROM.

Animating in 3D

Now that you've got a clear understanding of the 3D work environment, it's time to start animating layers in this new realm of the After Effects universe. Before we get ahead of ourselves, we should point out some of the peculiarities of pre-composing in 3D.

Pre-composing 3D layers

When you're doing 3D compositing, more often than not, you'll be working with large numbers of layers. Pre-composing them is especially helpful when you're trying to organize the various components of your composition. When you initially pre-compose a number of 3D layers, the newly created pre-comp layer sits in their place, but its 3D switch doesn't automatically get turned on. You might think you can easily remedy this by turning it on, but if you do, you'll see that the pre-comp's layers are flattened into the two-dimensional space of the new single pre-comp layer. Here's how to solve the problem: In addition to activating the pre-comp's 3D switch, you also have to turn on its Collapse Geometrics switch. After you do these two things, all of the 3D characteristics of the pre-comp's layers return.

Please excuse the long-winded explanation. If you find it to be confusing, here's an abbreviated recap. If you want to pre-compose a group of 3D layers, say a six-sided cube made from solids, here's what you do:

1. **Select the layers in the Timeline.**

2. **Press Command/Ctrl+Shift+C to pre-compose them and then click OK.**

3. **Turn on the new pre-comp's 3D switch.**

4. **Turn on the new pre-comp's Collapse Geometrics switch.**

Now the pre-comp behaves like a 3D cube that you can manipulate as a single object. Why do we mention this? Apart from being necessary for survival in the 3D environment, we find ourselves doing a lot of prep work before creating 3D animations. In other words, it's easier to set up your objects first and animate them later.

On the DVD-ROM

In order to better explain 3D, we created an After Effects project that includes a composition for each set of steps that we cover in the chapter. Just as a reminder, you need to copy the *Source Material* folder from the DVD-ROM to your hard drive. The After Effects project that corresponds to this chapter is called *Chapter 24.aep* and can be found in the *Project Files/Chapter 24* folder. The next exercise refers to the composition named *1-3DBox*.

STEPS: Creating a 3D Cube

1. **Create a new five second, 400 x 400, square pixel, 29.97 fps comp, and name it** *3DBox*.

2. **Create a new 200 x 200 solid.** Name it *Bottom* and color it white.

3. **Enable rulers by pressing Command/Ctrl+R and then position Guides in the comp, as shown in Figure 24-9.** You want them at the edges of the solid as well as in the center of the comp.

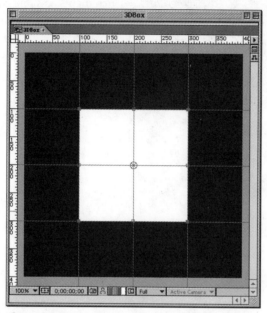

Figure 24-9: Position guides at the edges of the solid as well as in the center of the comp.

4. **In the Timeline, turn on the layer's 3D switch.**

5. **Using the Rotate tool, position the pointer over the layer's X-axis (the red arrow).** When the pointer turns into an X with an arrow circling around it, click and drag on the layer. Hold down the Shift key to limit the rotational change to 45-degree increments, and release the mouse after the layer appears to be edge-on and its Z-axis (the blue arrow) is pointing upward. See Figure 24-10 for reference.

6. **Using the Selection tool, position the pointer over the layer's Z-axis (the blue arrow).** When the pointer turns into a Z, click and drag down on the layer. Release the mouse after you move it down 100 pixels (the Anchor Point is centered on the lower guide, and the Info palette reflects the exact nature of the positional change). See Figure 24-11 for reference.

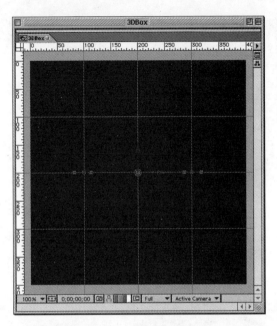

Figure 24-10: Rotate the layer around its X-axis while holding down the Shift key to limit the rotational change to 45-degree increments and release the mouse after the layer appears to be edge-on.

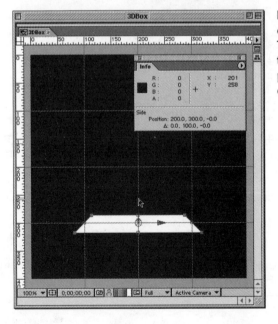

Figure 24-11: The layer moved down 100 pixels on its Z-axis. The Anchor Point is centered on the lower guide, and the Info palette reflects the exact nature of the positional change.

7. **Create another new 200 x 200 solid.** Name it *Back* and color it light red.

8. **In the Timeline, turn on the Back layer's 3D switch.**

9. **In the Comp window, change your view from Active Camera to Top.** This makes the new Side layer practically disappear because you are viewing it edge-on. If it's selected in the Timeline, it'll have a dotted outline and you'll be able to see its anchor point.

10. **Position the Selection tool over the Side layer's Z-axis (blue).** When the pointer turns into a Z, click and drag the layer up 100 pixels until its Anchor Point is centered on the guides. See Figure 24-12 for reference.

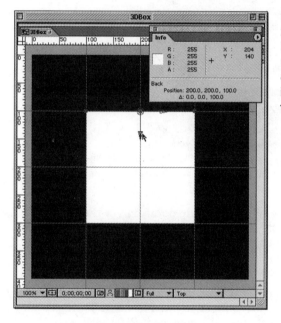

Figure 24-12: Position the Selection tool over the Back layer's Z-axis (blue). When the pointer turns into a Z, click and drag the layer up 100 pixels until its Anchor Point is centered on the guides.

11. **Duplicate the Back layer.**

12. **In the Comp window, which is still set to the Top view, drag the newly duplicated Back layer down 200 pixels on its Z-axis.** See Figure 24-13 for reference.

13. **In the Timeline, select the newly duplicated Back layer and press Command/Ctrl+Shift+Y to open its Solid Settings dialog Box.** Change its color to light blue, and rename it *Front.*

14. **Duplicate the Front layer.**

15. **In the Comp window, move the newly duplicated Front layer up 100 pixels along its Z-axis (the blue arrow) until it's centered in the comp.**

16. **Using the Rotate tool, position the pointer over the layer's Y-axis (the green "splotch").** When the pointer turns into a Y with an arrow circling around it, click and drag on the layer. Hold down the Shift key to limit the rotational change to 45-degree increments and release the mouse after the layer appears to be edge-on and its Z-axis (the blue arrow) is pointing to the left.

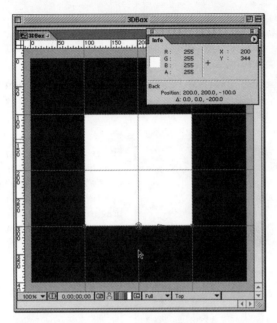

Figure 24-13: While you're still in the Top view, drag the newly duplicated Side layer down 200 pixels on its Z-axis. Again, use the guides and the Info palette for precision.

17. **Using the Selection tool, position the pointer over the layer's Z-axis (the blue arrow).** When the pointer turns into a Z, click and drag the layer to the right. Release the mouse after you move it right 100 pixels (the layer is positioned on the right guide, and the Info palette reflects the exact nature of the positional change). See Figure 24-14 for reference.

18. **In the Timeline, select the newly duplicated Front layer that you just moved and press Command/Ctrl+Shift+Y to open its Solid Settings dialog Box.** Change its color to light green and rename it *Right*.

19. **Duplicate the Right layer.**

20. **In the Comp window, move the newly duplicated Right layer to the left 200 pixels along its Z-axis (the blue arrow).** The layer is positioned on the left guide, and the Info palette reflects the exact nature of the positional change. See Figure 24-15.

21. **In the Timeline, select the newly duplicated Right layer that you just moved, and press Command/Ctrl+Shift+Y to open its Solid Settings dialog box.** Change its color to light purple and rename it *Left*. Congratulations! You just built a 3D box with an open top, a white bottom, and colored sides.

22. **In the Comp window, select Custom View 1.** Your box should resemble Figure 24-16. Move around it with the Camera tools to look at it from any angle that you want.

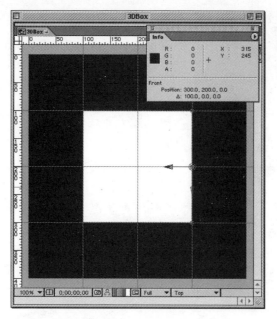

Figure 24-14: The layer is positioned on the right guide, and the Info palette reflects the exact nature of the positional change.

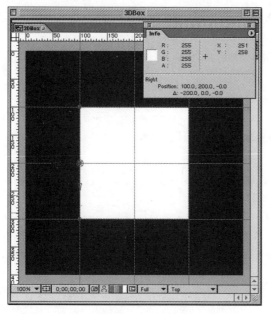

Figure 24-15: The layer is positioned on the left guide, and the Info palette reflects the exact nature of the positional change.

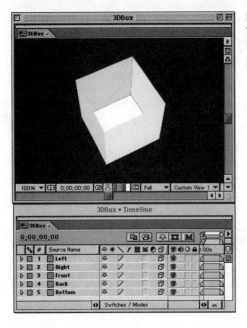

Figure 24-16: Congratulations! Custom View 1 should reveal the fact that you just built a 3D box with an open top, a white bottom, and colored sides.

Pretty nifty stuff, if you ask us. Now it's time to pre-compose the cube and make it move.

Tip   When we're working with 3D layers, we find it very useful to use all the keyboard shortcuts we can. We're especially fond of using the F10, F11, and F12 View toggling key functions in conjunction with the comma and period keys to zoom in on whatever view we've selected.

STEPS: Pre-Composing Your 3D Cube

1. **Open up your 3DBox comp again.**

2. **Click the Timeline to make it active and then press Command/Ctrl+A to select all the layers of the box.**

3. **Press Command/Ctrl+Shift+C and in the Pre-Compose dialog box that follows, name it *Pre-Comp Box,* and click OK.**

4. **Turn on the Pre-Comp Box layer's 3D and Collapse Geometrics switches.**

Bingo! Now it's time to animate this colorful, if empty box. Don't worry. As you make your way through the chapter, we throw lights and cameras in it.

STEPS: Making a Proud Parent of Your 3D Cube

1. **With your 3DBox comp open in the Comp and Timeline windows, press Command/Ctrl+K to look at your Composition settings.** Change its dimensions by selecting the NTSC D1, 720 x 486 option from the Preset pop-up menu. Click OK after you finish. This is so we have a bit more real estate to work with. Additionally, if you want to render it out to your video card, you have that option as well.

2. **In the Comp window, select the Active Camera view and use the Rotate tool to set the Orientation of the cube (Pre-Comp Box) at about 45, 315, and 0 degrees (X, Y, and Z-axes, respectively).** If you need to gauge the impact of your orientational change, watch the Info palette. Of course, you can always enter these numerical values directly into the number fields in the Timeline.

3. **In the Timeline, scale the Pre-Comp Box layer down to about 40%.**

4. **Using the Pan Behind tool, drag the cube's anchor point up and away from the cube.** The precise value is unimportant. You can adjust it later.

5. **In the Timeline, scrub the cube's Y-Rotation value while watching the Comp window.** Basically, you want to set up the cube so that adjustments to its Y-Rotation create a nicely pronounced 3D orbit around the anchor point. Take a moment here to adjust the cube's position and anchor point until you achieve the result that you want.

Tip

Toggle between the Active Camera and custom views to make adjustments to the anchor point along its Z-axis. Adjust the cube's position as well if you need to. We settled on the values shown in Figure 24-17. Remember to keep an eye on your axis modes. The Local Axis mode moves the cube relative to its Orientation. The World Axis mode moves the cube relative to the entire comp. Lastly, the View Axis mode moves the cube relative to the viewing angle that you select to look at the comp.

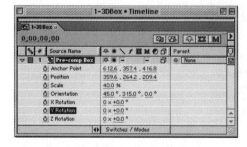

Figure 24-17: Using these values for the Pre-Comp Box layer produces the kind of Y-Rotation we want. Use these or come up with your own by experimenting with repositioning the cube and its anchor point by toggling between the Active Camera and Custom Views.

6. **Duplicate the Pre-Comp Box layer and change its Y-Rotation value to 45 degrees.**

7. **Repeat Step 6, adding 45 degrees to the cube's Y-Rotation (90 degrees).** Continue repeating this step until you get a total of eight cubes, each of whose Y-Rotation values are 0, 45, 90, 135, 180, 225, 270, and 315 degrees, respectively.

8. **Click the original Pre-Comp Box layer to select it, press Return, rename it** *Original Cube,* **and press Return again.**

9. **In the Timeline, make sure that the parenting column is visible.** If it isn't, Control+click/right-click any of the columns and select the Parent option to add it to your Timeline.

10. **Select all of the duplicated cubes and using the parent pop-up for any one of them, select Original Cube from the list of possible parents.** At this point, your comp should resemble Figure 24-18.

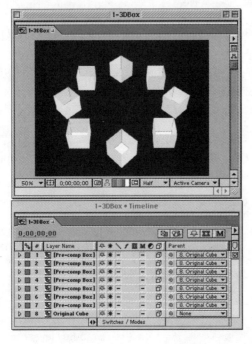

Figure 24-18: By duplicating the cube and offsetting the copies in increments of 45 degrees along the Y-axis, you get results such as this. Make one of the cubes a parent, and they all move together.

11. **Test the parenting relationship by scrubbing the Y-Rotation property for the Original Cube.** All the cubes should orbit around the anchor point.

12. **In the Timeline, make sure that you're on the first frame of the comp by pressing the Home key and then set an initial Y-Rotation keyframe for the Original Cube by clicking on that property's stopwatch.**

13. **Press the End key to go to the last frame of the comp (which should still be approximately five seconds long), press Page Down to go one frame past the last frame (to make an animation that loops cleanly), and change the Y-Rotation property so that it completes one full revolution (1 x 0.0 degrees).**

14. **Drag the playhead through the Timeline to preview the motion of your animation.**

Make whatever modifications you want to the orbiting cubes and render them out if you want. If you do render this comp, it will loop seamlessly because of the nifty trick in Step 13. Review what that was all about once again: Setting a keyframe cycle so that it starts at the first frame of a comp and ends *one frame after* the last frame of the comp sets up the animation to loop seamlessly.

What's new in After Effects 5.5: Enhancements to the 3D workspace

As we've already mentioned, Adobe launched After Effects into completely new territory with the release of version 5.0 when they added 3D-compositing capabilities to the application. Seasoned 3D artists who were used to certain kinds of interface conventions cried out for improvements, and with the advent of version 5.5, many features have been added to make designing in the third dimension a much more intuitive process.

First, and maybe most important of all, now you can view 3D objects from multiple angles simultaneously. In fact, you can choose from three different layouts by selecting Window ➪ Workspace ➪ One Comp View, Two Comp Views, or Four Comp Views, as shown in Figure SB 24-2. This comes as quite a relief, because it used to take a lot of hopping around from one view to another to get a sense of what a 3D project really looked like.

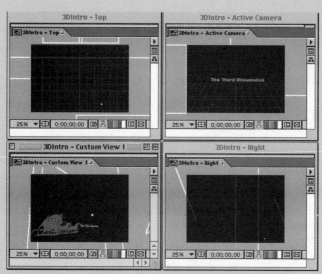

Figure SB 24-2: The new enhancements to 3D offer four simultaneous views of your comp from whatever angles you choose.

3D rendering

As of this writing, Adobe has developed a beta version of an Advanced 3D Render plug-in that handles layer intersections in a much more sophisticated fashion than the Basic 3D Render plug-in. You can get it from the Adobe Web site at www.adobe. com/aftereffects, and we strongly suggest that you do so. After you have it, drop it in the plug-ins folder inside the After Effects application folder and restart After Effects. Under the Advanced tab in the Composition Settings dialog box (which you can access by pressing Command/Ctrl+K), you can now choose between the Basic and Advanced 3D Render plug-in. The Basic version was developed to display complex diffused shadows created by lights. On the other hand, the Advanced version nicely renders layers intersecting in 3D space. Unfortunately, you have to choose between one and the other.

Note   Of course, if you have version 5.5 of After Effects, you already have both 3D Render plug-ins.

Applying 2D effects to 3D layers

Just so you know, if you apply an effect to a 3D layer, you'll only see it on the surface of the layer. In other words, there aren't any effects that work in 3D space. For example, say that you added and adjusted the Levels and Fast Blur effects to a 3D layer. The result is that the effects won't extend beyond the edges of the two-dimensional layer.

Don't throw in the towel though. Some interesting options are still at your disposal, and you should definitely experiment with them to see whether you can create something that you like. For example, transfer modes are just as functional in 3D space as they are in 2D. Another possible creative point of departure is the Fractal Noise filter. If you apply it to the layers that compose a polygon (such as the cube you've been working with), you can come up with some uncommonly stylish 3D animations.

Adding Cameras and Lights to the 3D Mix

Cameras and Lights are the features that make 3D in After Effects really special. As soon as you set up your 3D "set," you can place virtual cameras anywhere you want on it. You can animate the cameras so that they move through space while staying locked on a point of interest. For even more control, you can set an incredibly vast array of parameters for the mechanics of these virtual cameras. For example, you can adjust a virtual camera's focal length, focus distance, zoom, as well as many other sophisticated properties.

To make your 3D comps even more textured, you can position lights on your set. If you like, you can animate their position as well. You have four different types of lights to choose from, and each one has its own distinct properties. With the addition of lights and cameras, you can truly let your creative impulses out of the box.

Working with virtual cameras

To start working with cameras, duplicate your 3DBox comp in the Project window and name the copy *3DBox+Camera.* Choose Layer ➪ New ➪ Camera, and you'll see a rather gorgeous dialog box (see Figure 24-19). For the time being, accept the defaults and click OK.

As was the case with turning on a layer's 3D switch, nothing initially looks different in the Active Camera View of the Comp window. In fact, once again, you've enabled a huge number of creative possibilities; it's just that you can't see them yet. Take a look at the comp from the other views available, and the newly added camera is visible. Figure 24-20 shows the new comp from the Top View and Custom View 1.

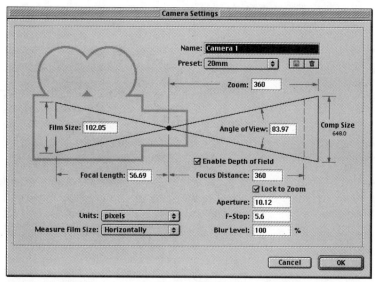

Figure 24-19: The Camera Settings dialog box contains more than a few parameters.

For a quick demonstration of the power of cameras, select the new camera in the Timeline and look at your comp from the Front View. Click and drag it to a new position that's up and to the left of its current location. Notice how its point of interest remains locked. Go back to the Active Camera view, and you see your comp from the camera's new location. After you finish with this example, you can delete the camera from the Timeline. See Figure 24-21.

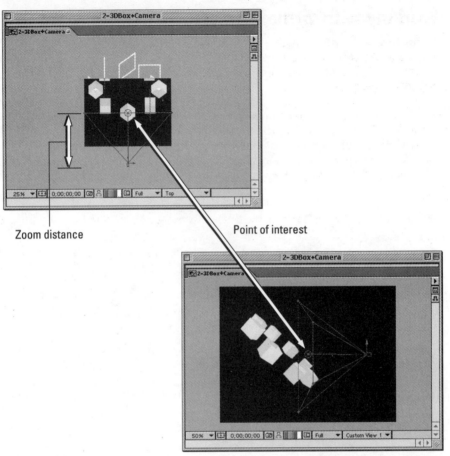

Zoom distance

Point of interest

Figure 24-20: The new camera layer is visible in the views beside the Active Camera View. In this case, you can see the 20mm camera from both the Top View and Custom View 1.

Note

At this point, the Active Camera view should make more sense. It works like this: The topmost camera in the stacking order of a comp is the Active Camera (provided that its visibility switch is turned on). If you want to jump between multiple camera views, you need to trim and/or split the camera layers as you would any other kind of layer.

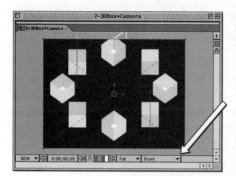 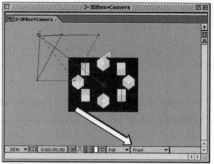

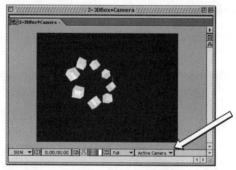

Figure 24-21: Using the Front View, move the new camera up and to the left of its original position. Notice how its point of interest remains locked. Go back to the Active Camera view, and you see your comp from the camera's new location.

Understanding the camera specs

The number of parameters in the Camera Settings dialog box is pretty intimidating at first. They're described in detail in the Online Help HTML document, which you can view by choosing Help ⇨ After Effects Help. We add to a few of those descriptions with our own pointers:

✦ **Preset:** This pop-up gives you a few presets to choose from. The presets are named relative to the different cameras' focal lengths. The greater the focal length, the greater the distance between the camera and the plane of view, which also happens to be the point of interest. If you use cameras with longer focal lengths, your view of a comp will be less distorted when you position the camera at extreme viewing angles. The initial default is the 50mm Camera.

✦ **Angle of View:** This determines the angle of the lens. The higher the value, the more you approximate a traditional wide angle lens. You can animate this property by animating the Zoom property in the Timeline. Obviously you can't go beyond 180 degrees. The higher you set this value, the greater the distortion of the image.

✦ **Enable Depth of Field:** This option enables the camera to behave more realistically. If you turn it on, you enable the Focus Distance, Aperture, F-Stop and Blur Level properties. Depending on the values you set for those properties, you can attain a high degree of photorealism in which parts of the image will blur because they're out of focus. This is great, but it also ups your render time considerably. If you're in Draft 3D mode, you won't see the results of these settings.

✦ **Aperture/F-Stop:** These fields offer different ways to alter the same property, which is really the width of the virtual camera shutter. As you increase the size of the aperture, you increase the blur in the part of the image that is out of focus.

✦ **Blur Level:** This field enables you to increase or decrease the amount by which a natural blur results from the aperture setting.

✦ **Film Size:** This field is initially set in relation to work properly according to the size of the comp.

There's a reason why nothing really happens to the appearance of the Active Camera View of your composition when you add a new camera. The new camera gets positioned so that the settings you specify for it are relative to the way that After Effects intelligently positions the camera so that your view of the composition remains unchanged.

When you alter a preset camera's settings, you're making your own custom camera, which you can save in much the same way that you save a custom composition's settings. After you save a custom camera, it appears in the Preset pop-up.

Try to name your cameras something other than the default. This helps you avoid getting confused, especially if you're using more than one; such as, *20mm Left Pan*.

Animating cameras

Cameras can be animated in much the same way that other 3D objects can. In addition to the methods that you acquired when learning how to manipulate regular 3D layers, you can also use the camera tools (Orbit Camera, Track XY Camera, and Track Z Camera) to change a camera's position. You can get stuck in a couple of places, and we address those in the exercises that follow.

Cameras have a point of interest or a spot on which they're focused. When you add a new camera, by default, it auto-orients itself to its Point of Interest. This can create problems when you're animating the camera's position. In the next set of steps, you animate a camera that flies through the ring of spinning cubes that you created in the last exercise.

STEPS: Using a Camera for a 3D Flythrough

1. **In case you haven't already, duplicate your 3DBox comp in the Project window and name the copy** *3DBox+Camera.*

2. **Choose Layer ➪ New ➪ Camera.** Opt for the 20mm preset, name it *20mm Camera,* and click OK.

3. **Set a Position keyframe for the 20mm Camera layer at the first frame of the comp.**

4. **Jump to the end of the comp by pressing the End key.**

5. **Select the Left View from the View options in the Comp window.** You may also want to set your comp's magnification so that you have command over a larger general area by pressing the comma key to zoom out and the period key to zoom in. See Figure 24-22 for reference.

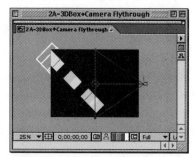

Figure 24-22: Animating the Camera Flythrough from one of the side views is the easiest way.

6. **Drag the camera along to the left.** Drag the camera without using the axis controls to keep it auto-oriented.

Caution

If you directly drag the camera's Z-axis, its orientation and point of interest won't stay fixed at their original values.

7. **Still viewing the comp from the Left View, drag the playhead through the animation and watch the camera as it moves through the rings.** You see that its orientation snaps suddenly as the camera crosses the image plane. This produces less than optimal results, and we fix this in the next couple of steps.

8. **Control+click/Right-click the 20mm Camera layer and choose Transform ⇨ Auto Orient.** Turn Auto-Orientation off in the Auto-Orientation dialog box and click OK. Now when you preview the animation, you see that the camera's point of interest travels with the camera and its orientation remains unchanged during the move.

9. **In the Timeline, make sure the 20mm Camera layer is selected and press R to solo its rotation properties.**

10. **Still viewing the comp from the Left View, drag the playhead through the animation and watch the camera once again as it moves through the rings.** Set an Orientation keyframe as it begins to move through the middle part of the positional animation.

11. **Drag the playhead to a point in time when the camera has sufficiently flown through the ring of spinning cubes and set an X-Orientation value of 180 degrees.** Drag the playhead through the middle of the animation and watch the camera's orientation. Adjust the timing of the keyframes to suit your own needs. If you want the Orientation animation to happen smoothly, select the two Orientation keyframes and press F9 to make them Easy Ease keyframes.

12. **Return the view of the comp to the Active Camera view and press the spacebar to play it back.** If you want to make further adjustments to the camera's path or orientation, feel free to. This initial animation is merely meant to serve as a point of departure.

Interesting, isn't it? Well, folks, that completes your introduction to the world of cameras in 3D space in After Effects.

Tip   Experiment wth the different Auto-Orient options by Control+clicking/right-clicking the 20mm Camera layer and choose Transform ⇨ Auto Orient. In the dialog box that follows, experiment with the different auto-orient options (Point of Interest, Path, and Off) when animating your camera moves. Utilize all of the different views to see how After Effects interpolates between the camera's position keyframes in the different auto-orient modes. Don't forget that you still have Bezier controls on your keyframes if you want to jazz up their interpolation. Actually, the Bezier controls for keyframes in the Comp window operate in 3D space, and this is a new and very cool phenomenon.

Note   You can also auto-orient regular layers towards the Active Camera. Awesome.

Tip   If you run into trouble animating a camera (read, *you're stuck with no visible way out*), look into changing your auto-orient options.

What's new in After Effects 5.5: Camera data import

Many 3D artists, modelers, and animators love After Effects for both its compositing capability and its rendering flexibility. With each release of After Effects, Adobe has added more support for working with 3D data from various applications.

After Effects 5.5 enables you to import 3D camera data from Maya and 3D Studio Max projects. Using this data, you can composite new elements into 3D compositions, create mattes for imported 3D elements, and perform color correction. When importing RPF (Rich Pixel Format) files from 3D Studio Max, you can also work with the camera data in After Effects.

Using a Null layer as a parent in 3D camera animations

Believe it or not, but the Orbit Camera tool is *not* the tool to use if you want to animate a camera's motion path in an orbital path around an image. The reason for this makes sense after you pull your hair out for a little while (not like we did). For example, say that you add a camera to a comp. Then you set it to auto-orient and create an initial positional keyframe for it. Jump forward in time, and then use the Orbit Camera tool to position the camera on the other side of the image plane. While it may work properly in your mind's eye, the fact is that the resulting interpolation between the two positional keyframes is based on the shortest distance between them. Instead of an orbital path, the camera animates along a ruler straight line through the middle of the comp. Not so hot, folks.

If you want to pull off a smooth camera orbit, the quickest and easiest way involves adding a null object layer to your comp.

STEPS: Animating a Clean Camera Orbit

1. **After you add a camera to your comp, choose Layer ➪ New ➪ Null Object.**

2. **Turn on the Null Object's 3D switch.**

3. **In the parent column, select the Null Object layer as the camera's parent.**

4. **Animate the 3D rotational properties of the Null Object layer.**

Problem solved. Smooth camera moves are easy after you know this trick.

Note

When you make the Null Object layer the parent of the camera, it acts as the camera's virtual anchor point. If you try to create a smooth orbital motion path for a camera without using a Null Object, it's practically impossible to get a perfect circle. In 2D space, you can paste a circular mask into a layer's motion path, but in 3D, that's not an option.

Throwing light

Lights provide even more realism when creating objects in 3D space. Similar to enabling Depth of Field for an Active Camera, render times can be absolutely deadly depending on the complexity of your comp. To add a light to your comp, choose Layer ➪ New ➪ Light. The Light Settings dialog box shown in Figure 24-23 opens.

We put together a brief rundown of what the different light settings can do for you by adding to the descriptions that already exist in the Online Help HTML document, which you can view by choosing Help ➪ After Effects Help.

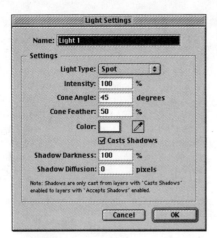

Figure 24-23: The Light Settings dialog box is a bit less taxing than its Camera Settings cousin.

✦ **Light type:** There are four light types, and each of them are considerably different from one another:

 • **Spot light:** As its name suggests, a spot light shines a beam of focused light on a point of interest. Unlike the others, a spot light has an adjustable Cone Angle and Cone Feather. The Cone Angle controls the diameter of the light beam, and the Cone Feather controls the softness of the spot light's edges.

 • **Point light:** Like the Online Help says, this light behaves like a bare light bulb. This is a great one for using within pre-composed shapes that have holes cut out of them. Think flashlights, slide projectors, lamps, and any other objects into which you might put a light bulb.

 • **Parallel light:** This light is good for a broad directional wash of light.

 • **Ambient light:** After you start working with lights, your entire comp can get pretty dark. You can control only the intensity and the color of ambient light, and it effects all surfaces consistently.

✦ **Intensity:** This property controls the brightness of the light. You can crank it way past 100%, and you can also set it below 0% to create what the Online Help calls *nonlight,* which subtracts the color and brightness from existing lights.

✦ **Color:** The swatch opens the picker, but more importantly, light is part of an additive color scheme. Specifically, if you mix multiple lights comprised of different colors, you move toward white in the blended areas.

✦ **Casts Shadows:** Enables the light's ability to throw shadows. Keep in mind that if you shine a light on a layer, that layer needs to have its Accepts Lights switch turned on in its Material Options.

✦ **Shadow Darkness/Shadow Diffusion:** These settings are obviously contingent on whether Casts Shadows is enabled. The Shadow Diffusion property only works by using the Basic 3D Render plug-in.

You can have a great time animating spot and point lights. If we want to use parallel lights, we tend to position them and leave them where they stand because you don't have a great deal of control over them when moving them through space. Ambient light controls the overall brightness of a 3D comp that contains lights and can't be positioned anywhere. We've put together some examples that are shown in Figure 24-24 and Color Plate 24.2.

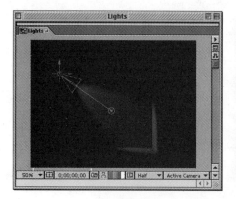
Spot light

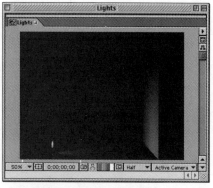
Point light in a box

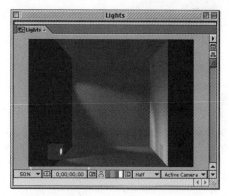
Spot, Point, Parallel, and Ambient lights

Figure 24-24: Spot lights can be tightly controlled, and Point lights are great for throwing shadows out of perforated objects. Parallel and Ambient lights are more general in their application.

What's new in After Effects 5.5: More enhancements to the 3D workspace

Well, lucky for us, the future has arrived a bit ahead of schedule. In addition to multiple views, there have been some nifty improvements done on the Material Options we just mentioned. All of them, specifically those properties geared toward reflecting highlights (Specular, Shininess, and Metal), work beautifully now.

Next, you might want to try out the new "stained glass" effect. In a 3D-enabled comp, create a new Spot light and enable it to Cast Shadows. Point it at a solid layer that you've enabled to Accept Shadows. Position a still image or a video clip between those two layers and enable it to both Accept Lights and Cast Shadows. Figure SB 24-3 shows a basic 3D projection setup like the one we just described.

Figure SB 24-3: A basic projection setup
contains a light, a projection layer of video,
and a solid layer acting as a projection "screen."
Footage Courtesy of ArtBeats (Starter Kit)

Once you've created your own similar setup, you can take advantage of the Light Transmission property, which is new in version 5.5. Crank up the middle layer's Light Transmission value to see what kinds of variation you can get in the projected image. The higher you raise the Light Transmission value, the more the projected shadow will mirror the projection layer. At lower Light Transmission levels, the projected shadow will be more diffuse.

There's one more notable improvement to After Effects' implementation of 3D in version 5.5. If you want, now you can designate any light as an "adjustment light." If you turn on a light's Adjustment Layer switch in the Timeline, it will shine only on the layers beneath it in the stacking order.

One final word about lights: After their 3D switches have been flipped on, regular layers contain the following Material Options: Casts Shadows, Accepts Shadows, and Accepts Lights. If lights are going to have an impact on the layers of your comp, those layers need to have these options turned on. That goes for the layers inside nested comps as well. Truth be told, the other parameters of the Material Options settings don't really work (Ambient, Diffuse, Specular, and Shininess). We're sure they'll improve in future builds of After Effects.

In short, After Effects has crossed over into new territory with the addition of 3D. Adobe's put together a great start in this area, and the future only promises more improvements in this realm.

✦   ✦   ✦

Adding Expressions to Your Arsenal

Expressions have become so popular with some motion graphic artists in the After Effects community that they swear they'll never use another keyframe if they can avoid it (in case you don't know, *expressions* are lines of JavaScript that control a layer's properties). Sounds extreme, doesn't it? Expressions are another example of one of the huge changes that constitute version 5.0. Taken on their own, expressions or 3D would have been more than enough to fully justify a new release (new version number), but lucky for us, we've managed to end up with both of these enhancements in this go-round.

What's up with expressions? First of all, expressions bear no relation to the kind of expression that you think of as a familiar manner of speaking; actually, quite the opposite is true. Many of us have based our enjoyment of After Effects on the fact that we didn't have to learn a programming language before we could start designing. Don't worry. This is still the case. Not only are expressions easy to use, but also you don't have to learn a lot of code to start getting results.

Explaining Expressions

Again, don't be scared of an overly code-heavy lesson. As soon as you begin to see how much you can enhance your work with such a small investment of your time, you'll see that expressions are nothing to fear.

For example, have you ever found it frustrating to set 10 sets of keyframes for 10 identically spinning objects? With the benefit of expressions, you can create one animation and use very simple expressions to make the remaining objects spin in unison. And you'll never have to type a single line of JavaScript. The act of using the expressions pick whip will "write" the

Expressions versus Motion Math

Many After Effects users point out that expressions seem just like Motion Math scripts. So when and why would you use expressions rather than Motion Math?

Here's a good way to think about it. Remember that Motion Math scripts, when applied, create *lots* of keyframes for your layers. In fact, keyframes are created for every frame of the comp, and after they've been set, they're hard to adjust as a whole. The only real way to modify keyframes made by a Motion Math script is to run the Motion Math script again. Say, for example, that you use the motion of one layer to affect the motion of another layer with Motion Math. What if you needed to change the motion of the first layer? You'd have to reapply the Motion Math script so that the revised motion of the first layer would affect the second layer.

By contrast, expressions are "live." They create a dynamic, real-time link between whatever properties you choose. Taking another look at the previous Motion Math example, recall that the motion of one layer affects the motion of another. If, instead of Motion Math, you were to use expressions to define this relationship, you could make any number of changes to either layer and not worry about revising anything because the expression is a live connection between the two elements.

code for you (the *pick whip* is an icon that you can drag to a property to automatically create an expression). As we mention throughout the book, the great thing about After Effects is the relatively short distance between your imagination and the results in the Comp window. Expressions add even greater control to the process of realizing your vision.

On the DVD-ROM

To better explain expressions, we created an After Effects project that includes a composition for each series of steps that we cover in the chapter. Just as a reminder, you need to copy the *Source Material* folder from the DVD-ROM to your hard drive. Our own corresponding After Effects project is named *Chapter 25.aep* and is found in the *Project Files/Chapter 25* folder.

Getting to Know the Expression Icons

Expressions are based on JavaScript language. As we mentioned earlier, Adobe has made it quite easy for users who don't know JavaScript to be able to create and use expressions. If you're revolted by the idea of code, you can use the pick whip to create expressions or use the pre-written commands from the basic expressions guide provided by Adobe.

To begin creating an expression, you need to select a property for a layer in the Timeline window and select Animation ⇨ Add Expression. Or, if you prefer, you can also choose to Option/Alt+click the property's stopwatch to begin creating an expression. Note that when you do so, After Effects automatically fills the expression field area with a default expression that notes the fixed value of the property or the value of keyframes, if any are present.

After you activate expressions in the previous manner, you can then use the pick whip by dragging it to another property in the Timeline. Using the pick whip results in an expression being written in the expression field. After it's written, you can easily modify it as you see fit.

Figure 25-1 shows the layout of the expression area.

Expression on/off switch

Numbers turn red when property is controlled by expressions

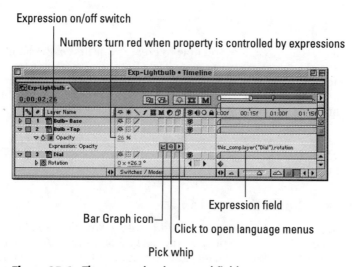

Expression field

Bar Graph icon

Click to open language menus

Pick whip

Figure 25-1: The expression icons and fields

Tip

To view all expressions for a layer, select the layer and press EE.

✦ **Expression on/off switch:** Click this button to turn the expression on or off. When expressions are turned on, the values for the property turn red. This indicates that the property is now being controlled by an expression. When the property values are red, don't try to change them as you would when working regularly with After Effects. When the expression is turned off, a slash appears through the switch.

✦ **Bar Graph icon:** Click this button to view the velocity or the value graph as it is modified by the expression. The graph modified by the expression appears in red, while the unmodified one appears in black.

✦ **Pick whip:** The pick whip can be used to create expressions. To use the pick whip, click the icon and drag it to another property. After you do so, After Effects automatically adds an expression in the expression field.

✦ **Language element menu:** The language element menu allows access to the elements that you can use to create expressions. Click the arrow and scroll down the menus to select the elements.

✦ **Expression field:** This is the area where expressions are added. You can freely write your own expressions in this area or edit the ones that are added automatically by After Effects. This field can be easily resized by dragging the bottom area of the field to a lower location. Resizing allows for a larger viewing area for any expression, and this can be useful if your expression contains multiple lines of text.

Creating Your First Expression

In the upcoming step exercise, we show you how to create your first expression. In this case, you use the pick whip. First, you create a few Rotation keyframes for a dial. Then you activate expressions and use the pick whip to attach the Rotation of the dial to the Opacity of a light bulb. The final result is that as the dial turns, the Opacity of the light bulb changes with it.

On the DVD-ROM

For the next series of steps, you should use the composition called *EXP-Dial and Bulb-Final* as a point of reference. Use the *Exp-Dial and Bulb-Clean* comp to work on creating your own expressions.

STEPS: Creating a Basic Expression

1. **Choose Composition ➪ New Composition and create a New Composition.** To facilitate this step exercise, we provide the comp *Exp-Dial and Bulb-Clean* in which the layers that make up the dial and the lightbulb are already laid out. We suggest that you start out with this comp to speed up the process. If you'd rather lay it out yourself, you need to drag in the four layers that make up the dial and the lightbulb. Their names are: Bulb-Top, Bulb-Base, Dial Plate and Dial/Dial.

2. **First, create keyframes to rotate the dial.** Try to use Rotation values that work well with the possible range of Opacity values, which can only run from 0 to 100%. For example, using negative Rotation values simply results in an Opacity of 0%.

3. **Select the Bulb-Top layer and press T to solo its Opacity property.** Then select the Opacity property by clicking it and choose Animation ➪ Add Expression. A default expression appears in the expression field for the Opacity of the bulb. Note that you can also use the keyboard shortcut of Option/Alt+Shift+=, but our favorite way of activating expressions is to Option/Alt+click the stopwatch of the property for which you want to activate expressions.

4. **Click the pick whip next to the Opacity expression and drag it to the Rotation property of the dial.** The following expression automatically appears:

```
this_comp.layer("Dial").rotation
```

This expression is basically saying that within "this" comp (meaning the comp we're working in), this expression will be looking at the layer called `"Dial"`, and it will be sampling the Rotation property of the Dial layer. Simple as that.

Figure 25-2 shows the process of using the pick whip to create an expression that sets the Opacity of a layer to match the Rotation of a different layer.

5. **Press enter on the numeric keypad to activate the expression.** This step is critical. If the insertion cursor remains active in the expression field, the expression is not yet active. You need to press the Enter key on your numeric keypad, or click somewhere outside the expression field to make the expression active.

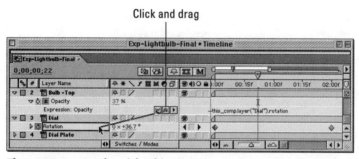

Figure 25-2: Use the pick whip to create an expression that sets the Opacity of a layer to match the Rotation of a different layer.

Play your comp and you see that the bulb glows and darkens in relationship to the turning of the dial. Remember that you never set any Opacity keyframes for the bulb. This is merely an introduction to the power you can derive from using expressions.

Tip

Expressions allows the user to access almost any parameter associated with a layer. One exception is accessing the amplitude information in an audio file.

Caution

When working with expressions, keeping in mind the dimensionality of the properties you are working with is important. For example, Rotation and Opacity are one-dimensional properties, whereas Scale, Position, and Anchor Point are two-dimensional because they have both an X- and a Y-component. When using the pick whip to create expressions, you should try and work within properties that have the same number of dimensions.

Converting expressions to keyframes

We just established that expressions provide flexibility by creating live connections between the values of different layers' properties, but you will have times when you may want to sever this connection. For example, after creating an expression that controls one layer's behavior by taking its property values from another, you may want to work with the layers independently. In that case, you can convert expressions to keyframes. This can also be handy if you're having trouble managing the expression. After you convert an expression to keyframes, you can edit the keyframes individually.

To convert an expression to keyframes, select the property in which the expression is written and then choose Animation ➪ Keyframe Assistant ➪ Convert Expression to Keyframes.

Creating and editing expressions

In the previous step exercise, we showed you how to create an expression by using the pick whip. After you create an expression this way, you can edit it freely. This gives those of you that aren't JavaScript gurus some flexibility in providing a way to change and control the behavior of the expressions.

For example, by adding the + (add), − (subtract), / (divide), and * (multiply) symbols and a number to the end of an expression, you can modify the expression's final effect by the mathematical function that results from combining whatever operator and number that you typed.

In the next set of steps, we give this method a spin.

The following exercise entails creating a clock with moving hands. First, we animate the hour hand by creating Rotation keyframes. Next, we add an expression to make the minute hand rotate with the hour hand. Because the minute hand of a clock moves a whole lot faster, we have to edit our expression just a bit to achieve the desired result. You'll see that all the expression needs is three additional characters from your numeric keypad.

On the DVD-ROM

For the next set of steps, you should use the composition called *EXP-Clock-Final* as a point of reference. Use the *Exp-Clock-Clean* comp to work on creating your own expressions.

STEPS: Creating and Editing a Basic Expression

1. **Choose Composition ➪ New Composition to create a New Composition.** To facilitate this step exercise, we provide you with the comp *Exp-Clock-Clean* in which the necessary layers are already laid out. We suggest that you skip this step of making a new comp and open up the *Exp-Clock-Clean* comp to speed up the process.

2. **Solo the Rotation properties for both the Hour and the Minute hand by selecting the two layers and pressing the R key.**

3. **Set two Rotation keyframes for the Hour Hand layer.** Set the first one at the first frame and the second one at the last frame of the comp. Change the Rotation settings for the second keyframe to one revolution. Hence, the hour hand should complete one revolution by the end of the comp.

4. **Select the Rotation property for the Minute Hand by clicking the property name and choose Animation ⇨ Add Expression.**

5. **Drag the pick whip from the Minute Hand's Rotation expression to the Hour Hand's Rotation property.** The following expression is automatically added to the expression field for the Minute hand:

```
this_comp.layer("Hour Hand").rotation
```

6. **Play your comp now by pressing the spacebar.** Notice that the two hands now complete a full revolution by the end of the comp. This is obviously not clocklike behavior. We need to edit the expression so that the minute hand completes 12 revolutions for every one of the hour hand.

7. **Edit the expression by changing it from**

```
this_comp.layer("Hour Hand").rotation
```

to

```
this_comp.layer("Hour Hand").rotation*12
```

by adding *12 to the end of it. Note that the asterisk stands for the multiply function.

Figure 25-3 shows where to add the *12 in the expression.

8. **Press Enter on the numeric keypad to activate the expression and then press the spacebar to play your comp.** Your minute hand should now complete 12 revolutions for every one completed by the hour hand.

Add *12 to make the minute hand move 12 times faster

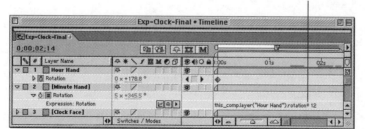

Figure 25-3: How to edit and modify an expression

Note here that what we have created is a "live" connection between the hour hand and the minute hand. At this point, if we were to go back and change the hour hand's rotation from one revolution to two or three, the minute hand would automatically adjust itself. Elegant timesaver, don't you think?

Saving expressions

After you have created or modified an expression, you may want to save it for future use. This is fairly easy to do because expressions are just text. You can highlight them in the expression field and choose Edit ➪ Copy. Then open a document in any word-processing utility, such as SimpleText, and choose Edit ➪ Paste. When you need to reuse these expressions, select and copy them in your word processing document, activate the expressions field in After Effects for any property and paste them into the expression field.

Bear in mind that expressions are sometimes only useful in the context for which they were created. For an expression of any length, its use and benefit may be tied to the mixture of layers and effects that's indigenous to a specific composition. If you do plan to save and reuse expressions, you may want to add comments to help clarify their function. To add comments to an expression, type // at the beginning of a comment. Any text between // and the end of a line is ignored by the expression.

In the next series of steps, we show you a very handy expression, which makes a circle for a layer.

On the DVD-ROM   For the next series of steps, look at the composition called *EXP-Circle*.

STEPS: Using and Saving an Expression

1. **Create a new composition by choosing Composition ➪ New Composition.**

2. **Create a new solid by using the Command/Ctrl+Y keyboard shortcut.** Set the dimensions of the solid to 20 x 20 pixels and make it any color that is clearly visible.

3. **Solo the Position property of the solid layer by selecting it and pressing the P key.**

4. **Activate the expressions for the Position property by Option/Alt+clicking the Position property's stopwatch.** The word `position` automatically appears in the expression field.

5. **Type the following expression into the expression field.** (You erase the word `position` that initially appeared automatically.)

   ```
   add([this_comp.width/2, this_comp.height/2],
   [Math.sin(time)*50, -Math.cos(time)*50])
   ```

6. **Press Enter on the numeric keypad to activate the expression.**

7. **Play your comp and you see that the small solid moves in a circle.**

8. **Type some comments so that you know what the various parts of the expression actually accomplish.** Click the expression field to make it active and before the expression, type the following lines:

```
//This expression makes a circle.
//Enter a smaller number where 50 is to make a smaller
//circle.
//Enter a larger number for a larger circle.
```

Remember that any lines that are preceded by // are not used by the expression. These are just expressions.

9. **You can save this expression (which is provided courtesy of Adobe Systems) and reuse it later.** To do so, simply highlight the expression field and then choose Edit ➪ Copy.

10. **Open any word-processing utility, such as SimpleText or Notepad, and create a new document.** Then choose Edit ➪ Paste to paste the expression into the document. You can create your own library of handy expressions this way.

Working with Arrays

So far, we have been working with straightforward expressions that generally deal with one-dimensional values. Understanding dimensions is critical to understanding arrays in expressions. Think of Position as a value. Position has two dimensions, X and Y. On the other hand, Opacity is a single dimension value that ranges from 0% to 100%. You may think that the Scale property is a single dimension, but it too has an X- and a Y-component.

Arrays in expressions describe multi-dimensional properties. So, here's how you spot an array in an expression. Its two distinguishing characteristics are that it has brackets [] around it, and it has commas between the members of the array.

Take, for example, the following array:

```
[this_comp.layer(1).rotation, this_comp.layer(1).rotation]
```

The preceding array can be viewed as following [x, y].

The brackets indicate the fact that we're looking at an array. Two members are in this array; we know that because there are just two, separated by a single comma. If there were three expressions separated by two commas, then we would view the array as three-dimensional [x, y, z].

When you create an expression for a multi-dimensional array, by default, any and all dimensions are affected. You have a few ways around that.

In the next set of steps, we show you how to work with the simple arrays and edit them to suit your needs.

On the DVD-ROM

For the next series of steps use the composition called *EXP-Scale Array-Final* as a point of reference. To work with your own comp, use *Exp-Scale Array-Clean*. If you want to view a comp containing the incorrect default values, take a look at *Exp-Scale Array-Wrong*.

STEPS: Handling Arrays in Expressions

1. **Choose Composition ⇨ New Composition to create a New Composition.** To facilitate this step exercise, we provide you with the comp *Exp-Scale Array-Clean* in which the layers for a dial and a solid have already been laid out. We suggest you skip this step and open up the *Exp-Scale Array-Clean* comp to speed up the process. If you need to refer to the correct final version, take a look at the *Exp-Scale Array-Final* comp.

2. **First, create three Rotation keyframes for the dial.** You can do so by selecting the Dial layer, soloing its Rotation property by pressing the R key, and then clicking the stopwatch to begin animating. In our comp, we keep it simple and set three keyframes, one at the first frame for 0 degrees, another at 0:00:02:15 set to 100 degrees, and a final one at 0:00:05:00 set to 0 degrees again.

3. **Select the solid comp called Level and solo its Scale property by pressing the S key.**

4. **Option/Alt+click the stopwatch for the Scale property of the Level layer to activate an expression.**

5. **Drag the pick whip from the Scale property of the Level layer to the Rotation property of the Dial.** The following expression automatically appears in the expression field:

```
[this_comp.layer("Dial").rotation,
this_comp.layer("Dial").rotation]
```

Figure 25-4 shows the array in the expression.

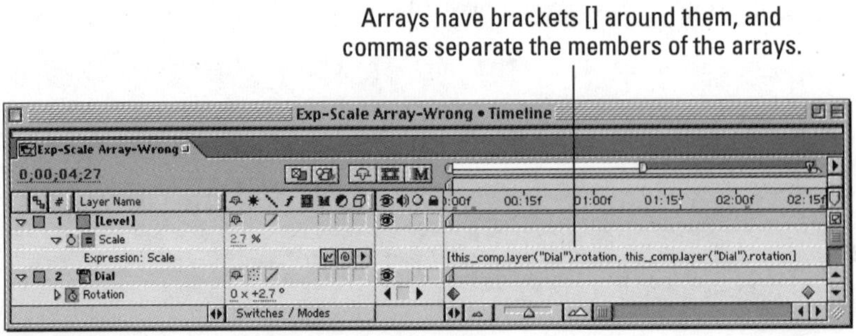

Arrays have brackets [] around them, and commas separate the members of the arrays.

Figure 25-4: The expression above shows an array that represents both the width and the height of the layer.

Here you are looking at an array. We know that because of the brackets [ ] around it. This array has two members that represent both the width and the height of the Level layer. The width of the layer is the first part of the expression that comes before the comma, whereas the height of the level layer is represented by the second equation, which follows the comma in the middle.

6. **Press the Enter key on the numeric keypad to activate the expression and then press the spacebar to play the comp.** Your level scales in both the X- and the Y-dimensions (read, width and height). That is not what we want. We only want the height to rise and fall without changing the width.

   To set this expression so that we only animate the height of the level, here is what we need to do: First, we need to know the default value of the member of the array that we want to leave unchanged. In this case, the default value of the width, or the first member of the array, is 100 percent.

7. **Highlight the expression and change it to**

   ```
   [100, this_comp.layer("Dial").rotation]
   ```

   Essentially, we've told the expression to hold the width of the layer to 100%.

8. **Press the Enter key to activate the expression and press the spacebar to play it.** Your level should rise and fall while its width remains fixed.

Using Expressions with Effects

So far, we have kept to the simpler geometrics of a layer: Scale, Position, Opacity, and so on. But bear in mind that expressions can work just as well with effects. By now, you know that effects simply appear as just more properties in the Timeline. Using the pick whip, you can associate the Effect properties of one layer to another layer's Transform or Effect properties.

In the next series of steps, we show you just such an exercise.

On the DVD-ROM

For the next series of steps, you should look at the composition called *EXP-Effects (text)*.

STEPS: Controlling Effects with Expressions

1. **Make a new comp by choosing Composition ➪ New Composition.**

2. **Create a new solid by pressing Command/Ctrl+Y and make it comp-sized.**

3. **Select the solid layer and choose Effect ➪ Text ➪ Basic Text.**

4. **Type any text into the text box and click OK.** In the Effect Controls window, you can select any color or font size that you want.

5. **Select your solid text layer again and choose Effect ⇨ Blur ⇨ Fast Blur to apply the effect.**

6. **Next, using the Tracking property of the Basic Text effect, create a tracking effect for the text by using keyframes.** This spreads the text apart over time.

7. **Open the text layer's Effect properties in the Timeline so that you can see both the Tracking and Blurriness properties from the two effects.**

8. **Option/Alt+click the Blurriness property stopwatch to activate an expression.**

9. **Click and drag the pick whip from the Blurriness channel to the Tracking property.** The following property is added to the expression field.

```
effect("Basic Text").param("Tracking")
```

Figure 25-5 shows the process of using the pick whip.

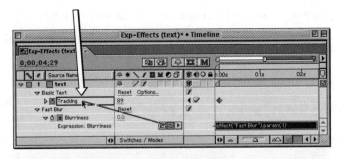

Figure 25-5: Drag the pick whip from the Blurriness property to the Tracking property of the text layer (top). A new expression is added (bottom).

10. **Press Enter on the numeric keypad to activate the expression and then press the spacebar to play your Comp.** You'll notice that the text blurs too fast and too much. We need to fix that, and we're going to do that by adding a very simple mathematical entry.

11. **Double-click in the expression field and edit the expression to read:**

```
effect("Basic Text").param("Tracking")/15
```

This reduces the magnitude of the Fast Blur by a factor of 15.

Note that all you need to do is to add /15 at the end of the expression. This cuts down the Blurriness by dividing it by 15.

We tried 5 and 10 before we settled on 15.

12. **Again, press Enter on your numeric keypad to activate the expression, and then press the spacebar to play the comp.** Your text blurs as it tracks outward.

Working with layers and time in expressions

We hope that at this stage your mind is exploding with the possibilities that expressions offer you. So far, we have linked properties to one another and even controlled effects by using expressions. Expressions can go quite a bit further than what we've shown you so far. In the next series of steps, we show you how to manage both time and layers using an expression provided by Adobe.

For the next series of steps, you should look at the composition called *EXP-Trail*.

STEPS: Creating a Trail of Images

1. **Make a new comp by choosing Composition ⇨ New Composition.**

2. **Drag the *Musical Note1.ai* footage item from your Project window into the Timeline.**

3. **Create some motion for this layer by setting Position keyframes.** Try to create a complex path that weaves around the comp.

4. **Next, drop the *Musical Note2.ai* footage item into the Timeline.** Make sure that the *Musical Note2.ai* layer goes on top of the *Musical Note1.ai* layer in the stacking order.

5. **Solo the Position properties for both the musical notes layers by selecting them and pressing the P key.**

6. **Option/Alt+click the Position property stopwatch for the *Musical Note2.ai* layer.** This activates an expression for this layer and a default expression is added in the expression field.

7. **Highlight the default expression to delete it and replace it with the following expression:**

```
this_comp.layer(this_layer, 1).position.value_at_time(time - .5)
```

8. **Press Enter on the numeric keypad to activate the expression and press the spacebar to play the comp.** The *Musical Note2.ai* layer should now follow the same path as the *Musical Note1.ai,* except with a lag of half a second. Note that the (time - .5) value represents the half-second delay. If you want the second note to follow closer, change this setting to .25 or less, perhaps even .10. To extend the lag, change the setting to 1. Also, in the (this layer, 1) section of the code, the number 1 implies that the *Musical Note2.ai* layer is looking at the layer below it. This setting should be –1 if you want the layer to look at the layer above it, or 2 if you want it to look two layers below.

9. **Drag the *Musical Note3.ai* from the Project window into the Timeline so that it lies above the previous two layers.**

10. **Select the *Musical Note3.ai* layer and press the P key to solo its Position property.**

11. **Option/Alt+click the stopwatch for the Position property for the *Musical Note3.ai* layer.** This activates an expression.

12. **Highlight the expression field for the *Musical Note2.ai* layer and select the text in the expression by dragging the pointer over the characters to highlight them.**

13. **Choose Edit ⇨ Copy to copy this expression.**

14. **Highlight the expression field for the *Musical Note3.ai* layer and select the expression in it.**

15. **Choose Edit ⇨ Paste to paste the expression into the *Musical Note3.ai* layer.**

16. **Press the Enter key on the numeric keypad to activate the expression.**

17. **Press the spacebar to play your comp.** The *Musical Note3.ai* layer follows the *Musical Note2.ai* layer, which in turn is following the *Musical Note1.ai* layer. Note that in the *Musical Note3.ai* layer's expression field, if you change the (this layer, 1) setting to (this layer, 2), then the *Musical Note3.ai* layer looks at the *Musical Note1.ai* layer. In that case, the *Musical Note3.ai* layer and the *Musical Note2.ai* layer will have the same timing and speed, because they will both be referring to the *Musical Note1.ai* layer.

You can feel free to arrange the Musical Note layers now, as long as you change the (this layer, 1) setting to control which layer they need to look at. You can also edit the (time - .5) setting to change how closely or how far apart you want the notes to follow one another.

Figure 25-6 shows the final results of our exercise.

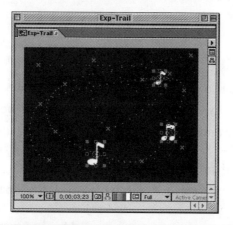

Figure 25-6: Here's the arrangement of the three layers and the expressions needed to make a trail of objects.

Using the element menus

To write expressions of any sophistication and length, you need to have a working knowledge of JavaScript in addition to some essential math functions. Adobe has provided many ways of creating and managing expressions, even if you know nothing about JavaScript or math.

Another way to make basic expressions in After Effects is to use the language element menu that is located in the Expressions buttons. This menu is located in the expressions icon area and becomes active when you activate expressions for a layer.

In the next series of steps, we show you a very simple way of using the menu to create a tiny expression that adds randomness to any property.

On the DVD-ROM   For the next series of steps, you should look at the composition called *EXP-Randomness*.

STEPS: Creating Randomness with Expressions

1. **Make a new comp by choosing Composition ⇨ New Composition.**

2. **Drag the Bulb-Top and Bulb-Base layers provided from the Project window into the Timeline of your new comp.** Arrange them to create a lightbulb.

3. **Select the Bulb-Top layer and press the T key to solo its Opacity.**

4. **Option/Alt+click the Opacity stopwatch on the Bulb-Top layer to activate an expression.**

5. **Open up the language element menu by clicking its arrow.** This arrow is the third icon to the left of the graph and the pick whip icons.

6. **From the language element menu, choose Random Numbers ⇨ random(.**

   Figure 25-7 shows this selection.

7. **The expression** `random(` **appears in the expression field.**

8. **At this point, you need to think of the upper value for the range of the random values that you want to use.** In this case, we're creating randomness for Opacity, and our upper limit is 100. Enter **100)** to complete the expression. Your expression should now read `random(100)`. This means that your Opacity now randomizes between 0 and 100.

9. **Press Enter on the numeric keypad to activate the expression.** Play your comp by pressing the spacebar, and you see that the bulb flickers on a random basis.

Note that you can add randomness to just about any property, such as Rotation, an effect point, or any other effect property for that matter. The key is knowing the upper limit. For example, for Rotation your upper limit is 360. If you were creating a random Rotation, you would simply add `random(360)` in the expression field for the maximum random Rotation range.

Controlling expressions by using Effect Controls

In the previous sections, we have shown you how to edit expressions and modify them to your needs. There is yet another way of controlling expressions that we want to show you before we wrap this chapter up. This method shows you a way of tying expression values to sliders and controllers found in the Effect Controls window. It may sound a bit weird at this stage. However, follow along with the steps, and you'll see what we mean.

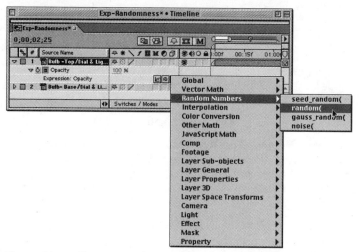

Figure 25-7: Choose Random Numbers ⇨ random(from the expression language element menu to add a small expression to your property.

We should note that you will find it easier to get through this section after you work your way through the rest of the step exercises in this chapter. In short, this section may be a bit advanced for some readers.

Note   Brian Maffit, a longtime guru of After Effects, must be credited here because he's the only person we've seen come up with this fabulous technique. Many people have used Brian's wonderful "Total After Effects" training tapes, and without him, not only would there be fewer users of After Effects, but there would also be a lot less fun in this world.

On the DVD-ROM   For the next series of steps, you should work with the composition called *EXP-Effect Controllers-Clean*. For reference, you can look at the completed comp called *EXP-Effect Controllers-Final*.

STEPS: Controlling Expressions with Effect Controls

1. **Double-click the *EXP-Effect Controllers-Clean* comp in the Project window to open it up.** This is the same comp used earlier where we created a trail of musical notes following each other. (If you are unclear on how this was done, refer to Chapter 18 and look at the exercise where we showed you how to do that.)

   You may notice that the layer at the bottom of the stacking order in the Timeline, *Musical Note1.ai,* has some Position keyframes applied to it, while the next layer, *Musical Note2.ai,* trails the bottom layer based on an expression. Then the top layer, *Musical Note3.ai,* trails the *Musical Note2.ai* layer based on a similar expression. In the expression

```
this_comp.layer(this_layer, 1).position.value_at_time(time - .5)
```

the .5 indicates the time of one-half second. The minus sign before the .5 indicates that the layer should lag behind by one-half second. Earlier, we showed you how you can change this –.5 to –.25 to make the layer lag by just one-quarter second, and so forth. However, changing numbers like that doesn't really feel like After Effects. In After Effects, we're more used to changing values with sliders, so we're going to bring some sliders into the mix. Don't worry; you'll see what we mean.

First, we need a set of "dummy" sliders to manipulate.

2. **Select the top layer, *Musical Note3.ai*, and choose Effect ⇨ Adjust ⇨ Brightness and Contrast to apply the effect.** Click the "f" icon in the upper-left corner of the Brightness and Contrast effect in the Effect Controls window to deactivate the effect. That's right, make the effect inactive; we just want to use the two sliders it provides.

3. **In your comp, highlight the value .5 for the *Musical Note2.ai* layer in the expression field.**

4. **Then select the pick whip for the *Musical Note2.ai* layer and drag it to the *Brightness* property, which is the topmost one in the Effect Controls window.**

Figure 25-8 shows this process.

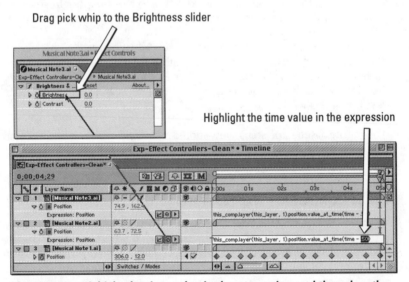

Figure 25-8: Highlight the time value in the expression and then drag the pick whip to an effects slider.

What's new in After Effects 5.5: Expressions enhancements

With version 5.5, Adobe has added two new enhancements to expressions. The first one is a minor one. The second enhancement has implications that blow our minds!

First, let's look at the minor enhancement: Expressions can now be looped. There are now four different loop types, as well as some options for controlling the timing of your loops. Loops can be set to go in one direction (forward or backward) or back and forth ("ping-pong").

The second enhancement to expressions has some major implications. In After Effects 5.5, Adobe has provided effects that add interface elements to your Effect Controls window. These interface elements (sliders, check boxes, and so on) can then be linked to expressions to control them. Think about this for a second. When you wrap your head around it, you'll realize that it's like being able to create your very own effects in After Effects. The first basic step toward accomplishing this is to create an expression in which there's a value that you want to control with a slider or any other interface control. Then select the layer in question and choose Effect ➪ Expression Controls, and select an interface element. This new element, a slider for example, will now appear in the Effect Controls window.

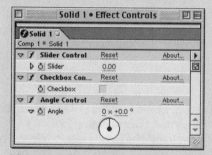

Figure SB 25-1: The Expression Controls group of effects offer interface elements that enable you to create your own effects based upon expressions.

Highlight the value in the expression you want to control and then drag the pick whip from the expression to the interface element in your Effect Controls window. Release the mouse, and you can move the slider around and control your expression. You can also rename the slider or the interface element by clicking its name and pressing Return.

5. **Press the Enter key on the numeric keypad to activate the expression.**

6. **Next, select the pick whip for the *Musical Note3.ai* layer and drag it to the Contrast property, second from the top in the Effect Controls window.**

7. **Control+click/Right-click the Brightness property in the Effect Controls window and choose Edit Value from the contextual menu.** In the Slider Control box that is presented, set the Slider Range from 0 to 5.

8. **Control+click/Right-click the Contrast property in the Effect Controls window and select Edit Value from the contextual menu.** In the Slider Control box that is presented, set the Slider Range from 0 to 5.

Figure 25-9 shows the Slider Control dialog box.

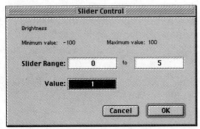

Figure 25-9: Change the Slider Range to better reflect the time values that you are using in your expression.

That's all there is to it. What we have just done is attach the time lag value of the *Musical Note2.ai* layer to the Brightness slider and the time lag value of the *Musical Note3.ai* layer to the Contrast slider. The Brightness and Contrast sliders won't result in any changes to the image because we turned off the actual effect. We also edited the range of the sliders so that they represent 0 to 5 seconds. Now you can move the Brightness slider to a value of one and the *Musical Note3.ai* layer will lag behind the *Musical Note2.ai* layer by one second. Similarly, you can change the value of the Contrast slider to two, and the *Musical Note2.ai* layer will lag behind the *Musical Note1.ai* layer by two seconds. No more need to fuss with your expressions. Simply use the sliders to control your lag time for the trail.

Remember what we said in the beginning? Some designers hope to virtually eliminate keyframes from their animations. By now, you can see why. The amount of work you need to put into creating keyframes for certain kinds of animations can be drastically reduced if you take the time to become familiar with expressions. If you've been working your way through the book from front to back, you've seen a little of what Parenting, Null Object layers, 3D, and now expressions can do for your animations. Folks, combine these, and you'll be cooking with fire.

✦   ✦   ✦

Improving Your Visuals with Sound

The world of audio presents quite a departure from the topics covered so far. Up until this point in the book, the entire focus has been on using After Effects as a visual post-production tool. That doesn't mean we've been neglecting an entire aspect of the software's potential application, because After Effects isn't really a fully sufficient solution when creating professional audio to complement professional video. While it's limited in some ways, After Effects still contains a number of useful ways of handling this particular area of media production.

The audio filters in After Effects are an interesting and mixed bag of offerings. Depending on your needs, you may find that they provide you with just enough sweetening control to not have to worry about looking into other software packages. If you're not familiar with the term *sweetening,* it refers to the process of cleaning up audio for production. When compared to After Effects, systems such as ProTools offer much greater control in this area, but if you're working in a broadcast situation where a lot of expertise is scattered across the multiple facets of production, you don't need to worry about the complexities of audio problems. On the other hand, if you're a freelancer who offers clients one-stop shopping for all their production needs, you'll definitely need to branch out and increase your knowledge base in this sector of the market and, in turn, make some informed decisions on software and hardware — if you haven't already.

Okay. Lecture's over. How about learning some audio techniques in After Effects? If that's what you're looking for, press ahead.

Mixing Sound in After Effects

After Effects works with numerous forms of audio. You can just as easily work with DV files containing audio along with video as you can with an AIF file ripped from an audio CD. In fact, the list of supported audio formats now includes the increasingly popular red-hot MP3 format. In addition to AIF and MP3, other notables include AU, WAV (Mac only) and Mac sound (obviously, Mac only).

Note   For those of you that have been living underground for the last couple of years, the MP3 audio compression format has revolutionized the music business. MP3 audio technology has enabled consumers to place their entire music library on a small handheld device, such as the Apple iPod MP3 player, for one. Not only can you rip and play whatever files whenever you want, the hardware consists of a tiny hard drive or, in other variants, a memory chip. Unlike a CD player, the playback doesn't skip if you're jogging on a treadmill! The files are small, but their quality is comparatively high. As a result, not only has the technology appeared on the desktop and in small playback devices, but Internet Radio is also huge. While it disappoints classical music purists on account of its clamped dynamic range, it's developed a huge following among a less exacting popular audience.

Our usual workflow involves cutting segments of a piece with editing software and then importing them into After Effects in order to add graphics and tweak the audio with some kind of effect or adjustment. After we finish the After Effects component, we export the bits back out to the edit suite. That's where we make our final edit and lay it off to tape, or if the video is meant for the Web or a CD-ROM, we compress it instead. Of course, there are a number of variations on this general setup, but that's basically it.

As far as audio is concerned, we actually do more work on it with the editing software than we do in After Effects. The reason for this is that After Effects doesn't allow for real-time playback of an audio track; as is its custom, it needs to load everything into RAM before you can see or hear a preview of your work. Still, even with that limitation, you find a number of well-designed audio features as well as some interesting filters, some of which we use on a pretty regular basis.

Previewing Audio

As soon as you bring audio into After Effects, it behaves a bit differently than other layers in the Timeline. To begin understanding the audio aspect of the application, place a file containing some audio into the Timeline of a new composition. Press L once to solo the audio Levels. Press LL (in fairly quick succession) to open up a graph of the audio waveform. As soon as the graph is visible, you can expand its viewing size by dragging the bottom edge to suit your needs. A *waveform* is a detailed "picture" of the sound, and it provides you with an excellent visual reference that you can take advantage of when timing your visual cues.

The amplitude of the audio is reflected in the highs and lows of the waveform as it progresses from left to right. Spikes indicate a lot of vibration (read, a loud noise), and low-lying areas are quieter. For example, a steady drumbeat appears as an easily identifiable pattern of evenly spaced apart peaks. We often use the waveform as a guide for edit and effect points. For example, explosions work well when timed with cymbal crashes. A slightly subtler example may involve fading an effect out as a track becomes more silent. You get the idea. In essence, it can be very handy to see what the audio's doing if you want your visual cues to match the audio track. Figure 26-1 displays an audio file and its waveform.

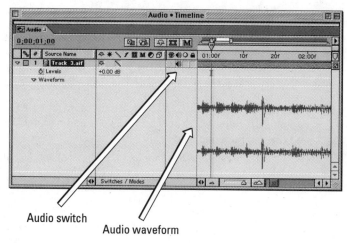

Audio switch

Audio waveform

Figure 26-1: Here's an audio file and its waveform. Drag the bottom edge of the graph to enlarge your view if you like.

Instead of a little eyeball indicating whether the layer is visible, a layer that contains audio has its own switch telling you whether you can hear the track if you want to preview or render it. While its speaker icon is clear enough, this is one of those interface quirks that can be fairly vexing until you get used to it. The audio switch column is positioned directly above any keyframe indicator for a layer, and sometimes beginning users of After Effects think that they're somehow related when, in fact, they're not (see Figure 26-2). The keyframe indicator tells you whether you're parked on a keyframe for any property in a layer. Again, the fact that it lies right under the audio switch column is irrelevant despite appearances to the contrary.

Understanding the sample rate of audio

What is the sample rate?

Audio tracks, such as image files, can contain varying amounts of data. In the same way that images have varying bit depths, the same parallel can be drawn when considering the sample rate of an audio track. Sample rates are measured in kHz, or thousands of cycles per second. CD quality audio is standardized to include 16-bit files sampled at 44.1 kHz (there are 8 bits per channel, and the combination of both is a 16-bit stereo file). High-end DV cameras operate at 48 kHz. The lower the sample rate of an audio file, the lower its audio resolution. It follows that a low sample rate provides less detail to your ear, resulting in fuzzy "noise" and an overall lack of quality.

How does an audio track's sample rate relate to its waveform?

Here's another fact: The more detail that's contained in an audio track, the more information you'll be able to see when you zoom in on a small portion of its waveform. This isn't unlike zooming in on a high-resolution image as compared to a highly compressed one.

Audio switch

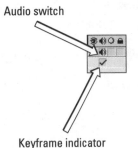

Keyframe indicator

Figure 26-2: Even though it looks like there might be a relationship, none exists between a layer's audio switch and the keyframe indicator.

So, how do you preview audio? Press the period key on the numeric keypad, and you hear an audio preview, the length of which is set in the preferences (see Figure 26-3). Most of the time, you're going to want a bigger audio preview than you get from the default setting of eight seconds. We usually set ours to at least double that, depending on the project. One more detail: The audio preview plays from the current time forward. Nothing's broken; that's just the way it works. However, there is a workaround for this. If you hold down the Option/Alt key and press zero on the numeric keypad, you'll preview the audio from the beginning of the work area.

If you want to scrub the audio in a comp, hold down the Command/Ctrl key as you drag the playhead.

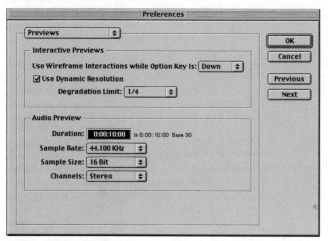

Figure 26-3: The Previews preferences dictate the length of your audio preview.

Editing Audio Levels

If you're going to make adjustments to the audio levels on a layer, you need to use the Audio palette to set them (see Figure 26-4). You can't scrub the numerical value for the levels in the Timeline, even though it looks as though you should be able to (see upcoming sidebar). For example, if you want to animate an audio fade-in, first you need to set keyframes for the Levels property at the points in time when you want the fade to start and finish; however, you can only adjust the values for those keyframes by tweaking the levels in the Audio palette.

What's new in After Effects 5.5: Scrubbable audio levels in the Timeline window

Now when you're working in After Effects 5.5, you can scrub the audio levels in the Timeline. Just as you would with any other property, position your pointer over the numerical value for the audio level in the Timeline, and then click and drag. If the Audio palette is open, you'll see that the changes in levels are dynamically updated.

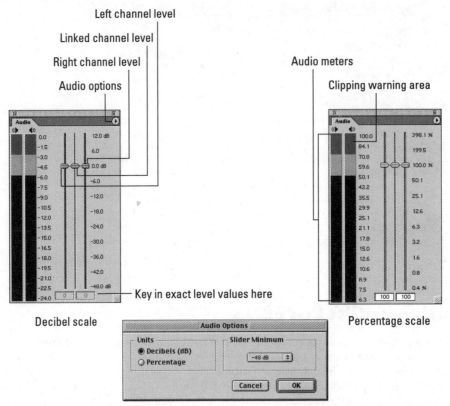

Figure 26-4: You need to use the Audio palette to adjust the audio levels on a layer. You can't make these adjustments in the Timeline unless you have version 5.5.

If you click the little arrow at the upper-right corner of the Audio palette, you can see the options for it (refer to Figure 26-4). Viewing the Audio palette in percentage units can be quite useful if you're not an audio guru by trade. If you select percentage as the unit of measurement for volume, you can see quite clearly that increases in audio levels are exponential. This fact isn't widely known, and it can be a big help in understanding why seemingly small increments of change that you make at the high and low ends of the spectrum are actually rather big, relatively speaking.

On the DVD-ROM

In order to better understand audio, we created an After Effects project that includes a composition for a step exercise in the chapter. Just as a reminder, you need to copy the *Source Material* folder from the DVD-ROM to your hard drive. Our own corresponding After Effects project is called *Chapter 26.aep* and is found in the *Project Files/Chapter 26* folder. For the following exercise, feel free to use the composition called *Audio*.

STEPS: Setting Audio Level Keyframes

1. **Create a new comp, and drag an audio file into the Timeline.** If you prefer, you can double-click the comp called *Audio* in the Project window of the *Chapter 26.aep* project.

2. **With the audio layer selected in the Timeline, press LL to solo the audio layer's Levels and Waveform.**

3. **Click the stopwatch next to the Levels property name to set a keyframe at the first frame of the comp.**

4. **Drag the middle slider of the Audio palette down to the bottom.** This sets the initial Levels keyframe to –48 db. You'll notice that the waveform turns into nondescript flat lines indicating that no audio can be heard if the comp is left in its current state.

Note You can also scrub the audio level in the Timeline. See preceding sidebar.

5. **Press Command/Ctrl+G to open the Go To Time dialog box, enter 100, and click OK.** This sets the Current Time to 0:00:01:00.

6. **Drag the middle slider of the Audio palette up to zero.** It may not land cleanly on zero, in which case you can click in the numerical fields at the bottom of the Audio palette and key in precise values. By the way, the Tab key jumps between the left and right channel fields. If you set them this way, press Return or Enter after you're done. This step returns the detail to the waveform because its levels have been raised.

7. **Make sure that the work area includes the opening fade-in for the audio track and press Option/Alt+0 on the numeric keypad to hear an audio preview of the work area.** The audio should fade in over the first second of the comp, and as it does so, the sliders on the Audio palette indicate the exact changes to the levels in real time, which is really pretty cool. It also displays the volume of the track by using the bars on the left. If the volume is clipping or otherwise dangerously high, you'll see its meters spiking into the red zone. If this is happening, you want to set the levels a bit lower to avoid distortion.

   More importantly, you may notice that the audio fades up in a way that sounds "wrong," for lack of a better word. Earlier, we discussed that changes in audio levels are exponential as you move in either direction away from 0 db. The gulf between 48 db and 0 db is a great deal bigger than the one from 0 to 10, for example. You may find that either the value of the first keyframe or the speed of the interpolation between the two keyframes would produce better results, if adjusted.

8. **Make adjustments to the audio level of the first keyframe.** Use the waveform graph as a guide. You may even want to consider making the first temporal keyframe Bezier instead of linear and adjusting its handles so that you get a better fade-in.

Admittedly, this is hardly a sexy exercise, but it explains the mechanics of this quirky aspect of After Effects. The distinguishing characteristic of making adjustments to an audio track is the lack of control in the Timeline. All changes must be made in the Audio palette, and that's a good thing to know. One other point worth mentioning is that you can set different levels for the left and right audio channels, should you desire.

Tip

Don't forget that you can set markers on a layer during a real-time audio preview by pressing the * (asterisk) key on the numeric keypad. Select the layer that you want to add markers to before you initiate the preview, and after the audio starts playing, press the asterisk key at the parts in the audio track that you want to mark for later reference. After you add markers to a layer in the Timeline, you can label them, reposition them, or delete them. You can label them by double-clicking directly on them to access their options.

Cross-Reference

There's a fun exercise in Chapter 23 that enables you to take the amplitude of an audio track and have it directly influence a property for another layer, such as scale. If you're curious, it's called called Modifying the *layeraud.mm* (Layer Audio) script.

Leveraging the Standard Audio Effects

The audio effects (see Figure 26-5) contain a number of interesting ways to mess around with an audio track. Some are practically grounded in their application, and others are more fun than they are imminently useful. For example, the audio filters in the Standard version include an intuitive Bass & Treble control, which can really help warm up a tinny track or bring out detail in a slightly muffled one. On the other hand, they also include Backwards, which, unless you want to see if Led Zeppelin's *Stairway to Heaven* really contains evidence of devil worship, is something you probably won't use that often. The same is true of the Production Bundle audio filters. For example, an effect, such as Tone is simply great. Tone is often considered to be the audio equivalent of a solid and can take on a number of helpful applications. On the other hand, there's the slightly less utilitarian Flange & Chorus, which produces cool-sounding results but probably isn't going to wind up in your day-to-day workflow. Nonetheless, filters such as Backwards and Flange & Chorus are an absolute blast to play with, and they can also lend an appropriately stylized feel to a project, so we're certainly not complaining. Keep moving forward and go check them out.

Cross-Reference

Chapter 8 describes working with effects in general. If you aren't familiar with applying effects or working in the Effect Controls window, take the time to read (or re-read) the beginning of Chapter 8.

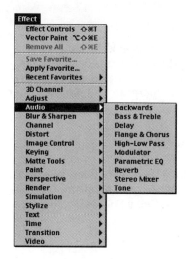

Figure 26-5: The Audio group of effects as they appear in the Effect menu

The Online Help (choose Help ➪ After Effects Help) is an HTML document that goes well beyond the printed User's Guide in explaining After Effects in detail. In addition to containing all of the information included in the User's Guide, the Online Help contains a lot of very useful basic information on all the effects that ship with After Efffects. Refer to it as often as you need to; our purpose in writing about these effects is to supplement that information rather than repeat it.

As far as the following explanations of effects are concerned, we created an After Effects project that includes a composition for each effect that we cover in the chapter. Just as a reminder, you need to copy the *Source Material* folder from the DVD-ROM to your hard drive. Our own corresponding After Effects project is called *Chapter 26.aep* and is found in the *Project Files/Chapter 26* folder. Feel free to substitute your own audio files with the examples shown in the figures and exercises.

Using the Backwards effect

Okay. Slap this onto an audio file by selecting the layer and choosing Effect ➪ Audio Backwards and see if you can hear the demon from *The Exorcist* talking. If you want to mix lots of audio tracks in the Timeline, you can try your hand as a George Martin style producer (you know, the fifth Beatle) and work on your own version of "Strawberry Fields" by reversing some of the audio tracks.

Don't forget that time-remapping and stretching a layer also affects the audio track. In truth, time-remapping and stretching completely nullify any need you may have for this filter. Not only can you play a track backwards with the time controls, but you can also control its speed by adding and modifying time-remapping keyframes.

Using the Bass & Treble effect

If you want to adjust the audio of a layer like you might tweak the controls on your stereo, select the audio layer in the Timeline and then choose Effect ➪ Audio ➪ Bass & Treble. That's about all there is to it. After you add the effect, move the appropriate sliders in the Effect Controls window to increase or decrease either the Bass or Treble of the audio track.

Using the Delay effect

Delay may as well be called Echo, but because there's a visual effect called Echo, that's probably how it ended up getting its name. When you initially apply this effect to a layer, you add an echo to your audio. The Delay Effect Controls are shown in Figure 26-6.

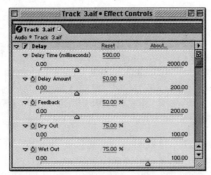

Figure 26-6: The Delay Effect Controls

By default, the echo begins 500 milliseconds (half a second) behind the audio track. You can adjust this using the Delay Time slider. The other properties in the Effect Controls that you should become familiar with are the Dry Out and Wet Out effect properties, because these terms are universal in the audio domain. Dry represents the unfiltered audio, and Wet represents the affected audio. The effect only really works when the two are partially combined. In this case, the default settings for these sliders are set to 75%. If you knock either one back to 0%, you'll be left with only the clean or the affected audio track. In essence, the combination of these sliders controls the overall intensity of the echo.

Caution   An echo goes beyond the actual duration of an audio clip. In other words, you may need to extend the out point you've trimmed for an audio layer because the Delay won't be finished playing until after the unaffected audio is finished.

Tip

Used in conjunction with time-remapping, you can abruptly stop the underlying audio while the effect continues to echo. You've probably seen (or heard) this in a million different movies.

Using the Stereo Mixer effect

Most audio tracks contain a left and right channel. Applying the Stereo Mixer effect (see Figure 26-7) enables you to mix these channels as you see fit. This can be a lot of fun. If you want to, you can put all of an audio track into one channel and keyframe it so that it all goes into the other. Don't be misled by the percentage values of the Pan sliders. By default, the Left Pan is set to –100% and the Right Pan is set to 100%, which means that everything is as it should be. If you want to put all of the audio into the right channel, leave the Right Pan at 100% and set the Left Pan to 100%. Conversely, if you want to put all of the audio into the left channel, set both the Left Pan and the Right Pan to –100%. Knowing this makes it a bit easier to understand.

Caution

If you put all of an audio file into one channel, you run the risk of clipping the output of the one channel. Check the meters on the Audio pallette during a preview to maker certain that your effect isn't producing distorted audio.

Figure 26-7: The Stereo Mixer Effect Controls. Notice the default Left Pan and Right Pan values.

Plying the Production Bundle Audio Effects

By now, you've probably grown accustomed to the fact that Production Bundle effects provide a good deal more power than their Standard cousins. In the realm of audio, this isn't as clearly demonstrated as it is in other categories. A couple of these filters are more fun than they are daily workhorses, but a few of them are actually pretty darned impressive.

Using the Flange & Chorus effect (PB Only)

Flange & Chorus can help you turn a simple track of audio into something approximating the sound of a modern-day rave. Apply it to a track containing a lot of synthesizers, and you see what we mean. Aesthetically speaking, this filter definitely has a futuristic industrial feel. Apart from that, you might be wondering what it's really good for. The Online Help contains some useful information on how to separate the Chorus from the Flange, if you're interested. This can be pretty neat if you want to make one voice or instrument sound as though they're part of a larger group.

Using the High-Low Pass effect (PB Only)

The High-Low Pass filter is a good sweetening tool. Sometimes, you want to cut out parts of the audio spectrum to clean up an audio track. For example, there may be a refrigerator humming beneath the dialogue, or your audio track could just as easily be suffering from tape hiss or a high-pitched squeal from a television. In cases such as these, the High-Low Pass effect can be quite helpful. You can use it to block out frequencies above and below the range where voices lie in the audio spectrum.

First, select the offending track and then choose Effect ⇨ Audio ⇨ High-Low Pass. In the Effect Controls, you need to specify whether you want a High or a Low Pass from the Filter Options pop-up menu. A High Pass actually sets a floor, whereas a Low Pass sets a ceiling. In other words, a High Pass filter lets frequencies through above a specified value, whereas a Low Pass filter lets frequencies through below a specified value. Practically speaking, you set a High Pass filter to block out unwanted sound at the lower parts of the audio spectrum, and you employ a Low Pass filter to block out undesirable frequencies in the higher ranges of the audio spectrum.

To get the most out of this filter, you want to experiment using the following guidelines:

✦ To use it as both a High and a Low Pass, apply the filter twice, specifying the alternate option in each case (see Figure 26-8).

✦ Voices run the gamut from approximately 100 Hz (a High Pass Frequency slider value of approximately 100) to 5 kHz (a Low Pass Frequency slider value of 5000). Make this a starting guideline. You may even want to save the pair as a favorite called something such as "Hi-Lo Voices Only."

✦ Remember that the default settings of 0% Dry Out and 100% Wet Out represent only the affected audio. If you're chopping out too much and can get the Frequency sliders to do your bidding, try adding in a little Dry Out.

✦ You can experiment with these filters to make people's voices sound as though they're calling long distance. The point is that there are also creative options here.

✦ Extreme use of this filter can drop your track's overall audio level. Compensate appropriately with the overall Levels control.

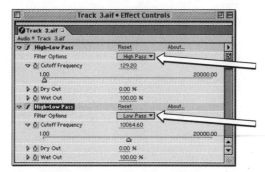

Figure 26-8: To cut out parts of both ends of the audio spectrum, apply the High-Low Pass filter twice and set each instance appropriately.

Using the Modulator effect (PB Only)

The Modulator filter takes the existing pitch of an audio track and gives it a watery, wobbly-sounding distortion. If you apply it to an unwavering pitch or tone, it applies a vibrato kind of effect to it. So, if you ever need an uninspiring flat-sounding note to sound more like an opera singer, or even better, a completely blitzed opera singer from another plane of existence, then the Modulator effect is yours to use and abuse.

Tip Once you apply the Modulator effect, the Modulation Rate property controls the frequency of the "wobble." A value of 1 produces one complete "wobble" per second. The Modulation Depth controls the extremity of the "wobble." Choosing Sine as the Modulation Type results in slide between the variations in pitch, whereas Triangle alternates between pitches without sliding in between.

Using the Parametric EQ effect (PB Only)

Earlier, we mentioned that the Bass & Treble filter is similar to the dials bearing the same names on your stereo. Those of you with nicer stereos have Parametric Equalizer settings on your amplifier, and the Parametric EQ filter mimics those kinds of controls (see Figure 26-9).

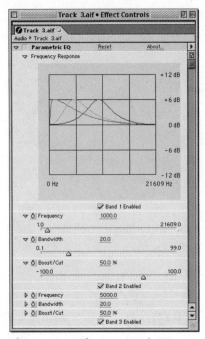

Figure 26-9: The Parametric EQ
Effect controls

If you enable all three bands in the Effect Controls, each of them is represented
on the Frequency Response graph, by a red (Band 1), a green (Band 2), and a blue
(Band 3) line. On the graph, the X-axis represents the audio spectrum, and the
Y-axis represents the volume level. If you experiment with the sliders, you'll notice
that the Frequency property affects the X-coordinate of the top of the bell curve,
the Bandwidth property affects the width of the bell curve, and the Boost/Cut
property affects the Y-coordinate of the top of the bell curve.

Great, but what does all that stuff really mean? As the properties suggest, you can
specify a range of the audio spectrum with the first two band sliders, and then you
can accentuate or diminish that range depending on your needs. The affected range
is represented by the range of values within the bell curve of the band on the
Frequency Response graph. For flexibility's sake, the filter provides you with three
sets of controls. As we said earlier, you can manipulate this like a similar set of controls on a good stereo system.

Tip   After you apply the High Low Pass filter to isolate the part of the audio spectrum
where voices lie, you can use the Parametric EQ effect to "warm" up the quality of
the voices in an audio track. Experimentation is key here.

Using the Reverb effect (PB Only)

The Reverb filter (see Figure 26-10) helps make your audio track sound as though it's being played in different types of physical space. Depending on how you tweak its settings, you can make a music track sound as though it's being played in a cavernous gym or a small garage. Creating the illusion of a specific space is a powerful tool in establishing the realism of an environment.

Figure 26-10: The Reverb Effect Controls

The following list describes the Reverb effect properties.

✦ **Reverb Time:** Crank this value up to increase the size of the virtual room in which the audio can be heard. Conversely, crank it down to place the sound in a smaller virtual space. The reason this property acts this way is that sound takes a longer time to bounce off the walls of a valley than it would if it were generated in a concert hall, for example.

✦ **Diffusion:** This property controls the randomness of the echoes generated within Reverb Time.

✦ **Decay:** This property controls how long each echo lasts. Short or small decay values approximate surfaces that absorb noise (such as foam or fabric). Long decays are indicative of hard surfaces that sharply reflect noise (such as concrete).

✦ **Brightness:** This property controls how "tinny" the echoes sound. Higher values accentuate this effect.

✦ **Dry Out/Wet Out:** Again, the Dry Out slider controls the unaffected audio, whereas the the Wet Out slider controls the affected audio.

Using the Tone effect (PB Only)

The Tone filter (see Figure 26-11) creates the audio equivalent of a solid layer. The reason we draw that comparison is that you don't need to start out with a preexisting sound in order for the filter to generate its own sound. It's similar to the way you can add a solid layer to a comp without needing any pre-made graphic elements.

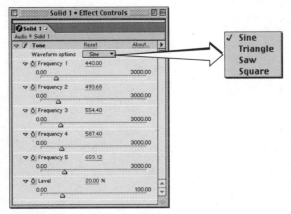

Figure 26-11: The Tone Effect Controls

If you add the Tone effect to preexisting audio, it cancels it out. Instead, it makes more sense to apply it to a new solid, which we show you how to do in the following steps.

STEPS: Generating Original Sound with the Tone Filter

1. **Create a New Composition by pressing Command/Ctrl+N.** Don't worry about its particulars too much, because you are working with sound.

2. **Press Command/Ctrl+Y to create a new solid and click OK.** Again, don't worry about its color or size.

3. **In the Timeline, turn off the solid's visibility by clicking the little eyeball in the switches column for the layer.**

4. **Click the solid to select it and then choose Effect ⇨ Audio ⇨ Tone.** The audio switch for the solid appears, and now your solid, invisible to the eye, generates a tone according to the settings of the effect properties. The Effect Controls reveal five Frequency sliders, each one representing a different pitch.

5. **To hear an audio preview of the work area, press Option/Alt+0 on the numeric keypad.** The five frequencies play as a chord at the level specified at the bottom of the Effect Controls menu.

With the solid still selected in the Timeline, go ahead and add the Modulator or Flange & Chorus Effect. Now that you know how to alter existing sound, you can experiment with all the different audio filters in modifying the newly generated Tone.

Tip The Tone filter gives the choice to play five frequencies simultaneously. If you want to turn any of them off, just set their frequency to zero.

Tip If you use the comp you made in this exercise as a pre-comp in another composition, you can select it as the basis for the Audio Spectrum and Audio Waveform effects.

True "Sweetening"

Before we leave the topic, we should mention that the most useful kind of professional audio work is concerned with "sweetening" dialogue and natural sound so that it's both warm-sounding and free of clicks, pops, and other random noises. In much the same way that you might use Photoshop to remove scratches and specks of dust from a scanned image, a ProTools audio editor can break down an audio track and remove any distracting irregularities. This kind of post-production skill goes well beyond blocking out ranges of frequencies as you might with the High Low Pass filter. So, it all depends. If your After Effects project involves creating visuals for a pre-selected music track, you probably won't have to worry too much about seeking outside help. If, by contrast, your project contains lots of spoken dialogue taped in different environments, there's almost no way you can avoid needing to get some assistance. With any luck, your budget allows for it.

So, bearing in mind that After Effects was never really designed to be a complete post-production solution for your audio, it still has its strengths. After you learn the quirks of keyframing audio levels, sometimes you find that's all the control you need to complete the audio component of a project. After you know the audio preview workarounds, you can leverage After Effects as a decent audio-editing tool. Lastly, after you've experimented with the audio filters, you can go forward with a clear understanding of what the application does well as compared to what you might want to leave to an audio specialist. Considering that After Effects is really a compositing application, you'll realize that its audio capabilities are pretty decent.

✦   ✦   ✦

Wiggling, Tracking, and Stabilizing

Once again, we return to the topic of control. Whether you're trying to perfect the movement of a layer along a motion path, map an effect point to an object traveling within a movie clip, or take shaky footage and keep it from moving, After Effects provides you with a number of tools to help you in your quest. There's a keyframe assistant that goes by the name of The Wiggler. We kid you not. Then again, that might not come as a surprise if you've already had experience with The Smoother. In addition to these joyfully named creations, there are also some tracking and stabilizing controls built into the Layer window. In this chapter, we examine the workings of these tools so that you can put them to good use.

The Wiggler is a keyframe assistant that creates randomization, and with a little input from you, its randomness can be made to order. Want fries with that wiggle? In addition to The Wiggler, After Effects now offers similar control over randomness in your animations with the addition to expressions, so this palette isn't as critical as it used to be, but it's still a great tool to keep handy.

The Motion Tracking and Stabilizing controls are built to address a number of specific production problems. Mapping certain effects on to jittery footage can be a particularly vexing problem, and the Motion Tracker makes life considerably easier if you're faced with that particular issue. Stabilizing works almost exactly like motion tracking, and after the Stabilizer has analyzed a clip, you can tweak its controls to take the jitter out of shaky footage if you want to get rid of it.

On the scale of complexity and sophistication, these aren't beginner topics, but then again, through solid and intuitively-based design, Adobe has kept these tools from being prohibitively complicated. See for yourself and enjoy.

Randomizing with The Wiggler (PB Only)

So it's randomness you want. No problem. First, we show you how to use The Wiggler (see Figure 27-1), and then we show you how to control it with some degree of finesse. You can access it by choosing Window ➪ The Wiggler.

Note   You need the Production Bundle to access this feature.

Figure 27-1: The Wiggler is a keyframe assistant that you can access by choosing Window ➪ The Wiggler.

So what is this little palette capable of doing? When you initially open it up, the chances are that its options will be grayed out. At least two keyframes need to be selected before The Wiggler's options become available to you. Complete the next set of steps to become familiar with the workings of this small, yet powerful, wonder.

In order to better explain The Wiggler, we created an After Effects project that includes a composition for the following set of steps. Just as a reminder, you need to copy the *Source Material* folder from the DVD-ROM to your hard drive. The After Effects project that corresponds to this chapter is called *Chapter 27.aep* and is found in the *Project Files/Chapter 27* folder. For the following exercise, refer to the comp that's called *Wiggling*.

STEPS: Introducing the Wiggler

1. **Create a new NTSC D1, 720 x 486 comp by choosing Composition ➪ New Composition (Command/Ctrl+N) and selecting the D1 preset.** Give yourself at least five seconds to work with it.

2. **Create a new solid by choosing Layer ➪ New ➪ Solid (Command/Ctrl+Y).** In the Solid Settings dialog box, name it *Wiggle,* specify a size of 100 x 100, and color it white.

3. **Making sure the solid layer is selected in the Timeline, press P to solo the layer's Position property.**

4. **Click the stopwatch next to the Position property name to set an initial keyframe for the layer at the first frame of the comp.**

5. **Press the End key to go to the last frame of the comp and click in the Keyframe Navigator to set another Position keyframe for the layer.** Alternatively, you can press Option/Alt+P to set the Position keyframe.

6. **Click the Position property name to select both of the keyframes that you just set.**

7. **Choose Window ➪ The Wiggler to open The Wiggler palette.**

Tip

The Wiggler behaves like any other palette. You can drag it into another open palette, or you can leave it out on its own.

8. **Specify the following Wiggler settings:**

   • **Apply To:** Spatial Path

   • **Noise Type:** Jagged

   • **Dimension:** All Dimensions Independently

   • **Frequency:** 10.0

   • **Magnitude:** 25.0

9. **In the lower-right corner of The Wiggler, click the Apply button.** This creates random position keyframes between the two keyframes that you selected in Step 6. Because of the settings you specified in Step 8, the keyframes will be set 10 times per second and will vary by as many as 25 pixels from the original position of the layer. See Figure 27-2.

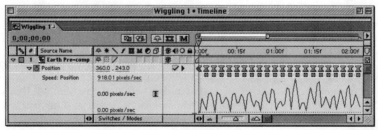

Figure 27-2: The Wiggler generates random keyframes within limits that you directly control. In this case, the Wiggler has created 10 keyframes per second, the values of which vary by as many as 25 pixels from the original position of the layer.

10. **Press 0 on the numeric keypad to preview the random movement of the Wiggle solid layer.**

11. **With the Wiggle solid layer selected in the Timeline, hold down the Option/Alt key and drag a footage item from the Project window into the Timeline.** After you release the mouse, your selection takes the place of the Wiggle solid. We used the Planet Earth movie provided to us by the creative gang at EyeWire. To make it a little more interesting, we scaled it down to 30% and placed a layer of animted EyeWire stars behind it.

Well done. Consider yourself introduced to The Wiggler. Pretty cool, right? Think past the basic nature of this exercise, and you'll probably start imagining all the different components of your animations that might benefit from a little wiggle, or if you prefer, randomness.

The following list describes The Wiggler's controls in detail:

✦ **Apply To:** This pop-up menu gives you the choice between Spatial Path and Temporal Graph. Spatial Path applies to properties with positional coordinates (X, Y, and Z, if applicable), whereas Temporal Graph applies to all other properties. The Temporal Graph option is critical, because this enables The Wiggler to extend its random keyframe creation to any property that can be keyframed.

✦ **Noise Type:** This pop-up menu gives you the choice between Smooth and Jagged. The descriptions of these choices pretty much speak for themselves; however, they're most profound when applied to a Spatial Path.

✦ **Dimension:** If you're using The Wiggler on a Spatial Path, you can opt to create randomness in any one dimension (X, Y, or Z, if applicable), or you can affect all of them at once. As far as affecting all dimensions is concerned, you can opt to create a different set of random keyframes for each axis (All Dimensions Independently), or you can create the same amount of randomness on each axis (All Dimensions The Same). If you're using The Wiggler on a Temporal Graph, you'll have as many options as the affected property has variables.

✦ **Frequency:** This value determines the number of keyframes that The Wiggler generates per second. After the keyframes have been created, they're adjustable like any others.

✦ **Magnitude:** This value determines the range of values within which The Wiggler generates randomness. In the last set of steps, you set this value to 25, which told the Wiggler to generate random positional keyframes that would not exceed more than 25 pixels above or below the original values of 360 (X) and 243 (Y). If you use The Wiggler on a property that allows for negative values (such as Rotation, for instance), depending on the Magnitude setting, the random values will swing into negative territory. Alternatively, if you use The Wiggler on a property that doesn't allow for values past a certain finite limit (such as 0% and 100% for Opacity), the random values will clip.

So, as you can see, this little palette is a rather valuable addition to the interface. Complete the next set of steps to see what The Wiggler can do for properties besides those with spatial coordinates.

STEPS: Wiggling Temporal Properties

1. **Picking up where you left off in the last exercise, select the Wiggling layer in the Timeline and press T to solo its Opacity property.**

2. **Set two 50% opacity keyframes for the layer at the first and last frames of the comp.**

3. **Select both of the newly created keyframes by clicking the Opacity property name.**

4. **Make sure that The Wiggler is visible.** If not, choose Window ➪ The Wiggler.

5. **Specify the following Wiggler settings:**

   - **Apply To:** Temporal Graph—This is your only option because opacity isn't a spatial property.

   - **Noise Type:** Jagged—Either way, in the case of a property such as opacity, choosing Jagged or Smooth isn't going to matter much. If you want to make dramatic and "jagged" looking jumps in opacity, it makes more sense to change the newly generated Bezier keyframes into Hold keyframes in the Timeline, but you can do that after you create them with The Wiggler first.

   - **Dimension:** Doesn't matter—Again, you're working with one property.

   - **Frequency:** 10.0—We only suggest 10 if you want to match the timing of the opacity keyframes to the position keyframes. If not, feel free to do what you like.

   - **Magnitude:** 50.0—Because the keyframes you set are at 50%, a magnitude or variance of 50% in either direction enables the random opacity values generated by The Wiggler to vary between 0 and 100%.

6. **In the lower-right corner of The Wiggler, click the Apply button.**

7. **Preview your animation by pressing 0 on the numeric keypad.** If you applied the random opacity keyframes to the Planet Earth layer, she probably looks a little nervous by now.

Not bad for a little palette called The Wiggler. After all, they could have called it the "Random Value Keyframe Generator," but it's much more fun using something that sounds like a failed character sketch for an archenemy in the old Batman series. It's safe to say that it's also a pleasure to not have to worry about setting all of those individual keyframes by hand, and The Wiggler works with just about any property for which you can set keyframes. If you move past 2D transformations and ponder the possibilities of wiggling effect properties or Z-depth values, it becomes clear just how great it is to have this little guy around.

The Wiggler generates truly random values. If you don't like the random values it creates, choose Undo (Command/Ctrl+Z) and click Apply on The Wiggler palette once again. Every time you do this, The Wiggler generates different random values, so you can keep repeating this process until you've got the randomness that you want. After the keyframes have been generated, you can change their position in time (and space, if applicable). Don't forget that you can change the Keyframe Interpolation methods as well. The effect of randomness can be greatly enhanced when you change Bezier keyframes to Linear keyframes in the Timeline, and even more so if you opt to convert them to Hold keyframes.

Note Actually, you can write very simple expressions to create randomness in your animations. Consequently, you've got a choice in terms of how you go about this process. Be sure to look up the following terms in the Expressions section of the Online Help (choose Help ➪ After Effects Help): random, wiggle, and temporal _wiggle.

Cross-Reference We cover the subject of Keyframe Interpolation in Chapter 6 as well as expressions in Chapter 25.

Tip If you're adding randomness to a motion path, turning on Motion Blur can produce some very good-looking photorealistic results.

Using the Motion Tracker/Stabilizer Controls (PB Only)

The Motion Tracker/Stabilizer controls enable you to take a clip of shaky footage and do any number of cool things with it. These controls can be very useful if you want to track the motion in a clip and apply it to another layer's position. You can just as easily apply the tracking data to an effect point. Better still, you can apply the tracking data to a layer's Corner Pin effect points. Of course, barring all the fancy stuff, you can simply stabilize the clip to make it appear as though it came from a locked down camera. All these tricks involve a good deal of fun provided that your footage isn't too shaky.

Fortunately for us, these controls have been greatly improved in version 5.0 of After Effects, so if you're new to this aspect of compositing, have fun. If you got used to the idiosyncrasies of earlier versions of the Motion Tracker, you might want to take a look at the revisions to this part of the interface. The rest of the chapter will focus on these particular features.

Note Perhaps this is obvious, but the Motion Tracking features only work on a layer that contains a movie, not a still. No one's skimping here; after all, there's no motion to track in a still image!

Tracking movement in footage

As we mentioned earlier, the Motion Tracker/Stabilizer controls are built into the Layer window. Without further ado, go ahead and drop a piece of footage into a new composition and double-click its layer in the Timeline to open it up in its own Layer window. Click the arrow in the upper-right corner of the Layer window and select Tracker/Stabilizer Controls. This will enhance the appearance of the layer window rather dramatically, as shown in Figure 27-3.

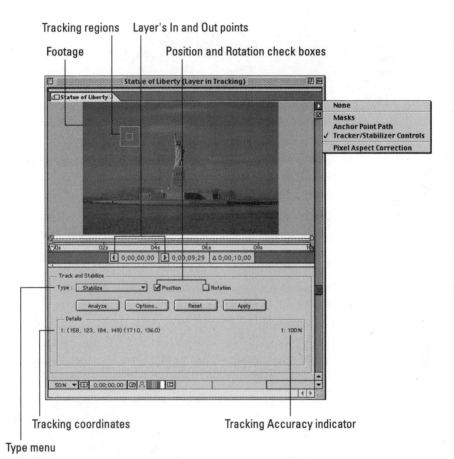

Figure 27-3: The Tracker/Stabilizer Controls are in the Layer window.
Image courtesy of Sekani (Corbis NY Vistas, Vol. 213)

Debunking the Tracker/Stabilizer controls

As you can see, this is an entire interface unto itself. Even the parts of it that look as though they're typical of the Layer window actually differ in some areas. You need to familiarize yourself with most of these basic components before you can understand what this part of After Effects is all about, so take a good look at the following descriptions:

✦ **Tracking regions:** Use these to track an object in the footage. See Figure 27-4.

Search region

Feature region

Track point

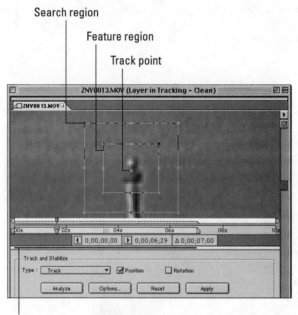

The Motion Tracker "Progress Meter"

Figure 27-4: The tracking regions consist of the search region, the feature region, and the track point.

Image courtesy of Sekani (Corbis NY Vistas, Vol. 213)

- **Search region:** The Tracker scans the outer box, or search region, for the object you defined in the feature region (see next). Consequently, you need to set the size of the search region carefully. If you want to track an object that flies through the frame at breakneck speed — say, a quickly moving hand — you would do well to set a large search region so that the hand is within the search region on a frame-by-frame basis. If you're tracking an object that doesn't move that much, you can set a smaller search region. You can move its control points by simply dragging on them.

- **Feature region:** Frame the object that you want to track as tightly as you can within the feature region. The area of the feature region is always within the search region. If the feature region "jumps" away from the object that you want to track halfway through the tracker/stabilizer's analysis of a clip, don't despair. Click Stop and use the Page Up key or drag the playhead back to the frame where the tracking went awry, place the feature region back over the object you were tracking, and click Analyze again. If you repeatedly strike out, you may need to resize the search region or adjust the tracker/stabilizer options. We go into more detail on the Tracker/Stabilizer options after the first exercise.

Tip

The feature region "likes" areas with high contrast. Look for corners, edges, and other areas that give the Tracker as much help as it can get.

- **Track point:** The track point is represented by small crosshairs, and you can drag it anywhere that you want in the image, even independently of the feature region if you prefer. The tracking data attaches the second layer to the track point, depending on how you're using the Tracker/Stabilizer controls. If you're using it on a layer's position, the track point represents the second layer's position. If you're using it on an effect, the track point represents the effect point. For example, you may want to track an area of high contrast with the search and feature regions, but at the same time, you want to place the layer somewhere other than the high contrast feature region. On a Perspective Corner Pin track, each of the four track points represents the position of the corner pin's four effect points. All of this is revealed in the folowing exercises.

Note

If you're using the Tracker/Stabilizer controls in Stabilize mode, you won't see any crosshairs because, in this case, the center of the feature region represents the track point.

✦ **Type menu:** This menu enables you to specify how you want to use the Tracker/Stabilizer controls. You have four options: You can track or stabilize the clip, or you can use the controls to map the coordinates of the Corner Pin effect on another layer.

✦ **Analyze button:** Clicking this button tells the tracker to get into gear and start following your feature region on its journey through the frame over time.

✦ **Tracking coordinates:** These numbers tell you the X- and Y-position of the feaure region as well as the X- and Y-position of the track point (in parentheses). The number of visible coordinates depends on the type of tracking you're doing. For example, if you're tracking a corner pin, there will be four sets of coordinates visible (one for each corner). If you're tracking a single object, then you'll only see one set of coordinates.

✦ **The Motion Tracker "Progress Meter":** Keep an eye trained on this little sliver of screen real estate. Areas in black indicate the portion of a clip that has been analyzed. This provides you with an easy way to tell exactly how much of your clip has been tracked.

✦ **Layer's In and Out points:** These are not your everyday in and out points. Instead, they tell the tracker/stabilizer which part of the clip to track. They don't reset the in and out point of the layer in the Timeline.

✦ **Position and Rotation check boxes:** These check boxes enable you to track both properties individually or simultaneously.

✦ **Tracking Accuracy indicator:** This percentage tells you how "sure" the tracker/stabilizer is that it's actually tracking what you told it to track. It changes frame-by-frame. Think of it as an honest self-evaluation, something so lacking in this cynical age.

✦ **Apply button:** Press the Apply button as soon as you're ready to convert the tracking data into keyframes for an effect point(s) or another layer's position.

✦ **Options button:** We cover this dialog box in greater detail following the first exercise. See the following section.

✦ **Reset button:** This button discards all tracking data and starts the process anew.

Complete the next set of exercises to see what all of the various controls can actually do for you. After you get your feet wet with the first tracking exercise, we'll go over all of the tracking options in detail so that you can continue working with a real understanding of the mechanics behind the Tracker/Stabilizer Controls.

On the DVD-ROM

In order to better explain the Tracker/Stabilizer Controls, we created an After Effects project that includes a composition for the following set of exercises. Just as a reminder, you need to copy the *Source Material* folder from the DVD-ROM to your hard drive. The After Effects project that corresponds to this chapter is called *Chapter 27.aep* and is found in the *Project Files/Chapter 27* folder. For the following exercise, work with the comp called *Tracking - Clean*. For reference, you may want to refer to our own comp called *Tracking*.

STEPS: Using Movement in a Clip to Track Another Layer

1. **Double-click the *Tracking - Clean* comp in the Project window.** In this composition, we laid out two elements for you. One is a pre-composed track matte of a burning flame from ArtBeats, and the other is a QuickTime movie of the Statue of Liberty from Sekani/Corbis. If you take a close look at the footage of the Statue of Liberty, you'll notice that the footage is somewhat shaky. The goal of this exercise is to track the shifting position of the torch and then place the flame in the comp according to the tracking data. As you can tell after you open the comp, the flame needs to be scaled down in order for this to look right.

Note

Before you continue, make sure that the playhead is positioned on the first frame of the comp.

Tip

When working with the Motion Tracker features in After Effects, make a point of occasionally viewing your comp at 100% magnification and Full resolution. This is the only way to tell whether the Motion Tracker is working precisely.

2. **Select the Matted Flame pre-comp layer and press S to solo its scale property.**

3. **Enter a value in the range of 15 to 20%.**

4. **Position the Matted Flame layer so that it looks as though flames are emanating from the statue's torch.**

5. **Select the Pan Behind tool from the Tools palette and reposition the Matted Flame layer's Anchor Point so that it sits directly on top of the torch (see Figure 27-5 for reference).** You may find that it's easier to do this once you zoom in on the comp by pressing the period key. You can zoom back out by pressing the comma key. If you're zoomed in on the comp and you want to change the view of your work area, hold down the spacebar and drag with the Hand tool to move to a different area.

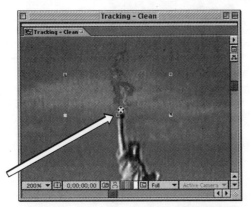

Figure 27-5: Using the Pan Behind tool from the Tools palette, reposition the Matted Flame layer's Anchor Point so that it sits directly on top of the torch.

Image courtesy of Sekani (Corbis NY Vistas, Vol. 213)

Note The reason you're moving the Anchor Point to the position of the torch is because the tracking data from the torch will be applied to the Anchor Point of the Matted Flame layer.

6. **In the Timeline, double-click the QuickTime movie layer to open it up in its own Layer window.**

7. **In the Layer window, click the arrow in the upper-right corner to view the Layer window options and choose Tracker/Stabilizer Controls.**

8. **From the Type menu, choose Tracking.**

9. **Click in the center of the two boxes that make up the Tracking Regions and drag them so that the center of the Feature Region (the inner box) is located over the position of the torch in the footage.**

10. **Drag the control points of the Search Region (the outer box) to include an area that loosely frames the torch.**

11. Position the crosshairs of the Track Point by dragging them to the base of the torch. After you complete Steps 9–11, your Layer window should resemble Figure 27-6.

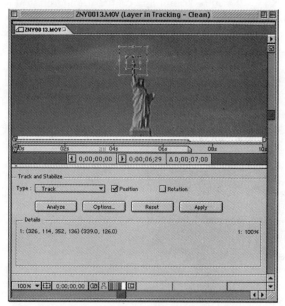

Figure 27-6: After you complete Steps 9–11, your Layer window should look something like this.
Image courtesy of Sekani (Corbis NY Vistas, Vol. 213)

Tip

If you experienced trouble moving the Tracking Regions around the Layer window, you can always press Reset to get a clean start. Remember that if you want to move both the Feature Region and the Search Region, drag inside the Search Region to move them both simultaneously.

12. Click the Options button in the Tracker/Stabilizer Controls.

13. Make the following selections in the Motion Tracker Options dialog box:

- **Layer menu:** Matted Flame is your only option.

- **Frames per Second:** Accept the default of 29.97 (to match the clip).

- **Track Fields:** Select this check box because the clip is interlaced.

- **Accept all the remaining default settings:** Because this clip is relatively low-maintenance, the default options should be acceptable.

14. Click OK.

15. Click the Analyze button in the Tracker/Stabilizer Controls. As it hums along, you'll notice that the Tracker follows the position of the torch.

16. **After it finishes, click the Apply button.**

17. **Close the Layer window.**

18. **Press 0 on the numeric keypad to preview your animation.** If things have gone smoothly, the flame will move with the torch for the duration of the comp. Check out Figure 27-7.

Figure 27-7: If things have gone smoothly, the flame will move with the torch for the duration of the comp.

Image courtesy of Sekani (Corbis NY Vistas, Vol. 213)

Note   In the Timeline, select the Matted Flame layer and press U to solo its animated properties. Look at the myriad of position keyframes. These were created when you clicked the Apply button in Step 16, and the positional data for these was gathered when you clicked the Analyze button in Step 15.

If you don't end up with what you want, you may have gotten tripped up in a couple of places. First of all, did you analyze the entire clip? Hopefully, you began your work from the first frame of the comp. If you didn't, keyframes will only have been generated going forward from the initial position of the playhead. Secondly, you may have set an inaccurate Anchor Point in Step 5, in which case the flame isn't lining up nicely with the torch. If so, there are a couple of fixes.

If you didn't analyze the whole clip, no need to worry. In the Tracker/Stabilizer controls of the Layer window, drag the playhead to the first frame of the layer, position the search and feature regions as well as the track point in the appropriate location over the torch, and click the Analyze button again. As soon as the entire clip's tracking "Progress Meter" is black, you can press Stop, and then click Apply once again.

Tip   On your way to mastering these controls, don't panic. No keyframes are applied to the layer until you click the Apply button.

If the tracking data is correct but all of the position keyframes seem to be similarly offset by just a few pixels, you can reposition, or "nudge" all of the keyframes rather easily. Click the Position property name for the "Matted Flame" layer to select all the keyframes, and then use the arrow keys on the keyboard to reposition them one pixel at a time.

Tip   To improve the overall look of the last exercise, consider adding the Remove Color Matting effect to the "Matted Flame" pre-comp layer. This removes darkened and multiplied black color from the flame's edges. For more kicks, try the Glow filter applied to the alpha channel of the layer and experiment with the effect properties until your flame starts looking even better.

Piece o' cake, right? Well, sadly, not quite. That clip happens to be a particularly easy piece of footage for the Tracker to analyze well. If only life were always so easy. The truth is, that motion tracking is almost always going to be a bit more difficult than that last exercise. If you manage to get stymied when tracking a complex piece of herky-jerky footage, a solid grasp of the Tracker/Stabilizer Options can provide you with the means to figure out a number of problems you may encounter.

Understanding the Tracker/Stabilizer options

Try to develop a solid working knowledge of the Motion Tracker Options (see Figure 27-8). If you get stuck and adjustments to the search region prove fruitless, the advanced section of the Motion Tracker Options dialog box may yield success. To access the options, click the Options button in the Tracker/Stabilizer controls.

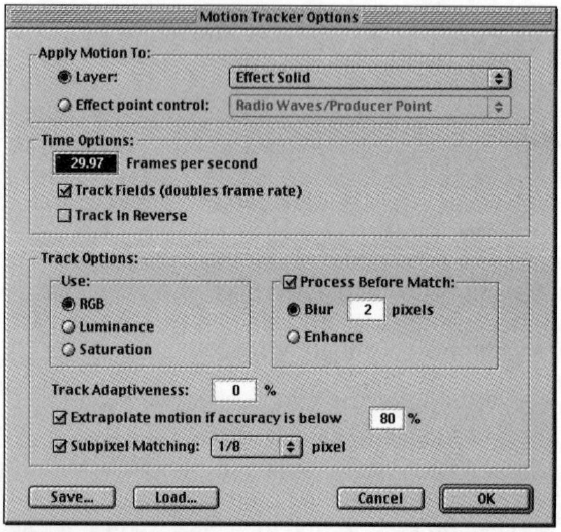

Figure 27-8: After you have an understanding of the parameters in the Motion Tracker Options, you can troubleshoot tracking problems more effectively.

Following is a list of the Motion Tracker Options dialog box options.

✦ **Apply Motion To:**

- **Layer and Effect point control menus:** Whatever you select from these menus determines either the layer or the effect point that you want to attach to the tracking data gathered from the tracked layer.

✦ **Time Options:**

- **Frames per second:** Make a point of matching the tracking frame rate to the frame rate of the footage being tracked. This way, the movement of the layer or the effect point that's attached to the tracked layer keeps the overall motion consistent within your comp.

- **Track Fields:** If the clip you're tracking is interlaced, make sure you select this option.

- **Track In Reverse:** Select this option if the object that you're tracking starts off-screen. Go to the last frame in the Layer window before you click Analyze, and the tracker works its magic in reverse so that you don't have to worry about its accuracy at the beginning of your comp when the object you're tracking hasn't yet entered the screen.

✦ **Track Options:**

- **Use:** Your selection in this menu tells the tracking regions to respond to your clip on the basis of its RGB values, its Luminance (overall brightness) values, or its Saturation (concentration of color) values. RGB usually works well, but in certain cases, the other options produce superior tracking results.

- **Process Before Match:** Click the check box if you want the Motion Tracker to simplify the image before gathering tracking data. By "simplify," we mean selecting the blur option to blur noisy footage by a specific number of pixels to isolate areas of contrast, or by selecting enhance, which sharpens the edges in a dull, flat image. Remember that this is only for the purpose of helping the tracker find its mark. These settings don't change the image as it exists in the comp.

- **Track Adaptiveness:** As its name suggests, the percentage you specify here determines how much the tracker "learns" as it continues building a track. For example, you want to set it relatively high if the image that you're tracking drastically changes shape or color. By contrast, you want to set it low if the object you're tracking remains visually consistent throughout the duration of the clip.

- **Extrapolate motion if accuracy is below *xx*% (where *xx* stands for the desired percentage):** This is an interesting and valuable parameter. When you initially define your tracking regions, for every additional frame that the Motion Tracker analyzes, the Tracker tells you how sure it is that it's looking at the feature region that you initially defined as indicated by the value shown in the Tracking Accuracy Indicator in the main Tracker/Stabilizer controls. By setting this value to 80%, for example, you're telling the Motion Tracker to make an educated guess as to the location of the feature region if it's less than 80% sure that it's successfully tracking it. The guess is based on the position and velocity of the feature region before the accuracy dipped below the 80% threshold. Pretty cool stuff, but you want to experiment with it to get a sense of how it works. For example, what if the man you're tracking walks behind a tree and disappears completely for a few frames? If you've set the Extrapolate Motion value above 0%, the Tracker's going to be sure that it lost sight of the guy, in which case it'll extrapolate the current position based on the tracking data it had already gathered. Assuming your man was walking at a constant rate of speed, the tracker will do a great job guessing his position behind the tree. If, however, the man stops behind the tree to get some rest and get that rock out of his shoe, then the extrapolation will be less than stellar.

- **Subpixel Matching:** This menu enables you to tell the Tracker how closely it will monitor the feature region you've defined. While it's great that you can split a pixel into 256 subpixels, the Analyze stage of the motion tracking process can take an overwhelmingly long time. You'll develop a feel for how much subpixel matching is necessary if you do a lot of tracking. Typically, we don't do much work beyond 64 subpixels, and that's a rare occurrence.

✦ **Save button:** If you like, you can click this button to save a group of tracking option settings if you know you want to use them again. The file includes all the options that you selected in addition to the position of the tracking regions as well as any tracking data that may have already been acquired.

✦ **Load button:** This button enables you to load a previously saved tracking options file (see previous section).

These otherwise unremarkable buttons belie the fact that they can be used to import tracking data from other applications, most notably Puffin Design's Commotion, an excellent rotoscoping, painting, tracking, and compositing application, and an extremely valuable addition to the digital video artist's toolbox if your work involves a lot of meticulous rotoscoping and tracking.

Tracking for effect

As we mentioned earlier, you can apply tracking data to realistically position the coordinates of an effect point. Essentially, it involves the same process involving any other application of the Motion Tracker. The next exercise picks up where the last one left off by adding a Lens Flare to the torch on of the Statue of Liberty.

STEPS: Using Movement in a Clip to Track an Effect

1. **Back in your *Tracking - Clean* comp, select the bottom layer containing the footage of the Statue of Liberty in the Timeline and choose Effect ⇨ Render ⇨ PS+Lens Flare.** For the moment, accept the Lens Flare dialog box defaults and click OK.

2. **In the Timeline, double-click the layer to open it up in its own Layer window.**

3. **Select the Tracker/Stabilizer Controls option from the Layer window menu located in the upper-right corner.**

4. **In the Tracker/Stabilizer Controls, make sure that Track is selected in the Type menu and then click the Options button.**

5. **In the Motion Tracker Options dialog box, click the Effect Point Control radio button.** Select the PS+Lens Flare.../Flare Center option in the pull-down menu. See Figure 27-9 for reference.

6. **Accept the defaults and click OK to close the the Motion Tracker Options dialog box.**

7. **In the Tracker/Stabilizer Controls, your tracking data should still exist from the last exercise.** If so, the "Progress Meter" should reveal a black strip indicating the frames that the Motion Tracker has already tracked. If the black strip is still there, all you need to do is click the Apply button to track the position of the center of the PS+Lens Flare effect. If the data is gone for some reason, you need to repeat Steps 9–11 from the last exercise. Following that, click the Analyze button, let the Tracker build its track, and then click the Apply button.

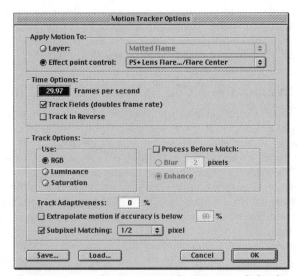

Figure 27-9: In the Motion Tracker Options dialog box, click the Effect point control radio button. Select the PS+ Lens Flare.../Flare Center option in the pull-down menu.

8. **Close the Layer window.**

9. **Press 0 on the numeric keypad to view a RAM Preview of the traveling lens flare.** You may want to reduce the brightness setting of the PS+Lens Flare effect (to approximately 50) and change the transfer mode of the Matted Flame layer to something that blends more effectively with the newly applied filter (we settled on Hard Light, but a number of them work well).

Basically, the only real difference to how you approach the two exercises is the selection of the effect point option in the Apply Motion To portion of the Motion Tracker options. That completes your basic introduction to the Motion Tracker. Keep going and check out some of the other functions you can do with it.

Tracking for the Corner Pin effect

Simply put, using the Motion Tracker for a corner pin effect can provide you with some high-quality entertainment. This is one of those enormously fun production tricks that provide you with the power to unleash your own brand of revisionist history upon the world. In the next exercise, you'll add an image to an old piece of film footage by using the Motion Tracker in conjunction with the Corner Pin effect.

On the DVD-ROM

In order to better explain the Tracker/Stabilizer Controls, we created an After Effects project that includes a composition for the following exercise. Just as a reminder, you need to copy the *Source Material* folder from the DVD-ROM to your hard drive. The After Effects project that corresponds to this chapter is called *Chapter 27.aep* and is found in the *Project Files/Chapter 27* folder. For the following exercise, work with the comp called *Track/Corner Pin - Clean*. For reference, you may want to refer to our comp called *Track/Corner Pin*.

STEPS: Using Movement in a Clip to Track a Corner Pin

1. **In the project window, double-click the comp called *Track/Corner Pin - Clean*.** You see that we laid out two elements for you in the Timeline. The bottom layer is some rather amusing film footage that's been digitized into a D1 QuickTime movie provided to us by the helpful folks at Sekani. The top layer is a very simple little PICT file that we made in Photoshop. In the interest of trying to understand the purpose of the exercise, preview the movie so that you get a sense of the motion in the clip. The goal here is to place the "Don't Jump!" sign in the window of the house regardless of the movement of the camera following the cat.

Tip

To avoid a potential headache, make sure the playhead is located on the first frame of the comp.

2. **In the Timeline, select the top layer and choose Effect ⇨ Distort ⇨ Corner Pin.** This enables the Perspective Corner Pin option in the Tracker/Stabilizer controls.

3. **Double-click the bottom layer containing the footage to open it up in its own Layer window.**

4. **Select the Tracker/Stabilizer Controls option from the Layer window menu located in the upper-right corner.**

5. **In the Tracker/Stabilizer Controls, select Perspective Corner Pin from the Type menu and then click the Options button.**

6. **In the Motion Tracker Options dialog box, you notice that After Effects has already figured out the Apply Motion To settings.** Still, you want to tweak the other settings a bit before proceeding. Set the remaining options, as shown in Figure 27-10, and after you finish, click OK. Remember, you can always go back and adjust the options as needed.

Note   Because this is black and white footage, we opted to use Luminance as the basis for the track.

7. **In the Tracker/Stabilizer Controls, position the four tracking regions over the general area of the first window to the right of the cat.** Click and drag inside each feature region to move each set of tracking regions where you want them.

8. **Using the period and comma keys to zoom in and out, focus your view on the area around the window of the house where you loosely positioned the four tracking regions.**

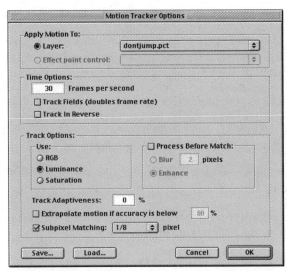

Figure 27-10: Tweak the Motion Tracker Options as shown here.

9. **Set the tracking regions carefully.** Set the search regions first, then set the feature regions. Lastly, set the position of the track points precisely at the corners of the window frame in the footage. When you're setting the tracking regions, remember the guidelines we suggested earlier. If you look at the footage, you'll see that the motion in the clip isn't overly extreme, so your search regions don't need to be too big. Look at Figure 27-11 for reference.

Figure 27-11: Use our tracking region selections as a guide when setting your own.
Image courtesy of Sekani (Funny and Furry 2)

Caution   If you adjust the feature region after you've set the track point, you'll move the track point whether or not you want to. Subsequently, you want to try and position your search and feature regions first.

10. **After you carefully set the tracking regions, click the Analyze button to track the position of the Corner Pin effect points.** Watch the Tracker carefully as it builds the track. Stop and start it as often as you like. If a tracking region starts to drift off target, stop the track and press the PageUp/PageDown keys or drag the playhead to go back to the frame where the offending tracking region went astray, reposition it, and click Analyze once again. If this doesn't fix the problem, go back into the Motion Tracker Options, set the subpixel matching to a higher resolution, and click OK. Return to the frame where the track got lost and click Analyze once again. Ultimately, you should be able to put together a good track; it just requires patience and persistence.

Tip   While the Motion Tracker is analyzing a layer, you can stop it either by clicking the Stop button or pressing any key.

Note   If you get way too muddled and confused, you always have the option of clicking the Reset button and starting the process anew.

11. **After the Tracker has finished analyzing the clip, click the Apply button.**

12. **Close the Layer window.**

13. **Press 0 on the numeric keypad to view a RAM Preview of the "Don't Jump!" sign moving in conjunction with the house in the clip.** See Figure 27-12.

14. **If you notice problems with the consistency of the track, go back into the Tracker/Stabilizer controls to tweak the spots where the track drifts using the methods explained in Step 10.**

Figure 27-12: If successful, the Corner Pin track realistically positions the "Don't Jump!" sign in the window of the house.

Image courtesy of Sekani (Funny and Furry 2)

15. **If you want to improve the overall quality of the sign in the window, we outlined a few additional tweaks.** Try adding the Noise filter to it so that it's consistent with the grainy noise in the footage. Going further, you may want to add a Fast Blur to match the focus of the image, and you can also enable Motion Blur and turn on the layer's Motion Blur switch to match the jerky camera movements that are quite noticeable when the cat jumps.

We hope that you had some fun with the exercise. As you can imagine, you can use this technique to do all kinds of things to your video assets. We should also mention that there are some helpful production techniques that make the prospect of motion tracking a lot easier. If you know that you'll be doing motion tracking before you begin shooting, you can mark the object that you're going to be tracking by affixing white tape or Ping-Pong balls on the corner of the object. The feature region then has a much easier time tracking the high contrast of your markers than it might otherwise.

Note

The Tracker/Stabilizer controls offer another corner pin option in the Type menu called an Affine Corner Pin. Our experience has shown that the Perspective Corner Pin usually handles all our needs in this department. The Online Help suggests that you use the Affine Corner Pin option in situations when you're working with footage in which the object that you need to track changes in scale that are the result of shifts in zoom. Even in these scenarios, the Perspective Corner Pin seems to work perfectly well. Experiment with the Affine Corner Pin option and make your own judgment. Its controls are almost exactly the same as those of the Perspective Corner Pin, except for the fact that you can't control the fourth tracking region.

Cross-Reference There are a couple of additional effects with corner pin effect points, and these work beautifully with the Corner Pin features in the Tracker/Stabilizer controls. Try your hand at corner pinning the following effects: Card Wipe, Card Dance, and Shatter. We cover these effects in detail in Chapters 15 and 16.

Stabilizing shaky footage

Occasionally, you may be required to stabilize a piece of shaky footage. The Tracker/Stabilizer controls employ the same basic tracking technology in this process, except that the tracking data is applied to the tracked layer's Anchor Point. By using the tracking data to generate Anchor Point keyframes, the layer moves around the composition while the contents of the layer remain in place, assuming the track is accurate. The next exercise involves stabilizing some film footage that was shot without a tripod.

On the DVD-ROM In order to better explain the Tracker/Stabilizer Controls, we created an After Effects project that includes a composition for the following exercise. Just as a reminder, you need to copy the *Source Material* folder from the DVD-ROM to your hard drive. The After Effects project that corresponds to this chapter is called *Chapter 27.aep* and is found in the *Project Files/Chapter 27* folder. For the following exercise, work with the comp called *Stabilize - Clean*. For reference, you may want to refer to our own comp called *Stabilize*.

Tip To avoid a potential headache, make sure the playhead is located on the first frame of the comp.

STEPS: "Locking Down" a Clip with the Stabilizer

1. **In the Project window, double-click the comp called *Stabilize - Clean*.** This one involves a single layer of film footage. Look at it by pressing the spacebar to get a sense of the camera's erratic movement. Nothing is intrinsically wrong with the footage because it was shot with specific stylistic considerations. Suppose, after the fact, that you wanted to isolate the girl in the frame so that she appeared to be relatively still. The remaining steps will show you how to do just that.

2. **In the Timeline, double-click the layer to open it up in its own Layer window.**

3. **Select the Tracker/Stabilizer Controls option from the Layer window menu located in the upper-right corner.**

4. **In the Tracker/Stabilizer Controls, choose Stabilize from the Type menu, check both the Position and Rotation check boxes, and then click the Options button.** In this instance, we also want to track the rotation in the footage.

5. **In the Motion Tracker Options dialog box, adjust the settings, as shown in Figure 27-13.** After you finish, click OK.

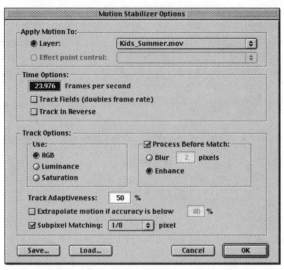

Figure 27-13: Start the stabilizing process by initially working with these settings in the Motion Stabilizer Options dialog box. If you need to, adjust them later.

6. **Using the Tracker/Stabilizer Controls, set the tracking regions, as shown in Figure 27-14.**

Rotation tracking region

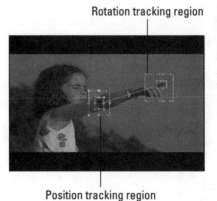

Position tracking region

Figure 27-14: Use these position and rotation tracking regions as a guide for stabilizing this piece of footage.
Image courtesy of Axel Baumann, Director of Photography

7. **After you set the tracking regions, click the Analyze button to begin tracking the layer and watch it carefully.** If the tracking regions drift at any point during the process, follow the troubleshooting guidelines in the following tip.

Tip   It's important that we repeat the key aspects of the troubleshooting process once more: If a tracking region starts to drift off target, stop the track, and press the PageUp/PageDown keys or drag the playhead to go back to the frame where the offending tracking region went astray, reposition it, and click Analyze once again. If this doesn't fix the problem, go back into the Motion Tracker Options, set the subpixel matching to a higher resolution, and click OK. Return to the frame where the track got lost, and click Analyze once again.

Tip   While the Motion Tracker is analyzing a layer, you can stop it either by clicking the Stop button or pressing any key.

8. **As soon as the Tracker has finished analyzing the clip, click the Apply button.**

9. **Close the Layer window.**

10. **Press 0 on the numeric keypad to see a RAM Preview of your efforts.** See Figure 27-15.

Is the footage stabilized? More specifically, does the girl remain in place while the edges of the layer travel all over the Comp window? Hopefully, the answer is, "Yes!"

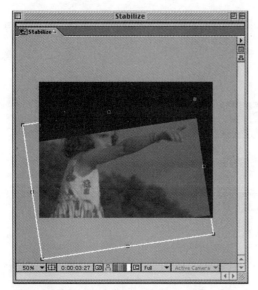

Figure 27-15: Stabilizing footage with a lot of camera movement results in moving the edges of the layer all over the Comp window.

Image courtesy of Axel Baumann, Director of Photography

Note One major drawback when stabilizing footage is the unavoidable and inconsistent softening of the image. Because the Motion Tracker is moving things around at the subpixel level, there's no workaround, unless you want to apply one of the Blur effects to the end result.

As you can tell, the results of all this effort wouldn't be all that useful if this comp was the end result. Now that you've stabilized the footage, a reasonable question might be something such as: "What can you do with it?"

The answer lies in nesting this comp into a new composition and masking it so that only the desired area remains visible. After you do that, you can use it as an element in your project.

On the DVD-ROM For reference, take a look at the comp called *Stabilize - Masked*. In it, we took the stabilized footage and masked it so that the edges of the layer are no longer visible. Granted, this greatly reduces the dimensions of the clip, but that's the trade-off with stabilizing footage.

Mastering the Tracker/Stabilizer controls is a matter of experimentation. Now that we've told you how they work, it's a fact that you're going to have varying degrees of success with them depending on the quality of the footage that you're using. Hopefully, you haven't gotten too tired of your usual refrain: "Test early and often."

Before telling an eager client that you can track and stabilize with ease, you should be diligent in your preparation of test shots to see if what's being proposed is actually within your capacity.

✦   ✦   ✦

Rendering for All Media

Juggling Format Issues

Some people say the Devil's in the details, while others claim that it's God that can be found in them. We're going to take a decidedly more secular approach to this idea, at least as far as it concerns video format issues as they relate to After Effects. Why write, much less read, a chapter on format issues? If it's that kind of fun you're looking for, why not get a job cleaning the elephant stables at the circus? In truth, it isn't that bad.

First of all, if you don't know how to deal with the technical issues surrounding video formats, you run a high risk of watching all your hard work go down the drain when a field-rendering glitch makes your final lay-off look like a disaster. Video professionals are loath to admit it, but nightmares like that one play out more often than you might think. Nothing is more heartbreaking than toiling to complete a beautiful spot for a client, only to find that the final output contains some strange glitch that you can't seem to fix — or worse, even begin to figure out.

This chapter addresses some of these quirks. If you're serious about broadcast design, it's necessary info. It also happens to be interesting, so trust that it's not excruciating to learn. A solid grounding in the technical aspects of video formats is really indispensable when it comes to delivering professional work, so if you know that you have some weak spots in this area, jump in and absorb the details.

What Are Formats?

Okay. Take this quick test: Describe the following terms in detail: NTSC, PAL, SECAM, DV, SD, HDTV, SDI, 3:2 Pulldown, progressive scan, alternating fields, and drop-frame timecode. If you don't know what these various terms and acronyms mean, you've come to the right place.

Since the advent of television, the engineers of the world have figured out more than a few ways to generate a video signal. In the sections that follow, we look at the various video formats that are important these days and do our best to tell you what we know.

Understanding NTSC Video

NTSC video is *interlaced video*. In an interlaced video format, two fields of video are combined to create one frame of video. NTSC video runs at 29.97 frames per second; therefore, it contains 59.94 fields per second.

To understand interlaced video, you have to look at the cathode ray tube inside a television. This tube is flared; it starts out as a slim electron gun and ends in the square format we all know as the good old television screen. For interlaced video, each field of video is drawn separately by the electron gun and combined to create one frame. For example, the gun first traces lines 1, 3, 7, 9, 11, and so on, and then it returns to the top to trace lines 2, 4, 6, 8, 10, and so on. Depending on the system, either the odd fields or the even fields get drawn first. This is known as the *field order* of the video, and the system is known as *upper field* or *lower field first*. Because NTSC video consists of 525 lines for each frame, 262.5 lines are drawn in each field.

For an After Effects artist, the field order of the video is very important. When bringing video footage into your After Effects project, you need to specify the field order that the footage was captured with, and you need to specify the order for the rendering phase as well.

Keep in mind that video interlacing is only relevant if you're creating video meant for broadcast or other interlaced systems such as an NTSC monitor. You don't need to concern yourself with interlacing for video that is being rendered for computer playback, because computer monitors don't use interlaced video. Instead, they use something called *progressive scanning*. In a progressive scan system, the video is drawn on the screen in a simple progressive fashion, one full frame at a time. In short, the lines are drawn in a linear (1, 2, 3, 4, 5) fashion.

Note   With the advent of digital television, issues of interlacing versus progressive scan have gotten a little mixed up. The specifications for digital television contain numerous formats that use both scanning methods. These formats are distinguished by the letters "i" (for interlaced) and "p" for progressive.

29.97 fps versus 30 fps

Okay. Let's clear something up here and now. NTSC video, the type used in both the United States and Japan, and the one you are most likely working with as you read this book, works only (and we repeat *only*) at 29.97 frames per second. There is no such thing is "30-frames-per-second" NTSC video.

There is a very common misunderstanding that somehow 29.97 fps represents "drop-frame" timecode and 30 fps represents "non-drop-frame" timecode. For the record, this is completely incorrect. Drop-frame versus non-drop-frame timecode has nothing whatsoever to do with the frame rate of video. Drop-frame timecode, represented by semicolons (;) between the numbers representing seconds and frames, is simply a different way of labeling video frames to make up for the discrepancy between real clock time and timecode time. Drop-frame timecode changes the numbering of *frames* at the start of each minute, except at every tenth minute. Hence, drop-frame timecode goes from 01:00:59;28 to 01:00:59;29 to 01:01:00;02. Notice that the frame numbers 01:01:00;00 and 01:01:00;01 are skipped, or dropped. It is critical to remember that only the frame numbers are dropped, not any video frames. Non-drop-frame timecode progresses in a linear fashion without skipping frames. Non-drop-frame timecode is represented by a colon (:) between the numbers representing seconds and frames.

Note Regardless of the type of timecode, colons always separate the numbers representing minutes and seconds and hours and minutes. A semicolon only gets added between the numbers represennting seconds and frames in drop-frame timecode; otherwise, every other number separator is a colon.

We cannot tell you how many times we've come across video editors, After Effects artists, and others who are convinced that drop-frame timecode means the video is actually running at 29.97 fps and that non-drop-frame timecode means the same video is actually running a bit faster at 30 fps. Rarely have so many believed something that is so completely wrong. Remember, forever, that NTSC video *always* runs at 29.97 fps. Drop-frame versus non-drop-frame timecode doesn't have anything to do with the actual frame rate of video. The timecode mode only affects how the frame numbers are displayed in the timecode format. Period.

So what does all that mean for a practical After Effects artist? Do you have to be careful what timecode mode you are in? Can you mix and match? Yes, actually you can. If you so desire, you can freely mix and match timecode modes in After Effects; however, we can think of at least one good reason not to. If you are working on an intricately timed project, that is, one that requires precise frame numbers when creating video that needs to match up with a pre-edited program or specifically timed sections of a program, you'll really want to use the timecode mode native to the project. This will help you think clearly and keep the frame count on track. When working with drop-frame timecode, just don't become confused by the fact that it skips two numbers every minute.

NTSC versus PAL and SECAM Video

NTSC, which stands for *National Television Standards Committee,* is just one of the video systems in use around the world. In addition to being the system used in the United States and Japan, NTSC is used in Canada and the Philippines, among other countries. NTSC, as we previously described, has a frame rate of 29.97 fps and has 525 total lines of resolution.

Phase Alternating Line, or *PAL,* as it's more commonly known, is the system that's most commonly used in Western Europe. PAL operates at 25 fps and has 625 lines of resolution. PAL's resolution is considered to be better than NTSC's because it has an extra 100 lines, but NTSC has a slight edge in that it has a higher frame rate. PAL's color and hue is also considered superior to NTSC's, and it's almost always the preferred format for filmmakers who plan on transferring the video to film. The reason for this is that PAL's 25 fps frame rate transfers well to film in terms of motion as well as sampling 25 fps down to 24 fps, which is film's native frame rate. By contrast, NTSC's 29.97 fps frame rate creates some problems when it is sampled down to the 24 fps frame rate of film.

SECAM stands for *Séquential Couleur Avec Memoire (*which translates from its native French as Sequential Color with Memory). This is the world's third most popular video system, and it's used in France, Eastern Europe, Greece, and Egypt. SECAM has a frame rate of 25 fps and contains 625 lines of resolution. We usually don't hear too much about the SECAM standard, but you should know that it exists because it's one of the most common video systems around the globe.

Understanding the DV format

The advent of the DV format has revolutionized the world of video. DV video cameras, tapes, and decks have been some of the hottest selling items for the past few years, and this segment of the market shows no sign of slowing down. You can recognize the DV format by the small but ubiquitous DV logo found on tapes and cameras in virtually every electronics store in the country.

Before the DV format took the market by storm, the only choices were formats such as BetaCam for professionals and VHS or 8mm for consumer or semi-professional work. Attempts at creating a "pro-sumer" market with such formats as S-VHS and Hi-8 never really got anywhere, whereas the DV format really has created a true pro-sumer market.

DV has allowed users with even the most restrictive budgets to create very high quality video, and it has even gained a measure of acceptance at some broadcast houses and networks, but not as much as everyone had hoped for. The interesting and important aspect regarding DV is that it's not only a tape and a recording format, but it's also a compression standard.

Understanding the multiple DV formats

The DV format is a set of specifications and standards agreed upon by a consortium of 55 companies around the world. It was released in 1995 and quickly went on to become the most popular video format in recent years. The resolution of DV is roughly twice that of VHS, and more importantly, it's an entirely digital format. This helps it retain its quality across multiple generations (as long as the path used happens to be digital as well). In other words, when you capture DV video to a desktop video-editing application, there is no degradation between what's on the tape versus what's captured on the computer's hard drive. Another standout feature of the DV format is the fact that it uses very high-quality digital audio.

The team of engineers that created the DV format focused its efforts with the computer and desktop video revolution in mind. Consequently, the DV format provides very high image quality at relatively lean data rates. The data rate of DV is fixed at 3.5MB per second, and at that rate, even the most common hard drives are capable of capturing it and playing it back without dropping frames. Early adopters of the technology might remember vexing sessions in which the first DV ready computers sometimes had trouble successfully capturing DV footage, but those times are happily becoming a distant memory.

The DV tape format has three common derivatives that are formats in themselves. These are MiniDV, DVCAM, and DVCPro. MiniDV is the smallest and the most common format among them. That's what's on those super small tapes that are typically used in consumer-level DV cameras.

Faced with the physical limitations of the MiniDV format and the unreliability of frame accuracy in editing, Sony invented the DVCAM format while Panasonic developed the DVCPro format. Both these formats use larger tape shells and a broader track of tape. The DVCAM and DVCPro tapes are physically larger, but they have the same compression and quality as MiniDV.

Working with DV compression

DV is a modern digital standard that was well thought out by the engineers who designed and implemented it. As we mentioned, DV compression is high quality, yet it works at a relatively small data rate of 3.5MB per second. This flexibility allows even the most common hard drives on the market to capture and play it back with ease.

DV cameras have built-in hardware compressors that use the DV compression standard. There are also software compressors and decompressors (called *codecs*) that are available for software playback of the DV format. QuickTime and other media architectures include the DV codec as part of their basic installation. See Figure 28-1.

When rendering in After Effects for a DV format, you must make sure to choose the DV codec in the QuickTime Compression Settings dialog box.

Bear in mind that rendering for DV requires more than just selecting the DV codec. The DV format has a native frame size of 720 x 480, and it also uses the D1/DV pixel aspect ratio. You need to match these settings in the output module dialog box in the Render Queue and make sure you select the appropriate frame rate (29.97 fps for NTSC and 25 fps for PAL). Only then will your After Effects render be compatible with the DV format.

Working with Standard Definition (SD) video

Standard definition is a general term that's used to loosely define video that is commonly used in editing systems and broadcast transmissions. This often encompasses everything ranging from BetaCam to VHS video captured with a video card. Because After Effects works with video captured into computers, it is essential that you are familiar with the data rate, frame size, and pixel aspect ratios of SD.

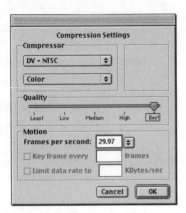

Figure 28-1: The DV codec is selected in the QuickTime Compression Settings dialog box for rendering output for DV.

SD commonly uses a frame size of 720 x 486, although you may come across 640 x 480-sized video as well. Almost all 720 x 486 video uses the D1 pixel aspect ratio, whereas 640 x 480 video uses a square pixel aspect ratio. The frame rate of video depends on the video system that you're using; again, NTSC runs at 29.97 fps while PAL and SECAM operate at 25 fps.

When working with SD, another important item that you want to be aware of is the compressor that was used to capture or prepare the video with which you're working. A fairly common codec used to capture SD is MJPEG. Whatever it is, it's essential that you use the same codec for your rendering needs. As always, from the very beginning, you want to build your project to the spec required by your final output.

Tip   Click a footage item in the Project window and After Effects displays its thumbnail as well as a whole lot of useful information about the video. Within this list of vitals, you can see the frame size, pixel aspect ratio, frame rate, and even the name of the compressor used to create the video footage. You should use the same settings for your comp, and a foolproof way to make sure you get it right is to drag the footage item onto the comp icon at the bottom of the project window. After Effects automatically sets the settings of the resulting comp to match that of the footage item. This is a great feature that can ward off a great deal of frustration. We recommend that you use it as often as you can.

SDI — Serial Digital Interconnect

SDI, or *Serial Digital Interconnect,* also known as *Serial Digital Interface,* is often confused with being some form of compression. It's actually simpler than that. SDI is an Input/Output standard, much like the composite signal or the S-Video signal. The SDI format can use all different kinds of compressors, such as MJPEG-A; however, SDI is most commonly used with uncompressed video.

SDI is used to transfer extremely high-quality video on very high-end (read *expensive*) video cards and other video equipment. SDI is commonly found on the Sony Digital BetaCam (DigiBeta) decks and on some Sony DVCAM and Panasonic DVCPro decks.

SDI is also used in situations where video has to be transported across long distances. Because the signal remains clear and doesn't degrade over long wires, production facilities prefer to use SDI to move a video signal around their buildings.

Numerous cards and decks use SDI, and it's very popular with a lot of After Effects users. If you're lucky enough to be working with this kind of hardware, the codec you use to render your After Effects projects depends on what the SDI hardware manufacturer provided. If you are buying an SDI-based editing system or capture card, you'll be provided with a software codec that you'll need to install before you start using it in conjunction with After Effects.

Understanding HD (High Definition) video

The promise of HDTV (High Definition Television) has been in the air for a while now. Like most miracle technologies that get a lot of hype, this one is taking its time becoming widespread. The problem stems from its complexity. HDTV represents a radical departure from preexisting technology, and despite a federal mandate to implement it, HDTV is still catching on pretty slowly.

HDTV can have a frame size of up to 1920 x 1080 pixels (as compared to the 720 x 480 frame size of the DV format, for example). This represents a quantum leap in the number of pixels. HDTV has almost six times more pixels than SD, and when captured, it can require a data rate of over 120MB per second, as compared to the data rate of 3.5MB per second of DV. These are huge numbers, but the resulting picture quality is exceptional indeed.

The Advanced Television Systems Committee (ATSC) has worked to create the ATSC DTV (for Digital Television) specifications that include a list of 18 picture compression formats. Note that only six of these formats qualify for the HD label.

Because After Effects works independently of any resolution, frame size, or frame rate, as After Effects artists, you should know that the app doesn't care much what kind of video with which you happen to be working. After Effects can accommodate just about any format and frame size that you might ever need to use. You can create a frame size of up to 30,000 x 30,000 pixels for a comp, and for that matter, you can enter any frame rate up to 99 fps. Still, it's important that you know about the different formats that the DTV revolution represents.

Table 28-1 shows the various formats that comprise the ATSC's DTV specifications.

Table 28-1
High Definition Formats

DTV Format	Scan Lines	Horizontal Pixels	Aspect Ratio	Picture Rate
HDTV	1080	1920	16:9	60i, 30p, 24p
HDTV	720	1280	16:9	60p, 30p, 24p
SDTV	480	704	16:9	60p, 60i, 30p, 24p
SDTV	480	704	4:3	60p, 60i, 30p, 24p
SDTV	480	640	4:3	60p, 60i, 30p, 24p

Note: i= interlaced, p= progressive

As we mentioned before, you needn't be confused when confronted with these 18 different variations. Only six formats from Table 28-1 qualify for the HD label; these are the Interlaced and Progressive variations of the 1080 x 1920 and 720 x 1280 frame sizes. Also, even though most HD monitors and TVs are capable of receiving and showing all 18 formats, not all broadcasters are going to be sending out signals in all 18 formats. Some networks have chosen the 1080i format, while others have settled for the 720p variants.

Troubleshooting Field Issues

Managing your field order in After Effects is critical for producing high-quality work. When you import a piece of video footage into After Effects, the application will often guess the field order of that footage and interpret it as such. If you know it to be incorrect, you can use the Command/Ctrl+F keyboard shortcut to bring up the Interpret Footage dialog box and change the interpretation.

Sometimes, you may not know the field order of the footage, or After Effects may not be able to guess it. If this ever happens, there's a fairly simple method for guessing the field order of the incoming footage; its only requirement is that the footage contain some motion in it, such as a person moving or a car passing by.

In the following step exercise, we show you how to interpret the field order of incoming footage.

On the
DVD-ROM

For the next series of steps, you need to work with the *Field Test.mov* footage provided in the *Chapter28.aep* After Effects project. No comp is necessary for this step exercise.

STEPS: Determining the Field Order of Incoming Footage

1. **Select the *Field Test.mov* footage item provided in the Project window by clicking it.** This displays its thumbnail as well as information on the frame size and frame rate of the QuickTime movie; however, no field order is specified.

2. **Keeping the footage item selected, use the Command/Ctrl+F keyboard shortcut to bring up the Interpret Footage dialog box.** Using the Separate Fields pull-down menu, select the Upper Field First setting, and click OK. Note that there are just two possible settings here: Upper or Lower.

3. **Option/Alt+double-click the *Field Test.mov* footage item.** This opens it up in the After Effects footage window. See Figure 28-2 for reference.

4. **Press the spacebar to play the movie.** The footage consists of a biker passing through the camera frame. Notice that the biker makes a jerky back and forth motion as it passes through the frame. This tell you that the Upper Field First setting represents the incorrect field setting for the incoming footage.

5. **Close the footage window.**

6. **Select the *Field Test.mov* footage item and use the Command/Ctrl+F keyboard shortcut to bring up the Interpret Footage dialog box once again.** This time, select the Lower Field First setting from the Separate Fields pull-down menu and click OK.

7. **Option/Alt+double-click the *Field Test.mov* footage item.** This opens it up in the After Effects footage window. Press the spacebar to play the clip again, and this time you'll notice that the unsightly back and forth motion is no longer an issue as the biker passes through the frame. This represents the correct field setting for this footage. You can leave this footage marked as Lower Field first.

Figure 28-2: Option/Alt+double-click on the *Field Test.mov* to open it in the After Effects footage window and play it by pressing the spacebar. The footage makes a back and forth motion if the field order is set incorrectly.

Tip   After determining the field order of the incoming footage, be sure to use the same field order when you render your comp as well. The output field order is set under the Field Render pull-down menu in the Render Settings dialog box in the Render Queue.

Determining the field order of outgoing footage

The test we just showed you relies on two conditions: one, that someone can give you a piece of footage captured from an editing system; two, that it has some motion in it. Unfortunately, there may come a time when you don't have access to a piece of footage captured with an editing system and still be required to determine that system's field order. Yikes! What then?

Assume that you're an After Effects artist who has to create a short promo for an editor. Sometime later on, the editor will insert your piece into a larger edited program. Furthermore, let's assume that the editor is working with a Media 100 or an Avid editing system. We're using these two as examples because no one ever seems too sure as to what their particular field order is. Believe it or not, this is not an uncommon experience.

The following steps teach you how to determine the field order of an editing system.

STEPS: Determining the Field Order of an Editing System

1. **Choose Composition ➪ New Composition.** Set the comp settings to what constitutes the best guess you can make for the editing system. For example, if the editing system is working with DV footage, you can guess a frame size of 720 x 480 and a frame rate of 29.97 (assuming that it's NTSC). If, for example, the editing system seems to be using SD (Standard Definition) video, you can choose a frame size of 720 x 486. Set the duration of the comp to one second.

2. **Make a new solid using the Command/Ctrl+Y keyboard shortcut.** Set the size of this solid to 100 x 100 pixels and make it white.

3. **Create a positional animation for the small white solid.** Set it to move from outside frame left to outside frame right over ½ a second or 15 frames.

4. **Choose Composition ➪ Make Movie.** Select a location for the final render and click OK. This opens up the Render Queue.

5. **Click the Render Settings and choose Upper Field First under the Field Order pull-down menu.** See Figure 28-3 for reference.

6. **In the Output To field, name your render *Upper.mov*.**

7. **Duplicate the comp in the Render Queue by selecting it and pressing Command/Ctrl+D.** In the Render Settings for the duplicate, select Lower Field First.

8. **In the Output To field for the duplicate, name your render *Lower.mov*.**

9. **Click Render in the Render Queue window.**

10. **After the renders are finished, send both of these renders to your editor on a Zip or other removable media.** Have the editor import these movies and play both of them on the editing system. The one with the correct field order will play smoothly, while the render with the incorrect field order will make the solid skip and flicker as it moves across the frame.

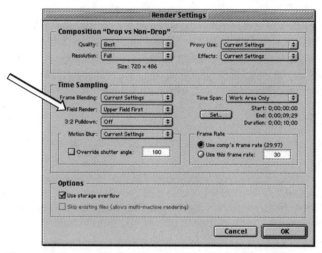

Figure 28-3: Set the Field Order in the Render Settings dialog box.

If you're working with interlaced video footage that you plan on rendering for play-back on a computer monitor, you must de-interlace this footage. To do so, first separate fields for the footage by using the Interpret Footage dialog box. Then during the render stage, set the Field Order in the Render Settings to Off.

Minimizing flicker with After Effects

Occasionally, when you render an After Effects comp for video, your output will suffer from a phenomenon known as *flicker*. A flicker is most commonly visible when you render a comp that contains artwork comprised of very thin lines. It can also be an issue when you move text across the screen. A flicker can result from many sources, but one of the most common reasons is that your comp includes lines that are thinner than one pixel. This results in the line getting displayed in only one field of an interlaced video frame. The tricky part about this sort of flicker is that you're only going to catch it if you're viewing your artwork on either a television or a broadcast monitor. If you only view your After Effects comp on a computer monitor, you won't notice any flicker because your computer monitor displays pixels by means of a progressive scan.

Here are some suggestions to help you minimize any flicker in your After Effects projects:

✦ **Use a broadcast monitor:** If you are preparing your After Effects work for eventual broadcast, always view your work on a broadcast or television monitor as you go along. This is the best way of catching flicker while your work is in progress.

✦ **Use a filter:** Select a layer that's flickering and choose Effect ⇨ Video ⇨ Reduce Interlace Flicker. Set the softness to .4 or .5. All this filter really does is blur your image a bit. You could actually achieve the same results by using a Gaussian or other blur filter at a very low Blurriness setting.

✦ **Avoid Serif fonts:** Serifs are the small curlies that some fonts contain at their edges and stems. These serifs are quite thin and tend to flicker on video created for broadcast. There are Serif fonts, and there are Sans Serif fonts. In short, you should always attempt to use Sans Serif fonts, such as Helvetica, Futura, and many others.

✦ **Use thicker lines:** Avoid using lines in your artwork that are thinner than one pixel.

✦ **Check your field order:** Incorrect field order can exacerbate flickering. Double-check the field order and make sure you have set it correctly across the board. This check includes checking the field order of any incoming footage as well as the field order set during the final render.

✦ **Use Motion Blur and a high shutter angle:** As a last resort, you can turn on Motion Blur for your flickering layer and change the shutter angle to 360 degrees. The 360 degree setting works especially well for horizontally moving items. Use a setting of 180 degrees if the motion is vertical.

Understanding the 3:2 Pulldown

Often times, you may receive footage that was transferred from film to video. Using this type of footage adds a potential trouble spot to your work. The process of converting a 24 fps film frame rate to the 29.97 fps frame rate of video is known as 3:2 Pulldown.

The trick in 3:2 Pulldown involves the manner in which four frames of film have to be spread across five frames of video. First, the film is slowed down 0.1% to make up for the difference between 30 fps and 29.97 fps.

Figure 28-4 explains the 3:2 Pulldown process.

Then the first film frame (f1) is used for the first three fields of video (v1.1, v1.2, and v2.1; in this numbering scheme, the first digit represents the frame number, and the second digit represents one of the two fields). The second frame of film (f2) is used for two fields of video (v2.2 and v3.1). Frame three (f3) of the film is then spread across the next three fields of video (v3.2, 4.1, and 4.2). Finally, the fourth frame of film (f4) is used for the last two fields of video (v5.1 and v5.2).

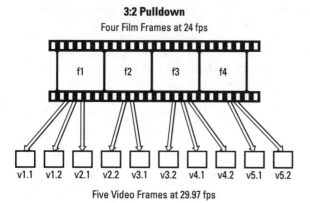

Figure 28-4: A diagram of the 3:2 Pulldown process

If you're working with video footage that was transferred from film, you will have to deal with the 3:2 Pulldown. In order for your final render to play properly without any distortion, you must set the proper pulldown for this imported footage. Later on, you'll need to add the pulldown back at the render stage. The main area in which a lack of proper 3:2 Pulldown manifests itself is if you have compressed or stretched your footage in After Effects.

STEPS: Determining the Pulldown

1. **Select your footage in the After Effects Project window.**

2. **Press Command/Ctrl+F to bring up the Interpret Footage dialog box.**

3. **Click on the Guess 3:2 Pulldown button.** After Effects analyzes the first 10 fields of the clip and suggests the best phase it can find. The "W" and "S" order in the final setting represents the series of "Whole" and "Split" frames as they occur in the final footage. If you know the order, you can manually set it as well, although After Effects does a pretty good job of figuring it out on its own.

Note that this same pulldown order has to be added back into your footage at the final render stage. This setting is found under the Render Settings dialog box, which is available for each item in the Render Queue window.

Mixing and Matching Frame Sizes and Pixel Aspect Ratios

Any digital image is composed of pixels. *Pixel,* by the way, is short for picture element, and it's the smallest unit that makes up any computer-based image. When we say 720 x 480 frame size, we're really talking about a frame that is 720 pixels wide and 480 pixels tall.

Each of these pixels has an aspect ratio, which means that the pixel has a fixed height and breadth. For example, computer-based images, such as the ones created in Adobe's Photoshop, are comprised of pixels that are square. On the other hand, video, such as SD or DV, often uses a pixel aspect ratio that is not 1:1. In fact, the pixels that make up a video image captured via FireWire or a video capture card are often rectangular. In those examples, the pixels' aspect ratio is 0.9:1. This may not seem like a big difference, but if these pixel aspect ratios are mixed and matched without care, you can have distortion in your final images. This distortion is especially visible when you're working with round objects such as a basketball, for instance.

Remember that pixel aspect ratios are never arbitrary; they're often tied to standardized frame sizes. For example, video cards that use the 640 x 480 frame size always use square pixels. The same is true for items that are displayed on a computer monitor. Other kinds of video, such as SD at 720 x 486 or DV at 720 x 480, use nonstandard or rectangular pixels. The pixel aspect ratio for DV and SD is often referred to as the *D1* standard, after the D1 digital format.

When creating a new composition in After Effects by choosing Composition ⇨ New Composition, you get a few choices for selecting pixel aspect ratios. Following are the settings you see in the New Composition dialog box.

Understanding pixel aspect ratio settings

Before we move on to explain the pixel aspect ratio settings found in After Effects, it is important to point out that these settings are meant to be set to the native pixel aspect ratio of the incoming footage, not necessarily for your rendered output.

- ✦ **Square Pixels:** This setting uses a 1:1 (or 1.0) pixel aspect ratio. The most common frame sizes that use this setting are 640 x 480 and 648 x 486.

- ✦ **D1/DV NTSC:** This is by far the most common pixel aspect ratio you need to use. This setting uses a 0.9 pixel aspect ratio. Frame sizes, such as 720 x 480 (DV) and 720 x 486 (D1) both use this setting. This setting is for a 4:3 frame aspect ratio output.

- ✦ **D1/DV NTSC Widescreen:** This setting uses a 1.2 pixel aspect ratio. Employ this setting if you are working with the frame sizes of either 720 x 480 or 720 x 486 and need to output for a 16:9 frame aspect ratio.

- ✦ **D1/DV PAL:** This D1/DV PAL setting uses a 1.0666 pixel aspect ratio. This setting is meant for the 720 x 576 frame size when a 4:3 output is your goal.

- ✦ **D1/DV PAL Widescreen:** If you are working with the 720 x 576 frame size and need a 16:9 frame size aspect ratio output, use this setting. The pixel aspect ratio for this setting is 1.422.

- ✦ **Anamorphic 2:1:** Selecting this setting uses a 2.0 pixel aspect ratio. Use this choice if your video was shot using an anamorphic film lens.

- ✦ **D4/D16 Standard:** Select this setting for a frame size of 1440 x 1024 or 2880 x 2048 when the output is intended for a 4:3 frame aspect ratio. The pixel aspect ratio for this setting is 0.948.

✦ **D4/D16 Anamorphic:** This setting uses a 1.896 pixel aspect ratio. Use this setting if your video footage has a 1440 x 1024 or 2880 x 2048 frame size and your final output is for an 8:3 frame aspect ratio.

Pixel aspect ratio for incoming footage

Each incoming item in After Effects has its own pixel aspect ratio. When you import a piece of footage into After Effects, the program makes some educated guesses as to its pixel aspect ratio. As we mentioned though, sometimes you need to go in and manually set the pixel aspect ratio for the footage.

Below are the series of steps that show you how to set the pixel aspect ratio for each item in the After Effects Project window.

STEPS: Setting the Pixel Aspect Ratio for Imported Footage

1. **Select your footage in the After Effects Project window.**

2. **Choose File ⇨ Interpret Footage ⇨ Main.** Alternatively, you can press Command/Ctrl+F to bring up the Interpret Footage dialog box.

3. **Use the Pixel Aspect Ratio pop-up menu to select a ratio and click OK.**

Figure 28-5 shows the menu in the dialog box.

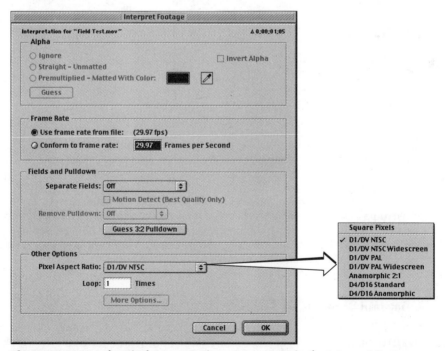

Figure 28-5: Use the Pixel Aspect Ratio pop-up menu in the Interpret Footage dialog box to set the pixel aspect ratio of your footage.

Setting pixel aspect ratio for compositions

In the last series of steps, we set the pixel aspect ratio for an item or footage in the After Effects Project window. Don't forget that each composition in After Effects also has its own pixel aspect ratio.

Follow these steps to select the pixel aspect ratio for compositions.

STEPS: Setting the Pixel Aspect Ratio for a Composition

1. **Create a new composition by choosing Composition ⇨ New Composition.**

2. **In the Composition Settings dialog box that is presented to you, select a ratio from the Pixel Aspect Ratio pop-up menu and click OK.**

Figure 28-6 shows the pop-up menu in the Composition Settings dialog box.

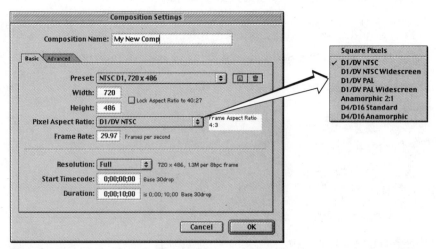

Figure 28-6: Shown here is the Pixel Aspect Ratio selection menu in the Composition Settings dialog box. Each composition can have its own pixel aspect ratio.

Tip   Note that the previous two steps show you how to set the pixel aspect ratio for a new composition. You can also choose a pixel aspect ratio for a preexisting composition. To do so, open the composition and choose Composition ⇨ Settings or press Command/Ctrl+K. At that point, you can select a different pixel aspect ratio from the Pixel Aspect Ratio pop-up menu.

Mixing pixel aspect ratios

Previously in this chapter, we described how computer-based graphics consist of square pixels, such as the ones created in Adobe Photoshop, for example. Video images such as DV (720 x 480 frame size) and D1 (720 x 486 frame size) consist of rectangular or non-square pixels. Mixing these pixels incorrectly often produces distortion in the final images.

In the following step exercise, we assume that you're preparing your still images in Adobe Photoshop (which uses square pixels) and are about to integrate them into a composition that uses either DV (at 720 x 480 frame size) or D1 (at 720 x 486 frame size).

STEPS: Using Square-Pixel Material When Outputting to D1 or DV NTSC:

1. **When working in Adobe Photoshop, set your image size to the following settings:**

   If you are planning to output for DV (which has a frame size of 720 x 480), set your image size in Photoshop to 720 x 534.

   If you are planning to output for D1 (which has a frame size of 720 x 486), set your image size in Photoshop to 720 x 540.

2. **Import your final Photoshop file into After Effects as a comp.**

3. **Create a new composition in After Effects by choosing Composition ➪ New Composition.** If your plan is to output DV, select the NTSC DV, 720 x 480 for frame size and D1/DV NTSC for pixel aspect ratio. However, if you plan to output to D1, select NTSC D1, 720 x 486 for frame size and D1/DV NTSC for pixel aspect ratio. Select the rest of the settings for your composition and click OK.

4. **Drag your Photoshop comp into the new composition.**

5. **Select the Photoshop comp containing the square-pixel graphics and use the Command/Ctrl+Option/Alt+F (Shrink to Fit) command to fit the layer into the comp.** Now you can design and render without fear. There won't be any distortion in your final render despite the disparate elements.

Knowing alternatives to mixing pixel aspect ratios

We just showed you one way to integrate square-pixel based artwork into a non-square pixel-based composition; however, that method requires that you create your artwork in Photoshop at weird image sizes, such as 720 x 534 or 720 x 540. Creating artwork at these sizes may not be a big deal if you only have to do it once in a while, but if you're an art director who spends your day preparing artwork in Photoshop for use in After Effects, these image sizes create a bizarre working situation. Why, you may wonder, if your final output format is 720 x 480 (for DV), can't you simply create your stills at the same 720 x 480 image size in Adobe Photoshop? Wouldn't that be so much simpler?

Well, it is. But there is a caveat as well as an added step you have to take. Check it out.

STEPS: Mixing Aspect Ratios: An Alternative Approach

1. **When working in Adobe Photoshop, create your image sizes to be exactly that of your final output.** If your final output is DV (at 720 x 480 frame size), set your Image Size in Adobe Photoshop at 720 x 480 pixels. If your final output is D1 (at 720 x 486 frame size), set your Image Size in Adobe Photoshop at exactly 720 x 486.

2. **Finish your artwork and import it into After Effects as a comp.** After Effects automatically interprets the size of your image (720 x 480 or 720 x 486) and, by default, assigns these stills the D1/DV NTSC pixel aspect ratio. This is incorrect. Remember, your stills weren't made at the D1/DV NTSC pixel aspect ratio; they're composed of square pixels.

3. **In the Project window, select one of the layers of your Photoshop comp from the folder containing the layers and choose File ⇨ Interpret Footage ⇨ Main.** Choose Square Pixels from the Pixel Aspect Ratio pop-up menu and then click OK.

4. **Control+click/Right-click the footage item that you just set to Square Pixels and choose Interpret Footage ⇨ Remember Interpretation.**

5. **Select the remaining layers of the Photoshop comp from the folder containing the layers, Control+click/right-click one of them and choose Interpret Footage ⇨ Apply Interpretation.**

6. **Create a new composition by choosing Composition ⇨ New Composition.** If your plan is to output DV, select the NTSC DV, 720 x 480 preset. However, if you plan to output to D1, select NTSC D1, 720 x 486 preset. Adjust the rest of the settings for your composition as you see fit and click OK.

7. **Drop your footage and your Photoshop comp into it and work away.** You may notice that your square pixel-based footage may look a bit distorted in the D1/DV NTSC pixel aspect ratio-based comp. This is actually correct. Go ahead and create your design and render without fear. The still layers and footage mix without any distortion in the final render.

Tip   As we mentioned in Step 7, your square-pixel based stills will appear to be distorted in the Comp window. If this really bothers you, click the small arrow located in the upper-right corner of the Comp window to open the flyout menu, and select Pixel Aspect Correction. While this compensates for the distortion, note that this setting is for viewing purposes only.

Working with Interpretation Rules

In the After Effects application folder, you may have noticed a text file called *interpretation rules.txt*. This is a file that tells After Effects how to interpret field order, alpha channel, frame rate, and pixel aspect ratio when importing footage.

The beauty of this file is that it is simply a text file that you can edit with any text editor, such as SimpleText or Notepad.

Armed with this kind of control, you can set all kinds of interpretation guidelines for your work in After Effects. For example, there are numerous variations of formats and field orders that After Effects doesn't know what to do with. Often, you may find that you're working with an editing system which generates output that After Effects doesn't automatically know how to handle in terms of its field order or correct pixel aspect ratio. In that case, you can create your own interpretation rules for After Effects to follow. This saves an enormous amount of work and thinking on your part. After you learn how to modify this file, After Effects follows your orders until you change them. Note that you can always override the Interpretation Rules by selecting a footage item in the Project window and choosing File ➪ Interpret ➪ Main (or by pressing Command/Ctrl+F).

Understanding Interpretation Rules

If you want to begin understanding Interpretation Rules, use SimpleText or Notepad to open up the *interpretation rules.txt* file that is located in the After Effects application folder. After it opens up, the first element that you see is a whole lot of # signs.

For example, the file starts out with the following:

```
# "Interpretation Rules.txt"
# Adobe After Effects Automatic Footage Interpretation
```

To find out what all those # signs mean, read on. The next line is as follows:

```
# lines beginning with "#" are comments
```

In other words, any line that starts with the # sign is just a comment line and is not read as an interpretation rule for After Effects. So far, so good.

So the only lines that contain active rules for After Effects are the ones *without* the # sign at the beginning. Another common symbol you will see is the * or the asterisk symbol. In the Interpretation Rules, this symbol stands for a wildcard. Just so you know: Wildcard values match anything and change nothing.

Check out some basic rules of the Interpretation Rules file.

✦ **Rule 1:** The Basic format of a rule is `{match requirements} = {set interpretation}`. That means that all settings shown to the left of the = sign are the ones that After Effects looks for. And all the settings shown on the right side of the = sign are what After Effects sets the interpretations to after it finds the matching requirements.

✦ **Rule 2:** The layout of the rule is width, height, frame-rate, file-type, codec = pixel aspect ratio/name, field order, conform frame-rate, alpha interp. In short, the matching requirements are listed in the order of width, height, frame-rate, file-type, and codec. After the equal sign, you tell After Effects what to do by listing what pixel aspect ratio it should set, what the field order should be and what to conform the frame-rate to as well as the alpha channel interpretation.

Check out one active line of a rule and see what it says:

```
# Avid 640x480 is square-pixel, upper-field first
640, 480, *, "MooV", "avr " = 1/1, U, *, *
```

Note here that rules always come listed with a comment line. In this case, the comment line (which is preceded by a # sign) tells us that the following rule will set Avid 640 x 480 video footage, regardless of its frame rate (because the * is a wildcard symbol that stands for "any value"), that contains the file code and the codec code to do the following:

✦ Use a square pixel aspect ratio (represented by 1/1).

✦ Use an Upper field first field order (U for upper, L for lower).

✦ Conform to the frame rate to whatever it might be.

✦ Maintain any alpha channel that exists.

Understanding the correct syntax of the rules language is important:

✦ Width & height are shown as integer numbers — for example 640, 480.

✦ The frame-rate is displayed as a decimal number — as in 29.97.

✦ File-type is displayed as four characters, which must be in quotes.

✦ Codec is also displayed as four characters, which must be in quotes.

Tip   The Interpretation Rules file requires you to specify both the file-type and the codec code for the file when creating rules. These are four character codes. To find out the file-type and codec code for a specific file, Opt+click (Mac) or Alt+click (Windows) on the footage in the Project window. The four character codes appear in the last line of text, next to the thumbnail.

✦ The pixel aspect ratio is shown as a ratio of integers (for example, 10/11). The ratio can also be followed by a name for that ratio, such as 10/11/"New Aspect". Note that giving it a name adds this name and the pixel aspect ratio choice to the Composition Settings and the Interpret Footage dialog boxes under the Pixel Aspect Ratio pop-up menus.

✦ The field order is displayed by a single character: F = Frame, U = Upper field, or L = Lower field.

✦ Use a decimal number for the conform rate — such as 29.97.

✦ The codes for the alpha interpretation are I = Ignore, S = Straight, P = Premultiplied with Black, and W = Premultiplied with White. Note that the alpha interpretation is ignored for footage that does not contain an alpha channel.

In light of what you have learned, look at another Interpretation rule.

```
# assume NTSC DV is D1 aspect, lower-field
720, 480, 29.97, "MooV", "dvc " = 648/720, L, *, *
720, 480, 29.97, "MooV", "dvpn" = 648/720, L, *, *
720, 480, 29.97, ".AVI", "dvsd" = 648/720, L, *, *
```

The preceding rule is meant to correctly interpret DV footage. It has three lines because DV may come in a few different flavors as far as file types and codecs are concerned. Very simply, the rules tell any footage that has a frame width of 720 and a height of 480 (which runs at a frame rate of 29.97 fps) and that uses the file code "MooV" and the codec code of "dvc " (the empty space after the dvc and the last quotation mark is *very* important) to do the following:

✦ Use a pixel aspect ratio of 648/720.

✦ Set the field order to L (or Lower field first).

✦ Use the wild card values (in short, do nothing) for the conform rate and the alpha channel interpretation.

Now you can make your own interpretation rules and force After Effects to live by *your* rules!

The information in this chapter is meant to help you ward off real-world production problems. If you're a designer, you want to prevent the otherwise wonderful world of digital video from becoming a minefield. If you really take the time to learn these quirks, your life will become a lot easier as your deadlines approach, especially if you work across different kinds of media.

✦   ✦   ✦

Prepping for Editors

After Effects wouldn't amount to much if not for the myriad of software applications on either side of the After Effects workflow. You need still image, vector, and video-editing programs to prepare elements for After Effects, and after you render the comps in your project, you almost always need to use additional software to put together the final deliverable goods. These "goods" often come in the form of video or film that needs to be cut together using a number of editing systems on the market. In essence, you typically prepare a number of elements with video-editing software, apply some magic to them in After Effects, and hand them off to the editing applications once again.

This chapter exists to shed some light on how After Effects works with some of the more popular editing suites in today's digital video market. You've already seen how Premiere, Adobe's own versatile editing solution, generates project files that import into After Effects with the layout of the Timeline intact. What if you're working with Avid, Media 100, or Final Cut Pro editing systems? Integrating these applications with After Effects involves a few more tricks. If you're a freelancer whose clients run the gamut from small production houses to large broadcast networks, it may not be a bad idea to learn something about how different editing systems dovetail with After Effects.

In the dynamic and changing world of digital video, it never hurts to keep an eye on trends and developments in the field. Which codecs work best for streaming video on the Web? What's the most cost-effective DVD-Video production workflow? More along the lines of this chapter, which editing suites work best in certain environments? Based on the demand for certain services, how quickly will capital improvements to your shop's video hardware pay for themselves? What's your magic bullet? Which VTR deck, capture board, editing application, and compositing software is going to provide you with the optimal solution? These are huge questions, the answers to which are specific to your position in the market, but at the very least, we can tell you something about how After Effects fits into different workflows.

Working with Non-Linear Editing Systems

Non-linear editing derives its name from the process of digitizing video assets and editing pieces of them together in any order you like. The benefits of such a system are pretty obvious. With a non-linear editing system, you can compose video sequences nondestructively, that is, without worrying about having to reedit a sequence on a tape if you want to add another clip to an otherwise perfect sequence. Before digital videographers enjoyed the benefits of such wonderful engineering, editors worked in tape-to-tape environments in which last minute changes prompted far more nervous breakdowns than they do today. Anyway, take a look at how After Effects fits into this relatively brave new non-linear world.

Working with Avid Editing Systems

Avids are the most popular editing systems in the world, and they come in many flavors. We should tell you that it's quite a challenge to attempt to condense the integration of Avid and After Effects into one section of a single chapter. That said, we suggest that you use this chapter as a general guideline when jumping between the two worlds. In truth, it's really impossible to keep up with all the new developments inside the Avid world, at least as far as this book is concerned. Because there have been so many changes to all the different models and makes, we suggest that you closely read the user manual that ships with your own particular Avid System.

The idea behind the information here is to present an overall perspective on the various stages of a generalized workflow between Avid and After Effects. Just know that some of the details may change by the time you're actually holding this book in your hands.

Understanding the Workflow

The basic workflow between Avid and After Effects is the same as it is between any NLE (Non-Linear Editing System) and After Effects.

The following list outlines the general stages of this process. Afterwards, we examine each stage in greater detail.

1. **Export from Avid:** The first stage of the workflow entails selecting your material in Avid and exporting it in preparation for work within After Effects.

2. **Import into After Effects:** The second phase of your work is to import this exported video material into an After Effects project.

3. **Layer and Design:** Next, you prepare comps in After Effects and use the Avid video material to layer and design your effects and compositions. This is where you set keyframes, apply effects, and build a composition along your own design.

4. **Render:** After you are satisfied with your layering and design in After Effects, you render your final movies.

5. **Import render into Avid:** These final renders are then imported back into your Avid. Here, you use these renders just as you would any other video clips.

6. **Output to tape:** Finally, you're ready to edit this final material back and lay it off to videotape to finish your program.

Exporting material from Avid

To prepare for exporting from Avid, you need to check on a few items before you proceed. First, make sure that your captures in Avid have been at the highest quality. Another detail to keep in mind is that some earlier versions of QuickTime and Video for Windows limit the largest file size to 2GB. If that's an issue, you may have to export your video in portions.

Here are the general steps to follow when you export material from Avid.

STEPS: Exporting from Avid

1. **Select your material in Avid.** You can do so by selecting a clip in the bin. If the clip that you want to export is loaded into a Source, Record, or Pop-Up monitor, you can mark an In and an Out point to select the area that you want to export.

2. **Choose File ➪ Export.** The Export File Type dialog box is presented to you.

   Figure 29-1 shows the Avid Export File Type dialog box.

3. **In the Export File Type dialog box, select your QuickTime settings.** You have the option of exporting just audio, video, or audio and video. Also, check the Export Full Frame box. This enables you to export both fields of the frame.

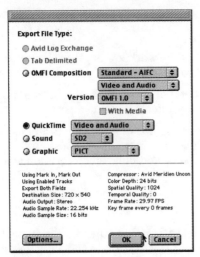

Figure 29-1: Here's the Avid Export File Type dialog box. Depending on your Avid's model and make, your settings and choices may vary.

4. **Click OK after you're done.** The File Save dialog box is presented to you.

5. **Type a name for your file, select a destination folder, and click Save.** A new QuickTime Export dialog box is presented to you.

6. **Select additional Size and Audio settings in this dialog box.** Maintaining the material's original frame size and native audio rate is essential for a clean export. In other words, don't rescale the video or resample the audio. Also, check the Cross Platform Movie option if you want to create an export that works on both the Mac and PC platforms.

7. **Click the Compression Settings button to open the QuickTime Compression Settings dialog box.**

    Figure 29-2 shows the QuickTime Compression Settings dialog box.

8. **Select an Avid codec from the codec pull-down menu.** An AVR (Avid Video Resolution) Selection dialog box appears in which you can select your AVR setting. Again, make sure that you maintain the original quality of your video when selecting the AVR setting.

9. **Click OK after you're done, and the file begins to export.**

Caution

If you have After Effects installed on the same workstation as the Avid, the previously outlined steps work just fine; however, if your After Effects workstation is separate from the Avid editing station, you need to make sure that you have the Avid codec installed on your After Effects workstation. (See the following sidebar, entitled "Choosing your codec.")

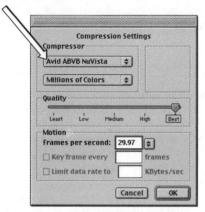

Figure 29-2: You use the QuickTime Compression Settings dialog box to select the codec for your export.

Importing Avid footage into After Effects

This part of the process is relatively painless. Importing Avid material into an After Effects project is no different than importing any other footage item(s). Drag and drop the items from the desktop onto the Project window, or within After Effects, choose File ➪ Import ➪ File or Multiple Files.

Choosing your codec

When exporting material from Avid for use in After Effects, you should always strive to use the Avid codec when selecting your export codec in the QuickTime Compression Settings dialog box. This Avid codec is automatically installed during the original installation of the Avid software. When you reach the rendering stage, you should select the Avid codec for rendering purposes again (in the QuickTime Compression Settings dialog box). If your copy of After Effects is installed on the same workstation as the Avid, the scenario we just outlined shouldn't present you with any problems.

The situation gets complicated if your After Effects workstation is a different machine than the Avid workstation. In that case, you may not have the Avid codec installed on your After Effects workstation. This situation can easily be remedied. Avid offers its codec free of cost on its Web site at http://support.avid.com. Simply download this small piece of software and drop it into the Extensions folder, located within your System folder, and then the Avid codec becomes available as an option in the QuickTime compression dialog box.

You always have the option of rendering with another codec (such as Animation or Component Video) and then importing the final renders into Avid. However, be warned that renders done with QuickTime codecs other than the Avid codec take a very (often very, very) long time to import into the Avid. So, avoid the headaches and make sure that you have the Avid codec available on the After Effects workstation.

Just be sure that you installed the Avid codec on the machine where you're doing your After Effects work. If you're not sure about this, consult the preceding sidebar, "Choosing your codec."

Separating fields for Avid

Upon importing the Avid material into After Effects, make sure that you separate the fields of the imported footage. This process is fairly simple. You just select your footage in the Project window and use the Command/Ctrl+F keyboard shortcut to bring up the Interpret Footage dialog box. Within the dialog box, you can specify the field order of the Avid footage. In some cases, After Effects automatically guesses the field order. In other cases, you have to set it manually.

Different breeds of Avid use different field orders. Table 29-1 should help you get started. As always, consult the Avid User Manual for precise information on the field order of your own particular Avid model.

Note   Some of the Avid literature may refer to the Upper Field as the Odd field and the Lower Field as the Even field.

Table 29-1		
Field Orders of Some Common Avid Systems		
Platform	*Avid System*	*Field Order*
Windows NT and Mac	MCXpress (NTSC)	U
Windows NT and Mac	Media Composer (Meridien) (NTSC)	L
Windows NT and Mac	Symphony (NTSC)	L
Windows NT	Xpress, NTSC	L
Windows NT	Xpress 2.2 and earlier(NTSC)	U
Windows NT	Xpress 2.5 and later (NTSC)	L
Windows NT	Media Composer 6.x and 7.x (ABVB) (NTSC)	U
Windows NT	Media Composer 8.x (Meridien) (NTSC)	L
Windows NT	All PAL systems	L
Mac OS	All PAL systems	U

Note: U= Upper Field First. L= Lower Field First.

Tip   To confirm that you have the correct field order, Option/Alt+double-click the footage in the Project window after you set the field order for it. Press the space-bar to play it. (You may have to reduce the magnification by pressing Option/Alt+period.) If the footage displays a "jerky" back and forth motion while playing, the order is set incorrectly. Change the field order in the Interpret Footage dialog box and test it using this method again. This test works best if the footage in question contains fast motion; otherwise, it might prove inconclusive.

Working with Avid material in After Effects

To begin working with Avid footage in After Effects, first you need to create a composition. In order for you to determine the frame size, frame rate, and other information about the Avid Material, you can simply click the footage in the After Effects Project window. This displays a small thumbnail of the footage at the top of the Project window. More importantly, all the vital statistics of the footage are listed next to the thumbnail, and these bits of info tell you how to set up your comp.

It's actually quite a bit easier to create a comp with the correct settings by dragging any of the Avid footage onto the New Composition button located at the bottom of the Project window. This method automatically creates a comp with the right frame size, frame rate, and duration and even names the comp based on the file you selected.

Rendering in After Effects for Avid

Now it's time to enter the rendering phase. At this point, you should have finished your layout and design within After Effects. There's really no big difference between rendering in After Effects and rendering for Avid in particular. The only major exception is that you select the Avid codec in the QuickTime Compression dialog box.

Follow these general guidelines when rendering your material for Avid.

STEPS: Rendering Material for Avid

1. **Choose Composition ⇨ Make Movie.**

2. **Select a name and destination for the final render in the dialog box that's presented to you.** After you're done, click Save.

3. **This opens the Render Queue.** Click the Render Settings for your comp and choose your settings with the following considerations in mind:

   Pay special attention when selecting the field order in the Field Render pull-down menu. Earlier in the chapter, we showed you Table 29-1. Use it to set the field order according to the model and platform specific to your Avid system. The rest of the settings in the Render Settings dialog box are fairly easy to figure out. Set the Quality and Resolution to Best and decide whether you want to render just the work area or the full length of the comp. Lastly, make sure that your frame rate is set to 29.97 for NTSC or 25 for PAL. After you're done, click OK.

4. **In the Render Queue, click the Output Module for your comp.** This opens the Output Settings dialog box.

5. **Under Format, select your output format (for example, QuickTime Movie).**

6. **Next, click the Format Options button.** This option opens up the QuickTime Compression dialog box. This is where you choose the codec for your final render. For Avid, select the Avid codec provided (for example, Media Composer). Macintosh based Avid systems display the Avid codec as either Avid QuickTime or Media Composer. On Windows-based machines, the options may be displayed as Avid AVI or Avid QuickTime.

Note When you select an Avid codec, a small dialog box appears asking you to choose the appropriate resolution for your Avid. Be sure to select the AVR setting that you were using when you captured and exported your material. Click OK after you're done. Figure 29-3 shows the AVR selection dialog box.

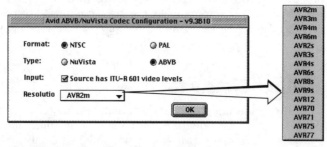

Figure 29-3: The AVR selection dialog box

7. **Back in the Output Module Settings dialog box, adjust any remaining settings if necessary (such as audio, if applicable).** Click OK and close the Output Module Settings dialog box.

Caution Be sure not to upsample or downsample your audio. Render the audio at the native rate at which you captured and exported the original Avid material.

8. **Click the Render button to begin rendering your comp.**

Note AVR (Avid Video Resolution) is a trademark of Avid, and the AVR settings are used to indicate the data rate—hence, the quality of the resulting video. To determine what the AVR settings translate to, check your Avid documentation.

Handling alpha channels with Avid material

Alpha channels provide transparency information. Computer image files have three channels (RGB) for color information purposes. A fourth channel, called the *alpha channel,* is often added to provide information that is used by After Effects, or Avid editing software, to composite images on top of one another.

Here you face a choice. If you need an alpha channel for your final render, you have two options. If you're using a newer version of the Avid codec (8.0.2 or later) you can render the alpha along with the RGB as a single file. However, if you're using an older version of the Avid codec or outputting an AVI file, you will need to render the alpha and the RGB as two separate files and combine them within Avid after you import the final renders into your Avid system.

In the following section, we outline both methods of rendering as well as the method for compositing the rendered output within the Avid system.

Any image file with an alpha channel is also known as a 32-bit file. This is because each of the channels (RGB and alpha) consists of eight bits of information, all of which add up to 32 bits. After Effects only works with 32-bit files and if you import image files that are 24-bit (meaning they lack an alpha channel), After Effects automatically assigns them one and treats them as 32-bit files. For a full frame of video, the alpha channel may be fully opaque, or solid, but it is there nevertheless.

STEPS: Rendering an Alpha with RGB as a Single File

1. **Choose Composition ⇨ Make Movie.**

2. **Select a destination and provide a name for your final render.**

3. **This opens up the Render Queue.** Click the Render Settings for your comp and choose your settings.

   Pay special attention when selecting the field order in the Field Render pull-down menu. Earlier in the chapter, we showed you Table 29-1. Use it to set the field order according to the model and platform specific to your Avid system. The rest of the settings in the Render Settings dialog box are fairly easy to figure out. Set the Quality and Resolution to Best and decide whether you want to render just the work area or the full length of the comp. Lastly, make sure your frame rate is set to 29.97 for NTSC or 25 for PAL. After you're done, click OK.

4. **In the Render Queue, click the Output Module for your comp.** This opens up the Output Settings dialog box.

5. **Under Format, select your output format (for example, QuickTime Movie).**

6. **Next, click the Format Options button.** This option opens up the QuickTime Compression dialog box. This is where you choose the codec for your final render. For Avid, select the Avid codec provided (for example, Media Composer). Macintosh-based Avid systems display the Avid codec as either Avid QuickTime or Media Composer. On Windows-based machines, the options may be displayed as Avid AVI or Avid QuickTime.

When you select an Avid codec, a small dialog box appears asking you to choose the appropriate resolution for your Avid. Be sure to select the AVR setting that you were using when you captured and exported your material. Click OK after you're done.

7. **Back in the Output Module Settings dialog box, under the Channels pull-down menu, select the RGB+Alpha setting.** Figure 29-4 shows the Channels setting in the Output Module Settings dialog box.

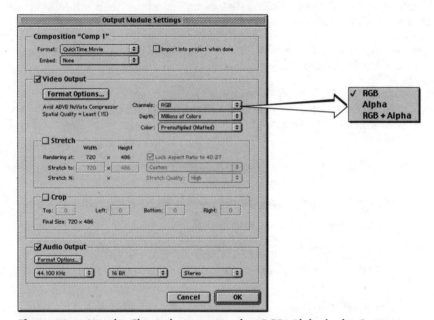

Figure 29-4: Use the Channels menu to select RGB+Alpha in the Output Module Settings dialog box.

This is where you tell After Effects to render a single file, which contains RGB as well as Alpha channel information. Bear in mind that if the RGB+Alpha setting is grayed out, it means your currently selected codec does not support alpha channels. Click OK after you are done.

8. **Click the Render button in the Render Queue to begin rendering your comp.** After the render is finished, import your final render into Avid.

Tip   If your alpha channel is not seen when you import the final render into Avid, select Invert Existing Alpha in the Import Settings dialog box in your Avid.

STEPS: Rendering an Alpha and an RGB as Two Files

1. **Choose Composition ➪ Make Movie.**

2. **Select a destination and provide a name for your final render.**

3. **This opens up the Render Queue.** Click the Render Settings for your comp and choose your settings.

Pay special attention when selecting the field order in the Field Render pull-down menu. Earlier in the chapter, we showed you Table 29-1. Use it to set the field order according to the model and platform specific to your Avid system. The rest of the settings in the Render Settings dialog box are fairly easy to figure out. Set the Quality and Resolution to Best and decide whether you want to render just the work area or the full length of the comp. Lastly, make sure your frame rate is set to 29.97 for NTSC or 25 for PAL. After you're done, click OK.

4. **In the Render Queue, click the Output Module for your comp.** This opens up the Output Settings dialog box.

5. **Under Format, select your output format (for example, QuickTime Movie).**

6. **Next, click the Format Options button.** This opens up the QuickTime Compression dialog box. This is where you choose the codec for your final render. For Avid, select the Avid codec provided (for example, Media Composer). Macintosh-based Avid systems display the Avid codec as either Avid QuickTime or Media Composer. On Windows-based machines, the options may be displayed as Avid AVI or Avid QuickTime.

7. **Back in the Output Module Settings dialog box, under the Channels pull-down menu, select the RGB setting.** This is where you tell After Effects to render the first file, which contains only the RGB channel information. Click OK after you're done.

8. **Choose Composition ⇨ Add Output Module.** A new output module is added in your Render Queue, below the queued comp.

9. **Open the Output Module Settings dialog box by clicking the Output Module setting name in the Render Queue.** Select Alpha from the Channels pop-up menu. Leave the format set to QuickTime (for Mac OS) or Video for Windows (for Windows) and the codec to the Avid codec. In short, leave all settings unchanged, except that for this go-round you select just Alpha in the Channels menu, not RGB or RGB+Alpha. Click OK after you're done.

10. **Back in the Render Queue, click the underlined word next to Output To.** This brings up the Save Movie As dialog box. Type a name and set a destination for it. Click OK after you're done.

11. **Click the Render button in the Render Queue to begin rendering your comp.** After the render is finished, import your final render into Avid.

Layering Alpha and RGB files within Avid

If you have created separate files for the RGB and the Alpha channels, you need to import these clips into Avid and combine the two files to create the desired transparency in your video.

Follow these general steps to combine the two files.

STEPS: Combining the RGB and the Alpha Renders in Avid

1. **Import both the RGB only and the Alpha only rendered movies into Avid.**

2. **Apply the Matte Key effect in your Avid.** Note that the Alpha only render will be employed as the foreground matte within your effect.

3. **Choose Reverse in the Matte Key effect to convert the alpha information correctly for the Alpha only layer.**

4. **Adjust your matte contrast as necessary to create the final transparency.**

Tip

If you do a whole lot of work between Avid and After Effects, we suggest that you look into purchasing a plug-in made by Automatic Duck. This plug-in enables you to import your entire layered Avid Timeline as an identically layered comp into After Effects, and vice versa. This way you can maintain your video tracks in Avid as layers in After Effects and skip the whole series of steps needed to export from Avid to After Effects. Go to its Web site at www.automaticduck.com for more information.

Working with the Final Cut Pro Editing System

Apple Computer's release of their Final Cut Pro editing software represents a milestone in the history of non-linear editing systems. Final Cut Pro has quickly become the choice of many for their editing needs. Most commonly, Final Cut Pro is used in DV-based setups. With an Apple G4, Final Cut Pro, a DV camera and a FireWire cable, you, too, can begin to capture and edit your video in no time flat. Make no mistake though; Final Cut Pro is a versatile and flexible system. Numerous companies make video cards that are certified by Apple to be compatible with Final Cut Pro. Using these capture cards, you can work with Standard Definition (SD) as well as High Definition (HD) video. Final Cut Pro is known as the "DV to HDTV" solution, and indeed it appears that this is an appropriate title.

In the next few sections, we discuss the process of working between Final Cut Pro and After Effects. Even though we discuss this particular workflow in the context of the DV format, don't lose sight of the fact that the general flow and logic of these steps remains the same whether you're working with SD or HD video. Whenever it's relevant, we'll point out the key issues you need to keep in mind when adapting these steps for SD or HD video.

Working between Final Cut Pro and After Effects

Not surprisingly, the workflow between Final Cut Pro and After Effects follows the steps that any other NLE (Non-Linear Editor) generally requires. The steps include exporting video from Final Cut Pro, importing it into After Effects, creating a layered comp with it, and finally, rendering the comp back out to Final Cut Pro.

Next, we outline each phase of this workflow in detail.

STEPS: Exporting Material from Final Cut Pro

1. **First, in Final Cut Pro, make a selection for export.** You can select a clip in a sequence or in the Browser. You can also double-click a clip in the Browser or the sequence to load it into the Viewer. Another way to make a selection is to set In and Out points in the Timeline to mark the section that will be exported.

2. **Choose File ➪ Export Final Cut Pro Movie.** The Exports dialog box is presented to you.

   Figure 29-5 shows the Exports dialog box in Final Cut Pro.

Figure 29-5: Final Cut Pro's Exports dialog box

3. **Next, select a location in the Exports dialog box where you want to save the exported movie and provide a name for your export.**

4. **In the Settings menu, choose Current Settings.** Checking this option box uses the current compression settings for your selection. Note that in Final Cut Pro, these current settings are found in the Item Properties dialog box if your selection is a clip, or in the Sequence Settings dialog box if your selection is a sequence.

5. **Next, in the Quality drop-down menu, choose Hi Res (1).** This setting determines the render settings that will be used (such as field rendering, motion blur, filters, and frame blending). Avoid lower render quality settings; while they might speed up the export process, the loss in image quality isn't worth the time saved. When exporting material from Final Cut Pro for After Effects, you should always strive to maintain the highest possible level of quality.

6. **In the Include menu in the Exports dialog box, choose Audio and Video.** If your selection only contains video, you should choose the setting for Video Only. Audio tracks with no sound or clips in them still take up some disk space.

7. **Be sure to uncheck the Make Movie Self-Contained check box.** This step ensures the making of a "reference" movie. Reference movies are faster to make and take up a whole lot less disk space than Self-Contained movies. There is one major caveat on that point, however: Reference files require that you do your After Effects work on the same workstation where you edit with Final Cut Pro. Reference movies taken to another workstation won't work without the supporting media from which they take their "reference." Self-contained movies take longer to export and are larger in size, but they can be moved from one workstation to another without the supporting media.

8. **Click the Save button to save your exported movie.**

At this point, you have successfully selected and exported a section of your video from Final Cut Pro. The next series of steps pertain to importing your Final Cut Pro material into After Effects and setting the correct field order.

STEPS: Importing Final Cut Pro Footage into After Effects

1. **In After Effects, choose File ➪ Import ➪ File.** You are presented with the Import File dialog box.

2. **Find your exported Final Cut Pro movie, select it and click Import.** The footage is imported and appears in the After Effects Project window. DV footage is automatically recognized by After Effects as having a field order of Lower Field First. You can check this by clicking your footage and reading the field order as it appears next to the thumbnail of your video.

3. **If you are working with non-DV video (SD or HD, perhaps), the field order for the video may not be recognized correctly.** To manually set the field order of the incoming footage, select the footage and choose File ➪ Interpret Footage ➪ Main (Command+F). The Interpret Footage dialog box appears.

4. **In the Fields and Pulldown section of the Interpret Footage dialog box, select Lower Field First from the Separate Fields pull-down menu (assuming that you know your material is DV).** Obviously, if you're working with different kinds of footage, make the appropriate selection here. You can also select the Pixel Aspect Ratio under the Other Options section.

5. **Click OK to close the Interpret Footage dialog box.**

By the end of this last series of steps, you should have imported your Final Cut Pro material into After Effects and set the correct field order for your footage. The next phase in your work entails creating a comp out of the material from Final Cut Pro.

Cross-Reference To learn how to determine the field order of incoming footage as well as set the pixel aspect ratio correctly, see Chapter 28.

STEPS: Creating Comps in After Effects for Final Cut Pro

1. In After Effects, choose Composition ➪ New Composition (Command/Ctrl+N).

2. In the Composition Settings dialog box, choose the following settings:

- Type a name for the composition.

- In the Preset pull-down menu, select NTSC DV, 720 x 480. We're assuming that you're working with DV here. For SD or HD video, select the appropriate Preset from this menu or enter the correct dimensions by clicking the footage in the Project window and noting the imported clip's dimensions (as well as its frame rate and pixel aspect ration), which will be printed next to the thumbnail.

- Next, in the Pixel Aspect Ratio pull-down menu, choose D1/DV NTSC. Again, we're assuming you're working with DV here.

- Set the Frame rate to 29.97 if you are working with NTSC. Set it to 25 if you're working with PAL. Note that drop-frame versus non-drop frame timecode has no effect on the actual frame rate of either NTSC or PAL video.

- Set the Resolution setting to Full.

- Select the proper starting timecode and duration.

3. Click OK after you're done.

Tip Though we have many times, we feel that we can't emphasize this enough: You can drag any footage item in the After Effects Project window onto the New Composition button (located at the bottom of the Project window) to create a composition with the correct frame size, frame rate, duration, and name of the footage.

Your comp is now ready for you to start building your After Effects masterpiece with your Final Cut Pro material. You can layer your video, add effects, and set keyframes "to taste."

The next and final phase of working between the two applications is to render your final After Effects composition as a movie that you can import into Final Cut Pro. In the following series of steps, we walk you through this process.

STEPS: Rendering in After Effects for Final Cut Pro

1. With your final composition selected in After Effects, choose Composition ➪ Make Movie (or press Command/Ctrl+M). You are presented with a dialog box where you can type a name and a location for your final rendered movie.

2. Click Save. This opens the Render Queue.

3. **Click Current Settings (to the right of the words Render Settings).** This opens the Render Settings dialog box.

4. **Make the following selections in the Render Settings dialog box:**

   - **Set Quality to Best.**

   - **Set Resolution to Full.**

   - **Set Field Render to Lower Field First (for DV video).** Of course, if you're working with SD or HD video, you need to make sure that the field order is set to the native field order of the SD/HD video.

   - **Select Length of Comp in the Time Span menu.** Alternatively, you can also elect to render only the work area portion of your comp.

5. **Click OK to close the Render Settings dialog box.**

6. **Back in the Render Queue, click the setting name next to the words Output Module.** This opens up the Output Module Settings dialog box.

7. **Click the Format Options button in the Output Module Settings dialog box.** This opens up the QuickTime Compression Settings dialog box.

8. **Select DV-NTSC from the Compressor pull-down menu.** The list of codecs in the Compressor menu vary depending on what codecs are installed on your machine. If you happen to be rendering for a proprietary video card, you will most likely have to use the particular codec provided with that video card. For example, if you are using Final Cut Pro in conjunction with the Aurora Igniter card, you will need to select the Aurora MJPEG codec. This codec is installed on your computer when you install the software drivers provided with your video card.

Note

The Quality slider in the QuickTime Compression Settings dialog box has no effect when working with the DV codec. The DV codec does not have a low resolution setting. It only works at high (and, more importantly, *fixed*) resolution and data rate.

9. **Click OK after you're done.**

10. **Back in the Output Module Settings dialog box, you can choose to include audio by checking the Audio Output check box at the bottom of the window.** Do not upsample or downsample the audio. Always attempt to maintain the original audio rate of your material.

Caution

After Effects settings always default to the 44.1 kHz setting in the Output Module Settings dialog box, but most DV audio is captured at either 32 kHz or 48 kHz. Be sure to keep the original sampling rate of your video material.

11. **Click OK after you're done.**

12. **Back in the Render Queue, click the Render button to begin rendering.**

When After Effects finishes rendering, you can import this rendered movie into the Final Cut Pro Project window and use it in your sequence.

Tip   With the popularity of Final Cut Pro soaring every day, you have more and more solutions for integration between After Effects and Final Cut Pro. Currently, a company named Automatic Duck has announced a plug-in that allows for a complete exchange between Final Cut Pro Timelines and After Effects compositions. Not only can you export video tracks as layers, you can also export effects, keyframes, and geometric properties. For more information visit: `www.automaticduck.com/products/auto_comp_import_fcp/index.html`.

Working with Media 100 Editing Systems

Media 100 editing systems are widespread and well regarded in the non-linear editing market. These systems provide extremely high-quality video at a very affordable price and are popular with independent producers and medium-sized production houses.

In this section of the chapter, we show you how to work between the Media 100 editing systems and After Effects. You can follow two different workflows when working between Media 100 and After Effects. In the first method, you simply export media from Media 100 and use it in After Effects, much like working with any other NLE, such as Final Cut Pro or Avid.

The second method involves using an After Effects plug-in offered free of charge by Media 100. This plug-in enables you to convert your Media 100 Timelines directly into identically layered After Effects compositions.

Next, we cover both of these workflows in detail.

STEPS: Exporting Material from Media 100 for After Effects

1. **Select the clip that you want to export in Media 100.** You have many ways to accomplish this while working within the interface of Media 100. You can select an entire clip by double-clicking it in the bin or in the Timeline. The clip will be loaded into the Edit Suite dialog box. You can also set a range in a Media 100 Timeline and simply export clips within that range. Alternatively, you can export the entire program by clicking anywhere in the Timeline.

2. **Make sure the Edit Suite dialog box is selected and choose File ⇨ Export.** The Media 100 Save Exported File as dialog box is presented to you.

   Figure 29-6 shows the Save Exported File as dialog box in Media 100.

3. **Enter a name for the exported file and select a destination for it.**

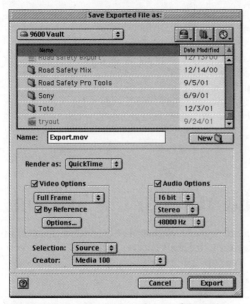

Figure 29-6: The settings for Media 100's Save Exported File as dialog box enables you to make a number of choices for your exports.

4. **Next, select what it is you want to export from the Selection menu.** The following is a list of the available settings that you can choose from:

   - **Program:** Exports entire Timeline.

   - **Range:** Exports only the clips under the range created.

   - **Frame:** Exports the current frame from the edit suite. Note that this setting is only for exporting a single frame.

   - **Source:** Exports the entire clip, even if the clip was trimmed in the Edit Suite dialog box.

   - **Select:** Exports just the selected portion of the clip as marked by an In and an Out point in the Edit Suite dialog box.

5. **Next, in the Save Exported File as dialog box, select the appropriate choices.** The settings are explained here:

   - **Self-Contained Movie:** Selecting this choice exports a self-contained movie using the Media 100 codec. This type of export is often large and takes more time to export, but a self-contained movie does have the advantage of not being dependent on any media. As a result, it can be moved off the Media 100 workstation and onto a separate After Effects workstation (as long as the separate workstation has the Media 100 codec installed).

- **By-Reference Movie:** Exports the selected item and creates a reference movie, using the Media 100 codec. This type of export is extremely fast and creates a tiny file. However, a reference movie is dependent on the media it "refers" to, and it cannot be used anywhere except on the workstation that contains the media. When working with After Effects, this is your best and first choice (assuming that it's an option).

- **Other:** Selecting the Other radio button then makes the menu next to it active. You can use that menu to export a QuickTime movie, DV Stream or AVI file. Note that if you select Other and proceed, you will be presented with other choices and a QuickTime dialog box to select a codec and other settings.

6. **Click the Export button to begin your export.** If by any chance your selection for export contains unrendered clips, the Render Confirmation dialog box will be presented to you. You have two choices here, Render All, which does *not* render the real-time transitions, and Force Render All, which force-renders everything. You want to select the Force Render All option to make sure all items are rendered and exported properly.

As you can see, like any other export dialog boxes for a non-linear editor, you have a choice between some basic elements when exporting from Media 100. Of course, you can select whether you want to export Audio only, Video only, or Audio and Video.

After you have exported from the Media 100, the next step involves working with the material in After Effects.

Working Between Media 100 and After Effects

At this stage in the chapter, we don't need to repeat what remains to be done. The next step, of course, is importing the Media 100 material into your After Effects project and creating comps by layering your video and adding effects. The last phase as always is the render process. Next, we briefly cover the remaining aspects of working in After Effects with Media 100 material.

Working in After Effects with Media 100 material

After importing the Media 100 material into After Effects, you need to set the Field Order for the video footage. As usual, the best guide for you to refer to is the User Manual that came with your own particular flavor of Media 100.

Within Media 100, you often have a choice of working in two modes:

✦ **640 x 480:** This frame size uses the M100NTSC codec and is Upper Field first. Note that this frame size uses a square pixel aspect ratio.

✦ **720 x 486:** You can elect to work in Media 100 at the 720 x 480 frame size. In this case, you will be using the M100NTSC 720 codec and work at Lower Field First. This frame size uses a D1/DV NTSC pixel aspect ratio.

After you set the field order for the footage using the Interpret Footage dialog box, the next item you should check is whether After Effects has correctly guessed the pixel aspect ratio of your footage. In certain formats of Media 100, you may be using the 640 x 480 frame size. Remember that the 640 x 480 frame size uses square pixels. You can check to see how After Effects interprets your pixel aspect ratio by clicking the footage and reading the information shown next to the thumbnail.

After you set the field order and the pixel aspect ratio, you're ready to create a comp and work with the material. Once more, the simplest method to create comps with Media 100 material is to drag the footage directly onto the New Composition button at the bottom of the After Effects Project window. This step auto-detects the frame size, the frame rate, and the other particulars of the clips (in addition to saving you the guesswork as well as the manual entry in the Composition Settings dialog box). Particularly with Media 100, make sure that you have set the correct pixel aspect ratio for your comp.

In certain versions of Media 100, you may need to install a Media 100 read-only codec (really a "transcoder") on your After Effects workstation, if it happens to be separate from where your Media 100 is located. Otherwise, After Effects may not be able to view your Media 100 files correctly. This caution does not apply if your copy of After Effects is installed on the same workstation that contains your Media 100 software and hardware. The Media 100 codec is available free with the Media 100 application. Just copy it to your system folder, and After Effects will happily view your Media 100 exports. Just note that this is a read-only codec, which means that it does not appear as a render codec in the QuickTime Compression dialog box.

To find out more information about pixel aspect ratios, see Chapter 28.

Rendering in After Effects for Media 100

After you have finished laying out your effects and keyframes, you are ready to render your comp for use in Media 100.

Rendering for Media 100 from After Effects is no different than other rendering. The only item to note is that you must select the Media 100 codec in the QuickTime Compression dialog box. This ensures that when you import the final render into Media 100, it will instantly be converted to a Media 100 file that requires no further conversion.

Just remember the caution previously mentioned. If your After Effects application happens to be installed on your Media 100 workstation, you'll see the Media 100 codec available in the QuickTime Compression dialog box during the render process. On the other hand, if your After Effects workstation is separate from your Media 100 workstation, then you won't find a Media 100 codec in your QuickTime compression dialog box. In that case, we suggest that you select another codec, such as Animation, for your renders. When selecting Animation, bear in mind that this codec is uncompressed when the slider is set to Best quality in the QuickTime Compression dialog box. Uncompressed video can result in extremely high data rates, so you may want to bring the quality slider to a medium setting to make the data rate compatible with the Media 100. Also, if you create a render using the Animation codec, Media 100 will have to rewrite this Animation file to a Media 100 file. Be forewarned: This conversion process takes some time, so if you can, install the Media 100 codec wherever you need it.

Using the Export Plug-In from Media 100

So far, we have described the process of working between Media 100 and After Effects as one that follows a general pattern of selection, export, creating comps, and then rendering. However, Media 100 has recently added a new feature that makes the whole process a lot easier when working between the two applications. If you're a Media 100 user or looking to be one, you need to know about this new feature.

Media 100 now provides an After Effects plug-in on its application install disk. This plug-in is called M100ProjectImporter. This enables new versions of Media 100 to convert a Media 100 Timeline directly into an After Effects project. No need to select, and no need to export. Simply drop the M100ProjectImporter into your After Effects Plug-ins folder (located in the After Effects application folder), and then when you export a Media 100 Timeline, you can import it into After Effects as an identically layered composition. Each clip of video is laid out as a separate layer and can be manipulated and altered in ways unimaginable before this feature was added.

Next, we outline the steps that you need to follow to export your Media 100 Timeline as an After Effects project, and then we outline the steps needed to import this file into After Effects.

Caution This method of working between Media 100 and After Effects only works on the Macintosh versions of After Effects and Media 100 and requires After Effects 4.0 or later.

STEPS: Exporting Media 100 Timelines for After Effects

1. **Make sure that the Program window is active in Media 100 and choose File ⇨ Export To ⇨ After Effects.**

2. **Name the file and select a location for it.**

3. **Click Export to begin exporting the file.** Media 100 creates a file with a MLA extension, such as, *First Export.m1a.* This is a file format specifically created by Media 100 to create files that can then be imported into After Effects. Keep in mind that when employing this export method, the entire Timeline gets exported. There is no way to just export a section or a range from Media 100 when exporting via this method. Also, be sure to render all your effects and clips before exporting your Timeline to After Effects.

When exporting a Media 100 Timeline using the method described previously, Media 100 creates a fast and small reference file that can later be imported into After Effects. This reference file has links to specific media files that are actively in use in your Media 100 Timeline. Here's an extremely important point: If by any chance you rename the media files or move them, these files will become unavailable in After Effects, and placeholders will be used in their place. Consequently, you want to organize all your media and material very carefully before exporting to After Effects.

STEPS: Importing Media 100 Timelines into After Effects

1. **In an After Effects project, choose File ⇨ Import ⇨ Foreign Project Files as Comp.** The Import File dialog box is presented to you.

2. **Locate and select the exported file from Media 100.** Remember that this file has a MLA extension.

3. **Click the Open button.** The exported Timeline from Media 100 appears as a comp in the After Effects project. The Project window also shows a folder that contains all the clips that you used in the Media 100 Timeline.

4. **In the Project window, double-click the comp to open and view it.**

After you follow the preceding steps, you have the entire Media 100 program Timeline as an After Effects comp in your project.

Before following the steps previously outlined, we remind you to make sure that you have installed the M100ProjectImporter plug-in into the After Effects Plug-ins folder. You can find this plug-in on the Media 100 Application Install CD-ROM, in the *After Effects Plug-In* folder. Simply add this plug-in to the After Effects Plug-ins folder (located in the After Effects application folder).

Understanding Exports from Media 100 to After Effects

If you follow the workflow previously outlined and convert your Media 100 Timelines to After Effects comps, you should be aware of how certain items are translated between the two applications.

✦ **Sound is exported:** The MLA file also automatically exports sound along with the video from your Media 100 Timelines.

✦ **Black is converted to solids:** If you have any black clips in your Media 100 Timeline, these are converted into solids.

✦ **Each clip is a layer:** Each clip from Media 100 is converted to a layer in After Effects. Each clip has a label, a number assigned by After Effects, and a source name. Note that the source name used is the name of the actual media file in Media 100. The time layout window accurately displays the time location and the duration for each clip.

✦ **Clips can be untrimmed:** Clips that appear as layers may have additional media that were suppressed during your edits in Media 100. This suppressed media is available to you if you drag the In and Out handles of your layers in After Effects.

As we mentioned at the beginning of the chapter, After Effects fits into the middle of a creative workflow. As an After Effects artist, whether or not you do the actual editing, you rely on video-editing applications to generate the video clips that serve as elements in your creative process. After your work is done, you'll almost always need to bring your rendered comps back into an editing environment before you can consider your efforts to be "finished." We trust that by now you know a little bit more about the integration of editing and compositing in a video production workflow.

✦   ✦   ✦

Appendixes

After Effects Resources

This appendix contains a list of resources that may be of interest to any After Effects user.

Adobe After Effects Sites

`www.adobe.com/products/aftereffects/main.html`: Adobe's main After Effects site. Contains links for downloads, training and users forums. Links here take you to numerous extensive sites managed by Adobe for After Effects users. Explore!

`www.adobe.com/support/database.html`: Having problems in After Effects? Start at this site and do a search.

`www.adobe.com/products/tips/aftereffects.html`: The Adobe site for After Effects tutorials.

`http://studio.adobe.com/expertcenter/aftereffects/main.html`: Adobe's Expert Center for After Effects. You have to register the first time, but it is well worth it. You find tutorials as well as tips and helpful explanations.

`www.adobe.com/products/aftereffects/community.html`: Site for locating an After Effects Users Group in your town.

`www.adobe.com/products/tryadobe/main.html`: Go here for numerous downloads of tryout versions of Adobe software.

`www.street-tree.com/nycaeug.html`: Home of New York City's After Effects Users Group.

`http://msp.sfsu.edu/Instructors/rey/aepage/aeportal.html`: The After Effects portal. The starting point for hundreds of links for After Effects. From here you find links to tutorials, plug-ins, information, and endless lists of sites devoted to After Effects.

`www.aefreemart.com`: True to its name, the After Effects Freemart contains more free and useful information about After Effects than anywhere else on the Web.

`www.cybmotion.com`: Trish and Chris Meyer's wonderful site has loads of valuable information about After Effects. It has links to every article by the dynamic duo of After Effects. Let's face it: Trish Meyer is a goddess.

`www.totaltraining.com`: Brian Maffitt's site for his training tapes for After Effects. Contains links and free tutorials.

`www.dv.com/magazine`: One of the few truly useful magazines on digital video, the DV magazine site is full of information and articles relevant to After Effects and digital video.

`www.wwug.com/forums/adobe_after-effects/index.htm`: The World Wide Users Group forum of After Effects. Hosted by none other than Mr. Guru himself, Brian Maffitt. Post your questions or help others who may have some.

`www.postforum.com/forums/list.php?f=11`: Another forum for After Effects users.

`www.toolfarm.com/aftereffects/plugin.shtml`: Perhaps the best site for locating, downloading, or purchasing any and all plug-ins for After Effects.

`www.creativecow.net`: Creative cow has a nice collection of articles and tutorials relevant to After Effects users.

`www.intelligentassistance.com/AfterEffects`: Site for makers of the Intelligent Assistant for After Effects.

`www.digitalanimators.com`: We don't know who designed this nightmare of a Web site, but it does have some useful After Effects tutorials.

`www.anglepark.com/AvidFAQ/AfterFXG.html`: A site devoted to working between After Effects and the Avid editing systems.

`www.learndynamicmedia.com/tips-techniques/index.html`: Information about working between After Effects and the Media 100 Editing systems.

`http://neosapien.net/flame`: A free plug-in distributed for After Effects. You can even download the code for the plug-in and modify it to suit your needs.

`www.walkersj.com/aeplugins/aeplugins_index.html`: Site for some more free plug-ins, courtesy of Steven Walker.

`www.lafcpug.org/porting_between_fcp_ae.html`: Information about working between After Effects and the Apple Final Cut Pro editing software.

`www.synthetic-ap.com/products/echofire`: Web site for EchoFire software, which allows you to view your After Effects work on an NTSC monitor.

✦   ✦   ✦

Keyboard Shortcuts for the Mac

Repetition is the way of life when working with After Effects, and without keyboard shortcuts, there would be no life in After Effects land.

This appendix provides the keyboard shortcuts found in After Effects. We added bold to the ones that we use most often.

Table B-1 **Working with Footage Items in the Project Window**	
Action	*Shortcut*
Open last project	Command + Option + Shift + P
Open Import File dialog box	Double-click a blank area in the Project window
When opening a project, suppress opening of all windows (except the Project window)	Hold down Shift
Reveal file creator ID	Option + click the element in the Project window
Open selected footage item or composition	Double-click or press Enter on numeric keypad
Open movie in an After Effects footage window	Option + double-click

Continued

Table B-1 *(continued)*

Action	Shortcut
Activate most recent composition	\
Add selected item to most recently activated composition	**Command + /**
Replace a selected layer's source footage in Comp window with selected footage	Command +Option + /
Replace a selected layer's footage item or composition	Option + drag footage item from Project window into composition
Replace footage file	Command + H
Set Interpret Footage options	Command + F
Scan for changed footage	Command +Option +Shift + Q
New folder	Command +Option +Shift + N
Remember footage interpretation	**Command +Option + C**
Apply footage interpretation	**Command +Option + V**
Set proxy file	Command + Option +P
Project Settings	Command + Option +Shift + K

Table B-2
Viewing Windows — Composition, Layer, and Footage Windows

Action	Shortcut
Display/hide title-safe and action-safe zones	' (apostrophe)
Display/hide grid	Command + ' (apostrophe)
Display/hide proportional grid	Option + ' (apostrophe)
Center active window	Command + Option + \
Suspend window updates	Caps Lock

Action	Shortcut
Cycle through tabs in the frontmost window	Shift + , (comma) and Shift + . (period) (Add Option to zoom window to fit)
Take multiple (up to four) snapshots	Shift + F5, F6, F7, and F8
Display snapshot in active window	F5, F6, F7, and F8
Purge snapshot	Command + Shift + F5, F6, F7 and F8
Purge all	Command + Option + / on numeric keypad
Display channel (RGBA)	Option + 1, 2, 3, or 4
Display channel (RGBA) in color	Option + Shift + 1, 2, 3, or 4
Display channel in color	Shift + click channel icon
Display unmatted color channels	Shift + click alpha channel icon
Display Project window	Command + 0
Display Project Flowchart view	Command + F11
Display/hide palettes	**Tab**
Hides all palettes, except Tools palette	**Shift + Tab**
Close active tab/window	Command + W
Close active window (all tabs)	Command + Shift + W
Close all windows (except Project window)	Command +Option + W

Table B-3
Moving Around the Timeline Window

Action	Shortcut
Go to beginning of work area	**Shift + Home**
Go to end of work area	**Shift + End**
Go to previous visible keyframe or layer marker	J
Go to next visible keyframe or layer marker	K
Go to a composition-time marker	0–9 on main keyboard
Scroll selected layer to top of Timeline window	X
Scroll current time to center of window	D
Go to time	**Command+ G**

Note
You can skip any punctuation in the Go To Time dialog box. Simply enter **600** to go to 6:00. The Go To Time entry box also supports relative time entry as well. For example, entering +15 in the Go To Time dialog box advances the playhead by 15 frames. Oddly enough, to go backwards, you also have to use the + sign first. So, for example, to go back by 15 frames, enter **+–15** in the Go To Time entry box. Simply entering –15 will take the playhead 15 frames before zero time, which is probably not what you want.

Table B-4
Footage and Layer Windows

Action	Shortcut
Go to beginning	Home or Command + Option + left arrow key
Go to end	End or Command + Option + right arrow key
Step forward one frame	Page Down or Command + right arrow key
Step forward 10 frames	Shift +Command + right arrow key or Shift + Page Down
Step backward one frame	Page Up or Command + left arrow key
Step backward 10 frames	Shift + Page Up or Command + Shift+ left arrow key
Go to layer In point	**i**
Go to layer Out point	**o**
Snap items (visible keyframes, time markers, and In and Out points, and so on) to each other on a time ruler	Shift + drag item

Table B-5
Previewing in the Timeline Window

Action	Shortcut
Start/pause playback	**Spacebar**
Preview audio from the current time	**. (period) on numeric keypad**
RAM Preview	**0 on numeric keypad**
RAM Preview every other frame	Shift + 0 on numeric keypad
Save RAM Preview	Command + 0 on numeric keypad

Action	Shortcut
Scrub video	Drag or Option + drag current-time marker (depending on Preview Preferences setting)
Scrub audio	Command + drag current-time marker
Wireframe preview	Option + 0 on numeric keypad
Display rectangle instead of alpha outline during wireframe preview	Command + Option + 0 on numeric keypad
Leave window contents during wireframe preview	Shift + Option +0 on numeric keypad
Leave window contents during rectangle preview	Command+ Shift + Option + 0 on numeric keypad

Note: If no layers are selected, these commands apply to all layers. Also, these commands honor the loop and audio settings in the Time Control palette.

Table B-6
Working with Layers in Composition and Timeline Windows

Action	Shortcut
Rename layer, composition, folder, or effect	Return
Select next layer back	Command + down arrow
Select next layer forward	Command + up arrow
Select a layer by its layer-outline number	1–9 on numeric keypad
Select noncontiguous layers	Command + click layers
Deselect all layers	Command + Shift + A, or F2
Lock selected layers	Command + L
Unlock all layers	Command + Shift + L
Split selected layer	Command + Shift + D
Activate Comp window with layer	\
Display selected layer in Layer window	Enter on numeric keypad
Show/hide video	Command + Option + Shift + V
Hide other video	Command + Shift + V

Continued

Table B-6 *(continued)*

Action	Shortcut
Display or close Effect Controls window for selected layers	Command + Shift + T or F3
Switch between Comp and Timeline windows	\
Open source of a layer	Option + double-click a layer or press Option + Enter on numeric keypad
Scale layer without dragging a handle in Comp window	Option + drag layer
Snap layer to edges or center of frame in Comp window	Command + Shift + drag layer (begin dragging before pressing keys)
Constrain layer movement along X-axis or Y-axis	Shift + drag layer (begin dragging before pressing keys)
Stretch layer to fit Comp window	Command + Option + F
Stretch layer to fit vertically, preserving frame aspect ratio	Command + Option + Shift + G
Stretch layer to fit horizontally, preserving frame aspect ratio	Command + Option + Shift + H
Reverse a layer's playback	Command + Option + R
Set In point	**[(left bracket)**
Set Out point	**] (right bracket)**
Trim In point of a layer	**Option + [(left bracket)**
Trim Out point of a layer	**Option +] (right bracket)**
New Solid	**Command + Y**
Display solid settings	Command +Shift + Y
Add/Remove expression	Option + click property stopwatch
Set In point by time-stretching	Command + Shift +, (comma)
Set Out point by time-stretching	Command + Option + , (comma)

Action	Shortcut
Move In point to beginning of composition	Option + Home
Move Out point to end of composition	Option + End
Constrain rotation to 45-degree increments	Shift + drag Rotate tool
Constrain scaling to footage frame aspect ratio	Shift + drag layer handle
Constrain movement along X- or Y-axis	Shift + drag layer
Reset rotation angle to 0 degrees	Double-click Rotate tool
Reset scale to 100%	Double-click Selection tool
Change property value	Drag underlined values in Switches/Modes panel
Change property value x 10	Shift + drag underlined values
Change property value / 10	Command + drag underlined values

Table B-7
Zooming in Composition, Layer, and Footage Windows

Action	Shortcut
Zoom in	. (period) or Command + Option + =
Zoom out	, (comma) or Command + Option + - (hyphen) on main keyboard
Zoom in and resize window	Option + . (period) or Command + = on main keyboard
Zoom out and resize window	Option + , (comma) or Command + - (hyphen) on main keyboard
Zoom to 100%	/ (on main keyboard) or double-click zoom tool
Zoom to 100% and resize window	Option + / on main keyboard
Zoom window	Command + \
Zoom window to fill monitor	Command +Shift + \

Table B-8
Viewing Layer Properties in the Timeline Window

Action	Shortcut
Anchor Point	A
Audio Levels	L
Audio Waveform	LL
Effects	E
Expressions	EE
Mask Feather	F
Mask Shape	M
Mask Opacity	TT
Mask properties	MM
Material Options (3D)	AA
Opacity	T
Position	P
Rotation	R
Time-remapping	RR
Scale	S
Show all animating values	**U**
Show all modified values	**UU**
Set layer property value in dialog box (works with P, S, R, F, and M)	Command + Shift + property shortcut
Hide property or category	Option + Shift + click property or category name
Display/hide Parent column	Shift + F4
Add/remove property	Shift + property shortcut
Toggle switches/modes	F4
Turn off all other solo switches	Option + click solo switch
Change a setting (such as video or lock) for all selected layers	Click a layer switch
Open Opacity dialog box	Command + Shift + O
Open Anchor Point dialog box	Command + Option + Shift + A
Zoom to or from frame view	; (semicolon)
Zoom in time	= on main keyboard
Zoom out time	- (hyphen) on main keyboard

Table B-9
Working with Compositions in the Comp Window

Action	Shortcut
Set composition resolution to custom	Command + Option + J
Composition Flowchart view	Command + Shift + F11
Toggle window display options in Palette menu	Command + Shift + H

Table B-10
Working with the Tools Palette

Action	Shortcut
Selection tool: Selects, moves, and resizes layers, masks, and controls	V
Rotation tool: Rotates layers in the Comp window	W
Camera tools (3D): Orbit, Track XY, and Track Z	C, or Shift + C to cycle through tools
Rectangle tool or Oval tool: Draws a rectangular or elliptical mask in the Layer window; double-click to reset the mask	Q, or Shift + Q to toggle between tools
Pen tool: Edits Bezier masks, motion paths, and Value graphs	G
Pan Behind tool: Moves a layer behind a mask, or moves the anchor point without moving the layer	Y
Hand tool: Scrolls window to reveal areas beyond window edge; hold down spacebar to use Hand tool in any window	H or hold down spacebar
Zoom tool: Magnifies (or reduces, if used with Option) an area of a page	Z

Table B-11
Manipulating Keyframes in the Timeline Window

Action	Shortcut
Add or remove keyframe (if stopwatch is on) or turn on time-vary stopwatch (if off)	Option + Shift + property display shortcut
Select all keyframes for a property	Click property name
Deselect all keyframes	Shift + F2

Continued

Table B-11 (continued)

Action	Shortcut
Snap keyframe to significant times	Shift + drag keyframe
Nudge keyframe one frame forward	Option + right arrow
Nudge keyframe one frame backward	Option + left arrow
Select all visible keyframes	**Command + Option + A**
Go to previous visible keyframe	J
Go to next visible keyframe	K
Switch interpolation between Linear and Auto Bezier	Command + click keyframe
Change Auto Bezier interpolation to Continuous Bezier	Drag keyframe handle
Toggle between Continuous Bezier and Bezier interpolation	Command + drag keyframe handle
Easy ease	**F9**
Easy ease in	Shift + F9
Easy ease out	Command + Shift + F9

Table B-12
Nudging Layers in Comp and Timeline Windows

Action	Shortcut
Nudge layer 1 pixel in specific direction	Arrow key (nudges in direction of arrow)
Nudge layer 1 frame earlier	Command + Page Up
Nudge layer 1 frame later	Command + Page Down
Nudge layer rotation +1 degree	+ (plus) on numeric keypad
Nudge layer rotation −1 degree	− (minus) on numeric keypad
Nudge layer scaling +1%	Option + + (plus) on numeric keypad
Nudge layer scaling −1%	Option + − (minus) on numeric keypad

Note that nudging counts pixels at the current magnification, not at current size. For example, nudging an item one pixel at 50% magnification is the same as nudging the item two pixels at 100% magnification. Also, hold down the Shift key to amplify nudging, scaling, or rotation by 10.

Table B-13
Managing Work Area in the Timeline Window

Action	Shortcut
Set beginning of work area to current time	B
Set end of work area to current time	N
Set work area to selected layers	Command + Option + B (sets work area to comp duration if no layer is selected)

Table B-14
Working with Masks in Comp and Layer Windows

Action	Shortcut
Reset oval or rectangle mask to fill window	Double-click tool
Scale around center point in Free Transform mode	Command + drag
Select all points on a mask	Option + click mask
Free transform mask	Command + T or double-click mask
Exit free transform mode	Return

Table B-15
Working with Effects in the Effect Controls Window

Action	Shortcut
Expand/collapse effect controls	` (grave accent)
Add keyframe for effect property	Click stopwatch next to effect property name
Activate Comp window containing layer	\
Make goat sound	Control + click the star icon at top of window

Table B-16
Working with 3D animation in Comp and Timeline Windows

Action	Shortcut
New camera	Command + Option + Shift + C
New light	Command + Option + Shift + L
Orientation (for 3D layer)	Command + Option + Shift + R
Remember view A	Shift + F10
View stored view A (defaults to Front)	F10
Remember view B	Shift + F11
View stored view B (defaults to Custom View 1)	F11
Remember view C	Shift + F12
View stored view C (defaults to Active Camera)	F12
Return to previous view	Esc
Toggle Casts Shadows property	Command + Shift + C

Table B-17
Using Markers in Comp and Timeline Windows

Action	Shortcut
Set layer-time marker	* on numeric keypad
Remove layer-time marker	Command + click marker
Go to previous visible layer-time marker or keyframe	J
Go to next visible layer-time marker or keyframe	K
Go to a composition-time marker	0–9 on main keyboard
Set and number a composition-time marker at the current time	Shift + 0–9 on main keyboard

Table B-18
Using Other Palettes

Action	Shortcut
Switch from Selection tool to Pen tool	Hold down Command
Switch from Pen tool to Selection tool	Hold down Command
Display filename in Info palette	Command + Option + E

Table B-19
Keyboard Shortcuts in Motion Tracker Window

Action	Shortcut
Enlarge magnification	Command + plus symbol on main keypad
Reduce Magnification	Command + minus symbol on main keypad
Move feature region	Option + drag
Make region inactive in affine corner pinning	Option + click region

Table B-20
Keyboard Shortcut in Motion Math Window

Action	Shortcut
Return to default script	Option + click Cancel button

Table B-21
Keyboard Shortcuts for Vector Paint

General

Action	Shortcut
Undo	Shift + Z
Bypass Paint	Option/Alt + click
Access the After Effects contextual menus	Command + Option + click

Selections

Action	Shortcut
Selects all strokes	Shift + A
De-selects strokes	Shift + D
Select visible strokes	Shift + W
Select current time	Shift + T
Deletes all selected strokes	Backspace
Toggle selection	Shift + select
Deselect	Command + select
Add to selection	Command + Shift + select

Continued

Table B-21 *(continued)*

Tools

Action	Shortcut
Switch to Eyedropper tool (returns to the previous tool when done)	Shift + C
Set Radius and Feather for Brush Settings	Command + click and drag
QuickPaint using the selected mode in Vector Paint's contextual menus	Shift + Painting

Transformations

Scale Selected Strokes

Action	Shortcut
Scale up by 1%	Option + (plus, on the numeric keypad)
Scale down by 1%	Option – (minus, on the numeric keypad)
Increases the vertical scale (height) by 1%	Option + up arrow
Decreases the vertical scale (height) by 1%	Option + down arrow
Increases the horizontal scale (width) by 1%	Option + right arrow
Increases the horizontal scale (width) by 1%	Option + left arrow

Rotate Selected Strokes

Action	Shortcut
Rotates clockwise by 1 degree	+ (on the numeric keypad)
Rotates counter-clockwise by 1 degree	– (on the numeric keypad)

Reposition Selected Strokes

Action	Shortcut
Nudges the position up, down, right, or left by one pixel	Arrow keys

Note the following when using the Transformation keyboard shortcuts: All the geometrical transformations listed require a current selection; holding down Shift increments all geometric transformations by 10 times; holding down Command performs scaling/rotation on selected strokes individually as opposed to a group; holding down both Shift and Command performs transformations on strokes individually by increments of 10.

✦   ✦   ✦

Keyboard Shortcuts for Windows

Repetition is the way of life when working with After Effects, and without keyboard shortcuts, there would be no life in After Effects land.

Following are the keyboard shortcuts found in After Effects. The ones shown in bold are the shortcuts that we find ourselves using most often.

Table C-1 Working with Footage Items in the Project Window	
Action	**Shortcut**
Open last project	Ctrl + Alt + Shift + P
When opening a project, suppress opening of all windows (except the Project window)	Hold down Shift
Open selected footage item or composition	Double-click or press Enter on numeric keypad
Open movie in an After Effects footage window	Alt + double-click
Activate most recent composition	\
Add selected item to most recently activated composition	**Ctrl + /**
Replace a selected layer's source footage in Comp window with selected footage	Ctrl + Alt + /

Continued

Table C-1 *(continued)*

Action	Shortcut
Replace a selected layer's footage item or composition	Alt + drag footage item from Project window into composition
Replace footage file	Ctrl + H
Set Interpret Footage Alts	Ctrl + F
Scan for changed footage	Ctrl + Alt + Shift + Q
New folder	Ctrl + Alt + Shift + N
Remember footage interpretation	**Ctrl + Alt + C**
Apply footage interpretation	**Ctrl + Alt + V**
Set proxy file	Ctrl + Alt + P
Project Settings	Ctrl + Alt + Shift + K

Table C-2
Viewing Windows — Comp, Layer, and Footage Windows

Action	Shortcut
Display/hide title-safe and action-safe zones	' (apostrophe)
Display/hide grid	Ctrl + ' (apostrophe)
Display/hide proportional grid	Alt + ' (apostrophe)
Center active window	Ctrl + Alt + \
Suspend window updates	Caps Lock
Cycle through tabs in the frontmost window	Shift + , (comma) and Shift + . (period) (add Alt to zoom window to fit)
Take multiple (up to four) snapshots	Shift + F5, F6, F7, and F8
Display snapshot in active window	F5, F6, F7, and F8
Purge snapshot	Ctrl + Shift + F5, F6, F7, and F8
Purge all	Ctrl + Alt + / on numeric keypad
Display channel (RGBA)	Alt + 1, 2, 3, or 4
Display channel (RGBA) in color	Alt + Shift + 1, 2, 3, or 4
Display channel in color	Shift + click channel icon
Display unmatted color channels	Shift + click alpha channel icon
Display Project window	Ctrl + 0

Action	Shortcut
Display Project Flowchart view	Ctrl + F11
Display/hide palettes	**Tab**
Hides all palettes, except Tools palette	**Shift + Tab**
Close active tab/window	Ctrl + W
Close active window (all tabs)	Ctrl + Shift + W
Close all windows (except Project window)	Ctrl + Alt + W

Table C-3
Moving Around the Timeline Window

Action	Shortcut
Go to beginning of work area	**Shift + Home**
Go to end of work area	**Shift + End**
Go to previous visible keyframe or layer marker	J
Go to next visible keyframe or layer marker	K
Go to a composition-time marker	0–9 on main keyboard
Scroll selected layer to top of Timeline window	X
Scroll current time to center of window	D
Go to time	**Ctrl+ G**

Table C-4
Footage and Layer Windows

Action	Shortcut
Go to beginning	Home or Ctrl + Alt + left arrow key
Go to end	End or Ctrl + Alt + right arrow key
Step forward one frame	Page Down or Ctrl + right arrow key

Continued

Table C-4 (continued)

Action	Shortcut
Step forward 10 frames	Shift + Ctrl + right arrow key or Shift + Page Down
Step backward one frame	Page Up or Ctrl + left arrow key
Step backward 10 frames	Shift + Page Up or Ctrl + Shift + left arrow key
Go to layer In point	**i**
Go to layer Out point	**o**
Snap items (visible keyframes, time markers, and In and Out points, and so on) to each other on a time ruler	Shift + drag item

Table C-5
Previewing in the Timeline Window

Action	Shortcut
Start/pause playback	**Spacebar**
Preview audio from the current time	**. (period) on numeric keypad**
RAM Preview	**0 on numeric keypad**
RAM Preview every other frame	Shift + 0 on numeric keypad
Save RAM Preview	Ctrl + 0 on numeric keypad
Scrub video	Drag or Alt + drag current-time marker (depending on Preview Preferences setting)
Scrub audio	Ctrl + drag current-time marker
Wireframe preview	Alt + 0 on numeric keypad
Display rectangle instead of alpha outline during wireframe preview	Ctrl + Alt + 0 on numeric keypad
Leave window contents during wireframe preview	Shift + Alt + 0 on numeric keypad
Leave window contents during rectangle preview	Ctrl + Shift + Alt + 0 on numeric keypad

Note: If no layers are selected, these Controls apply to all layers. Also, these Controls honor the loop and audio settings in the Time Control palette.

Table C-6
Working with Layers in the Comp and Timeline Windows

Action	Shortcut
Rename layer, composition, folder, or effect	Return
Select next layer back	Ctrl + down arrow
Select next layer forward	Ctrl + up arrow
Select a layer by its layer-outline number	1–9 on numeric keypad
Select noncontiguous layers	Ctrl + click layers
Deselect all layers	Ctrl + Shift + A or F2
Lock selected layers	Ctrl + L
Unlock all layers	Ctrl + Shift + L
Split selected layer	Ctrl + Shift + D
Activate Comp window with layer	\
Display selected layer in Layer window	Enter on numeric keypad
Show/hide video	Ctrl + Alt + Shift + V
Hide other video	Ctrl + Shift + V
Display or close Effect Controls window for selected layers	Ctrl + Shift + T, or F3
Switch between Comp and Timeline windows	\
Open source of a layer	Alt+ double-click a layer or press Alt + Enter on numeric keypad
Scale layer without dragging a handle in Comp window	Alt + drag layer
Snap layer to edges or center of frame in Comp window	Ctrl + Shift + drag layer (begin dragging before pressing keys)
Constrain layer movement along X-axis or Y-axis	Shift + drag layer (begin dragging before pressing keys)

Continued

Table C-6 (continued)

Action	Shortcut
Stretch layer to fit Comp window	Ctrl + Alt + F
Stretch layer to fit vertically, preserving frame aspect ratio	Ctrl + Alt + Shift + G
Stretch layer to fit horizontally, preserving frame aspect ratio	Ctrl + Alt + Shift + H
Reverse a layer's playback	Ctrl + Alt + R
Set In point	**[(left bracket)**
Set Out point	**] (right bracket)**
Trim In point of a layer	**Alt + [(left bracket)**
Trim Out point of a layer	**Alt +] (right bracket)**
New Solid	**Ctrl + Y**
Display solid settings	Ctrl + Shift + Y
Add/Remove expression	Alt + click property stopwatch
Set In point by time-stretching	Ctrl + Shift + , (comma)
Set Out point by time-stretching	Ctrl + Alt + , (comma)
Move In point to beginning of composition	Alt + Home
Move Out point to end of composition	Alt + End
Constrain rotation to 45-degree increments	Shift + drag Rotate tool
Constrain scaling to footage frame aspect ratio	Shift + drag layer handle
Constrain movement along X- or Y-axis	Shift + drag layer
Reset rotation angle to 0 degrees	Double-click Rotate tool
Reset scale to 100%	Double-click Selection tool
Change property value	Drag underlined values in Switches/Modes panel
Change property value x 10	Shift + drag underlined values
Change property value / 10	Ctrl + drag underlined values

Table C-7
Zooming in Comp, Layer, and Footage Windows

Action	Shortcut
Zoom in	. (period) or Ctrl + Alt + =
Zoom out	, (comma) or Ctrl + Alt + - (hyphen) on main keyboard
Zoom in and resize window	Alt + . (period) or Ctrl + = on main keyboard
Zoom out and resize window	Alt + , (comma) or Ctrl + - (hyphen) on main keyboard
Zoom to 100%	/ (on main keyboard) or double-click zoom tool
Zoom to 100% and resize window	Alt + / on main keyboard
Zoom window	Ctrl + \
Zoom window to fill monitor	Ctrl + Shift + \

Table C-8
Viewing Layer Properties in the Timeline Window

Action	Shortcut
Anchor Point	A
Audio Levels	L
Audio Waveform	LL
Effects	E
Expressions	EE
Mask Feather	F
Mask Shape	M
Mask Opacity	TT
Mask properties	MM
Material Alts (3D)	AA
Opacity	T

Continued

Table C-8 *(continued)*

Action	Shortcut
Position	P
Rotation	R
Time-remapping	RR
Scale	S
Show all animating values	**U**
Show all modified values	**UU**
Set layer property value in dialog box (works with P, S, R, F, and M)	Ctrl + Shift + property shortcut
Hide property or category	Alt + Shift + click property or category name
Display/hide Parent column	Shift + F4
Add/remove property	Shift + property shortcut
Toggle switches/modes	F4
Turn off all other solo switches	Alt + click solo switch
Change a setting (such as video or lock) for all selected layers	Click a layer switch
Open Opacity dialog box	Ctrl + Shift + O
Open Anchor Point dialog box	Ctrl + Alt + Shift + A
Zoom to or from frame view	; (semicolon)
Zoom in time	= on main keyboard
Zoom out time	- (hyphen) on main keyboard

Table C-9
Working with Compositions in a Comp Window

Action	Shortcut
Set composition resolution to custom	Ctrl + Alt + J
Composition Flowchart view	Ctrl + Shift + F11
Toggle window display Alts in Palette menu	Ctrl + Shift + H

Table C-10
Working with the Tools Palette

Action	Shortcut
Selection tool: Selects, moves, and resizes layers, masks, and controls	V
Rotation tool: Rotates layers in the Comp window	W
Camera tools (3D): Orbit, Track XY, and Track Z	C, or Shift + C to cycle through tools
Rectangle tool or Oval tool: Draws a rectangular or elliptical mask in the Layer window; double-click to reset the mask	Q, or Shift + Q to toggle between tools
Pen tool: Edits Bezier masks, motion paths, and Value graphs	G
Pan Behind tool: Moves a layer behind a mask or moves the anchor point without moving the layer	Y
Hand tool: Scrolls window to reveal areas beyond window edge; hold down spacebar to use Hand tool in any window	H, or hold down spacebar
Zoom tool: Magnifies (or reduces, if used with Alt) an area of a page	Z

Table C-11
Manipulating Keyframes in the Timeline Window

Action	Shortcut
Add or remove keyframe (if stopwatch is on) or turn on time-vary stopwatch (if off)	Alt + Shift + property display shortcut
Select all keyframes for a property	Click property name
Deselect all keyframes	Shift + F2
Snap keyframe to significant times	Shift + drag keyframe
Nudge keyframe one frame forward	Alt + right arrow

Continued

Table C-11 *(continued)*

Action	Shortcut
Nudge keyframe one frame backward	Alt + left arrow
Select all visible keyframes	**Ctrl + Alt + A**
Go to previous visible keyframe	J
Go to next visible keyframe	K
Switch interpolation between Linear and Auto Bezier	Ctrl + click keyframe
Change Auto Bezier interpolation to Continuous Bezier	Drag keyframe handle
Toggle between Continuous Bezier and Bezier interpolation	Ctrl + drag keyframe handle
Easy ease	**F9**
Easy ease in	Shift + F9
Easy ease out	Ctrl + Shift + F9

Table C-12
Nudging Layers in the Comp and Timeline Windows

Action	Shortcut
Nudge layer one pixel in specific direction	Arrow key (nudges in direction of arrow)
Nudge layer one frame earlier	Ctrl + Page Up
Nudge layer one frame later	Ctrl + Page Down
Nudge layer rotation +1 degree	+ (plus) on numeric keypad
Nudge layer rotation −1 degree	− (minus) on numeric keypad
Nudge layer scaling +1%	Alt + + (plus) on numeric keypad
Nudge layer scaling −1%	Alt + − (minus) on numeric keypad

Note that nudging counts pixels at the current magnification, not at current size. For example, nudging an item one pixel at 50% magnification is the same as nudging the item two pixels at 100% magnification. Also, hold down the Shift key to amplify nudging, scaling, or rotation by 10.

Table C-13
Managing Work Area in the Timeline Window

Action	Shortcut
Set beginning of work area to current time	B
Set end of work area to current time	N
Set work area to selected layers	Ctrl + Alt + B (sets work area to comp duration if no layer is selected)

Table C-14
Working with Masks in the Comp and Layer Windows

Action	Shortcut
Reset oval or rectangle mask to fill window	Double-click tool
Scale around center point in Free Transform mode	Ctrl + drag
Select all points on a mask	Alt + click mask
Free transform mask	Ctrl + T or double-click mask
Exit free transform mode	Return

Table C-15
Working with Effects in the Effect Controls Window

Action	Shortcut
Expand/collapse effect controls	` (grave accent)
Add keyframe for effect control	Alt + click effect property name
Activate Comp window containing layer	\
Make goat sound	Right-click on the star icon at top of window

Table C-16
Working with 3D Animation in the Comp and Timeline Windows

Action	Shortcut
New camera	Ctrl + Alt + Shift + C
New light	Ctrl + Alt + Shift + L
Orientation (for 3D layer)	Ctrl + Alt + Shift + R
Remember view A	Shift + F10
View stored view A (defaults to Front)	F10
Remember view B	Shift + F11
View stored view B (defaults to Custom View 1)	F11
Remember view C	Shift + F12
View stored view C (defaults to Active Camera)	F12
Return to previous view	Esc
Toggle Casts Shadows property	Ctrl + Shift + C

Table C-17
Using Markers in the Comp and Timeline Windows

Action	Shortcut
Set layer-time marker	* on numeric keypad
Remove layer-time marker	Ctrl + click marker
Go to previous visible layer-time marker or keyframe	J
Go to next visible layer-time marker or keyframe	K
Go to a composition-time marker	0–9 on main keyboard
Set and number a composition-time marker at the current time	Shift + 0–9 on main keyboard

Table C-18
Using Other Palettes

Action	Shortcut
Switch from Selection tool to Pen tool	Hold down Ctrl
Switch from Pen tool to Selection tool	Hold down Ctrl
Display filename in Info palette	Ctrl + Alt + E

Table C-19
Keyboard Shortcuts in the Motion Tracker Window

Action	Shortcut
Enlarge magnification	Ctrl + plus symbol on main keypad
Reduce Magnification	Ctrl + minus symbol on main keypad
Move feature region	Alt + Drag
Make region inactive in affine corner pinning	Alt + click region

Table C-20
Keyboard Shortcut in the Motion Math Window

Action	Shortcut
Return to default script	Alt + click Cancel button

Table C-21
Keyboard shortcuts for Vector Paint

General

Action	Shortcut
Undo	Shift + Z
Bypass Paint	Alt + click
Access the After Effects Contextual Menus	Ctrl + Alt + click

Selections

Action	Shortcut
Selects all strokes	Shift + A
De-selects strokes	Shift + D
Select visible strokes	Shift + W
Select current time	Shift + T
Deletes all selected strokes	Backspace
Toggle selection	Shift + select
Deselect	Ctrl + select
Add to selection	Ctrl + Shift + select

Continued

Table C-21 *(continued)*

Tools

Action	Shortcut
Switch to Eyedropper tool (returns to the previous tool when done)	Shift + C
Set Radius and Feather for Brush Settings	Ctrl + click + drag
QuickPaint using the selected mode in Vector's Paint's Contextual Menus	Shift + Painting

Transformations

Scale Selected Strokes

Action	Shortcut
Scale up by 1%	Alt + (plus sign on the numeric keypad)
Scale down by 1%	Alt – (minus sign on the numeric keypad)
Increases the vertical scale (height) by 1%	Alt + up arrow
Decreases the vertical scale (height) by 1%	Alt + down arrow
Increases the horizontal scale (width) by 1%	Alt + right arrow
Increases the horizontal scale (width) by 1%	Alt + left arrow

Rotate Selected Strokes

Action	Shortcut
Rotates clockwise by 1 degree	+ (on the numeric keypad)
Rotates counter-clockwise by 1 degree	– (on the numeric keypad)

Reposition Selected Strokes

Action	Shortcut
Nudges the position up, down, right, or left by one pixel	Arrow keys

Note the following when using the upcoming transformation keyboard shortcuts: All geometrical Transformations require a current selection. Holding down Shift increments all geometric transformations by 10 times. Holding down Ctrl performs scaling/rotation on selected strokes individually as opposed to a group. Holding down both Shift and Ctrl performs transformations on strokes individually by increments of 10.

✦   ✦   ✦

What's on the DVD-ROM

This appendix contains information about the resources included on the DVD-ROM. First of all, don't be misled by the letters *DVD,* because they don't refer to the kind of disc that you can pop into your home entertainment DVD player. In fact, it's easier to think of this disc as a CD-ROM with a lot more room for data. Instead of the typical CD-ROM ceiling of about 650MB, this DVD-ROM contains up to 4.7GB of storage space!

Here are some of the things you'll find on this cross-platform disc:

◆ All the files related to the step exercises in each chapter

◆ Trial versions of applications, including Adobe After Effects

◆ Demo versions of After Effects plug-ins

System Requirements

Hopefully, most of you won't have an issue accessing the data on the DVD-ROM. If you've acquired your workstation in the past couple of years, the chances are that the manufacturer loaded your machine with a DVD drive capable of reading this kind of disc. In fact, this should be standard issue by the time you're reading this sentence.

For Macintosh:

◆ Power PC Processor (G4 recommended).

◆ Mac OS 9.1 or 9.21; if you're running After Effects 5.5, it will work on OSX (10.1) as well.

For Windows:

✦ Pentium II, III, or 4 Processor.

✦ Windows 98, Windows Millenium Edition, or Windows 2000; or if you're running After Effects 5.5, it will work on Windows XP as well.

✦ Microsoft DirectX 8.1 software (recommended).

For either platform:

✦ At least 128MB of RAM. (When it comes to After Effects, you can never really have too much RAM. You'll have an easier time getting more out of the application if you start with at least 256MB.)

✦ Apple QuickTime software (version 5.0 recommended).

✦ 24-bit color display adapter.

✦ You should run the After Effects projects and their related footage from your hard drive, in which case, you may want to have as much as 4GB free. If that presents you with a problem, you can copy items to your hard drive on a project-by-project basis.

Using the DVD-ROM

To get the most out of the DVD-ROM, follow these steps:

1. **Insert the DVD-ROM into your computer's DVD drive.**

2. **Double-click the DVD icon that appears on your desktop to display its contents.**

3. **Double-click the ReadMe file.**

4. **For optimal results, you may find it easier to copy the Project Files and Source materials folders to your hard drive.** If this presents you with space constraint problems, you can also copy files to your hard drive on a project-by-project basis.

These are After Effects version 5.0 project files. This means that you'll be able to open them in case you haven't yet upgraded to version 5.5. If you have made the move to 5.5, when you initially open these projects, you'll get a message saying that "this project must be converted from an earlier version and will open as *Untitled*." That's okay; just save the project to update the file's format to version 5.5.

5. **Regarding the demos or trial versions of software included on the DVD-ROM, double-click their individual Install or Installer icons to install the plug-ins or applications that you want to try out.**

What's on the DVD-ROM

The DVD-ROM contains chapter project files (as well as their source materials), supplemental material from some other folks in the After Effects community, a PDF version of this book, and plenty of goodies such as demo versions of third-party After Effects plug-ins. What follows is a description of the contents of each folder at the root of the DVD-ROM.

Project files

With the exception of Chapters 4 and 29, every chapter in the book has its own After Effects (.aep) project file located in the Project Files folder on the DVD-ROM. Each of these projects includes examples of the concepts covered in the given chapter. We suggest that you copy this folder to your hard drive.

Source materials

Each project relies on source material that we've provided in this folder. In it, you'll find audio files, an Adobe Premiere project, QuickTime files, and still images of both the bitmap (Photoshop) and vector (Illustrator) variety. We also recommend that you copy this folder to your hard drive, but you may find that space is a bit tight (it's approximately 4GB). If this is the case, collect the files from any of the projects to your hard drive on an as-needed basis.

Cross-Reference   We cover the Collect Files command in Chapter 7.

In the QuickTime folder, we've included watermarked high-resolution video clips from the following stock footage companies. If you need high-quality footage for your After Effects projects, go to their Web sites:

✦ ArtBeats: www.artbeats.com

✦ Bestshot.com, Inc.: www.bestshot.com

✦ Creatas: www.creatas.com

Note   Creatas also provided us with some beautiful line art in the form of EPS files, which you can find in the *Stills* folder.

✦ Digital Juice: www.digitaljuice.com

✦ EyeWire by Getty Images: www.gettyimages.com

✦ Sekani: www.sekani.com

✦ Videometry: www.videometry.com

✦ We've also included several audio tracks in the *Audio* folder, most of which were kindly provided to us by Narrator Tracks, a division of Gungor Productions. If you need royalty-free music to complement your video productions, visit them at www.ntracks.com.

PDF

For your digital enjoyment, we've included a PDF version of the book on the DVD-ROM.

More AE art and techniques

Some very generous and talented After Effects artists donated their time and effort to this project, and you should definitely check out each of their contributions in the folders contained here. If you like what you see, you can find out more about these motion graphic designers:

✦ Steve Fein, CEO of Big Ripple Multimedia and a creator of digital elegance, has created a lot more work that you can find at //www.bigripple.com/.

✦ Adam Helfet Hilliker, cofounder of HHG Designs and a brilliant artist, has showcased more of his work at //www.helfet.com/ and at //www.hhgdesigns.com/.

✦ An extraordinarily gifted as well as prodigious AE artist, Mark Magnus can be reached at this e-mail address: mmagnus@worldnet.att.net.

Goodies

You'll find the following folders inside the Goodies folder.

Applications

We've included tryout versions of Adobe's entire Digital Video Collection:

✦ **Adobe After Effects:** Need we say more about this particular product?

✦ **Adobe Premiere:** Adobe's own video editing software.

✦ **Adobe Photoshop:** The world's greatest image editing application.

✦ **Adobe Illustrator:** Another indispensable tool when it comes to motion graphic design. At the very least, you'll need it if you're at all serious about typography, and that's saying nothing about everything else it can do.

After Effects plug-ins

We've included demo versions from a number of excellent third-party plug-in developers. The following list details some of the offerings:

✦ **The Foundry:** Tinderbox 1 & 2 are truly amazing filters that cover a variety of production needs. In many ways, these are an application unto themselves. First-rate stuff.

✦ **DigiEffects:** Check out the excellent CineLook, CineMotion, Delirium, Aurorix, Berserk, and Cyclonist filters. CineLook and CineMotion are industry-leading effects that make your video look like film.

✦ **Trapcode:** We've included both the Shine and 3D Stroke filters. They are excellent, cost-effective, and quick to render. Shine has earned high marks from AE users who need a quick turnaround from a volumetric light effect.

✦ **Alias | Wavefront:** Maya Paint Effects.

✦ **Visual Infinity Inc.:** Grain Surgery.

✦ **neosapien.net:** aeFlame.

✦ **Alien Skin Software:** Eye Candy 3.1.

✦ **Digital Film Tools, LLC:** Compositre Suite 2.0.

✦ **StageTools:** MovingPicture for After Effects.

Utilities

Just in case you need it, we've provided you with Acrobat Reader:

✦ **Adobe Acrobat Reader 5.0:** If you don't have it already, you'll need this program to view PDF files.

Troubleshooting

If you have difficulty installing any of the material from the DVD-ROM, try the following solutions:

✦ **Turn off any anti-virus software that you may have running.** Installers sometimes mimic virus activity and can put your computer on the defensive. Of course, if you do disable your anti-virus software, make sure that you turn it back on later.

✦ **Close any open applications.** There may not be any memory left for the installers. Also, some installers automatically update applications, and this may cause additional problems.

If you still have trouble with the DVD-ROM, please call the Hungry Minds, Inc., Customer Care telephone number: (800) 762-2974. Outside the United States, call (317) 572-3994. Hungry Minds, Inc., will provide technical support only for installation and other general quality items; for technical support on the applications themselves, consult the program's vendor or author.

✦   ✦   ✦

Index

Your CD-ROM is protected by **FileOpen Publisher**™

Do you have information worth protecting? If you are distributing documents on the Web or CD-ROM, they can be copied, changed, and redistributed ad infinitem.

FileOpen Publisher works with Adobe Acrobat ™ to put you in control of your digital content. Using strong encryption and sophisticated logic handling, FileOpen Publisher lets you decide who may see your PDF documents, for how long, and how they may use them. If you are selling your publication, you can be sure that only users who have paid can open it.

Best of all, FileOpen Publisher allows you to retain control over your workflow and your business—you process your own documents, host them on your website or CD-ROM, and collect all revenues from your customers. FileOpen Systems will never monitor your usage of the software or charge any royalty beyond the basic license fee.

Distribute your electronic publications with confidence—find out more about FileOpen Publisher by visiting www.fileopen.com.

- Batch encrypt PDF files
- Set expiration dates on documents
- Prevent "re-distilling" of PDFs
- Control how many times a document may be opened or printed
- Authorize users from your website
- Easily create CD-ROM installers
- Available in 12 languages
- Free, unlimited distribution of client

As featured in:
* The Acrobat 5 Bible *
The Seybold Report * Publish Magazine
Electronic Publishing * Emedia Professional
Desktop Publishers Journal * InfoWorld

Adobe®Solutions Network
Developer Program

Adobe and Acrobat are registered trademarks of Adobe Systems, Inc.

FileOpen Systems Inc.   www.fileopen.com   email: info@fileopen.com

Hungry Minds, Inc.
End-User License Agreement

READ THIS. You should carefully read these terms and conditions before opening the software packet(s) included with this book ("Book"). This is a license agreement ("Agreement") between you and Hungry Minds, Inc. ("HMI"). By opening the accompanying software packet(s), you acknowledge that you have read and accept the following terms and conditions. If you do not agree and do not want to be bound by such terms and conditions, promptly return the Book and the unopened software packet(s) to the place you obtained them for a full refund.

1. **License Grant.** HMI grants to you (either an individual or entity) a nonexclusive license to use one copy of the enclosed software program(s) (collectively, the "Software") solely for your own personal or business purposes on a single computer (whether a standard computer or a workstation component of a multi-user network). The Software is in use on a computer when it is loaded into temporary memory (RAM) or installed into permanent memory (hard disk, CD-ROM, or other storage device). HMI reserves all rights not expressly granted herein.

2. **Ownership.** HMI is the owner of all right, title, and interest, including copyright, in and to the compilation of the Software recorded on the disk(s) or CD-ROM ("Software Media"). Copyright to the individual programs recorded on the Software Media is owned by the author or other authorized copyright owner of each program. Ownership of the Software and all proprietary rights relating thereto remain with HMI and its licensers.

3. **Restrictions On Use and Transfer.**

    (a) You may only (i) make one copy of the Software for backup or archival purposes, or (ii) transfer the Software to a single hard disk, provided that you keep the original for backup or archival purposes. You may not (i) rent or lease the Software, (ii) copy or reproduce the Software through a LAN or other network system or through any computer subscriber system or bulletin-board system, or (iii) modify, adapt, or create derivative works based on the Software.

    (b) You may not reverse engineer, decompile, or disassemble the Software. You may transfer the Software and user documentation on a permanent basis, provided that the transferee agrees to accept the terms and conditions of this Agreement and you retain no copies. If the Software is an update or has been updated, any transfer must include the most recent update and all prior versions.

4. **Restrictions on Use of Individual Programs.** You must follow the individual requirements and restrictions detailed for each individual program in Appendix D of this Book. These limitations are also contained in the individual license agreements recorded on the Software Media. These limitations may include a requirement that after using the program for a specified period of time, the user must pay a registration fee or discontinue use. By opening the Software packet(s), you will be agreeing to abide by the licenses and restrictions for these individual programs that are detailed in Appendix D and on the Software Media. None of the material on this Software Media or listed in this Book may ever be redistributed, in original or modified form, for commercial purposes.